TALLEYRAND
A Biography

By the same author:

UP FROM CAESAR

TALLEYRAND

A Biography

by J. F. BERNARD

G. P. Putnam's Sons, New York

Copyright © 1973 by J. F. Bernard

SBN: 399–11022–4

Library of Congress Catalog
Card Number: 72–80242

PRINTED IN THE UNITED STATES OF AMERICA

For my mother and father,
in continuing gratitude

Contents

Part One

The Formative Years (1754–1789)   11

1. The Beginnings   13
2. A Priest in Spite of Himself   34
3. The Abbé de Périgord in the Great World   45

Part Two

Revolution and Exile (1789–1797)   71

4. The Assembly   73
5. Monseigneur d'Autun Retires   93
6. Exile: England and America   131

Part Three

Talleyrand and Napoleon (1797–1814)   167

7. The Directory   169
8. The Consulate   220
9. The Empire   256
10. Erfurt and Beyond   282

7

Part Four

THE RECONSTRUCTION OF EUROPE (1814–1815)   321

11. The Treaty of Paris and the First Restoration   323
12. London Interlude   350
13. The Congress of Vienna   367
14. The Confidential Approach   384
15. Crisis and Solution: The Triple Alliance   398
16. Italy and the Hundred Days   412

Part Five

RESTORATION, RETIREMENT, AND REVOLUTION (1815–1830)

421

17. Talleyrand's Hundred Days   423
18. The Years of Retirement   458

Part Six

THE LONDON EMBASSY (1830–1834)   525

Part Seven

THE FINAL YEARS (1834–1838)   583

Bibliography   621

Index   639

Illustrations

FOLLOWING PAGE 328

Talleyrand at the Age of Sixteen
Catherine Grand, Princess de Talleyrand
Dorothea of Courland, Duchess de Dino
Napoleon at Erfurt
Signing of the Final Act of the Congress of Vienna
Talleyrand, by Gérard
Chateau of Valençay
Talleyrand (terra-cotta)
Hôtel Talleyrand, in the rue St.-Florentin (U.S. Embassy Building)

Maps

Europe on the Eve of the French Revolution   68

The Napoleonic Empire at Its Greatest Extent (1811)   279

Europe After the Congress of Vienna   419

Part One

THE FORMATIVE YEARS

(1754–1789)

*I am perhaps the only man of distinguished birth,
belonging to a numerous and esteemed family,
who has not, for a single week of his life, enjoyed
the sweetness of being under his father's roof.*

—*Mémoires*, Vol. I, p. 13

1

The Beginnings

"H E WAS a strange man," Victor Hugo wrote, "feared and respected. His name was Charles-Maurice de Périgord. He was noble, like Machiavelli; a priest, like Gondi; defrocked, like Fouché; and he limped like the devil himself." Men greater than Hugo had been even less kind to Talleyrand. "Shit in a silk stocking," Napoleon called him. Mirabeau, in the same vein, noted that "he would exchange his soul for a pile of dung, and he would be right to do so." Even his parents thought him "fit for nothing." Yet in his lifetime he helped create and then came to control a world undreamed of before his birth. He charmed Bonaparte and transformed him into a new Charlemagne, and then he led him to Waterloo and sent him to die in exile on St. Helena. Kings and princes he made and unmade with equal facility. Twice he gave the crown of France to the Bourbons, and once he took it away. He was a priest, a bishop, an aristocrat, and a confirmed libertine, gossip, gambler, and revolutionary. Scorning hypocrisy, admiring virtue, he cultivated every vice of his own time and some of a later age. A patriot and champion of the people, he betrayed his country and pulled down its regimes whenever it suited his own designs. Then he died, and Prosper de Barante spoke his eulogy: "These are the things that we have seen. We shall not live to see the like again." And France wept.

Charles-Maurice de Talleyrand-Périgord was born in Paris, on the second day of February, in the year of grace 1754, and in the reign of Louis XV the thirty-ninth. As was customary in that time of exalted religious principles and equally high infant mortality, he was christened on the same day, in the parish church of St.-Sulpice.

The infant was the second child of Charles-Daniel de Périgord, Count de Talleyrand, lieutenant general in the armies of France and *menin*, or personal attendant, to the dauphin. His mother was Alexandrine-Marie-Victoire-Eléonore de Damas d'Antigny. His parents were a handsome couple, young—the count was nineteen, and the countess, twenty-five—proud, the descendants of ancient dynasties, and related to the greatest houses of France. And they had this in common with much of the most illustrious nobility of the kingdom, that they had hardly a sou to their name.

Alexandrine de Damas, at the time of her marriage in 1751, had brought to her husband a modest dowry of 15,000 francs,* but at the time of Charles-Maurice's birth the couple were in such reduced circumstances that the countess was compelled to appeal to her father, the Marquis d'Antigny, for funds to purchase the linen that was necessary for her confinement.

Annoying as this poverty was and as important as it was to be in forming the character of Charles-Maurice, it was not a catastrophe. To be poor, in the France of the *ancien régime,* was a disaster only when one belonged to the lower orders of society. Money was a great convenience and sometimes even a necessity, but it was not the standard by which one was judged. The truly important thing was not wealth, but a noble name, and, if possible, an ancient one into the bargain. To such credentials, one had only to add a modicum of talent and ambition in order to live comfortably and even, if circumstances were auspicious, luxuriously. The newborn son of the Count and Countess de Périgord was to write, many years later, with a candor that was not unusual at a time when self-enrichment at the expense of the state was regarded as being in the very nature of things, that his parents "had only a small fortune but held a position at court that, if used properly, was sufficient to secure the highest offices for themselves and their children."

The count and countess, in fact, were themselves the beneficiaries of that same system of familial self-perpetuation at court, for, as Talleyrand explained, no one in the eighteenth century "could conceive of any power or glory other than that which derived from the king's majesty." Since the time of Richelieu, there had been members of the family in the royal entourage, "where they willingly surrendered their independence and, by exhibiting the utmost devotion, endeavored to make up for having been among the last to arrive." The infant's parents were in an ideal position to

---

* The franc of the *ancien régime* had, in the mid-eighteenth century, approximately the same purchasing power as the American dollar in the mid-twentieth century.

profit from the devotion of their ancestors,* and they—and many of their relatives—did so, not only without being compelled to feel guilt over it, but even with the approbation and envy of other, less fortunate members of society.

This opportunity the dynasty of Talleyrand-Périgord owed to the fact that it was as ancient as it was noble. It traced its remote origins to one Wilgrin, Count of Périgord, a contemporary of Charles the Bald, who died toward the end of the ninth century and whose immediate successors bore the surname of Taillefer, or Tallerang. By the twelfth century the Tallerangs were already well established as counts de Grignols and princes de Chalais and were reigning as sovereigns—albeit petty ones—in the vicinity of Périgord, in southwestern France. The elder branch of the family was extinguished in the male line in the mid-fifteenth century. A cadet branch had been founded in 1166, by Hélie de Périgord, Count de Grignols, and it was to Hélie that, from 1440 onward, the family of Talleyrand-Périgord traced its descendance.

The family tree and the dynastic pretensions of the house had been strengthened in 1613, when King Louis XIII issued letters patent recognizing the descent of this cadet branch from the Carolingian counts de Périgord, and again, unofficially, in 1815, when Louis XVIII was to remark to the newborn scion of the family that "our houses date from the same era." Nonetheless, countless contemporary genealogists—and everyone at the court of France regarded himself as a genealogist—were skeptical about the soundness of this doubly royal grafting of the Talleyrand branch onto the Périgord tree. In years to come, Louis XVIII himself, when he was especially annoyed, would be heard to remark that the Talleyrands were *du Périgord, et non de Périgord*—"from Périgord, but not *de* Périgord." For biographical purposes, King Louis' prepositional distinction is of no great importance. What matters—and what is known for certain—is that the Talleyrand-Périgords were universally regarded by their contemporaries, both within France and without, as bearing one of the great names of the realm. This consideration was sufficient to assure the family honor, esteem, and a living. That there had been no Talleyrand of distinction for several centuries was a fact of little interest either to the family itself or to French society, just as the family's relative poverty in the eighteenth century had little effect upon their self-respect and their standing in the world. Birth and family were, if not all, then at least the key to all. The *ancien régime*

---

* "My relatives," Talleyrand said, "held various situations with the royal family." Most of these situations were relatively modest ones, such as those enjoyed by his parents. A few relatives, however, had known how to take optimum advantage of the royal presence. Talleyrand's great-great aunt, for example, had captured the heart of Louis XIV and, as the Marquise de Montespan, had reigned over Versailles for a dozen years.

regarded a name as a negotiable instrument and a title as a more than adequate substitute for wealth.

There were some fine stories told in the Talleyrand family to demonstrate that it was extraordinarily endowed with both these precious commodities. The most famous of these tales concerned Adalbert, tenth-century Count de Périgord, who, after a bit of intentional insolence toward Hugues Capet, King of France and ancestor of the Bourbon dynasty, was angrily asked by his sovereign, "Who, then, has made you a count?" Adalbert retorted, just as angrily, "Who, then, has made you a king?"

Adalbert's hair-trigger temper seems to have been a characteristic inherited by many of his descendants. The story of the counts de Périgord is one of rapacity, greed, and misgovernment, and their victims were most often not their own enemies or those of France, but their vassals and servants. In the twelfth century, for example, Hélie I, on a whim, ordered the Bishop of Limoges' eyes to be gouged out. The Viscount de Limoges then had Hélie arrested and thrown into a dungeon, with the intention of exacting an eye for an eye. Hélie escaped a short time later, but not before tasting the sweetness of vengeance in his own way: He impregnated the viscount's only daughter. Another Hélie gave evidence of a different temperament, and one which was to prefigure that of a Talleyrand in a later age. He was a churchman and Dean of Richmond in the diocese of York. Pope John XXII made him a cardinal in 1331, and thereafter this Talleyrand reigned as the power behind the papal throne. Of him, Petrarch noted: "It amuses him to make popes rather than to be Pope."

In the early seventeenth century another Talleyrand—Henri, Count de Chalais—took an opposite tack and twice attempted to assassinate Cardinal Richelieu, omnipotent minister of Louis XIII. On the first occasion, the cardinal nobly forgave the count this aberration. On the second, he had him beheaded, by an apprentice executioner who took thirty-four strokes of the ax to do the job. Thereafter the representatives of the dynasty of Talleyrand-Périgord settled into less dangerous ways and became useful servants of church and state: soldiers, diplomats, and prelates.

The truth is that this conversion was not entirely of their own making, nor was it one that made them stand out from their contemporaries among the nobility. France, under the iron fist of Richelieu, was undergoing a great change in the first part of the century. Until then the most ancient nobility of the kingdom, including the Talleyrands, had held themselves aloof from the royal court. "Though they did not actually disdain to hold offices attached to the person of the sovereign," Prince Talleyrand was to explain many years later, "they displayed little eagerness to obtain them. They were content to believe, or at least to pretend to believe, that they themselves were the greatest personages in the land. Thus, the descendants of the ancient great vassals of the crown were less known to the king than the descendants of some minor barons. . . . The pride which induced most families of high lineage to keep aloof from the court caused the king to view them with less favor." Actually, it was not so much the aloofness of the ancient nobility that caused king and cardinal to "view them with less favor" as the independence from the crown and the defiance of royal authority that this attitude symbolized. Richelieu's goals, as he defined them, were "first, the glory of the king and, second, the power of the state." Neither of these could permit a virtually autonomous and semifeudal nobility. So, "in order to enhance the royal power, Cardinal Richelieu summoned the heads of the great families before the king, and they settled at court." Thus, the Montmorencys, Noailles, and Talleyrands of France, as well as other ancient dynasties of semisovereign princelings, were induced, by threats and blandishments, to forsake their independence and move into the royal orbit. The reign of Louis XIV and the glory thereof completed the process of taming the nobility. These men, whose forebears had thought nothing of challenging one King of France to his face—or of attempting to assassinate the chief minister of another—now could not "conceive any power or glory other than that which proceeded from the king's majesty" and "all men's dreams were centered within the limits of the chateau of Versailles." The motto of the House of Talleyrand-Périgord, *Ré qué Diou*—"No King but God"—remained; but its meaning was now forgotten in a whirl of court ceremonies, and its significance was dimmed by the luster of ten thousand candles glistening in the great Hall of Mirrors at Versailles. The Sun King was at his zenith, and lesser lights had to be content simply to reflect his splendor.

The Talleyrands, while they basked with their peers in the radiance of the throne, did not forget how to fight. It was not by low bows and polite conversation that they had won and held, since time immemorial, their many titles: counts of Grignols, princes of Chalais, marquis d'Excideuil, marquis de Talleyrand-Périgord. But now they fought not against other Frenchmen, but against the king's enemies and under the king's command. One Talleyrand, Gabriel, was killed at the siege of Barcelona in 1714, and Gabriel's son, Louis-Charles, met the same fate at the Battle of Tournai, in 1745. Before his death Gabriel, with the instinct for survival that had characterized his ancestors for almost a thousand years, had contracted a fortunate, if not a felicitous, marriage with one of France's great heiresses: Marie-Elizabeth Chamillart, granddaughter of Colbert, illustrious and ingenious Minister of Finance under Louis XIV. Marie-Elizabeth's mother was Marie-François de Rochechouart, daughter of the Duke de Mortemart, who had married Colbert's daughter. In addition to her dowry, the new Marquise de Talleyrand had contributed several qualities to her husband's family: From her father came a nobility as illustrious as that of the Talleyrands and an intellectual and verbal agility that was so pronounced and so famous as to pass into the language of the era as *l'esprit Mortemart* —"the Mortemart wit." From her mother's side, she had brought a talent, equally famous and somewhat more practical, for accumulating money. There were some who would say, in later years, that the infant Charles-Maurice de Talleyrand had come by his repartee and his cupidity honestly enough.

The Marquis de Talleyrand and his wife, Charles-Maurice's grandparents, had several children, two of whom would leave their marks on history, though for different reasons. One, Charles-Daniel, Count de Périgord, would, in 1751, marry Mademoiselle de Damas d'Antigny and, three years later, sire Charles-Maurice de Talleyrand. The other was named Alexandre-Angélique, and he, through his family's connections and a natural tendency toward piety, was to become Duke-Archbishop of Rheims and, later, Cardinal-Archbishop of Paris.

Talleyrand's parents, as has been remarked, were comparatively poor. Despite their distinguished lineage and their resounding titles, their income was not sufficient to maintain them in the style which their obligations, at least in their own judgment, required of them. This inconvenience, however, was made tolerable to the count and countess by their possession of something even rarer, in that era of prearranged marriages, than money: conjugal bliss. So close was their union, and so obvious their mutual fidelity and affection, that the couple were almost an embarrassment to their friends at court. Love, let alone happiness in marriage, while perhaps appropriate to the solid bourgeoisie of France, was considered by the nobles to be inappropriate, if not actually alien, to their own rank and station.* It is possible that their attachment to each other was so all-absorbing as to make it difficult for them to feel or to show real parental affection for their children. What is certain is that Charles-Maurice, from the day of his birth, was virtually ignored by the Count and Countess de Périgord. The reason may have been, at least in part, that it was not yet the fashion for parents to pretend to live solely for the sake of their children. Romanticism and "sensibility" were as yet virtually unknown, and it would have seemed un-

* The memoirs of the period abound with maxims and anecdotes illustrating this wholly eighteenth-century concept of marriage. One duke, on his wedding day, instructed the new duchess as follows: "I will allow you every possible latitude, except footmen and princes of the blood." (The nonroyal dukes were engaged in a century-old battle with the princes over their respective prerogatives.) Another duke, upon finding his wife *in flagrante* with her lover, upbraided her for her lack of discretion. "What," he asked, "if someone else had found you like this?" And the Duke de Richelieu, one of the great rakes of his time, upon refusing permission for his daughter to marry a nobleman of no distinction, consoled the girl by pointing out that "If you truly love each other, there is no reason why, after your marriage to someone of your own rank, you should not continue to see each other."

usual for parents to occupy themselves unduly with the upbringing and education of their offspring. This was particularly true of the nobility and,
above all, of the court nobility. The children of the wealthier nobles were
usually raised in the houses of their parents but, very frequently, were entrusted entirely to the care of servants—which meant, in effect, that they
were left to shift for themselves.* The less affluent lords and ladies of the
court made use of another expedient: They entrusted their offspring to the
care of *une femme du peuple*—"a woman of the people"—or a peasant or
bourgeois family. In neither instance were the parents regarded as remiss
in their duties or as lacking in love toward their children. Family sentiment
in France at that time was as strong as, or stronger than, in later ages, but
it was a sentiment which embraced the family as a whole and as a group
rather than any particular individual within the familial group. Parental
obligation required not that the mother and father lavish attention and
love upon a child, but that they advance the fortunes and position of the
family by "providing for" the child. That is, by arranging an advantageous
marriage and, as Talleyrand explained, by securing for their child the highest offices within their reach.

Whatever the justification in the case of little Charles-Maurice, the fact
remains that no sooner had he been christened on February 2, 1754, than
he was turned over to someone whom Talleyrand identifies only as "a
woman," adding that she lived in "an outlying district of Paris"—probably
the Faubourg St.-Jacques. The child remained there until the age of four,
and of that period of his life very little is known. Talleyrand himself records only one incident: "At the age of four, I was still there, when I acci-
dentally fell from the top of a chest and dislocated my foot." This, in all
probability, was the origin of the pronounced limp that was to become a
source of so much anguish to the child, and later to the man, and of so
much amusement to his enemies. "Talleyrand's talons," Sainte-Beuve was
to call his feet. Even this, however, is somewhat uncertain. A cousin, the
Abbé Maurice de Périgord, asserted, years later, that Charles-Maurice had
been born lame and, indeed, that each generation of the family produced
at least one clubfoot. It seems unlikely that the good abbé would know
more about it than Talleyrand's mother, and the latter, in describing her
children† to her own mother only a year after Charles-Maurice's birth,

* The same Duke de Richelieu whose advice to his daughter on marital fidelity seemed so strikingly modern tells us that, though heir to one of France's grandest and richest dukedoms, he was
brought up almost entirely under the lackadaisical supervision of one of his father's footmen. He
often went hungry, he records, and suffered bitterly from lack of adequate clothing in winter. But,
he adds, this was no worse than what was endured by most of his friends of the same rank and
age.

† Another child, a boy, had been born before Charles-Maurice, but he died at some point while
the latter was still an infant. The countess bore two children after Charles-Maurice: Archambaud

pointed out that they "are very lively and good-natured." There is no mention of a defect of any sort—and no hint of an infirmity that one might hope to conceal from the child's grandmother.*

It is possible that the woman to whose care Charles-Maurice had been entrusted was indifferent to or ignorant of the seriousness of the injury. It is more likely that she was simply a member of that social and economic class whose experience and means did not include the ministrations of medical science. The foot was left to heal itself as best it could, and the woman did not even inform the child's parents of the accident until several months afterward—that is, until it had become obvious that the injury was permanent.

The Count and Countess de Périgord, once informed of their son's accident, seem to have been genuinely concerned,† and after a series of consultations with various medical authorities, a belated attempt was made to correct the child's defect or at least to make it less painful for him to walk.** But it was too late. "The dislocation of my foot," Talleyrand remembered, "was already too far gone to be corrected. Even my other foot, since it had to bear the entire weight of my body, had grown weaker. Thus, I have remained lame for life."

Other than this reference to the accident that crippled him, Talleyrand has only this to say of the time immediately following his birth: "My early years were spent cheerlessly." The bleakness of these four years was to remain vivid in his memory all of his life. Many years later, in London, he was to recall that he had received one visit from his family during that time—from an uncle, who found him "dressed in rags, out in the snow chasing swallows."

(1762), who was to become his parents' heir, and Boson (1764). Both these younger sons were reared by their parents in the house belonging to the countess' father and mother, in the rue Garancière.

* A number of early historians and biographers believed, or at least wrote, that Talleyrand's infirmity was congenital and hereditary and that it was thus the result of a family weakness rather than of an accident. It is worth noting that these scholars, whose ideas were all formed at a time when it was generally believed that any deformity of the body was the reflection of a spiritual deficiency—a belief not entirely eradicated in the twentieth century—were uniformly unsympathetic to Talleyrand both as a man and as a statesman. One may recall that in the 1930's Franklin D. Roosevelt's crippled legs figured largely not only in scurrilous pamphlets circulated by his enemies, but even in cartoons occasionally published by supposedly reputable newspapers.

† Talleyrand's eminent biographer G. Lacour-Gayet refers to letters from the Countess de Talleyrand to a female relative in which she expresses her concern and describes the various corrective devices employed ("L'enfance de Talleyrand," *Revue de Paris,* 16 août 1926). Lacour-Gayet quotes only fragments of these letters, however, and to this date the originals have remained both unpublished and inaccessible.

** As a child Talleyrand was apparently unable to walk without the aid of a crutch. In later years he always carried a cane, upon which he leaned heavily, and wore a large rounded shoe with a metal frame which extended up his leg to the knee, where it was attached with a leather strap. This device is presently on display at the château of Valençay.

Shortly after his parents' discovery of his lameness, Charles-Maurice was removed from the care of his foster mother and sent to stay with his great-grandmother, the Princess de Chalais,* at her chateau in Chalais,† in the Périgord region of France. This lady, perhaps moved by news of his lameness, had asked for the boy—an act of thoughtfulness for which her great-grandson never ceased to be grateful. He was dispatched directly to her by coach without having even the opportunity to visit his own parents, who were still living in the rue Garancière, in the very shadow of St.-Sulpice in Paris, only a few miles distant from the Faubourg St.-Jacques. In the coach, a public conveyance, he was given over to a Madame Charlemagne for supervision during the journey—"a kindly woman," Talleyrand described her, many years later. The coach was bound for Bordeaux, and it was to deposit its young passenger at Chalais en route. The journey, some 300 miles, over rough roads, lasted for seventeen days. At the end of that time Madame Charlemagne released the boy into the arms of the waiting Princess de Chalais.

Until the time of his visit to Chalais, Charles-Maurice had known nothing of familial affection or of the warmth and security deemed necessary to the proper development of a child. Toward his parents, in later years, he seems to have felt little bitterness for this neglect. In speaking of his childhood, he remarks only that "My father held the same views as his mother concerning the upbringing of children whose parents enjoyed a position at court. Thus, mine was left more or less to take care of itself. Not through any indifference toward me, but owing to the attitude some people have that the best course is to do what everyone else does." Of his great-grandmother, however, he speaks only in the warmest terms. "Madame de Chalais was a most refined and distinguished lady. Her mind, her language, the dignity of her manners, the sound of her voice were enchanting." But his appreciation of her and of her place in his life went beyond these superficial qualities. Many years later, when he was an old man, he could not write of her in the *Mémoires* without being moved or without allowing his emotion to be seen through his words:

> She was the first member of my family who displayed any affection toward me and also the first who taught me the sweetness of filial love. God bless her for it. . . . To this day, her memory is precious to me. How often have I regretted her death. How many times, and with what bitterness,

* This was Marie-Françoise de Rochechouart, daughter of the Duke de Mortemart. She had first married the Marquis de Cany, by whom she had a daughter—the Countess de Périgord's mother. After the death of Cany, she had married Louis-Charles de Talleyrand, Prince de Chalais, Grandee of Spain, and head of the House of Talleyrand-Périgord. She was thus doubly related to Charles-Maurice.

† A small town in southwestern France, in the *département* of Charante south of Angoulême.

have I understood the importance of sincere affection from a member of one's own family. Such affection provides great comfort through the trials and troubles of life, when those who inspire it are near to us.

Indeed, between the great lady of seventy-two years and the crippled, lonely boy of four there sprang up an immediate and intense attachment and affection which, on the part of Charles-Maurice, was evoked by the simple fact of his acceptance by his great-grandmother. He himself, who had barely known his parents, who had been entrusted to the care of strangers since his birth, whose most important formative years had been "cheerless," was now given the affectionate approval for which he yearned. "I pleased her," he says simply, and "I always called her *grand'mère*, although she was my great-grandmother, because, I think, this made me feel closer to her."

The love which he was now free to give was sufficiently abundant to encompass not only Madame de Chalais, but her way of life and her environs. The child delighted in all that he saw and heard, and the memories of the two years spent at Chalais were to remain with him and influence him for the rest of his life. He noted with approval the courtesy and consideration with which his relative's friends and neighbors treated one another and their tenants. "In the provinces distant from the capital," Talleyrand explains, "a certain attention to dignity and position rules the relations between the members of the old aristocracy residing on their estates and the lesser nobles and the tenants on those estates. The chief nobleman of a province would have thought it unbecoming for him not to have been kind and polite. . . . As for the peasantry, their lord visited them only to assist them and to speak kind and comforting words . . . and the minor nobility endeavored to follow the example set for them by the leading aristocracy of their province. The manners of the Périgord nobility resembled their ancient castles. They were imposing and set upon firm foundations." This graciousness of manner and consideration of the dignity of his inferiors was a lesson which the boy would learn and retain the whole of his life. Napoleon was to say of him, "He had a gentle bearing, one that attached people to him." It was the example that he saw at Chalais, in the house of his great-grandmother, which had first sown the seed of this graceful quality in him. It was there, in the midst of portraits of his ancestors, warriors and churchmen and diplomats, that the future courtier, whose bearing and seigneurial air were to become a legend in Europe, was initiated into the social graces required by his rank and demanded by the usages of his time: how to enter and leave a room, how to bow with grace, how to compliment a lady, how to dress with elegance, and, above all, how never to bore one's companions.

The time I passed at Chalais [he wrote] made a lasting impression on me. The things that first impress the minds and eyes of children are those which determine their disposition and their inclinations in later life. . . . I am probably indebted to these years for the general lines of my conduct in life. If I have been capable of displaying affection and even tenderness without too much familiarity, if I have been able to give the impression of superiority without haughtiness, if I show consideration for age, then it was at Chalais, at the side of my grandmother, that I absorbed all these sentiments which surrounded my relatives in that district, and which they enjoyed with delight.

The life led by the household at Chalais has been vividly described in one of the few genuinely moving chapters of the *Mémoires,* in terms that evoke the love and admiration of the child for the aged relative who had given him a home. His grandmother, he tells us, surrounded herself by a miniature court composed of several gentlemen of ancient family, "whose deference and refined manners were mingled with the loftiest feelings." On Sunday these gentlemen accompanied the princess to mass, and each of them, as befitted noblemen of subordinate rank in the presence of a Princess de Chalais, "discharged toward her duties dignified by exquisite politeness." None of these gentlemen in attendance, however, were allowed to forget that the princess was not the only Talleyrand at mass. "A little chair, close to my grandmother's prie-dieu, was reserved for me," Talleyrand recalled.

After church, the princess, her great-grandson, and the gentlemen all returned to the chateau and went directly to a large room called the *apothécairerie*—the "healing room." Madame de Chalais installed herself in a large velvet armchair, behind a black lacquered table. Around her, on shelves "which were kept scrupulously clean," were jars filled with various curative ointments and potions. "The recipes for these," the *Mémoires* assure us, "had always been faithfully preserved at the castle, and every year they were prepared with the greatest care by the village surgeon and the pastor." Once everything was ready, Madame de Chalais gave the signal, and a chambermaid introduced into the room, one by one, "all the sick persons who required assistance and who had assembled in the next room."

As they entered, they were questioned by two Sisters of Mercy concerning their ailments. The sisters then prescribed the medication suited to the complaint, and the princess pointed out where that particular remedy was stored. Throughout all this, little Charles-Maurice stood next to Madame de Chalais, "as was my right, because of the closeness of our relationship." He was responsible for removing the linen for bandages from its drawer, "from which my grandmother herself cut what was required." In addition to the medicine prescribed, each patient then received some herbs from which to prepare a potion, some wine, "and always some other substantial relief, but that which most touched his heart were the kind and considerate words from the good lady who endeavored to alleviate his sufferings." The health of the peasants of Chalais must have been vigorous indeed to withstand the combined assault of the priest, the barber-surgeon, and the chatelaine. Yet it was not the curative effects of the lotions, potions, and bandages that was prized.

> More learned and elaborate drugs [Talleyrand points out] even if they had been distributed without charge by famous doctors, would have failed to attract so many of the poor and especially to do them so much good. Gentleness, respect, faith and gratitude, the chief means of cure for the lower classes, would have been absent. . . . Confidence is the most efficient of all remedies, and it is strongest when it proceeds from the solicitude of a lady of rank with whom all ideas of power and protection are connected.

That Talleyrand's ideas on psychogenic cures were considerably ahead of his time is interesting, but unimportant. What matters is the vividness of the impressions that he retained, when writing the *Mémoires* sixty years later, of the gentleness, goodness, and dignity of the first woman whom he had ever loved and respected. "The recollection of what I saw and heard during these early years of my life is extremely pleasant to my mind," he confesses. But the pleasure that he derived from life at Chalais was perhaps the least of it. It was there, at the side of Madame de Chalais, as a member of her little "court," that he first witnessed the sweetness of friendship and that he first experienced a strong attachment to women. Both these qualities were to combine, in later years, into a tenacity of affection which enabled him to calculate the duration of his attachments, to both friends and lovers, not in months or years, but in decades and half centuries. At Chalais, he had seen his *grand'mère* surrounded by the respectful admiration and love of neighbors and friends whom she had known all her life and whose sentiments she reciprocated until the day she died. Like the woman whom he loved with the purity and intensity of childhood's first love, he too would have friends whom he would cherish, with a curious indifference to their faults and failings, throughout his long life.

Under the Princess de Chalais' direction, Charles-Maurice's education for life took on a more formal aspect. During the time that he was there, he "learned at Chalais all that could possibly be learned in that place—that is, to read and write and, to a certain extent, to speak the *patois* of the province." It is not known who Talleyrand's first teacher was. It is unlikely that it was the princess herself, as pleasing as the picture thus conjured up might be of the elderly lady with her great-grandson at her knee. Such tasks were not undertaken by mothers, or even great-grandmothers, in the noble houses of the time. Sometimes a servant was entrusted with this responsibility. More often, the local curé was called upon to impart what he knew to the offspring of the house. It is more likely than not that, at Chalais, the priest, when not preaching or filling prescriptions, initiated the boy into the mysteries of the written language.

The years of Charles-Maurice's idyllic existence at Chalais ended as abruptly and unexpectedly as they had begun. When he had been there slightly more than two years, word arrived from Paris that the boy was to return to the city—not to live in his parents' house, as he might have wished, but to attend school at the Collège d'Harcourt.* The boy was desolate, and his grief was shared by the lady who had become his dearest relative on earth. "When we parted," he tells us, "I cried, and so did she, so great was her love for me." Then he climbed into the Bordeaux coach and was driven away. He and the princess were not to see each other again, for she died while he was at the *collège.*

The journey to Paris took seventeen days, and on the seventeenth day he disembarked in the city at the station in the rue d'Enfer—the Street of Hell. This was at eleven o'clock in the morning. He was met by a servant of his family and taken directly to the Collège d'Harcourt, "where by noon I was seated at dinner."

The agony of leaving Chalais and the old princess apparently had been made bearable for the boy by the thought that at the end of the seemingly endless journey, he would find his parents waiting. His reaction at being met by a stranger and thrust immediately into the midst of other strangers had not abated by the time that he recorded his recollections more than half a century later: "I had been painfully impressed by being hurriedly sent to the school without first having been taken to my mother and father. I was then eight years old, and my father had never seen me. I was told—and I believed it—that all this hurry was due to some unforeseen and unavoidable circumstance." The Count and Countess de Périgord, it seemed, were prevented by their obligations elsewhere from meeting their son. There is no indication that they expressed or felt the least interest in the appearance of this son, his health, or his character. The child, with all of a child's willingness to believe that he was loved, could not but be overwhelmed by this rejection. "I felt myself isolated," he said, "helpless, shut up within myself." It is a theme that recurs throughout the chapters of the *Mémoires* dealing with Talleyrand's childhood and youth: cheerlessness, sadness, isolation, rejection.

* The Collège d'Harcourt was, at the time, one of the most distinguished schools in Paris. It was also the oldest, having been founded in 1280. Except for a quarter-century interval during and after the Revolution, when its building served as a prison, the institution has had an unbroken existence to this day. It is presently known as the Lycée St.-Louis.

This is not to say the Collège d'Harcourt had no consolations to offer to a boy whose mind and emotions had just been awakened by the experience of Chalais. "I got on pretty well," he says, with a touch of pride. "My schoolmates liked me, and I adjusted cheerfully to my new situation." He was helped along by the presence in the *collège* of one of his Talleyrand cousins, the son of the Count de la Suze,* whose lodgings and tutor he shared. This help seems to have been of a purely social nature, for neither La Suze nor his tutor, the Abbé Hardi, were equipped to enjoy or transmit the pleasures of the mind. "If I succeeded at all in my studies," Talleyrand said, "that result cannot be attributed either to the example of my cousin or to the talents of my teacher." The deficiencies of his cousin, however, were more than compensated for by Charles-Maurice's discovery at the *collège* of another boy, Auguste de Choiseul-Beaupré,† the first real friendship of his own age. This mutual attraction was to endure until Choiseul's death almost sixty years later, and the two friends were to remain constantly in touch, although the pursuit of their respective careers would deprive them of each other's company for long periods of time. Charles-Maurice had found a replacement, at a different level, for the love with which he had been surrounded at Chalais, and with the tenacity that characterized all his attachments, he was to cherish and preserve one as carefully as he did the other. Of Choiseul, Talleyrand wrote in 1815: "He shared, and still shares, all the cares, pleasures, and dreams of my life."

Charles-Maurice was fortunate in his relationship with Choiseul, for if he had had to depend on the affection and attention of his parents, his years at the Collège d'Harcourt would have been very bleak indeed. There is no evidence that the Count and Countess de Périgord ever visited the school or even that they made any special effort to find the means with which to pay the costs entailed by the education of their son and heir. So far as these expenses were concerned, it is significant that years later, when Charles-Maurice first had an income of his own, he immediately began sending sums to his former teacher at the *collège* in payment for the instruction received there. The boy did, however, have the opportunity at least to see his parents on a regular basis. "Once a week, the Abbé Hardi called with me on my parents, and we dined with them." Of such visits, Talleyrand says very little. It would not be unfair to assume that these dinners were formal and ritualistic affairs, in which the boy, like all children of

* The Count de la Suze was the son of Talleyrand's paternal grandmother by her earlier marriage to Louis-Michel Chamillard. Upon Chamillard's death, she married Daniel-Marie, Prince de Talleyrand, Charles-Maurice's grandfather.

† Choiseul was the nephew of the Duke de Choiseul, who was then chief minister to King Louis XV. In later life the boy was to add the name of his wife to his own and become known in history as Choiseul-Gouffier, ambassador to Constantinople, peer of France, minister of state, and member of the Council of Louis XVIII until his death in 1817.

his age, was expected to sit quietly and speak only when addressed directly. The only words of his parents that he recalls were admonitory in nature: "On leaving, I regularly heard the very same words: 'Be a good boy, and try to please M. l'Abbé.' "

For the first three years at the *collège,* life followed the same pattern. The boy seemed happy enough with the friendship of Choiseul and the approbation of his schoolmates, and his natural keenness of mind enabled him to overcome both the ineptitude of some of his teachers* and the tendency, common among children of his rank, not to regard his studies as a serious preparation for life. Indeed, he immersed himself in his work with such eagerness and such contentment that in later years he seems to have looked back nostalgically upon this period of his life and to have experienced a very mild sort of regret that he had been obliged to forsake the tranquillity of Academe for the rigors of public life. "I might have been a successful scholar," he said. "My natural inclinations lead me to think so, and this opinion, I notice, is shared by almost all of my [former] schoolmates. The little encouragement given me, for fear that I should become too clever a boy, is the reason why the first years of my life were spent in a rather dull and insignificant manner." His success was so brilliant that he seems, for the most part, to have escaped the sting of the whip which was at that time the universal stimulus applied to recalcitrant students. The first time that he was threatened with this punishment he was so mortified that he ran away from the school and turned up a short time later at his parents' house. "My pride as a nobleman," he said, "would not allow me to endure such an indignity." He therefore turned to the only person who he thought was in a position to offer both understanding and protection: his father. In this, he was disappointed. "My son," the Count de Périgord said, "one of our ancestors, Henri de Talleyrand,† Count de Chalais, became the favorite of Louis XIII because the king remembered that in his youth your ancestor had allowed himself to be whipped in his place." So the boy was returned to the *collège* to face his whipping. If a Count de Chalais and,

---

* Talleyrand was not very fortunate in his teachers at the Collège d'Harcourt. After the Abbé Hardi, of whom the boy had a low opinion, he was turned over to a tutor named Hullot, who soon gave signs of advanced dementia and had to be put away. The madman was replaced by a M. Langlois, "who was a perfect gentleman, but who knew nothing but French history." So taken was Langlois by the glories of France's nobility that he seems to have spent much of his time conniving to obtain a share of it for himself. Since Talleyrand's uncle, the Count de la Suze, was Grand Marshal of the Royal Household at this period, M. Langlois was able to secure for himself, through his charge at the *collège,* the patent that he desired so avidly. Thereafter he seems to have thought teaching to be beneath his newfound dignity. "It may be concluded," noted Talleyrand, "that if I have since then succumbed to the temptation to play a part in public affairs, the responsibility is in no way that of M. Langlois."

† This was the same Count de Chalais who was beheaded in 1626 for plotting to assassinate Richelieu—a detail to which Talleyrand's father, in his eagerness to explain the value of a whipping, seems not to have alluded.

indeed, a King of France could bear the humiliation of a beating, a scion of the House of Talleyrand must do no less.

At the end of Charles-Maurice's third year his studies were brusquely interrupted by an attack of one of the most dreaded and fatal diseases of the time: smallpox. Since it was contagious, he was required to leave the school. But it was not to his parents that he went. The Count and Countess de Périgord, upon learning of Charles-Maurice's condition, sent word that he was not to come to the rue Garancière. If he could not remain at the school, then he must be taken to the house of a Madame Lerond in the rue St.-Jacques, where he would be cared for. Neither parent thought it necessary to visit the stricken child. Instead, they sent two servants, carrying a sedan chair, to convey the boy to the woman who was to nurse him. Charles-Maurice, once there, was subjected to the treatment customary at that time, which seemed to consist chiefly in an attempt to suffocate the patient. "In those days, victims of smallpox slept in beds surrounded by double curtains. The windows of their room were kept closed and sealed against air, and a blazing fire was kept up." The boy's constitution, however, seemed proof even against the medical science of his age. "In spite of this murderous treatment—which killed many other people—I recovered from the disease. I was not even marked."

During the long period of convalescence, Charles-Maurice had much time to think, and his thoughts were not happy. "My mind was full of concern at the little interest aroused by my illness, by the fact of my having been sent to college without ever having seen my parents, and by other sad memories." This theme of resentment for the indifference of his parents was one that recurred occasionally during his life. Yet he is guarded in expressing too openly the bitterness that he obviously felt over this continuous rejection, and the *Mémoires* touch on the subject with a brevity that is itself revealing. "I may say, once and for all, without ever allowing myself to think of it again, that I am perhaps the only member of a large and distinguished family who never, in his entire life, had the good fortune to spend one single night under the same roof as his parents." He never really forgave his mother and father for this neglect. In the *Mémoires*, however, which were written for posterity, Talleyrand's bitterness is minimized, and he even attempts to explain the sins of his parents in terms favorable to them:

> In my later life, it has occurred to me that my parents, having decided, out of family considerations, that I was to be trained for a profession for which I had demonstrated no aptitude, were afraid that they would not be able to carry out this plan if they saw me too often. This fear is a proof of their affection for me, and I am grateful for it.

He was even willing, in this public expression of gratitude for neglect, generously to outline the benefits that he had derived from it:

> I do not complain of it, for I believe that my early impressions developed and strengthened my intellectual powers. My sad and dreary childhood caused me to exercise these powers at an early age and to think more deeply than perhaps I would have done had my early years been filled with happiness and joy. It may also be that these first disappointments of my life taught me to bear misfortune and disappointment with indifference, and to meet such things with the resources which my self-knowledge taught me that I possessed.

This generous posture, dictated no doubt by Talleyrand's strong sense of family loyalty, was not always sustained in private in the years to come. The resentment, frustration, and bitterness of the child were so strong that they occasionally erupted in the adult. A Swiss gentleman named Dumont, who knew Talleyrand rather well during the revolutionary epoch, records:

> I heard him say many times that since he had been rejected by his parents and since he was regarded by them as a burden and a good-for-nothing, he had turned into a sad and taciturn child. He said that he had never in his life spent a night in his parents' house and that they had forced him to renounce his rights as the eldest child in favor of his younger brother.

Family loyalty, a natural generosity of spirit, and an understandable tendency to minimize the unpleasantness of his experiences with his parents— all these things would, in later years, perhaps enable Talleyrand to forgive the Count and Countess de Périgord for the slights he had suffered at their hands. But to forget these injuries was beyond his power. He saw their vestiges in the depths of his character and their imprint on every significant act of his life.

In 1769, Charles-Maurice was still unaware of the extent to which his parents would affect that life. He was in his fifteenth year, and it was a time of decision. He had reached, as he put it, "the time of what is called the *conclusion of studies.*" A decision had to be made concerning his future. Or rather, a decision had already been made, and it was now time for it to be implemented. Of the course to be followed, Charles-Maurice had only a general idea. "I had received the first intimations through certain vague references that I heard about me." But these hints had not prepared him for the suddenness or for the reality of what lay in store. Talleyrand's parents, in consultation with the boy's uncle, Alexandre-Angélique, who was then Coadjutor Archbishop of Rheims, had determined that their eldest son must enter the church. "Since my lame foot made me incapable of serving in the army," Talleyrand explained, "I must necessarily enter holy orders. No other career was open to a man of my rank." This, of course, necessitated that Talleyrand relinquish his prerogatives as the eldest son of the House of Talleyrand. These rights must go to one who would perpetuate the dynasty through legitimate issue—a task to which an ordained priest, vowed to eternal chastity, was clearly unequal. So the family conclave had decided the matter: Charles-Maurice would enter the church, and his younger brother Archambaud would become the family heir.

None of this was communicated immediately to the boy, who was thus stripped of his rights. Instead, he was ordered by his parents, as soon as his studies had been terminated, to go to Rheims, on an extended visit to the house of his uncle. And "since it was not fitting for me to arrive at the archbishop's palace in a public conveyance, my journey to Rheims was more comfortable than that to Chalais had been. A post chaise called for me at the Collège d'Harcourt and drove me to my destination in a couple of days. My parents did not ask me to visit them before I left." It was at Rheims, upon his arrival, that the boy was informed of what the future held for him. He was to prepare himself to take holy orders, and he was to begin by donning the soutane—the cassock, which would officially and formally set him apart from the world of which he had as yet learned nothing.

There was logic of a sort behind the decision of the Count and Countess de Périgord to send their son to Rheims. Charles-Maurice, although the eldest of their children, because of his lameness had been relegated to the status of a younger son and, as such, destined for the church. The boy had shown no interest in such a career, no natural tendency toward it, and no particular aptitude for it. He must therefore be presented with an object lesson. He must be shown that the church was a means of realizing the highest ambitions and of satisfying the grandest designs. He must also come to know that the apparent austerity demanded in theory of priests did not, in practice, apply to every priest in every case. Nowhere in France was there a city better suited than Rheims to impress all these things upon the mind of a boy of fifteen. And there was no prelate who embodied and illustrated all the advantages and privileges of the ecclesiastical state more strikingly than the reigning Duke-Archbishop of Rheims, Charles-Antoine de la Roche-Aymon.*

The venerable duke-archbishop had attained his rank by the means customary in his time. He was the youngest son of a family as distinguished and almost as ancient as that of young Charles-Maurice. He had entered the church because he had little taste for the comparative rigors of military

---

* Talleyrand's uncle, Alexandre-Angélique, was coadjutor to this prelate—that is, he had been named archbishop with the right of succession—a right which he was to exercise upon the death of Roche-Aymon in 1777.

life and notwithstanding a preference, manifested early in life, for the pleasures of bed and board rather than for those of the divine office. The influence of his family and his own assiduous pursuit of advancement had given him a bishopric in 1725, at the age of twenty-seven. He was Archbishop of Toulouse in 1740 and Grand Almonier of France in 1760. The see of Rheims, the wealthiest, most prestigious diocese of France, had fallen to him in 1762. And he was destined in his old age to wear the scarlet multitasseled hat of a prince of the church. All this he achieved without making so much as a pretense of cultivating the sacerdotal virtues of poverty and chastity. In the luxury of his house and the magnificence of his life he rivaled and outshone the princes of the blood. No fewer than fifty guests sat down to dinner with the archbishop every day of the week, and they feasted from vessels of silver and gold in each of the several palaces that he owned. When he traveled, it was in the style of a sovereign, surrounded by a great retinue of outriders, guards, secretaries, and chaplains and with eight horses drawing his carriage. His time was spent, not in meditation and prayer or even in discharging his vast responsibilities to his church, but in hunting in his forests, organizing entertainments for his guests, and devising compliments for one or the other of the ladies who had caught his fancy. For this great prelate's chastity was as fictive as his love of poverty. The lady of his house, as well as of his heart, as everyone in France knew, was a certain Madame de Rothe, who could come and go in the palace without compromising herself too openly—for she was the archbishop's niece.

This was the ecclesiastical household into which Charles-Maurice was thrust by his parents so that he might contemplate the advantages offered by a career in the church. There he found every element that might appeal to his senses or excite his ambition—two approaches to which the various representatives of the family had, through the centuries, seemed especially partial. All that he had to do in order to open the door to such a world for himself was to enter the seminary and, in a few years, offer himself for ordination to the priesthood. Yet the boy seemed immune to it all:

> My frame of mind was such that I looked upon my new residence as a poorly disguised place of exile, notwithstanding all the care taken to make it attractive to me. The opulence, the rank, and the very pleasures of the Archbishop of Rheims and of his coadjutor were a matter of indifference to me. At the age of fifteen, when all our instincts are still in their natural state, we can hardly believe that circumspection—that is, the art of revealing only a part of one's actions, thoughts, feelings, and impressions—is the most important of all qualities. So, in my opinion, all the wealth and pomp of the Cardinal de la Roche-Aymon could not justify the sacrifice of my sincerity that was required of me.

His apparent indifference must have become evident to his uncle or to his parents (for they occasionally took the trouble to visit Rheims to study the progress of their son along the path that they had laid out for him); they therefore tried another tack, one calculated to appeal less to his passions and more to his mind:

> The only plan then was to hold out to me the attraction of public life and to point out the advantages that were to be obtained from it. They thus sought to appeal to the talents that I happened to possess, and with this end in view I was induced to read the *Mémoires* of Cardinal de Retz,* those of Cardinal Ximenes,† and of Hincmar, a former Cardinal of Rheims.** My parents were willing to agree to any path that I chose—so long as I entered upon it by crossing the threshold of the church."

The example of great prelates who had also been great statesmen was, no doubt, impressive and opened up an avenue of thought that had not yet occurred to Charles-Maurice. "Youth," he confesses, "is the time when we are most honest. I could not understand at that time what it was to embrace one profession with the intention of following another, to assume a mask of constant self-denial so as to succeed in one's ambitions, to enter the church in order to become a Minister of Finance. Such understanding required too great a knowledge of the society that I was entering and of the times in which I was living for me to be able to accept this as a matter of course." He was, to put it simply, confused, and the elaborate scheme prepared by his parents and the Coadjutor Archbishop of Rheims, "rather than enabling me to make up my mind, had the opposite effect." Worse yet, there was no one to whom Charles-Maurice could turn for disinterested advice. The stage had been carefully set, and the actors well chosen. "All the persons who surrounded me spoke a conventional language and carefully concealed from me any way by which I might avoid carrying out the plan that my parents had for my future." He must therefore depend upon his own resources and observations for guidance. Madame de Genlis, who was a guest in the archiepiscopal palace during the boy's sojourn there, was perceptive enough to sense something of the moral quandary in which he found himself. "He limped a little," she wrote, "and he was pale

* Archbishop of Paris, rival and eventually victim, of Cardinal Mazarin. He played a leading part in the Fronde, the uprisings against the authority of the crown that characterized the minority of Louis XIV in the mid-seventeenth century.

† Ximenes, or Jiménez, was regent of Castile (1506) and grand inquisitor of Spain. He is remembered as a great and just, if remarkably bloodthirsty, administrator and statesman.

** A close friend, adviser, and defender of Charlemagne's immediate successors, Hincmar is regarded as one of the most influential figures in the history of Carolingian France. (He was not, however, a cardinal as Talleyrand claims. The Sacred College was founded in 1069—almost two centuries after Hincmar's death.)

and silent. But what struck me most was the impression that he gave of being an *observer*." His own mother was less acute in sensing his confusion and his aloofness. "My son is very happy in his new surroundings," she wrote gaily to her relatives.

The struggle between Talleyrand's native integrity and his natural wish to please his family lasted for a year. It was, in truth, an unequal contest. However revolted he might be at the prospect of assuming "a mask of self-denial so as to succeed in one's ambitions," however bitter might be his resentment at the society which decreed that "I must necessarily enter holy orders, as no other career was open to a man of my name," there was never any real possibility that he might refuse to follow the orders of the Count and Countess de Périgord. There was, in fact, no alternative to the church for the "younger" son of an illustrious, but impoverished, dynasty. And there is no doubt that, unconsciously, the boy was profoundly impressed by the splendor and gaiety that he had seen in the life of the Duke-Archbishop of Rheims. His own later life was to furnish ample proof that despite his protestations, the lesson devised by his family had not been wasted.

So, at the end of a year in his uncle's care, he submitted. He would enter the seminary: "Seeing that my fate could not be avoided, my wearied mind surrendered, and I allowed myself to be taken to the Collège of St.-Sulpice." *

* The theological seminary of the Parisian archdiocese, founded in the middle of the sixteenth century by the pastor of the parish of St.-Sulpice, Jean-Jacques Ollier. It was (and is) conducted by the society, also founded by M. Ollier, known as the Priests of St.-Sulpice and is known now, as it was in Talleyrand's time, for both the excellence of its instruction and the conservatism of its faculty.

2

A Priest
in Spite of Himself

TALLEYRAND remained at St.-Sulpice for five years, from 1769 to
1774. They were uniformly miserable years. "I was so unhappy," he
told the Duchess de Dino many decades later, "that for my first two
years in the seminary I hardly spoke to anyone." The *Mémoires* say that he
spent three years without speaking. Whatever the case, it is certain that he
was profoundly unhappy and that his unhappiness had the effect of depriving him of the one consolation that was available to him within the walls of
St.-Sulpice: the companionship of his confreres. He was not accepted by
his classmates as he had been at the Collège d'Harcourt. "People thought I
was haughty and often reproached me for it. When they did, I did not
bother to reply, for it seemed to me if they had known me better, they
would not have thought so. But then they said that my arrogance was
beyond endurance. Good God! I was neither haughty or arrogant. I was
merely an innocent adolescent, and an extremely miserable and confused
one." He was also rebellious, and this, perhaps more than unhappiness,
was at the root of his isolation from his fellows. "I had a grudge against my
teachers, my parents, and against institutions generally—but especially
against the concept of 'social propriety' to which I had been forced to surrender."

His frustration and resentment against the system which had forced him
to don the cassock did not cloud his judgment. He was a seminarian
against his will, and he would be a priest against his will. So be it. Since his
fate was, to all appearances, irrevocably decided, he must make the best of
it. He therefore devoted himself seriously to his studies and acquired a rep-

34

utation within the seminary as a gifted student. His mind, however, was not satisfied with the intellectual exercises provided for in the curriculum of St.-Sulpice. There is no evidence that he ever exhibited anything more than an academic interest in theology, either as a science or as an art. His formal studies were a key—a key to the great world that lay beyond the Place de St.-Sulpice; a key which, once his courses had been completed, would open doors leading to high places. Despite Talleyrand's protestations to the contrary, the seed planted so clumsily at Rheims had taken root. "People said, I often thought to myself, that I was fit for nothing. Then, after giving way to despondency for a few moments, a strong and comforting feeling would come over me, and I would feel that I was indeed fit for something—even for good and noble deeds!"

Both his intellectual hunger and his dreams of noble deeds found satisfaction in the library of the college. "Its works were numerous and carefully selected, and I spent my days there reading the works of the great historians, the private lives of statesmen and moralists, and a few poets . . . the description of a country bearing traces of great changes, sometimes of upheavals, had great interest for me." In later years, he explained to the Duchess de Dino precisely the sort of inspiration that he derived from these books:

> I lived silently and alone, spending my hours of recreation in the library, where I chose and devoured the most revolutionary books I could find. I fed my mind with histories of revolts, seditions, and revolutions in every land. I was myself rebelling against society, for I could not understand why, because I had been afflicted with an infirmity from childhood, I should be debarred from occupying my natural position.

Tallyrand's choice of books is revealing. He was ambitious, and he was rebellious. Ambition he nurtured by studying the careers of men who had, like himself, aspired to great and noble acts—and who, moreover, had found the means to fulfill those aspirations. His resentment and rebelliousness against society led him to the study of revolts and revolutions in every land, and from these books he carefully selected that which his own, heretofore limited experience told him was useful and applicable to his own time: "My third and really useful education," he tells us, "dates from this time. It was self-taught, in lonely silence. I was always face to face with the author whose work I was reading, and I had only my own judgment to rely on. It nearly always happened that when my opinion differed from that of an author, I concluded that mine was correct. My ideas thus remained my own. The books I read enlightened my mind but never enslaved it." Thus were spent Talleyrand's years of apprenticeship in preparing for a career of which he still dreamed only vaguely. He was gathering ammunition and forging his armor for the future. It was a future that still remained distant, inscrutable, but nonetheless exciting. "A feeling of hope, nebulous and indescribable, like all youthful passions, excited my mind. I never allowed it to rest."

There was another youthful passion, more basic than hope, which also excited the young seminarian's mind at this time. His training at the archiepiscopal court of Rheims and his sense of isolation at St.-Sulpice led to a logical, if not wholly inevitable, result: Talleyrand fell in love.

"By the merest chance," he confesses, "I met a person who had some influence in modifying my state of mind. I recall this meeting with pleasure, because I probably owe to it the fact that I was spared the effects of melancholy in its most acute form." At the time Talleyrand was eighteen and in his second year at St.-Sulpice. He had reached the age at which his passions and emotions were ripe and ready to "break forth in superabundant and full activity." It was in this state that he had noticed, not once but several times, in one of the chapels of the Church of St.-Sulpice, "a handsome young lady whose simple and modest appearance pleased me extremely." The sight of the girl had a predictable effect upon Talleyrand, and he, who had never shown signs of unusual piety, now began to manifest remarkable diligence in attending services at St.-Sulpice. Still, he could not bring himself to speak to the girl. A cassock-clad seminarian, even a Talleyrand and even under the *ancien régime,* could not approach a strange young lady in a place of worship, at least not without some plausible pretext.

The pretext so assiduously sought was soon found. "One day, as she left the church, a severe shower began, and I found the courage to offer to see her home, provided she did not live too far. She agreed to share my umbrella. I accompanied her to the rue Férou." The distance between the rue Férou and St.-Sulpice is very slight, and apparently the two young people had more to say to one another than could be encompassed in that span, for the girl—Dorothée was her name*—invited her escort into her apartment. "And since she was a very proper young lady, she proposed that I come to call again."

Thereafter Talleyrand called at the rue Férou often; twice a week at first, he tells us, and "more often thereafter"—probably every day. The couple, aside from their obvious differences in rank and their stations in life, had a great deal in common. Dorothée, Talleyrand discovered, had been forced onto the stage, against her will, by her parents, out of ambition

* The *Mémoires* do not, of course, give the girl's name. On the basis of the information actually provided, however, combined with a bit of ingenious detective work, Lacour-Gayet was able to ascertain that she was called Dorothée Dorinville and that she was a minor player at the Théâtre Française where she was known under the professional name of Lurzy, or Luzy (*Talleyrand,* Vol. I, p. 88).

and out of the desire to be rid of her. He, for related motives, was being forced unto the altar. "This situation brought about unreserved and mutual confidence between us. All the troubles of my life, my fits of ill humor, her own disappointments and tribulations were the subject of our conversations." The emotional release provided by Dorothée's affection and the need satisfied by the presence of one in whom Talleyrand could at last confide were the basis of this first and perhaps sweetest of all his loves. In his old age, he recalled it with fondness and delight and even with a touch of loyalty to the girl who, almost a half century before, had taught him that there was more to life than books, or family, or even ambition. "I have been told since that time that she was not clever," he wrote, "but I never had occasion to notice it myself."

The effect of this new relationship, which lasted for two years—that is, for the remainder of his stay at St.-Sulpice—was immediate and obvious. "I became, even in college, more amiable or, at any rate, better-tempered. My superiors cannot have failed to have had some suspicion of what had reconciled me to my position and even made me almost cheerful." Indeed, they could hardly avoid having such suspicions, for it seems that, at the age of eighteen, Talleyrand had already acquired that total lack of regard for the approval of his associates that was to become so marked in his later career. He did what seemed necessary and left it to others to argue over whether it was right or wrong. In this case, he made no attempt to conceal his liaison from his superiors at the seminary or from his confreres. He went openly to his rendezvous with Dorothée in the Church of St.-Sulpice, and openly he accompanied her back to her apartment in the rue Férou, wearing his soutane. If this be sin, he seemed to feel, then let them make the best of it. And make the best of it they did. The superior of St.-Sulpice a few years previously had been a man named Couturier, who was wise and experienced in the ways of the world. From the Abbé Couturier, the priests of St.-Sulpice had learned "the art of being blind when it was necessary to be so. He had taught them that they must never find fault with a student who was regarded as destined to fill high posts, to become coadjutor to the Archbishop of Rheims, perhaps a cardinal, perhaps even *Ministre de la Feuille*." * So Talleyrand explains, and it was doubtless so, to some extent. It is also reasonable to believe that the priests of St.-Sulpice cast an eye on the present at least as much as on the future and that they did not relish the prospect of dismissing or even of reprimanding the nephew of the Coadjutor Archbishop of Rheims for, of all things, an illicit liaison. A large number of the bishops and archbishops of the realm—

* The *Ministre de la Feuille* was the royal official—always a prelate—to whom was delegated the king's authority to distribute benefices. It was he who made and unmade bishops and archbishops in France.

upon whose benevolence the Collège of St.-Sulpice depended for its very existence—were too vulnerable in this respect to be pleased at the thought of the scandal that would ensue. In any event, the matter was passed over in silence, so far as official reaction was concerned, and the faculty and students of St.-Sulpice were relieved to note that young Talleyrand seemed to have overcome his tendency toward "haughtiness" and "arrogance." The social vices of silence and solitude had been overcome at the moment in which the reluctant seminarian's virtue had been lost. A few of his professors, it is true, expressed some private doubts about Talleyrand's total fitness for the priesthood; but the boy's sponsor and protector at Rheims dismissed these reports as irrelevant. With the family's goal already in sight, no boyish peccadillo could be allowed to impede Talleyrand's progress toward the altar and, eventually, toward the episcopal purple and perhaps even farther, to the scarlet robes of the Sacred College.

The first step in this ambitious progress was already at hand. In September, 1774, Talleyrand's formal thesis in theology was accepted by the faculty of the Sorbonne and he was awarded the degree of Bachelor of Sacred Theology. Thus fortified with the proper credentials, it was time for him to take the decisive step over the threshold of the church—that is, to receive the subdiaconate, the lowest of the major orders, and, simultaneously, as required by canon law, to pronounce the vows that would bind him, forever, to the virtues of chastity and obedience. Accordingly, early in April, 1775, he stood in the sanctuary of the Church of St.-Nicolas-du-Chardonnet in Paris, clad, for the first time, in the long white alb of his order and holding the subdiaconal tunic with which the officiating bishop was to invest him. The bishop, in a solemn tone, addressed to Talleyrand the ancient words required by the church: "This order, once received, can never be cast off, and you will be bound over forever to the service of God. Reflect, while there is yet time. But, if you persist in your holy resolution, then, in the name of the Lord, step forward."

Talleyrand took one step and then knelt at the prelate's feet. It was done. The vows had been taken, the doors to preferment had been opened, and the Count and Countess de Périgord had been victorious over the scruples of their overly sensitive son. But the parents seemed as indifferent to their victory as they had been to their son's misery. They did not choose to be present at their son's formal entry into the consecrated ranks of the clergy, and they sent no member of the family as their representative. The Abbé de Périgord, as Talleyrand was now called, was as alone as he had been when turned over to the "woman of the people" in the Faubourg St.-Jacques.

The *Mémoires* relate nothing of Talleyrand's feelings at this critical mo-

ment in his life. He says only that he "left college some time before the coronation of the king." * Of his attitude toward the irretraceable step that he
had just taken we know little for certain. It is highly unlikely, however, that
he was as phlegmatic as the single sentence in the *Mémoires* might lead one
to believe. The Bishop of Blois, a respectable and respected prelate, assures
us that Talleyrand was "in a devil of a mood on the day that he received
the subdiaconate." But the Bishop of Blois, so far as can be established,
was not present at the ceremony. A Sulpician priest, Monsieur de Cussac,
reports that Talleyrand told him: "They are forcing me to become a cleric,
but they will regret their decision." It is not impossible that the good Sulpician was trying at once to excuse Talleyrand's later conduct and to mitigate the guilt that he may have felt, as the new subdeacon's superior, for
allowing the ceremony to take place. All things considered, it is not farfetched to believe that the newly minted Abbé de Périgord was as actively
resentful as ever of the yoke imposed upon his unwilling neck. The very
brevity with which he passes over so important a moment in his life may
lead one to conclude that far from having finally consented in his heart to
embrace the clerical state, he had reached a pitch of disgust and disenchantment that permitted him to ignore the vows themselves with the same
aplomb with which he passes over the ceremony at which they were taken.
Certainly, there is not the slightest evidence in his behavior, either immediately after April, 1774, or in the following sixty years, that he ever gave a
serious thought to his vow of obedience and even less to that of chastity.

The next words in the *Mémoires* relate that Talleyrand's parents sent
him to Rheims to attend the coronation of King Louis XVI. Of corona-
tions, Talleyrand was to see aplenty in his long life; but this was the first
that he saw, and it was the last that France was to witness under the old regime, when the rite of coronation was regarded in much the same light as
the consecration of a bishop—that is, as a religious rite which placed the
indelible mark of divine approval upon the anointed of God. Louis XVI
was to be the last of the kings of France "by divine right." Yet the Abbé de
Périgord seems to have been wholly indifferent to the religious significance
of the splendid ceremony. He notes that the young king was "scrupulously
moral and uncommonly modest"; that Queen Marie-Antoinette's "affability, grace, and kindness tempered the austere virtues of her consort"; and
that "the heart of every subject overflowed with affection for the young
sovereigns." Then he explains what he found most significant in the ceremonies at Rheims: "My acquaintance with several women, remarkable in

* Louis XVI, who was crowned on June 11, 1775, thirteen months after the death of his grandfather, King Louis XV.

different ways and whose friendship never ceased to add enchantment to my life, dates from the coronation of Louis XVI." *

Talleyrand's ordination as a subdeacon had indeed changed his life, and it was not a change that limited itself to the freedom to make the acquaintance of remarkable and accommodating women of his own class. Now a permanent member of the clergy, he was in a position to take advantage of the opportunities of advancement that his parents and his archiepiscopal uncle of Rheims had described so glowingly in earlier years. Both, in fact, had already begun to redeem their promises. First, there came from the newly crowned King Louis XVI † a benefice—and a truly magnificent one —the Abbey of St.-Rémy at Rheims. The income of 18,000 livres was enough to provide the Abbé de Périgord with the necessities of life, and it was sufficient for him not to have to depend on the generosity of his parents—to his great relief and theirs. His uncle, too, did his share by causing Talleyrand to be elected a member of the Assembly of the Clergy from the province of Rheims, the purpose of which was to regulate the financial relations between church and state in France. Almost simultaneously, the coadjutor archbishop appointed him Promoter of the Assembly—which meant that it was now his duty to expose and prosecute delinquent clerics and generally to promote the rights, freedom, and discipline of the clergy.

As soon as the Assembly of 1775 was over—during which Talleyrand seems to have occupied himself, prudently, in listening to the opinions of his elders and not taking his new duties too literally—he entered the Sorbonne. For although he was the titular of benefices and Promoter of the Assembly, he had not yet completed the course of theological studies that were necessary for him if he was to be ordained a priest.

Talleyrand remained enrolled as a student at the Sorbonne for two years, until 1777, when he received his license in Sacred Theology, *nobilissimus*—with the greatest distinction. That he was able to do so was a tribute to the quality of the instruction he had received at St.-Sulpice, for, as he readily admits, his two years at the Sorbonne "were taken up with everything except theology, for pleasures occupy most of the time of a young graduate student." But, he adds, not all his time was spent in dissipation, for "ambition also takes up a share of one's days, and the memory of Car-

* The three women were Elizabeth de Montmorency-Laval, Duchess de Luynes; Marie de Thiard, Duchess de Fitz-James; and Catherine de Boullongne, Viscountess de Laval. Initially all three were to be something more than friends to Talleyrand, and he was, as he said, later to treasure their friendship into his old age and theirs.

† Some biographers—Orieux among them (p. 103)—seem to believe that these benefices were conferred upon Talleyrand through the intercession of the Countess du Barry, mistress of Louis XV. According to this imaginative tale, they were his recompense for an amusing retort to the effect that "Paris is a city in which it is easier to find a woman than a benefice." The story is entirely in character, both for Talleyrand and for the countess. It lacks credibility only because Du Barry fell from power too soon (April, 1774) to have had the opportunity to encounter the young man at Versailles.

dinal Richelieu, whose fine mausoleum was in the church of the Sorbonne, was not without a certain suggestiveness in this respect. At that time, I knew only ambition in its most noble sense, and I was eager to undertake anything in which I thought I could succeed." When he left the Sorbonne, the new licentiate felt that, at last, he could begin to realize his ambitions: "I found myself at last completely free to do as I pleased."

He had more than simple freedom. As titular Abbot of St.-Rémy and even as Promoter of the Assembly of the Clergy, he had very few real duties. The purpose of such benefices and offices was not to impose responsibility, but to confer income. The actual administrative work was left to subordinates less fortunate in their family connections who, if they were wise, swallowed or at least concealed their resentment and contented themselves with whatever share of the revenues of the benefice they could obtain in return for their services. Talleyrand, therefore, after years of confinement, first at Harcourt and then at St.-Sulpice, suddenly found sufficient time to amuse himself and with adequate funds to finance those amusements. As soon as he was able, he acquired a small house in Paris— "little, but comfortable," he says—in the Faubourg St.-Germain, rue de Verneuil, and there he indulged himself in the two pleasures that he treasured most. He collected books, and he entertained his friends. And he delighted in every moment of "the proud pleasure of being indebted to myself alone for my position." He was, at long last, master of himself and of his fate.

His friends, like his books, were chosen on the basis of their rarity and elegance. The dearest and most prominent of them was Auguste de Choiseul, the "charming boy" who had been Talleyrand's first friend at the Collège d'Harcourt and the one who was to remain "the man I have most loved." After Choiseul, at least superficially, it appears that Talleyrand preferred Louis de Narbonne, a young man of very ancient family. But "although in society the names of M. de Choiseul, M. de Narbonne, and the Abbé de Périgord were often linked, our intimacy with M. de Narbonne did not possess entirely the character of friendship." There was too much about Narbonne that Talleyrand disliked: "his humor often violates good taste, and his character does not inspire the confidence required for a close relationship." Talleyrand, when he gave of himself, gave unstintingly, but he did not give of himself carelessly or indiscriminately.

There were many others who gathered in the house in the rue de Verneuil and who formed the coterie of which Talleyrand, Choiseul, and Narbonne were regarded as the nucleus. They were, as the *Mémoires* point out, "a singular mixture." The old nobility was represented by Armand de Gontaut, Duke de Lauzun; finance, by a Swiss banker named Panchaud; philosophy, by Joseph Barthès, who enjoyed a great reputation at the time;

the arts, by the Abbé Delille, whose poetry enjoyed wide, if brief, renown, and by Sébastien Chamfort, also a poet and a tragedian. The future was present in the persons of Mirabeau, who was to become the great orator of the Constituent Assembly, and, somewhat less dramatically, by Pierre du Pont de Nemours, who was to emigrate to America in 1815 and found a princely dynasty of his own in that democracy. Not all these intimates of Talleyrand were men of aristocratic or even of respectable antecedents. The Abbé Delille was the illegitimate son of a middle-class father, and Chamfort attempted to disguise the fact that his father was a grocer by calling himself *De* Chamfort and pretending that he, too, was a bastard. There were others, of course: the Abbé Louis, of bourgeois origins, who was later to be transformed into the Baron Louis and a Minister of State; Rulhière, a historian, son of a policeman; Marmontel, a peasant-turned-philosopher. "We touched," Talleyrand says, "upon every subject and with the greatest possible liberty. It was the spirit and fashion of the time. . . . It was a marvelous way of spending our mornings."

The freedom of thought and of expression which Talleyrand relished was indeed, as he said, the fashion of the day. France was at the pinnacle of the age of the *philosophes*—the freethinkers who, condemned by the church and execrated by all respectable Christians, had nonetheless succeeded in planting the acorn that was shortly to bring forth the pagan oak of Liberty, Equality, and Fraternity. Under their influence, no subject on earth or in heaven was so sacred as to be unsuitable for discussion in the salons of Paris. The person who was responsible, more than any other, for this new spirit of freedom was a man named Arouet, who called himself Voltaire and who, for his unshakable belief in human liberty, had been forced to live in exile in Switzerland. In 1778, Voltaire, at the age of eighty-four and in the last year of his life, returned to Paris and was accorded a triumph the like of which had not been seen within living memory. Everyone flocked to do him homage—everyone, that is, except those who were prevented from doing so out of respect for the opinions of respectable society. Talleyrand was not one of the latter. The good opinion of society remained, as always, a matter of consummate indifference to him. The good opinion of the church mattered hardly more. He sought out the author of *Candide*, knelt before him, and implored his blessing. The old apostate and excommunicate, whose works were (to his delight) all on the Index of Forbidden Books, stretched out his hand and touched the head of the young subdeacon of the church, and the spectators burst into applause.

The story spread through Paris rapidly and soon came to the ears of the Archbishop, Monseigneur de Beaumont. He had already heard tales of the comings and goings of the Abbé de Périgord. He had heard that his subdeacon kept company with freethinkers and other persons of ill repute, that he was greatly admired by the fashionable ladies of Paris, and that he reciprocated this sentiment with a most unbecoming warmth. All these things might be forgiven, if not entirely ignored, for the abbé in question was the nephew of the reigning Duke-Archbishop of Rheims* and therefore entitled to more latitude in his conduct than clerics with less influential relatives. But Talleyrand's public obeisance before the archenemy of the church was too much, too great a scandal, to be passed over in silence. The archbishop himself summoned Talleyrand and administered a severe reprimand.

Monseigneur de Beaumont's pious rage had little effect upon Talleyrand except to persuade him that if he were ever to receive the preferment for which he hoped, it would have to be elsewhere than in his own archdiocese of Paris. He would therefore have to have himself transferred to a diocese ruled by a prelate more given to tolerance and of greater understanding. The matter was soon arranged. In September, 1779, he was received into the archdiocese of Rheims by his uncle. And as though to seal the bargain, he was at the same time ordained a deacon.

Talleyrand was now but one step away from the priesthood. But it was a most important step. Within the reach of the priest lay bishoprics and archbishops' thrones and palaces, power and splendor, and, for a man of sufficient ambition and talent, even the place occupied, with varying degrees of distinction, by a long line of French cardinals which included the great Richelieu and the less impressive Mazarin. The priesthood was then a necessity, and it was as a necessity, and a rather painful one, that Talleyrand viewed it. Still, the step had to be taken. He had completed his theological studies, and he was now twenty-five, the proper canonical age for ordination. To delay the ordeal would only delay any chance of further advancement.

It was in truth an ordeal. The ceremony was set for December 18, 1779. Although Talleyrand treats the occasion in the same way as his ordinations to the subdiaconate and diaconate—which is to say that he hardly mentions it—there is more than ample evidence that despite his dreams of power, he was still at war with his conscience and with his heart. During the evening preceding the ceremony, Choiseul called upon his friend and found him in tears. Talleyrand confessed his anguish. In the morning, he would become a priest forever, and he must thenceforth bear the sacerdotal burden. He loved the world, and he would be set apart from it. He loved freedom, and he would be obliged to bind himself to obedience. He loved to question, and he would be compelled to promise reverence and re-

---

* Talleyrand's uncle, Alexandre-Angélique, had at last succeeded to the see of Rheims in 1777, upon the death of Cardinal de la Roche-Aymon.

spect for his superiors and their opinions. He loved the society of women, and he would now cut himself off forever from the possibility of marriage. Subdeacons and even deacons, if they were clever enough, might occasionally obtain dispensations from their vows, but priests, never. In a few hours, when the ordaining bishop imposed his hands upon the head of the Abbé de Périgord, these things, which he treasured above all others, would be lost to him forever.

Along with despair over the future, there came a final surge of bitter resentment and of fierce rebellion against the forces that he felt himself too weak to oppose. When Choiseul, greatly shocked at the state of his friend, pleaded with him, in the name of God, to refuse ordination, Talleyrand replied in a cold voice: "I cannot. It is too late. I cannot refuse." When Choiseul attempted to find arguments that would move him, Talleyrand replied "that he could not go against his mother's wishes," that her urging was more insistent than ever, and that he was weary of attempting to do battle alone against all the pressures that were brought to bear on him. Finally, he repeated the argument that he had heard from his mother and uncle with such bewilderment, many years before: Since no career other than the church was open to him and since he had no resources other than those provided by the church, he had to resign himself to his fate. Choiseul, in a state of despair almost equal to that of Talleyrand, withdrew and left his friend to his thoughts.

Talleyrand had surrendered. The strength of will, which was to become the dominant trait of his mature years, had not yet been fully formed, and what there was of it had been weakened by his years of forced submission in the seminary. The will to resist, the urge to be free and, above all, to be true to himself had been bent and then broken. His education at the court of Rheims, his training at St.-Sulpice, the insistence of his parents, and the hard school of his childhood had done their work. If he was to avoid total rejection by his family, if he was to conquer the specter of poverty, if he was to attain a position that would put him forever beyond the reach of those who esteemed him as "fit for nothing," he had no choice but to surrender. He must tread the one path that lay open to him.

The day of December 18 dawned gray and bleak. By midmorning the Count-Bishop of Noyon had spoken the final words of the sacred rite: "Thou art a priest forever." Not by a look or gesture did Talleyrand betray the agony that he must have experienced at that moment. But there was no one to congratulate him on his fortitude, for neither of his parents attended the ceremony.

3

The Abbé de Périgord in the Great World

T HE INCARDINATION of Talleyrand into his uncle's diocese of Rheims did not mean that as a cleric of that place he would be required to reside in that city. Canon law stipulated only that every cleric must be accredited to a diocese, not that he actually live there, which was just as well, for there was only one city in France in which an intelligent, clever, and ambitious young man might live happily, and that city was not Rheims, but Paris.

The holy chrism of ordination was no sooner dry on his hands, therefore, than Talleyrand was back in Paris. The pretext he used for leaving Rheims was that his uncle had promised him the post of Agent-General of the Clergy* and that it was only in the capital that he could cultivate the persons who would be useful to him in discharging the duties of this office. It was an ideal situation, for it afforded him the opportunity to do what he had wished to do all along—that is, to come and go in the society of city and court without hindrance from his superiors. "A public career being open to me," he says, "I rather cleverly took advantage of the position of agent-general of the clergy, which had been promised to me, to widen the circle of my acquaintances."

His reputation as a wit, based upon the reports of his circle of intimates, had preceded him into the great salons of his day—a reputation which Tal-

---

* The Agents-General of the Clergy, of which there were two, were elected for a term of five years by the Assemblies of the Clergy. Their duties were serious and consisted in acting as liaison officers between the church and the government in all that related to the income and expenditures of the church and to the maintenance of the privileges of the church and the clergy.

leyrand modestly attributes to his "cold manners and apparent reserve."
He explains precisely how these factors opened to him doors that might
have remained forever closed to a more garrulous abbé:

> At the time I first went out into society, Madame de Gramont,* who did
> not like any reputation that she had not made herself, rendered me a serv-
> ice by seeking to embarrass me. I was having supper for the first time at
> Madame de Boufflers', and I was seated at one end of the table, hardly
> speaking to my neighbors. Madame de Gramont, in a loud, harsh voice,
> called me by name and asked me why, on entering the drawing room after
> her, I had said "Ah! Ah!" I replied: 'Your Grace did not hear correctly
> what I said. My words were not "Ah! Ah!" They were "Oh! Oh!" That
> silly reply provoked much hilarity. I continued to eat and said not another
> word; but when we left the table, several persons came up to me, and I re-
> ceived invitations which enabled me to make the acquaintance of those
> persons whom I was most eager to meet.

Measured against Talleyrand's stated purpose of widening his circle of
acquaintances, his active social life not only was "very pleasant," but also
"was not too much a waste of time." There were houses in which to be a
guest was considered so important that an invitation caused one to be
"ranked among the distinguished men of the day. I might say that many
people whom I did not know spoke highly of me simply because they had
met me at these dinner parties to which an invitation made one's reputation."

There were other kinds of houses, of course, and a young man slated for
advancement had to be careful in choosing precisely which invitations he
should accept and which refuse. Salons which were open to all comers
were to be shunned unless one was "willing to be ranked with the crowd."
There were some houses that one avoided so as not to seem too indiscrimi-
nate in accepting invitations. In this respect, it was best to "affect estrangement from, and even dislike for, some prominent member of society." As
his target, Talleyrand selected Jacques Necker, Minister of Finance to
Louis XVI, and then proceeded to criticize him openly for his public policies, his character, his appearance ("I said that, with his fantastic hat, his
long head, his big body, burly and ill-shaped . . . he had all the earmarks
of a charlatan"), and the poor state of his health. There is no evidence that
M. Necker was aware of the contempt of the obscure young abbé, and that
is perhaps why Talleyrand concludes his recital of the minister's faults by
claiming that he said "a thousand other things that it would be useless to
repeat, because today [1815] everyone is saying them."

Another kind of salon to be avoided or to flee from was that with gran-

---

* She was the daughter of the Duke de Choiseul, first minister to the king, and therefore a close
relative of Talleyrand's dearest friend, Auguste de Choiseul.

diose literary pretensions. One such was presided over by Count von Creutz, minister of Sweden, "who thought to please his master by pretending to be considered a wit in France." Creutz's habit was to invite the poets of the day to give readings at his house. "We went there three or four times," Talleyrand says, "but Marmontel read so many of his tragedies that he drove away all the guests. I held out until he came to *Numitor.*"

One of the houses that Talleyrand frequented during this period, which he found particularly agreeable "and which was kept just on the verge of decency," was that of the Marquise de Montesson who was the wife of the Duke d'Orléans.* Since Orléans was famous for the ease with which he could be bored into stupefaction, Madame de Montesson's chief aim in life became to keep him amused. To that end, she had plays performed in her house, several of which she wrote herself. And, to interest as well as entertain Orléans, she invited everyone with any claim to distinction in Paris. In her theater, "a special box was reserved for the use of the more worldly members of the clergy, to which I had secured admission. . . ."

Talleyrand, as an adult, seems also to have found pleasure in the company of his mother, whom he visited for herself rather than for the purpose of making new friends:

> I preferred to call upon my mother when she was alone so that I could better enjoy the graces of her mind. No one ever seemed to me to possess such fascinating conversation. She was without pretense. She spoke only by allusions. She never made a pun, for that would have been too direct. Puns are remembered, whereas her only wish was to please—that is, to please her audience for the moment and then to be forgotten. A richness of easy expressions, new and always delicate, enabled her to express the various things in her mind.

The admiration thus expressed was that of a man of the world for a woman of some social attainment. He wrote almost as a stranger about a lady whom he knew only casually, not as a son about his mother. Too much had happened for that accidental relationship to be able any longer to influence Talleyrand's judgment either in favor of or against the Countess de Périgord.

The abbé, gregarious as he was, succeeded in combining business with pleasure or ambition with enjoyment by cultivating the acquaintance of a large number of men prominent in public affairs and of an even larger number of ladies who were, in a large measure, responsible for that promi-

* Madame de Montesson's husband had died in 1769. She married Orléans secretly in 1773, after having been his mistress openly for several years. This was the Duke d'Orléans who was to play an important part in the Revolution under the style of "Philippe-Egalité" and "the Red Prince." He was the father of that Louis-Philippe, Duke d'Orléans, whom Talleyrand would one day transform into Louis-Philippe, King of the French.

nence. For, as he tells us candidly, "everyone who sought office began by frequenting some of the chief families of Paris, whose opinions and language they formed." Thus, early in his life, Talleyrand came to know Maurepas, Louis XVI's Minister of State who held all the power of a prime minister; Turgot, the Comptroller General of France; Malesherbes, president of the Cour des Aides (Tax Court) and, later, Minister of State; Castries, Secretary of State and soon to be Marshal of France; and Charles-Alexandre de Calonne, Turgot's successor as Comptroller General. Among the ladies whom he cultivated, with varying degrees of intimacy but with an eye fixed on the future, was Louise de Rohan, Countess de Brionne, who, in addition to her own charm and the fact that "on certain days, the best society in Paris met" at her house, had two lovely daughters and a daughter-in-law, the Princess de Vaudémont, whose elegant beauty was justly famous. The younger of the daughters, Princess Charlotte de Lorraine, pleased Talleyrand enormously and was pleased by him in turn, and their brief and tender liaison received the Countess de Brionne's indulgent blessing. Charlotte was succeeded in Talleyrand's affections by the striking Madame de Vaudémont, who, once passion had been satisfied, was to remain Talleyrand's most loyal and most cherished friend until her death almost a half century later.

The abbé also made the acquaintance at this time of the Duke de Choiseul, the famous uncle of Auguste de Choiseul, who had gained the double distinction of becoming Minister-Secretary of State under Louis XV (1758–1770) and the bitterest enemy of Louis' mistress, the Countess du Barry. His battle with the countess had ended, perhaps inevitably, given Louis' character, in his defeat and exile to his estate at Chanteloup. But rather than detract from his stature, this denouement had increased it, for Du Barry was universally despised, and her enmity conferred upon her principal victims something of the aura of martyr-heroes. Everyone in Paris and Versailles therefore made a point of beating a path to the gates of Chanteloup. Among them was Talleyrand, who, for his trouble, was given this piece of advice by the elder statesman:

> When I was a minister, I made a practice of having others do more work than I did myself. One must never allow oneself to be buried under paper work; instead, one should hire men who are good at that sort of thing. The ideal is to be able to control a situation by means of nothing more complicated than a gesture or a sign. . . . A minister who moves about in society is in a position to read the signs of the times even in a festive gathering, but one who remains shut up in his office learns nothing.

This was a counsel that Talleyrand never forgot, for it suited him perfectly. In later years, he was to emulate the great Choiseul to the point that his enemies would accuse him of laziness and draw some startling conclusions from his apparently lackadaisical work habits. Molé would say that "the busiest and most laborious moments of his day" were those spent in dressing and that "he is incapable of prolonged reflection or work and has none of the qualities of a statesman." Fifty years after his visit to Chanteloup, Talleyrand would be ambassador in London, and his secretary would note that "M. de Talleyrand faithfully observed this rule: a superior should never do anything that a subordinate can do for him. It was a rule given him, he said, by the Duke de Choiseul at Chanteloup."

In May, 1780, in the midst of this exhilarating plunge into the political and social world of the old regime, the promise of the Duke-Archbishop of Rheims was fulfilled, and the Abbé de Périgord received his appointment as Agent-General of the Clergy. It is not unlikely that the announcement provoked smiles in the halls of Versailles as in the salons of Paris. The Abbé de Périgord was a clever and charming young man, to be sure. But an Agent-General? Amusement quickly changed to astonishment, for Talleyrand threw himself like a demon into his new responsibilities. He who in later years would constantly preach to his subordinates the ancient maxim of the Greeks and the philosophy of Choiseul, "Above all, not too much zeal," now showed himself extraordinarily zealous, and the energy he manifested evoked amazement even among his superiors. "It is the result of his youth," they said. "With a little more experience, it will soon pass." But it did not pass, any more than the post of Agent-General satisfied his ambitions. "I was anxious not to remain forever Agent-General of the Clergy," Talleyrand wrote, "but I took all necessary precautions not to let anyone suspect my ambition. Thus, in order to attract notice, I did work which, while it did not exactly belong to my post, was connected with it." Among the duties that he thus took on were those of his fellow Agent-General, the Abbé de Boisgelin, who "because of a rather too public adventure had been deprived of the confidence of the clergy." * In truth, Talleyrand welcomed the activity necessitated by his new mission. He had too keen a mind and too driving an ambition to be long content with the mere conversation, however pleasing, of his friends and acquaintances. Moreover, he was aware that since he had to forge his way to success through ecclesiastical preferment, it was time that he begin to work at it in earnest.

The first serious reform that he proposed, in an effort to regain the public esteem that the clergy, under the hammerblows of the *philosophes,* were rapidly losing, was the abolition of the national lottery. "This," he says, "was one of my favorite ideas, for I had investigated all the chances and all

* Boisgelin's "adventure" was his public liaison with Madame de Cavanac—who, before her marriage to Monsieur de Cavanac, had been famous, under the name of Mademoiselle de Romans, as a mistress of Louis XV and as the mother of one of his sons (the Abbé de Bourbon).

the consequences of that baneful institution." His proposal, as he presented it to the clergy, was that the church of France, out of its revenues, should buy the lottery from the state and then abolish it. The continuing revenue thus lost by the state would be made up out of ecclesiastical income, in the form of a voluntary annual donation. "I was eager," Talleyrand explains, "to hold up the clergy as the protectors of strict morality. And by inducing the clergy to accept some financial sacrifice in support of that principle, I should have rendered a service both to public morals and to the order to which I belonged." But the pious clergy were not as willing as the worldly abbé to sacrifice a portion of their income, and Talleyrand's proposal received no support at all. "Even those upon whom I most depended to second my motion refused to do so," he says. "It may be said that this, my first political campaign, was not very successful. The reason, I believe, is that my ideas were far too radical for the men to whom they were offered."

His next proposal, the effect of which would also be to deprive the higher clergy of a portion of their income, met with no more success. The ordinary curé of France, without family connections and friends at court to plead his cause and obtain profitable sinecures for him, received a sum of 500 livres with which to maintain himself, and the *vicaires,* or assistant pastors, were paid 200 livres*—amounts which, Talleyrand points out, "were far from sufficient." He therefore asked the bishops and archbishops to petition the state for an increase—which meant, inevitably, that the state had to receive more revenue from the church in order to meet these costs. In order to persuade the prelates to part with some of their money, Talleyrand cleverly appealed to their sense of justice. There was an error, he said, which had caused the intentions of King Louis XIV concerning clerical salaries to be misinterpreted. "I confined myself to requesting the redress of this error, of which, I said, the higher clergy must surely be happy to be informed." But they were not happy, and another of Talleyrand's ideas was voted down.

The most humane of his efforts at this time was related to the situation of women in the maritime province of Brittany whose husbands had been lost at sea but whom canon law prevented from ever remarrying on the grounds that it was impossible to ascertain whether or not their husbands were truly dead. "I employed theological principles—which, when handled properly, are elastic enough to serve any purpose—to show it was desirable that after a certain number of years sufficient to prevent social scandal,

---

* In order to establish a basis of comparison, it may be noted that at the time of Talleyrand's proposal the higher clergy and various religious communities had annual incomes ranging from 100,000 to 2,000,000 livres. Here are a few figures, taken at random: the Abbot of Clairvaux, 400,000; Cardinal de Rohan, 1,000,000; the monastery of Cluny, 1,800,000.

these poor women should be allowed to remarry." He set forth this argument in a memorandum, which eventually fell into the hands of the Bishop of Arras, who, "after denouncing it in the strongest possible terms, threw it into the fire. Thereafter," Talleyrand concludes, "it required nothing less than the Revolution to enable all these poor Breton women (who, I should imagine, were no longer young) to marry again if they chose to do so."

The fact that Talleyrand's proposals were voted down and, occasionally, thrown into the fire did no serious harm to his reputation. These "little reforms," as he called them, were not actually part of his assigned duties, and they were regarded merely as the well-intentioned proposals of a zealous, but naïve, young priest. His proper work as Agent-General was not only not neglected, but indeed performed with such diligence and intelligence as to excite general admiration among his superiors, and there was much talk of his remarkable abilities as an administrator and of his talent for organization. "I enjoyed a certain reputation," Talleyrand notes, "but not yet being sufficiently acquainted with the world, I was happy to think that I had still some years before me during which I might share the life and pleasures of society." So, while, as his position required, he surrounded himself "with persons of learned and sound views" and while, with an eye to the future, he was pleased that his performance "had attracted to me the attention of men who, by profession, were in a position to further my ambitions," he was careful to keep a discreet distance between himself and these newfound admirers and advisers. "It was advantageous to be on good terms with them," he explains, "but somewhat dangerous to be too closely identified with these men." Moreover, since he was in no hurry, he did not feel really obliged "to arrange any of the deep combinations [of relationships] that are necessary to satisfy one's serious ambitions."

It is possible that Talleyrand's protest that he was "in no hurry" to advance in the church had something to do with his nonecclesiastical activities in the period during which his superiors were so impressed with his zeal and intelligence. The truth was that the young abbé had embarked on several adventures which were every bit as "public" as that which he asserted had deprived his fellow Agent-General, Boisgelin, of the confidence of the clergy. The only difference between the two seemed to be that Talleyrand was energetic, and Boisgelin was, as Talleyrand remarked, afflicted with "a natural indolence." Certainly, Talleyrand was no more discreet in his private life than Boisgelin. On his trips to Brittany, to investigate the situation of the sailors' widows, he habitually visited with Madame de Girac, sister-in-law of the Bishop of Rennes. It was commonly believed in Paris, and it was probably true, that the relationship between the abbé and the bishop's sister-in-law was not wholly spiritual.

The putative affair with Madame de Girac, however, was a minor aspect in the overall context of Talleyrand's life at this time. His conduct was, even taking into account the considerable latitude allowed to the clergy at the time, nothing less than a public scandal. In the winter of 1782–83, he had formed a liaison with the beautiful and clever Countess Adélaïde de Flahaut. They met at Versailles and were immediately attracted to each other. A short time later they were living together openly—so openly that the countess soon bore a child, whom she named Charles, after the boy's father. Her husband, the Count de Flahaut, seems not to have been particularly disturbed, either by his wife's relationship with Talleyrand or by the mysterious appearance of an heir. The marriage between the Count and Countess de Flahaut had been "arranged" between their families, and it existed in name only. He was in his fifties when they first met; and she, seventeen years of age. He had interests other than his wife and seemed immune to the charms that Talleyrand found so irresistible. With no outraged husband on the scene to make matters awkward, Talleyrand, quite typically, refused to pretend that his relations with the countess were anything other than what they were in fact. They went about together so guilelessly that even the gossips of Versailles were shocked into silence, and their intimacy ceased even to be a subject of conversation. So far as their son, Charles de Flahaut, was concerned, it was taken for granted that Talleyrand was his father—an assumption which Talleyrand never bothered to deny, but which he confirmed, for all practical purposes, by the extraordinary care which he was to exercise, in later years, in furthering the boy's career.

The intimacy between Talleyrand and Adélaïde de Flahaut lasted for almost ten years, during which time their mutual regard gradually deteriorated until it had run the gamut from the height of passion to the depths of indifference. Madame de Flahaut, indeed, was one of the very few women Talleyrand loved whom he did not retain as a devoted friend after passion had cooled. The cause of their eventual and mutual disenchantment seems to have been those very qualities of the countess that had attracted Talleyrand to her in the first place. Gouverneur Morris, who was soon to become American ambassador in Paris, describes her in the following terms:

> She was at this time in the glory of her youth and attraction, with possibly a touch of sadness about her, and certainly a rare sympathy, which, added to her thoroughly trained mind, with its decided philosophic cast, gave her an uncommon power over men.

Morris himself had experienced this power, for he was one of her most devoted, though unsuccessful, admirers. Others, however, were more fortunate than he. Once the countess had seen the effect of her beauty, wit, cleverness, and charm on Talleyrand—who, we are assured, was the first man to benefit from her husband's neglect—she could not resist the temptation to discover if she could exercise the same power over other men. Talleyrand, being Talleyrand, rather than make a scene and play the deceived lover, regarded the countess' weakness as permission to engage in peripheral amatory adventures of his own. From that point, their relationship declined in both intensity and cordiality until, in 1791, it was to disintegrate altogether, with the countess and Talleyrand going their separate ways— she into the arms of an English admirer, Lord Wycombe, and he into the generous bed of Germaine de Staël (daughter of M. Necker, Minister of Finance, whom Talleyrand had attacked so brutally and so recently), later to become as famous for her amatory appetites as for her contributions to the romanticism of the nineteenth century.

In spite of the intensity of Talleyrand's social and emotional life since his ordination to the priesthood, he never permitted himself to lose sight of the goals that he had set for himself. Sensuous and sensual he might be, but he never allowed his liaisons or his pleasures to blur the outlines of his purpose. He was in his thirtieth year, he had talent, he was a Périgord, and he had already attracted the favorable notice of his ecclesiastical superiors. Yet it seemed that advancement was as remote as ever. Then, in 1785, he was given the opportunity to recall his existence to the Assembly of the Clergy—especially to those who guarded the doors to power in the church. To the Assembly of that year he presented a series of reports on the works of public assistance—schools, hospitals, orphanages, poorhouses—which the church maintained in France. Some of the information contained in these reports, he had gathered in the course of his work as Agent-General. The rest came to him as the result of an elaborate questionnaire that he had circulated among the bishops and superiors of religious houses throughout the kingdom. All this data had been collated and compared, and from it emerged, under Talleyrand's expert hand, a vast picture of the financial state of the church in France: its income, its expenses, its fixed assets. Nothing so comprehensive or so precise had ever been attempted before, and the bishops of France were struck with amazement, both at the extent of their wealth and at the vast amount of work and thought that the Abbé de Périgord, even in the midst of his well-known distractions, had expended. The Archbishop of Bordeaux publicly expressed the Assembly's gratitude: "It is a monument of talent and of zeal, and our everlasting gratitude is extended to the able hands that prepared it." And then, since they could now afford it, the Assembly voted to put into those same hands a practical expression of that gratitude: a gift of 24,000 livres.

Talleyrand was pleased, but not entirely satisfied. Rhetoric was fine, in its place, and money was even better; but there was something finer yet: a miter and a bishop's throne. A priest of the Périgord family, especially one whose "talent and zeal" had been publicly acclaimed by the most important clerics in France, was long overdue for a bishopric at the age of thirty-one. Talleyrand's uncle, the Duke-Archbishop of Rheims, had received the miter at the age of twenty-seven, and he possessed not half the ability or half the ambition of his nephew. There were many bishops, archbishops, and cardinals who had been able to exchange the somber black cassock of an ordinary priest for the violet of the bishop and occasionally for the sacred purple itself at an even earlier age.

The explanation, of which Talleyrand was perfectly aware, was that these prelates and princes of the church, while they might lack most of his virtues, possessed the one vice of which he himself was conspicuously innocent: hypocrisy. They might have their ladies and lovers, and some might even worship Voltaire from a distance; but they did so discreetly and without scandal. Their sins were usually played out in their episcopal salons and bedrooms, and they did not flaunt their mistresses in Paris and still less at the court of Versailles. Of these men the church asked, or at least expected, only that they avoid scandalizing the faithful. But this was too stringent a requirement for a man who, flexible though he might be in all else, could never bring himself to pretend to be what he was not or not to be what he was. The result was that in 1785, the year in which the bishops of France were praising his intelligence and devotion, his name was stricken from the list of names of those eligible for bishoprics.*

King Louis XVI was a moral and upright man, devout and, on occasion, generous. His generosity, however, did not extend to the weaknesses of others. Or rather, his devotion took the form of the strictest possible interpretation of the commandments of God and of the church. He had heard reports on the life led by the Abbé de Périgord. The Bishop of Autun, Talleyrand explained later to Choiseul, had been carrying tales to the king. It is not impossible that Louis had little need of the bishop's gossip. It was well known that Talleyrand frequented houses that were less than respectable; that he had friends whose political and religious opinions were, to say the least, unorthodox; that he had spent entire nights at the house of Madame de Genlis—at the gambling tables, some said, and others said even more scandalous things. (The latter were probably right. It is of Madame de Genlis that Talleyrand remarked, "In order to avoid the scandal

---

* Since before the time of Charlemagne, the rulers of France had enjoyed, and had occasionally fought to protect, the right to name candidates for the bishoprics, abbeys, and other major benefices of their realm. The prerogative of naming bishops to vacant sees, as exercised by King Louis, dated formally from the Concordat of 1516 and had been reinforced by a further agreement between Henri IV and Rome at the end of the sixteenth century.

of flirting, she consents immediately.") His various liaisons, especially the current one with Madame de Flahaut, were open and therefore inexcusable. Perhaps even more serious was the charge that Talleyrand had used his friendship with Charles-Alexandre de Calonne, Comptroller General of the Finances, to obtain information which he used in speculation. This abuse of confidence would, of itself, have been enough to offend a man as honest as Louis XVI.

It is not known for certain whether Talleyrand was aware that he was *persona non grata* in the king's eyes, at least so far as the distribution of bishoprics was concerned. It seems that he was not, for in 1786 he believed that he was on the point of realizing his ambitions. The Archbishop of Bourges was gravely ill, and it was expected momentarily that he would, by his death, render vacant his see, which was one of the wealthiest and most prestigious in France. As the archbishop lay in his bed, growing weaker by the minute, the gossips of Paris and Versailles had already appointed the Abbé de Périgord his successor. It is not known how the rumor began. It is not impossible that Talleyrand himself invented and propagated it in the hope that once repeated by his friends at court, it would inspire the king to forgive and to act. In any case, we find him writing to his friend Mirabeau: "I am the only one who is being mentioned for the archbishopric of Bourges. It is a fine position. . . . The archbishop has had an attack of apoplexy, and no one thinks that he can last more than two or three weeks." But to everyone's chagrin, the ailing archbishop seemed now to grow stronger rather than weaker, and he lingered, in the limbo of quasi-convalescence, well into 1787. Then he had another seizure. Talleyrand, barely able to conceal his relief, wrote to Choiseul:

> My archbishop is getting worse by the day. It is said that he is actually going to die this time and that even the most potent medicines are doing no good. This time my fate will be decided. It seems to me that it will be difficult not to give me the archbishopric of Bourges. Even the malice of the Bishop of Autun cannot find a way to deprive me of it.

But deprived he was. The archbishop did, in fact, die, but his throne was given to the Bishop of Nancy. It was all done so quickly that one may believe the king had had no difficulty in reaching a decision.

Talleyrand, of course, was greatly disappointed and very puzzled. "What will happen now?" he asked Choiseul. "It seems to me that there will be no more opening for a long while yet, and even then, will I be given a place that is suitable to me and to which I myself am suited? Nothing that I want turns out as I wish, and I must tell you, my friend, that this is not a happy time for me. But things will change, and I will wait."

The fact is that, along with the loss of the archbishopric of Bourges, Tal-

leyrand had been dealt an even heavier blow. He had, for a glorious moment, been on the verge of receiving a far rarer prize than the pallium of an
archbishop: the red hat of a cardinal of the Holy Roman Church.

This glittering promise had been extended, as were so many of the delights in Talleyrand's life, by a woman, the Countess de Brionne. The
countess was descended from one of France's princely families, the House
of Rohan, and she had married into another, that of Lorraine. Her influence at the royal court was great, for she was on terms of intimacy with
several of the king's ministers and of friendship with the rest. In addition,
she cultivated religiously those monarchs of Europe whose awe of French
culture and French thought made them eager to have the friendship of a
lady as renowned for the brilliance of her salon as the Countess de
Brionne. Among these foreign princes were Frederick II of Prussia and
Gustavus III, King of Sweden.

Knowing Talleyrand's great ambitions, as well as his first disappointment in 1785, when the incumbent Archbishop of Bourges had refused to
expire, this lady determined to bring all her influence to bear in order to
satisfy the abbé, who had succeeded in captivating both herself and the
fairest part of her family. In keeping with her station in life, however, what
she determined to acquire for her friend was no mere bishopric, but a car-
dinalatial seat. Hearing that King Gustavus was about to begin a voyage to
the south of Europe, which would take him to Rome, she immediately
wrote soliciting his good offices on behalf of Talleyrand. The Protestant
King of Sweden, while in Rome, was to ask a favor of Pope Pius VI: a cardinal's hat for the distinguished Abbé de Périgord.

As it happened, the Pope accorded a particularly gracious reception to
the King of Sweden in Rome. Pius was a man of great amiability, and he
was disposed to grant any reasonable favor, especially to a visiting, albeit
Protestant, monarch. Accordingly, Gustavus had only to mention Talleyrand for the Pope to reply that he would be very pleased indeed to number
among his cardinals a man reputed to be as brilliant as the Abbé de Périgord. Gustavus immediately conveyed the Pope's words to the Countess de
Brionne, who, no less rapidly, passed them on to Talleyrand himself. It was
as good as done. Talleyrand accepted the congratulations of his friends
and settled back to await the official communication of his elevation from
the nuncio of His Holiness in Paris.* At that moment, however, a greater
force than the King of Sweden intervened in Talleyrand's affairs. News of

---

* According to canon law and ancient custom, one became a cardinal at the moment that the
reigning Pope decided upon his elevation, whether the Pope expressed that decision explicitly or
kept it locked *in petto*—in his breast. In either case, the cardinal-designate was not permitted to exercise his prerogatives until his elevation had been officially communicated to him, but in the case
of cardinals designated *in petto,* their seniority was calculated from the date of the Pope's decision.

the Countess de Brionne's intrigue with King Gustavus was not slow in reaching Paris from Rome, and Marie-Antoinette, Queen of France, swore that the countess' protégé would never wear his red hat. She had reasons of her own for this decision. She had recently been implicated in an ugly scandal, the famous Affair of the Diamond Necklace,* by the Cardinal de Rohan—the Countess de Brionne's cousin. At his trial, the cardinal had cast serious doubts on Marie-Antionette's complete innocence in this intrigue, and the countess had heatedly defended the cardinal's story in her salon. The queen therefore instructed the Austrian ambassador in Paris, Count Mercy, that the representative of her brother (the Emperor of Austria) in Rome was to oppose, in the strongest terms, the elevation of any candidate put forward by the Countess de Brionne, the King of Sweden, or the Cardinal de Rohan. The queen's "petty revenge extended even to me," Talleyrand explained later, "and I had some difficulty in obtaining the position to which I was naturally called. But the affection of Madame de Brionne and her daughters comforted me greatly for the opposition I experienced in my career. . . . The nomination of the Pope was withdrawn, and it is probable that my cardinal's hat was left to molder for many years in some French fortress."

The opposition of Marie-Antoinette, the disapproval of the king, the talebearing of the Bishop of Autun—all of which Talleyrand described modestly as "my disfavor at court"—were soon neutralized by events over which not even monarchs by divine right could exercise any control. On May 2, 1788, the Archbishop of Lyons died. Talleyrand's hopes rocketed, and Madame de Brionne spent her days and nights soliciting the support of her friends at court for the candidacy of her protégé. But King Louis refused to be moved. Even worse, his choice for the archbishopric that Tal-

---

* The Affair of the Diamond Necklace, which completed the disenchantment of the people of France with "the Austrian woman," as Marie-Antoinette was called, was a blow to the prestige of the crown from which it never recovered. Yet it seems that the queen was entirely innocent of any wrongdoing in this matter. Her jeweler, Boehmer, had offered her a splendid diamond necklace for the price of 1,600,000 francs. Since the state was on the verge of bankruptcy, Marie-Antoinette felt compelled to refuse. By then, however, news of the necklace's existence had become known, and a plan was devised, by a lady called the Countess de la Motte-Valois, to obtain the necklace for herself. She succeeded in persuading the Cardinal de Rohan, who was in disgrace at the court, that Marie-Antoinette had forgiven him and that, as a sign of his reinstatement in favor, he would be allowed to act as the go-between in the purchase of the necklace for the queen. It seems that the cardinal's doubts were dispelled by a midnight confrontation, in the gardens of Versailles, between himself and a lady whom he took to be the queen but who was in fact a woman who resembled her closely. The cardinal, now convinced, bought the necklace on credit, and handed it to Madame de la Motte-Valois to carry to the queen. Instead, she sent it to England, where it was broken down and the individual stones were sold. The whole bizarre affair came to light when Boehmer began to complain that the queen had not paid him the full amount for the necklace. The Cardinal de Rohan and the Countess de la Motte-Valois were arrested and tried before the Parlement of Paris, where he was aquitted as a dupe, and she convicted as a felon. The verdict, however, was so worded as to cast grave doubt on the innocence of the queen.

leyrand desired so desperately fell upon Talleyrand's worst enemy among the higher clergy, the influential and well-informed Monseigneur de Marboeuf, Bishop of Autun.

Yet all was not lost. Marboeuf's promotion was hard to accept, but the burden was made somewhat lighter by the thought that if Lyons now had a new prelate, Autun had none at all. Talleyrand's friends therefore set to work with renewed vigor. Even the clergy of Autun were induced to join in persuading the king to name the Abbé de Périgord as their new bishop. They pointed to the splendid work that he had done as Agent-General of the Clergy. They spoke of his eloquence, his learning, and his energy. His public sins they dismissed as the result of youth and human frailty, and they gathered proofs of his doctrinal orthodoxy to impress the Most Christian King of France. But Louis was no fool. He had heard these arguments before, and despite any evidence to the contrary that might be adduced, he knew that this was the same Abbé de Périgord, unchanged, whom he had ordered dropped from consideration a few years before. Talleyrand's friends persisted, but Louis was more stubborn than they. Moreover, he had a conscience, and that conscience told him that the faithful of Autun and the church of France deserved better than the Abbé de Périgord.

At this critical point, fate intervened once more in Talleyrand's career. His father, the Count de Périgord, lay dying, and for the first time in his life, so far as is known, he asked to see his son. Talleyrand came, and the two spoke softly and briefly. It may be, as some whispered, that the count, on his deathbed, had implored his son to reform his life and to give up his dissolute friends. Or it may be, as others said, that he begged his son's forgiveness for the wrong he had done him in forcing him into a life for which, as had by now become all too obvious, he was in no way suited. Then, perhaps out of conviction, perhaps out of guilt, the Count de Périgord made a promise to Talleyrand: He would speak to the king about the bishopric of Autun.

Charles-Daniel de Périgord-Talleyrand was the representative of an ancient family, one whose origins stretched back into the dimness of Carolingian France, as did those of King Louis. The Talleyrands were therefore, according to the usages of the time, the "cousins" of the king. This nonorific relationship entailed certain prerogatives denied to lesser mortals. One such was that the King of France might, without demeaning himself, call upon his cousin of Périgord in circumstances of sufficient gravity to warrant such a visit. And so Louis, who had always had a certain affection for Talleyrand's father and who knew, moreover, that the count had been an attendant and a dear friend of his own father, came to comfort him in his final moments on earth. The funereal circumstances of his visit, the memory of his own father whom he had loved dearly, and the words of the count which no doubt evoked the remembrance of both caused Louis' attitude to soften. When the dying man spoke his request for his son's elevation, the king could not refuse. He promised that Talleyrand would become Bishop of Autun.

Two days before the count's death, Louis XVI signed the document nominating Talleyrand to Autun. The text read:

> . . . the king, being at Versailles, and knowing full well the saintly life and morals, the piety, teaching, and sufficiency, as well as the other laudable and virtuous qualities united in the person of the lord Charles-Maurice de Talleyrand-Périgord . . . has given and made over to him the bishopric of Autun on the 10th day of the month of December, 1788.

Louis, no doubt, was unhappy over the promise he had made to the moribund Count de Périgord. But he was an honorable man, and his word was sacred. When Talleyrand's mother, who deplored her son's way of life, asked the king to reconsider his decision, Louis proved as stubborn then as he had earlier. He could not dishonor himself by reneging on a promise made to a dying man. So he signed, and made Talleyrand a bishop. *Cela le corrigera,* he said—"he will grow into the job."

Talleyrand himself was not unreservedly happy about his bishopric of Autun. It was hardly a fair exchange for Bourges or Lyons, let alone for a seat in the Sacred College. The city was small and provincial—a town, actually, distinguished only by some interesting ruins dating from Roman times and by its cathedral, planned originally as a Byzantine basilica, with its famous porch and its graceful towers rising against the clear Autunois skies. Its population was small—under 10,000 people—and, worse, its revenues amounted to only 22,000 livres. Still, there were certain compensations for the relative obscurity of his see. Along with the bishopric itself, the Bishop of Autun received a fine string of titles: Count de Saulien, and Baron d'Issy-Leveque, Lucenay, Grosme, and Touillon. None of these, it is true, approached the style of a Count de Périgord or a Prince de Chalais. But they were Talleyrand's own, held independently of his family, and that lent them a resonance that was pleasing to a man who found that to be responsible for one's own position was life's proudest pleasure. The final consideration that made Autun acceptable as Talleyrand's see was the fact that by custom, the incumbent of that diocese was generally regarded as the prime candidate for the archbishopric of Lyons—as Monseigneur de Marboeuf had just demonstrated. And Marboeuf was well along in years, while Talleyrand was only thirty-four.

According to the discipline of the church, a newly appointed bishop had to spend three days in prayer and solitude before being consecrated. As offhandedly as Talleyrand accepted the see which had come to him, so to speak, as a bequest from his father, he felt that he had to conform to this regulation. He retired to the Seminary of Issy (which belonged to St.-Sulpice), there to prepare himself for the sacred order that he was about to receive. If we can believe the Abbé Ducloux, who had been appointed Talleyrand's spiritual director for the length of his stay at Issy, the retreat was little short of a disaster. Never, the abbé related, had he had so difficult a retreatant. In the midst of his exhortations to Talleyrand, the door would open and a group of "frivolous people of the world" would rush in and begin exchanging gossip with the bishop-elect, although the worst of it was the latter's continual irreverence and inattention, which the Abbé Ducloux found "shocking" and "outrageous."

The ceremony of consecration which followed this ordeal took place on January 16, 1789, in the chapel at Issy. Not a single member of his family was in attendance. It may have been just as well. A witness to the ceremony, a Sulpician priest, who had been a seminarian at the time, related that the new bishop's attitude throughout the ceremony was *inconvenant*— unbecoming. Talleyrand, he recalled, was unmoved, distracted, and seemed to be going through the rites mechanically, like an actor who is bored with a role. But when it came time for him to take his oath of office, his voice was clear and steady: "I, Charles-Maurice, chosen for the Church of Autun, from this day forward will be faithful and obedient to St. Peter the Apostle, to the Holy Roman Church, to our Holy Father the Pope and his legitimate successors. I shall do all in my power to preserve, defend, increase, and promote the rights, honors, privileges, and authority of the Holy Roman Church and of our Holy Father the Pope and his successors." Once Talleyrand had been sworn and anointed, he received the regalia of his new office: the miter, the crozier or pastoral staff, and the ring. The choir then sang the antiphon, *Ecce sacerdos magnus*—"Behold a great priest, who in his time has pleased the Lord."

After several false starts, Talleyrand was now a bishop and launched on the road to his extraordinary future. His bored compliance with the regulations and rites of the church indicated, to those who could interpret his indifference, his skeptical attitude to the religious aspects of his new office. It was not the episcopal prerogatives that he coveted and certainly not the power to ordain priests and to confer the sacrament of confirmation. His ambition was not for place, titles, or apostolic authority; it was for power. Autun, obscure and poor as it was, marked his entry into the precincts of power. It would be used, to the extent that it could, to promote and further that quest.

The manner in which Talleyrand played his role of bishop was typical of what was to come in later years. Immediately after his consecration, he left Issy—not to visit Autun, concerning which he had not the slightest interest, but to return to Paris. Autun was his by law both canon and civil, and there was no need for him to be physically present in his see in order to confirm his right to it. But the clergy and faithful of the diocese must learn at once that they had a master. He therefore instructed the Abbé de Grandchamps, archpriest of his cathedral, to take possession of the see in his name, and then, from Paris, he set about putting Autun in proper order so that it might serve his purposes. He named several trustworthy priests as officials in his chancery and appointed wise and prudent clerics as his rural deans. To preside over them all, he dispatched to Autun a new vicar-general who would rule with the authority of the bishop himself: Borie Desrenaudes, an old and trusted friend who had been ordained on the same day as himself. Then, still from Paris, he spent the next months winning the minds and hearts of his faithful by means of letters.

In the first of these, he quotes Paul's Epistle to the Romans: *Desidero videre vos*—"I am impatient to see you." This was not entirely accurate; if there was impatience, it was on the part of the people of Autun, who had not yet laid eyes on their bishop. But it served the purpose for which it was intended by keeping the people in a state of growing and expectant curiosity concerning their hitherto invisible shepherd. He then goes on to assure the Autunois of their importance to him: "You, our very dear brothers, have become our beloved and only concern. All our thoughts, our desires and sentiments go out to you." And so that no one might think that a scion of the House of Talleyrand-Périgord was far removed from the cares and troubles of simple folk, he opens his heart to his people and tells them of his father's longing to have his son made Bishop of Autun; of the fact that Autun was his mother's birthplace; and of his father's joy when, on his deathbed, he learned that his son had indeed been appointed to "our beloved diocese. . . . And then, after that sad moment had come, it seemed that it was among you, among my mother's people, that my grief might find refuge and among you that I might seek consolation." The letter ends, as do all of Talleyrand's pastoral letters, with an exhortation to prayer, so that "your days may be filled with a holy communion with God."

The letters were read from every pulpit of the diocese, and they produced an immediate and unanimous effect among the people. The humanity and apostolic zeal conveyed by his letters won their hearts. Rumors of Talleyrand's dissolute life in Paris, which had drifted down to these simple Christians, were not only discounted, but indignantly rejected. Even the clergy, who were not so naïve as their parishioners, were persuaded that they were fortunate in having such a man as their bishop, for the wisdom and judgment which he had already shown in administering his diocese—albeit from Paris—had gained their universal approbation and respect. Then, later in February, 1789, in the midst of this outpouring of goodwill, important and exciting news arrived from Paris for the people of Autun: Their bishop, no longer able to restrain his eagerness, would arrive within a few days for a prolonged visit.

Talleyrand had not been untruthful when he wrote of his impatience to see the people of Autun. The energy with which, as soon as he had returned to Paris after his consecration, he had set to work organizing his diocese demonstrated, if it was not literally true that the diocese occupied "all our thoughts," that he nonetheless took his responsibilities seriously enough to win the approval of a clergy understandably skeptical about the effectiveness of absentee bishops. Even the ease with which he preached the importance of prayer, though he himself, so far as is known, never prayed, is understandable within the overall context of Talleyrand's background and training. In that part of the *Mémoires* relating to his childhood at Chalais, he dwells at length on the responsibilities to the people which devolve upon the nobility, particularly the ancient nobility, of France—responsibilities which include the duty to offer aid and counsel in terms intelligible to the people. Talleyrand himself may not have believed; but he recognized that others believed, and he conceded their right to do so. So long as he was Bishop of Autun, he would employ his talents not only in administering his diocese to the best of his ability, but also in instructing and edifying the faithful—at least by his words, if not by his example. There was, in Talleyrand's mind, no question of hypocrisy. He had, not for the first time in his life or for the last, taken on responsibilities which, however uncongenial he might find them, he would meet with all the resources at his disposal.

At the same time, there is no doubt that Talleyrand's letter to Autun had about it something of the spirit and the purpose of a public relations campaign. But it was not so much the approval of the clergy and the people that he desired as their support. From Paris, he had been following closely the momentous changes then being worked in public opinion and in the political world. Paris was in the ferment of that political upheaval which, only a few months after Talleyrand's elevation to the bishopric of Autun, was to erupt into the Revolution. Everywhere, at every level, there was an air of expectancy. Those irreversible forces which precede revolutions were making themselves felt, and everyone, from the king to the common laborer to the cleverest conversationalist in the salon of Madame de Brionne, was conscious that great changes were in the air. The talk in the salons had shifted from the sands of gossip, scandal, and entertainments onto the more ominous ground of politics and economics. All, Talleyrand reports, "considered themselves able to rule the country. They criticized all the measures adopted by the ministers. The personal conduct of the king and queen was discussed and almost always incurred the disapproval of the salons of Paris. Young women spoke pertinently of all the branches of the administration." The throne, everyone felt, was tottering, and Paris was oppressed by a strong sense of approaching disaster. Misery, want, financial depression, and financial deficit were like warning fingers pointing to an ominous shape lurking in the shadows.

That shape, which by 1789 had assumed such definite lines that it could no longer be ignored, was the specter of national bankruptcy. It was not a sudden and unexpected crisis, but it was one which, under the *ancien régime,* there seemed to be no way of solving. The cost of France's participation in the American Revolution,* added to the enormous debts inherited from the reigns of Louis XIV and Louis XV and to the excessive and virtually unregulated expenditures of the state and the wastefulness of the court, had thrown the nation's finances into complete confusion. King Louis XVI, at the beginning of his reign, had done the best he could with the means at his disposal. He had entrusted the financial administration of the country to Jacques Turgot, a friend of Talleyrand's and a man of rare ability and courage. To King Louis, Turgot had explained his program in the simplest and most forceful terms: "There will be no bankruptcy, there will be no increase in taxation, and there will be no borrowing." He hoped to extricate the nation from its dilemma by two methods: first, by reducing expenditures and, second, by virtually abolishing government regulation of agriculture, commerce, and industry. The latter expedient was intended to increase the gross national product and therefore yield larger revenues for the state.

Turgot's methods had already been proved effective in one of France's poorer provinces, but applied on a national scale, they had created more problems than they solved. By abolishing needless expenditures, Turgot had offended everyone (and there were many) who enjoyed pensions and sinecures from the state. By doing away with state control of commerce, he had outraged the speculators. By suppressing the guilds, which limited production by limiting the number of workers in each industry, he had earned the hatred of organized labor. When he freed the peasants from the obligation to repair public roads (the *corvée*), he had drawn upon himself the vengeance of the landowners who were now saddled with the expense of such maintenance. Thus, all those who had prospered under the old system—the nobility, the clergy, and the bourgeoisie—were combined in opposition to Turgot and, reinforced by the provincial parlements and by the queen herself, brought great pressure upon King Louis to dismiss Turgot. The minister warned Louis: "Do not forget, your majesty, that it was

* The total deficit, in 1780, had already been 47,000,000 francs—of which 40,000,000 had gone, in one form or another, to support the American Revolution.

weakness which brought Charles I to the block." And Louis replied sadly, "Ah, Turgot and I are the only ones who love the people." But he yielded to the importunities of the queen and dismissed the man who might have saved the throne.

Turgot's fall threw a flood of light upon the nature of the *ancien régime*. All reformers were given notice that no changes affecting the privileged classes would be tolerated. Since the national finances could be saved only by reforms affecting those classes, there was no way out. From that time on, the fate of the system was sealed, and all that could now be done was to postpone the inevitable storm.

Turgot's successor had been Jacques Necker, a Genevan banker, whom Talleyrand despised for himself rather than for his policies. Necker succeeded nonetheless in attracting a great number of sincere enemies by proposing strict economy in state and court expenditures. The step which had particularly infuriated the court was his decision to publish a financial report showing the revenues and expenses of the state. This had never been done before, and the court was outraged that such great mysteries should be unveiled before the masses—particularly since the report showed how much was spent annually for pensions to the courtiers. Once more King Louis yielded to pressure, and Necker fell.

As the next minister, the court party had secured the appointment of Charles-Alexandre de Calonne. No one could have been more agreeable. His sole purpose seemed to be to please as many people as possible, and, for a while, he had succeeded. The members of the court had only to make their wishes known to have them gratified. For Calonne, a man of charm, wit, and intelligence, had an approach to the art of spending which was greatly appreciated by those around him. "A man who wishes to borrow must appear to be rich," he said, "and to appear rich, he must dazzle by spending freely." Talleyrand's verdict was to the point: Calonne was "like the clever steward of some ruined spendthrift." In this spirit, money flowed freely in those halcyon years. In three years, in a time of peace, Calonne borrowed nearly 300,000,000 livres—and spent twice that amount.

It had seemed too good to be true, and it was. In August, 1786, the time arrived for an accounting. The treasury was empty, money was urgently needed, and there was no one willing to lend to the state. In the face of this crisis, Calonne had made a sensible, though impolitic, move. He proposed a general tax, which should fall upon the nobles, as well as upon the lower classes. Predictably, the tax had aroused the same opposition as the measures proposed by Turgot and Necker. Calonne therefore had had to resign.

Loménie de Brienne, who followed him in office, had met the same fate. Since there had been nothing to do but propose new taxes, he had proposed them. The Parlement of Paris immediately protested and refused to

register the new tax law. The king himself appeared and attempted to overawe the deputies, but as soon as he had left the building, they revoked the
approval exacted by the king's presence. The provincial parlements had
followed the lead of Paris and refused to register any fiscal law not approved by the Parlement of Paris. Everywhere was heard the principle
enunciated in the capital: Taxes can be imposed only by those who are to
pay them. Everywhere, beginning with the Parlement of Paris, there were
demands for the convocation of the States-General of France. Finally, in
December, 1788, the king had been forced to acquiesce. For the first time
since 1614, the States-General was convoked. The representatives of the
three estates—the commoners, the clergy, and the nobility—were to meet
at Versailles, on May 4, 1789. King Louis, who had learned nothing in his
fifteen years on the throne, but who seemed to have forgotten the past, recalled to office the banker Necker—whom Talleyrand considered "the last
man who should have been chosen to fill as important a post as that of a
Minister of France at so critical a time."

All these events Talleyrand had followed intently during the years after
his ordination. He had known the ministers who, one after another, had
been compelled to resign as their proposals were rejected by the two
classes to which he belonged—the clergy and the nobility. He had seen
failure after failure in their attempts to restore order to a situation that was
beyond order. "It was not yet recognized," he explains, "that a few incontestable principles of political economy, and a reasonable use of public
credit, constitute the whole science of financial administration." Now the
unexpected had occurred. The States-General was to meet. His political
activities heretofore had been behind the scenes, in the salons, through the
medium of conversation and suggestion. Now a broad avenue to direct political power was being opened up to him, one that suited perfectly his talents and ambitions. He had, in 1783, met William Pitt in the house of the
Duke-Archbishop of Rheims. Talleyrand was, at the time, twenty-nine
years of age, and he as yet lived only on the fringes of power as Agent-
General of the Clergy. Pitt was twenty-five, but he had already been Chancellor of the Exchequer and, in a few months, would become Prime Minister. The differences between the English and French systems were no
doubt striking to a man as perceptive and ambitious as Talleyrand. In one
country, power was open to men of ability, regardless of age, by way of
Parliament. In the other, it was open only to age, by way of court intrigue.
Or rather, that had been the situation in France until Louis' decision to
convoke the States-General. Now opportunity was at hand. France was
about to convene its own approximate equivalent of Parliament, and it was
as a deputy to the assembly that one would find the means to satisfy ambition. In these circumstances, Talleyrand's mind had discerned the value of

Autun even before his consecration. He must be sent to the States-General as a deputy from his diocese. His efforts to win over the clergy and people of Autun had been more than a mere exercise in public relations. It had been a political campaign, one that was to be brought to its logical culmination during Talleyrand's announced sojourn in Autun.

On March 12, 1789, before dawn, the narrow streets of the town were already packed with people eager to see their bishop. Lookouts had been posted, and by midmorning Talleyrand's coach had been sighted on the approach to Autun. The bells of the churches began to ring as the bishop rode through the crowded streets, smiling and blessing his people with ready grace as the coach carried him to the cathedral, where a *Te Deum* was sung to celebrate his coming.

Talleyrand neglected none of the arts of the politician on campaign. He gave frequent dinners at the Bishop's Palace to which almost everyone was invited, and these entertainments were long remembered as having been one of the delights of his brief tenure as Bishop of Autun. At such gatherings, talk turned naturally to the problems of the town, secular as well as religious, and to the needs and aspirations of the people, both political and spiritual. During the day Talleyrand campaigned with equal and tireless skill, walking through the streets, conversing familiarly with respectable tradesmen's wives and families and discussing more serious matters with the men. To everyone his message was the same: Tell me what you wish me to do, and I will do it.

Occasionally, what the people wanted him to do was not precisely what he himself might have wished, but even then, he listened courteously and, if possible, acquiesced. There were times when he should have followed his own judgment rather than the opinions of others. One such instance occurred on March 25, the Feast of the Annunciation. The chapter of the cathedral had expressed a strong desire to have the pontifical mass celebrated by their bishop. It was not an unreasonable request, and so, after some hesitation, Talleyrand assented. It was the single mistake of his visit to Autun. Because of his lameness, he stumbled over the trailing vestments that he was required to wear, and because he had never before presided at so complex a ceremony, he stumbled over the rubrics, giving the wrong responses and generally showing himself so unfamiliar with the elaborate rites that several members of the chapter were moved to laugh so loudly as to be heard at the altar.

Talleyrand may not have known precisely how to celebrate a pontifical mass, but he knew how to conduct a campaign. He depended on good food, good wine, good conversation, and good public relations to the extent that these were the everyday tools of a man in search of office. But to those who were in a position to understand the situation of France he

offered more solid fare. In an address to the assembled clergy of his diocese, he set out an explicit program of social and economic reform that, for
its time, was amazingly radical. "No public act shall be the general law of
the land unless the people shall have solemnly consented to it," he said,
"and no taxes shall be imposed in violation of the inalienable and exclusive right of the people to establish taxes, to modify, limit, or revoke them,
and to legislate as to their use." Public order must be restored to France,
and public order rests on two foundations: liberty and property. Both are
sacred, but the time had come to consider whether or not certain things
had been unjustly designated as "property" which, in fact, belonged to the
nation as a whole rather than to any individual or group. The second basis
of public order, liberty, must be proclaimed anew and reinforced. Freedom
of speech and of the press must be guaranteed by law. Citizens must be
granted the right to trial by jury, and they must be protected from unjust
prosecution by habeas corpus. The right to education must be extended to
all classes of citizens. The finances of the nation must be reformed, not
with new taxes, but by abolishing old exemptions, by selling crown lands,
by organizing a sinking fund, and by establishing a national bank. Finally,
the fundamental right of every man to work must be recognized and implemented. To this end, government control of agriculture, industry, and
commerce must be done away with; only then would the opportunity to
earn a living be open to every Frenchman.

These were the things he had discussed, and heard discussed, in the salons of Paris. They were the things which he sincerely believed offered the
only possibility of salvation for France. His sincerity and his skill in presenting his ideas carried the day. On April 2, he was elected, by an overwhelming majority, deputy of the clergy from the bailliage* of Autun. Talleyrand was now one of the men chosen to reform France and, eventually,
to give it a constitution. He was in a position from which he could, and
would, rise to heights unforeseen by anyone except perhaps himself.

Even though he had obtained what he had come for, Talleyrand showed
no signs of being in a great hurry to leave Autun. Instead, he lingered for
ten days after the election, conferring with his new constituents and attending to his diocese as though the votes had not yet been cast and the
matter of a deputy not yet decided. Perhaps too hurried an exit after the
election would have raised doubts in the minds of the Autunois about the
sincerity of their bishop. Or it may have been that Talleyrand was not
eager to relinquish so soon the universal respect, admiration, and even

---

* The basic unit of representation in the States-General, which had its origin in medieval France
and which, by force of custom, had been used in the States-General of 1614 and therefore in that
of 1789.

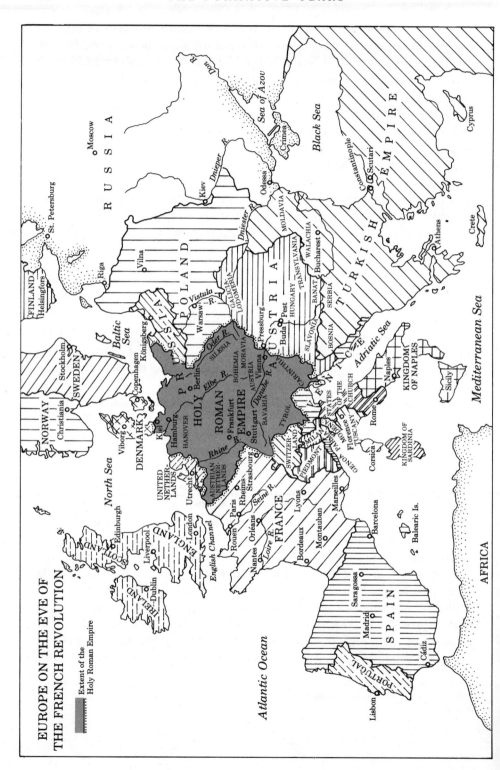

EUROPE ON THE EVE OF
THE FRENCH REVOLUTION

Extent of the
Holy Roman Empire

affection with which, for the first time in his life, he was surrounded. Yet he could not remain indefinitely. The States-General was to meet on May 4, and he had to be in Paris beforehand to lay the groundwork for his participation. Moreover, Easter was approaching, and the bishop would no doubt be expected to undergo once more the ordeal of a pontifical mass.

By April 12, Easter Day, he was on the road to Paris, to the States-General and to his destiny. He was never again to set foot in his diocese of Autun.

Part Two
REVOLUTION AND EXILE

(1789–1797)

The torrent formed by ignorance and passion was so violent that it was impossible for any man to stem it.

—Mémoires, Vol. I, p. 102

4

The Assembly

T HE STATES-GENERAL of France was convened on Sunday, May 4, 1789, at Versailles. It was a mild spring day, and the streets of the town were packed with people—Parisians, mostly—who had come to watch the deputies as they went in procession to the Church of St. Louis to pray for the guidance of the Holy Spirit. The Bishop of Autun was there, among his fellow representatives of the first estate, in his episcopal robes, stately and distinguished despite his limp. One observer who saw him at this time—but who recorded his recollections under the Restoration, when Talleyrand was in disgrace—remembered that "his appearance was not without a certain attraction. I was struck less by his good features than by his posture of indifference combined with malevolence, which had the effect of giving him a certain air—as though I were looking at the head of an angel, animated by the spirit of a demon." The figure which drew all eyes, however, was not that of Talleyrand, but of Talleyrand's friend, Philippe, Duke d'Orléans. It was whispered that Orléans' ambition was to displace his Bourbon cousin on the throne of France and to reign as a constitutional monarch.

Orléans had already won great popularity among the people by his widely publicized liberalism and by his open opposition in 1788 to King Louis' new taxes. He was conspicuous among the 289 deputies of the second estate,* who "glittered in gorgeous dresses and orders." Last in the

* The deputies representing the three traditional orders (states, or estates) were divided as follows: the clergy, 293; the nobility, 289; and the commons, or third estate, 595.

procession came the third estate. Gouverneur Morris, who was watching from a balcony in company with Madame de Flahaut, noted that, in contrast with the first estate, "superb in violet robes," and the flamboyant nobles, the commoners were somberly dressed "in black mantles, very plain, and hats without feathers." For all three orders, there were cheers and applause. And when the king was sighted, shouts of *Vive le roi!* resounded in the streets. Only Marie-Antoinette was regarded as a villain that day. When she left her carriage to enter the church, there was silence, broken by a few cries of *Vive le Duc d'Orléans.*

After the mass of the Holy Spirit, the deputies, led by the first order, repaired to the Salle des Menus Plaisirs at Versailles, where the Assembly was to be convened. Symbolically, the clergy and the nobles were seated on upholstered chairs to the left of the throne. To the right were the dignitaries and officials of the royal court and the princes of the blood, comfortable, according to their rank, on stools, chairs, or armchairs. Opposite the throne were the representatives of the third estate, on hard benches "with neither cushions nor backs."

The king opened the proceedings by a short address, in which he noted that "the day that I have desired in my heart for so long a time has finally arrived, and I am now surrounded by the representatives of the nation that it is my glory to command." His words were received with loud applause and, by some, with tears of joy. The good impression thus made, however, was mitigated by Necker, who rose to deliver a report on the financial state of the realm. He went on for one hour, then two, then three. By the end of the first hour the deputies were conversing in low tones among themselves. By the end of the second some were asleep and others were nodding. It was noted that the Bishop of Autun, almost alone among the representatives of his order, never wavered in his attention to the minister's report. But it hardly mattered. Necker, a firm liberal, was regarded as the man of the hour, the man who would save France. "The audience," Morris says, "saluted him with a long plaudit." When the applause had subsided, the King made ready to depart and received "a long and affecting *Vive le Roi.* The Queen rose, and to my great satisfaction, she heard for the first time in several months the sound of *Vive la Reine!* She made a low curtsey, and this produced a louder acclamation; and that, a lower curtsey."

The sovereigns having withdrawn, the deputies filed out of the hall in the order prescribed by etiquette: the clergy, the nobles, and then the representatives of the people. The men of the States-General returned to their houses in groups to plan for the coming sessions. The king returned to his hounds and horses; the queen, to her balls and dresses. And Necker to his columns of figures, his hopes, and his illusions. The great adventure had begun.

The States-General was, from the very beginning, confronted by difficulties that seem, at least in retrospect, almost insurmountable. To the casual observer, the nation—with the exception of the court—seemed united in the determination to effect radical reforms. So it was in fact. But the spirit which had animated the higher clergy and the nobility in the time of Richelieu was not yet dead. These two orders were determined on reform. But it had to be a reform which left their ancient privileges and powers intact. This determination was symbolized dramatically by the fact that after the opening ceremonies of the Assembly, the nobles and the clergy declared that they would exercise their ancient prerogative of holding themselves separate from the third estate. The implication was clear: Since the three estates were to deliberate separately and vote separately, the fact that the representatives of the people outnumbered those of the clergy and nobles—595 to 582—was irrelevant. Any matter on which the first and second estates differed from the third would be carried by the former—with two estates voting for approval (or disapproval) and one voting in a contrary sense. The effect of this arrangement, hallowed as it was by time and tradition, was to deprive the third estate of any real voice in the decisions of the Assembly. Its sessions were to be no more than a forum for the expression of opinions which the clergy and the nobles, in their wisdom, might choose either to consider or to ignore. On May 6, at the very first session of the States-General, the first and second estates made known their intentions, and on that same day, the third estate declared that it would not accept this procedure. The Assembly was therefore paralyzed. Worse, it seemed that there was no cure, for, at this stage, each estate maintained that its position was irreversible. Two parties were thus automatically created: the aristocrats and the people.

There is no doubt that Talleyrand, at this moment, was wholly of the opinion of his peers that the conduct of the affairs of France was the privilege, indeed the right, of the upper classes. His background, his training, and his own thinking made it impossible for him to feel otherwise. The liberal opinions that he had stated to his clergy of Autun, concerning the rights of the people to liberty, prosperity, and protection from oppression, were perfectly sincere. But it was the prerogative of the aristocracy to recognize and implement these rights, not that of the people to claim them unilaterally. Paternalism, or rather benevolent despotism, was an integral part of his heritage, and it had been passed on to him at Chalais, by his great-grandmother. These attitudes he cherished throughout his life, under every form of government and in every circumstance. They were attitudes, he declared in his old age, that "increase from generation to generation. For a long time to come, people whose fame or fortune are of recent origin will be unable to appreciate their sweetness."

In this frame of mind, he was bewildered by the vehemence with which the leaders of the third estate—Mirabeau, Bailly, Sieyès, Malouet, and others—were demanding their "rights." He was then, as he was to remain, a man of order, compromise, and moderation. Extremism in any form he abhorred, and violence, even in rhetoric, he found incomprehensible. "He was," wrote Aimée de Coigny, who knew him well, "preoccupied solely with neutralizing violence."

There was a great deal for him to do in this respect. He had opposed from the first the plan adopted by Necker for the composition of the States-General, which, he felt, gave to the third estate an "almost unlimited latitude" in the right to elect or be elected. Even worse, it caused "the representatives of the third estate to be composed almost exclusively of lawyers*—a class of men whose method of thinking, as necessarily results from their profession, generally makes them dangerous" in public affairs. The harm, however, had already been done: "The greatest mistake was to authorize the third estate to elect as many deputies as the other two orders together. This concession could be useful only if the three orders were combined into a single body. And therefore, by granting it, this fusion was made inevitable and consented to implicitly." The fault was, no doubt, that of Necker. But the solution would have to be found by the Assembly itself, and it would have to be found with as little delay as possible. The vehemence of the "lawyers" was beginning to communicate itself to the people, and already it was being said publicly that the arrogance of the first and second estates was preventing the fiscal relief of which the nation was so desperately in need.

The struggle over the question of whether the three estates would deliberate jointly or separately continued from May 5 to June 9. As the days went by, apparently in fruitless debate, there was a constant displacement of opinion in favor of the third estate. Necker's opening address, in retrospect, had left much to be desired; he had avoided entirely the critical question of constitutional reform, for one thing, and, for another, he had made dangerous allusions to his "confidence in the generosity" of the privileged classes. Finally, the two higher orders had hoped for strong intervention by the government in favor of their privilege of separate deliberation, and Necker had responded only by a feeble and ineffectual recommendation. It had begun to appear that the clergy and the nobles, rather than having placed themselves in opposition to the representatives of the people and on the side of their natural allies, the government and

---

* There were, in fact, 365 lawyers out of 595 deputies of the third estate. Of the remainder, 179 were government employees of one kind or another; small businessmen (merchants, landlords, etc.), 142; and farmers, 142. On the whole, it was a thoroughly middle-class representation. (*Liste Complète de Messieurs les Députés*, British Museum F 828 [3].)

the crown, were instead isolated, if not alienated, from both in their determination to maintain their ancient privileges.

Despite the ferocity of the debate which raged around him, Talleyrand,
during the weeks following the convening of the Assembly, seemed peculiarly inactive. He had, no doubt, been shocked by the violence of the passions unleashed among the representatives of the third estate. But this
reaction did not affect him as it did some of his noble and reverend associates. Rather than awaken in him the determination to resist, at any cost,
the pretensions of the third estate, it evoked a recognition of reality. It was
obvious that Mirabeau and the other leaders of the commons* had not the
slightest intention of giving way. Indeed, they had refused even to allow
the credentials of their members to be verified or any officials to be elected
other than a *doyen*, or dean, on the grounds that any decision reached by
one estate independently of the other two was invalid. In the face of this
situation, discretion and moderation came to the fore. "So violent," Talleyrand says, "was the torrent of ignorance and passion that it was impossible
to control it. Those who foresaw most clearly where this was all leading
therefore adopted, to the extent that prudence permitted, a passive role.
This, generally, was the course that I followed."

There were some among Talleyrand's associates who were not so prudent. The nobles, it is true, despite the presence among them of a small
group of liberals—the Duke d'Orléans and his party—were vociferously
opposed to any concession which might compromise their privileged position with respect to the commons. Among the members of the first estate,
however, there were men who, by birth and by sentiment, belonged among
the commons rather than among the clergy. These were the members of
the lower clergy—the country pastors—who had been elected by their parishioners. They were the weak link in the solid front of the first two orders. To them the commons found an adroit way of appealing. On June 10
the Abbé Sieyès moved, and his motion was seconded by Mirabeau, that
the clergy and the nobles be summoned formally to join the commons, and
that, on June 12, the credentials of all deputies be verified.

Two days passed, and there was no response from the higher orders.
But, on the thirteenth, when the commons had already begun verification
of its deputies' mandates, three members of the first estate, country priests,
appeared and requested admission. They were received with wild enthusiasm. On the fourteenth, a large number of the clergy, also from the lower

* At the inception of the Assembly, the third estate had taken the name of communes, or commons. The term, which had enjoyed an honorable history in medieval France, connoted, above all,
resistance to feudal privilege. This, considered in connection with the meaning that "Commons"
had acquired in England, was intended as an expression of the third estate's refusal to accept subordinate rank in France's social or political hierarchy.

ranks, were admitted, and the commons, thus encouraged, on June 15, took a bold step and proclaimed itself *the* National Assembly. It had, in a stroke, gathered all power into its own hands and proclaimed that the clergy and nobles had ceased to exist in the political life of France. Four days later the clergy formally voted to join the commons.

The growing strength of the commons had been the cause of much speculation among the members of the royal court, and now the defection of the first estate turned that unease into alarm. The king's youngest brother, the Count d'Artois,* was, at this time, on good terms with Marie-Antoinette, and together they were able to persuade King Louis that he must put an end to the mischief before it went further. On the morning of June 20, therefore, in a downpour, the deputies arrived at their hall to find the doors closed and workmen in possession. The hall was being prepared, they were told, for a royal session two days later. The deputies, indignant, then withdrew to the tennis courts nearby (the *Jeu de Paume*) and, after rejecting a motion by Sieyès to adjourn to Paris, pledged themselves by a solemn oath "never to separate, but to meet wherever circumstances may dictate, until the constitution of the realm and public reform are established and implemented."

It was nothing less than a solemn, direct, and public challenge to the king. But Louis was too convinced of his divine right and too much dependent upon his queen and his brother to be daunted. The royal session convened, a day late, on June 23, and the king's address was read. For two months past, the deputies were told, they had accomplished nothing, and now the time had come for them to return to their duties. The king therefore commanded that the separation between the three orders be maintained. After announcing a number of reforms, mostly of a fiscal nature, he ordered the deputies to separate immediately into their respective estates and to attend to their duties. Then he withdrew, followed by the royal party. The deputies, however, refused to move. The royal master of ceremonies, noting this, repeated the king's command to Bailly, president of the Assembly, and Bailly replied firmly that since the Assembly was in session, he could not adjourn it without a motion and a vote. When the master of ceremonies persisted, Mirabeau stood and, in his thundering voice, spoke the deputies' defiance: "We are here by the will of the people, and we will leave only at the point of the bayonet." When this was reported to Louis, he could say only that if the deputies refused to leave the hall, then the best course, obviously, was to allow them to remain.

The Assembly's display of strength and the king's weakness provoked

* Artois' eldest brother, the Count de Provence, would succeed to the throne as Louis XVIII, through Talleyrand's influence, in 1814. Artois would eventually succeed him (1824) and reign as Charles X.

great consternation in Talleyrand's mind. He was a reformer, but not yet a revolutionary, and he saw that, if the commons was allowed to defy the crown with impunity, revolution was inevitable. The Assembly would not be able to resist the constantly increased pressure of the people of Paris for drastic and perhaps fatal changes at the social and economic levels. The previous winter had been one of unparalleled severity, bread had been difficult to obtain, and the city's inhabitants had suffered intensely. They had formed the habit, from the opening day of the States-General, of making the journey to Versailles, at first to listen and then to assemble in the streets and to demonstrate. Mirabeau, Sieyès, Mounier, and other popular members were constantly receiving ovations, which they soon learned to convert into political weapons, and as the people became jaded, the leaders' rhetoric of necessity became more and more extravagant so as to elicit the public support that they now found indispensable. All this—as both the court and the Assembly knew—was but the faint echo of a great and dangerous force, rumbling ominously twelve miles away in the city of Paris, a force which, if not controlled, might sweep away not only the evils of the system, but the system itself.

Talleyrand's own belief was that France's only reasonable hope of salvation lay in the establishment of a two-chamber system similar to that of England, in which the commons would correspond to the lower house of the British Parliament and in which "a peerage, composed of members of the episcopacy and of heads of noble families of the oldest nobility, greatest wealth and lustre" would have powers similar to those enjoyed at that time by the House of Lords. It was a moderate and prudent course, which would have at once preserved the monarchy, though in constitutional form, and made possible the reforms so essential to the nation. In pursuit of it, Talleyrand decided to act. He was on amicable terms with the Count d'Artois, who, he says, "was then displaying kindness and even (if I may quote his own words) friendship toward me," and he asked for an interview, in which he suggested that Artois relay to the king the suggestion that "the States-General be dissolved, but that, circumstances being what they were, they then be reconvoked according to one of the plans I have described"—that is, in the form of an upper and a lower chamber. Talleyrand's advice, however, was thought to be "too risky." It was a course, he explains sadly, "which required strength, and there was no one in the king's party capable of strength."

Talleyrand now drew the inevitable conclusion: The monarchy was lost. Or rather, it had assented, through inaction, to its own destruction. All that could now be done was to save what could be saved of France as he knew it:

> There was but one reasonable course to take, and that was to yield without being forced to do so and while there was still some credit in doing so.

This might prevent matters from being carried to extremes. It compelled the third estate to be circumspect, and it enabled the other two orders to retain some influence over the common deliberations and to gain time—which often means to gain everything. If there was still a chance to recover lost ground, this was the only one. I did not hesitate, therefore, to join the men who set this example.

The men who set the example for the first estate were the very large group of humble curés who, on June 24, joined the commons. On June 25, forty-seven of the nobles followed them, led by the king's cousin and the first prince of the blood, the Duke d'Orléans. On June 26, Talleyrand, in company with several other bishops, did likewise. And on June 27, the king, seeing that he had been presented with a *fait accompli*, commanded the deputies of the first and second estates to join themselves to their fellows in the third. There was now, legally and officially, but one order, and that was the National Assembly.

Talleyrand was in a better position by far to exercise some influence over the course of the Assembly than he had been when his field of action had been limited to the first and second estates. For one thing, he was very well acquainted with the leaders of the commons, especially with Mirabeau, the renegade nobleman who had had himself elected as a deputy of the third estate. In the years before the convocation of the States-General, Mirabeau had been one of Talleyrand's circle of intimates and, probably through Talleyrand's intercession with friends at court, had been given a post as a secret agent of the foreign service in Berlin. In gratitude, Mirabeau had used his limited influence with the government in support of Talleyrand's candidacy for the bishopric of Autun. There had been a violent rupture between the two men, to which gossip assigned two possible causes: a letter to Calonne, Minister of Finance, from Mirabeau, containing uncomplimentary remarks about Talleyrand, which Calonne showed to the latter, or—and this was the more common belief—the fact that as soon as Mirabeau was safely in Berlin, Talleyrand had replaced him in the affections of his mistress. Whatever the cause of the quarrel, Talleyrand and Mirabeau had quickly made it up, so much so that profiting from Mirabeau's friendship with Calonne, Talleyrand had been initiated by the minister into the mysteries of government finance and had thus been enabled to speculate, to great advantage, in the state funds and to lay the cornerstone of his later fortune. (It was this activity that Louis XVI had found so reprehensible as to cause Talleyrand's name to be struck from the list of men eligible for the episcopacy.) Mirabeau himself had reaped much profit from this sort of adventure, and there were many other aspects of his life, as Talleyrand very well knew, that would not bear too close scrutiny. But the two men were drawn together by the bond which unites friends, as well as by that which joins together accomplices. They seemed to have had a genuine respect for each other's talents and a mutual delight in each other's wit.

With Mirabeau, Talleyrand felt very much at home, and their intimacy was confirmed when the two met in the now duly constituted Assembly. The leader of the commons went often to Talleyrand's house,* where, in addition to Choiseul and Narbonne, a partially new circle of friends had begun to gather. It was comprised of the leaders of the militant wing of the Assembly, hardly any of whom were themselves very representative of "the people": the Duke de Biron,† the Duke de La Rochefoucauld, the Abbé Sieyès, the Abbé Grégoire, the Marquis de Lafayette (who, having never forgotten the glory he had reaped in America, was determined to repeat his performance in France), the Marquis de Sillery, the Viscount de Noailles, and a host of journalists, economists, merchants, and authors. The center of this group, though not actually its leader, was the Duke d'Orléans, who was often present in the company of his henchman and confidential agent, Choderlos de Laclos, author of *Liaisons Dangereuses*. Orléans' liberalism seemed to offer some hope of averting the storm that Talleyrand and his noble friends now perceived as imminent. If the intransigence of Louis XVI should cost him his throne, Orléans, as head of the cadet branch of the royal dynasty, might advance his own candidacy and give to France that constitutional monarchy which was now, in Talleyrand's opinion, the indispensable minimum for the survival of the throne.

Precisely how far this group was committed to Orléans is not clear. There is no doubt that they were generally regarded as hostile to Louis XVI, which is not wholly true, and that they were looked upon and spoken of as a sort of shadow government of opposition, which, in the light of later developments, appears probable.**

Given the rapidity with which matters were moving in the last days of June and the first days of July, this hope, rather than subversive, seemed only moderate, for the leaders of the Assembly were obviously losing their

---

* Soon after the convocation of the States-General, Talleyrand had given up his house in the Faubourg St.-Germain and taken another in the rue de l'Université.

† Biron had fought with Washington in America, where he was known as the Duke de Lauzun, and from which he had imported a revolutionary zeal equal to that of his friend, Lafayette.

** It was, and still is, commonly believed that both Talleyrand and his friend Mirabeau had accepted sums of money from the court in exchange for the use of their influence in defending the monarchy. There is no real evidence to support this allegation—a fact which signifies very little, since the nature of the transaction and the prudence of Talleyrand would preclude written evidence. It would not have been out of character for Talleyrand to accept payment for acting on his own convictions—as was amply demonstrated in his later career. To someone who once remonstrated with him for this practice, Talleyrand replied: "Your honesty and my honesty are not the same honesty."

control over events. The restlessness of the Parisians had reached fever pitch just at the moment that the commons had won its victory over the first and second estates. The working classes were demanding food; the middle classes, who saw in the Assembly their only hope of avoiding bankruptcy, were demanding reforms; and the intellectual and professional classes were agitating among both these groups. By the end of June the army itself—French Guards quartered in the capital—had registered its sympathy with the people by rising in mutiny and refusing the order of their commander to return to their barracks. The Assembly had accomplished its revolt. In Paris, another revolt was in its first stages. And now the troops in the capital were in open mutiny. Something, obviously, had to be done. What the court party—that is, the queen and the Count d'Artois—undertook was to persuade King Louis that in the use of force lay his only hope of saving the situation. By using the army, he could simultaneously rid himself of the liberal and ineffectual Necker, dissolve the National Assembly, and reduce Paris to order. Louis listened and, as always, acquiesced. New commanders were appointed for the Parisian troops, and other regiments were ordered to move on the city. By the first week of July it had become clear, as Talleyrand pointed out, that it was the king's intention "to arrest by force a movement which the government had failed utterly to foresee." The Assembly then voted a resolution asking the king to withdraw his troops and to authorize instead the establishment of a civic guard in Paris. The king's answer reflected a firmness of purpose which, if it had been employed a month earlier, might have saved his throne. He would not order his troops to withdraw; he would use them instead to put down disorder.

When news of the king's decision reached Paris, on July 11, the representatives of the various sections of the city voted immediately to defy the royal order and, on their own authority, to establish a civic guard. Bailly was elected mayor of Paris, and the Marquis de Lafayette was appointed commander of the newly formed body called the National Guard. In answer, Louis, on the same day, dismissed the popular Necker, appointed in his place a highly unpopular reactionary, the Baron de Breteuil, and ordered his troops to move into the city. The following day Paris rose in open revolt. On July 14 the people stormed the Bastille, the state prison and therefore the symbol of royal oppression. Late in the afternoon it fell, and its commander and his officers were massacred. The king's troops had not been ordered to resist the people, and therefore, drawn by the excitement, a great number of them had joined sides with the people and directed the assault. "The instrument of force thus escaped from the hands which tried to make use of it" were the words, like an epitaph, which Talleyrand used to describe the collapse of the crown's authority in the capital of France. "From this moment, the government is powerless."

It appeared to Talleyrand that there was still a chance to save the throne and perhaps even the king. On July 15 he asked to be received by the latter. He had no doubt consulted with Mirabeau and with some of his other friends from the rue de l'Université, and he had a plan to offer. Since his overtures to Artois for the dissolution of the Assembly and its reconstitution in the form of a true parliament had been rejected, he was determined to appeal directly to Louis' innate good sense and to his undoubted love for his people. The answer that he received, however, was that his majesty had designated his brother, the Count d'Artois, to receive the Bishop of Autun.

The interview took place on the night of July 16, at the royal residence of Marly. Talleyrand was accompanied by several friends, "members of the National Assembly, and of that minority of the nobility who were representatives of the third estate." It is not improbable that Mirabeau was among them.*

> When we were in the presence of the Count d'Artois, we explained to him, in all frankness, the situation of affairs and of the state as it appeared to us. We said to him that it was a great mistake to believe that the agitation that was stirring all minds could be easily calmed. The time was past when delays, caution, and a few concessions might avert the dangers which threatened France, the throne, and the king himself. Only an energetic display of royal authority, wisely and skillfully employed, could do so.

What Talleyrand suggested to Artois was nothing less than that he and his friends be asked by the king to form a government. "We know," he assured the count, "the ways and the means and the position which would enable us to undertake this and which guarantee our success if the confidence of the king should entrust us with it."

Artois listened attentively. "He fully understood us," Talleyrand noted, "but was perhaps inclined to think that we were exaggerating the danger of the situation and our own importance in being able to remedy it." In any event, the king's brother had been instructed only to listen to Talleyrand's proposal and to report to Louis on its nature.† "The Count d'Artois was

---

* The account of the interview is that given by Talleyrand to the Baron de Vitrolles, in 1814. "M. de Talleyrand named to me the friends who accompanied him," Vitrolles comments, but he does not transcribe those names. Artois himself confirmed the accuracy of Talleyrand's report to Vitrolles by assuring the latter that it was "the exact truth." (Letter of Vitrolles dated April 6, 1852, transcribed in the Mémoires, Vol. I, pp. 106–8.)

† The remainder of the exchange between Artois and Talleyrand follows the account given by the latter to the Count de Baucourt and reproduced by Baucourt in the Mémoires as an appendix (Vol. I, pp. 104–6). It agrees in almost every detail with that of Vitrolles.

much affected, rose, and went to the king. After a prolonged absence, he returned to declare to M. de Talleyrand that nothing could be done with the king, who was determined to yield rather than to cause a single drop of blood to be shed by resisting the popular uprisings."

Artois himself saw no hope of saving the monarchy, and he was therefore determined to save at least himself. "As for me," he told Talleyrand, "my decision is made. I depart tomorrow. I am leaving France." Talleyrand pleaded with Artois to remain, pointing out that emigration at such a time might well jeopardize his own claim to the throne and that of his children; but Artois held firm. Matters had gone too far for a prince of the blood now to be concerned about rights of accession to a throne that would soon cease to exist. Talleyrand then reminded Artois that "since the king and the princes are determined to desert their own interests and those of the monarchy, it now becomes necessary for each of us to think of his own interests." *

"Indeed," Artois replied, "that is what I advise you to do. Whatever happens, I shall never hold you at fault, and you may always rely on my friendship."

It is beyond doubt that Talleyrand was perfectly sincere in this effort to preserve the monarchy and King Louis. To the institution he was attached by the strongest ties of both tradition and personal conviction, and to the man he was bound by the sense of loyalty to legitimate succession that was of such importance in the France of the *ancien régime*. For a nobleman to attack a monarch's character, ability, or performance of his duties was regarded as his privilege, provided he was willing to accept the risks involved, but to desert the sovereign in the hour of peril would have been a dishonor too horrible to be borne by a "cousin" of the king. Honor required that Talleyrand stand firm at least until the king himself had signified his intention of deserting his "own interests and those of the monarchy." This aristocratic requirement had now been fulfilled, and Talleyrand had therefore served notice that he would thenceforward look to his own interests.

These interests left only two courses open to him. Either he must follow the example set by Artois and emigrate, or he must, as he himself had said, "support the new state of affairs." The possibility of emigration was not considered lightly. "The Count d'Artois was the first to give the signal for it," he said, "and his departure caused me much grief. I loved him, and it needed all the force of my reason to keep me from following him." The

* According to Vitrolles' account, "we begged of the Count d'Artois permission to add that if the application we now made conscientiously and in good faith was not appreciated and if it had no effect and led to no result, Monseigneur must not be astonished if, not being able to resist the torrent that threatened to carry all before it, we should support the new state of affairs."

temptation was very strong to follow the man who might conceivably be the next King of France, if, as now seemed certain, Louis XVI were to lose his throne. The aristocrat's loyalty to a legitimate heir to the crown was basic, absolute, and almost natural; with respect to the Duke d'Orléans, who might become king through expediency rather than through the right of succession, loyalty would wax and wane according to circumstances. To these honorable sentiments were joined the entreaties of Talleyrand's friends, Madame de Brionne and her daughter, the Princess de Carignan, and the example set by several of the princes of the blood and by many of the aristocrats, and perhaps also his own interior doubts about whether he would be able successfully to meet and to control "the torrent which threatened to carry all before it."

Finally, he decided against emigration. "There could have been a necessity for emigrating only if there had been a personal danger against which France could have afforded no refuge. . . . This danger did not exist at that time, and it might have been prevented altogether; but the first effect of emigration was to create it." Most of the nobility were unable to leave the kingdom because of age, sickness, or poverty, and, he points out, those who remained were inevitably and seriously compromised by those who went abroad. "The nobles who could not leave became objects of suspicion, which soon degenerated into hatred; they were compelled therefore to join the ruling party out of fear or to become its victims." Another serious consideration was that emigration might entail the loss of titles and of estates. The former might be repaired, but "property, once lost, could not be restored as easily as titles. . . . The loss of property would then be an incurable disease, not only for the nobles themselves, but for the entire state. . . ." Thus, in Talleyrand's opinion, Artois and his friends who had fled France had been guilty of a form of betrayal of themselves, their class, and their country. "Far from being a duty, emigration could be excused only by the immensity of a personal danger from which there is no other way of escaping."

The elaborate rationale against emigration, written in Talleyrand's old age, very likely reflected, at least to some extent, his true reasons for deciding, as he put it, "not to leave France until constrained to do so by personal danger, to do nothing to provoke such danger, not to struggle against a torrent which must be allowed to pass." The danger to himself seemed slight. His position in the Assembly, his friendship with Mirabeau and with Orléans, and his own record as a supporter of liberal measures would protect him, at least for the moment, from attack. There was no point in abandoning his position, his rank, his titles because of what might be. The part of a prudent man was to remain and to retain a position which might allow him "to save those who could be saved, to take advantage of any opportunity which presented itself, and to hold myself in readiness for such an opportunity."

For another three years, he was to remain in France and to play an important role in the momentous events of that extraordinary era, while all those of his class who were able fled to the safety of England, Germany, and Italy, abandoning their less fortunate friends and relatives and their possessions to the fury of the rising storm.

The three years which followed the fall of the Bastille were a time of intense activity for Talleyrand. Although he adhered closely to his self-imposed rule of prudence, as he says, "on most questions," he felt that he could not ignore the great issue which had originally brought France to the brink of revolution: that of fiscal reform. So he confined his active intervention, he says, to "matters relative to the finances of the state."

That is not entirely accurate. On July 14, the day of the Bastille's fall, he had been appointed to the Constitutional Committee of the Assembly. His reputation as a man of intelligence and moreover of liberal opinions, together with his close ties to Mirabeau, was responsible for this important appointment; and he was determined that this stepping-stone to higher positions should not be wasted. The report of the committee was intended to be the basis on which the Assembly was to give to France what all classes of citizens earnestly desired: a constitution. Its duty, therefore, was to define the rights of the citizens and the responsibilities and organization of the government. It was, in other words, to re-create France. Throughout the month of August, the committee's preliminary recommendations were debated at length, not only in the Assembly, but also in the streets of Versailles and of Paris. Then, on the twenty-seventh, by unanimous vote, a motion was passed adopting the document known to history as the Declaration of the Rights of Man.* It is known for certain that Talleyrand was the author of the sixth of the Declaration's twenty-two articles. It was on his motion that it was adopted by the Assembly. And it had applications that went far beyond "the finances of the state":

> VI. The law is an expression of the will of the community. All citizens have a right to concur, either personally or by their representatives, in its formation. It should be the same to all, whether it protects or punishes; and all being equal in its sight, are equally eligible to all honors, places, and employments, according to their different abilities, without any other distinction than that created by their virtues and talents.†

* The original title, reflected in Tom Paine's classic translation of the document, was "Declaration of the Rights of Man and of the Citizen by the National Assembly of France."

† This is the text of Paine's translation. Despite the wide acceptance of the translator's language, it lacks something of the elegant simplicity of Talleyrand's idiom.

It was as though Talleyrand himself, having personally been the victim of the injustice of the old system, having been compelled to give up his rightful place as the Périgord heir and forced into a profession for which he had neither qualifications nor liking, having been deprived of honors and employments for which he was preeminently qualified, had composed Article VI within the framework of his own experience. What to later generations were to be self-evident principles were, in the France of 1789, a daring and vigorous assertion of the most radical revolutionary beliefs, and as such it threatened the foundations of every regime in Europe. It was intended as such by the Constitutional Committee which framed it. Two members of the committee tell us that, upon first hearing Talleyrand read the draft of his Article VI, they shivered with emotion and excitement. Its nature was immediately obvious to the Assembly, which gave Talleyrand an ovation when the article was presented and moved.

Within that context, Talleyrand's modest assertion that he limited his activities to "matters relating to the finances of the State" takes on new significance. The Declaration, as a whole, reflects precisely the same principles and remedies that he had preached to his clergy in Autun while soliciting their support for himself as their deputy to the States-General and that had been incorporated, verbatim, into the *cahier*, or instructions, handed him by his constituents upon his departure from Autun: human liberty, freedom from oppression, habeas corpus, freedom of speech and of the press, representative taxation, and, what was most important at that particular moment, the right of the citizens or their representatives "in cases of evident public necessity" to suspend property rights.

The unanimous adoption of the Declaration signaled the beginning of Talleyrand's attempts to remedy the economic disorder of the state by the careful application of its principles. On August 27, he spoke to the Assembly to recommend authorization for the government to borrow 80,000,000 livres in order to meet its day-to-day expenses. This, it is true, was no more than Calonne had done, or Brienne, or Necker. The difference was that in this instance, it was not the government which required the people to find the necessary funds. It was the people themselves, through their representatives, who voted to accept this responsibility. Even so, the mere voting of new monies could be nothing more than a temporary expedient. The resources and the credit of the state were exhausted, and the people could not be expected to bear indefinitely the fiscal burden imposed upon them by decades of incompetent and wasteful administration under the old regime. A new source of revenue must be found, and quickly.

On October 10, 1789, Talleyrand asked the president of the Assembly for permission to speak. The hall became quiet. It was rare that Talleyrand spoke. Unlike his confreres, he mounted the dais only when he had something of importance to say. On this occasion, even the men of the Assembly which had proclaimed the Declaration of the Rights of Man listened in astonishment as the Bishop of Autun proposed radical surgery to restore France to fiscal health. "The ordinary means of revenue are now exhausted," he declared. "The people are in the direst of straits and are unable to bear the smallest increase in taxes, however justifiable such an increase might be. There is, however, another source of revenue, as immense as it is as yet untapped, which, in my opinion, may be utilized without offending the rights of property even in their strictest sense." Then he loosed the thunderbolt: "This source, it seems to me, is the property of the church."

The Assembly was instantly in an uproar. The Bishop of Autun was proposing nothing less than the despoliation of the greatest landowner in Europe, the church of France, which—as Talleyrand well knew from his days as Agent-General of the Clergy—owned perhaps one-fifth of the land of the kingdom. Talleyrand waited until the noise had subsided and then continued as though he had heard nothing. "It seems to me," he said quietly, "that there is no need to discuss at great length this question of ecclesiastical property. It is evident that the clergy is not a proprietor in the same sense that others are, since the goods of which they have the use and of which they cannot dispose were given to them not for their personal benefit, but for use in the performance of their functions."

What he proposed, therefore, was not merely that church property be stripped of its exemption from taxation, but that it be transferred to the state—"nationalized." He then offered the motion that:

> The National Assembly declares that all ecclesiastical property is at the disposal of the nation, with the charge of providing in a suitable manner for the expenses of worship, support of ministers and relief of the poor, under the surveillance, and following the instructions of the provinces.
>
> That, in the measures to be taken to provide for the support of ministers of religion, revenues [for each individual minister] must be not less than 1,200 livres per annum, exclusive of house and gardens therewith.

The motion was promptly seconded, and Talleyrand retired to his seat in the Assembly. The debate raged until November 2, when the question was called, the votes cast, and the motion passed by a large majority. Not once during the debate is it recorded that Talleyrand again spoke for the measure. After preparing the motion and presenting it, he turned the matter over to Mirabeau and occupied himself with other things. He knew his strength; and he knew his weaknesses also. He was too cool, too detached, and too logical to be effective in the give-and-take of open discussion in an Assembly of several hundred persons, whereas Mirabeau, with his booming voice and total willingness to sacrifice logic and reason to rhetoric, was able to answer all arguments, confound all adversaries, and, if necessary, outshout all opponents, for days on end without showing the slightest trace of confusion, weariness, or remorse.

The motion authorizing the confiscation of ecclesiastical property was one of the most significant acts of Talleyrand's career in the Assembly and one of the most controversial accomplishments of his career. He was, literally, never to hear the end of it. It began with letters from his own clergy of Autun protesting their bishop's part in the loss of "their property." Talleyrand answered, reminding them that so far as he was able to ascertain, the clergy had never owned property. "You must know, gentlemen, that we are only administrators and that as individuals we have no real right to whatever property may be necessary to our existence." The answer of the cathedral chapter of Autun was to circulate a letter among the priests of the diocese, asking them "while showing every sign of respect due to the dignity of our bishop, and with appropriate regard for his great talents, to try to do battle against his system to the very end."

The reaction of the clergy in the rest of France was, predictably, less muted. It was said openly that Talleyrand, "having enriched himself by the most vile means possible, now dares propose to strip the clergy of its goods while he poses before the abused people of France as a model of generosity." The frustrated rage of the clerics carried them so far as to declare that Talleyrand had entered the church solely with the intention of robbing it: "Having decided at an early age to sacrifice the clergy to the nation, he felt that the most effective way to betray it was to have himself consecrated a bishop."

Such words Talleyrand bore with as much patience, or rather indifference, as he did the respectful solicitations of his clergy of Autun. In later years, when he was to be reproached for having been responsible for the church's loss of its wealth in France, he would pretend not to have heard. So total did his deafness become in this respect that he did not even bother, in the *Mémoires*, to mention the confiscation of clerical riches by the nation. It may be that, having himself devoted much effort to the accumulation of money, he understood too well the greed of others to feel that a comment was necessary.

The passage of the confiscation act strengthened Talleyrand's position in the Assembly, and whatever harm it may have done him among the clergy, it spread his fame among the people. He now moved on to other work which, though less controversial, had at least as much substance for the long-range welfare of France. "I opposed the creation of paper money," he says, "and the reduction of the interest on the national debt. I established, in a rather extensive essay, the principles on which I believed a national bank should be founded. I proposed the establishment of universal weights and measures." This modest summary, given in the *Mémoires*, omits a great deal that is to Talleyrand's credit. Among other things, he drew up the police regulations for Paris, supported the suppression of the feudal revenues of the church (the tithes), proposed the enfranchisement of Jews in France, and devised a method for the insuring of loans—in addition to his work on the Constitutional Committee and on the confiscation act. All this he did within the space of five months. He had learned to follow the rule of the Duke de Choiseul and did nothing himself that he could delegate to others. "In this way," he explained later, "one's day has more than twenty-four hours."

The single accomplishment of which Talleyrand was proudest during his membership in the Assembly was the *Report on Public Education* which he prepared for the Constitutional Committee. "To accomplish this great work," he explains, "I consulted the most learned men and the most prominent scholars of the time. . . . Everyone assisted me, and the fame that this work enjoys now requires that I name them." * The *Report* was indeed a landmark in public education in Europe, and its influence, particularly in the schools of France, was to survive Talleyrand himself by more than a century.†

By the beginning of 1790 Talleyrand's reputation as a careful observer, diligent worker, and liberal thinker had spread among his associates in the Assembly to the point that he had fully emerged as one of their recognized and most influential leaders. When criticism of the Assembly's methods, of its confiscation of the property of the church and of some of its more prominent members, became too open to be ignored, it was Talleyrand who was chosen to prepare an address designed to calm the people. It was delivered on February 9, 1790, amid great bursts of applause, and was widely acclaimed as a magnificent defense of the accomplishments of the Assembly. "We are told that we have destroyed everything," he declared. "But how can we build unless we first destroy? We are blamed because our assemblies are disorderly, but what does it matter so long as our decrees are wise?" Having worked through the catalogue of complaints and refuted them, to the delight of the Assembly, he concluded on a note of warning, cloaked in his habitual language of prudence: "Let us beware of impetuosity and of too much activity. And above all, let us shun violence, for nothing is more fatal to freedom than disorder."

* Some of the names are not unknown in the twentieth century: Lagrange, the mathematician; Lavoisier, the chemist; Gaspard Monge, who was to be Bonaparte's chief engineer during the Egyptian campaign; Vicq-d'Azyr, the anatomist; and La Harpe, the literary critic and lecturer.
†Some of Talleyrand's enemies claimed that the *Report* was entirely the work of other persons—secretaries, some said, or the learned men and scholars to whom Talleyrand referred, or even Borie Desrenaudes, Talleyrand's vicar-general at Autun. It is interesting, and perhaps significant, that none of the people to whom authorship was attributed bothered to claim it for themselves.

A week later Talleyrand was nominated for the office of President of the Assembly. His opponent was his friend, one of the early and most prestigious leaders of the Assembly, the Abbé Sieyès. On February 26, when the votes had been counted, it was announced that, by a majority of 373 to 125, the Bishop of Autun had been elected to preside over the governing body of France for the customary term of a fortnight.

The election was no mere compliment, and the duties it implied were, in this instance, more than honorific. Talleyrand, at the time of his election, enjoyed a popularity in France, particularly in Paris, that he had never known before and that he would never know again. His work in the Assembly, combined with the intense interest in public affairs which characterized Paris, had created for him a following such as existed for no one else in the Assembly. The newspapers of the time record that in the streets, people would gather in groups when Talleyrand's carriage appeared and applaud until it was out of sight. When he attended public functions, such as banquets, mobs would gather in the streets and call his name until he appeared at a window, with Sieyès at his right and Mirabeau at his left, and then there would be "a storm of shouts and applause." For the moment, he was the most popular man in France. Even Mirabeau had been eclipsed.

Popularity was, in 1790, precisely what the Assembly needed most. Much of the criticism that Talleyrand's oration had so skillfully deflected had, in fact, been justified. The work of the members had been, to date, largely one of words. As Talleyrand had worked away at the task of transforming the *ancien régime* into a society of free and equal men, many of his colleagues had whiled away their hours in contriving and delivering extravagant speeches on the equality of man and the blessings of freedom. For the rest, the Assembly had been largely occupied with the framing of a constitution for France and had given its attention almost exclusively to the theory of government rather than to its practice. This meant, in effect, that France, with an elected assembly and a reigning king, had no effective government. The royal administration had been discredited and dismissed; but the revolutionary administration had not yet come into existence, and the result was an interval of virtual anarchy. In Paris the mob felt free to slaughter any unpopular official who happened to fall into its hands. In the provinces the castles of the nobility were burned and tax offices were demolished. "There no longer exist executive powers, laws, magistrates, or police," the Venetian ambassador reported in horror. In August the Viscount de Noailles, one of Talleyrand's circle, had stated to the Assembly that the cause of this disorder was the retention by the nobility of their feudal rights and that these rights must therefore be abolished. The measure was voted upon and passed. But still the disturbances continued. The

Duke d'Orléans, who had become disenchanted with his friends of the Assembly when it appeared that France would, after all, have a constitutional monarchy, but with Louis XVI as its king, was now employing dozens of *agents-provocateurs* to stir up the people of Paris, rousing the citizens against his cousin at Versailles. Jean-Paul Marat, a doctor from England, who had written a booklet on the evils of English-style constitutionalism, was loudly attacking the advocates of constitutional monarchy—that is, the Assembly—as "traitors." Finally, the people, under the double stimulus of these extremists, had lost all restraint. A mob of Parisians had marched to Versailles on October 4 and, despite the protection by Lafayette of the king and queen, had stormed the palace. When the mob returned to Paris in the evening, it was leading the royal carriage, in which cowered King Louis, Marie-Antoinette, and their young son, the dauphin. The people of Paris were bringing their king to Paris, and he would never return to Versailles. In the wake of the procession came the Assembly, which had promised also to transfer its deliberations to the capital. It had placed itself under the thumb of the mob.

Talleyrand's role throughout the violent drama had been one of passivity. The rage of the people had been part of the "torrent which must be allowed to pass." But he had also said that he would "raise no obstacle between opportunity and myself, and I would hold myself in readiness for it." The opportunity had come, finally, when Talleyrand was elected President of the Assembly. But it had come almost too late. The Assembly had stripped the king of power but, as Talleyrand notes, had been "too fascinated by the chimerical ideas of equality and of the sovereignty of the people" to exercise that power itself. Therefore, the nation was sliding to the brink of ruin; the throne, which Talleyrand still hoped to save by transforming it into a constitutional monarchy, was tottering; daily Paris grew more restless and more demanding. All this the men of the Assembly hoped somehow to correct by electing a president who was acceptable to Paris and thereby gain time to correct its errors. "Those who had been most eager to destroy the royal power," Talleyrand explains, "perceived at last that they had gone too far, and they attempted to retrace their steps."

Mirabeau had pointed out that "the problem with revolutions is not to get them under way, but to stop them when they have gone far enough." But Talleyrand was the wiser of the two. He had already seen where the road taken by the Assembly had to lead, and he knew that matters had gone beyond the point where they could be controlled by any group of men, however dedicated they might be. "The torrent formed by ignorance and passion was so violent that it was impossible for any man to stem it." His verdict was like the death knell of reason in the Revolution.

5

Monseigneur d'Autun Retires

T HE SAD state of the Revolution that had begun so gloriously was illustrated, for all the world to see, on July 14, 1790. To celebrate the
anniversary of the storming of the Bastille, the Assembly had decreed that a festival must be held. Since France was still Catholic, the celebration must take the form of a mass.

The problem was that only two months before, the Assembly had
adopted a measure known as the Civil Constitution of the Clergy, which
was a logical extension of Talleyrand's motion of October, 1789, allowing
the state to appropriate church goods. The effect of the Constitution was to
place the church under the control of the state, rather than of Rome. To
this, not even the most liberal of the bishops of the Assembly could assent;
Talleyrand, alone of the episcopal brethren, had supported the measure.
And by June Talleyrand was the only bishop left in the Assembly. There
was therefore little choice when it came time for King Louis to select a
bishop loyal to the new Constitution as celebrant of the projected Feast of
the Federation, as it was called. The fact that Talleyrand, whose fondness
for gambling, speculation, and women was public knowledge, should be
selected as the "chaplain of the Revolution" was indicative of the depths to
which that Revolution had sunk, and the irony of it was not lost upon Talleyrand himself. Nonetheless, he could not refuse the king's command,
much less offend either the Assembly or the people of Paris, who were
looking forward to a magnificent spectacle.

The day of the feast dawned gray, and the rain fell in torrents on the
thousands who had assembled before daybreak in the Champs de Mars.

There was laughter, and songs rose from the crowd. Then there was silence, and everyone turned toward the entrance of the enclosure to watch King Louis and Queen Marie-Antoinette enter and take their seats upon the royal tribune. There was not a cheer, not a *Vive le roi*.

The mood of the crowd improved somewhat upon Talleyrand's appearance a few minutes later, in magnificent vestments, his head held high, his face impassive. Accompanying him were sixty chaplains from Paris and various *départements*. He climbed the steps of the altar carefully, supported by two of the chaplains, and the mass began. When it was over, he blessed the banners of the eighty-three *départements* of France. Then the king spoke a few words, assuring his people of his paternal affection, and a few cries of *Vive le roi* were heard for the first time that day. Madame de Staël, who was present, said later that the cheers had sounded like cries of farewell.

The plan of the ceremony called next for the oath of allegiance to the nation, the Constitution, and the king. Lafayette was the first to swear, and as he did so, Talleyrand whispered: *"Pourvu qu'on ne me fasse pas rire"*—"Please don't make me laugh."

The ceremony ended with the singing of a hymn, as sheets of rain continued to fall and the celebrant and his assistants, the King and Queen of France and their attendants, and thousands of patriotic Parisians stood dripping in their finery. When the last note had sounded, the king and queen withdrew and returned to the Tuileries, which had now replaced Versailles as the royal residence. The people returned to their homes. Talleyrand, as soon as he had removed his vestments, hurried off to one of his favorite gambling places, where he promptly broke the bank.

There is no doubt that the ceremony was little to Talleyrand's liking. In his own mind, it seems, his ties—or rather his bondage—to the church had been voided with the passage of the Civil Constitution of the Clergy. He had not, it is true, done more than merely vote for approval of the Constitution. Although acknowledged as one of the most influential speakers of the Assembly, he had carefully avoided adding his voice to those who spoke either for or against the act. Actively to support passage would have been scandalous for a bishop, even so reluctant a bishop as Talleyrand. For this bill went far beyond the mere nationalization of the property of the clergy. It struck at the roots of Roman Catholicism by permitting the state to usurp powers that since time immemorial had been exercised by the Pontiff: control over the fifty-three bishops of the French hierarchy and over their confirmation in office; control over the policies and practices of the church of France; and control even over what was taught and preached in the village churches of the nation.

Such radical measures, unheard of since the great investiture conflicts of the Middle Ages, could not but draw the wrath of Rome upon the heads of those who supported them. Thus, the bishops of the Assembly had fought the Civil Constitution every inch of the way, determined to preserve whatever they might of Rome's authority in France. When they saw that there was no chance of success, they withdrew and returned to their dioceses. The Bishop of Autun alone had remained seated, and when the king's approval had been obtained for the Constitution, he was among the first to take the oath of fidelity: "I swear, with uplifted hand, diligently to fulfill my duties; to be faithful to the law, to the nation, and to the king; to uphold the Constitution, and especially the decree relating to the Civil Constitution of the Clergy." Only three other bishops could be found who would consent to take the oath.*

It seems likely that Talleyrand's reticence during the debate over the Civil Constitution and his subsequent willingness to take the oath required of him were not without purpose. Since the creation of bishops now rested entirely in the hands of the state, it must follow that the state could relieve a bishop—particularly one who had taken the oath—of his episcopal character. Yet such a bishop, to avoid the accusation of acting out of self-interest, would sit silent while it was debated whether or not the state should assume such powers. Whatever the case, it was on December 28, 1790, that Talleyrand took the oath to the Constitution "and especially to the decree relating to the Civil Constitution of the Clergy." During the first week of January, 1791, he wrote to the king, the chief of state, formally resigning the bishopric which he now had held, for a few days, at the sole pleasure of the state. There was no letter of resignation addressed to Rome, and according to the new state of affairs in France, there was no need for one.

It was an unexpectedly simple way to be rid of a profession that he had been compelled to follow, that he had always detested, and that now no longer was necessary to him as a stepping-stone to greater things. He wrote:

> I resigned the bishopric of Autun, and I thought only of abandoning the first career I had followed. I put myself at the disposition of events, and provided I remained a Frenchman, all else was of indifference to me. The Revolution promised new destinies for the nation. I followed its course and took my chances.

Talleyrand's resignation seems contemporaneous with his appointment,

* They were the Bishop of Orléans, who subsequently resigned his see and married; Loménie de Brienne, Archbishop of Sens and former minister of Louis XVI, who, despite his adherence to the Constitution, was beheaded in 1794; and the Bishop of Viviers, who, after having sampled amply the joys of the world, sought and obtained absolution from Rome for both his apostasy and his sins.

in early January, to the post of an administrator of the Department of the Seine (Paris), and this was the pretext that he used to be rid of his unwanted miter. On January 20, we find him writing to the clergy of Autun that he had been offered an advantageous position in the capital which made it necessary for him to relinquish his diocese and encouraging them to proceed as soon as possible to the choice of a successor. For according to the new Constitution, the bishops of France were now freely elected by the clergy of a vacant diocese rather than appointed by the king and confirmed by the Pope.

Having resigned as a bishop and having notified his former subordinates of his resignation, Talleyrand was once more forced to don his episcopal robes on behalf of the Revolution. It was, ironically, the very Constitution that had dispensed Talleyrand which now made it necessary for him to officiate at a final ceremony. The new law provided for the consecration of bishops and the ordination of priests to replace those who had not taken the oath. But it did not specify how, with only four constitutionalist bishops in the kingdom, the consecrations and ordinations could take place. The law itself forbade bishops who had not taken the oath to perform these ceremonies, and Rome had threatened with excommunication any bishop, constitutionalist or not, who dared do so. It therefore became necessary for the state once more to call upon Talleyrand for his services. He confesses:

> . . . in spite of all the repugnance I felt, I thought it necessary to come forward. Here are the motives which decided me. . . . If no one could be found to confer it upon them [consecration upon the new constitutionalist bishops], it was greatly to be feared, not that all religion would be forbidden, as came to pass a few years later, but—what seemed even more dangerous, since it might have been more lasting—that the Assembly, by the doctrines it had sanctioned, might soon force the country into Protestantism, which was more in accord with the ruling opinions, and that France would not then be able to be drawn back to Catholicism, whose hierarchy and forms are in harmony with those of the monarchical system.

These motives may not be so farfetched as they at first appear. It is difficult to believe that Talleyrand, who had never in his career as a clergyman willingly performed a religious ceremony, should, once he had officially and formally renounced that profession, consent to do so without some reason based upon conviction. All the more so since there was actual physical danger involved if he performed the ceremony. He had been threatened with assassination by supporters of Rome, and he took the threat seriously enough to prepare his last will and testament and deposit it with Madame de Flahaut before proceeding with the consecration. It is also possible that he was motivated by nothing more lofty than a desire to appear to be at the disposition of the state, a desire so strong as to relegate the risk of bodily harm to secondary rank.

Whatever the reason and despite his revulsion, he performed the ceremony on February 24, 1791, in the Oratoire of the rue St.-Honoré. The priests of the house had left in a state of outrage, to protest the desecration of the premises by what they considered a sacrilegious and immoral act. But as Lafayette and some of his troops stood guard outside, two priests were raised to the episcopal dignity through the ministrations of the former Bishop of Autun, assisted by two other constitutionalist bishops who had, somehow, been turned up by the government.* The assassins did not put in an appearance, and Talleyrand, after he had removed his sacred vestments for the last time in his life, went to the house of Madame de Flahaut and collected his last will and testament.

Talleyrand may have been through with the church, but the church was not quite through with Talleyrand. Pius VI, in 1791, had launched a sentence of excommunication against any priest who took the oath to the Constitution, and against any bishop who ordained or consecrated a constitutionalist candidate for the priesthood or the episcopacy. Talleyrand was guilty on both counts. And he was delighted. Excommunication, to his way of thinking, meant that both Paris and Rome agreed that he was no longer a member of the clergy. A sentence in the Pope's letter had lent strength to this interpretation: "Nothing more desirable can come to pass than to see one renounce the church who, for so many reasons, merits to be thrust out."

A year later, in March, 1792, one month before the decree of excommunication was to be final, Pius VI addressed a private letter to Talleyrand, pleading with him to take advantage of the "inexhaustible patience of Holy Mother Church" and giving him sixty days in which to retract his errors and repent for his sins. If he did not do so, then the awful sentence would be pronounced, and Talleyrand (whom the letter described, inaccurately, as the "Author of the Schism"—that is, of the Civil Constitution of the Clergy) would be cut off from the communion of the faithful forever. When the sixty days of grace had passed, Pius carried out his threat, but by then Talleyrand was no longer in France.†

There were few moments in Talleyrand's clerical career in which he would not gladly have surrendered his soutane. That he did so at the time in which he did is due to the conjunction of several factors, the most obvi-

---

* Three bishops are required for the validity of the ceremony of the consecration of a bishop.
† The formal reduction to the lay state, which Talleyrand assumed was implied in the sentence of excommunication, was not actually forthcoming until 1802, when Bonaparte was First Consul and Talleyrand was Foreign Minister.

ous being the opportunity presented by the Civil Constitution. This, however, was the occasion of, rather than the reason for, his decision. It is reasonable to believe that given the stipulations of the Civil Constitution and Rome's reaction to them, Talleyrand, by taking the oath, had cut himself off from further advancement in the church. And since his leadership in the Assembly had been attained independently of his rank of bishop, and presumably would be preserved independently of it, it was no longer necessary for him "to embrace one profession with the intention of following another." The latter—public affairs—could be, and indeed was actually being, pursued openly.

Another consideration was that while Talleyrand's episcopal rank would have been no hindrance and indeed would have been helpful in the executive branch of government—that is, as a minister of the crown—it had now become legally impossible for him to accept any appointment to a ministry. On November 12, 1790, it had been voted that no deputy could become a minister until three years had elapsed between his resignation from the Assembly and his appointment to office by the king.* If Talleyrand were to make his way, therefore, it would have to be as a member of the Assembly. And in the Assembly, as in the eyes of the Parisians, bishops were increasingly suspect because of the reactionary outbursts that had greeted the nationalization of church goods and the promulgation of the Civil Constitution.

Finally, by the end of 1790 and the first months of 1791, it had become clear that Talleyrand must prepare himself by all possible means, including the relinquishment of his episcopal dignity, to assume a greater share of the leadership of the Assembly. For Mirabeau, his friend, collaborator, and chief competitor for domination at that time, was dying.

The two men had been intimates since the days of Talleyrand's "circle" in the Faubourg St.-Germain, "where we gathered every morning and where my friends shared my frugal meals." Drawn to each other by the talents, wit, friends, and interests which they shared, they had also in common a strength of character and a flexibility of practice that made it difficult for them to refrain from criticizing each other publicly and then of quarreling violently in private. There had been several such altercations, the most famous being that which had taken place while Mirabeau was in Berlin and Talleyrand in Paris—with Mirabeau's mistress. Their relationship in the Assembly was predictably uneven. They cooperated continually in their work, and they had no real differences of opinion concerning what must be done or left undone. They were united in their determination to

---

* This had been aimed chiefly at Mirabeau by one of the rightist Jacobin members, who, when he proposed the measure (November 7, 1790), had said: "You have already been tamed and subjugated by a genius of eloquence. What would he not be able to do to you as a minister?"

keep the Revolution from being precipitated into the chaos of anarchy by the destruction of the monarchy. Their respective ambitions, however, were the cause of constant friction. It was no secret that Mirabeau coveted above all the chair of the presidency, and that it came as a blow to him that Talleyrand rather than he was elected at a critical juncture in the Assembly's existence. "No party loves me," Mirabeau said despondently, shaking his leonine head, tears coursing down his pockmarked cheeks, "not even the party to which I have been able to be useful." It was not his ambition, but the fact that he did not bother to conceal it, which seemed most to irritate Talleyrand. On one occasion, after Mirabeau had declaimed at length from the tribune on the qualities which a president of the Assembly must possess, enumerating one by one the qualifications with which, as all the world knew, he himself was most conspicuously endowed, Talleyrand rose in his seat and demolished the great orator by observing that "There is only one virtue that has not been mentioned in the address of M. de Mirabeau—that the president should be heavily pockmarked." On another occasion, after Talleyrand had opposed him on a minor point in the Assembly, Mirabeau roared a string of threats at him, ending with: "I shall surround you with a circle of viciousness such as you have never seen!" Talleyrand answered quietly from his seat, "Am I to understand that M. de Mirabeau proposes to embrace me?"

Despite such clashes, the two men were genuinely fond of each other, and reconciliation always followed quickly upon the heels of their quarrels. Talleyrand was deeply affected when, in December, 1790, it became obvious that his friend's health, never robust, was declining rapidly. By January Mirabeau had to be helped to the tribune. At the end of March he was dying. Knowing that the end was imminent, he asked for Talleyrand. When he came, Mirabeau confided to him his most valued possession. "I have here," he said, "a great many papers. In them is to be found whatever honor will be associated with my memory. Promise me that these papers shall one day be known and that, for the sake of our friendship, you will vindicate my memory by seeing that these documents are published." * Talleyrand swore that he would do what the dying man asked, and a few hours later Mirabeau was gone.

The following day, April 3, 1791, Talleyrand pronounced a eulogy before the Assembly:

> Yesterday I went to see Mirabeau. A great crowd of people filled the house, but I had brought with me a sadness more poignant than that felt

---

* These papers were entrusted by Talleyrand to Étienne Dumont, a friend and collaborator, as well as a journalist of some renown, who edited them and supervised their publication, in 1833, under the title of *Souvenirs de Mirabeau.*

by the public. A sentiment of desolation, which filled my soul with the reality of death, was everywhere—everywhere but in the spirit of the man who
was at that moment facing the greatest trial. . . . I will not dwell on the
emotion excited by some of his addresses. Monsieur de Mirabeau, even at
that moment, remained the statesman. From that point of view, we must
look upon his words as a precious relic snatched from death's tremendous
prey.

The relic to which Talleyrand referred were the thoughts contained in the
papers that had been handed him by his friend. But what he himself remembered most vividly was Mirabeau's final, despairing declaration to
him: "My friend, I take with me into the grave the last shreds of the monarchy."

It would be easy to conclude, from the vast amount of work turned out
by Talleyrand in the first years of the Revolution, that the man whose dissipation had become a scandal in an age difficult to scandalize had resolved to abandon his customary amusements and devote his energies exclusively to the work of the Assembly and to the nurturing of his
ambitions. Nothing could be further from the truth; and nothing would
have been more foreign to Talleyrand's nature. His passion for public
affairs had come to the fore with his election to the States-General in 1789,
but his other passions remained intact, nonetheless, and were indulged
with an intensity which, in a less devoted man, would have required the
business of state to accept second place.

The stage on which Talleyrand's predilections were played out remained, as always, Paris. There had been, and were to be, momentous
changes in the life of the capital between 1789 and 1792. The smell of revolution pervaded the atmosphere, and nothing escaped its touch. The king
was a virtual prisoner in the Tuileries and later would become an actual
prisoner in the Temple. The splendor of the court had vanished, and many
of the great names which had illustrated the glories of the *ancien régime*
and animated the life of the city were now seen only on the ever-growing
list of émigrés. Still, the existence of the ordinary Parisian as yet had been
little affected by the flow of events; and that of the social stratum in which
Talleyrand moved, hardly more. Gambling and lovemaking continued as
before, and there were dinner parties, and above all, there were still the salons of the great ladies. The wife of the British ambassador, Lady Sutherland, wrote home explaining that "the tranquility of France is but little disturbed." And she concluded with the complaint that "this world is grown
very dull." Gouverneur Morris added only that the potatoes he saw in the
marketplaces "are what we consider as the worst kind" and that Paris was
"as large and stinking" as ever.

Talleyrand himself recorded very little concerning his personal life during the three years which followed the first assembly of the States-General. For what can be known of it, posterity is indebted largely to that astute foreign observer Gouverneur Morris, an American whose early dream it had been to live in the French capital in order "to rub off in the gay circles of foreign life some of the many barbarisms which characterize a provincial education." He had realized that dream in 1789, at the age of thirty-seven. Despite his dislike of the size and stench of Paris, the city had lived up to his expectations. To the minister of France in the United States, he wrote upon arrival: "The more I see of Paris, the more sensible I am of your sacrifice in leaving it to traverse a great ocean and establish yourself with a people as yet too new to relish that society which forms here the delight of life."

Morris' purpose in Paris at this time was profit rather than delight. He was there as a business agent, to look after tobacco and flour contracts with the French on behalf of the family firm of which he and his cousin, Robert Morris, were the principals.* He was young, single, clever, experienced in financial matters, spoke excellent French, and he had arrived fortified with letters of introduction to members of the highest nobility of France and to leaders in public affairs. All these things combined to secure his immediate admittance into the most exclusive social and political circles, and there he met Talleyrand almost daily. They also met with equal frequency in the apartment of the Countess Adélaïde de Flahaut in the Palace of the Louvre,† for Morris, in addition to his interest in financial matters, his love of good conversation, and a decided limp,** had in common with Talleyrand a great passion for the countess.

It was in Adélaïde de Flahaut's drawing room that Talleyrand and Mor-

---

* Robert Morris had been named Superintendent of Finance by the Congress of the United States, and Gouverneur Morris had been appointed assistant superintendent. Together, they had founded the first bank in the new nation, the Bank of North America. Gouverneur, in addition, had had a hand in the framing of the American Constitution, but he is remembered chiefly for having devised the monetary system of the United States and, as such, for being the father of the American dollar.

† The royal palaces of France were filled with families of indigent nobles who, through some connection at court, had obtained a "place" at the expense of the state—that is, a modest income, supplemented by lodgings, in exchange for services that were more nominal than real. Thus, Adélaïde's husband, the day after their marriage, had been named Intendant des Jardins du Roi (Superintendent of the royal gardens), through the influence of the Princess de Polignac, Marie-Antoinette's favorite. Madame de Flahaut's elder sister had married a brother of the princess, and this was sufficient to give her husband a claim to royal patronage.

** Morris had a wooden leg, which he once used to save his life when attacked by a Paris mob during the Terror. Mistaken for an English spy, he had removed the appendage and waved it above his head, shouting that he was an American who had lost his limb in his nation's struggle against tyranny. Whereupon the mob's threats turned to loud cheers. Actually, Morris had never struggled against anything more dangerous than a deficit. His leg had been amputated as the result of a carriage accident.

ris first encountered each other in October, 1789. On October 14, Morris went to the countess' apartment for dinner, but while they were talking, she was handed "a note from the Bishop of Autun. He is to dine with her at half-past five. She insists that I shall leave her at five. I put on a decent show of coldness." The following day, however, we find Adélaïde de Flahaut and Morris "dining *a trio* with the Bishop." Thereafter, hardly a day goes by that there is not some mention of "the Bishop" in Morris' journal.

A degree of intimacy seems quickly to have developed among the three of them. Late in October, Morris noted: "I go to the Louvre, and I find the Bishop with Madame de Flahaut. He asked to have dinner with his son today, and it is a family affair. When he has left, I express my regret to Madame de Flahaut at having interrupted such a charming scene. She speaks a great deal about her child, and she weeps with abandon. I dry her tears as they fall." Morris' "provincial education," however, apparently had not prepared him adequately for a relationship in which hypocrisy or even reticence played no part. "I go to the Louvre," he writes, "where the Bishop of Autun is waiting for me. . . . Madame being ill, I find her with her feet in warm water, and when she is about to take them out, one of her women being engaged in that operation, the Bishop employed himself in warming her bed with a warming-pan. It is curious enough to see a reverend father of the Church engaged in this pious operation." Yet the American is determined to learn. A short time later, "Madame, being ill, goes into the bath, and when placed therein sends for me. It is a strange place to receive a visit, but there is milk mixed with the water, making it opaque. She tells me that it is usual to receive in the bath, and I suppose it is, for otherwise I should have been the last person to whom it would have been permitted."

By the time that Talleyrand had met Morris the American was already in love with Adélaïde de Flahaut. It was in the countess' nature not only simultaneously to captivate as many men as she could, but to require, or at least to contrive, that the competitors for her favors should accept one another and, if possible, like one another. Thus, she was able to amuse herself in the company of both at the same time. There was, of course, an initial resentment between the two men; and there are several entries by Morris which seem indicative of a certain jealousy on Talleyrand's part: "Go to the Louvre. Immediately after my arrival, the Bishop comes in, who seems not at all content to find me here." Yet shortly thereafter Talleyrand overcame this emotion, either because he considered it unworthy of him or because he had decided, for reasons of his own, to abandon the field to the American. By then Morris is noting that Adélaïde's "countenance glows with satisfaction in looking at the Bishop and myself as we sit together, agreeing in sentiment and supporting the opinions of each other. What a triumph for a woman. I leave her to go home with him."

Jealousy was not an emotion that Talleyrand was capable of sustaining for long or one that he could display gracefully and convincingly, given his own imperfect fidelity. And the Countess de Flahaut, for her part, was too good-natured to expect the impossible of the Bishop of Autun. She was famous in court society for her kindness and cheer. The consensus of her friends was enshrined in a widely repeated remark of François de Montesquiou to her: "Your character is such that you are able to destroy more unhappiness than fate is able to create." Given Adélaïde de Flahaut's complaisancy and Talleyrand's weakness so far as other women were concerned, it was understandable that by the time Gouverneur Morris appeared in Paris their relationship had ripened from passionate attraction to tender attachment. Adélaïde was Talleyrand's mistress, formally and officially; and he, her lover, in the same sense. They were accepted as such everywhere in society. Yet the countess was not compelled to restrain her taste for coquetry, and it is not known that Talleyrand ever was obliged to refuse an invitation to dalliance. Hence, his calm acceptance of Gouverneur Morris in the countess' life; and hers of the long list of ladies with whom Talleyrand's name was linked, for brief periods, during their liaison. The arrangement suited Talleyrand perfectly. Incapable of fidelity himself, he never required the appearances of that virtue in his mistresses or allowed the reality of it to be required of himself.

It is likely that Adélaïde de Flahaut's coquetry was no more than that. The homage of men was sufficient for her at that time, and she did not allow or even encourage their embraces. Morris, unaccustomed as he was to the peculiar morality of court ladies, was hard put to understand why he must fail where the Bishop of Autun had succeeded so conspicuously, and he pressed his suit with unrelenting ardor and great ingenuity. On one occasion, he was dining at the house of Jacques Necker, the Minister of Finance. Talleyrand had already become interested in Necker's daughter, Germaine de Staël, and had made his intentions quite clear to everyone concerned. Morris fell into conversation with Madame de Staël concerning Talleyrand's advances to her and put forth a suggestion which demonstrated that his social education had advanced rapidly: "I desire her to let me know if he succeeds," he noted, "because I will, in such case, take advantage of such intelligence in making my court to Madame de F." Morris' talebearing, however, did him no good. When he begged Madame de Flahaut to be at least as kind to him as Germaine de Staël was to Talleyrand, Adélaïde replied simply: "I cannot, for, in my heart, I am married." This was in November, 1789. By the first part of 1791, however, her attitude had changed drastically. She asked Morris one day: "If I should suddenly become a widow, whom do you think I should marry?" He answered cautiously that he assumed her choice should fall upon "the Bishop," since he had heard it said that the French clergy would soon be allowed to marry. Adélaïde rejected the idea emphatically: "Oh, I will never marry Monseigneur d'Autun, for before going to the altar with him I would have to mention my liaison with someone else." The reason for this complete change of heart was not entirely of her own doing. As Talleyrand's fascination with Germaine de Staël had waxed, his interest in Adélaïde had waned. It was not that the countess had lost her charm, her goodness, or her beauty, but that Necker's daughter had virtues perfectly suited to wean away first the attention and then the affection of a man whose values were broader than those that could be contained in the comparatively modest life of Madame de Flahaut. Madame de Staël had, by the time of the States-General, emerged as one of the cleverest, most learned and entertaining women in France, and her salon* was the recognized meeting place of France's political and social elite. "She is capable of infusing life into solitude," one of her contemporaries wrote, "of substituting herself for the world, and, indeed, of becoming the whole world herself." Moreover, she had the gift of unreserved admiration, freely expressed, for any man who should capture her fancy. It did not displease Talleyrand to hear repeated everywhere Germaine's compliment: "If Talleyrand's conversation could be purchased, I would gladly go into bankruptcy." It did not lessen her attraction that whenever he was attacked for his work in the Assembly or for his lack of morals, she would defend him heatedly and capably in the face of all comers. The obvious devotion of so celebrated a woman was impossible to discount and difficult to resist. To these credentials, Germaine added others which, if her intelligence and loyalty alone had been insufficient to attract Talleyrand, would have assured his attention. Though not beautiful in a conventional sense and somewhat careless in her dress, she had, nonetheless, features which drew the universal admiration of her contemporaries. Her eyes were said to be the finest in Europe, and her hands, which she used constantly to enhance her words, were exquisitely shaped. In addition, she was the confidante and adviser, as well as the daughter, of France's most powerful and popular minister.

It was widely believed that Talleyrand's ardent pursuit of Madame de Staël—which was the subject of universal gossip—was founded more upon ambition than passion and that his ultimate designs centered more on a ministerial portfolio than the lady's virtue. It was true that in the early stages of Talleyrand's courtship, members of the Assembly had not yet been barred from office in the government and that Germaine, clever as she was, might well have secured such a prize from her father on behalf of

---

* She maintained two salons, actually, one in the house of M. Necker and the other in that of her husband, the Baron de Staël, Swedish ambassador to Paris, in the rue du Bac.

a lover. But it is also true that after it had become illegal for a member of the Assembly to accept such a post, Talleyrand's ardor continued unabated,* until the lady finally succumbed to Talleyrand's importunities early in 1791, to the delight and amusement of all Paris and especially of Mr. Morris.

Only Adélaïde de Flahaut, it seemed, and possibly the Baron de Staël were less than pleased at the news. The pursuit had been so extended, so public, and therefore so humiliating to her that the countess' legendary forbearance was exhausted. There had been scenes with Talleyrand, which he could never endure, and reports by Morris: "Go to the Louvre and find Madame has quarrelled with the Bishop. . . . In consequence of the quarrel, she is very ill, and surrounded by friends and servants." In January 1791, just as Talleyrand's new quarry was about to be taken, Adélaïde opened her heart to Morris, "complaining bitterly of the Bishop of Autun's cold cruelty." Yet she was to prove that by nature she was as flexible as Talleyrand himself, though more content to follow where others led. Her reference, in Morris' presence, to "my liaison with someone else" was almost simultaneous with her complaints about Talleyrand's cruelty. And Morris' sympathy was no doubt tempered when Madame de Flahaut's new lover, a son of the Marquess of Lansdowne, was introduced into the scene. "Lord Wycombe *est enniché ici* [is ensconced here]," he notes acidly. And soon he is complaining that Wycombe had replaced not only Talleyrand, but Morris himself, in Adélaïde de Flahaut's life. "She is," he concludes, "a coquette, and very fickle."

The relationship between Talleyrand and the countess was not to degenerate into recriminations and total disenchantment for a while yet; but from the beginning of 1791, it was clear that, of what remained to him of the delights of this *ancien régime,* Talleyrand had shed more than his bishopric of Autun.

The disintegration of Talleyrand's liaison with Madame de Flahaut, the resignation of his bishopric of Autun, and his self-imposed laicization all contributed, in varying degrees, to the changes that were to be worked in his life during 1791 and 1792. The most immediately significant factors in these changes were those over which he was in no position to exercise any control—that is, the events attending the progress of the Revolution in those critical years.

Talleyrand has described that concatenation of acts and circumstances

---

* It was perhaps just as well. Jacques Necker had not forgotten and never forgiven Talleyrand's earlier and public criticism of him, and he turned a carefully deaf ear to the praise that he heard daily of his daughter's friend. "He is a clever man," Necker wrote to the King of Sweden, "and an able politician, but he is too ambitious."

as a torrent so violent that no one could have hoped to abate it. Up to the
end of 1790, however, he and Mirabeau together had been able, if not to
control it, then at least to guide it. The work of the Assembly, which had
now occupied almost two years, was to prepare a constitution for France
which, while embodying the ideals of liberty and equality, was intended to
preserve, in recognizable form, an institution basic to French political and
social life: the monarchy. To this ideal, Mirabeau had been committed,
and to it Talleyrand remained committed. Yet in the course of 1791, not
only the monarchy itself, but even the democratic principles which it had
been the purpose of the Revolution to substitute for the absolutism of the
Bourbon kings, were to be swept away in a storm of "ignorance and passion."

Mirabeau's death signaled the crumbling of the defenses which he and
Talleyrand had attempted to build against the forces of extremism among
the men of the Revolution. It not only deprived the throne of one of its
champions, but also brought to the fore, to fill the vacancy in the active
leadership of the Assembly created by his passing, a group of men whom
Mirabeau had always succeeded in holding down by his vigor and his rhetorical gifts: Danton and Robespierre, the leaders, respectively, of two influential and, for that time, radically republican revolutionary clubs,* the
Cordeliers and the Jacobins. The rise of such men, and the power of their
factions during 1791 was not accidental. Discontent with the Assembly
and its work had been spreading both to the right and to the left, and an
important cause had been the Civil Constitution on the Clergy: Pope Pius
VI, after some delay and at the same time that he had proceeded against
Talleyrand and the other constitutionalist bishops, had declared that the
enforcement of the Civil Constitution in France would amount to heresy

---

* The history of France's revolutionary clubs—which, by the time of Mirabeau's death, had
evolved into political parties rather than clubs—is complex and confusing because of the rapidity
with which their leaders shifted their own and their followers' positions. The most important of
these organizations were: the *Cordeliers* led by Danton and Desmoulins, who were initially republicans of the extreme left, but with the rise of other extremists led by Robespierre, Danton gradually adopted more moderate views—until he himself was replaced in the club's leadership by such
extremists as Marat and Hébert. The *Jacobins*, likewise, were moderates under the leadership of
Mirabeau, Lafayette, and Sieyès but, after Mirabeau's death, became increasingly radical and republican under Danton and Robespierre. In the Assembly, the Jacobins and the Cordeliers together were designated as *la Montagne* (the Mountain), from the raised seats which they occupied,
and the individuals were known as Montagnards. The *Girondists*, led by Brissot de Warville, Condorcet, Dumouriez, and Vergniaud, were moderate republicans and were regarded as being in opposition to the Jacobins and Cordeliers. The *Feuillants* were a splinter group of the Jacobins who
retained the original moderate policies of that club and who advocated a constitutional monarchy.
Their leader was Barnave. The independent members of the Assembly—that is, those who were attached to none of the clubs—were known as *la Plaine* (the Plain) since the benches they occupied
in the chamber were lower than those of the Mountain. Though the Plain easily constituted the
majority of the deputies, they were virtually leaderless and came to be dominated by the radical
Mountain.

and schism, and he had transmitted this opinion directly to King Louis XVI. Now Louis was a devout Catholic, a firm believer in the primacy of the Roman Pontiff. He had struggled as long as he could to withhold his consent from the Constitution,* and after several weeks, he had given in under protest. From that moment, as he made perfectly clear, he regarded himself as a man acting under compulsion, and he ascribed no binding force to any act to which he agreed but to which he could not consent in good conscience. But the king's acceptance of the Civil Constitution did not conclude the matter. Furious protests arose throughout the provinces, and in the south of France there was a serious threat of insurrection.

In this situation, as in all revolutions and times of unrest, the army was an important factor. The Assembly, in order to detach the armed forces from their allegiance to the king, had, in early 1790, ordered the troops to swear a new oath: to the law and to the king, in that order, and not to act against the citizens of France. Even so, the regiments stationed along France's northeastern frontier, commanded by General Bouillé, a staunch royalist, were regarded as loyal to the king, and it was feared that if Louis summoned them to his aid, they would obey. This fear was stimulated and exacerbated by a member of the Cordeliers, Jean-Paul Marat, who published a violent pamphlet, *C'en est fait de nous*—"It's all over for us"—in which he demanded the execution of all "traitors" and "conspirators" as the sole means of preserving Paris from the vengeance of the king and the operations of his army. On August 31, within a few days of the pamphlet's appearance, several regiments, stationed at Nancy, demoralized by democratic propaganda (it is not clear whether or not Marat's pamphlet had a direct bearing), rose in mutiny. Order was restored by Bouillé's vigorous action, but the uprising caused great excitement. The Assembly denounced Marat's pamphlet and passed a formal vote of thanks to Bouillé. The republicans, however, led by Danton and his Cordeliers, strongly opposed both acts, and there were noisy demonstrations in Paris in favor of the mutinous soldiers. This, more than anything else, resulted in a large number of resignations of their commissions by professional (*i.e.,* royalist) officers in the infantry and calvary regiments and in their subsequent emigration to Germany and England. The armed forces were therefore left in the command largely of officers sympathetic to the republican cause.

On the heels of this radical change in the position of the military, there

---

* As yet, there was no formal Constitution granting the king a power of veto. It had been assumed by the Assembly, however, as well as by the court, that the Constitution would embody such power, and by tacit accord, the king was allowed to exercise it from the early stages of the Assembly. In reality, the veto, both before and after the promulgation of the Constitution, was a sham. The king could exercise it only in the full realization that to do so might well result in the abolition of the monarchy and perhaps even in the gravest danger to himself and his family.

came another in the executive branch. Necker, although still a minister of the crown, was now discredited and ignored. Since his power depended on that of King Louis and since Louis' power had been largely usurped by the Assembly, he now served merely as the head of a cabinet without substance or influence. Early in September, 1790, he was mobbed in the streets of Paris and offered his resignation to the king. Then he fled back to his native Switzerland.

Except for extremist elements in the Jacobin and Cordelier clubs, the Revolution, until the winter of 1790, had shown little sign of being antimonarchical in sentiment. By December, however, the various causes of unrest in the nation and the growing—and, to some extent, self-imposed—isolation of the king from the true sentiments of the people congealed into a movement that was distinctly toward a republic. The work of the Assembly itself left the door open to diatribes from journalists, such as Camille Desmoulins, against a constitutional monarchy. It was pointed out that the constitution being drafted by the Assembly limited the vote to some 2,000,000 Frenchmen, all of middle- and upper-class status. Why, it was asked, should there continue to be such distinction between classes? Why should not the poor, as well as the rich, have the opportunity to determine their own destinies? Why should women not have the same rights as men?

By the first part of 1791 France was flooded with pamphlets in favor of the abolition of the monarchy and the establishment of a truly egalitarian republic. Popular societies with a program of universal suffrage were formed and became very fashionable. In a few months, the antimonarchical concept had been transformed from the idea of a few extremists into a powerful force in French politics. It was a concept propagated by demagogic methods and the rhetorical pyrotechnics which characterize any mass movement. As such, it might have been defeated, by the same means, if the cause of constitutional monarchy had had as its leader an inspired demagogue of its own. But it had none. Mirabeau was dead, and Talleyrand, for all his popularity in the Assembly and among the people and for all his talent, was incapable of the calculated illogic, to say nothing of the personal flamboyance, required by such a role. Mirabeau's place, therefore, was quickly filled by men attuned to the changing sentiments of the people and to the opportunities offered by the situation: Danton, leader of the republican Cordeliers, and Maximilien Robespierre, a deputy of the Assembly and a leader of the Jacobins. Only a few days after Mirabeau's death, Robespierre had published a pamphlet in which he argued, with the considerable gifts at his command, the case for democratic suffrage. Coming at the moment that it did, the pamphlet catapulted its author to instant fame, and everywhere Robespierre was hailed as the champion of the poor, the friend of the oppressed, and the apostle of equality.

With the rise of republicanism, the situation of King Louis was rendered even more untenable. Behind him lay the abdication of his spiritual powers through the Civil Constitution of the Clergy. Ahead lay the specter of a constitution which would formally strip him of the secular powers of which the Assembly had already, in practice, deprived him. And with the voices of Danton, Robespierre, and Marat becoming louder by the day, it was doubtful that the Assembly, which had now become a force for comparative moderation, would be able to resist increasing public pressure, not to constitutionalize the monarchy, but to abolish it. By the spring of 1791 it seemed that the only way out of the dilemma lay in escape from Paris. Louis' hopes centered on the northeastern frontier, at Metz, 200 miles from Paris, where the energetic and royalist Bouillé was still in command of his regiments and where, beyond the Rhine, Louis' brother-in-law, the Emperor Leopold of Austria, was already assembling troops to intervene, if necessary, on behalf of Marie-Antoinette, his sister. On June 20, 1791, the attempt was made. The arrangements were in the hands of a Swedish nobleman attached to the queen, Axel Fernsen, who had procured false passports, devised disguises for the royal family, and secured an enormous coach for their use. All went well until the royal party reached Varennes, a village in the frontier district not more than 15 miles from Verdun where Bouillé had a strong garrison of troops. At this point, however, the scheme broke down. Bouillé had planned to have a large cavalry escort meet the king at Varennes, but his arrangements went awry, and King Louis, Queen Marie-Antoinette, and the dauphin were left to wait in the village. Meanwhile, the postmaster of Ste.-Menehould, a village on the itinerary of the royal fugitives, had recognized the occupants and ridden ahead to rouse the National Guard at Varennes. The game was obviously up. After a slight skirmish between a detachment of Bouillé's cavalry and the National Guard of Varennes, Louis was sent back to Paris, surrounded by armed and hostile contingents from all the surrounding villages.* Meanwhile, in Paris, the news of the king's flight had resulted in great excitement. Nowhere, not in the Assembly or in the streets, was there the slightest doubt about the significance of the event. Indeed, Louis himself had taken care that there should be none. Before leaving the city, he had signed a proclamation declaring that all the decrees he had signed since the convocation of the States-General had been obtained under compulsion and were therefore null and void. The people responded to this act of apparent perfidy in the way that might be expected: Every emblem of the monarchy in Paris was torn down or demolished. Even Louis, never the most acute

* Louis' brother the Count de Provence, who left Paris at the same time, managed his escape differently and more successfully and made his way into the Netherlands. (In 1815 he was to repeat the experience and the journey as King Louis XVIII.)

observer of events, knew precisely what his abortive attempt at escape implied for himself and the throne. At Varennes, speaking to one of the officials guarding him, he had said, "If we return to Paris, we shall die."

In the Assembly, there was great unrest and even greater indecision about what to do. Marat declared that a military dictatorship was the only solution to the situation, but except for a few personal supporters, the proposal was barely listened to. Danton, who was not a member of the Assembly, led a deputation from his Cordeliers Club and presented a petition demanding the deposition of Louis XVI, but this met with hardly more enthusiasm. The men of the Assembly were, for all intents and purposes, a thoroughly middle-class body. They had labored long and lovingly to bring into being a Constitution, and their work was nearly completed. It mattered not at all that, under attack from the republicans, the proposed Constitution had become as unpopular with the people as it was with the court or that far from being a reconciliation of the pretensions of absolutism with the principle of popular government, it had become merely an instrument to protect the privileges of the middle classes from infringement by either the people or the crown. In the Assembly's view, the important thing was that the Constitution be promulgated. Louis' flight had meant that it was endangered, and his return to Paris meant merely that the deputies' Constitution was safe, after all. September 3, Louis, now totally discredited and a virtual prisoner in his palace of the Tuileries, was sent the document and directed to sign it. He did so, and the Constitution immediately went into effect.

So far as Talleyrand was concerned, the promulgation of the Constitution had an instantaneous effect. The Assembly, which had evolved out of the States-General, was now dissolved by the provisions of the document. It had regarded the Constitution as its proper work, and once that work was done, it was willing to retire and make room for the election of a new Assembly, which was to be known as la Législatif. (The original Assembly was later to become known as la Constituante—the Constituent Assembly.) It would be up to the deputies of the new Assembly to implement the provisions of the Constitution, and elections to this Assembly were called for September. The members of the old Assembly, however, had also stipulated that they themselves could not be elected to the new body. In practice, this meant that in the midst of great events, Talleyrand was unemployed. As a deputy, he had been barred first from accepting office under the crown, and now he was prevented from seeking reelection as a deputy.

But the situation was not entirely hopeless. Louis' act of signing the Constitution, unwilling though it may have been, and the call for the election of a new Assembly had evoked a somewhat sympathetic reaction from certain classes in favor of the king. There were even several demonstrations on his behalf—which, if Louis had been more adept as a politician, might have been turned to the advantage of the crown. Moreover, since the new Constitution granted the franchise only to the middle and upper classes of society, it was not entirely unexpected that the deputies of the new Legislative Assembly would reflect a moderate rather than a radical viewpoint. So it was that when the deputies met on October 1, it was found that the republican Jacobins had only 136 representatives. The Feuillants, who inclined generally toward a policy of rehabilitating rather than restricting the royal power, numbered 264. And in the center, there were some 400 deputies, more or less uncommitted, who would vote now with the Jacobins on the left and now with the Feuillants on the right.

Talleyrand himself belonged to the party of the Feuillants, and his membership was a matter simultaneously of expediency and of conviction. The government summoned to office in November, 1791, by Louis under the provisions of the new Constitution was, predictably, composed of Feuillants. Moreover, his old friend Narbonne had been made Minister of War. Talleyrand could therefore hope that some use would be found for his talent under the new regime. The guiding principles of the Feuillants, however, were essentially his own. He was convinced that the Constitution offered by the Assembly contained "endless faults," in that it conferred upon the king the semblance rather than the substance of power* and that, as such, the Constitution was alien (as indeed it was) to the history and traditions of France and basically incompatible with the concept of a hereditary monarchy.

That Talleyrand was right was quickly demonstrated. Although the Feuillants greatly outnumbered the Jacobins in the Assembly, they had neither the leaders naturally to attract the support of the uncommitted deputies of the center nor the excitement of a radical program to elicit that support spontaneously. The Jacobins therefore quickly established their influence over this rather amorphous part of the Assembly, and, through their club organization, they packed the public galleries of the hall and thereby came to direct the current of opinion among the deputies by the judicious application of applause or vocal disapproval. To such pressure

* The provisions that Talleyrand cites in support of this assertion are that the king no longer enjoyed the right to convene and dissolve the legislative body; that the power to nominate bishops, judges and public officials now was vested in the constituencies rather than in the crown; that the king could no longer dismiss public officials; that the Legislative Assembly alone could declare war and make peace; that while the king was granted a power of veto, the Assembly could override it and enact any law regardless of the king's wish; and other restrictions which, as ordinary as they would seem to later ages, in 1791 went far beyond what was provided for in the two working models of constitutions known to informed Frenchmen, those of Britain and America. (*Mémoires*, Vol. I, p. 101.)

the Feuillants could oppose nothing more effective than the inertia of a powerless king and an equally powerless government. The Jacobins therefore dominated not only the Assembly, but also public opinion, and the latter was now visibly polarizing against the monarchy. In this, the Jacobins were aided by Louis himself, who had now given up any hope of help from within France and was looking to foreign intervention to save the situation. No course could have been more fatal, for the more threatening that intervention became, the more the Jacobins seemed a patriotic party and the more the king and queen appeared traitors to the cause of France.

The antimonarchical rage of the republicans, the powerlessness of the Feuillant government, the intrigues of the court—that is, of Marie-Antoinette—with the Austrians, and the threatening posture of the conservative monarchies of Europe with respect to the Revolution*—all suggested to the leaders of the various parties a single solution: war. The Jacobins† were for war because, as Talleyrand explained, "they thought that, if war were delcared, the king, since he would be responsible for operations, would be at their mercy. That is, he would be able to employ only those means that they would choose to place at his disposal. Thus, by holding the sovereign responsible for disasters that their own actions would make inevitable, they would be able to incite the army and the people to rebellion." The Feuillants were also for war, though for war of a different kind and for a different reason. Their leader, Lafayette, in October, 1791, had resigned his post as commander of the National Guard. In November, he had been defeated by a Jacobin candidate, Jérôme Pétion, for the mayoralty of Paris. Now he hoped for a military command and, along with his fellow Feuillants, saw in war the opportunity for building a victorious army by means of which the king and constitution might definitively be imposed on Paris and the Jacobins cowed. For this, a small war would do perfectly well. While the Jacobins were agitating to take on Austria, Lafayette and his party aimed at no greater target than the Elector of Trier, in

* In the Declaration of Pillnitz in August, 1791, following the news of King Louis' capture at Varennes, the King of Prussia had joined the Emperor of Austria in inviting the other sovereigns of Europe to combine with them to reestablish order in France—which, they stated, was a matter of concern to all of Europe. Only Catherine of Russia and Gustavus of Sweden offered their support. George of England sent a message explaining that despite his personal concern for Louis XVI, Britain would remain neutral. Spain and Sardinia, after an initial token expression of bellicosity, preferred to wait before committing themselves so as to reap the fruits of intervention without incurring its initial risks.

† Marat and Robespierre were conspicuous dissenters in this instance, and prophets as well. Both feared the success of some soldier of fortune who might, with a stroke of his sword, convert the Revolution to his own purposes. "We have more to fear from success than from defeat," Marat wrote in l'Ami du peuple on April 24, 1792. "The danger is that one of our generals, crowned with victory . . . lead his army against the capital." The man whom they both foresaw and feared was, at that moment, a lieutenant of the French artillery, on extended leave on his native island of Corsica.

whose city of Coblenz the Count d'Artois and the Count de Provence had gathered a miniature court and an army of several thousand soldiers.

Talleyrand was opposed to both these plans. "In 1790," he wrote, "war would have been useful to the monarchy" by rallying the people to the throne. "But in 1792 it could only have resulted in the overthrow of the monarchy." His own preference was for a plan calling upon the armed émigrés to withdraw their forces from the frontiers and placing French troops on a footing of peace. "This course," he says, "was not adopted. Or rather the steps resorted to were so indecisive as to render them utterly useless."

The steps to which he referred were indeed useless. At the end of October the Legislative Assembly issued decrees ordering the Count de Provence, the Count d'Artois, and the other émigrés to return to France before January 1, 1792; those failing to obey were subject to the penalty of death. The king naturally vetoed the measure, being unwilling to assent to the death of his brothers and his nobles. Instead, he agreed to summon the Elector of Trier to ask him to require his guests to disband their troops. If he did not, it was to be made clear, the armies of France would be required to take matters into their own hands. It was foreseen that the elector, as a vassal of the Emperor Leopold, would seek advice in Vienna and that he would be told to refuse such demands. This would give the Jacobins the pretext that they wanted for war. Instead, and to everyone's surprise, the emperor instructed the elector that he was to have his lands cleared of émigré troops no later than December 31. If this were done, Leopold continued, he would protect the elector's territory from attack by the French. At the same time, Vienna made it clear that while Austria would not be dragged into war by the military posturing of Provence and Artois, it fully intended to take whatever action was necessary to preserve the good order of Europe and to protect the King and Queen of France from their own people.

The Assembly's efforts to make a declaration of war necessary had, for the moment, come to naught. Yet it was clear that sooner or later, the Revolution would have to defend itself from the onslaught of the foreign monarchies. Prussia, Austria, and Russia were gathering troops, and it was only a matter of time before France would have to choose: It must either wait until it was attacked and then defend itself, or it must attack first and trust that an offensive was the best possible defense against its enemies.

In this situation, it was imperative that France, if it were to face the armies of the three great Continental powers, be assured that it would not simultaneously have to contend with an enemy to the west—that is, with Great Britain. By the end of December Count Louis de Narbonne, Minister of War, and Antoine de Lessart, a nonentity who had been appointed

Minister of Foreign Affairs, had decided that a special envoy must be sent to London to exact a promise of neutrality from the British government and even, if possible, to promote an alliance between the British and the French.

Narbonne had not forgotten his friends. Talleyrand was appointed to undertake the task, and King Louis duly approved the choice. In mid-January, 1792, Talleyrand left Paris on the first mission of a diplomatic career that was to span almost half a century and that would be remembered when the men on whose instructions he acted would have sunk into oblivion.

Talleyrand's career as a diplomat and statesman was consistently to be crowned with the most brilliant and sometimes unexpected successes. It is striking that his first undertaking, the mission to London, far from being an adumbration of those accomplishments, was instead something of a failure at every level. Talleyrand himself had not hoped that it could be otherwise. "Though I felt that my mission had little chance of success, I accepted it," he said.

It is not that Talleyrand was not suited to the job. His friendship with Narbonne would have been hardly sufficient to qualify him if he had not already demonstrated his grasp of France's needs and his ability to convey those needs persuasively and with fitting subtlety and flexibility. Moreover, Talleyrand was already acquainted with the younger William Pitt, the British Prime Minister, whom he had met at Rheims in 1783, and with a number of other men prominent in British life, such as Lord Holland and Lord Lansdowne, the latter being the father of that Lord Wycombe who had succeeded Talleyrand in Madame de Flahaut's favor.

The mission had come at an auspicious moment so far as Talleyrand himself was concerned. "I had been anxious to leave France for some time, for I was tired and disgusted." He had, only a short time before, on the advice of Gouverneur Morris, suggested himself to Narbonne for the post of minister to Vienna and had been disappointed when De Lessart, the Foreign Minister, had refused him the appointment—very possibly at the insistence of Marie-Antoinette, who undoubtedly would have preferred a friend and confidant to represent France in her native land. It is also likely that the Feuillant ministry was not insensitive to the effect that the presence of a renegade and excommunicated bishop might produce at the court of his Apostolic Majesty of Austria. The mission to London, coming as it did upon the heels of this rejection, had been warmly received by Talleyrand. It presented the opportunity not only to undertake a task of considerable importance for France, but also to renew acquaintances among the émigrés with which England, especially London, was filled. And not least was the consideration that peace, and the possibility of an alliance with England, were matters to which he himself was wholly committed and for which he had spoken and worked since his entry into public life. "It is now, at this moment," he had said in the Assembly in 1791, "that we must begin to lay the groundwork for lasting brotherhood between France and England." In 1786, he had spoken in the salons and written in favor of the Commercial Treaty between France and England. And to De Lessart he wrote a succinct statement of the convictions on which his mission was predicated: "Two neighboring nations, the prosperity of one being founded on commerce and of the other on agriculture, are compelled by the very nature of things to reach a mutual understanding and to reap a mutual profit." The necessity of friendship and cooperation between the two nations was to be the cornerstone of Talleyrand's diplomacy through-out his life; he would preach it to Napoleon, to the Bourbon kings of the Restoration, and to the July Monarchy as readily as he did to the Assembly of the Revolution and the Feuillant ministry. His conviction of this necessity would grow as his experience with England increased his admiration for the English and their institutions. But it was never to be a purely theoretical conviction, founded on abstract principles and speculative considerations. In every instance, Talleyrand's support of an Anglo-French entente was dictated by a single, eminently practical consideration: France would never be really secure in Europe unless Great Britain was bound to it by the closest ties possible in the circumstances. Under the Orléans monarchy, it was to be because the new dynasty required British recognition and support if it was to survive; under the Restoration, to achieve a balance of power against Russia, Prussia, and Austria; and under the Empire, for similar reasons. The mission to London in 1792 was inspired by the same motive that was to dictate his preaching over the years, in and out of season, of the imperative nature of a rapprochement between England and France: the desire for peace. For Talleyrand, formed in the school of Voltaire, peace was the natural, indeed the only possible, state of man. War represented not the conquest of one nation by another, but the victory of irrationality over reason. Conflict, he always regarded with horror and revulsion; and peace, as the first duty of the state. He was to say in later years that he never abandoned a regime until it had abandoned itself. He would abandon the Restoration when its blindness brought France to the brink of civil war. He would abandon Napoleon when his errors made war inevitable. And he would abandon the Revolution when it began to spill the blood of Frenchmen. For the moment, however, everything must be done in the cause of peace while peace was still possible. "The Revolution," he wrote, "promised new destinies for the nation. . . . I devoted to it all my energies, being resolved to serve my country for herself."

The journey to London, thus undertaken in a spirit of high purpose, had also the air of a holiday about it. Traveling with Talleyrand was his old and intimate friend, Lauzun, Duke de Biron—fun-loving, quick-witted, and, as Talleyrand remarked, "romantic and courageous"—to whom Narbonne had confided a commission to buy horses for the army with the advice that "a little tour in England will be just the thing for your jaundice."

Neither the festive spirit of the travelers nor Talleyrand's dim hopes for the mission survived their arrival in England. There had already been announcements in the newspapers of the coming of Talleyrand and Lauzun, both of whom were not unknown in London society. Lauzun was a colorful and romantic figure and excited much interest. His fame as a rake exceeded even Talleyrand's, and it was said that among his many distinguished mistresses had been Marie-Antoinette herself (which was untrue) and Catherine of Russia (which was true). His strikingly handsome appearance, his intelligence, and the fact that he had been one of the young French nobles who had deserted Versailles to fight against England in the American wilderness—all assured him of the attention, if not of the affection, of London society. That he bore one of the most ancient and honored names in France and that he was a duke were interesting, but not relevant. When it came to titles and lineage, the English tended to regard as suspect anything that had its origins beyond the Channel. (This sentiment had been immortalized in a maxim, one which English ladies and gentlemen of fashion did not hesitate to repeat among themselves: "The niggers begin at Calais.")

The social credentials of a Talleyrand-Périgord, therefore, were not sufficient of themselves to entitle a representative of the Revolution to the respect and consideration of London. The very fact that Talleyrand was a representative of the Revolution hardly added to his chances of acceptance. The English, as a whole, had taken an unfriendly view of the upheavals in France and were surprisingly unsympathetic to the struggles of the French to throw off the yoke of absolutism which they themselves took such pride in having shed. This reaction, perhaps to be expected among the upper classes, which were conservative by nature, was common even among the ordinary shopkeepers and laborers of London. The source of such an attitude could be traced to the presence in England of so many thousands of émigrés, whose view of the Revolution was understandably condemnatory and whose plight as exiles had evoked first the sympathy and then the support of the hospitable English. So bitter was the hostility of the émigrés that they regarded as a traitor to the monarchy any member of their class who had chosen to remain in France with the embattled king rather than flee to the safety of a foreign land. The epithets of "traitor, renegade, and defrocked priest" were the least unkind of the terms reserved by the émigrés for Talleyrand.

The opinions of the French nobility residing in England were given substance among the English by the rumors concerning Talleyrand which had preceded him to England. That a man might have a weakness for women, even for many women, might be understandable in a prime minister or foreign secretary or occasionally in a King of England; but in a bishop, even a bishop of the idolatrous Roman Church, it was infamous (though not necessarily unspeakable). That he might speculate in state funds was only to be expected of such a man. And that such a man would be sent by the revolutionaries to infect England with pernicious antimonarchical and antireligious doctrines was not surprising, particularly not to Englishmen who had read—and who had not?—Edmund Burke's *Reflections on the Revolution in France*, published in 1790, which had made Burke the spokesman of reactionary conservatism in Europe.

Talleyrand's reception in London was therefore, to say the least of it, not cordial. The émigrés, of course, would have nothing to do with him, and their friends among the English nobility followed suit. Horace Walpole, Earl of Orford (and son of the great statesman of the same name), declared loudly that he could not bring himself to look upon "the viper that has cast his skin, the Bishop of Autun." The King and Queen of England were hardly better disposed or better mannered than their subjects. Upon his arrival on September 24, Talleyrand asked for an audience for himself and Lauzun with their majesties, which was granted with obvious reluctance. Lauzun was received with civility; but when Talleyrand was presented, King George could hardly bring himself to nod to the profligate ex-bishop, and Queen Charlotte slowly and deliberately turned so that the emissary of the French might see only her back. Reports of this treatment were received with great hilarity in the great houses of London, as was, a short time later, the news of Lauzun's arrest and imprisonment for debt. Some said that the French duke had been the victim of a vicious practical joke arranged by some of the émigrés; others, that he had attempted to defraud a horse dealer in a transaction to purchase animals for the army of the Revolution. What is certain is that Lauzun ended up in jail, from which he was liberated only after Talleyrand, with a great deal of trouble, managed to scrape together sufficient cash and influence to pay what was allegedly owed. The incident, whether or not Lauzun was innocent and coming soon after Talleyrand's royal snub, did little to enhance the prestige of the French mission. To all appearances, revolutionary France was represented in London by two renegade noblemen, one of whom was a lascivious ex-bishop and the other a horse thief.

At the political and diplomatic level, Talleyrand fared hardly better than at the social. In truth, he had come poorly prepared from a bureaucratic standpoint. He was merely a "personal representative" of the French government; not a minister and not an ambassador. Instead of credentials that might properly be presented at the Court of St. James's, he had only a letter from De Lessart to Lord Grenville, the Foreign Secretary, introducing Talleyrand in fulsome terms, and a note from King Louis expressing France's desire to "preserve and increase the good understanding that presently unites our two kingdoms." At his first interview with Grenville, he presented the letters, and being aware that Britain might have reservations about any arrangement with a country in which power might shift so unpredictably and in which public order, so dear to the English soul, had been virtually nonexistent for almost three years, he assured the secretary at length that the convulsions necessarily accompanying the process of reform were at an end and that France would now begin to reap the benefits of those reforms and enter into a new stage of peace and prosperity. In this interview, Talleyrand was listened to in almost absolute silence. His wholly unofficial status, the suspicion that his mission was one of propaganda rather than of peace, and the daily reports of increased unrest in France led Grenville to exercise a caution even more extreme than that which he habitually employed. Talleyrand, unaware that the sphinxlike demeanor of Grenville was the one he presented daily to the world, and not knowing that the policy of strict neutrality with respect to the affairs of France was one to which Pitt's government had determined to adhere in any case, attempted to inject some warmth into the interview by reminding the Secretary that as a man of public affairs he had always maintained that France and England were natural allies. When this evoked no response, he appealed to Grenville's pride, saying that so young a statesman (Grenville was thirty-two) must surely have a more sympathetic and enlightened view of events in France than an older man deaf to new ideas.* This was also received in glacial silence.

The interview concluded with Talleyrand offering certain considerations for British neutrality in the event of a Continental war, including the suggestion that France and England might reach an agreement which would enable them mutually to guarantee each other's colonies.† But this, he said, was a matter on which the government might prefer to reflect before returning an answer, and he suggested that they meet again shortly. To this, Grenville agreed, and the two men parted civilly enough.

* Duff Cooper conveys Grenville's response and his character perfectly in a single phrase: "Talleyrand did not know that Grenville had never been young." (*Talleyrand*, p. 45.)

† This was a matter of some importance to Britain in 1792, since it was at that moment undergoing one of the most violent of the regular upheavals in Ireland.

In the interim, Talleyrand paid a brief courtesy call on William Pitt. If he had expected the Prime Minister to show more warmth than Grenville, he was disappointed. Pitt, after a curt allusion to their meeting at Rheims in 1783, went directly to the point. Since Talleyrand was not officially accredited to his majesty's government, he said, he could hope for no official response to the proposals he had made to Grenville. The same message was repeated by Grenville himself in his second meeting with Talleyrand. He added, however, that although he could not negotiate with an envoy who had no credentials, he was in a position to assure Talleyrand and, through him, the French government that Britain had every intention of adhering to its stated policy of neutrality with respect to Continental affairs.

It was a victory, of a sort, to the extent that Talleyrand had received the assurance which had been the primary object of his mission. He had not, however, the satisfaction of knowing that he had been able to persuade the British government to alter by a hairsbreadth the course that it had set for itself independently of his arguments. Of course, his fondest ambition, for a treaty of alliance with Britain, was impossible to realize or even to discuss until France had an accredited ambassador in London. He therefore wrote to De Lessart in Paris, suggesting the appointment of such an envoy* and offering for the post the name of the Marquis de Chauvelin, a young nobleman of attractive appearance, splendid lineage, impeccable manners, irreproachable revolutionary sentiments, and total innocence in foreign affairs. The nominal ambassador was to be a figurehead, and Talleyrand wanted no one who would try to be more than that. Chauvelin "is young enough," he explained, "not to be indignant that someone else will do the work."

It is possible that Talleyrand, acute observer that he was, also foresaw a certain social value in having the personable Marquis de Chauvelin in London. That he had not found a warm welcome in society had been due to sins which might be forgiven Chauvelin: his reputation and the cause with which he had associated himself.

> His reception was bad [Gouverneur Morris reported to Washington], for three reasons. First, that the Court looked with horror and apprehension at the scenes being enacted in France of which they consider him the prime mover. Secondly, that his reputation is offensive to those who pique themselves on decency of manners and deportment. And lastly, as to propagate the idea that he should corrupt the members of the administration.†

* Talleyrand's own appointment, as he had discovered when he requested the embassy in Vienna, was not possible legally. The same decree of the Assembly which barred deputies from accepting ministerial portfolios excluded them equally from ambassadorial appointments.

† The third reason cited refers to a rumor that Talleyrand had at his disposal some 40,000

Even his utter calm, the wit, and conversational powers through which "by amusing others, he amused himself," which in Paris had won such approval, in London had precisely the opposite effect. Étienne Dumont, a Swiss national who was in London at the time, reported:

> The English, whose whole attitude toward Frenchmen is made up of preconceived notions, found him lacking in the [putatively French] national characteristics of vivacity, familiarity, indiscretion, and gaiety. Instead, they thought his manner sententious, his demeanor cold, and his air that of an observant critic—all of which were his defenses in the role of diplomat.

The English, in other words, did not know what to make of this French nobleman who, in England, exhibited all the characteristics of an English nobleman on tour in France.

The little social success Talleyrand enjoyed during his first sojourn in England came to him in the houses of a few Englishmen of liberal convictions such as the Marquess of Lansdowne and Fox, who were part of the Whig opposition to Pitt's Tory government. These connections, however, rather than being to Talleyrand's benefit, contributed to the mistrust with which he and his mission were viewed. "He also allied himself with leading characters among the Dissenters," Morris duly recorded, "and renewed the impression, made before his departure from Paris, that he meant to intrigue with the discontented."

In these circumstances, it was Talleyrand's hope that, by securing the appointment of a straw ambassador such as Chauvelin, who was too young and inexperienced to have acquired either a manner or a reputation that the English would find distressing (he was only twenty-five), he, and France, might regain some of the ground that had been lost. With this in mind, he decided to return briefly to Paris in order to make a full explanation of the situation to De Lessart and Narbonne and, since he had as yet had no response to his suggestion for Chauvelin's appointment, personally to argue his case.

Talleyrand landed in France on March 15, and was met by friends who had driven from Paris with disturbing news. On March 10, King Louis had dismissed Narbonne from office. "I was surprised to learn that the king is still in a position to be able to dismiss anyone," one of the men observed. What had provoked the phlegmatic Louis to action had been Narbonne's intrigues against the king's favorite minister, Moleville, but Narbonne's dismissal had consequences far beyond what Louis was able to foresee. The Girondists, under Brissot de Warville, had seized the pretext for ac-

---

pounds, to be used in purchasing the favor of government officials. Whether or not the report was true (which seems doubtful) was irrelevant. Morris' point was that the British believed it to be true.

cusing De Lessart of treason and impeaching him* and for denouncing the other members of the Feuillant government. Thus, the ministers had been compelled to resign, and Louis to ask the Girondists—or, more accurately, the Brissotins—to form a government. The Ministry of Foreign Affairs went to Charles-François Dumouriez, a capable and intelligent man, but one fanatically anti-Austrian and determined on war, who was to emerge as the leading figure in the Brissotin ministry.

When Talleyrand arrived in Paris, therefore, the situation was uncertain. With Narbonne dismissed and De Lessart awaiting trial for treason in Orléans, there was more than a little reason to fear that he himself might be implicated in the disgrace that had fallen upon the Feuillant ministry which he had supported and with which he was associated. But as it turned out, Dumouriez's aims and policies were not essentially different from those of the man he had replaced. Like De Lessart and Narbonne, he regarded war as the only effective means of restoring order in France by restoring authority to the crown. But whereas the Feuillant government had contemplated a limited war along the French frontier, directed at the lands of the Elector of Trier, Dumouriez was determined to strike directly at Austria by invading its province of the Netherlands. His object, however, was not to annex the Netherlands (that would have been unacceptable to the British), but to establish a Belgian republic. Almost the first act of Dumouriez's ministry, therefore, was to dispatch a special agent, Hugues Maret,† to incite the Belgians to revolt. The second was to ask Talleyrand to visit him in order to discuss how an attack against the Netherlands might be justified to the British.

Neither Dumouriez's decision to make use of Talleyrand's talents nor Talleyrand's acceptance of Dumouriez's invitation was based upon mutual attraction. The two men, in fact, had little affection for each other. Dumouriez resented Talleyrand's aristocratic background, and he was intimidated by his reputation for intelligence and subtlety. A soldier by training and a general by virtue of the Revolution, he had a military man's suspicion of the intangible qualities of statecraft and diplomacy, and he subsequently acted in accordance with these suspicions by filling his embassies with men who lacked both the ambition and the intelligence to do more than transmit Dumouriez's messages to the governments of Europe. Britain, however, presented special problems, because of its power and be-

---

* De Lessart was thrown into prison. During the summer of 1792, Danton ordered him brought to Paris. En route, he was strangled by a Parisian mob at Versailles. The specific accusation against him was that he had intrigued with the Austrian court, and there is considerable evidence that he had done so, in cooperation with the queen.

† Maret was to play a significant role during the Napoleonic period under the title of Duke de Bassano.

cause it regarded the Netherlands as a commercial and strategic territory of special interest. Since war was imminent, he had little choice but to call on the man, perhaps the only man, who knew the situation in England from firsthand experience and who had the intelligence to draw the proper conclusions from it. Talleyrand, for his part, was more than willing to overcome his dislike for Dumouriez in order to return to London. He still hoped for an alliance, and Dumouriez was willing to give him what Talleyrand thought was necessary to lay the groundwork for that alliance.

During the early weeks of April, Talleyrand and Dumouriez hammered out a number of bold and imaginative suggestions to put to Pitt and Grenville. As the basis of an alliance, there would be a new commercial treaty between Britain and France which would be highly advantageous to the English. In addition, France would cooperate with England if the latter decided to intervene in the New World in order to liberate the Spanish colonies there—and thus open up immense commercial possibilities to both the British and the French. Finally, France would surrender to England the island of Tobago and, as a sign of its faith in the peaceful intentions of the British, demolish its fortress at Cherbourg. These, however, were merely the immediate benefits to be derived from an understanding between France and England. The effective purpose of such an entente would be to check the ambitions of Austria, Prussia, and Russia on the Continent and to guarantee the peace of Europe by establishing a balance between the liberal powers of the West and the conservative autocracies of the East. Though the terms would change, the substance of this policy would remain the same throughout Talleyrand's career: peace in Europe through an Anglo-French alliance.

As this grand design for peace was being articulated, war was in the making. The sensible Leopold of Austria had died in March and had been succeeded by his son, Francis II, a hotheaded and reactionary prince obsessed with the ambition to crush the spirit of revolution by destroying its manifestation in France. In this, he was supported by his chief minister, Prince Wenzel Anton von Kaunitz. With the new emperor and Kaunitz determined on war on the one side, and Dumouriez equally bellicose on the other, matters took a fatal turn. An increasingly acrimonious exchange of notes between Vienna and Paris, beginning on March 18, ended, on April 20, with the Legislative Assembly voting overwhelmingly for a declaration of war "against the King of Bohemia and Hungary"—that is, against Austria, though not against the Holy Roman Empire from which Francis II derived his title of Emperor. In retrospect, this fine distinction between Austria and the Empire, and Dumouriez's attempt to localize his war, would seem ludicrous. April 20, 1792, would mark the beginning of a conflagration which would continue, with only a brief interruption, for almost a quarter century and which would convulse the whole of Europe.

For the moment, there was some slight hope in Talleyrand's mind that peace might still be possible or at least that the war might be kept from spreading. If the alliance between France and England could be worked out immediately in London, then Austria might be brought to moderate its hostility toward France, and Prussia and Russia might choose to remain neutral in the conflict. The wheels had already been set in motion for his return to England. On March 28, Dumouriez had informed the king that "M. de Talleyrand should depart at once for London, where he has already begun a negotiation which he conducted with much skill. . . . As, according to the decrees, he cannot go to England with an accredited title, I propose that he be given an associate with the title of Minister Plenipotentiary." Thereupon, in accordance with Talleyrand's wish, Chauvelin was appointed Minister Plenipotentiary. Immediately after the Assembly's declaration of war, Talleyrand and Chauvelin left for England and arrived in London on April 30.

The news of the opening of hostilities between France and Austria and of the French invasion of the Netherlands, had preceded them, and the reception they were accorded was one of open and violent disapproval. Talleyrand was jeered at in the streets, and Chauvelin, when he presented himself at court on May 2, was treated hardly better than Talleyrand had been earlier in the year. The British, as a nation, were indignant at the French action and alarmed at its possible consequences. Even the leaders of the Whig opposition, such as Fox, whom Talleyrand had found sympathetic only three months before, had suddenly lost their enthusiasm for a revolution that proposed to spread itself by force of arms. As for the Tory government, it was equally unenthusiastic over the possibility that France might, through its representatives in London, attempt to disseminate its revolutionary ideas on British soil. Talleyrand's protests that the mission of the embassy was not to proselytize but to negotiate were rejected with derision by the press. In these circumstances, it was clear, an alliance with England was impossible. The government would never consider it, and if it did, public opinion would never allow it. Nonetheless, the effort had to be made.

In the first week of May, Talleyrand communicated to Grenville, through Chauvelin, the basis for the proposed alliance between the two countries. And then he waited. As the days and weeks passed, news arrived from the Continent. Antwerp and the whole of Belgium had fallen to the armies of the Revolution. In these places, it was reported, the institutions of France were being imposed upon the people—brutally, if necessary. "Since the arrival of this news," Talleyrand complained to Paris, "our mission has become very difficult."

Finally, on May 25, Grenville gave an answer to France's proposals, but it was given in the Foreign Secretary's own fashion, by being released to the newspapers rather than communicated directly to the Minister Plenipotentiary.* The substance of it was that while England regretted that war had broken out, it hoped to be able to remain at peace with France, and it trusted that France would do its share in maintaining that peace. What Pitt's government was saying, in effect, was that so long as France respected English interests, England would remain neutral in Continental affairs. And with this Talleyrand had to be satisfied for the moment. It was hardly more than he had been able to obtain from Grenville earlier in the year, the sole difference being that the promise of neutrality had now been given publicly and officially rather than privately and unofficially.

Grenville's response seems to have satisfied the Brissotin government, whose immediate goal, like that of the Feuillants, had been a firm declaration of British neutrality. Dumouriez dispatched a message of congratulations to "the Minister Plenipotentiary and his esteemed collaborators," praising Talleyrand's accomplishment—which was not really much of an accomplishment and which, as Talleyrand knew, would have been achieved no matter who was representing France in London. The simple fact was that England's treasury was still suffering from the expenditures incurred ten years earlier in fighting its former colonies, as well as France, in the New World and could not afford a major Continental involvement in 1792. Pitt, moreover, in his nine years in office, had gone far in his program of reform. He had succeeded in balancing the budget, in reducing armaments, and in passing important electoral legislation. A war would have imperiled these successes, made impossible other reforms contemplated for the immediate future, and wreaked havoc in the exchequer. Talleyrand was aware of the reasons for the government's declaration of neutrality, and unlike Dumouriez, he was not satisfied with it. Or at least he felt that nothing could be lost by continuing to pursue the faint possibility of an alliance that would not only benefit France, but, by creating a balance of power in Europe, allow Pitt to continue his reform program in relative security.

Given Talleyrand's persuasiveness and tenacity and Pitt's intelligence, it is not impossible that if the internal situation of France had not worsened drastically at that precise moment, something might have come of Talleyrand's plan. By the end of June, however, news arrived in London that

---

* Grenville and Pitt had been outraged when a letter handed to Chauvelin by King Louis, declaring the latter's belief that "the alliance is necessary to the stability of our two states and to their internal tranquility, as well as to the peace of Europe," was given out to the newspapers before being delivered in London. Talleyrand therefore could not (and did not) complain of Grenville's action.

brought all negotiations, and all hope of negotiations, to an abrupt halt. On June 15, Dumouriez's government, forced from office by a conflict with the king over the use of the veto, had been replaced by a new Feuillant ministry headed by Lafayette. The Jacobins, furious at this defeat, decided on a monster demonstration against the king on June 20. On the appointed day a vast mob assembled out of the working-class faubourgs of St.-Antoine and St.-Marceaux. Armed with axes, pikes, clubs, and a few firearms, they went first to the Assembly, where they noisily presented a petition demanding that "the king must observe the law." The crowd, estimated at some 8,000 people, then roared through the streets to the Tuileries, where, despite some resistance put up by the National Guard, they stormed the palace, invaded the king's apartments, and for four hours upbraided the trapped king and insulted the queen in the most violent terms. Louis, to his credit, refused to be cowed. His coolness no doubt saved at least the life of the detested Marie-Antoinette, if not his own. To please the men of the faubourgs, he placed the red cap of the Revolution—the "liberty cap"—on his head, while the queen, in a gesture of conciliation did the same to the young dauphin. Then the king emptied a bottle of red wine as a sign of fraternization with the mob. Finally, Jérôme Pétion, the Mayor of Paris, succeeded in having the palace cleared. The assassination of the king and queen, which many had feared and for which a few had hoped, had been averted.

The events of June 20 had an immediate effect throughout Europe and in England. The assault upon Louis' dignity and privacy awakened universal revulsion for the cause of the Revolution, and Louis' humiliation at the hands of the mob won for him instantly the wholehearted sympathy and support even of the English working classes. Étienne Dumont relates that Talleyrand and he, along with a half dozen other members of the French mission, were regarded with such hostility when they went for a walk at Ranelagh that the crowds actually separated so as to avoid infectious contact with them: "People withdrew to the right and the left as we approached, as though they thought that the very air we breathed was contagious." The attitude of the court and the government was no less hostile and no less openly expressed. Even Talleyrand was brought to the realization that any hope of an alliance between the revolutionary government of France and that of England was, for the moment, dead and that there was no longer any reason for his presence in London. The representative of a king who had been stripped of all authority and dignity by a mob from the streets was no longer in a position to negotiate.

Talleyrand returned to Paris on July 5. By July 6 he had taken his seat on the Constitutional Committee of the Department of the Seine, a position which he had held since his days in the Assembly but which he had occupied only rarely in those less hectic times. The business before the committee was significant. A motion had been introduced to suspend Pétion from his mayoral office on the ground that he had been derelict in not preventing the storming of the Tuileries on June 20. The committee, in other words, must now choose to side either with the mob or with the monarchy. Perhaps surprisingly under the circumstances, they chose the latter. On July 7, Talleyrand, along with most of his colleagues, voted to suspend Pétion. On July 13, however, the Assembly, led by the Jacobins, quashed the suspension and reinstated Pétion. Whereupon Talleyrand, followed by other members of the committee, resigned in protest against this attempted legalization of anarchy. Given the ascendancy of the Jacobins in Paris and the now total discredit of the monarchy, the resignation and the protest were nothing less than an act of courageous defiance of mob rule.

The next day, July 14, was Federation Day, and as usual, a public celebration took place in the Champ de Mars. As Talleyrand appeared in the company of the other former members of the Constitutional Committee, shouts of *Vive Pétion!* rose from the crowd, and those who had voted for the suspension were subjected to insults and epithets. To make matters worse, as Talleyrand and his companions passed in front of the royal tribune, Marie-Antoinette smiled and nodded in response to their respectful bows. She no doubt intended to show her gratitude for the committee's efforts to restore some semblance of dignity to the crown; instead, it roused the fury of the people to a new pitch. Talleyrand was perhaps understating the people's reaction when he wrote later that "the marks of approval given us by the queen when we passed under the balcony where she was with the king further excited the populace against us." The most prominent members of the committee, especially Talleyrand and the Duke de la Rochefoucauld d'Enville, chairman of the committee, were immediately accused of being "favorites of the court"—that is, enemies of the people. That smile was to cost Rochefoucauld dearly. The next day he left Paris in disguise but was recognized at Gisors and was stoned to death by the people of that city.

For the moment, Talleyrand remained in Paris. Having lost all official position and, worse, having forfeited his good standing in the Revolution, he occupied his time by calling upon his friends, upon Madame de Staël, and even by renewing his relations with Madame de Flahaut, with whom he dined on August 6—in company with the inevitable Gouverneur Morris. There was, in fact, little else that he could do. Powerless, in disgrace, and even in danger of his life, he was reduced to watching and hoping for an improvement in the situation and for a return to reason when the people, as they must, should tire of upheaval and disorder. But he was not optimistic:

After the events of that day [July 14] and the rout of the Prussians in Champagne,* the revolutionists flattered themselves that they had abolished the monarchy forever. They were blinded by their fanaticism, but no more so than the men who were of the opinion that royalty could soon be restored and Louis XVI replaced on his throne by force. At this stage, it was no longer a question of whether the king should reign, but whether he himself, the queen, their children, and his sister might still be saved.

The question expressed by Talleyrand was answered on August 10. Once more the palace of the Tuileries was stormed by the people, but this time their prey had escaped. Louis and Marie-Antoinette had been awakened at dawn by shrieks of *Vive la nation!* in the streets, and knowing what was to come, they had fled to the Legislative Assembly and begged for protection. The mob, in frustrated rage, turned upon the king's household troops— about 1,000 Swiss infantrymen—butchered them, and then mutilated their bodies. As the massacre went on and as the palace was being sacked, Louis and his family remained unmolested in the Assembly. They were there for three days, living as best they could in a tiny room provided for their use, while the deputies debated their fate. Finally, on August 13, Louis, Marie-Antoinette, the dauphin, and Madame Elizabeth, the king's sister, were sent under guard to imprisonment in the Temple, a small medieval dungeon in the center of Paris. The king was suspended from his functions, and the assembly elected a provisional Executive Council to assume his duties and responsibilities. This council was composed entirely of Jacobins, and its membership was almost the same as that of the former Brissotin ministry. There was one exception. The Ministry of Justice was given to Georges Danton, with whom Talleyrand was acquainted, and it was Danton who was the dominant figure in the new government.

The dramatic deposition of the king and the appointment of the Executive Council, with Danton at its head, at once realized Talleyrand's worst fears and provided him with the possibility, now that the king's cause was irretrievably lost, at least of saving himself. He wrote:

> After August 10 I solicited a temporary mission to London from the provisional Executive Council. As the pretext of my mission, I chose a scientific question with which I was somewhat qualified to deal, seeing that it related to a motion previously made by me in the Constituent Assembly. . . . My real object, however, was to leave France, where it seemed to me useless and indeed dangerous to stay any longer.

It would have been possible, of course, for Talleyrand to become an émigré—that is, simply to leave France without authorization. But emigration

---

* The victory of the French army, under General Dumouriez, against the forces of the Duke of Brunswick, which took place at Valmy on September 20.

had been forbidden by the Assembly, and all émigrés had been proscribed. Talleyrand was too prudent a man to burn bridges unless it was absolutely necessary: "I wished to leave the country with a regular passport, so that I would not be barred forever from returning to it."

The opportunity to present his proposal to Danton came without delay. The new Minister of Justice summoned Talleyrand immediately after taking office. Danton, magnetic, eloquent, audacious, and brilliant, was above all a realist, and as such he was aware—even in the confused period following the abolition of the monarchy—first, of the necessity of offering a plausible explanation to the courts of Europe for the events of August and, second, of his own lack of knowledge of how to go about making that justification. He needed advice, and he knew that in Talleyrand he had a man experienced in negotiations. The two men had, at one time, been fellow members of the Department of the Seine, and it seems that even in the hectic days following Talleyrand's return from London, Danton had had occasion to ask his advice on foreign affairs. In any event, when it would be Danton's turn, two years later, to be accused of betraying the Revolution, one of the charges to be made against him was that of "having been constantly in the company of the Bishop of Autun."

Danton's proposition was straightforward enough. Talleyrand was asked to compose an official note to the British government justifying the assault on the Tuileries and the deposition of the King of France, extolling the Legislative Assembly as the savior and guarantor of peace and public order, and requesting recognition of the new regime. Talleyrand's answer was equally unequivocal: He would do so, in exchange for a passport enabling him to travel to England in an official capacity. His mission, he explained to Danton, was part of a plan "to establish a uniform system of weights and measures. In order for this system to be adopted by the different nations, however, it would have to be vouched for by the most competent men of Europe, and it was therefore expedient to confer with England on the subject." It was not for nothing that Danton had become famous in France as "the Mirabeau of the Marketplace." He had, in addition to the latter's oratorical gifts and gift of leadership, an equal understanding of men. He knew that in Talleyrand, he had met his match in determination and in cold calculation. The bargain was made without further discussion.

The resulting note to England is characterized by that delicacy of expression which was habitual to Talleyrand, and by that ability to modify reality through a judicious choice of words, which was, and remains, the hallmark of the born diplomat. The king, he explained, who had been guaranteed a preeminent position under the new Constitution, had secretly intrigued against that Constitution and had attempted to corrupt patriotic

Frenchmen through bribery. The people, therefore, exasperated at the king's unwillingness to follow the light of reason, had taken matters into their own hands and marched on the Tuileries. (There is no mention of the slaughter of the Swiss guards or of the sacking of the palace.) Therefore, "there must be no misunderstanding between England and France. George III and his ministers must not interpret as a threat and an insult to all kings the overthrow of the King of France." Indeed, the note goes on to express the most "candid expression of the friendship of the provisional government of France for the government of England." Talleyrand concludes the note with the writer's personal "assurance of his friendship, confidence, and esteem for the people who, before any other nation of Europe, was able to obtain and preserve its own independence . . . and that when the English nation recovered its sovereignty, the powers of Europe, and France in particular, did not hesitate to recognize the new government which the nation had accepted."

Talleyrand's references to the Revolution of 1648 and to the subsequent death of Charles I on the scaffold were, in the circumstances, unfortunate. It had the result of provoking indignation among the English by reminding them of their own sins committed in the cause of liberty. As for the rest of the note, it was not altogether a distortion of the actual events of August. There is no doubt that the king and queen had been intriguing with the Austrians and that they hoped fervently for the defeat of the revolutionary armies of France. It was also true that they had attempted to win support among certain of the leaders of the Assembly by offering large sums of money. (Mirabeau, for one, had accepted the offer. And there was some evidence—which had not yet come to light—that Talleyrand himself had been approached but had, for reasons of his own, declined.) Since this was so, it would not have been unreasonable to assume that England, if violent emotions had not already been brought into play, might accept the *fait accompli* of the provisional government and, after a decent interval, extend recognition—just as the France of Richelieu had recognized the government of Oliver Cromwell in England almost 150 years earlier.

Certainly, Talleyrand was sincere in his efforts, on Danton's behalf, to save whatever could be saved of the work he had so recently begun in England. From that standpoint, the note is perhaps justifiable. It seems certain, however, that given Talleyrand's strong reaction, as a member of the Constitutional Committee, to the events of June 20, he would never have consented to excuse, let alone to applaud, the behavior of the mob if it had not seemed to him absolutely imperative that he do so for the sake of his own survival.

The events following the election of the provisional government indicated that the survival not only of Talleyrand himself, but of a great number of the nobles and clergy of France was extremely precarious. Beginning in mid-August, hundreds of persons belonging to those suspect classes were arrested by order of the Commune of Paris, which had been declared the final authority on all matters of internal security. The prisons were filled to overflowing, and convents and monasteries were designated as places of confinement for those whom the official dungeons could not hold: the "aristocrats, bishops and priests" who had been declared enemies of the people.

Talleyrand, who was both an aristocrat and an ex-bishop, was in imminent danger. By the end of August he was daily expecting his passport from Danton, and daily he was disappointed. On September 1 the situation in Paris had become desperate. At midday, Danton spoke in the Assembly, calling on the people to save themselves and the nation by their own courage. At two o'clock the tocsin was sounded. And at four o'clock, as the Assembly adjourned, the people attacked the prisons of the "aristocrats, bishops and priests" and began to massacre those held in them. Between September 1 and September 4, it is estimated that 1,200 people lost their lives—about half of the prison population of Paris. The atrocities of the *septembriseurs,* as the mobs were called, continued for two weeks. In the midst of the massacres, Talleyrand was still trying desperately to secure his passport from Danton. On September 1, a Jacobin deputy, Bertrand Barère, had met him in the Ministry of Justice late at night, where he was waiting for Danton. "*M. l'évêque* [the bishop]," Barère noted in his *Mémoires,* "was in a pair of leather knee breeches, booted, with a round hat, a short coat, and with his hair tied in a queue. I had known him quite well for three years in the Assembly, and he greeted me cordially. When I expressed surprise at finding him at the ministry so late, he answered, 'It is because I expect to leave in the morning for London, on a mission for the Executive Council. I am waiting for the papers that Danton is supposed to bring me after the meeting of the council which is presently under way.'" Talleyrand had waited until amost two o'clock in the morning, but when Danton finally came, it was with empty hands. The other business of the council had been too pressing to bring up the matter of the passport. Talleyrand would have to wait.

For six more days he waited, literally not knowing whether each day might be his last, for the people had now turned from the prisons and were attacking suspected "enemies of the Revolution" in the streets or dragging them from their homes to the rapidly emptying prisons to provide more victims for the mob. Then, on the seventh day, the passport arrived, properly signed by Danton and duly countersigned by five other members of the council. "Let Talleyrand pass," it read, "en route to London by our orders.—Danton, 1792—*République.*"

6

Exile: England and America

I N MID-SEPTEMBER, 1792, a brief notice appeared in London's *Morning Chronicle*:

> Messieurs de Talleyrand-Périgord . . . and several others have been obliged to seek here a refuge against the fury of the faction which now in France violates all principles of justice and humanity: Their sole crime appears to have been to content themselves with abolishing the abuses of the old government and to establish a sort of monarchy, and of their unwillingness to cooperate in establishing anarchy and proscription in the name of the Republic.

Thus, London and the community of French émigrés in London were informed of the arrival in their midst of the former deputy to the States-General, former Bishop of Autun, former member of the Constituent Assembly, former diplomat-without-portfolio of the Legislative Assembly, and recent apologist for the Commune.

The news was not received with universal joy. London was already filled to overflowing with refugees, and the initial hospitable attitude of the English was changing to one of thinly veiled exasperation. Sir James Bland Burges, Under-Secretary at the Foreign Office, wrote, at the time of Talleyrand's arrival in England:

> The late horrors in France have at least been attended with one good consequence, for they have turned the tide of general opinions here very suddenly. French principles and French men are daily becoming more unpopular, and I think it is not impossible that in a short time the imprudence of

some of these levellers will work so much on the temper of our people as to
make England neither a pleasant nor a secure residence for them.

The advent of revolutionary leaders such as Talleyrand and of less prominent former members of the Assembly such as Jaucourt, Beaumetz, and
Montmorency—all friends of Talleyrand—was particularly distressing:

> Of those who are known, [Burges went on] I am sure not one, except a few
> harmless old women, deserve anything; for the whole class were Jacobins
> and persecutors so long as they were in power, and would be so still, were
> they not supplanted by others of the same stamp. . . . I sincerely hope that
> some means may be found of getting rid of them before any bad conse-
> quences may come from their residence among us.

The émigrés themselves were even less kind, and perhaps with less reason, than Burges. Talleyrand and his friends, as well as the hundreds of
others who had fled the horror of the September Massacres and the Terror,
were regarded as *constitutionnels* and *monarchiens* and were blamed for
having supported a monarchy which had been stripped of its authentic
character. Those who had fled France at the first signs of what was to come
in 1789—*les purs* ("the pure ones") they called themselves—regarded Talleyrand and his friends, who had, after all, aided and abetted the Revolution, as the cause of all their misfortunes, and they could scarcely conceal
their delight when these "traitors" were forced finally into exile by the
Revolution that they had helped create. Narbonne, when he first appeared
in England late in 1792, was greeted by the Duke de la Châtre with the
words: "You and your damned Constitution have ruined everything. You
are the primary cause of all our misfortunes. Now we can all starve happily
together."

Talleyrand was not insensitive to such attitudes, nor did he find them
wholly without some justification in fact. "It would be a great mistake," he
wrote, "for anyone to conclude . . . that I found fault with those who emigrated. . . . Nearly all the émigrés were motivated by a nobility of sentiment and by a deep devotion to the royal cause." He had always thought
that the mass emigration at the beginning of the Revolution had been the
"wrong step" and that it had been an important cause—perhaps the most
important one—of those very same "misfortunes" for which he and his
friends were blamed. Emigration, he maintained, "compromised everything, relatives, friends, possessions, and the throne with them. And not
only the throne itself, but the life of the monarch as well, and that of his
family, which, perhaps one day on the brink of the abyss, or already in the
abyss, could account for its misfortunes only by crying out: 'Look and see
where emigrations had led us.' "*

---

* That this was actually the opinion, if not the very words, of Louis XVI, is illustrated in the
Mémoires of the Marquis de Clermont-Gallerande, who was sent by Louis to Coblenz in order to

That Talleyrand made no secret of such opinions and that the course of events in France now lent credibility to them in no way helped mitigate the bitterness of the émigrés toward *Monsieur l'abbé,* as they sometimes referred to him contemptuously. This, however, Talleyrand accepted with his customary nonchalance. He was confident that despite the coldness of the British government and its refugee guests, he would find ample company and sufficient amusement in England.

Talleyrand's first necessity was a place to live, and he quickly found a small house in Kensington, in Woodstock Street. Since, for the first time in his adult life, he had no servants to care for his needs, the supervision of his bachelor establishment was placed in the willing hands of Madame de la Châtre, wife of one of the most vehement of the early émigrés. She was also the mistress (and eventually the wife) of Count de Jaucourt. Jaucourt, one of Talleyrand's closest friends in the early days of the Assembly, had come to England at the time of the September massacres, and Madame de la Châtre, to her husband's embarrassment, had followed him. She then proved her devotion further by employing her domestic skills on behalf of any of Jaucourt's friends—and there were several, in addition to Talleyrand—whose experience had not included the management of a household.

Hardly had Talleyrand settled into Woodstock Street and begun to enjoy the safety of England when he discovered that the Channel, while it might protect him from physical harm, was no guarantee against either the winds of fortune or the attacks of his enemies. On August 10, during the sack of the Tuileries, a safe (known as the Iron Cupboard) had been discovered in the king's chambers, and its contents subsequently had been turned over to the Minister of the Interior. Among these papers were discovered several items of correspondence which, in varying degrees, compromised both the king and the persons mentioned in the letters. One such item was a note to the king, dated April 22, 1791, from Arnaud Laporte, secretary of the King's Civil List:

> Sire, I am sending to your majesty a letter written the day before yesterday, and which I received only yesterday afternoon. It is from the Bishop of Autun, who wishes to be of service to your majesty. He asks me to inform you that you may count on his zeal and discretion, and that you have only to point out to him how you wish him to act. The new faction which has arisen among the Jacobins [*i.e.,* the Feuillants, of which Talleyrand was a member] desires the reestablishment of public order, the maintenance of the monarchy, the downfall of the democratic sect, and the safety of your person.

---

describe to the Count d'Artois and the Count de Provence "the personal danger in which his life had been placed by the emigration" (*Mémoires,* Vol. I, p. 97. Charles, Marquis de Clermont-Gallerande).

The letter to which Laporte's note refers was not found. From the intendant's wording, it is possible to conclude that, for some reason, it was not
enclosed. Perhaps it did not even exist. But this consideration did not
cause the members of the Convention* to hesitate. They had been elected
precisely to rid France of "royalist accomplices" and "traitors." On December 5, therefore, the Convention found that there were indeed
"grounds for accusation against Talleyrand-Périgord, former Bishop of
Autun, and that all relevant documents are to be seized immediately." Despite Danton's protests that the accused man was officially "accredited to
the London embassy," the Convention then proceeded to place Talleyrand's name on the list of proscribed émigrés.† With this done, an order
for Talleyrand's arrest was issued, and citizens were warned to be on the
lookout for a man "five feet three inches tall [he was actually two and one-
half inches taller], with a long face, blue eyes, and an ordinary nose slightly
retroussé . . . [who] limps on one foot, either the right or the left."

When the news of these proceedings reached London, Talleyrand
dashed off a vehement letter to the Convention, denying all allegations: "I
have never said or done anything of the kind. I have had no dealings with
the king, either directly or indirectly, or with M. Laporte." The letter,
which went on for several pages in the same vein, did not impress the Convention—which, however, allowed it to be printed in the *Moniteur* of December 24, 1792.

A week earlier, the *Moniteur* had printed another document for the defense, written by a man who signed himself only as "D," which constituted
an able and resourceful vindication of the pristine purity of Talleyrand's
revolutionary beliefs and pointed out that despite all the accusations that
had been made, there was not one shred of firsthand evidence against Talleyrand: "In all the compromising papers belonging to the former king,
there is not a single line, not a single word, written by him." Moreover, the
anonymous author** continues, on the very day that the Convention voted

* Following the suspension of the King on August 13, the Legislative Assembly had voted to
dissolve itself and make way for a new body whose function it would be formally to determine
whether or not the monarchy should be abolished. This body—in reality, a new constituent assembly—was to be known as the National Convention. It was convened on September 20, 1792, and
in it were vested, both by law and in fact, dictatorial powers.

† At the same time was inscribed the name of "the Talleyrand woman, the widow Damas"—
Talleyrand's mother who, along with her other sons, Archambaud and Boson, had taken refuge at
Coblenz in September.

** Authorities are in disagreement on this point, as on others. Lacour-Gayet believes that the
"D" refers to Desrenaudes, Talleyrand's former vicar-general at Autun, who had remained in
Paris; but then Lacour-Gayet also attributes most of Talleyrand's writing (*The Report on Public
Education,* for instance) during the revolutionary period to Desrenaudes—an attribution based
upon flimsy external critical data. It seems more likely, if somewhat more melodramatic, that the
"D" stood for Danton. The author's manner of presenting evidence and the reference to Talley-
rand's memorandum to the Foreign Ministry indicate that the author was a lawyer well versed in

to condemn Talleyrand, the Ministry of Foreign Affairs in Paris had received from him a memorandum which attested, beyond dispute, to his undiminished devotion to the ideals of the Revolution.

The Convention, having already made up its mind, was not interested in evidence, and though both Talleyrand's letter and the anonymous defense were widely read and commented upon, the proscription stood.

The question of whether or not Talleyrand actually wrote the letter mentioned in Laporte's note to the king—that is, whether he was guilty as charged—is one that has been hotly debated on all sides. The answer, however, is of no particular importance. The principles set out in Laporte's note—that "The new faction which has arisen among the Jacobins desires the reestablishment of public order, the preservation of the monarchy, the overthrow of the democratic sect, and the safety of your person"—were those that it was still safe openly to profess in 1791; indeed, they were the recognized principles not only of the Feuillants, but also of the majority of the Assembly at that time. Nor was it a crime, early in 1791, to offer one's services to the king—though by the end of 1792 the mere suspicion that such an offer had been made would have been sufficient to send anyone to prison, if not to the newfangled guillotine that had just been installed in the Place du Carrousel opposite the Tuileries. That Talleyrand denied having written such a letter, whether or not he actually did, is not surprising under the circumstances, for proscription meant that a person forfeited not only his civil rights (and his liberty, if he was apprehended), but also his property, his reputation, and his chances of returning to France. It is significant, however, that under the Restoration, when it would have been to his credit to have admitted authorship of the letter, he never once alluded to it—although he made a point of reminding the Count d'Artois, during that period, of the midnight interview in which he had offered his services and those of his friends to the royal cause.

It is more likely than not, all things considered, that Talleyrand did not write a letter to Laporte, or anyone else, offering his services to the king. But it is certain that the principles expressed in the fictive letter were those which Talleyrand professed from the very beginning of the Revolution, that they were the principles to which he adhered throughout that upheaval, and that they were the very same principles that he would incorpo-

---

the rules of evidence (as Danton was and as Desrenaudes was not) and that he was sufficiently highly placed in the government to have had knowledge of and access to the memorandum in question. Finally, after Danton's death, a copy of this memorandum, dated November 25, 1792, was found among his papers. The chief argument for Desrenaudes has been that Danton was absent from Paris from early December until the end of the month and that he could not then have authored the defense published in the *Moniteur*. Danton's latest biographer has demonstrated beyond a reasonable doubt that this was not the case. See *Danton* by Robert Christophe, pp. 320–21.

rate into the Constitution of France under the Restoration. It was not coincidental that the collapse of the monarchy in 1792 and Talleyrand's disenchantment with the Revolution were contemporaneous. Shortly after his arrival in England, he described to Lord Lansdowne what had become of the Revolution that had begun with such great promise:

> Only an absurdly small number of men still remain faithful to the ideal of liberty, and these do so despite the blood and filth of the horrible atrocities which now obscure its features. Trapped for two years now between terror and defiance, the French have become slaves—that is, they say only what it is safe to say. Initiative has been destroyed by clubs and pikes, and the people have become accustomed to dissimulation and corruption—a habit which, once acquired, will make it possible for them to find happiness only in exchanging one tyrant for another. Everyone quakes before the head cutters, from the leaders of the Jacobins down to the ordinary honest citizen; and today there is a chain of vileness and falsehood the first link of which is hidden in filth.

It was not that Talleyrand had abandoned his principles along with the Revolution. It was rather that the Revolution had abandoned both Talleyrand and his principles.

Talleyrand's condemnation by the Convention, for all its unpleasant implications, produced at least one welcome side effect: It removed from his shoulders the burden of being accredited to a government whose excesses were daily exciting horror and mistrust among the English. After the September massacres, even those who had supported the Revolution in its early stages were aghast at the thought that their own country might easily be contaminated by the madness which had shown itself, in so virulent a form, only a few miles from the shores of England, and there was great agitation for the government to take steps against the "French propaganda" that might be disseminated by refugees who, as Burges of the Foreign Office had pointed out, were themselves nothing more than "Jacobins and persecutors so long as they were in power." Edmund Burke, who in 1789 had hailed the Revolution as a new day for mankind, by the end of 1792 was declaring in the Commons that it was the duty of every English patriot "to keep the French infection from this country; their principles from our minds, and their daggers from our hearts." And in December, Pitt's government asked for, and received, the authority to supervise the activities of foreigners in England and to expel any émigrés whose acts or words were deemed dangerous to the security and good order of England.* The threat was clear, and it was one to which Talleyrand was particularly sensitive

---

* This action of Parliament, known as the Alien Bill of 1792, was introduced by Grenville; its purpose was to make an earlier measure (the Alien Bill of 1782) more immediately applicable to French refugees; as such, it was strongly opposed by Fox but passed over his objections.

and, given his previous mission in England, especially vulnerable. He lost no time in writing to Grenville, assuring him of his good intentions and even offering his services in a limited capacity:

> I greatly desire that you be aware that I have no mission of any kind in England. I have come solely to find peace and to enjoy, among true friends, true liberty. If, however, my Lord Grenville should wish to become informed on the state of France today, which are the parties responsible for her present turmoil, what is the extent of the actual power of the provisional Executive Council, and what conjectures may reasonably be formed on the basis of the terrible and fearsome events to which I have been an eyewitness, then I should be pleased to give him an account of these things.

To this offer, Grenville made no reply. Nothing that Talleyrand could say or do would alter his belief, or Pitt's, that the former representative of the Revolution was anything but *un homme profond et dangereux*—"a deep and dangerous man," as Grenville called him.

In truth, events in France, after the passage of Grenville's Alien Bill, did nothing to lessen the consternation of the government and people of Britain or to mitigate their distrust of such men as Talleyrand. Early in December, the Convention had voted to bring King Louis to trial for his crimes against the people of France and on December 11, Louis, mild, dignified, and somewhat bewildered, had listened to a litany of the charges against him, the most serious of which accused him of having conspired with General Bouillé against his subjects and of having broken his oath to the Constitution. The king, after denying all the charges, had been granted two weeks in which to prepare his defense. On December 26 the trial was resumed and, except for the rendering of a verdict, concluded. Until January 3, 1793, Louis' life hung in the balance. The most cautious of the members were for Louis' deposition; the most vehement, for his death. On that day, however, Bertrand Barère, a leader of the center, mounted the tribune and, in an impassioned tirade, demanded the life of the king as an indispensable "measure of public safety." From that moment, though the debates continued, all attempts to save Louis were doomed. On January 15, two questions were put to the Convention for a vote: Was Louis guilty as charged? And, if so, what should be his punishment? To the first, 683 members—almost everyone present—voted affirmatively. To the second, the vote was split among death, imprisonment, and exile. Finally, after thirty-six hours of discussion, the president of the Convention, Pierre Vergniaud, announced that the sentence to be imposed was death. On January 18 the date of execution was fixed for January 21. On that day Louis,

dressed in royal white, was driven from the Temple to the Place de la Révolution* and guillotined.

With Louis' death was ended any chance of reconciliation between England and revolutionary France. News of the execution fell upon London
like a thunderbolt. It was received first with stupefied disbelief, then with
horror, and finally with a burst of rage. Cries of "War with France!" were
heard both in the streets and in Parliament. All public places were closed,
and the court and Parliament went into deep mourning. "Everyone who
had a black coat," wrote one of the émigrés, "or who could somehow procure one put it on." Talleyrand, like everyone else, mourned Louis' death,
but, more than Louis, he mourned the death of constitutional law and
order in the Revolution. The king's execution signaled the end of any hope
that he may have retained. "The reign of illusion has ended in France," he
wrote. As though to confirm his words, on January 31, ten days after King
Louis' death, England declared war on France.

In these circumstances, it is understandable that the circles in which Talleyrand moved in London were somewhat restricted. With Grenville and
Pitt hostile to him, the doors of the great Tory houses were shut, and remained shut, for the two years that he lived in England. To the ladies of
these houses, who knew him only by reputation, he was a Mephistophelian
figure, though perhaps an intriguing one, whom one might discuss but
never receive. "The Duchess of Gordon," Gouverneur Morris noted on a
visit to London, "asks my opinion of Bishop d'Autun, who is, she is told, a
very profligate fellow." And Lady Stafford wrote, in mingled delight and
horror, that "the Évêque d'Autun is here, by the name of Mons. Talleyrand-Périgord. . . . He is a disagreeable-looking man, has a baddish, trick-
ing character, and supposed not very upright in disposition or heart."

In this respect, Talleyrand's social situation in London was not very different from what it had been during his mission early in 1792, and because
it was expected, the reaction of these ladies did not trouble him unduly. He
had friends enough among the Whigs to occupy his evenings. "I was immediately received with the utmost kindness by the Marquess of Lansdowne,"† he wrote, "whom I had known in Paris." Lansdowne's thoughtfulness was such that he not only entertained Talleyrand frequently, but
"sent me word every time he received a visit from some distinguished per-

---

* Before the Revolution, it was known as the Place Louis XV and, after the Revolution, as the
Place de la Concord.

† Lansdowne never wavered in his sympathy for France or in his opposition to Pitt. He had
been First Lord of the Treasury until 1783, but had resigned upon the latter's ascension to power
and had never been recalled to office because, Talleyrand pointed out, "some people brought
against him the accusation of being *too clever,* which, in England as well as in France, is what people accuse a man of when his superiority offends them" (*Mémoires,* Vol. I, p. 170).

son whose acquaintance he thought I might be pleased to make." Through Lansdowne's courtesy, Talleyrand came to know, with some degree of intimacy, several of the most illustrious men of the time and some who were yet to achieve distinction within Talleyrand's lifetime: George Canning, the future Secretary of Foreign Affairs; Jeremy Bentham, the social philosopher and moralist; Joseph Priestley, philosopher and pioneer in electrical research; Lord Hastings, later governor-general of India; and, of course, Lord Shelburne, Lansdowne's son, who would be Chancellor of the Exchequer in 1809, Home Secretary in Canning's Cabinet (1827), and a member of the government during Talleyrand's London embassy in the 1830's. Charles Fox also opened his house to Talleyrand and shared his friends with him and generally did his best "to make my stay in London as pleasant as possible."

It was not, however, among the English, kind though they may have been, that Talleyrand sought his chief pleasure and consolation. His own house in Woodstock Street soon became a meeting place for the many friends from France who had fled the Terror—Narbonne, Montmorency, Beaumetz, and many others. Narbonne and Talleyrand in England remained, as ever, inseparable companions. A friend of the former, Dr. Justus Erich Bollman, who had accompanied Narbonne from Paris, has left a descriptive assessment of the two friends at this time:

> Narbonne is a rather big man, a bit heavy, but vigorous, and his head impresses one with its arresting and superior air. His mind contains an inexhaustible wealth of ideas. He possesses all the social virtues in a supreme degree, and to the most arid of subjects he communicates an incomparable charm. When he wishes to do so, he can attract irresistibly, and even intoxicate, a single person as well as a roomful of people.

Even this incredible paragon, however, is surpassed by Talleyrand, who apparently was able to work a spell of his own on the awestruck German:

> There was only one other man in France who is worthy, from this point of view, to be compared to him [Narbonne]—one who, in my opinion, greatly surpasses him. This is his friend, Talleyrand, ex-Bishop of Autun. Narbonne pleases, but in the end he tires one; to Talleyrand, however, one could listen for years. Narbonne seeks to please, but one is conscious of the effort involved; when Talleyrand speaks, it is without the slightest effort, and he lives constantly in an atmosphere of perfect relaxation. Narbonne's language is more brilliant, but that of Talleyrand is more gracious, more incisive, more intriguing. Narbonne is not the kind of man who is capable of pleasing everyone; sentimental people cannot abide him, and over them he has no power. But Talleyrand, who is no less morally corrupt than Narbonne, can move to tears even those who hate him.

The qualities of Talleyrand and Narbonne described by Bollman were

such as to overwhelm mortals who might be required by convention to prefer one or the other as their friend. Germaine de Staël, for one, did not try.
Early in 1792, Narbonne had been permitted to become her lover, so that
she might enjoy the company of both men without being compelled to
make the impossible choice. For the time being, however, the lady was deprived of both her friends. After Narbonne's flight from Paris, where she
had hidden him in the Swedish embassy, Germaine had joined her father
and husband in Switzerland, and there, to the dismay of M. Necker and
the Baron de Staël, she was occupying her days with devising pretexts and
means for a journey to London, where she might, in an excess of civilized
generosity, divide her favors between Talleyrand and Narbonne.

At that moment, Talleyrand was not lacking in feminine company. Madame de la Châtre, in addition to her domestic skills, possessed qualities
which made her a charming companion, not the least of these being, one of
her admirers remarked, that her virtue was not of the sort that men found
depressing. Madame de Genlis, too, was there, making careful notes of everything she saw and heard for inclusion in her memoirs; "that scribbling
trollop," Horace Walpole called her. In her care was Adélaïde d'Orléans,
daughter of the Duke d'Orléans, who had been orphaned when her father,
having voted for the death of Louis XVI, was himself beheaded for aspiring to succeed his cousin as King of France. Though only sixteen at the
time, Adélaïde was already exhibiting that strength, intelligence, and prudence which, with Talleyrand's blessing, was to enable her brother, Louis-
Philippe, in 1830 to acquire the crown that her father had coveted.

To Madame de Genlis, Talleyrand was strongly attached, not only by
habit—for hers was one of the houses that he had frequented in Paris—but
also by admiration. She had long been mistress to the Duke d'Orléans and
had played admirably the role of mother to his children by the duchess.
Her loyalty to the duke and to his family had never wavered, even when
his path had led to the guillotine and when it seemed that her loyalty
would lead only to destruction. Now, penniless in London, she was bur-
dened with the responsibility for the care and education not only of Adélaïde d'Orléans, but also of one of the duke's natural daughters. In misfortune, she lost nothing of her gaiety and charm, and though her sharp
tongue made her less than popular in some circles, Talleyrand's devotion
to her never faltered. With hardly a shilling to his name, he managed
somehow to share what he had with her. She, in turn, used her slender resources to organize little dinner parties where the principal fare was the
liveliness of Talleyrand's mind. As for the food, there was usually little,
and that rather poor, though Talleyrand was careful to describe Madame
de Genlis' table as being "charming in its commendable frugality." When
it happened on one occasion that, somehow or other, she was able to

scrape together the means to invite a large group of people for a more adequate meal, Talleyrand found it necessary to reassure his hostess. Upon entering the house, he whispered to her: "I promise not to look surprised."

The charm of Madame de Genlis' company was supplemented by that of the Countess de Flahaut, who, having fled France shortly after Talleyrand's hasty departure, had established herself in London, in Half Moon Street. She was among the more fortunate of the émigrés, having succeeded in escaping with a satisfactory amount of cash. But with no experience in the management of money, she had soon frittered away the entire amount on dresses and hats and entertainment and was reduced to supporting herself by weaving and selling straw hats.* Such a menial occupation and its poor return could not long satisfy someone of Adélaïde de Flahaut's talents. She resurrected a novel which she had begun in Paris and, with Talleyrand's encouragement, set to work in earnest. Her days were now spent writing; and Talleyrand's nights, in correcting and proofreading her copy. The novel, *Adèle de Senange*, was shortly finished, published by subscription, and met with great success. The countess, who had always lived on the verge of poverty in her tiny Louvre apartment, earned herself the considerable sum of 40,000 francs. Talleyrand promptly asked her for the loan of 12,000—which, just as promptly, she refused.

Talleyrand's own writing occupied a fair part of his time. "My mornings," he says, "were spent in recording my impressions of the previous day"—no doubt with a view toward the eventual compilation of his memoirs. He was later to conclude, however, that this had been time wasted. "After my return to France . . . my friends sent to me all the notes taken during the time I resided in England. I was astonished to see that they could be of no use to me at all in the work I am now writing [the *Mémoires*]. It would be impossible for me to narrate the events of this period. I simply do not remember them. Their connecting link is lost for me." More durable was a biography of the Duke d'Orléans, *Philippe-Égalité*, on which Talleyrand spent considerable time and effort. Although it was never published separately, it was eventually revised and incorporated into the *Mémoires*, where it paints a portrait of a prince who, reprehensible as his conduct may have been in betraying his royal cousin and in aspiring to succeed him, cannot be blamed either for the Revolution or for its consequences (though many in Talleyrand's time did blame him). It was not that Philippe-Égalité lacked the ambition to be a villain or the character for it, for he was a paragon of the vices: "immorality, extreme frivolity, want of

_____

* This had become a favorite occupation for the émigrés who were forced to support themselves—that is to say, for most of them. The hats, woven of a special straw, became quite popular (particularly in America, to which they were exported) and in London sold for 25 shillings apiece. However, it took between fifteen and twenty hours of work to produce one such hat.

reflection, and weakness." It was not one man, but the spirit of an age, which unleashed the torrent: "It had no authors, leaders, or guides. It was sown by the writers who, in an enlightened and venturesome century, wished to attack prejudices, but instead subverted religious and social principles, and by incompetent ministers who, in increasing the deficit of the treasury, aggravated the discontent of the people."

Since Talleyrand, unlike Madame de Flahaut, derived no income from his writing and since he had no other possible source of revenue during his stay in England, he existed continually on the edge of poverty. Indeed, how he managed to make ends meet remains a mystery. He had been entered on the list of émigrés and proscribed, and his properties in France were therefore forfeited to the state. It seemed unlikely that he had been able to salvage more than a few jewels to take with him to England and a small amount of cash, for by the end of 1792 it was obvious that he was in desperate straits. The ordinary expense of living, added to the innate generosity of character which made him turn his house into a temporary hotel and boardinghouse for the stream of friends who were constantly arriving, homeless and penniless, from the Continent, required money far in excess of what he had. His solution, however, was not to curtail his kindness to his friends, but to give up the house in Woodstock Street and move to a smaller one nearby, in Kensington Square. Even there, new émigrés could be sure of finding a bed and modest fare until they were able to establish themselves. From this new house, Talleyrand wrote to Lansdowne, late in 1792, that he had hoped "to spend in your company some days of wit, reason, instruction, and tranquillity, but some of my French friends, devoted to the cause of liberty and chased away by pikes, have arrived in England. I wish to offer to them their first shelter, but by the middle of next week they will, I believe, have arranged their winter quarters, and I will then have the honor of seeing you at Bowood."

Even in more modest quarters, Talleyrand's obligations, or at least his hospitality, were more than his extremely limited means could bear. In March, 1793, he reached a painful decision. The only possession of value that remained to him was his library, which he had taken the precaution of shipping to England during the summer of the preceding year. If he were to be able to meet his expenses and continue to alleviate the needs of his friends, it would have to be sold. Only those among his friends who themselves loved fine books could have appreciated the enormousness of Talleyrand's sacrifice or known what it cost him to look at his treasures and realize that they were to be his no more. Yet the books were offered at auction, in nine sections, between April 12 and April 23. The return realized on the sale seemed hardly worth the loss of his books. "Today, with my books sold," he wrote to Madame de Staël, "I am worth, outside France,

750 pounds sterling. What good is it?" This sum, small as it was, served temporarily to relieve his own most immediate wants; some of it, in addition, went to Madame de Genlis, and to other friends in even greater distress than he.

Such sums could bring nothing more than temporary relief, given the almost desperate poverty of friends such as Madame de Genlis, Beaumetz, Montmorency, and Jaucourt. (Narbonne seems to have had either greater resources or greater ingenuity than the others. He kept a house in London, two servants, and a coach.) The sharing of houses and food among this small group of émigrés would lose its effectiveness when the dwindling resources on which those things depended vanished, as eventually they must, leaving them with nothing save their great names and resounding titles. What was needed was a wealthy benefactor. Providentially, one was not long in coming. An English gentleman named Locke, of unknown political beliefs but of great sympathy for the victims of the Revolution, placed at their disposal his estate of Juniper Hall in Surrey, near the village of Mickleham.

Juniper Hall was not one of England's "great houses." Yet it had a certain elegance of style and decoration that lent it an air of luxury. More important, it was sufficiently spacious to accommodate virtually the entire group of Talleyrand's friends, as well as an occasional guest. They therefore accepted the offer with delight, and for several months in 1793, they managed to rediscover the charm of the life that they had known in France. Talleyrand chose to keep his house in Kensington Square rather than move to Juniper Hall, but he paid frequent and extended visits to the little émigré colony.

In Mickleham there lived at this time a Mrs. Susanna Phillips, a gentlewoman of great curiosity concerning events in the great world beyond Surrey. Her inquisitiveness quickly extended to the exotic foreigners with magnificent names and mysterious histories who had ensconced themselves in Mr. Locke's house, and she came to call. The excitement of her discovery was communicated by letter to a sister, Miss Fanny Burney, who forthwith arrived in Mickleham for an extended visit. The two ladies' unreserved friendliness and undisguised curiosity enchanted the émigrés, who praised their "knowledge, wit, grace, and intelligence." Miss Burney, in turn, in her letters to her father and friends, could scarcely express her unbounded enthusiasm for the elegance, amiability, and talent of Talleyrand's friends. "There can be nothing imagined more charming, more fascinating than this colony," she wrote. Most charming and fascinating of all was Talleyrand himself, whom Miss Burney met shortly after Germaine de Staël's arrival in February, 1793. The Englishwoman had been prepared to dislike him for his reputed wickedness. "M. de Talleyrand," she noted, upon this first encounter, "opened last night with infinite wit and capacity. Madame de Staël whispered to me, 'How do you like him?' 'Not very much,' I answered. 'Oh, I assure you,' cried she, 'he is the best of men.' I was happy not to agree." But after a few days the lady had had a complete change of mind: "It is inconceivable what a convert M. de Talleyrand has made of me. I think him now one of the finest members and one of the most charming of this exquisite set. Susanna is completely a proselyte. His powers of entertainment are astonishing, both in information and in raillery."

The arrival of Madame de Staël at Juniper Hall, several weeks after the refugees had established themselves there, was a cause of particular exaltation for Miss Burney and Mrs. Phillips. But their pleasure was short-lived, for their father, when Fanny asked his permission to accept Germaine's invitation to stay at Juniper Hall, replied immediately, warning his daughters against this lady, who, he said, "has been accused of partiality to M. de Narbonne." This, Fanny rejected with great, if blind, indignation. "I do firmly believe it a gross calumny," she replied. "She loves him even tenderly, but so openly, so simply, so unaffectedly, and with such utter freedom from all coquetry, that, if they were two men or two women, the affection could not, I think, be more obviously undesigning. She is very plain; he is very handsome. Her intellectual endowments must be with him her sole attraction." Moreover, as proof of the innocence of the relationship between Germaine and Narbonne, Miss Burney cites the fact that "M. de Talleyrand is of their society. She appears to be equally attached to him. She loves M. de Montmorency . . . in fact, all this little colony lives together like brothers and sisters. Indeed, I think you could not spend a day with them and not see that their commerce is that of pure but exalted and most elegant friendship."

Dr. Burney's warning had been merely an echo of what was being said among his neighbors of Surrey. There were as many rumors as there were ladies at Juniper Hall, and all the rumors were true. Madame de Staël was indeed partial to M. de Narbonne—and to more than Narbonne. The affair between Madame de la Châtre and Jaucourt was notorious. Talleyrand's name also was coupled with that of Germaine de Staël, and the scandal of his liaison with Adélaïde de Flahaut had long caused English tongues to wag. The Princess de Hénin, former lady-in-waiting to Marie-Antoinette, was in the throes of a heated liaison with the Marquis de Lally-Tollendal (which, eventually, was to end in marriage). Miss Burney and her sister, once their eyes were opened to the true state of affairs, were dismayed. The émigrés, being French, were perhaps entitled to a certain laxity of conduct, but their sins must never be allowed to infect English womanhood. Now that she had heard what was being said, Fanny hastened to assure her father, "I would give the world to avoid being a guest under their roof." So the two ladies departed, leaving the émigrés to speculate on the vagaries of Britannic virtue; but not until Miss Burney had laid a firm hold on the affections of General d'Arblay, who, Frenchman or not, was single, eligible, lonely, eminently available, and rather a catch for a middle-aged English spinster. The pair were married in 1794 and, to all appearances, lived happily.

Germaine de Staël's arrival in England, as disastrous as it may have been for Miss Burney's great adventure, was the cause of rejoicing among the colony at Juniper Hall, where gaiety and keenness of wit were treasured above all things. But she was also welcome for another reason: She was immensely rich, and she was royally generous, and her ready assumption of the financial burdens of Juniper Hall came as a tonic to spirits depressed by privation and want. Her advent was the signal for four months of happiness. One of the favorite diversions on sunny days was to go for long drives in a dilapidated cabriolet belonging to Mr. Locke, with Germaine riding inside on one of the two seats and the groom's seat on the outside occupied, in turn, by Talleyrand, Narbonne, and Mathieu de Montmorency. The evenings were taken up with conversation and reading—the latter a fashionable pastime in which one of the company read viva voce to the rest. Madame de Staël herself declaimed parts of her essay "The Influence of the Passions on the Happiness of Men and Nations." Talleyrand, like his friends, was struck both by the strength of the piece and by its style, but in his enthusiasm, he succeeded in reducing the author to tears by remarking that her delivery left something to be desired: "You read prose very badly. . . . You make it sound like verse, and this produces a bad effect."

Despite these occasional minor contretemps, the months that Germaine de Staël spent at Juniper Hall served only to strengthen the ties between herself and Talleyrand. At the end of August, 1793, when she had returned to Switzerland, Talleyrand wrote: "I do not know what to do with myself. I am bored here, and worn out. . . . There is absolutely no one here in accordance with my mind and heart." And again: "It is absolutely certain that whatever I have been able to preserve of decency and good humor is due entirely to our union—and you know what I mean by *our*." It was clear that the Juniper Hall interval had marked the final parting of the ways between Talleyrand and Adélaïde de Flahaut* and that Germaine de

---

* It is not clear whether the breach was sudden, as the result of a particular incident, or a gradual drifting apart as the result of Germaine de Staël's presence. Talleyrand mentions the Countess de Flahaut only once in the *Mémoires*, and then in a different context, and the other memoirs and diaries of the period, such as that of Madame de Genlis, are no more helpful. All that can be known for certain is that at the beginning of Talleyrand's exile in England he and Adélaïde were

Staël not only had emerged victorious from the contest with her rival, but also had tasted amply of the fruits of victory. In later life, she was to recall the time spent with Talleyrand and Narbonne at the house in Surrey as "the four months salvaged from the shipwreck of my life."

The kindness of English friends, the distractions of Juniper Hall, the intellectual charms of Germaine de Staël, and the pleasant company of Narbonne, Beaumetz, Jaucourt, and Montmorency made it possible for Talleyrand to bear "the whole of the terrible year of 1793." Yet the events of that year—the waning of Danton's influence and the rise of Robespierre, the execution of Marie-Antoinette, the wholesale slaughter of aristocrats, priests, and ordinary citizens on the slightest pretext—were too much in direct contradiction to his own moderate and liberal principles not to awaken in him a sense of frustration and rage at his own helplessness. He had hardly reached the safety of England when he was writing: "In all honor, we cannot remain peaceful émigrés for very long." And "if there is a counterrevolution, we must take an active part in it." Man of peace that Talleyrand was, he could not endure peaceably the agony of France as the armies of the Revolution fell back and those of Prussia advanced into the heart of the country, as the Vendée rose in revolt against the excesses of the Convention and as the Convention itself tottered toward dissolution in the struggle among its factions. "I long to fight," he told Narbonne during the summer of 1793. "I can't tell you how much pleasure it would give me to give a good beating to those disgusting wretches [vilains gueux]!"

For a while in September it seemed that Talleyrand might be given the opportunity, if not to beat the wretches, then at least to take an active part once more in the affairs of France. The astonishing news came that Toulon, the great French port, had rebelled against the Convention and that the insurrectionists, hoping to incite the entire country against the tyrants in Paris, had proclaimed Louis XVI's young son King of France as Louis XVII. Seizing upon the opportunity, Talleyrand's hopes rose, and his mind began to lay plans for the reestablishment of constitutional government if the rebels should succeed. "The constitutionalists," he wrote to Madame de Staël, "are the only ones who can hope to do things, and undo things. . . . The Constitution is the only means of rousing men's spirits." For a time, his expectations were great, particularly when it was learned that England intended to reinforce the defenders of Toulon against the forces of the Convention. But two months later he was in despair: "I am in a frightful state of mind," he informed Germaine de Staël. "I no longer know

on friendly, though probably wholly platonic, terms. By the time that he left England for America there had been a definite cooling in their relationship, and when he returned from America, coolness had been replaced by indifference and near hostility.

what to hope for. Moria's attempt* has been useless. . . . This [failure] will excite the republicans against the unhappy Vendée, and then there will be countless massacres. One hears news of battles in which 20,000 or 30,000 men have been killed—and yet things remain as they were." His fears for the insurgents of Toulon were realized. The raising of the British siege of the port, owing largely to the skill and daring of a young artillery captain whose name, as it appears in the official reports, was Napoleone Bona-Parte, had marked the end of any real hope for success. By December the city had fallen into the hands of the Paris government, and the rebels had been slaughtered.

The defeat of the English at Toulon and the successes of the Revolution in putting down similar uprisings elsewhere in France, coupled with the re-alization that the tides of war were already turning in favor of the armies of France and against those of the Coalition (as the alliance among Prussia, Russia, Austria, and Britain was known), had serious repercussions in London. The government, especially Grenville, now thought it necessary, in Talleyrand's words, "to show zeal for the general cause." Since military victory had thus far eluded the English, Grenville determined to proceed against those whom he suspected of agitating on behalf of the enemies of England. The first victims of this determination were the more recent émi-grés—the *constitutionnels* and the *monarchiens*—and of these, Talleyrand was the most prominent and the most controversial, the "deep and danger-ous man."

A month after the news of Toulon's fall, on January 24, 1794, Talley-rand was visited in Kensington Square by two men who announced them-selves as agents of the government. One of them informed Talleyrand, rather brusquely, that under the terms of the Alien Act of 1793, he was no longer eligible for residence in England and had to leave the country within five days.†

Talleyrand was not a man to submit to arbitrary expulsion without pro-test. Immediately, he fired off a letter to Pitt, arguing that "I came to Eng-land to enjoy peace and personal security under the shelter of institutions protecting liberty and property. I am living here, as I have always lived here—that is, as a stranger to all discussion and to partisan interests. I have never attempted to conceal from just men any of my political opin-ions, any more than any of my actions." He goes on to note that far from being a partisan of the Convention, he has been its victim: "proscribed, ac-cused, declared an outlaw because of my support of the monarchy." And

---

* Lord Moria's fleet, after a long delay at Plymouth, had finally sailed for Toulon but had been beaten off by French artillery.

† Three other émigrés received the same treatment at this time; none of them were members of Talleyrand's circle or, so far as can be established, known to him.

yet, he continues, "I am suspected of the most outrageous ingratitude, of attempting to subvert the only country whose hospitality has given me a place to lay my head." The appeal went unanswered, and others, to Lord Melville (the Home Secretary) and even to the king, met with no success. When he saw that it was not possible to have the government's decision withdrawn, Talleyrand asked for a month's delay in order to settle his affairs in London. The answer came back that he might have three weeks —until February 15.

Even this concession could hardly have provided much comfort. Yet Talleyrand accepted his sentence calmly and even with good humor. On January 30 he wrote to Madame de Staël: "At the age of thirty-nine, I am on the threshold of a new life." And Narbonne, who was outraged at the injustice being visited upon his friend, wrote to Mrs. Susanna Phillips: "Nothing can equal his calm and his courage. He is almost gay."

Having accepted his fate with dignity, Talleyrand had now to decide where he would go. The countries of the Coalition other than Britain—that is, Austria, Prussia, and Russia—were obviously closed to him. Even neutral Switzerland, when he had asked for permission to visit Madame de Staël at Coppet late in 1792, had refused to allow him across its frontiers. The staid Swiss might have suffered a mere ex-revolutionary, but one who was also an ex-bishop was beyond endurance. After some consideration, his choice fell upon the United States of America. No doubt, his long acquaintance with Gouverneur Morris had awakened his curiosity about the infant Republic. Moreover, he had had enough of repression and persecution, even in so liberal a country as Britain, and he longed, as he confided to Madame de Staël, to be able "to proclaim, and proclaim aloud, what I have desired, what I have done, what I have prevented, and what I have regretted. I must prove that I have loved liberty, that I love it still." Finally, it obviously occurred to Talleyrand that a new country would offer some degree of opportunity to a clever man, not only to proclaim and defend his principles openly, but also to repair the fortune that the upheavals in France had destroyed. With this in mind, he spent the two weeks before his departure in visiting various banking and shipping firms in London, to offer his services as their representative in the United States. His background in the financial affairs of France and his prominence apparently were sufficient to permit these institutions to ignore Talleyrand's political heterodoxy, for by the middle of February he had in his possession a letter of credit for more than 8,000 American dollars.

On February 15, Talleyrand went aboard an American ship moored in the Thames, the *William Penn*, which was expected to sail momentarily. With him were his faithful valet, Courtiade, who refused to be separated from his master, and the Chevalier de Beaumetz, a friend from the Constituent Assembly and from the happy days at Juniper Hall, who had decided to try his luck in the New World with Talleyrand. The weather, however, was abominable; the ship's cargo could not be loaded, and the captain was detained on shore by business. For two weeks, Talleyrand slept aboard the ship as it remained in the Thames, refusing offers of hospitality from friends ashore. He explains: "I experienced some satisfaction in refusing such offers. Even unjust persecution entails some compensation. I never fully understood what my feelings were at this time, but there is no doubt that I was somewhat pleased with myself. I think that in those days of general suffering I would have regretted not having suffered also."

On March 2, the *William Penn* hoisted her sails and began the forty-day journey from London, across the Atlantic to Philadelphia, in the New World. The night before, Talleyrand had written a parting note to Germaine de Staël: "This is the last time I shall write from London. Tomorrow, I will be gone. . . . Let us hope that we will not be apart for more than a year. Adieu, dear friend. I love you with all my soul."

The *William Penn* had been under sail for less than two days and had just left the Thames when a violent storm arose. There were two separate dangers, both imminent. The ship might sink, or it might be blown out into the Channel and have to take refuge in a French port. The latter seemed hardly preferable to the former. "I was then between England and France," Talleyrand writes, "which indeed constituted one of the most critical positions in which anyone could be placed. I could see France, and my head was in danger there." The third possibility, a return to Britain, was the least undesirable solution, although "it would have been greatly repugnant to me to solicit the hospitality of a government which had tried to ruin me." Nonetheless, it was with a sense of relief that Talleyrand stepped ashore at Falmouth Harbor, where the captain of the *William Penn*, after an epic struggle, had succeeded in mooring his ship. Talleyrand and Beaumetz were delayed there for several days, while the rigging was repaired. During that time, they took their meals at a local inn, where an incident occurred which was to remain engraved in Talleyrand's memory.

The innkeeper, upon being informed that Talleyrand was bound for America, mentioned that one of his lodgers was an American general and, when Talleyrand expressed interest in meeting him, arranged for the two men to meet. "After the usual exchange of greetings," Talleyrand records, "I asked him several questions about his country. But from the very first it seemed to me that my curiosity annoyed him." Several times, Talleyrand attempted to engage the mysterious general in conversation but each time met with the same discouraging response. "Finally," he writes, "I ventured to request from him some letters of introduction to his friends in America."

The stranger's answer was: "I am perhaps the only American who cannot give you letters for his own country. All the relations I had there are now severed. I must never return to the States."

"He did not dare tell me his name," Talleyrand concludes. "It was General Arnold."

It seemed to matter very little to Talleyrand that Benedict Arnold, for having betrayed his country—or for having been loyal to the mother country, depending upon one's point of view—had been sentenced to death and was living out his life in desolate exile, shunned even by those who had benefited from his treason. Talleyrand knew how ephemeral were such considerations and how arbitrary such values. He himself had been condemned, outlawed, deprived of his property, forbidden to return to his native land. And now he was being expelled even from his place of exile. "I must admit that I felt much pity for him," Talleyrand adds. "Perhaps political purists will blame me for this. But I do not blame myself, for I was a witness to his agony."

The sense of isolation from the rest of the world, perhaps increased by his conversation with Arnold, persisted even after the *William Penn*, her repairs completed and taking advantage of a favorable wind, set out once more across the Atlantic:

> All the passengers were on deck, and looking in the direction of the shore, they all said, with evident pleasure: "I still see the land." I was the only one who felt relieved when we could see it no longer. At this moment, the sea possessed special charms for me. The sensations I derived from it were peculiarly suited to my mood.

The effect of the open water upon Talleyrand was instant and enduring. He was enamored of it. His passion survived even stormy seas, when the *William Penn* rolled and pitched, and Talleyrand remained below in mute anguish, the tongue that had been the delight of Paris stilled by needs more primal than the articulation of epigrams.

The voyage lasted for thirty-eight days. On the final day, Talleyrand was wakened by shouts of "Land! Land!" This, he says, was "the word I dreaded. However, the captain, the crew and the passengers all displayed the liveliest joy. On reaching the deck, I saw the pilot who was to take us up the Delaware. And at the same time, I noticed an outbound ship steering around the headland." Instantly, he was seized with the urge to remain on the water. Having learned from the pilot that the ship was bound for Calcutta—a voyage of some three or four months—he sent a boat out to the ship to ask if there was room for one more passenger. "The ship's destination," he explains, "was of no importance. All that mattered was that she was going on a long voyage, and my purpose was, if possible, to avoid setting foot on land." But when the captain sent back word that he was unable to take on passengers, Talleyrand resigned himself. "There was no alternative, and so I submitted to being taken to Philadelphia."

Philadelphia was then the capital of the new country, a bustling little metropolis of some 80,000 souls. The chief industry was government; but the shops were filled with luxuries from Europe, the streets and broad sidewalks were meticulously clean, and the crowds in the streets presented an assortment that, even to the sophisticated Frenchman, must have appeared exotic: merchants, farmers, Quakers, blacks and whites, elegantly casual Southern planters, and no-nonsense Yankee traders. To all this, Talleyrand's first reaction was one of peculiar indifference. "My mind was totally immune to the novelties which, as a rule, excite the interest of travelers. I had the greatest difficulty in rousing my curiosity." But he was fortunate enough to make contact with a man whom he had known in Paris, a M. Casenove, "who never pressed me to do anything, and himself felt interested in few things. . . . Thus, meeting with neither opposition, advice, nor direction, my instinct alone guided me, and I was therefore led to contemplate more attentively the grand sight under my eyes."

This initial indifference to the sights, sounds, and colors of the New World is perhaps understandable. Tastes formed in a great city gifted with the irregular charm of picturesque streets and built in an incredible variety of styles might find little attraction in the row upon row of identical houses of brick and wood, set out on unvarying blocks formed by streets running at right angles to avenues so similar as to be, to the unpracticed eye, almost indistinguishable. To one accustomed to the grandeur of Versailles, to the great *hôtels* of Paris and the magnificent chateaus of the French countryside, the provincial splendors of Philadelphia in 1794 must have seemed pale indeed. Moreover, Talleyrand had not chosen America as his place of refuge for a study of its street plans and its architecture. He was, and was to remain, interested not in things, but in people, and his attention focused on institutions rather than on buildings.

His first wish was to meet the persons who had succeeded in achieving, in the United States, what thus far had proved impossible in France: the establishment of a workable liberal constitution. Alexander Hamilton, who, in addition to his involvement in that area, was now Secretary of the Treasury in President Washington's Cabinet, was the first of these men whom he encountered. An immediate friendship sprang up between the two statesmen who had such a similarity of interests in both the constitutional and financial areas. In the two years that Talleyrand spent in the United States, he developed a great admiration for Hamilton,* "whose

---

* Talleyrand's loyalty to this new friend was to endure, as his personal loyalties usually did, throughout his life. It was a cause of great regret to him when Hamilton was killed in a duel with

mind and character placed him, in my opinion, on a par with the most distinguished statesmen of Europe, not even excepting Mr. Pitt and Mr. Fox."

It was Talleyrand's hope at this time, with Hamilton's help, to arrange a
meeting with President Washington. For that purpose, he had arrived in
Philadelphia armed with a letter from Lord Lansdowne, and he now entrusted it to Hamilton, who promised to hand it personally to the President. Hamilton did so, but to Talleyrand's great disappointment and Hamilton's embarrassment, nothing more was heard from Washington. In a
letter from the President to Lord Lansdowne, however, there is an allusion
to the reason: "It is a matter of no small regret to me that considerations of
a public nature, which you will easily conjecture, have not hitherto permitted me to manifest toward that gentleman the sense I entertain of his personal character, and of your Lordship's recommendation."

The "considerations of a public nature" to which Washington referred
are known, and they were very much the same as the considerations which
had barred Talleyrand from the great Tory houses in London. Talleyrand's
reputation had preceded him to the United States or at least to the President's Palace (as the executive residence in Philadelphia was called) in reports from Gouverneur Morris: ". . . with respect to morals, none of
them [Talleyrand, Narbonne, and Choiseul] is exemplary. The Bishop is
particularly blamed on that score. Not so much for adultery, because that
was common enough among the clergy of high rank, but for the variety
and publicity of his amours, for gambling, and, above all, for stock-jobbing
during the Ministry of M. de Calonne. . . ." Morris' righteous appraisal
might have been countered by Lansdowne's letter, which conveys unlimited admiration of Talleyrand's talents, emphasizes the unvarying rectitude
of his conduct in England, and describes him as "a very honorable man
who has suffered from a combination of persecutions." Washington's
"public considerations," however, were founded on something less speculative than Talleyrand's morals. They had to do with his politics, and they
had been created by the minister plenipotentiary of France in the United
States, Joseph Fauchet, an appointee and rabid supporter of Robespierre's
Committee of Public Safety. In June, 1794, Fauchet reported to Paris that
"Beaumetz and Talleyrand are in Philadelphia with a letter of recommendation from Lord Lansdowne. . . . M. Hamilton wished that they be presented to the President of the United States; but I was informed beforehand of what was planned, and I was able to prevent it. . . ." Fauchet had
addressed himself to the Secretary of State in the most violent terms, main-

---

the Vice President of the United States, Aaron Burr, in 1804. Years afterward, when Burr came to
call on him in Paris, Talleyrand instructed his majordomo to inform Mr. Burr "that the portrait of
Alexander Hamilton hangs over my mantelpiece" (Edward Everett, *The Mount Vernon Papers* p.
359.)

taining that his own mission as France's official representative would become impossible if a traitor such as Talleyrand were received by President Washington. "If Talleyrand is received at the President's Palace," he stated categorically, "I will never set foot in it again. You must now choose between an émigré and me." There seems to have been some hesitancy about the choice proposed by M. Fauchet, for it was only "because I stood firm that Washington finally replied, in writing, that he would never receive them, either in public or in private."

Talleyrand's humiliation was carefully masked. In the *Mémoires*, he does not even mention the episode. He was too well schooled in the exigencies of statecraft not to appreciate the difficulty of the position in which Washington found himself, and Washington apparently knew enough about Talleyrand to feel that his decision would not be taken amiss. "Time must naturally be favorable to him everywhere," the President wrote to Lansdowne, "and may be expected to raise a man of his talents and merit above temporary disadvantages which, in revolutions, result from differences in political opinion."

Washington also noted that "the reception he [Talleyrand] has met with in general has been such as to console him, as far as the state of society will admit of it, for what he relinquished in leaving Europe." This observation, though well meant, was not entirely justified. The small, exclusive social world which focused on the President's Palace was as sensitive to official opinions as that which opened and closed its doors at the nod of the Court of St. James's in London. Mrs. Bingham, the leader of that society, would not recieve Talleyrand, and lesser lights followed suit. There were, of course, houses which delighted in entertaining foreigners, particularly foreigners with a background of intriguing scandal. Talleyrand and Beaumetz, though they accepted invitations from such houses, seemed to find life in Philadelphia too restrained, conversation too dull, and the company too provincial to console them, as George Washington had hoped, for what they had "relinquished in leaving Europe."

There were places in Philadelphia, nonetheless, where Talleyrand felt perfectly at home, and his favorite among them was the bookstore of Moreau de St.-Méry, a former deputy to the Constituent Assembly from Martinique who had emigrated to Philadelphia. Moreau's shop, on First Street, became the meeting place for a half-dozen French refugees other than Talleyrand and Beaumetz: the Viscount de Noailles, the Marquis de Blacons and Omer Talon (both former deputies), the Duke de La Rochefoucauld-Liancourt, and the Count de Moré, as well as two or three others. The group met there almost nightly, in a small room behind the store, to discuss news from France, to talk, to laugh, to tease one another. By each contributing a small amount, they were able to have an ample supper, pre-

pared by Madame Moreau, and a bottle of Madeira—Talleyrand's favorite
wine—sold as "warranted to have passed the Cape." Sometimes their
voices grew so loud and their laughter so boisterous that staid Philadelphi-
ans were driven to complain to Moreau de St.-Méry, and the enterprising
bookseller and host noted that he lost customers because of his friends.
But it seemed to matter little. "How many times it happened that Talleyrand, having reached the little courtyard in front of my shop, would turn
and run up the stairs, and then sit down to spend the night. . . . We
opened our hearts to one another, our most intimate sentiments were exposed, our thoughts confessed, our experiences avowed." There were times
when Talleyrand, caught up in the joys of sympathetic companionship, appeared determined to spend the entire night in Moreau's shop. "Finally,"
Moreau recalled, "he would leave; but only when my wife said to him: 'It's
all very well for you, since you can stay in bed until noon if you like; but
remember that your friend here has to get up at seven o'clock to open the
store.' "

These cozily informal evenings at Moreau's home were Talleyrand's
chief entertainment during the two winters he spent in Philadelphia. There,
among Frenchmen of his own background and tastes, he could be himself,
unreservedly and without pretense. He had already learned that, elsewhere
in Philadelphia, this was impossible. The new society of America, being
new, required of its members an absolute degree of "respectability," and
this was a quality alien to Talleyrand at every stage of his life. He seemed
constitutionally incapable of appearing more virtuous than he really was,
and the reality of his virtues was not what, in Philadelphia, would have
been termed adequate. He therefore was made to pay for it. "Despite his
great amiability," the Count de Moré noted, "Talleyrand never attained in
Philadelphia society the success merited by his tone and manners. He
scandalized everyone by his total contempt for the 'respectability' of
America." Whether this contempt was studied or spontaneous is not
known. It was nonetheless real. And it manifested itself in a public demonstration of indifference to public opinion that outraged Philadelphia as
much as it must have delighted Talleyrand himself, who, Moré says, "was
not even remotely concerned about the present, and even less about the future." This demonstration—or rather, this series of demonstrations—consisted in a liaison, which seems to have lasted for over a year, with a handsome young woman of black antecedents. Talleyrand not only visited the
lady's rooms, but sometimes entertained her in his own small apartment on
North Third Street, and he took special delight in promenading with her
through the busy streets, supremely indifferent to the looks and words of
shocked surprise on the faces and lips of his virtuous Quaker hosts. "He

did whatever he wanted," Moré wrote, "and was supremely contemptuous of everyone and everything."

That was not quite true. Talleyrand had never been, was not then, and never would be contemptuous of money. It would have been strange if he, of all people, had not been infected by the American spirit of commercial enterprise that had flourished long before the break between Great Britain and its colonies in the New World and that existed, in a particularly virulent form among the French refugees in America, who were determined, one and all, to replenish the fortunes destroyed by the upheavals in their own country. Within a few months of his arrival in the United States, he was writing to Madame de Staël that "instinct tells me I must attempt to make a small fortune here, so that, when I am older, I shall not be in want or in dependence on others. This idea occupies my mind, but up to now I have not discovered the way to do it. There is much money to be made here, of course, but it is necessary already to have money in order to make it." Even so, there were ways for a man of ingenuity and initiative to advance himself, and Talleyrand was not lacking in either of those qualities. Shortly, he was soliciting Germaine de Staël's help in obtaining commissions from Europe:

> There are more chances to make one's fortune here than in any other place. I am arranging to get commissions from Europe, and anything that I can get will be a great help to me. If some of the friends of your father* would send ships to America or if some Swedes† send over goods to be sold, either to New York or to Philadelphia, I am in a position to do good business for those who would place themselves entirely in my hands. I beg of you to use a little of your energy to procure me some commissions. . . . In a little time, one can make a great deal, either by commissions in public funds or by commissions in the purchase of land. The reputations of American agents are so uncertain that European merchants are always at a disadvantage in trying to find someone to represent them here, and I offer myself for the job, since I have some qualifications in that line.

It was entirely in accordance with Talleyrand's experience and qualifications that his efforts to build a fortune should be of a speculative nature. He was, by nature and inclination, a gambler, and he was willing to take his chances in America, not on the turn of a card, but on the availability of vast tracts of virgin land and on the willingness of Europeans, especially Frenchmen, to invest in that land. Soon his efforts seem to have centered

* M. Necker, although retired from public affairs, was still one of Europe's most eminent bankers and the possessor of one of the Continent's great fortunes. He was therefore in a position to be most useful to Talleyrand.

† The Baron de Staël had thought it wise to take refuge in Switzerland during the Terror. However, he had considerable influence at the court of Sweden, and as ambassador to France he had had some experience in commercial affairs.

on these "commissions in the purchase of land" of which he had written to
Madame de Staël, and he asks her to let him know "if you know people
who have any desire to invest in the purchase of farms here, I would willingly attend to their affairs."

He seems to have had some success in this venture, at least if one may
judge by the alarm expressed by M. Fauchet in an indignant dispatch to
Paris late in 1794:

> The speculations of these stockjobbers and their hope of success are
> founded solely on the misfortunes of their former country. Their hope is
> that the lack of good laws and the impossibility of establishing order in the
> Republic will make a large portion of France desert her in search of peace,
> and they are preparing to receive them. These disastrous conjectures are
> expressed almost word for word in a letter recently addressed to Bishop
> Talleyrand from London. . . .

The "speculations" which Fauchet mentioned in this instance no doubt
referred to Talleyrand's earliest effort, which involved the purchase by
himself and Beaumetz of some undeveloped land in the state of Maine,
from Henry Knox, Washington's secretary of war. Talleyrand intended to
divide this acreage into smaller plots in order to provide land at low cost
for indigent émigrés and for his friends. By the beginning of 1795, however, he had begun to undertake the purchase of land, as an agent, in association with his Dutch friend Casenove, who was the American representative of two land development companies based in Holland. In this
capacity, he was required, or at least he felt it necessary, not only to handle
the actual arrangements of purchase, but also to visit the property in question and report on it to prospective buyers. Strangely enough, this man of
the salons was overcome with pleasure at the sight of the great forests
which bore no traces of man's presence. "I was still haunted by my love for
the sea," he explains, "and I almost forgot I was no longer sailing on it
when I found myself in that vast wilderness, where whatever I saw reminded me of nothing I had ever seen before."

His companions on one of his extended expeditions into the hinterlands
were Beaumetz; a Dutch gentleman—no doubt a business associate—
named Heydecoper; and, of course Talleyrand's friend and valet, Courtiade, who much preferred to follow his master into the unexplored vastness of America than to be abandoned to the perils of Philadelphia.

> I must confess [Talleyrand wrote] that I was delighted with the under-
> taking from the very beginning. . . . There were forests as old as the world
> itself . . . green and luxuriant grass decking the banks of rivers; large natu-
> ral meadows; strange and delicate flowers quite new to me. And here and
> there the traces of tornadoes that had carried everything before them. . . .

In the face of these immense solitudes, we gave free vent to our imagination. Our minds built cities, villages, and hamlets. . . . There is an inexpressible charm in thinking of the future when traveling in such a country. . . . It is impossible to move a step without feeling convinced that the irresistible progressive march of nature requires that an immense population will someday till the land which now lies idle but which requires only the touch of the human hand to produce everything in abundance.

His travels took him through the wilderness of upper New York State, to Connecticut, to Massachusetts, to Maine, and he noted his reactions, not only to the beauty and the potential of the land, but also to attitudes and customs which astonished and often scandalized him. He was particularly struck by the great disparity between the relative sophistication of the centers of commerce and the primitive character of society in the hinterlands, which he regarded as the result of disproportionate emphasis in America on trade and an inadequate interest in agriculture:

You have only to travel a hundred miles inland to see people bartering for whatever they buy, while others are drawing bills on the great markets of Europe. The contrast is too shocking. It is the symptom of a social disease. Sixty miles south of Boston, I saw six thousand feet of timber traded for a single bullock, while in Boston itself, a Florence straw hat easily brings twenty pounds.

The American attitude toward wealth was as puzzling to Talleyrand as it would be to later generations of Europeans. His own interest in money was purely utilitarian; it served only to buy the things that pleased him: luxurious surroundings, books, paintings, fine clothing, presents for his friends. The idea that it might serve to purchase social standing was foreign to a man accustomed to a society in which position was inherited rather than bought and in which rank was an inalienable quality which had always, and would always, exist independently of the inventory of one's material possessions. In Maine, he visited a man who had land for sale. "It was the best house in the district," he writes, "and the landlord was *a most respectable man,* as people say in this country." When they had settled their business, the talk turned to other matters, and Talleyrand inquired whether the man had ever been to Philadelphia. When he replied that he had not, Talleyrand mentioned Washington and asked him whether he was not curious "to see that great man. 'Why, yes,' his host answered, but then he added in great excitement, 'I should very much like to see Mr. Bingham, who, they say, is very wealthy.' " (This response could not have been very pleasing to Talleyrand. Mr. Bingham's wife was the lady who, as the leader of Philadelphia society, had set the example for that city by ignoring his presence.)

This exaggerated reverence for money as an end unto itself seemed one of the characteristics of America. "I met it everywhere in the States," Talleyrand says, "and very often as coarsely expressed." If this attitude toward money had been more practical and had expressed itself in terms of comfort and convenience, Talleyrand might have found it less mysterious. Instead, he noted that "the country has become acquainted with luxuries too soon. Luxuries are ridiculous when a man can hardly provide himself with the necessities. I remember having seen, in the drawing room of Mrs. Robert Morris,* a hat manufactured in the birthplace of the master of the house, carefully laid on an elegant Sèvres china table which had been purchased at Trianon by an American. A European peasant would not have been caught dead wearing such a hat." After similar examples, Talleyrand concludes:

> To us inhabitants of old Europe, there is something unbecoming in the luxury displayed by Americans. I admit that our own luxury often demonstrates our own improvidence and frivolity, but in America luxury only serves to emphasize defects which prove that refinement does not exist in that country—either in the conduct of life or even in its incidentals.

Talleyrand's treks through the American wilderness, for all his criticism of what he found, were not without their moments of hilarity and even of adventure. One night he and Courtiade became hopelessly lost in the middle of a dense forest. After hacking a path through the underbrush for what seemed hours and making no apparent progress, Talleyrand called out to Courtiade that they should stop and rest awhile. When he heard no answer from the valet, he stood and listened for a moment. There was not a sound. Unable to see more than a few feet, he called out, "Courtiade, are you here?" And out of the blackness, a few feet away, came the sad answer: "Unfortunately I am, my lord." The two men collapsed in laughter. Lost in the middle of a wild forest in total darkness, their clothing ripped to shreds, their faces unshaved, Courtiade's answer and its rigidly correct "my lord" had suddenly brought home to them the utter absurdity of both their predicament and their relationship.

On another occasion, Talleyrand, Beaumetz, and Heydecoper stayed at a Connecticut farmhouse where the two grown sons of the house spent the evening explaining to the travelers a scheme for hunting beavers and selling their pelts. "At each question that we put to our hosts," Talleyrand remembers, "they filled our glasses." By the end of the evening the youths' proposal had become so exciting and the glasses had been so often filled

---

* The wife of Robert Morris, brother of Gouverneur Morris and one of the wealthiest men of the new Republic. It was Robert, it appears, who provided the financial backing, as an investment, for the purchase by Talleyrand and Beaumetz of their acreage in Maine, though the details of the transaction and its terms are not clear.

"that M. de Beaumetz, M. Heydecoper, and myself were dying to join them. . . . M. de Beaumetz proposed to our hosts that they allow us to accompany them on their expedition. They both consented, and we were, without further formality, initiated into the brotherhood of Connecticut beaver hunters. . . . When morning came, the effect of the brandy had worn off, and we began to realize that the various things that each of us would have to carry would be an impossible burden. The provisions also, I think, weighed about forty pounds. We also thought that spending two or three months in the woods and marshes was really too much of a good thing. So we asked our partners not to hold us to our commitments of the evening before, and we were able to get free by handing over a few dollars. We resumed our journey feeling quite ashamed of what we had done."

Not all of Talleyrand's journeys in America were into the wilds. In New York, where he spent part of the summer, he came to know Aaron Burr, though he left no record of his impressions of that most dexterous of America's early politicians. Here, too, Talleyrand found a new friend, the French consul general, Antoine de la Forest, an aristocrat who had been minister to the United States before the Revolution and, successively, consul in Savannah, Charleston, and finally New York. He had been sufficiently astute to avoid the notice of the Committee of Public Safety—no small achievement, since he was a member of the old nobility—and not only had retained his diplomatic post, but had managed to acquire vast tracts of land in Virginia, which he turned into a very profitable plantation. De la Forest's intelligence and business acumen commended him to Talleyrand, and the two became fast friends. In his career as an agent, Talleyrand often benefited from the consul's advice and experience, and occasionally De la Forest contributed financial backing for one or another of Talleyrand's ventures.* (One of these was a scheme that promised vast profits: a trading expedition to India, which would sail from Philadelphia to Calcutta and back again. It had been done before—Talleyrand, in fact, had been in Philadelphia when the first such expedition had returned to that city—and it was said that the profits of the investors had been in excess of 500 percent of their outlay. With Count de la Forest's backing, and perhaps that of Robert Morris, Talleyrand and Beaumetz had outfitted a ship and were loading it with cargo. It appears that until the last moment, Talleyrand himself was planning to make the voyage which, to his great re-

---

* In later years, Talleyrand showed his gratitude to Count de la Forest by assuring his steady advancement under the Directory, the Consulate, the Empire, and the Restoration. In Talleyrand's provisional government after the fall of Napoleon in 1814, he was Minister of Foreign Affairs. His unaided abilities seem sufficient to have enabled him to survive Talleyrand's own disgrace under the Restoration, for he was a Minister of State and member of the Privy Council under Charles X.

gret, he had missed almost two years earlier. But by the end of the summer of 1795 he would change his mind. Events in France by then would look too promising for him to risk a long absence in the Orient. To Madame de Staël he wrote: "Either there will be a universal earthquake in Europe, or I shall return there next May." Beaumetz, however, needed wealth more than he needed Paris. He had married a penniless widow with three children—a step which Talleyrand described as "an act of folly which he alone does not recognize as such"—and the Indian expedition held out the promise of enabling him to support his ready-made family in comfort. So Beaumetz would sail, only to die a few months later, shortly after reaching Calcutta.)

Talleyrand's summer in New York was interrupted, in July, by an outbreak of yellow fever, which, in conjunction with the almost tropical heat, sent him on a jaunt northward to Albany, where Alexander Hamilton, having resigned as Secretary of the Treasury, had just opened a law office. This was a step which had puzzled Talleyrand exceedingly, and his bewilderment had only increased when Hamilton explained to him in Philadelphia that his financial needs were such that he could no longer afford to remain in public life. In France, rich men became richer in office. But in America, where money was worshiped with a devotion that astounded and shocked even Talleyrand, public servants had to resign and seek employment in order to support their families. One of the ladies who heard Talleyrand expound on the theme of Hamilton's decision noted that he "found this a very strange reason, and one that was perhaps a bit silly."

At Albany, the travelers—Talleyrand, Beaumetz, and an English associate, John Law—were received by Hamilton's father-in-law, General Schuyler, at his house, where Hamilton was spending some time. The day after their arrival, Talleyrand and Beaumetz were asked by General Schuyler to carry a message to nearby Troy: an invitation to Monsieur and Madame de la Tour du Pin,* to spend the day with him and his guests in Albany. Madame de la Tour du Pin recorded the story of Talleyrand's visit:

> One day, at the end of September, I was in my yard, hatchet in hand, busy cutting the bone of a leg of mutton which I intended to roast on a spit for dinner. . . . Suddenly, behind me, I heard a deep voice: "It is not possible to thrust a spit through a leg of mutton with an air of greater majesty." I turned around quickly and saw M. de Talleyrand and M. de Beaumetz. Having arrived the day before at Albany, they had found out from General Schuyler where we lived, and they had come to invite us, in his name, to

---

* The La Tour du Pin couple had fled the Terror in Bordeaux and settled in New York State, where they bought a farm near Albany in the summer of 1795. Since they could not take possession of the land until spring, however, they had rented a modest house in Troy.

dine and pass the following day at his house. . . . However, as M. de Talleyrand was greatly amused at the sight of my leg of mutton, I insisted that
they must come back the next day and eat it with us.

Madame de la Tour du Pin was a virtuous woman, and she prided herself
greatly on the fact. In her *Journal*, she speaks not infrequently of Talleyrand, whom she had known since her childhood, and she is uniformly cen-
sorious of his amatory adventures, his gambling, and above all of his having abandoned his clerical state. Even so, on this occasion, when face to
face with the man whose vices she deplored, she could not withhold her
admiration:

> M. de Talleyrand was kind, as he has always been and in every circum-
> stance, and to his kindness is added that charm in conversation that no one
> possesses in the same degree as he. He had known me since my childhood,
> and because of this, he assumed toward me a sort of paternal and gracious
> attitude that was enchanting. One cannot help regretting in secret that
> there are so many reasons for not esteeming him, for it was impossible to
> remember his vices once one had spent an hour in his company. Depraved
> as he was, he could not abide wickedness of any sort in other people. If one
> did not know him, one would think him the most virtuous of men.

Upon their return to General Schuyler's house, Talleyrand and Beaumetz found their host waiting for them on the porch, waving his hands and
shouting, "Hurry! There is great news from France!"

The great news was the death of Robespierre, who, after having sent
hundreds upon hundreds of men and women to their deaths under the
knife of the guillotine, had been obliged to suffer the same punishment. He
had simply overreached himself. The river of blood that flowed in Paris
and in the provinces had frightened the members of the Convention, or
rather, they had become frightened that Robespierre's famous "list" of
those to be executed included their own names. On July 27—Ninth Thermidor, according to the calendar of the Revolution—they had overwhelmed him with shouts of "Down with the tyrant!" and "Death!
Death!" Robespierre had been arrested and, one day later, guillotined.

After General Schuyler and his guests had pored over the details of
Robespierre's fall in the newspapers which had just arrived, the Frenchmen turned to the list of the tyrant's most recent and final victims and were
overjoyed to find no one named whom they knew. Later in the evening,
however, Talleyrand picked up a paper that he had not yet seen and read
there the name of the Countess de Périgord,* his sister-in-law. She had

---

* Madelaine de Senozan, the wife of Archambaud de Talleyrand-Périgord, Talleyrand's
brother. Archambaud had emigrated to Germany in 1790, but since all their property was in her
name, he had ordered her to remain in Paris so as to prevent confiscation by the state. Inevitably,
she had been arrested as an aristocrat and condemned.

been one of the last of Robespierre's victims, having been executed on the Ninth Thermidor—only a few hours before Robespierre's own arrest. Archambaud's wife had shared the prejudices of her husband's family against Talleyrand, the renegade bishop and friend of the Revolution. Yet, a few weeks before hearing of her death, he had written to Germaine de Staël, asking her to use her influence to protect the Countess' children:*

> In my last letter, which may well be at the bottom of the sea, I mentioned the children of Madame de Périgord and asked you to do whatever you can for them. As you know, my family and I do not share the same opinions—but that is all the more reason why I should be concerned about them.

Talleyrand's own cheerless years in the Faubourg St.-Jacques were still vivid in his mind.

The death of Robespierre in 1794 marked the beginning of the last phase of the Revolution in France. The people were now exhausted by tyranny and disgusted at the excessive and brutal shedding of blood. There was a universal cry for peace and order. The moderate Girondins, who had been expelled from the Convention, were now recalled. Local government was restored to the *départements,* and the autonomous Paris Commune was abolished. State support was withdrawn from the "constitutional" clergy, and the virtual separation of church and state was proclaimed. The Committee of Public Safety, which had exercised so energetically its power of life and death over the citizens, was stripped of jurisdiction. The Jacobin Club was closed, and in May, 1795, the Revolutionary Tribunal was abolished in order to open the way for negotiating a general peace.

As these changes were being worked in the year following Robespierre's fall, the émigrés had begun to filter back into France, more or less with official connivance, timidly at first and then in larger and ever larger numbers. By the spring of 1795 word had reached America that one might re-enter France at no great risk to one's life—though, of course, the property of the émigrés remained, and would remain, in the possession of the state.

In August, 1795, a Frenchman newly arrived in New York confirmed current rumors by allowing Talleyrand to read some of the speeches that had been made in the Convention regarding the reestablishment of the rights of the people and of the independence of the Republic. The events of the Ninth Thermidor, Boissy d'Anglas had said, "enabled the reign of

---

* Archambaud had three children: Mélanie, who married one of the De Noailles family and became Princess de Poix; Louis, Baron de Talleyrand, who was killed in Germany in 1808, during the Napoleonic Wars; and Edmond, who would, after his marriage to Dorothea of Courland, become successively Duke de Dino and Duke de Talleyrand.

happiness and virtue to be reborn in France." Thus encouraged, Talleyrand matured his plans. His hopes for building a fortune in America, the
projected expedition to India—all had become unimportant in the light of
the opportunity offered by the changed situation in France. Almost immediately, he dispatched to Paris a petition addressed to the Convention:

> I am not an émigré, and it is unjust that I be regarded as one. A man
> condemned in his absence must not be likened to an émigré. Flight owing
> to an accusation and, still more, absence for such a cause bear no resem-
> blance to the voluntary departure which constitutes the crime of emigra-
> tion. The National Convention had ruled that all those convicted by war-
> rant of arrest and denunciation since May 31 are authorized to return. I
> submit that the case of Talleyrand is absolutely identical to these.

The letter, however, was not sent directly to the Convention itself, but to
Desrenaudes, Talleyrand's friend and the former vicar-general of Autun,
with the instruction that he was to submit it at the opportune moment.

Meanwhile, Talleyrand appealed to the one other friend in France on
whom he knew he could count. Madame de Staël was back in Paris. The
Swedish embassy had been reopened, and her husband was again installed
as Swedish ambassador. Germaine's salon had reopened its doors, and as
always, she had the ear of the men in power—Tallien and Barras, especially—and she was eager to use her influence for the benefit of her friend
in Philadelphia, who had addressed a piteous appeal to her: "If I must
spend another year here, I shall die."

Both Desrenaudes and Germaine de Staël did their work diligently and
effectively. Desrenaudes delivered Talleyrand's petition to the Convention,
where it was read at the session of September 3, 1795, and then published
in the *Moniteur*. It was announced to Paris and to France at large that Talleyrand was asking to be allowed to come home; that he, like the rest of
France, had been a victim of the tyrants whom France had rejected on
Ninth Thermidor; and that he wished now to return and place himself at
the disposal of the Republic. Desrenaudes had chosen precisely the right
moment to submit the petition. Boissy d' Anglas had just published a bro-
chure establishing a distinction between fugitives from the September massacres and true émigrés and citing Talleyrand specifically as an example of
a fugitive who, although wronged by the Convention, had never ceased to
defend the Republic both in England and in America.

Germaine also made a contribution that day, through her friend, Jean-
Lambert Tallien, who, though involved in the excesses of the Terror, had
survived the Ninth Thermidor and emerged as one of the leaders of the
new spirit in the Convention. After Talleyrand's petition had been read,
Tallien rose to declare that "justice had not been done to Talleyrand-Péri-

gord," for far from being an émigré, he had left France at Danton's orders, upon an official mission for the Convention. The statement was received with applause.

The scene was now set for Germaine's *coup*. It was necessary that a motion be made in the Convention to the effect that the injustice cited by Tallien be remedied, and that Talleyrand's name be removed from the list of émigrés so that he might legally return to France. For this important role, she chose another of her friends, Marie-Joseph Chénier, member of the Convention and poet (and the brother of André Chénier), whom she alternately bullied and charmed in the attempt to persuade him to use his eloquence on Talleyrand's behalf. When Chénier held fast, pleading that he did not trust Talleyrand, Germaine enlisted in her cause a young woman who was simultaneously her friend and Chénier's mistress. In these new circumstances, Madame de Staël's arguments began to make themselves felt, and Chénier was compelled to admit that Talleyrand had indeed taken a firm stand in the Assembly against his own order, the clergy, and that he had showed statesmanlike qualities to the Revolution's benefit in persuading England to remain neutral during the first part of the conflict with the Coalition. By the end of August, 1795, he had surrendered, and when he mounted the tribune, on September 4, he made an impassioned plea for justice to be done to a man who had been greatly wronged, one who had rendered great services to the Revolution "in consolidating the Republic . . . and in the great services he rendered the Republic in London, on the diverse missions entrusted to him." Rather than the gratitude of the Convention, however, Talleyrand had been condemned for his patriotism: "He was proscribed in France by Robespierre and Marat, and Pitt proscribed him in England. But it was in the heart of a Republic, the land of Benjamin Franklin, that, contemplating the spectacle of a free people, he awaited the time when France should have, not assassins, but judges; not anarchy, but a Republic." Then, in conclusion: "I ask you for Talleyrand. I claim him in the name of his many services. I claim him in the name of national justice. I claim him on behalf of the Republic in whose service his talents may be employed. I claim him in the name of the hatred you bear the émigrés, whose victim he would be, like yourselves, if cowards were allowed to triumph!"

It was a masterful oration, one worthy of Talleyrand himself. But not everyone had been won over. A hostile deputy named Legendre moved that Talleyrand's petition, which was the formal basis of Chénier's plea, be "referred to the Legislative Committee for study." It was obvious that once in committee, the petition might never be heard of again; But Germaine had foreseen this stratagem and taken precautions. Three more of her friends—

Boissy d'Anglas, Brivals, and Génisson—rushed to the tribune to argue against Legendre's motion, which was defeated by a large majority. Then, amid cheers and enthusiastic applause, it was moved and voted to reinstate Talleyrand in all the rights of French citizenship. The official decree read:

> The National Convention decrees that Talleyrand-Périgord, former Bishop of Autun, is authorized to reenter the territory of the French Republic and that his name shall be removed from the lists of émigrés. Accordingly, the Convention rescinds the decree of accusation issued against him.

The news did not reach Talleyrand until two months later, on November 2. He rushed to Moreau de St.-Méry's bookshop to tell his friend, and there was a joyful feast there that night. Yet Talleyrand did not board ship immediately for France. For seven months until June, 1796, he remained in the United States—in Philadelphia, for the most part.

The reasons for this delay are not difficult to find. At that time no one in full possession of his senses would choose to cross the Atlantic during the winter if it could possibly be avoided. Traveling was always done in the spring or summer. Also, Talleyrand's business affairs had to be concluded before he could return to France, for as eager as he was to return, he was determined not to do so with empty pockets.* And finally, a new government had come into being in France during the last months of 1795. The Convention had voted itself out of existence and had been replaced by the Directory, which comprised an executive branch composed of five members who were elected by two legislative chambers: the Council of Five Hundred and the Council of the Ancients. Given the problems faced by this newly formed regime,† it seemed wise to wait and see what would happen in France; or, as Talleyrand wrote to Madame de Staël, "to allow time to do its work."

During the winter months of 1795–96, much of Talleyrand's energy seems to have been occupied in writing letters, both of obligation and of friendship. The first of these was a letter to the new Minister of Foreign

---

* Despite Talleyrand's strenuous commercial activities, especially during the period from June, 1794, to the summer of 1795, he does not seem to have done remarkably well in building up his fortune. His total assets, when he returned to Europe from America, amounted to 50,000 francs in cash—and there is reason to believe that at least part of this money was a loan from Madame de Staël.

† Throughout the fall and winter, there were demonstrations in Paris, demanding food. But there was no food, because the lands had been left largely untilled during the Terror, and there was no money in the treasury with which to buy food for the people. Moreover, the war with the Coalition was still being waged—and the Directors, upon taking office, had discovered that the government was entirely without means to pay the army, let alone purchase the matériel necessary to continue hostilities. Even the ministers of the new government were unable to draw their salaries during the first few months of the regime.

Affairs under the Directory, expressing Talleyrand's gratitude for his reinstatement as a citizen. The second, however, was to his true advocate, Germaine de Staël:

> Thanks to you, dear friend, this matter is finally resolved. You have done everything that I could have wished; and it was my desire that the decree be withdrawn by the same Convention that had passed it originally. In the spring, I shall leave here for any port that you wish. The remainder of my life will be spent near you, wherever you may be. . . . There are a thousand reasons for choosing May as the month during which to sail. . . . Do you think that M. de Staël will let me have a small room? It is to your house that I should like to come as soon as I arrive.

As the winter wore on, the news from France became better. The Directory was succeeding gradually, to everyone's surprise, in establishing a degree of order in the country and a corresponding degree of confidence in the Directors and the two legislative chambers. Thus encouraged, Talleyrand applied for and was granted a passport in New York by M. Fauchet's successor, a courteous man named Adat, who seemed to personify the new spirit that reigned in France. He then booked passage on a Dutch ship bound for Hamburg from Philadelphia and scheduled to sail on June 13.

On that day Talleyrand had dinner with Moreau de St.-Méry and his family. Afterward Moreau and his son accompanied Talleyrand to the dock where his ship, *Den Ny Proeve*—"The New Ordeal"—was moored. After a long farewell, Talleyrand went aboard. But the wind had died, and the ship remained at dock for two days. On the fifteenth, the sails were hoisted once more, and *Den Ny Proeve* moved slowly down the Delaware River toward the Atlantic. Before it reached the open sea, on the eighteenth, Talleyrand had a letter to Moreau taken ashore and mailed. "We have reached the sea, my friend, and the wind, though rather feeble, is holding out. No pirates have been seen for several days. Adieu."

Part Three

TALLEYRAND AND NAPOLEON

(1797–1814)

> *It is Talleyrand, after all, who best*
> *understands this age and this society,*
> *both the governments and the peoples.*
> *He deserted me—but then, I myself*
> *had deserted him somewhat abruptly.*
>
> —NAPOLEON

7

The Directory

TALLEYRAND, immediately upon landing in Hamburg, wrote to Moreau announcing his safe arrival on July 31: "Forty days from port to port. No pirates . . . but rain every single day. As yet, I know nothing of this city, since I've paid no visits. The cockade is very much in vogue, and I put one on as soon as I arrived." No sooner was the letter posted than a vistor was announced: an émigré named Ricci, who bore a message from Madame de Flahaut. Ricci "was simple enough to deliver the message: not to land, but to go back to America." Adélaïde, it seems, after a series of adventures, had installed herself in Hamburg, where she succeeded in capturing the heart of a Portuguese gentleman, M. de Souza, the ambassador to Denmark. "Since it was rumored that she had been on rather intimate terms with me, she feared that my presence would be an obstacle to her marriage with M. de Souza." This, Talleyrand thought, was asking too much. He had not spent forty days on his "wretched Danish ship" to turn around and go back to Philadelphia as a favor to Adélaïde de Flahaut. "I thought," he says in the *Mémoires,* "I might, without the slightest impropriety, take no notice of the extraordinary message brought by M. de Ricci, and so I spent a month in Hamburg, in the society of persons who, like myself, tried to do nothing to interfere with the marriage of Madame de Flahaut with dear M. de Souza." To Madame de Genlis, he described the situation more candidly: "'It is very simply no more than an attack of jealousy. But women do not die of jealousy, and men do not even get sick from it." From that day forward, however, there was no longer any warmth between Talleyrand and his former mistress (who did indeed marry De Souza and, to all appearances, made him an excellent wife).

The contretemps with Madame de Flahaut was more than made up for by Madame de Genlis, whom Talleyrand found in Hamburg to be "exactly the same as I had known her. . . . The unchangeableness of complex natures is a result of their flexibility." This was true, at least insofar as Madame de Genlis' political beliefs were concerned. She had always been a partisan of the Duke d'Orléans, as well as his mistress, and she remained a partisan still. At her insistence, Talleyrand was taken to meet her Orléanist circle, but, he reported to Madame de Staël, he could not make heads or tails out of their beliefs:

> I don't understand a word about what is called French politics in Hamburg. . . . The only thing I can gather is that everyone hates England and wants to return to France. The sale [of emigrés' goods in France] seems to create many republicans. For the rest, there is an Orléanist party the head of which, according to what my physician tells me, has only one ambition, and that is to go to America. There is a Lambeth party, composed of two members, of which one is the hapless Duke d'Aiguillon, and there is a Dumouriez party, which also has two members—Dumouriez's valet, Baptiste, and his physician. If Switzerland cannot come up with anything more dangerous than this group, then I see that we shall have a very quiet winter in Paris.

After a month in Hamburg—half of it spent in the company of Madame de Genlis and the other half in bed of a fever—he traveled to Paris by way of Amsterdam and Brussels, arriving in the French capital in the latter part of September, 1796. "M. de Talleyrand-Périgord," announced the *Courrier républicain*, "former Bishop of Autun and privileged émigré, has arrived in Paris."

The city to which Talleyrand returned bore only a superficial resemblance to that which he had left four years earlier. The picturesque grandeur that the monarchy and the life of the court had conferred upon the city was gone. There were no great coaches in the streets, no glittering lords and ladies in graceful carriages, and mud flowed in rivers in the principal thoroughfares. The statues of the kings had been pulled down, the monuments to their victories demolished. Many of the splendid *hôtels* of the nobles had been transformed into warehouses or public buildings; and, in the windows of many of the shops and open-air booths that had sprung up, the returning émigrés were able to recognize furniture, silver, china, and even family portraits that had formed part of the loot from their houses. Alongside these items were vestments and sacred vessels from the plundered churches and convents. It was as though a great storm had swept through the city, half demolishing it and spreading the goods of its citizens haphazardly through the streets and alleys.

There was a change in the people also. Gone was the restraint of the *ancien régime*, but gone too was the oppressiveness of the Terror. There was an air of gaiety and frivolity in the city; and, in the people, a reaction against the dreariness and misery of the Revolution, which manifested itself in an almost uncontrollable outburst of joy. Paris had gone from a state of shock into a frenzy of merrymaking. Everyone was seized with a mania for dancing. "Next to money, everyone in Paris loves, adores, idolizes dancing," wrote one observer, "and every class, rich or poor, high or low, dances everywhere." The poor danced in abandoned churches and even in the cemetery of Talleyrand's former parish, St.-Sulpice. "Balls and spectacles and fireworks have replaced prisons and revolutionary committees," Talleyrand wrote.

Extravagant fashions in dress mirrored the excesses in entertainment. Conventionality of style was as unfashionable as political convention, and the fashions were set by *les merveilleuses*—"the marvelous ones"—whom Talleyrand defined as "the wives of the *nouveaux riches* who took the place of the vanished ladies of the court and who, like the latter, were imitated by sluts competing for the prize in luxury and extravagance." The rage among the ladies was seminudity thinly overlaid with transparent muslin. The arms and legs were bare—"It gives one a chill simply to see it," Henry Swinburne complained—and the feet were sometimes bare and sometimes sandaled. In either case, rings on the toes were *de rigueur*. Among the men, styles were more restrained, but only slightly. Hats were pulled down over the eyebrows, and gigantic cravats were pulled up over the lower lip, so that, of a gentleman's face, only the nose and the eyes were visible; and sometimes not the latter, for lorgnettes were also fashionable. If the ladies were *merveilleuses* in their dresses of gauze, the men were incredible in their own right—and so they were called: *les incroyables*—"the unbelievable ones."

The wives of the *nouveaux riches* and the sluts, having displaced the ladies of Versailles in fashion, also had assumed their place as the leaders of Parisian society. Chief among these, at the time of Talleyrand's return, was Thérèse Cabarrús, mistress of a succession of lovers (the incumbent, in the summer of 1796, was Paul Barras, most powerful of the Directors) and wife of Madame de Staël's great and good friend Jean-Lambert Tallien. It was the "divine Thérèse" who was undisputed leader of society in Paris; but she was not a selfish woman, and she gladly shared the honors and the burdens of leadership with two close friends, Juliette Récamier and Josephine de Beauharnais. Madame Récamier, the wife of an exceedingly (*nouveau*) rich banker, was, by relaxed standards, the most decorous of the three. And Madame de Beauharnais was the most delightful. A Creole aristocrat by birth, she had married the Viscount Alexandre de Beauharnais, who, for his constitutionalist fervor, had been elected President of the Assembly, and who later, for his constitutionalist fervor, had been guillotined. Josephine had barely escaped the same fate, having been released from prison only upon the death of Robespierre. Thereafter she had consoled herself in the arms, successively, of Barras and General Hoche until she was swept off her feet by young General Bonaparte, who had, through his daring, in the preceding year put down an insurrection against the Convention and been made commander of the Army of the Interior. Josephine's husband— they were married in March, 1796—was presently commander of the victorious Army of Italy and, at his insistence and after many excuses, Josephine had left Paris, a month before Talleyrand's arrival, to join Bonaparte in his headquarters in Milan. Her salon, therefore, was temporarily closed.

These three, then, were the queens of society, *les merveilleuses* "who talked politics while dancing," Talleyrand noted, "and sighed after royalty while nibbling ices or gaping at fireworks." But their talk was not mere prattle, for when they spoke, the men who ruled France listened. Bonaparte, while in Paris, had been astounded at the influence played by these ladies. "A woman must come to Paris for six months," he wrote, "to learn her place in the world and to understand her own power. Here only, of all places in the world, do they wield such influence. And of course, the men are mad about them, think of nothing else, and live only by and for them."

"The men" were primarily the leaders of the two councils—Tallien, Chénier, and General Jean-Baptiste Jourdan—and, most important of all, Paul Barras, one of the five Directors and leader of the other four and, therefore, in practice, the ruler of France. Barras, an army officer by profession and a regicide by choice, was a Gascon, and he embodied all the traits generally, and often erroneously, attributed to the natives of Gascony. Unlike his fellow Directors, he was a nobleman by birth, and he could on occasion exhibit a gentlemanly comportment, though usually the mask he presented was that of a jovial man of the people. His intelligence was tempered by great cunning, and his judgment by a flexibility that was indistinguishable from a total lack of either principle or conviction. He had several consuming interests in life, and his responsibilities as Director were allowed to interfere with none of them. His mistresses, real and putative, were counted in the dozens, though, to his credit, it must be said that he required of them all that they be ladies of refinement and some distinction. With his male lovers he was less exigent, and he surrounded himself, even publicly, with riffraff from the streets. His greed was proverbial, and his four years in office, when he was not debauching or gambling, were spent in filling his pockets with both hands from the treasury.

Under Barras and his associates, France had been freed from the Terror, and its people could breathe again in comparative freedom. From that standpoint, the Directory was an improvement over the "Republic of Virtue" which had obtained under the Convention and Robespierre's Committee of Public Safety. For the rest, it can be said in all fairness that the Directory was the most corrupt regime with which France, in a long history of governmental corruption, had ever been saddled. It was not solely that the Directory was self-perpetuating, as every regime tends to be, in order to assure the ascendancy of its principles by any means in its power; it was rather that the Directory had no principles, unless profit can be counted as a principle. The Directory had risen out of the ruins of revolution, and its leaders were the men who had survived the Revolution and made a handsome profit from it. Their policies were therefore aimed, first, at protecting and increasing those profits and, second, at preventing the return of the Bourbons or the establishment of any other regime that might endanger them by such means as a redistribution of national property.

This was the Paris and the France to which Talleyrand returned in July, 1796. It is no surprise that he had made up his mind to have no part of it: "Since I perceived no element of order, and no guarantee of stability in the various political factions whose struggles I witnessed, I took care to keep aloof from active politics." He settled down to watch and wait.*

In accordance with this decision, Talleyrand's first bow to the new society of the Directory was a carefully noncommittal one. Before leaving America, he had been elected a member of the Institute of Sciences and Arts.† It was a great honor, and not one entirely undeserved—for Talleyrand's *Report on Public Education*, delivered to the Constituent Assembly in May, 1791, had proposed the creation of the institute and was directly responsible for its existence. His formal reception took place on September 23, 1796, only two days after his arrival in Paris, and on that occasion, he was asked by his associates to prepare two papers** to be read to the membership in the following year.

This was an obvious opportunity for Talleyrand to bring his name to the

* Madame de Staël was away from Paris at the time of his arrival. Talleyrand therefore stayed with an old friend from prerevolutionary days, Madame de Boufflers, at Auteuil, near the Bois de Boulogne, for a time. He later moved to a house belonging to an obscure general named Arcon in the rue de l'Assomption, near the Tuileries.

† The royal academies of the monarchy had been abolished in 1792 and replaced with a National Institute "entrusted with the responsibility for collating the various discoveries and improving the arts and sciences." This organization, the Institut des Sciences et des Arts, was organized in 1795 into four sections, comprising altogether 144 full members and 144 associate members. Talleyrand's appointment was to the second section, the Institute of Moral and Political Sciences, under the heading of Political Economy.

** The first, titled "On Commercial Relations Between England and the United States," was delivered on April 4, 1797; the second, "On the Advantages of Acquiring New Colonies," on July 3. Both were subsequently published in the official *Receuil des Mémoires de l'Institut* (t.ii, 1ere série, 1799). Their conclusions were incorporated by Talleyrand into the *Mémoires*, Parts I and II, *passim*.

attention of the public, not by associating it with the corrupt politics of the Directory, but under the auspices of the prestigious institute. "To pay my debt as an academician," Talleyrand relates, "I read at two public sessions papers which attracted a certain amount of attention. The first of these related to the United States, and the second to the necessity for France of acquiring colonies."

Both sessions of the institute were attended, not only by members, but also by the whole of the diplomatic corps accredited to the Directory and by as many of the public as could be admitted. The memory of Talleyrand's work in the Assembly, the highly praised success—which really had been no success at all—of his missions to England, the fact of his absolution from the guilt of which the Convention had accused him, all made of him, in the eyes of the people, a man to watch and one to hear. They were not disappointed. The first paper, on commercial relations between England and America, gave a general description of the state of society in the United States, its comparatively tranquil character, its varied and original customs, and the remarkable nature of its spirit of religious toleration. Talleyrand pointed out that "all the habits of the American make an Englishman of him. . . . The fact that the English language is common to both countries gives the English a certain proprietary right over American inclinations." Since this was so, he stated, England gained more than it lost by its separation from America, for the needs of America attached it to English interests, while their language, education, history and laws created attitudes which, if properly used, were and would remain English. Therefore, despite America's pronounced affection for France and for the French and notwithstanding that "the very name of England is mentioned with aversion, America is entirely English—which is to say that England, not France, is in a position to derive from that country all the advantages that one country can obtain from another." The English, in other words, were in an unassailable position with respect to the vast commercial potential of America, and French dreams of a mighty combine between themselves and the sister Republic in the New World were doomed to failure.

The second paper, read three months later, in July, completed the basic theme of the first. In discoursing on "the advantages of obtaining colonies in the present circumstances," he pointed out that after the turmoil of the Revolution, the citizens of France must be offered hope for the future and that hope lay primarily in colonial expansion—that is, in implanting French citizens in new lands and thus exporting the blessings of liberty and of justice. This would open up not only new horizons for French industry and culture, but also an unlimited opportunity for French enterprise and ingenuity, as well as for "those men who are unable to live in harmony with their fellows and who are unable to bear the notion of dependence" upon society. The message implied was perfectly clear: France's current troubles were the result of the ascendancy gained by adventurers, misfits, and malcontents who, rather than being allowed to victimize the people of France, should be permitted—or perhaps compelled— to expend their energies in a way that would benefit the mother country: by founding and developing French colonies. These colonies, however, were not to be imposed upon the New World, which would always remain a sphere of Anglo-American interest, but in France's new sphere of interest: along the coast of the Mediterranean. This, he pointed out, had been foreseen by "one of the great men of our time, who had most an eye on the future, M. le duc de Choiseul," minister of Louis XV, who, knowing that France would one day lose its colonies in America, had advised the opening of negotiations for the cession of Egypt to France by the Turkish Empire. In this way, France might compete commercially with England, though without coming into conflict with it, and indeed in a spirit of cooperation created by common interests.

The "certain amount of attention" which Talleyrand says was won by his papers was, in fact, much more than that. The breadth of his perspective in international relations and in the interplay of cultural values among nations, and the boldness of his vision of the future in proposing solutions to France's current problems, excited the admiration and acclaim of both Frenchmen and foreigners. Moreover, the interval between the two readings—one on April 4, the second on July 3—was designed carefully to keep his name before the public for as long a period as possible. The stratagem was a complete success. For almost three months, praise of Talleyrand's brilliance and of his obvious ability as a statesman was heard everywhere in Paris.

In the particular circumstances which existed at this juncture in the history of the Directory, Talleyrand's revived and growing prominence was of special significance. In the period immediately following his return to Paris, he had, according to his original decision, carefully avoided taking any part in active politics. After several months had passed, it is apparent that he had had a change of heart, a change occasioned, certainly, by resurgent ambition. Or rather, by an ambition that revived in the measure that its possibilities of satisfaction soared with the spread of Talleyrand's reputation as a statesman. Of at least equal importance was the fact that a major governmental crisis was imminent and that France was rapidly approaching the point where a radical choice must be made between the restoration of the Bourbon monarchy and the establishment of a strong and truly viable republican government. Discontent with the Directory was too universal, poverty and ruin too widespread, and the yearning for order and peace too strong for the regime to survive, in its current form, for very long.

The crisis came, or rather was provoked, by a combination of military and political events. The war against the Coalition was not going well. An attempt by General Hoche, in February, 1797, to land a force in Ireland so as to spark a revolt against England failed miserably. In the process, the supporting Spanish fleet was destroyed, and England was left in undisputed command of the sea. The French armies in Germany, under Jourdan and Moreau, were in full retreat. Only the Army of Italy, under the command of General Bonaparte, was meeting with success. In September, 1796, he had defeated the Austrians at Bassano; in November, at Arcola; in January, 1797, at Rivoli; in February, at Mantua. In less than a year, Bonaparte had disposed of five Austrian armies and captured the stronghold of the Hapsburgs in Italy. Finally, in April, he had advanced to within a short distance of Vienna, and Austria asked for peace, offering to cede the Netherlands and Lombardy to France. Bonaparte was the man of the hour, the hero of France, the savior of the Republic. He was also perhaps the "man with the sword" who Robespierre had feared might convert the Revolution to his purposes and whom Marat had foreseen: "the danger is that one of our generals be crowned with victory . . . and lead his victorious army against the capital."

It did not help the peace of mind of the Directors that concurrently with the rise of this messiah figure who overshadowed them all, they were forced to fight for their political life and for the continued existence of the Directory (that is, of their profits) in Paris. In March and April, 1797, as Bonaparte was bringing the Austrians to their knees, France was doing the same to the Directors. During those months, the first elections were held for seats in the Council of the Ancients and the Council of the Five Hundred. Both chambers had, up to this time, been controlled by former members of the Convention. By the end of April it was clear that France had risen up not only against the incompetence and corruption of the Directory, but also against the revolutionary principles which had continued to inspire the legislation of the councils. Out of 216 outgoing ex-conventionals who appealed to the electorate, 205 were defeated at the polls; and to make matters worse, or better, they were replaced, for the most part, by royalists of various coloration, from constitutional-monarchists to ultraconservatives. The stage was now set for a confrontation of major proportions. On one side stood the royalist-controlled chambers; on the other, the Directors, who were determined to retain power regardless of the chambers. And watching both sides stood Bonaparte, the conqueror of Italy, the god of the army, and the idol of the people, who, by a mere rattling of the sword, might give victory to either side—or to neither.

It is difficult to know whether Talleyrand's decision, expressed upon his return to France, to avoid "active politics" was wholly sincere or, granting its sincerity, to determine whether he intended merely to abstain from political activity only until he had familiarized himself with the situation sufficiently to intervene effectively. It is more likely that by the beginning of 1797 the state of French politics, the ever-present threat of a strong reaction to the excesses of the Directory, and the rising star of Bonaparte caused him to abandon his initial caution. Whatever the truth, by early 1797 he was not only actively engaged in politics, but was also determined to acquire some public office by means of which he might exercise control over events.

The papers read before the institute were but a single expression of that determination, one calculated to crown his efforts to enter the government. That he was successful is beyond doubt. The second paper of his "debt as an academician" was read on July 3. Fifteen days later he received a note from Lazare Carnot, one of the Directors:

> The Executive Directory invites you, citizen, to present yourself tomorrow, at 10 o'clock in the morning, at the offices of the Department of Foreign Relations. At that time, Citizen Delacroix, minister of the department, will turn over to you his responsibilities.

For the most part, the circumstances that led directly to Talleyrand's appointment are uncertain. It is known that having decided to reenter the political arena and to seek office, he became a member of one of the most influential of the many political groups in Paris, the Constitutional Club. The club's membership was composed of moderate progressives and moderate Jacobins—the Abbé Sieyès, Talleyrand's friend from almost twenty years earlier and his former rival in the Assembly; Chénier, who had moved for Talleyrand's recall from America; Montesquiou, a moderate leader of the royalist party; Hughes Maret, future Duke de Bassano; Benjamin Constant, author and political theorist; and, among others, Pierre-Louis Roederer, former *syndic*, or attorney general, of the Department of the Seine under the Constituent Assembly. Most of these men were on cordial terms with Talleyrand, and all of them were known to him, either from his days in the Assembly or through Madame de Staël. (Benjamin Constant, in fact, had lately become Germaine's lover, a fact which Talleyrand either ignored or accepted with his usual complacency.) Within the club, Talleyrand, by virtue of his reputation, his accomplishments, and his intelligence, quickly gained an ascendancy over the other members and thus emerged

as one of the leaders, along with Sieyès and Constant, of the moderate constitutionalist "party" which had great influence among the members of the
center in both chambers. From this vantage point, apparently, he had determined to step into the Ministry of Foreign Affairs—an ambitious step
for an ex-bishop, ex-noble, and former émigré in the France of the Directory. But it was precisely the unsettled condition of the country and the
precarious state of the government which placed this ambition within the
bounds of possibility. It was the responsibility of the Directory to appoint
the various ministers, and yet the number of candidates available was incredibly limited. The members of the councils were excluded from ministerial office by the Constitution. The army had need in the field of every one
of its competent and experienced generals. Returned émigrés who had
served under the *ancien régime* or under Louis XVI during the short-lived
constitutional monarchy were either unacceptable to the Directors or unwilling to take office in a government that might at any moment either be
replaced by a monarchy or fall victim to the displeasure of the enigmatic
commander of the Army of Italy. And relatives of émigrés who had not returned to France were excluded by law from office. Talleyrand's leverage,
on the other hand, was his proved competence as a diplomat and statesman, combined with his thinly disguised availability. In those circumstances, it seemed only a matter of time before the Directors, in an effort to
strengthen their government, had to make use of his abilities in an official
capacity.

There had been some discussion of this possibility in the spring of 1797
shortly after Talleyrand had begun making his political presence felt in
Paris. With the defeat of the Austrians in Italy by Bonaparte, the English
were virtually isolated in their war with France, with no obvious chance either of achieving a decisive victory or of prodding their remaining allies to
take a more active part in the conflict. In consequence, there was violent
agitation in England against Pitt's government, in Parliament as well as
among the public. This was accompanied by a series of mutinies in the
navy, which were put down only by offering amnesties and concessions;
but then the army began to show signs of serious unrest. Pitt was compelled to seek peace, and he scheduled a meeting with the French at Lille
early in July.

In Paris the question arose of naming a negotiator for the French delegation, one of sufficient experience, wit, and intelligence to contend with
the formidable English envoy, Lord Malmesbury. Talleyrand's name was
one of three suggested to the Directory, and it was the one to which Barras
inclined. Talleyrand had had experience with the English; moreover, he
was the talk of Paris, and it would not be to the Directors' discredit to take
advantage of his reputation in pursuing their own policies. But one of Bar-

ras' fellow Directors, Jean-François Reubell, was vehemently opposed to the idea and attacked Talleyrand's abilities and character in the most violent terms: "If you want honesty and ability," he concluded his diatribe, "then Talleyrand should not even be mentioned." Barras therefore let the matter drop, and Étienne Le Tourneur was appointed to negotiate with the English.*

This was a bitter disappointment to Talleyrand, and it came at a time when his chances of success had seemed particularly promising. The current minister of foreign affairs, Charles Delacroix, was highly unpopular. His ineffectual performance was universally criticized in the councils and universally ridiculed in the salons. It was already being rumored, while the peace conference with England was being discussed, that Delacroix would shortly be replaced and that his probable successor was Talleyrand. Then it became known that Talleyrand had been rejected by the Directors for a comparatively subordinate, though undoubtedly important, role in the English negotiations. Under a regime in which careers were made and unmade in the salons of Madame Tallien, Madame Récamier, and Josephine de Beauharnais, this was a great blow. Its apparent significance was that if the Directors had rejected Talleyrand for the post of negotiator with the English, in which he had had solid experience, it was highly unlikely that they would consider him a suitable candidate for the Ministry of Foreign Affairs.

Those who accepted this situation at face value underestimated Talleyrand's determination and his resources. He was disappointed but not discouraged. Barras, he knew, had proposed his name for the peace conference and might therefore be expected to support him for the ministry—particularly if Germaine de Staël's influence with Barras were utilized to its maximum extent. One of the other Directors, Louis-Marie La Revellière-Lépeaux, had been a colleague of Talleyrand's in the Constituent Assembly, and they had established an amicable, though not warm, relationship since Talleyrand's return to Paris. He, too, could probably be counted on to support Talleyrand for office. The other three Directors, however, were openly and bitterly hostile to Talleyrand. Reubell had already expressed himself on the subject—though Reubell, along with Barras and La Revellière, constituted the working majority of the Directors, the triumvirate that was united in opposition to the two remaining Directors, Lazare Carnot and François Barthélemy. Carnot, a *parvenu* and a Jacobin of extremist tendencies—he had been one of the earliest supporters of Robespierre—despised Talleyrand as a moderate, a former supporter of a

---

* The French and English delegates met on July 7, and the conference immediately deadlocked over the cession to England of the Cape of Good Hope and Ceylon. It was not until Talleyrand became Foreign Minister that a way was found around this problem.

constitutional monarchy, an aristocrat of the *ancien régime*, a dangerously prominent statesman, and as a friend of La Revellière, whose mortal enemy Carnot was. Barthélemy's dislike of Talleyrand was less complex. Himself a nobleman by birth and a diplomat under the old monarchy, he had always remained a conservative and a reactionary at heart, and he was never able to forgive Talleyrand his double sin of having abandoned first the church and then the king.

The opposition to Talleyrand displayed by three of the five Directors was one that the government, as a whole, could ill afford. The Council of Ancients and the Council of Five Hundred, now purged of its majority of *conventionnels* and led by the newly elected royalists and moderates, were in full revolt against the revolutionary legislation of their predecessors. By the early summer of 1797 they had embarked on a program of repealing all laws directed against the former nobility, the émigrés, and the church. Not content with this, a party of extremists, known as the Club de Clichy, led by Charles Pichegru, president of the Council of Five Hundred, had initiated a campaign to oust the incumbent Directors, replace them with men of their own choosing, and thus neutralize the power of the executive branch. Their first victory, in fact, had been the election of Barthélemy to the Directory, and this success was sufficient threat to impel the triumvirs to action. Barras was more than sufficiently astute to recognize that unless drastic steps were taken, the Directors' powers would be stripped from them one by one. Pichegru's first move was made quickly, on June 18, when it was proposed in the Council of Five Hundred to transfer all financial administration from the Directors to the treasury; and the treasury was, and had been since the earliest days of the Revolution, a nest of counterrevolutionaries. Once deprived of the power of the purse, the Directors would lose effective control of virtually the whole of the machinery of administration and also of military operations. The way would then be open to a restoration of the monarchy. Concurrently with the action of the council, a violent attack was mounted on the ministries of the government by Pichegru's party and supported by two of the Directors, Barthélemy and Carnot, who insisted that the Club de Clichy must be conciliated by a thorough overhaul of the ministries—that is, by the appointment of royalist ministers. In this, Barras pretended to acquiesce. Meanwhile, he appealed to General Hoche, who was now in command of the Army of the Sambre and Meuse, to send troops to Paris to be used by the Directors if it became necessary. By July 1 the troops had been dispatched—ostensibly bound for Brest, as reinforcements for an army bound for Ireland, but actually en route to Paris. By mid-July Hoche's troops were within striking distance of the capital, and Barras proceeded to play his cards. In a stormy session in the Luxembourg Palace,* the Directors proceeded, in accordance with the wishes of Barthélemy and Carnot, to discuss the dismissal of current ministers and the appointment of replacements. The results were totally unexpected. Barras, with troops within reach, was determined not only to defy the Club de Clichy but apparently also to provoke its adherents into open revolt against the government. Supported by La Revellière and Reubell, he announced first the retention in the ministry of Merlin de Douai and Dominique Ramel—the two ministers most odious to the royalists. The ministers dear to the right—Bénézach, Cochon, and Petiet—were dismissed and replaced by men loyal only to Barras. The moderate ministers—Delacroix, at Foreign Affairs, and Truguet, at the Ministry of War, were also dismissed, for these were the two against whom public opinion had been most aroused in recent months by France's military setback. General Hoche, who had heeded Barras' plea for support, was named Minister of War, amid a great uproar. The most violent debate, however, took place when Barras named his candidate for the Ministry of Foreign Affairs: Citizen Talleyrand-Périgord.

"This little priest of yours," Carnot shouted, "will sell us all down the river, one by one, for any amount that he can get!"

"What has he sold, thus far?" La Revellière asked.

"His God, to begin with," answered Carnot.

"How is that possible, since he does not believe in God?"

Carnot, trapped in his own illogic, responded that Talleyrand was a traitor to his class and that he had "sold out" the king. But Barras had a ready answer: "It seems to me," he said, "that we are the last ones who can hold that against him."

The debate went on at great length, but by the time that the votes were cast it was already clear that the triumvirs would win. The tally was two against Talleyrand, and three for him. Reubell had voted with Barras and La Revellière. It is not known how he managed to overcome his personal aversion to Talleyrand to such an extent. He may have decided that a moderate and gifted Talleyrand, however detestable, was preferable to an incompetent revolutionary or an intractable royalist. He may also have had his mind made up for him by a few words from Barras beforehand.

The mystery that remains behind Talleyrand's appointment as Foreign Minister is the explanation of why Barras was moved to nominate him and to support his nomination in the face of such strong opposition from Carnot and Barthélemy and, certainly, despite the reluctance of Reubell. It is not that there is too little information on this point, but rather that there is

* The former palace of Marie de Médicis, the Luxembourg had become the official residence of the five Directors and the seat of the executive branch.

too much. Talleyrand, Barras, and Madame de Staël each give a different account of the events preceding the nomination, none of them entirely accurate, and none of them wholly false.

Talleyrand's explanation is as follows:

> Madame de Staël, who had already acquired a certain influence, insisted on my going with her to visit Barras, one of the members of the Directory. I refused at first, for I could not call on one Director without asking to see all of the others, especially the ones who had been my colleagues in the Constituent Assembly [La Revellière and Reubell]. The reasons alleged to justify my refusal did not seem valid; besides, they had to be conveyed through Madame de Staël, who, being eager that I become personally known to Barras, arranged for Barras to send me a note inviting me to dine with him. . . . I had no alternative but to accept. On the appointed day, I was there at three o'clock in the afternoon. In the dining room, which I had to cross to reach the drawing room, I noticed covers laid for five persons. Much to my surprise, Madame de Staël was not invited. . . . While I was engaged in reading [Barras had not yet returned home] . . . two young men came in to ascertain the time by the drawing room clock and, seeing that it was only half past three, they said to each other, "We have time to go for a swim." They had not been gone twenty minutes when one of them returned asking for immediate help. I ran, with everyone in the house, to the riverbank . . . one of the young men had drowned.

Talleyrand was greatly distressed. Although he did not know Raymond, as the drowned man was called, he was told by one of the servants that "Barras was very fond of him. He had brought him up and, since he had been appointed a Director, he had made him his aide-de-camp." Talleyrand returned to the drawing room, pondering the awkwardness of his position. "I was alone, not knowing exactly what to do. Who was to tell Barras the misfortune that had befallen him? I had never seen the Director. My position was acutely unpleasant."

A short time later Barras' carriage drove up to the house, and a servant ran out, shouting, "M. Raymond has just been drowned, Citizen Director! He has just been drowned!" Whereupon, Talleyrand records:

> Barras ran across the front yard and rushed upstairs to his room, crying out aloud. After waiting some little time, one of his servants told him I was in the drawing room. He sent me word to excuse his not coming down and requesting me to sit down to dinner at once. The secretary who accompanied him remained upstairs. Thus I was alone at Barras' table. A quarter of an hour later, a servant came to request me to go up to the Director's room. I felt thankful for his supposing that under the circumstances the dinner served to me could have no attraction. I felt quite upset. As I entered his room, he took hold of both my hands and embraced me. He was weeping. I said to him all the kind things that the position in which I saw him, and my own position, could dictate. The embarrassment which he at

first displayed with me, a perfect stranger to him, gradually disappeared, and the share I took in his grief seemed to do him good. He begged me to ride back to Paris with him, and I readily accepted. From that day, I never had the occasion to regret having made his acquaintance. He was a man of excitable and impulsive nature, easily moved one way or the other. I had known him scarcely a couple of hours, and yet it might have been supposed that I was the person whom he liked best in the whole world.

Shortly after this first meeting, the Directory wished to make a change in the ministry. To this Barras consented, on condition that his new friend be appointed Minister of Foreign Relations. He defended his proposal with great warmth and so effectively that it was adopted. . . . The absolute character of the measures taken by the Directory, the pressing requests of Madame de Staël, and, above all, the belief that I might possibly work some good caused me to dismiss any idea of declining the post. On the following day, therefore, I called at the Luxembourg in order to thank Barras, after which, I went to the Foreign Ministry.

Fantastic as this account may seem, it probably contains a great deal of truth. A man did not become Foreign Minister, even under the Directory, simply because he was able to express sympathy at the proper moment. But when that man enjoys a reputation as a statesman and a diplomat and is widely regarded as a candidate for a ministry, when the proper groundwork has been laid by a Madame de Staël, and when circumstances absolutely require a new Minister of Foreign Affairs in any event, then Talleyrand's account becomes less incredible. It is highly probable, moreover, that at least the meeting between Barras and Talleyrand took place as Talleyrand describes. There were moments in his career when Talleyrand was certainly capable of lying; that he did so rarely is a tribute to his skill as a diplomat rather than to his moral sense. In the *Mémoires*, however, outright falsehood is almost totally absent, and so is the complete truth. In recording his experiences for posterity, Talleyrand's sin is not one of commission, but of omission. Those things in his career of which he was not proud were simply not mentioned. It is reasonable to conclude, therefore, that while Talleyrand's account of his meeting with Barras and his subsequent appointment may be wholly true, it is not the whole truth.

Barras' version of the same event, recorded in his own memoirs many years later, supplies some of what is missing in Talleyrand's narrative. Here it must be said that Barras' recollections are almost invariably colored by a desire for vengeance on those whom he regarded as responsible for his eventual downfall; which is to say that he lied a great deal. And since Talleyrand was, along with Bonaparte, the chief engineer of Barras' retirement from public life, he is not treated with conspicuous fairness. It did not help that what Barras did not know of his own experience regarding Talleyrand's rise, he relied upon Benjamin Constant and Madame

de Staël to tell him; and Constant was to become one of Talleyrand's bitterest and most vindictive enemies. Even so, there are undoubtedly elements of truth in Barras' explanations.

According to the Director's *Mémoires*, from the time of Talleyrand's return to Paris until the time of the appointment, he was under constant
siege from Madame de Staël, who insisted that a place must be made in the
government for Talleyrand. Day and night, in frequent visits, she sang the
praises of her friend, dwelling eloquently on his talents, his ability to man-
age difficult situations, his knowledge of courts, kings, ministers, and embassies. What, she asked, was a bourgeois like Delacroix, the then Foreign
Minister, compared to a Talleyrand? Yet, Barras insists, he remained unmoved. The counterattacks of Carnot and Reubell, which described Talleyrand as a "vile, licentious, unfrocked priestling," moved him to the
point where he was able to tell the importunate Germaine that he wished
to hear no more on the subject of Talleyrand. She was silent for two days
and then reappeared in Barras' office with ammunition designed both to
flatter the Director and to promise him a devoted ally in his struggle with
the councils and with his sometimes rebellious fellow Directors: "Talleyrand is devoted to you. He considers you something more than human.
. . . He would throw himself into the fire for you. . . . He has contacts in
every party and would be an incomparable source of information for you."
When Barras mentioned the objections of Carnot and Reubell, Germaine
replied, "So much the better! The more they oppose Talleyrand, the more
Talleyrand will be obligated to you. He will be your watchdog—and the
most faithful watchdog that you could possibly have!" Barras, incorruptible man that he was, refused to listen. However, he says, Germaine had not
yet played her final and most dramatic scene. Several nights later she reappeared at the Luxembourg in a state of great agitation. Talleyrand, she
said, had just visited her and threatened to kill himself. After describing
the scene, she went on, Barras says, to declaim, with great emotion: "Oh,
Barras, Barras, my friend, it is possible that at this very moment he is no
longer alive! It was only a few moments ago that he swore to me that he
would throw himself into the Seine unless he were made Minister of Foreign Affairs! He is so poor—he has only ten louis left! If only you would
receive him."

In describing the scene, Barras lingers lovingly on its truly spectacular
climax and describes Madame de Staël as being in such an emotional state
as to be beside herself. She clasped his hands in hers, he claims, and, with
tears streaming down her cheeks, recounted the pitiful story of Talleyrand's neglected childhood and of his horror at being forced into the
priesthood. Sobbing and on the verge of collapse, she admitted that Talleyrand had been often accused of some of the vices prevalent under the old

monarchy and that perhaps some of those accusations were even justified. She recovered sufficiently, however, to be able vigorously to describe Talleyrand's unparalleled services during the Constituent Assembly, his brilliant successes in England, and his devotion to France even when in exile in strange and barbarous lands. Finally, near hysteria, she offered to Barras, as surety for the truth of the things she said, the gift of her undoubted, if overly ample, charms. This overture, Barras exclaims righteously, he rejected: "Never have I emerged so innocent and so pure from such an ordeal."

Finally, Barras confesses, he could stand no more. "Tell your friend," he advised Germaine, "not to drown himself. Otherwise, it will not be possible for us to do anything for him. Meanwhile, we will try to find some way to make use of his talents on behalf of the Republic and his goodwill on our own behalf." He does not explain why, having resisted so firmly both the supplications and the advances of Germaine de Staël, he succumbed at last to the former and, with great difficulty, proceeded immediately to force Talleyrand upon the other Directors.

The third version of Talleyrand's appointment is that of Germaine herself, which was written some time after their friendship had cooled to the point where they were both privately indulging in recriminations:

> The friends of the Directory hoped that the Directory would consolidate constitutional measures and that, for this purpose, ministers would be chosen who would strengthen and support the government. M. de Talleyrand was willing to accept the post, and since he seemed the best possible choice for the Ministry of Foreign Affairs, I furthered his cause effectively by having him presented to Barras by one of my friends, and by strongly recommending him myself to Barras. M. de Talleyrand needed help in order to attain this high position, but once he had attained it, he needed no help to retain it.

It is probably unimportant that, of the three persons who described the circumstances of Talleyrand's rise to the ministry, one was an utterly corrupt and completely charming liar, who was removed from office through Talleyrand's efforts; one was, by profession, a writer of romantic tales and, into the bargain, a woman whose love for Talleyrand had turned, not into a friendship or into indifference, but into bitterness; and, finally, one was Talleyrand himself, who seldom prevaricated, but who conscientiously edited his *Mémoires* with both eyes fixed firmly on the verdict of history. Given the nature of the Directorial regime in France and the characters of the three persons involved, none of these versions is unbelievable, and none totally believable. All that is certain is that Talleyrand's entry into the Ministry of Foreign Affairs under the Directory, which was the formal beginning of his lengthy career as Europe's most eminent diplomat and statesman, was due to Barras' support of his candidacy and, in some measure, to Madame de Staël's influence with Barras.

As Minister of Foreign Affairs, Talleyrand quickly discovered that although he had gained admittance to the councils of power, that power was to be shared by him in a very limited fashion. Under Jean Delacroix, his predecessor, he writes:

> . . . all state matters concerning the department were settled beforehand by the Directors. And, like those of the previous minister, my duties were confined to signing passports and other administrative documents and to forwarding to the proper quarters the dispatches and other communications already drafted by the executive branch. Yet I often delayed these communications, which enabled me to mitigate their terms when the impulse under which they had been written had passed. I tried to impart dignity to this odd situation by trying to convince people—and perhaps myself, to some extent—that we would never have true order at home until we could have true peace abroad. And I added that since I had been called upon to contribute to the restoration of peace, I ought to devote myself wholeheartedly to its pursuit.

The weaknesses of the Directory and of the Directors were known to Talleyrand from the start. Government by impulse, like foreign relations by impulse, was alien and incomprehensible to him, who, above all things, prized reflection and deliberation. Any illusions that he may have had before taking office, to the effect that as a member of the government he might be able to play a role in establishing order in France's internal affairs, were quickly dispelled. "All business relative to home affairs," he says, "were kept from me." Thus excluded from a voice in the decisions taken by the Directors concerning both France's relations with foreign powers and its internal problems, Talleyrand became quickly disenchanted with what he terms "the ways of the Directors," which outraged his sense of order and decorum. "To give a clear idea of what I have termed 'the ways of the Directors,' I think it will be sufficient to relate the incidents that characterized the first council at which I was present. A quarrel took place between Carnot and Barras. The latter accused his colleague of having destroyed a letter which should have been submitted to the Directors. They were both standing. Carnot, raising his hand, said: 'I give you my word of honor that it is not so!' Barras replied, 'Do not dare raise your hand. Blood will drip from it.' " At another meeting a few days later, Barras and Carnot actually came to blows before they were separated by La Revellière—while Talleyrand stood aside, immobilized by astonishment and disgust.

What the *Mémoires* do not mention is that the Directors were even less gentle in their treatment of the various ministers than they were with one another. Talleyrand, in particular, seemed the special target of the brutal Reubell. "The existence of Talleyrand as a minister," the Prussian ambassador reported to Berlin, "is, as I reported earlier, precarious. If he is able to survive, it will be only through a miracle of intelligence and discretion. Among the Directors, everyone is opposed to him. Barras is the only one who even pretends to side with him. I am told that the other Directors hardly even speak to him." The ambassador's words were not to be taken literally. Reubell was constantly addressing Talleyrand on the subject of his imagined faults in precisely the terms that a teacher would use to reprimand a delinquent child. When the minister submitted a report to the Directors on a new commercial treaty between Spain and England, Reubell returned it to him with a note scribbled across the top: "Very poor. Do it over. And this time give us some detail." Talleyrand's only immediate weapon against such onslaughts on his dignity was his irony. But this proved too subtle a tool to be effective against Reubell's bullying disposition. On one occasion, after being taken to task by the Director for saying that he preferred not to reply to a particular question on foreign relations until he had had the opportunity to study it more deeply, Talleyrand replied coolly: "Even if I were able to give an answer immediately, I would not be able to engage in a discussion of the question with Citizen Reubell, who, as all the world knows, is Europe's most illustrious diplomat and administrator." Reubell appeared not to have grasped Talleyrand's meaning. Completely free of embarrassment, he ordered Talleyrand to go into an adjoining room and not emerge until he was able to answer the question. At the end of an hour, Reubell called him out and demanded his answer. Talleyrand politely informed the Director that he had a headache, bowed, and withdrew.

Talleyrand's contempt for such men, and such methods, was unbounded. "These were the sort of men who ruled France," he wrote. "And it was my task to try to obtain the readmission of France to the councils of Europe while they were in power."

Of the Directory, Talleyrand wrote: "All was done with violence, and, as a natural consequence, nothing could last." He himself was in an advantageous position to appraise and to draw conclusions from this "natural consequence." At the time that he became minister, he pointed out, it had proved impossible to conclude a peace with England.* It is true that the

* As early as 1796, Pitt had been forced, as Talleyrand points out, "to feign entering into negotiations with us, in order to overcome difficulties at home" (*Mémoires*, Vol. I, p. 193). These negotiations had been broken off in December, 1796, and resumed by Lord Malmesbury at Lille, as al-

other allies of the Coalition, with the exception of Austria—which, as the result of Bonaparte's campaigns in Italy, was on the point of withdrawing —and Portugal, which was bound to England, had signed treaties of peace with France.* These treaties, it is true, had been advantageous for France; they had been "bought and paid for with territorial cessions or pecuniary considerations" on the part of the Allies. But these gains were more than offset by deteriorating internal conditions in France at the time of Talleyrand's appointment. There was civil war, in the form of a royalist uprising, in the western provinces—in the Vendée, particularly—and poverty everywhere, with concomitant unrest. The hopes of the people, roused by the Revolution, had been frustrated by the indifference of the Directorial regime to the welfare of the people. "Liberty, Equality, and Fraternity were written everywhere on the walls," Talleyrand notes, "but the ideas and feelings they expressed were nowhere to be found. From the very highest agencies of the government to the lowest, there was scarcely one which was not completely arbitrary in its concept, organization, and operation."

That the Directory was incompetent, wasteful, and corrupt was a matter of general knowledge among those who followed the course of events. That it was a corpse waiting to be buried—"the destiny of all despotisms," Talleyrand notes—was no secret, especially among those who, like Talleyrand, were intimate witnesses to its day-by-day operations and victims to the whims of the Directors. In such a situation, a prudent man had to look to the future and guide himself accordingly. If the Directory were to fall, what would replace it? The royalists were strong, and their strength in the councils daily was being used in an increasingly heated campaign against the Directors and therefore against the Directory itself. If events continued along this path, it was likely, perhaps even inevitable, that there would be a restoration of the Bourbons. This, Talleyrand wished to avoid at all costs. His part in the Revolution had been such that if the royalist reactionaries came to power, the kindest fate he could expect would be, once again, exile. Equally to be feared was a resurgence of extreme Jacobinism in reaction to the increasing strength of the royalists. Talleyrand and France had already suffered enough at their hands. Between these two poles, public opinion was vacillating, and the moderates and the liberals, who were neither royalists nor Jacobins, were daily losing ground to both extremes.

In this predicament, France required a leader who could reconcile, or at

---

ready mentioned, in July, 1797. The excessive demands of the English prevented any agreement from being reached.

* Tuscany, in February, 1795; Prussia, April, 1795; Spain, July, 1795; Hesse-Kassel, August, 1795; Sardinia, May, 1796; Württemberg, August, 1796; Baden, August, 1796; the Two Sicilies, October, 1796; Parma, November, 1796; the Papal States, February, 1797; Venice, May, 1797. Austria, in May, 1797, had signed an armistice at Leoben and was now engaged in negotiating the preliminary peace treaty of Campo Formio.

least dominate, all parties. Talleyrand, with the talent, almost the genius, which he was always to demonstrate for choosing the winning side before it became clear to others who would be the victor, believed that such a leader was at hand. He had been in office only a week when he wrote his first letter to General Bonaparte:

> I have the honor to inform you, General, that the Executive Directory has appointed me Minister of Foreign Affairs. Fully aware of the fearful responsibility that my duties entail, I gain confidence from the knowledge that your glory cannot fail to facilitate any negotiations that I may be required to undertake. The mere name of Bonaparte will remove all obstacles.
>
> I shall diligently acquaint you with all matters which the Directory may instruct me to bring to your attention, though your fame, which so quickly spreads news of your achievements, will often deprive me of the pleasure of informing the Directors of the manner in which you will have executed their policies.

The letter depended for its effect upon the intelligence and character of the recipient. To a man without ambition and without the gift of subtlety, it would seem merely an obsequious acknowledgment, by a newly appointed minister, of the military successes of the Directory's most brilliant commander. But Talleyrand was counting on more than that from the young general whom he had never met but of whom he had heard a great deal. "Bonaparte," he wrote, ". . . feared a situation in which he would be defenseless against the very dangers to which his fame gave birth"—that is, to the jealousy and vindictiveness of the five men who were his masters. "He was ambitious enough to wish himself to be at the head of affairs, but he was not so blind as to believe this possible in France, at least not unless matters took a course which could not be regarded as imminent or even as probable."

Talleyrand's guarded appeal to Bonaparte's ambition, to his need for an ally in Paris to protect him against the "dangers to which his fame gave birth" and, perhaps above all, for an informant in the councils of the Directory, met with gratifying success. An immediate answer arrived from Italy:

> The government's choice of yourself as Minister of Foreign Relations is a tribute to its good judgment. It demonstrates that you possess great talents, a pure civic spirit, and that you are a stranger to the aberrations that have dishonored the Revolution.
>
> I will be flattered to exchange letters with you often, so as to keep you fully informed and also to persuade you of my esteem and respect for you.*

---

* Talleyrand says of this letter that it "is of sufficient interest to insert it at the end of these

Talleyrand's message to Bonaparte had been clearly understood, and it had evoked a response as satisfactory, yet as prudent and as guarded, as Talleyrand could have wished. The praise of Talleyrand's "pure civic spirit" was an admission that Bonaparte's sentiments, like the Foreign Minister's, lay with the undiluted revolutionary spirit of the Constituent Assembly and in opposition to the royalists of the right, who had now risen to power in the councils of the Directory. The reference to the "aberrations which have dishonored the Revolution" was an overt rejection of the policies of the extremists of the left, the new Jacobins. Talleyrand had been correct. The brilliant young general was a man of the center, like himself. Moreover, he would welcome, as Talleyrand had suspected, the presence of a reliable informant and ally in Paris.

The advantages to both parties of such an arrangement quickly became evident, as France, in the weeks following Talleyrand's appointment, edged near to civil war. Concurrently with that appointment and the dismissal of the ministers favored by the royalists, it was learned that Hoche's troops, summoned by Barras, were approaching the capital. On July 18 the two deputies whose duty it was to guard the constitutional privileges of the councils reported that these regiments—cavalry, mostly—were at La Ferté-Alais, a place which appeared to be within the radius from which the Constitution excluded troops which might threaten the independence of the councils. This caused a great uproar. Pichegru and some of his partisans made a formal demand for an explanation from the Directors, and heated discussions followed, in the course of which it was declared that the only effective countermeasure was the indictment of Barras, Reubell, and La Revellière by the councils. It seems that Pichegru had come to an arrangement with Carnot, whereby the latter would throw the blame for this violation of the Constitution on his three associates, and this, in turn, would make possible the indictment. In the meantime, Pichegru had demanded a formal explanation from the Directors, and when the answer arrived on July 20, explaining only that the presence of the troops so close to Paris was a mistake, it was noted that the message was signed by Carnot. What had happened was that a dispatch from Bonaparte had arrived in Paris, reporting that among the papers found in a trunk belonging to an émigré in Trieste were letters proving conclusively that Pichegru was involved in an elaborate conspiracy aimed at the restoration of the Bourbons in the person of Louis XVIII.* Carnot, shocked, shortly afterward made it

Mémoires" (Vol. I, pp. 195–196). But he did not do so, nor was the letter found among his papers after his death. It is reproduced, however, in the *Correspondance inédite de Napoléon Bonaparte avec le Directoire, le Ministère* . . . , Vol. II, p. 127.

* The son of Louis XVI and Marie-Antoinette, who had been acclaimed as Louis XVII by royalist factions, had died in the Temple in June, 1795. Later in the same month the Count de Pro-

clear in a public address that he would never lend himself to such a restoration.

The forces of the right were now in utter confusion, but they were saved,
at least for the moment, by the fact that the Directors were no more clear-
headed than they. Hoche, leaving his troops to assume his ministerial chair
in Paris, had been outraged upon learning that Barras' order, to bring his
regiments to within striking distance of Paris, had not had the approval of
the Directors, and a bitter quarrel ensued between himself and Barras. It
did not help matters when the leaders of the right began attacking Hoche's
appointment, asserting—correctly—that since the general had not yet
reached his fortieth birthday, he was not eligible, under the Constitution,
for appointment as a minister. The appointment was withdrawn, and
Hoche was sent back to his troops. Meanwhile, the councils had enacted a
decree, dear to the hearts of the royalists, ordering the suppression of the
political clubs—including, of course, Talleyrand's Constitutional Club.

The right, momentarily appeased by these easy victories, now granted
the Directors a brief interlude of peace. And this was precisely what the executive branch needed to complete its plans. It was obvious that the fanaticism of the right, as demonstrated by Pichegru's involvement with Louis
XVIII, must result eventually in a *coup* which would simultaneously restore the throne and, even worse, inaugurate another Terror—but this time
it would be a White Terror, the first victims of which would be every prominent regicide (among whom Barras, Reubell, Carnot, and La Revellière
were conspicuous), as well as the former members of the Assembly and the
Convention. In these circumstances, something must be done, and done
immediately.

While the Directors were puzzling out their plans in the days following
Hoche's fall from the Ministry of War, another message arrived from Bonaparte. This was a manifesto and a threat rather than a report, and it was
addressed to the two councils, which had been complaining, in an obvious
attempt to discredit the Directors, of Bonaparte's juggling of territories in
Italy. This, coming upon the heels of the discovery of Pichegru's treachery,
was too much. "Speaking in the name of eighty thousand men," Bonaparte
thundered from across the Alps, "I warn you that the days when cowardly
lawyers and contemptible chatterers could send valiant soldiers to be
butchered are over and done with!" A similar message arrived from
Hoche's Army of the Sambre and Meuse, even more threatening in tone.

---

vence, then in Verona, had taken the title of Louis XVIII and, on June 24, issued a proclamation
threatening punishment of the revolutionaries and the reestablishment of the *ancien régime*. Louis
XVIII, therefore, as legitimate pretender to the throne of France, was the figure around whom rallied the royalists of France in their plans for a restoration, and for the benefit of whom Pichegru's
intrigue had been inaugurated.

When the councils complained to the Directors of these threats, they were told flatly that while such statements by the military might be illegal, the complaints that they expressed were legitimate.

The stage was now set for the confrontation between the councils and the Directors. Or rather for the confrontation between the Bourbon partisans on the one side and Talleyrand and Bonaparte on the other. For the Minister of Foreign Affairs seemed to be the one member of the government who was not unduly concerned about the course taken by events. Madame de la Tour du Pin, who had left Albany and returned to France, noted in her *Journal* both the loud boasting of the royalists and the reaction of Talleyrand at this time: "People thought me absurd when I told them, as I knew perfectly well to be the case, that Monsieur de Talleyrand knew everything that was being plotted and that he was laughing up his sleeve at it."

Though Madame de la Tour's statement perhaps attributes an exaggerated degree of self-confidence to the Foreign Minister, the fact was that Talleyrand had already appraised the situation and decided upon a course of action to counter the growing power of the right. In this, he was of one mind with Barras, La Revellière, and even Reubell. But the problem was not so much to come up with a plan as to find a man capable of executing it. Hoche was approached first. He was, after all, a sincere republican, but he was a simple soldier, straightforward and guileless, with no noticeable ambitions and therefore with no taste for intrigue. A hurried exchange of letters between Talleyrand and Bonaparte produced a name acceptable to both, and to Barras: General Pierre-François Augereau. A rabid Jacobin and vehement antiaristocrat, who was in due course to become Duke de Castiglione, Augereau could be counted upon to take merciless action against any royalist plot, real or imagined.

The events of the early days of September, 1797, are given only a few lines in the *Mémoires*:

> At home, a faction was plotting the overthrow of the existing order of things . . . what soon became evident was the weakness of this faction, easily overcome, and whose real or pretended leaders were, in the course of a few hours, arrested for the most part, charged with plotting against the established government, convicted without being heard, and transported to Cayenne, by virtue of what was then termed a law.

Thus Talleyrand describes what was in effect the first *coup d'état* of his career, the Eighteenth Fructidor, Year V, according to the revolutionary calendar; September 4, 1797, following the computations of the rest of Europe. The truth was that the *coup* was not entirely of his own doing. That it was conceived with the cooperation of the triumvirs of the Directorate is likely; that it was planned by Talleyrand and Barras is probable. But that it was essentially a *coup* engineered jointly by Talleyrand and Bonaparte is certain. It was the first effort in a collaboration which was to continue, though not always smoothly, for years. And it set the pattern for success which was to continue until the final rift between the two men would send Bonaparte off to exile and death on St. Helena, and Talleyrand on to power under the Restoration.

The plan evolved in discussions with Augereau, who was now commander of the Paris military district, and his friend Louis Chérin, commander of the guard of the Directory, was simple, and effective. At dawn of the Eighteenth Fructidor, Paris was declared to be under martial law. Posters were displayed throughout the city, denouncing an "Anglo-royalist plot" to overthrow the Republic, and a decree was promulgated to the effect that anyone who tried to instigate the restoration of the monarchy or of the Constitution of 1793 would be shot without trial. A group of deputies presented itself at the Tuileries to protest but was dispersed by Augereau's troops. The leaders of the right—Pichegru, Dominique Ramel, and Amédée Willot—had been arrested when martial law was proclaimed, and the royalists, without leaders, were also without any plan of resistance. Barthélemy and Carnot, it was hoped, would save themselves by flight and spare the government the embarrassment of arresting them. Carnot did so, but Barthélemy, for some reason, had remained in Paris and was therefore arrested and sent to the Temple. Meanwhile, small groups of Barras' supporters from the two councils met and annulled the elections which had resulted in the packing of the two bodies with royalists.* By noon of the Nineteenth Fructidor the royalists were either in prison or hiding in fear of their lives, and the government was in full control. "Paris is quiet," Talleyrand immediately reported to Bonaparte. "Augereau has conducted himself perfectly. One can see that he has had a good teacher. A group of terrorists attempted to create a disturbance, but a few words from Augereau, spoken in a firm tone, sent them back to the *faubourgs*, and nothing has been heard of them since." Augereau's report, in keeping with its author's reputation, was laconic: "General: my mission is accomplished. The crisis, which it was feared would be terrible, has passed off like a holiday."

Talleyrand had spent the Eighteenth Fructidor as though it were indeed a holiday, playing cards with his friends at home. Two or three times every hour, a messenger would arrive from Barras or from Augereau with news of events. Talleyrand listened attentively, nodded, and occasionally smiled, and then he continued with his game of whist. The day held no surprises

---

* Forty-nine *départements* had their elections totally annulled, and others had them partially set aside. Altogether, 214 deputies were eliminated, 65 of them being deported, under the new law, to French Guiana, along with Pichegru, Barthélemy, Ramel, and Carnot.

for him, and knowing that it would not, he had arranged to spend it as comfortably as possible, among friends.

There is some evidence that following the *coup d'état*, Talleyrand had hoped that he and Bonaparte would be elected to replace Barthélemy and Carnot as Directors,* but he was disappointed in this ambition. Barras, Reubell, and La Revellière, having just rid themselves of a pair of difficult colleagues, were reluctant to take on new Directors who might well prove even more intractable. They therefore filled the vacant places with two nonentities, François de Neufchâteau, a poet, and Merlin de Douai, a lawyer. This, while a disappointment to Talleyrand, was hardly a disaster. The Directory, he knew, had not been given new life; it had merely been granted a reprieve from death, one which would last until the particular "concurrence of events" which might bring a more capable regime to power should be realized. "One must be willing to act," he explained years later, "not in order to place oneself at the service of unworthy men or of unworthy causes, but in order to make use of such men and such causes in such a way as to make the future better than the present."

It appears that, by the time of the *coup* of the Eighteenth Fructidor, Talleyrand and Bonaparte had reached a degree of mutual confidence which allowed each to glimpse the inner feelings of the other. Bonaparte's letters to Paris, Talleyrand notes, were now "carefully worded, in such a way that it was obvious he wished to appear in a role different from that which he had hitherto played on the stage of public life." While explaining to Talleyrand the peace negotiations which he was conducting with the Austrians, Bonaparte put forward candidly his entire political program, all predicated upon his intense discontent with the makeshift and therefore unsatisfactory and temporary nature of the Directory: "Despite our good opinion of ourselves," he wrote, "we Frenchmen are amateurs in the political arena. We do not even understand, as yet, the difference between the executive, legislative, and judiciary functions. In a state such as ours, where all authority issues from the nation—where the people are sovereign—the power of the government must be regarded as representative of the people, who rule in accordance with the Constitution." Having dared express his disenchantment with the Directors, Bonaparte proceeded, a week later, to lift the veil still higher: "Our actions must be guided by sound policy, and such a policy is nothing more than that which results from the calculation of combinations and chances. If we adopt such a policy, then, for a long time to come, we shall be both the greatest nation, and the arbiter, of Europe." Such expressions of ambition may be interpreted as either national

---

* The letter on this subject to Bonaparte has been lost. Talleyrand's hopes and his disappointment are known only from Bonaparte's answer.

or personal in scope, but Bonaparte's concluding sentence was intended to leave no doubt in Talleyrand's mind either of their true meaning, or of the part which Bonaparte himself, and Talleyrand, might play in such great events: "Today these may seem the vague expectations of a visionary zealot. Yet the means are in our hands, and should fate be kind, within a few years there may be momentous happenings. A cold, tenacious, and far-sighted man will know how to translate them into reality."

Bonaparte knew he had found the man he required to understand his ambitions and "translate them into reality." Until the Italian campaign, he had been merely a soldier, though a very capable one. In Italy, however, he had been required by circumstances to assume the functions also of negotiator, statesman, and ruler. On his own, he decided on peace and war, destroyed ancient principalities and created new ones, and treated with sovereigns as an equal. In his decisions, Paris was not consulted; it was merely informed. In Milan, his headquarters, he had created a court, where he was waited upon by representatives of Italy's most ancient families who came seeking the conqueror's indulgence and favor. He posed as the liberator of Italy, promising the people the blessings of the Revolution and establishing republics whose constitutions seemed to redeem those promises. The Italians responded, at least at first, by applauding their liberator. Having tasted such power, Talleyrand knew, Bonaparte would never again be content merely to execute the orders of a far-off government, particularly a government such as the Directory, which Bonaparte described to his fellow generals as "fit only to piss on."

That Bonaparte not develop a craving for power was the last thing that Talleyrand wished. The general's "vague expectations" were no more visionary than Talleyrand's own. Nothing less than a Herculean effort would be required if France were once more to be reestablished as the dominant power of Europe and regain admission to the European family. That the Directory was incapable of that effort was obvious beyond a doubt, but that Bonaparte and Talleyrand together could bring both sufficient energy and adequate genius to the task was certain. From the beginnings of his relationship with Bonaparte, therefore, Talleyrand saw opening up a glorious road into the future, both for France and for himself. The old bourgeoisie of the *ancien régime* and the new bourgeoisie created by the Revolution had now triumphed over both the right and the left. At the same time, a star was rising in France which seemed to embody the aspirations and interests of that bourgeoisie. This was the "concurrence of events" of which Talleyrand spoke and which had been realized perhaps sooner than he had hoped. It was also the beginning of the series of "combinations and chances" which Bonaparte recognized as the foundations of proper policy.

Talleyrand was perhaps the first, outside of Bonaparte's own family, to discern that the general was something more, and something infinitely more complex, than a soldier, and he was the first to tie his own fortunes to those of Bonaparte. At first glance, it is difficult to see what the two men had in common to make such a relationship viable or even possible. Talleyrand was the product of the ancient aristocratic traditions of France, while Bonaparte was the offspring of an impoverished family of dubious nobility, the native of a remote and savage island known only for the ubiquity of its bandits and the poverty of its inhabitants. Talleyrand was outwardly cold, reserved, and withdrawn. The most tragic and stupendous events could, at best, evoke a few words, and then the curtain of ice descended again. It was a role, assumed as the *persona* which he found most useful in public life and which he abandoned to some extent only in his personal relations. Bonaparte, however, was a man of raging passions, impulsive, often arbitrary in his judgments, and unpredictable even to his most intimate associates. He gave the impression of a volcano constantly on the point of erupting. Moreover, the differences between the two men ran deep beneath the surface. Talleyrand lived for pleasure—for the pleasures that power could bring and for those that money could buy. His delight lay in the company of his friends, in sparkling conversation, in the creature comforts with which he surrounded himself. Power was nothing more than a means, a tool to be wielded for the good of France and the peace of Europe, but also for his own benefit, as the means to pleasure. From that perspective, politics became preeminently the "science of the possible"—the art of attaining, with the least possible expenditure of effort, the best possible result. Bonaparte, however, conceived of power and glory as the purpose of his being, and the pursuit of those qualities as overriding all considerations, political as well as moral. Within the context of his megalomania, the distinction between the possible and the impossible did not exist and could never exist. This final divergence of views alone would one day bring Talleyrand and Bonaparte to a parting of the ways. At this stage in their relationship, however, each was what the other needed, and this consideration was sufficient to ensure mutual confidence and to create a spirit of collaboration. Bonaparte had military fame. At the age of twenty-eight, he had conquered Italy and brought Austria to its knees. For this, his sword alone had been sufficient. But he also had political ambitions, and for the realization of these he had need of Talleyrand, a statesman and politician of proved ability and discretion. And Talleyrand, for his part, saw in Bonaparte the soldier who had both the means and the will to impose order in France and to make peace in Europe. The encounter of Talleyrand and Bonaparte in history was that rare event, the confluence of complementary forces at the moment of perfect opportunity. Both recognized it as such, and both were determined to take advantage of it.

The correspondence between Talleyrand and Bonaparte during the latter months of 1797, after the *coup* of the Eighteenth Fructidor, was no longer that of a Foreign Minister with a victorious general in the field, but of
men united in a common cause, bound together by common ambitions,
and therefore indulgent of each other's faults. Bonaparte was, at that time,
negotiating the Treaty of Campo Formio with Austria, and Talleyrand,
recognizing that his correspondent was not a man to follow the dictates of
distant governments, offered only advice, and not instructions. "If we have
the Rhine as a boundary," he wrote, "and if Venice does not fall into Austrian hands, then we shall have a peace worthy of Bonaparte." But when
Bonaparte, on his own and against the wishes of both Talleyrand and the
Directors, handed over Venice to the Emperor of Austria, the Foreign
Minister could see that no purpose would be served by contesting the *fait
accompli*. The Directors did not dare protest their volatile general's action,
let alone reprimand him, and Talleyrand did not find it politic to do so.
"You have concluded the peace," he wrote on hearing of Campo Formio,
"and it is a peace in the best style of Bonaparte. You have my heartfelt
congratulations. Words do not suffice to express what I feel at this moment. The Directors are content, and the people are delighted. There may
be some outcry in Italy [over Venice], but that is not important. . . ."

Bonaparte's sacrifice of Venice contrary to Talleyrand's advice—"we are
not in Italy to become traffickers in nations," he had written—was, nonetheless, something of a blow. Talleyrand knew the power of public opinion,
and while he was perfectly willing to disregard it with respect to his private
life, he was and would remain reluctant to do so at the political level. Bonaparte's action, undertaken so as to obtain territorial concessions from
Austria in other parts of Europe, destroyed the posture, so carefully maintained until then, of France as a liberator and placed it, in the eyes of the
Italians and of the whole of Europe, on the level of the autocratic states
whose diplomacy was characterized by a willingness and even an eagerness
to "traffic in nations." Such an action, compromising as it was to France's
true interests, was alarming. Also alarming was the ambition to increase
the territory of France, which Talleyrand had always opposed. "We now
have learned," he had written in 1792, "that the only true, useful, and reasonable superiority, the only one which is worthy of free and enlightened
men, is that of being master of one's own nation and of never making the
ridiculous claim that one is master of other nations." This was a principle
to which Talleyrand adhered throughout his long career, and it must have
distressed him to see his newly found collaborator so unmindful of it at the
very beginning, and to realize that, as he was planning for the restoration
of order in France and the maintenance of peace in Europe, Bonaparte
was dreaming of territories and conquest and the extension of France's

boundaries. Yet it was, as with the Directory, necessary "to make use of such men and such events in such a way as to make the future better than the present." He therefore swallowed his disappointment, and perhaps his pride; for Bonaparte had announced that he would visit Paris, and Talleyrand was determined that nothing must disturb the harmony of his first meeting with the man who held the sword that France, and Talleyrand, needed.

Bonaparte reached Paris on December 5, 1797, and went immediately to Josephine's house in the rue Chantereine, which a grateful Directory was shortly to rebaptize the rue de la Victoire in honor of its chief resident. Early in the evening—he had arrived at 5 P.M.—he sent a message to Talleyrand, asking if the Foreign Minister would receive him the following morning. Talleyrand replied that he awaited the general's pleasure, and an appointment was made for the next day, at 11 A.M. Madame de Staël was agog with curiosity to meet the phenomenal general who was the hero of the hour; and Talleyrand, still on intimate terms with her and in her debt, moreover, for her intervention with Barras only a few months before, immediately sent her a note inviting her to meet Bonaparte. "By 10 A.M. she was in my drawing room," Talleyrand reports. "There were also some other persons, whom curiosity had attracted to my house. I remember that Bougainville* was there.

"When the general was announced, I went to meet him. While crossing the room, I introduced Madame de Staël to him, but he paid very little attention to her. Bougainville was the only one he was interested in. . . ." This was the first of several cuts which Bonaparte was to bestow upon Germaine de Staël, the accumulation of which was eventually to earn him her enmity.

Talleyrand's *Mémoires* contain only the briefest report of this first meeting, yet it appears that the initial impression was a favorable one: "At first sight, he seemed to me to have a charming face. Victory is most becoming in a young hero with fine eyes, a pale and almost consumptive look. We entered my study. Our first conversation was quite confidential on his part. He spoke in kind terms of my appointment as Foreign Minister, and he insisted on the pleasure it gave him to correspond with a person so different from the Directors." Then, as though intimidated by Talleyrand's name and reputation, the general made an attempt to establish their relationship on a more personal basis. "Almost abruptly," Talleyrand notes, "he said to me: 'You are the nephew of the Archbishop of Rheims, who is with Louis

---

* Louis de Bougainville, the diplomat, navigator, and explorer whose three-month journey around the world, in 1766, had made him something of a hero.

XVIII.' (I noticed that he did not say, 'with the Count de Lille.' *) Then he added, 'I also have an uncle who is an archdeacon in Corsica.† It was he who helped educate me. You know that, in Corsica, an archdeacon is the same as a bishop in France.' "

After this exchange, Talleyrand and Bonaparte returned to the drawing room, which was now packed with visitors, and then went together for the general to pay his respects to the Directors. "The hesitations and jealousy of the Directors caused Bonaparte a certain annoyance," Talleyrand reports. No doubt, Talleyrand would have been astonished if Barras and his associates had reacted otherwise. At a moment when no one in Paris had anything good to say about the Directors, Bonaparte was the idol of the city. "All Paris rang with his name," wrote Hortense de Beauharnais, Josephine's daughter. "The people thronged in such vast numbers to cheer 'the Conqueror of Italy' that the sentries stationed at the gateway to the house on the rue de la Victoire could hardly hold them back." But both Talleyrand and Bonaparte had had too much experience with "the people" to have any illusions about their support. The Directory, having been propped up by Augereau's intervention, had not yet run its course, and any attempt to replace it at that moment would have been premature. "Bah," Bonaparte said, "the people would flock just as eagerly to see me if I were on my way to the guillotine." In order to avoid precisely that possibility, Talleyrand and Bonaparte, throughout the conqueror's stay in Paris, emphasized not his victories, but his modesty and his lack of ambition. On December 10 a ceremony was held at the Luxembourg in which Talleyrand formally presented the general to the Directors and to the nation. Of the man, standing in a simple uniform before the crowd, Talleyrand said, "Ah, far from fearing what some would call his ambition, I feel the time will perhaps come when we will find it necessary to tear him from his studious retreat." It was noted with approval by the people that throughout his address Talleyrand never referred to Bonaparte by any title other than "Citizen." Bonaparte himself took his cue from Talleyrand's prudence and avoided public appearances. He barely ventured out of his house, and there he received only a small circle of relatives and friends. On the few occasions when he went to the theater and was cheered by the audience, he drew back into the recesses of his box so as not to be seen. The plan seems to have worked. By December 20 the official *Moniteur* reported that Bonaparte was "staying at his wife's house in the rue Chantereine, which is

* The title used by Louis XVIII as an émigré.

† This was Joseph Fesch, brother of Napoleon's mother, who was archdeacon of the cathedral at Ajaccio. Fesch, however, was not an archdeacon in 1797. Being unwilling to swear to the Constitution of the Clergy, he had put aside his cassock and was then serving as a purveyor of supplies to his nephew's army in Italy. He would later become Archbishop of Lyons and cardinal.

small, modest, and unpretentious. He goes out rarely and, when he does, it is alone in a carriage drawn by two horses. He can be seen frequently walking in his little garden."

One of his rare outings was to a magnificent dinner given by Talleyrand at the Hôtel Galliffet, his official residence in the rue du Bac, in honor of Madame Bonaparte. The affair was originally scheduled for December 25. But, as Josephine tarried on the road between Moulins and Paris,* it had to be postponed until January 3, 1798, and the hundreds of trees, shrubs, and flowers with which the residence had been festooned had to be changed three times in the interval. "I spared no trouble to make the fete brilliant and attractive," Talleyrand confesses, "although, in this, I experienced some difficulty on account of the vulgarity of the Directors' wives." At ten o'clock Bonaparte entered, and the 500 guests fell instantly silent as the orchestra struck up a new quadrille, the Bonaparte.

Madame de Staël, of course, was one of the guests, and she was as determined as ever to add Bonaparte to her collection of protégés. Seeing the general so surrounded as to be unapproachable, she turned to a mutual friend, Vincent Arnault, and asked him to take her to the general. Arnault, knowing Bonaparte's abhorrence of learned ladies, attempted to dissuade her, but she would not listen. Taking the helpless man's arm, she pushed through the crowd, and at last confronted Bonaparte. Arnault recorded the scene:

> A crowd instantly collected to catch the exchange between these two illustrious protagonists, as if it had been an encounter between the Queen of Sheba and King Solomon. Making it clear that she considered him the most eminent man of the age, and undeterred by the hostility and reserve obvious in the eminent man's face and voice, Madame de Staël persisted in plying him with questions:
> "Who is the woman, General, whom you could love the most?"
> "My wife, madame."
> "Yes, of course. But who is the one whom you could most admire?"
> "The one who is the best housekeeper."
> "Very well. But who is the woman whom you would consider most distinguished among her sex?"
> "The one who bears the greatest number of children."

This time, the general won his release. He bowed, kissed Germaine's hand, and left the group.

The encounter set all Paris talking, and Germaine was bitterly humiliated. She could not understand that while her mind might captivate such men as Talleyrand, Narbonne, and Benjamin Constant, Bonaparte's pas-

---

* She was in the company, it was later discovered, of a young man named Hippolyte Charles, a lover who had followed her from Italy.

sions were of a more elementary sort. Josephine's lovely face and empty head were precisely what suited him best. Nor could she comprehend that by attempting to thrust herself upon Bonaparte and thus forcing him to reject her, she was placing Talleyrand in the position of having to choose between herself and Bonaparte. There was not much doubt, in the circumstances, of where his choice would fall.

In describing Bonaparte's visit to Paris, Talleyrand says that his purpose was "to propose the conquest of Egypt to the Directors." It is certain that the two men had discussed the project in their letters. "Why should we not make sure of Malta?" Bonaparte had asked. "With Malta and Corfu in our hands, we should be masters of the Mediterranean. If we cannot dislodge England from the Cape, we must take Egypt." Talleyrand, whose paper, read before the institute, on "Advantages to Be Derived from New Colonies" had proposed, or rather resurrected, precisely this idea, had wholly agreed. He had, upon receipt of Bonaparte's letter in October, 1797, brought the idea before the Directors, with the comment that although great commercial advantages would accrue to France from such an undertaking, "the leader of this expedition would not have to be a man of exceptional military talent." It seems that Talleyrand's purpose was to have Egypt, but at the same time not be deprived of Bonaparte's presence in Europe. The Directors had neither agreed nor disagreed to the plan at that time, and Bonaparte's visit was no doubt connected in some way with the project. Having subdued Italy, redivided it according to his satisfaction, and made peace with the Austrians, he was eager for new employment. The Directors at first offered him command of the Army of England, which he declined on the ground that the chance of success was too slender to warrant an invasion of that country. As an alternate plan, he suggested instead that England be attacked in a vital spot, its commercial lifeline to India, and for this purpose, an attack against Malta and Egypt was essential.

Talleyrand made a formal presentation of this proposal to the Directors on March 5, 1798, after many days and nights spent with Bonaparte in its preparation. Having described the advantages of a colony on the opposite shores of the Mediterranean, he pointed out that Egypt, though nominally a part of the Turkish Empire, was in fact the property of no one, since the sultan's authority over it was virtually nonexistent. Moreover, if France did not take Egypt, Austria or Russia would certainly move into the breach and make impossible French domination of the Mediterranean. Finally, he noted, the Mameluke beys who ruled Egypt as feudal warlords had subjected French merchants to intolerable harassment, and military intervention under the color of protecting French interests would be easily justifiable. The Directors, after some discussion, approved. The expedition would sail at the beginning of summer, with Bonaparte as its commander.

It is not difficult to guess the reasons for the Directors' eagerness to see Bonaparte in Egypt. The dangerously popular general and his equally dangerous Jacobin veterans of Italy—most of whom would accompany him to Egypt—would be comfortably out of the way on the banks of the Nile. Moreover, the Directory, during 1796 and 1797, had managed to avoid bankruptcy only because of massive infusions of Italian booty thoughtfully dispatched by Bonaparte to Paris. It was hoped that Egypt would prove as profitable as Italy. Talleyrand's motives, however, are not as easy to discern. Joseph Fouché stated later that Talleyrand simply wished to be rid of Bonaparte and that he had conceived the Egyptian campaign as "a brilliant exile." There would come a time when Talleyrand might wish to be conveniently rid of Bonaparte, but that time was not yet. The Foreign Minister had everything to lose and nothing to gain from the prolonged absence of his collaborator on a campaign which, as Bonaparte himself pointed out, would "take anywhere from six months to six years." Talleyrand's reason both for proposing the expedition and supporting it was much subtler than that. His task as Foreign Minister, as he had described it, was "to try to obtain the readmission of France to the councils of Europe." With Italy prostrate at France's feet, Austria ingloriously defeated, Britain swept by a wave of invasion hysteria, and Bonaparte perhaps poised for another blow at an objective the identity of which the sovereigns of Europe could only surmise, France was perhaps as far away from acceptance among the law-abiding nations of Europe as it had been during the heyday of the Convention. It had not helped that Bonaparte had struck terror into the hearts of Europe's legitimate regimes by not only conquering Italy, but also, and more ominously, by dispossessing several ancient dynasties in order to create French-style democracies—the Cisalpine and Transpadane republics—in the northern part of the peninsula. If Europe was to have peace, and France the opportunity to reestablish order at home, the minds of the sovereigns must be set at rest; and the most effective way to do this was to remove the man whose presence seemed a continual threat to the monarchies of Europe. The Prussian ambassador in Paris, Sandoz Rollin, who was a friend of Talleyrand, reported to Berlin that the Foreign Minister had explained to him, in confidence, the real reason for the Egyptian expedition: ". . . to distract the [French] government and its military forces from those revolutionary ideas which are creating such an uproar in Europe. For the concept of a universal republic is as much an impossibility as was that of a universal monarchy." The thought is entirely Talleyrand's. So is its studied communication "in confidence" to the Prussian ambassador, who, as foreseen, immediately passed it on to Berlin, where, as Talleyrand knew, it would do the most good.

In mid-May, before sailing from Toulon, Bonaparte paid Talleyrand a final visit. He found the Foreign Minister in bed, ill. As he was making his farewell, the general suddenly blurted that he had not a franc to his name and that he had no idea of how he would live during the few days that remained to him in Paris. Talleyrand, no doubt thunderstruck that the conqueror of Italy, who had so generously filled the coffers of the government and the pockets of the Directors, had neglected to provide for himself, said, "Open my desk, and you will find 100,000 francs. Take them. You may repay me when you return." Thereupon, Talleyrand recorded, Bonaparte "threw his arms around my neck. I was greatly moved at the sight of his joy." *

Bonaparte sailed, with 50,000 men, on May 19, 1798. Before leaving, however, he and Talleyrand had discussed the latter's role during Bonaparte's absence and had arrived at an agreement—one which hinged on Talleyrand's resignation of his ministry.

> I had ascertained by then [Talleyrand explains] that what little evil I could prevent was insignificant, and if any real good could be worked, it could not be until later. The intention I had of resigning had induced me to take certain precautions. I had acquainted General Bonaparte with my resolution before his departure for Egypt. He fully approved the reasons which led me to take it and kindly used his influence with the Directors to solicit for me the appointment of ambassador to Constantinople, in the event that it was possible to come to some understanding with the sultan.

Bonaparte's recollection is slightly different:

> It had been agreed with the Directors and Talleyrand that immediately after the departure of the expedition to Egypt, negotiations should be opened with the sultan concerning the object of this expedition. Talleyrand himself was to be the negotiator and *was to start for Constantinople twenty-four hours after the expeditionary corps to Egypt had left the port of Toulon.* This promise, expressly requested and positively given, was forgotten. Not only did Talleyrand remain in Paris, but no negotiation took place.

There is little doubt that Talleyrand promised to go immediately to Constantinople to justify the French invasion of Egypt to the Turkish sultan

---

* "When Bonaparte had become First Consul, he repaid the loan and, at the same time, asked Talleyrand, "What was your reason for lending me this money? I tried a hundred times to decide what your motive was." Talleyrand replied, "I had no motive. I was feeling very ill, and I realized that I might never see you again. You were young, and you had made a great impression on me. I therefore decided, without any ulterior motive whatever, to help you." "In that case," Bonaparte said, "you were a fool."

and thereby, it was hoped, to forestall possible Turkish intervention. And there is no doubt at all that he did not fulfill his promise. Many reasons have been alleged for this apparent breach of faith on Talleyrand's part. The most common—and that which has most often passed into the history books—is that Talleyrand's sin of omission was a deliberate betrayal of Bonaparte, an abandonment of his associate to his fate on the sands of North Africa. That, certainly, is the explanation put forward by Bonaparte himself, twenty years later, when embittered by defeat and exile. It is also the least likely explanation. Again, there is no acceptable motive for betrayal and no evidence for it. There is, however, much evidence to show that Talleyrand, whether or not he was willing to go to Constantinople, was prevented from doing so. First, the ship, the *Badine*, sent by Bonaparte from Malta to transport Talleyrand to Constantinople, was captured en route to Toulon by the British. More important, however, was the fact that, immediately upon Bonaparte's departure, the position of France, both internally and at the level of international relations, began to deteriorate alarmingly. Talleyrand, as some of his contemporaries pointed out gleefully, was hardly master of his own actions, and self-appointment to a far-off embassy when France was faced with a serious threat of war, not only from England but also from Russia and once again from Austria, was clearly out of the question. The Directors, Barras particularly, would not permit it. Weighing the evidence on both sides of the question, the explanation for Talleyrand's "first betrayal" of Bonaparte seems simply to have been that he was not allowed, either by circumstances or by the Directors, to go to Constantinople. There was unfinished work to be done in France, and Talleyrand was the man most qualified to do it.

Much of this unfinished business had to do with the United States, with which France's relations had worsened to the point where it seemed almost inevitable that war would be declared. Since 1793, in fact, hostilities of a sort had existed on the high seas, with the ships of the Directory, manned by red-bonneted ruffians claiming to be Jacobins, seizing American ships under the pretext that they were trading with England (as they were). By the time of Talleyrand's appointment in 1797, the American Secretary of State could report to the Congress that more than 300 American vessels had been captured by French warships and privateers, mostly in the West Indies but also in the Atlantic. President John Adams, hoping to be able to maintain the United States' neutrality in the war between France and England, had sent a mission to Paris whose purpose it was to reach some sort of agreement with the Directory. The three delegates—Elbridge Gerry, John Marshall, and Charles Cotesworth Pinckney—arrived in Paris at a moment which, for them, was most unpropitious. It was October, 1797;

Austria had just been beaten; and the Directors, unaccustomed as they were to success in any form, were drunk with victory. It did not make the emissaries' task any more pleasant that immediately upon establishing contact with the new Minister of Foreign Affairs, they were informed by his agents that it would be useless to pursue negotiations until they had both made a substantial gift of cash to M. de Talleyrand and agreed to a loan which was clearly to the profit solely of the individual Directors.

The agents in question became so well known that they gave their pseudonyms to the ensuing embroglio, which was thereafter remembered as the X Y Z Affair. The amount of the "gift" solicited was 50,000 pounds sterling, and it was well understood that the money would be used to ensure the sympathetic understanding not only of Talleyrand himself, but of the five Directors. The American envoys, outraged at this manifestation of Old World corruption, refused indignantly to negotiate under such circumstances, and shortly afterward Marshall and Pinckney left Paris.* Since this was considered sufficient to save American honor, Gerry stayed on in Europe in a semiofficial capacity, to see whether Talleyrand could not be made to see reason or at least to lower his price.

Marshall and Pinckney, upon arrival in the United States, made a detailed written report to President Adams, who presented it to the Congress in April, 1798. The "X Y Z dispatches," as they were called, were subsequently published and created a great stir in the United States and a lesser one in France, where such episodes were viewed in a different light. Germaine de Staël, alarmed at criticism of the man whom she considered her creature, defended him valiantly in the salons of Paris, even though his position was clearly indefensible. Finally, in the throes of great emotion, she presented herself at the ministry and, with tears and loud cries alternating with ultimatums, demanded that Talleyrand clear himself of the charges being made against him. Otherwise, she insisted, his enemies would have a golden opportunity to force his resignation. He listened quietly to Germaine, uttering not a word himself, as she declaimed on the topics of honor and responsibility. Finally, he excused himself politely and left the room. He did not return. In Talleyrand's world, there was a sole unforgivable sin: bad taste. Germaine had sinned once in thrusting herself un-

---

* The American negotiators seemed unaware of a peculiar precedent for the exchange of "gifts" in Franco-American relations. In 1776 an American named Silas Deane was sent to Paris by Congress to purchase a huge amount of arms, clothing, and ammunition for Washington's army. According to documents in the Ministry of Foreign Affairs, Deane received a payment of 24,000 livres as a *secours extraordinaire*, or "extraordinary aid," from the king's private funds. (*Décisions du roi, 1760–1792*, "Affaires de l'Amérique," 7 décembre 1780.) Though Deane's "sweetness," as Talleyrand's euphemism has it, was considerably less than that demanded by Talleyrand, it should be remembered that he was not required, so far as is known, to share it with the members of Congress.

wanted upon Bonaparte in an encounter that had made her the butt of the gossips' jokes. This, for the sake of the services that Germaine had rendered him, Talleyrand was willing, not to forgive, but perhaps to ignore. Her intrusion not only into his ministry, but also into his private affairs, he could not forgive, and the incident marked the end of their amicable relationship. Talleyrand composed its epitaph when he related Germaine's behavior to a friend, remarking: "Madame de Staël has only one fault: She is unbearable."

Talleyrand did unbend to the extent of inserting an unsigned article in the *Moniteur* of June 9, 1798, pointing out that no minister could reasonably be expected to accept responsibility for the indiscretions of his agents. There he was content to let the matter of the 50,000 pounds rest. So far as the negotiations themselves were concerned, he had already contacted Gerry and succeeded in persuading him of France's good intentions. Bonaparte had just sailed for his Egyptian adventure with the cream of France's armies, England was becoming increasingly active in the Mediterranean, and Russia and Austria seemed on the point of forming a new coalition against France. The last thing the Directors now wanted was a war with America, and Talleyrand was instructed to bring to a happy conclusion the negotiations that had begun so inauspiciously. By the fall of 1798 the matter had been patched up, with French ships being ordered to respect the vessels of neutral countries. An official explanation of the X Y Z Affair was offered, in which it was suggested that the naïve American representatives in Paris had been the victims of charlatans and that Pinckney and Marshall had first cloistered themselves in a hotel and then left France before they could be received by Talleyrand or by the Directors. As transparent as Talleyrand's explanation was, it was accepted by a large part of the American public. It was an election year in the United States, and Talleyrand's communication, couched in terms of injured dignity, was seized upon by the Republican Party as proof that the entire X Y Z Affair had been a hoax perpetrated by warmongering Federalists.

The Republicans were in error. Talleyrand had never made a secret of the fact that he accepted money from foreign powers, and he would have been amused—or offended, as he was at Madame de Staël's reproaches— at any suggestion that the nature of his office required him to refuse gifts offered by, or even solicited from, governments eager for his consideration. "The Minister of Foreign Relations," Sandoz Rollin wrote to Berlin, "has declared loftily that he loves money and that he is determined, when he retires from office, not to be forced to go on the public dole. . . . I suggest therefore that it might be useful to present him with a gift. It is difficult, at this time, to estimate the size of it, but I should think that it would have to be no less than 300,000 francs." In the same dispatch, the Prussian ambas-

sador also lists the gifts suggested for the other ministers and major functionaries of the Directory, and they come to a goodly total. But Prussia did
not complain. Compared to other European powers, Prussia was expected
to make only a modest contribution. The conclusion of the peace negotiations with Lisbon, in August, 1797, brought with it 8,000,000 francs from
the grateful Portuguese, of which the Directors received a million apiece
and Talleyrand the balance. This, however, was an extraordinary stroke of
luck. Spain, for the Foreign Minister's benevolent attention, had to pay
only a million and a half, which was distributed in the same manner. If one
may believe Barras, and usually one cannot, and Germaine de Staël, who
is hardly more reliable, during the two years of his ministry, Talleyrand, by
virtue of his insistence upon gifts, took in between 12,000,000 and
15,000,000 francs from as many governments.* Though the true figure may
not have been so large, there is no doubt that it was sufficient to constitute
the foundation and to set the precedent for the tremendous fortune that
Talleyrand was to accumulate during his lifetime.

It is perhaps impossible for later generations, or even the generation immediately following Talleyrand's own, to understand or to forgive the peculiar habits of men in public life before, during, and shortly after, the
Revolution. By the standards of posterity, the era was one of unbelievable
corruption, and the men who rose above venality—Robespierre and Bonaparte in France, Pitt in Britain—were so rare as to be regarded as curiosities, and rather embarrassing curiosities at that. The custom of statesmen,
public figures, and even sovereigns receiving "pensions" and "considerations" from foreign governments was so widespread as to be not merely a
fact of public life, but an institution hallowed by ancient traditions and
rendered acceptable by long usage. There was no implication that the recipients of these monies had sold their consciences or abandoned their
principles, but merely that they claimed remuneration for the advantages

---

* Barras, whose knowledge of Talleyrand's affairs came to him from Madame de Staël, is very
explicit in listing the amounts received by Talleyrand and their respective sources. Curiously
enough, he neglects to record either the collections that he made on his own initiative or the per-
centages that he received from Talleyrand's collections. There were sufficient witnesses available
to compensate for the Director's forgetfulness.

According to figures published in various articles and pamphlets during Talleyrand's lifetime,
between 1797 and 1804, as Minister of Foreign Affairs, he received more than 30,000,000 francs in
"gifts" from foreign powers. Talleyrand never contested or commented upon these estimates; indeed, it would have been out of character for him to have done so. His silence, therefore, is indicative of nothing. Chateaubriand, though undependable in so many respects, exaggerated only
slightly when he wrote that "Talleyrand, when he is not conspiring, is bargaining." To those of his
contemporaries who were familiar with Talleyrand's extraordinary venality, the figure of
30,000,000 francs did not seem unrealistic. Even his friends did not protest when, only a few
months after his death in 1838, Louis Bastide, in his *Vie politique et religieuse de Talleyrand-Périgord*, collated all these published figures into a long list of the countries that had contributed to
Talleyrand's wealth, with the amount of their respective contributions.

which their talents and the interests of the state had secured for foreign countries. Even Barras does not reproach Talleyrand in principle for accepting such compensation, but only for the excessive amounts of it. For there is no denying that Talleyrand was venal to a degree uncommon even in an age of venality or that he was so, and would remain so, until the day of his death.

Benjamin Constant reports that Talleyrand's words, upon receiving the news of his appointment to the Ministry of Foreign Relations had been: "An immense fortune! An immense fortune!" Given Constant's hatred of Talleyrand and Talleyrand's own temperament, the anecdote is almost certainly spurious. Yet it expresses accurately the view of public office which Talleyrand adopted and which, to his credit, he would never condescend to disguise. In the same spirit, it is never recorded that he accepted "gifts" except in exchange for real services rendered. Under the Empire, for example, he once received 4,000,000 florins from a group of Polish noblemen for the exercise of his influence in the restoration of their country to independence. When it transpired that owing to circumstances, he could not guide Napoleon in the proper direction, Talleyrand promptly returned the entire sum to its donors. Even in venality, Talleyrand possessed an honesty that was all his own.

The name of Count Casimir de Montrond figures prominently for the first time in Talleyrand's life in the course of the X Y Z Affair, as one of the agents more or less implicated in the scandal. Neither Montrond nor the men actually known as X, Y, and Z took amiss Talleyrand's disavowal of them. Montrond, though he seemed to have no official capacity, either at the ministry or elsewhere, was Talleyrand's "confidential man"—the one to whom he entrusted the most delicate matters in his professional, personal, and financial affairs. Montrond and Talleyrand at this time became the closest of friends, and they would remain so throughout their long and eventful lives. It was a relationship that alternately puzzled and repelled Talleyrand's other friends. (Montrond himself seemed to have no other friends.) Montrond was already notorious as a rake, gambler, duelist, and black sheep, in whose company no respectable woman, and few men, cared to be seen. He was remarkably handsome—*le beau Montrond,* he was called—and though he had a certain wit about him, his talents were not on an order that would excuse vices which, in a man of position and accomplishment, might be forgiven. One day, many years later, Madame de Laval asked Talleyrand, in Montrond's presence, to explain the basis of their friendship. "If you wish to know," Talleyrand answered, "then I should say that I am fond of Montrond because he has so few scruples." Montrond, not to be outdone, interjected: "You should also know, madame, that I, for my part, am fond of Talleyrand because he has no scruples at all." Montrond offered a similar explanation to one of his mistresses, who complained that he seemed excessively attached to Talleyrand: "Good heavens, madame. Who could resist loving a man with so many vices?" Talleyrand's approach was different. He remarked not so much on Montrond's vices, which were known to the whole world, as on his cleverness, and he offered as proof the fact that his friend "has not a franc to his name, he has no income at all, and yet he is able to spend 60,000 francs a year without incurring a single debt." In recognition of this apparently miraculous power to multiply money endlessly, Talleyrand dubbed his friend *l'Enfant Jesus de l'Enfer*—the Infant Jesus of Hell. At a more practical level, he opened both his heart and his house to this amiable, charming, worthless, clever scoundrel, whose sole virtue seems to have been absolute loyalty to Talleyrand alone and total discretion in all of the latter's affairs.

There were friends other than Montrond, of course, many of them dating from before the Revolution and from the days of the Legislative Assembly. For many of these, Talleyrand had found places in his ministry, not only because, being friends, they could be trusted, but also because, in choosing his friends, he had always been selective, insisting equally on intelligence and refinement. There, predictably, was Desrenaudes, former vicar-general of the diocese of Autun, who had served Talleyrand so well while the latter was in America and who now was responsible for preparing drafts of all of the ministry's reports, memorandums, and circulars. It sufficed for Talleyrand to outline a communication in the broadest lines for Desrenaudes, a few hours later, to be able to place a masterful draft on the minister's desk. There was also Count Alexandre Blanc d'Hauterive, formerly one of Talleyrand's circle in Philadelphia and now chief of one of the divisions of the ministry, who would himself, through Talleyrand's influence, one day become Minister of Foreign Affairs. These, as well as a few others such as La Besnardière, Talleyrand's secretary, Osmond, his aide, and Durand de Mareuil, head of a division, all were joined in a common loyalty to Talleyrand which would endure until either their deaths or his. He had the ability to evoke complete devotion in men as well as women, and it was rare, once friendship was given or received by Talleyrand, that it was ever withdrawn by either party.

There were exceptions, of course, such as Adélaïde de Flahaut and, more recently, Germaine de Staël. And the principles of loyalty did not necessarily extend, in every case, to the light-o'-loves who entered Talleyrand's life hurriedly and left just as hurriedly, often on the same night. It happened only once, however, that Talleyrand, after an affair, forgot both his principles and his background to such an extent as to embarrass, apparently with all deliberation, the lady who had been the recipient of his affections. The woman in question was Madame Delacroix, wife of Charles Delacroix, Talleyrand's ineffectual predecessor in the Ministry of Foreign Affairs. Talleyrand, upon his appointment, had designated Delacroix to be ambassador to Batavia, an honorable post, but one which necessitated Delacroix's removal to The Hague. In his absence, Talleyrand had, after replacing Delacroix in his ministerial chair, proceeded almost immediately to replace him also in his conjugal bed. Madame Delacroix, a mature beauty of thirty-nine, was ripe for adventure. Her husband for years had suffered from an infirmity which made it impossible for him to fulfill his marital duties, and as soon as he had been dispatched to The Hague, it seems that Madame Delacroix was unable to resist temptation in the form of the new minister. It is not likely that the affair was of long duration, for, in any event, Delacroix returned to Paris in early September, 1797, and underwent a surgical procedure which, though dangerous, was successful. At the end of November he was once more in perfect health. By then, however, Madame Delacroix gave every sign of being several months advanced in pregnancy, and, in April, 1798, she presented her puzzled husband with a son, Eugène Delacroix, who was to attain considerable fame in later years as a painter. The child's paternity, of course, was immediately ascribed to Talleyrand. It seems that this was indeed the case. Eugène grew up to bear a strong physical resemblance to his mother's lover and even exhibited many of his behavioral traits. Moreover, as a young artist, Eugène was in constant receipt of money and support, usually in the form of commissions, from a powerful source who insisted on anonymity.

The singular circumstance accompanying Eugène's birth, however, was that shortly before the event, an unprecedented article appeared in the *Moniteur*—the official gazette over which Talleyrand exercised great influence—explaining to "the friends of humanity" and under the pretext of a public service, the precise nature of Delacroix's ailment and giving full details of the operation which, as the article stated, had restored the former minister "to the full enjoyment of his virility." Even to the casual reader, the dates given in the article illustrate that it was clearly impossible for Delacroix to have been the father of his wife's child. It seems probable that Talleyrand, if not directly responsible for the insertion of the article, at least knew of its planned publication and did nothing to prevent it. Not even the most devoted of Talleyrand's friends or the least critical of his biographers have ever attempted to offer a reason or even an excuse for this apparently vindictive behavior on Talleyrand's part. So far as is known, there was no reason for hostility toward Delacroix and no sign that the parting between Madame Delacroix and Talleyrand, at the end of their brief intimacy, was anything but amicable. It is not impossible that one of

Talleyrand's enemies among the Directors—Reubell, for instance—was responsible for the article or that one of his friends, such as Montrond, had conceived it as an elaborate, if cruel, practical joke. There is, however, no evidence of any kind to support this theory, except the purely circumstantial consideration that such an act was contrary to Talleyrand's standard of personal conduct. But in the absence of such evidence the implication is clear that for reasons which remain mysterious, Talleyrand either initiated or permitted the publication of the article, the sole purpose of which seems to have been to embarrass both Delacroix and his wife.

Talleyrand's dalliance with Madame Charles Delacroix, whatever its consequences, was but one in a series of distractions which he took no more, or less, seriously than required by the occasion, which is to say that they were numerous, transitory, and quickly dismissed from his mind. At about the time of the Delacroix affair, however, there entered his life a woman who was to have a more lasting effect: Catherine-Noël Worlée Grand, who would, within a few years, become Princess de Talleyrand.

It is not known precisely when Catherine and Talleyrand met. Barras says that it was *à l'étranger*—abroad—which may mean London, Hamburg, or Philadelphia. Other contemporaries, who knew Talleyrand well, state that Montrond introduced them; or that Catherine was a friend of the Marquise de Ste.-Croix, who presented her protégée to the Foreign Minister; or that Catherine, without ever having met Talleyrand, appeared at his house late one night to ask his protection for her fortune, which was in English banks, in the event of a French invasion of the British Isles. (The latter version is the most colorful one and, for that reason, the one most commonly believed.) These are all theories favored by one or another of Talleyrand's biographers, or Catherine's, according to the degree of romanticism with which they are affected. The fact is that the circumstances of their meeting are unknown and may very well have been less dramatic than generally believed. Catherine Grand, as she was commonly known, moved about quickly, both in London and in Paris, and it is not unlikely that she and Talleyrand were ordinary social acquaintances long before they were lovers. Certainly, opportunity was not lacking. In Paris, during the days of the Constituent Assembly and the Legislative Assembly, the lady had enjoyed the protection of a number of eminent and influential lovers, among them the M. de Lessart (who was Foreign Minister during Talleyrand's mission to London in 1792), Louis Monneron, a rich banker, and Édouard Dillon, one of Marie-Antoinette's favorites—all of whom were well known to Talleyrand and any one of whom might have presented his mistress to the then Bishop of Autun.

Catherine's amatory successes in Paris were of a pattern with her earlier life. She had been born in India—at Tranquebar, a Danish possession—in

1762, the daughter of a French official. In 1777, the family moved to Chandernagore, where Catherine at the age of fifteen, became the mistress of George Francis Grand, an English civil servant, who married her the following year. In 1778, Grand was transferred to Calcutta, where Madame Grand's beauty soon attracted considerable attention, and great admiration on the part of Sir Philip Francis, a member of the King's Council. Sir Philip had the habit of jotting down in his diary the chief episode of each day, and on November 24, 1778, there is the entry *omnia vincit amor*— "love conquers all." A less happy incident is found under December 8: "This night, the devil to pay in the house of G. F. Grand, Esq." Sir Philip and Madame Grand had been caught *in flagrante* by the outraged husband. As a result, the lady was sent home to her parents, where Sir Philip came looking for her and persuaded her to return to Calcutta with him. They seemed to have lived more or less happily in the same house with Sir Philip's wife, Lady Francis, until 1782. In that year Catherine, for reasons unknown, sailed from India for Europe. She was in France, and in the arms of her several lovers, until August, 1792, when the horrors of the incipient Terror caused her to flee to England. There she enjoyed generous, though somewhat obscure, patronage, which, nonetheless, she abandoned to return to France in 1795. With her was a handsome young Genoese diplomat named Cristofero Spinola.

It seems to have been at some time in late 1796 or early 1797 that Talleyrand's attention was drawn, in one way or another, to Madame Grand. In any event, by the time of his appointment as Foreign Minister in July of that year, Talleyrand and Catherine were regarded as lovers, and he had set her up in a house of her own at Montmorency, where he visited her several days a month. In March of the following year, Barras tells us, Talleyrand intervened, and caused a great uproar among the Directors, as well as in the press, to quash the arrest of Catherine, whose earlier association with Spinola had resulted in an accusation of conspiracy being lodged against them. There is, however, no official record either of the arrest or of Talleyrand's intercession.*

Certainly, by 1798, arrest or not, there was a strong bond of affection between Talleyrand and Catherine Grand, one which would have easily influenced the minister to expose himself to public attack on behalf of his mistress. Catherine was wholly unlike any of Talleyrand's previous mistresses. Of comparatively low birth, with little education and, according to all reports, even less intelligence, she had, nonetheless, certain qualities which were designed to appeal strongly to a man fatigued by the brilliantly

---

* It is not impossible that the lack of documentation on much of Madame Grand's life in Paris is due to Talleyrand's best efforts after the lady became Princess de Talleyrand in 1802.

imperious Germaine de Staël. These were Catherine's comparative youth, her unwavering good humor, and her incontestable beauty. Less engaging, but perhaps even more novel for Talleyrand, was Catherine's stupidity. It was such as to have become a legend in its own time. Paris was full of gossip about her *gaffes* and *gaucheries*. One of the most famous of these tidbits was that in answer to a question regarding the place of her birth, Catherine—who seemed to have some mysterious difficulty with prepositions and articles—had replied *Je suis d'Inde* ("I am a goose") instead of *Je suis de l'Inde* ("I am from India"). Except for a few staunch friends, who claimed that she was misunderstood, everyone agreed that Talleyrand's new mistress was something less than brilliant. They were also agreed that she was one of the reigning beauties of her time. Catherine was, in fact, endowed with physical perfection characterized by flawless form, thick masses of blond hair, blue eyes accented by black eyebrows, superbly delicate skin, and incomparable grace of movement. Had she been mute, Paris would have been at her feet. As it was, her purely decorative qualities would have made her an ornament to any ministerial household. And this she was given the opportunity to be. In the spring of 1798, through Talleyrand's influence, Catherine was granted a divorce from M. Grand, and thereafter she lived openly in the Hôtel Galliffet, where, to Talleyrand's amusement —and to the horror of some of the foreign ambassadors—she took quite seriously, or as seriously as her abilities allowed, her duties as the lady of the Minister of Foreign Affairs.

By the beginning of the summer the Minister of Foreign Affairs was occupied with more serious matters than Madame Grand's pretensions or their effect on the diplomatic community. Bonaparte's departure for Egypt seemed the signal for a flood of misfortunes which, in the aggregate, threatened once more to overwhelm the Directory. Elections had been held in the spring of 1798, and the results, from the Directors' point of view, again had been disastrous. Of the 400 new deputies elected, the majority by far were either militant royalists or, worse, even more militant Jacobins. The Directors, by a decree of the Twenty-second Floréal (May 4), had succeeded in excluding a number of these representatives. But this drastic measure had not been sufficient. The temper of the two councils was solidly hostile to the executive branch, and ominously, this hostility came more from the Jacobins than from any other part of the assembly. It appeared that the Directors now had few supporters beyond those who either held office by appointment or who hoped to hold such offices.

One reason for this strong and growing reaction was that the venality, extravagance, and incompetence of the Directors had brought France to the verge of bankruptcy. Already, 140,000,000 francs' worth of assignats had been issued, and their value had deteriorated to the point where they were worth only a small percentage of their face value. The costs of the war were enormous, and an army of more than 1,000,000 men had doubled the expenses of the state since 1795. By the last months of 1798 there was a deficit estimated at 150,000,000 francs. Had not Bonaparte systematically bled Italy, the Directory could not have survived so long as it already had. But Bonaparte was in Italy no longer, and, from Egypt, there came bulletins of victory, but no gold. New taxes were imposed, but since their collection devolved upon the communes, most of what was collected, either by design or through incompetence, never reached Paris; and the Directors received all of the blame, and none of the benefits, of these exactions. The Directors therefore borrowed heavily, with the inevitable consequence that the fianciers became virtually their proprietors, and corruption among both functionaries and politicians was endemic. There were scandals involving ministers, and every day new instances of fraudulent dealings were revealed.

To make matters worse, if anything were needed, the new coalition against France, which had loomed on the horizon since the spring of 1798, in the fall began to take on solid form. The Turkish Empire, provoked beyond endurance by Bonaparte's Egyptian expedition, declared war. Austria, incensed by France's insistence upon propagating republican institutions in Italy beyond what had been agreed to by Bonaparte at Campo Formio, now broke off negotiations for a permanent treaty of peace. The French delegates, when they attempted to leave the town of Rastatt, where the peace conference was being held, were assaulted and slaughtered by Austrian hussars. Austrian and Russian forces then moved into northern Italy and captured Milan—the very city from which Bonaparte, imperial in all but name, so recently had imposed a new form upon the ancient principalities of the peninsula. From the south, the troops of the Queen of Naples advanced northward. There were reports that the English, supreme upon the sea, were about to invade Holland. The Swiss were in rebellion against their French masters, and, in Germany General Jourdan had fallen back across the Rhine.

Thus faced with bankruptcy both financial and political, the Directory was tottering. The Jacobins in the councils attacked relentlessly, and criticism in the streets and salons was no less virulent. The Directors hardly dared show their faces in public for fear of being insulted or worse. "So long as their armies were victorious," Talleyrand observed, "people hated their rule but feared their power. But when the hour of defeat arrived, the government met with universal contempt."

Governments, Talleyrand knew, might survive opposition, defeat, and even revolution. But no government ever long survived the contempt of the governed. With this in mind, he decided upon a course of action. The problem, as always, was to select a man whose particular talents would enable him to implement that action; and, for such a man, Talleyrand did not have to look far. Emmanuel Joseph Sieyès, a friend from Talleyrand's earliest days as a young man newly liberated from the seminary, his associate in the Assembly, and now—by Talleyrand's appointment—French ambassador in Berlin, was perfectly suited to the task. A clever man, reserved, an astute politician, Sieyès was one of those public figures who exist in a state of interior dissatisfaction because they are always employed far below the level of their abilities. In Sieyès' case, this was quite true. The fault, however, was not that of Sieyès' employers, but his own. His single vice was cowardice, which he carried to such a degree that he had always been afraid to choose any side for fear of choosing the wrong one. This characteristic, which he no doubt interpreted as prudence, had often served him well enough. Despite his prominence during the first months of the National Assembly, by the time of the Terror he had succeeded in making himself so inconspicuous that he disarmed even the enmity of Robespierre. When once he was asked what role he had played in those terrible days, Sieyès replied simply and proudly, "I survived."

It was such a man that Talleyrand needed—one sufficiently identified with the Revolution to be acceptable to the less rabid Jacobins, and yet not so much so as to be unacceptable to the royalists. The wisdom of Talleyrand's choice was made evident in the spring of 1799, upon the annual retirement of one of the Directors. In May of each year the names of the five Directors were written on slips of paper, and one was chosen at random. In the current year the name of Reubell was found upon the chosen slip. It was probably not by accident. All the directors were unpopular, but the most unpopular of them was the violent, verbose Reubell, Talleyrand's enemy. It is hardly beyond belief that Barras' fine hand, with perhaps a bit of encouragement, had guided the uncertain finger of chance. Reubell himself seems to have suspected as much, since his acquiescence had to be purchased by a substantial bribe—it was called a parting gift—from the remaining Directors.

Talleyrand and his friends, meanwhile, had been at work among the members of the Council of Ancients, whose duty it was to elect Reubell's replacement, and when, at a propitious moment in the proceedings, Sieyès' name was put forward, it was opposed only by the extremist fringe of the Jacobins and the most unreconstructed of the royalists. Talleyrand's friend and colleague, by virtue of some adroit maneuvering on the part of the Minister of Foreign Affairs, thereupon replaced Talleyrand's bitterest opponent as one of the Directors. It was a victory thoroughly in Talleyrand's style and one quite in keeping with the new Director's own tastes. It was not for nothing that Robespierre had called Sieyès "the mole of the Revolution." The only one of those immediately involved, other than Reubell, who did not take it well, was Barras, who had hoped to replace Reubell with a creature of his own.

The genius of Talleyrand's plan was that the man he had placed in a Director's chair was, to the marrow of his bones, a revisionist. His true profession, his unique compulsion, his only love, was the devising of constitutions. It was said of him that he always had one in his pocket. And, as it happened, this was so. Almost the first act of his office was to announce to the councils that the only hope of the Republic lay in the radical reformation of the executive branch. To this end, he proposed, and the Jacobins voted, at the end of June, the removal of three of the Directors: Merlin, La Revellière, and Treilhard. This left only Barras and Sieyès himself. Together, they suggested as new Directors, and at Sieyès' urging, the Council of Ancients voted to install three new members. These were Roger Ducos, Barras' appointee, who was thought to be a partisan of the latter, but who was in fact the tool of Talleyrand and Sieyès; General Moulin, an obscure soldier of no special talent either civil or military; and Louis Gohier, a lawyer so undistinguished that as little is known of him after his election as before. It was a respectable accomplishment. By perfectly constitutional means, the number of Directors had been reduced, for all practical purposes, from five to two, and one of the two was committed to the overthrow of the Directory. Of the Directors of the Eighteen Thermidor, now only Barras remained, and after five years of uninterrupted power and luxury, he was used up as a man of action and was ready to come to reasonable terms with Sieyès and Talleyrand—or, if matters should require, with the Count de Provence, whose agents were in touch with him.

Then the one thing occurred which perhaps Talleyrand had not foreseen or, if he had foreseen it, had hoped it could be circumvented. The success of Talleyrand's "backstairs maneuver," as it became known, to acquire a Director's chair for Sieyès, had been due largely to the support of the Jacobins. Now these same supporters in the councils became an obstacle. The defeats of the armies were making them unruly. They had formed a club, meeting in the *Manège,* which threatened to develop all the characteristics of the old Jacobin Club. The *Manège* was closed—but the Jacobins, led by Jourdan, General Bernadotte (the Minister of War), and others, continued their meetings in new quarters. They began to clamor for a new Committee of Public Safety. When the government did not accede to their wishes, they began a virtual committee of their own, and the danger grew of a new Red Terror.

Simultaneously the Jacobin press launched a violent and sustained attack on the Directory, particularly on the morals and competence of the

Directors and the ministers. Thus encouraged, writers of scurrilous pamphlets scribbled night and day and then distributed their works in the streets, denouncing the government, its works and its pomps, and particularly its Minister of Foreign Relations, whose aristocratic connections, ecclesiastical background, and morals, public and private, made him particularly vulnerable. "The man responsible for our situation," one journalist wrote, "is none other than the everlasting Bishop of Autun, who, being a great nobleman, seems to know everything, even though he has never troubled to learn anything. . . . One must be even more stupid than this vile, vicious, intriguing pervert not to see that he had himself named a minister under Barthélemy and Carnot solely for the purpose of destroying the Republic from within. . . . He is a lover of the English, an émigré, the betrayer and the assassin of his country." And these were some of the less offensive things of which the minister was accused. The attack went on for weeks, and Talleyrand—though not he alone—was charged with being a royalist, an adulterer, a thief, an English spy and a perjurer. A young adventurer named Jorry brought a suit against him for false accusation, an action which had no foundation but which, supported by the Jacobins, created a sensation in the press, and Talleyrand was sentenced to pay Jorry 100,000 francs in reparation for the harm done to the "good name" of the latter.* Almost at the same time, Delacroix, Talleyrand's predecessor as Foreign Minister and the putative father of Talleyrand's son by Madame Delacroix, issued a public statement blaming Talleyrand for Bonaparte's situation in Egypt. It had been four months since news had arrived from the expedition, for the English, having destroyed Bonaparte's ships, were supreme in the Mediterranean. No one knew but that the most brilliant of the Republic's commanders, and the elite of its troops, might be lying dead on the endless sands of the African deserts—all, Delacroix pointed out, because of the bad advice given by Talleyrand.

These things Talleyrand, according to his custom, pretended to ignore. He could afford to do so, for he had already made his plans. Indeed, he may have welcomed the pretext that these attacks presented. It was now time to sink into the background, to extricate himself from a government which, as he and Sieyès knew better than their Jacobin enemies, was on the verge of collapse. On July 20 he presented a letter to the Directors: "It would be inexcusable on my part if, despite the certainty that I have accomplished for the Republic whatever good it has been in my power to do,

---

* Later in the year, under the Consulate, when Jorry was arrested and sentenced to deportation, Talleyrand asked Fouché, the Minister of Police, "as a personal favor," to obtain the culprit's pardon from the Consuls. "Since Jorry has never, so far as I know," he wrote to Fouché, "offended anyone other than myself, I feel I have a right to ask this of you." Thereupon, Jorry was pardoned, and he disappeared from history. (*Citoyen français,* 10 novembre 1799.)

the outrageous attacks upon me, which seem daily to increase in vehemence, should hinder the government in its work. . . . The time has therefore come for me to offer my resignation." Barras accepted the resignation
with "regret," and the Directors—to the fury of the Jacobins—expressed
their "gratitude for the departing minister's unceasing zeal, public spirit,
and extraordinary effectiveness" during his term of office.

The virtues which Barras extolled so unstintingly were perhaps greater
than he knew. Before resigning, Talleyrand had carefully prepared the way
for his return. In his place as minister, he caused to be appointed Charles
Reinhard, a mediocre statesman, but one who had accompanied Talleyrand on his mission to England in 1792 and whom Talleyrand knew to be
loyal to him. Reinhard was to be, so to speak, the minister ad interim,
who, during Talleyrand's absence, would follow his instructions and carry
out his established policies.

Almost the last official act of Talleyrand as a member of the government
was to recommend to Sieyès, as a candidate for the post of Minister of Police, a man who was at that time a minor functionary of the Ministry of
Foreign Affairs: Joseph Fouché. "At this moment," Talleyrand told Sieyès,
"when we are being attacked so daringly and so violently by the Jacobins,
we must make use of a Jacobin as our weapon—a Jacobin capable of
storming into battle, coming to grips with the enemy, and wrestling them
to a standstill. For such a man, you need look no further. There is
Fouché." Joseph Fouché was not the kind of man whom Talleyrand might
be expected to recommend. He was one of the most sinister figures of his
age, a regicide and one of the most fanatical of the Terrorists, uncouth in
manner, brutal in his relationships, filthy in dress and in personal habits,
loud and coarse in conversation. For Talleyrand, politics was the art of the
possible. For Fouché, it was the assassination or imprisonment of one's
enemies. Even Fouché's virtues were counted as vices in Talleyrand's eyes,
for this foul and disreputable Jacobin was a model and devoted father to a
large brood of children and the utterly faithful husband of a woman noted
equally for her gentle nature and her ugliness. Yet Fouché was precisely
the man needed by Talleyrand and Sieyès at that moment. Irreproachable
in both his private and public life, he was impervious to attack from the
Jacobins. At the same time, as a minister and as a man concerned above
all with his own survival, his talents would be at the service of Sieyès—that
is, of Talleyrand. Fouché was, in other words, the perfect hatchet man.
Sieyès saw Talleyrand's point immediately, and on the same day that Talleyrand's resignation was accepted by the Directors, Fouché became Minister of Police. From that moment, anything of importance that happened
in France, especially in Paris, immediately reached the ears of the two conspirators.

Having secured their flank, Talleyrand and Sieyès turned to the task once more of finding a man with a sword. Bonaparte, obviously, would have been ideal; but Bonaparte was in Egypt, and there was no time to bring him back. If Talleyrand and Sieyès did not act soon, the Jacobins might strike first. Any morning might see the guillotine installed once more in the Place de la Révolution, and the first heads to fall in a new Terror would undoubtedly be that of the Directors and ministers, former or incumbent. Various generals were sounded out—Bernadotte (who, Sieyès said, "looks like an eagle, but is actually a goose"), Moreau, Joubert, and Macdonald. All were unsuitable or unwilling, or both. As time was growing short, Talleyrand and Sieyès became desperate. All other possibilities having been eliminated, there still remained only one: Bonaparte. Finally, Talleyrand suggested that since no other means were available, action must be delayed until the commander of the Egyptian expedition could be brought home. He proposed therefore that negotiations be opened with Turkey for a treaty whereby, in return for the restitution of Egypt, Bonaparte and his army should be allowed to return to France. At Sieyès' insistence, the Directors approved the plan, and Talleyrand was now hopeful that Bonaparte's sword would be available by spring of the following year —if the *coup d'état* could be postponed for so long.

No one knew at that moment that Bonaparte was already making straight for France, having sailed from Alexandria when he had learned that France had been decisively defeated in Italy by the Austrians and the Russians. He landed at Fréjus on October 9, 1799, and the news was speedily brought to Paris.

"There," General Moreau told Sieyès, "is your man."

8

The Consulate

ON OCTOBER 16, Bonaparte was in Paris. The news of his arrival
had preceded him. Bourrienne, the general's secretary, assures us
that the citizens greeted him "with an outburst of affection which
had to be seen to be believed, and which will never be equaled." In the
course of the following morning, Talleyrand visited Bonaparte in the rue
de la Victoire. Those who expected recriminations over Talleyrand's alleged part in the Egyptian fiasco were disappointed: The general embraced
him warmly, as an old friend, and the two men spent a long time in conversation. Later in the day, Bonaparte called on Barras at the Palais Luxembourg, where the Parisians "packed the rooms and courtyards in order
to be able to see him."

This, of course, was perfect. Bonaparte, in addition to being the sword of
the *coup,* was the idol of the nation, and Talleyrand smiled and congratulated himself upon his choice. But he knew that idols are evanescent and
that the French quickly grow tired of heroes. Bonaparte therefore was
counseled to assume once more the mask of modesty which he had exhibited after his return from Italy. Soon, Bourrienne says, "the citizens were
complaining about the general's incognito. He was never seen at the theater or in the streets where they were waiting for him." Much of his time, in
fact, was spent at his house, in the company of Josephine—with whom he
had been quickly reconciled after a terrible scene over her affair with Hippolyte Charles. His evenings, however, were given over to political affairs
and to the discussion of the *coup* planned by Talleyrand and Sieyès. Sometimes in the rue de la Victoire and sometimes in Talleyrand's own house in

the rue de Taitbourt, they met, with an ever-changing group of soldiers, statesmen, and politicians, to discuss means and ends.

One of these participants describes Talleyrand as "nonchalantly lounging on a sofa," with "his face immobile, undecipherable, his hair powdered, saying little, occasionally interjecting a subtle or telling phrase, and then lapsing into his posture of distinguished lassitude and indifference"— an attitude which, though customary, was, in this instance, particularly indicative of Talleyrand's part in the stroke that was being planned. As in each of the many *coups* that were to punctuate his career, he seems to have had no definite, direct role. His permanent function was to serve as a source of plans and as a liaison agent among the conspirators. He was, by nature and preference, both a conciliator and a catalyst of men and of their ideas. He knew everyone, and he was aware of everything; moreover, many people were in his debt for favors rendered during his tenure as minister. Bonaparte was the strong man of the plot, the one who could be vaulted to power over the prostrate form of the Directory. Sieyès, Fouché, and the general's brother Lucien Bonaparte were the ones who assumed active parts in the execution of the plot. But it was Talleyrand alone who held in his hands the end of every strand in the vast web of intrigue that others were engaged actively in weaving.

Nonetheless, in the days of frantic planning that followed Bonaparte's return to Paris, there were certain problems, the solution of which devolved more or less naturally upon Talleyrand, not necessarily because he wished it, but because no one was as well qualified as he. One such difficulty was created by the fact that all five Directors lived in the Luxembourg, and that it was therefore very difficult to meet with Sieyès without arousing the suspicions of Barras. Talleyrand not only suggested the happy plan of allowing Barras to believe that he himself was a party to the conspiracy, but undertook to persuade him of it. His task was made easier, as he explains, because Bonaparte's prestige was such that the mere invocation of his name was sufficient of itself to evoke Barras' assent to almost any plan, for "the political parties of France saw in Bonaparte not a man who could be called to account for his actions, but one whom circumstances made indispensable and whose favor it was essential to win." In any event, Talleyrand explained carefully to Barras that Bonaparte greatly desired a reformation of the Directorial government and that what he had in mind particularly was the reduction of the number of Directors from an unwieldy five to a more powerful one—a sole Director who would thenceforth act as undisputed ruler of France. And that Director, he said, would be Paul Barras. A week later, on November 6, Talleyrand called upon Barras once more, this time accompanied by Lucien Bonaparte, president of the Council of Five Hundred, and the Minister of Police, the sinister

Fouché. With these imposing allies at his side, Talleyrand reiterated Bonaparte's plan—but this time, Barras tells us, no mention was made of the man who was to be the single Director left in office. Even so, it appears that Barras' suspicions were hardly aroused, so that, until the very moment of the *coup,* he regarded himself as a conspirator in the very plot that was being engineered to remove him from office on November 9.

The interval of more than three weeks between the time of Bonaparte's arrival in Paris and the striking of the blow was due in part to the amount of time consumed by Talleyrand's attempts to establish a degree of understanding between the various elements in the plot, and in part to the pettiness of the individuals involved. One of the most time-consuming problems, for instance, was the antipathy which existed, for no good reason, between Bonaparte and Sieyès. Almost a week was wasted while Talleyrand argued with the general in an attempt to persuade him to pay a visit to Sieyès. Bonaparte apparently believed that Sieyès, though a Director, should anticipate the *coup* and pay the first call. Sieyès, no less adamant, insisted that so long as he was a Director, he could not be expected to call upon a mere general. Talleyrand, when told of this impasse, had been horrified. The most important quality of any successful *coup,* he knew, was speed—it must be over before those who are likely to oppose it have time to gather their forces to resist. He hurried to the rue de la Victoire, where he had a candid discussion with Bonaparte and reproached him severely for his pettiness and folly. Then he suggested a solution. The next day Bonaparte called upon Sieyès and upon Ducos—on the principle that while one Director was not worth the trouble, two were. The day after, as suggested by Talleyrand, Sieyès and Ducos called upon Bonaparte. As the final part in this matter of great moment, the news of the visits was published simultaneously in the *Moniteur,* in such a way that it was not clear who had first called upon whom. Bonaparte grumbled, it is true, that he had been kept waiting at the Luxembourg and that only one of the two great folding doors had been opened for him; but the dilemma had been solved, and nothing now remained but to decide upon the details of the *coup d'état.*

On the eve of that day which, in revolutionary jargon, was known as the Eighteenth Brumaire of the Year VIII, Talleyrand spent the evening quietly at home, with a few friends, playing whist. Occasionally, a messenger would arrive, and there would be a whispered conversation, but apart from these not unusual interruptions, an innocent observer might have seen nothing to lead him to believe that anything was afoot. Nothing, that is, except that the master of the house retired at a surprisingly early hour. For at six o'clock the morning of November 9 a visitor was expected, and arrived punctually: Pierre-Louis Roederer. Roederer was a colleague of both

Talleyrand and Bonaparte in the institute and a deputy. More important, he was in Talleyrand's debt, for after the Eighteenth Fructidor he had been condemned to deportation to Guiana—a fate, known as the "dry guillotine," from which he had been saved by Talleyrand's intervention. In the present affair, Roederer had been entrusted with the preparation, under Talleyrand's supervision, of the texts of the various pamphlets, posters, and decrees with which the *coup* was to be launched. Once drafted, the documents were printed by Roederer's son, who, for this purpose, was posing as an apprentice in a printer's shop. Roederer and his son, when they arrived at Talleyrand's house on the morning of November 9, had been working for hours. The fruit of their labors was visible in the streets of Paris: The walls had been plastered with the notices composed by the father and printed by the son. Talleyrand, who had not yet completed his toilette, suggested that since they had some time to spare, they might sit down and compose a letter of special importance: the resignation of Director Barras. This Roederer dictated to his son and then handed it to Talleyrand, who, after making a few changes, slipped the paper into his pocket.

By eight o'clock Talleyrand and Roederer, along with General Macdonald, who had joined them, were at Bonaparte's house in the rue de la Victoire. A last-minute conference took place which lasted until late in the morning. As they talked, the army was taking up positions throughout the city, with an especially large number of troops being stationed around the Luxembourg and the Tuileries. When a message arrived confirming the execution of this part of the plan, it was time for Talleyrand to undertake the task which he had reserved for himself: to persuade Barras to resign. For this, he needed two things. One was a companion whose presence would have some significance. Barras, and all France, were already aware that the army and almost all its commanders would support Bonaparte in any undertaking. Moreover, Barras had already had evidence that the police, led by Fouché, and the Council of Five Hundred, presided over by Lucien Bonaparte, were involved in the plot. There remained only one force upon which Barras might believe he could depend: the navy. Talleyrand therefore took with him to the Luxembourg Admiral Bruix, a distinguished and highly regarded marine commander. The second item, and the more important, was a letter of credit for 3,000,000 francs. It was essential that Barras consent to disappear with as little fuss as possible, and while he could not be counted on to listen to reason, he could always be depended on to listen to money. Thus armed, Talleyrand and Bruix set out for the Palais Luxembourg.

Barras, meanwhile, had not been having an easy time of it. That this was the day of the *coup,* he was perfectly aware, having been informed of it by Talleyrand. Moreover, he could see soldiers surrounding the Directors' residence and, beyond them, a crowd of increasingly noisy citizens. He found it difficult to believe, however, that a plot, of which he had believed himself to be the cornerstone, could actually be taking place without his knowledge or active cooperation. The whole truth did not dawn upon him until he sent his secretary to fetch Sieyès and Ducos and learned that these two Directors were nowhere to be found and that no one knew where they had gone. That the two remaining Directors, Gohier and Moulin, were present was small consolation, for they were so insignificant that it was of no importance whether or not they were involved in the *coup*. In fact, when these two, alarmed by the growing mob in the streets, came to ask Barras' advice, he had them told that he was in his bath and could not be disturbed. Then he sat down to a melancholy lunch with the single guest who had come of the thirty who were expected, Gabriel Ouvrard—the banker who was financing the *coup d'état*.

They were at table when Talleyrand and Bruix were announced. Barras, to his credit, immediately recognized the situation for what it was. He did not resist or attempt to argue when Talleyrand led him to the window and pointed to the citizens milling in the street and to the soldiers fraternizing with the people. He listened almost in silence to the arguments of Talleyrand, Bruix, and Ouvrard, appealing to his love of his country, to his intelligence, and, finally and more satisfactorily, to his greed. At this point, Talleyrand produced the letter of resignation which, knowing Barras, he had caused to be phrased in the loftiest terms of high principle and self-sacrifice. Barras read, and signed, and promised to make no trouble. Talleyrand took the letter, bowed, told Barras he was "the first patriot of France," and handed over the 3,000,000 francs.* Within an hour, Barras was on his way to his country house at Grosbois—escorted by a company of dragoons which Talleyrand sent to "protect" the fallen ruler of France.

This was Talleyrand's only active participation in the events of the Eighteenth and Nineteenth Brumaire. From the Luxembourg, he returned home to spend the day receiving his friends and listening to news of the progress of the *coup*. It was uniformly good news. For the moment, all parts of the complicated intrigue were going as smoothly as had the resignation of Barras. The Council of Ancients, the majority of which were susceptible to Sieyès' influence, had been convened early in the morning in emergency session. Curiously, the notice of the meeting had failed to reach

---

* In his memoirs, Barras denies having received any money and suggests that if it had indeed been intended for him, it must have somehow remained in Talleyrand's pocket. It is highly unlikely that this was so. Barras, who had sold himself throughout his life, had never had a more valuable item to offer than on November 9, 1799, when his acquiescence in the *coup* was of great importance to its success. It is almost inconceivable that he would have surrendered so easily unless he were paid to do so—or that Talleyrand could have believed that he might be induced to resign without a stupendous bribe.

those members whose support was less than certain. Once the deputies had assembled, they were informed of the existence of a plot, inspired by the Jacobins, to overthrow the Republic. They had thereupon voted that both chambers should meet the following day, at St.-Cloud, where they would be safe from the threat of force which the Jacobins might be expected to exercise in the capital.* At the same time, the council appointed Bonaparte to command the troops in the area and delegated to him the responsibility for the protection of the councils from the "Jacobin conspirators." The Council of Five Hundred, when it met later in the day, had been taken completely by surprise. The decree of the Ancients was read to them, and Lucien Bonaparte, before any discussion could take place, declared the session adjourned until the next day at St.-Cloud.

Late in the morning, while Talleyrand had been with Barras, Bonaparte had gone to the Tuileries to take the oath as commander before the Council of Ancients. Along the way, he was surrounded by crowds, cheering "Long live the liberator!" He was cheered by the council and cheered again as he reviewed his troops. "It quickly became known," Bonaparte said later, "that Napoleon was at the Tuileries and that he alone was to be obeyed in France." To make certain that this was truly understood, Fouché ordered that the city's barriers be closed and that no coaches or couriers be allowed to enter or leave without the permission of the Minister of Police. Thus far all had gone well. The Directory had collapsed,† and all legal authority was now in the hands of the two councils. Before retiring late that night, Bonaparte said to Bourrienne, "All in all, today wasn't too bad. We'll see what happens tomorrow."

The next day, the Nineteenth Brumaire, the scene shifted to St.-Cloud. Talleyrand, with the faithful Desrenaudes and Roederer, drove out very early to a house which he had arranged to have placed at the disposal of himself and his friends. A steady stream of messengers kept him informed of what was taking place in the councils, and the news was not encouraging. Bonaparte had attempted to address the Council of Ancients but had blundered badly, provoked open hostility among some of the deputies, and therefore had done more harm than good. He had then gone to the Council of Five Hundred, presided over by Lucien Bonaparte. But Lucien had been unable to overcome the members' indignation at the presence at St.-Cloud of Bonaparte's troops and cannon, which they regarded as a display of force designed more to intimidate than to protect them. He was greeted

---

* Article III of the Constitution of the Year III (1795) empowered the Council of Ancients to transfer both themselves and the Council of Five Hundred to any location outside Paris.

† Gohier and Moulin, after a confrontation with Bonaparte at the Tuileries, had hastily submitted the resignations demanded by the general. Sieyès and Ducos, as Bonaparte informed Gohier and Moulin, had promised to resign on the Nineteenth Brumaire.

by shouts of "No dictatorship!" "No bayonets!" and "Down with the tyrant!" Some of the deputies became so threatening that Bonaparte had to
be escorted from the Orangerie, where the Five Hundred were meeting, by
a troop of his grenadiers. Word was quickly brought to Talleyrand that,
after the general's departure, the Five Hundred began debating whether or
not Bonaparte should be outlawed for conspiring against the Republic.
Immediately, Talleyrand sent Montrond, who had joined him in the course
of the morning, to Bonaparte with word of this development. The general
turned pale as a ghost. The cry of *hors la loi* had been sufficient to bring
down even the terrible Robespierre and send him to his doom. It was
Sieyès, the timid one, the coward, who infused courage into France's hero.
"If they try to outlaw you," he said, "then they themselves are outlaws.
They are having visions of 1793. Well, General, the only thing left for you
to do now is to order your men to throw them out."

A few minutes later a message arrived from Lucien Bonaparte: "Unless
the session is broken up within ten minutes, I can no longer be responsible
for anything." Whereupon Bonaparte sent in his soldiers, first, ostensibly
to rescue Lucien—who, since he had now stepped down from the chair,
was in no danger whatever. With Lucien at his side, he told Joachim
Murat, one of his commanders, to clear the hall. "Throw them all out of
here," Murat roared to his men, and then he charged in at the head of a
column, shouting to the deputies, "You are dissolved! You are dissolved!"
One of the commanders of the grenadiers recalled that "fat gentlemen
crawled through doors and windows, and coats, splendid hats, and plumes
were scattered about the floor." The few hardy souls who clung to their
dignity were hurried on their way by jabs of the grenadiers' bayonets, and
they vanished with their frightened colleagues into the deepening shades of
dusk.

Now that the recalcitrant Council of Five Hundred had been "dissolved" by Murat's men, the Council of Ancients was willing to reconsider
its hasty judgment of that morning. Declaring that in view of the flight of
the Five Hundred, the Ancients "now embody *ipso facto* the whole of the
national representation," they decreed that "four of the Directors having
resigned, and the fifth being under surveillance [Sieyès was at that moment
closeted with Bonaparte], a temporary executive body of three members
will be appointed." Then, upon the motion of a deputy who was a creature
of Sieyès, it was voted "temporarily to create a consular executive committee composed of Citizens Sieyès and Roger Ducos, former Directors, and
General Bonaparte. They will bear the titles of Consuls of the Republic."

When this news was relayed to Bonaparte, he said to Bourrienne, "Take
a note. I must issue a proclamation to the Parisians tonight." When it
reached Talleyrand, he said, "Now, my friends, we can have our dinner."

He took the two Roederers and Montrond to a house nearby, where a lady, Madame Simons, the wife of a Belgian banker, was waiting with a splendid hot meal. Talleyrand, as usual, had arranged beforehand to spend the evening as agreeably as possible, among friends. It did not detract from his pleasure that Madame Simons, famous on the stage as Mademoiselle Lange, had, until the day before, been Barras' mistress.

By November 14 Bonaparte was established in the Luxembourg Palace. One of his first official acts was to receive Talleyrand, thank him for his help in the difficult hours of the Eighteenth and Nineteenth Brumaire, and signify his intention of reinstating him as Minister of Foreign Affairs. "Talleyrand has everything that is required for negotiations," the Consul explained to Bourrienne. "He understands the world; he knows thoroughly the courts of Europe; he has *finesse*, to say the least of it; he never shows what he is thinking; and, finally, he bears a great name." All this was very gratifying, but not unexpected. It had been perfectly well understood by everyone concerned—except perhaps Barras—that Reinhard's appointment as minister the preceding July was an interim one, and that Talleyrand would soon return. On November 21, when Talleyrand was officially appointed, Reinhard gracefully—indeed, gratefully—returned to his former position as ambassador in Berne, and Talleyrand moved into the rue du Bac once more, for all the world as though he, the master of the house, had merely taken a vacation and were now home again. The event merits but a single sentence in the *Mémoires*: "I again became Foreign Minister."

A few days afterward Talleyrand again presented himself at the Luxembourg. This time it was to render formal thanks to Bonaparte for the appointment and, at the same time, to plant a seed. A new constitution was in preparation (which, according to one of Bonaparte's quips, must be "short and confusing"), and Talleyrand had his own ideas concerning the proper distribution of power under the new consular regime. "It is necessary," he told Bonaparte, "that you be first among the Consuls and that the first among the Consuls have all responsibility for anything relating directly to policy—that is, to the Ministry of the Interior and the Ministry of Police for internal affairs and to my ministry for external affairs, as well as the two principal means of implementing policy: the army and the navy. . . . Thus, you will have control of the essential branches of government and will thereby be enabled to attain a noble end: the reconstruction of France." As soon as Talleyrand had left, Bourrienne relates, Bonaparte said to him, "You know, Bourrienne, Talleyrand is an extraordinarily intelligent man. He gives me excellent advice."

On December 13, 1799, the new Constitution was promulgated. Bonaparte was named First Consul, to hold office for a period of ten years, and was invested, as Talleyrand explains—and as he had proposed—"with that share of authority which, in limited or constitutional monarchies, is in the hands of the sovereign. The only essential difference was that instead of limiting his power to the sanction of laws, he was also empowered to propose them." To assist the First Consul, there was to be a Second Consul and a Third Consul, with little more to do than supply the First Consul with advice—upon request. These two subordinates Bonaparte appointed with Talleyrand's customary discretion and prudence. As Second Consul, he chose Jean-Jacques Cambacérès who, though trustworthy, was widely regarded as a defender of the purest principles of the Revolution. As Third Consul, Charles-François Lebrun was to represent, or at least to symbolize, the interests of the right.

The problem had been, Talleyrand observes, "how to go about making Bonaparte a temporary sovereign. If one had proposed to appoint him sole Consul, this would have revealed an ambition which it would have been better carefully to conceal. Yet, if one had given him colleagues equal to him in rank and power, the government would have remained a polygarchy"—that is, a new Directory, with all the evils implied by such a regime. There is little doubt that the new Constitution, hurriedly drafted though it was by other hands, was the outcome, at least in its main lines, of Talleyrand's remarks to Bonaparte. Its result in practice, as Talleyrand remarked, was virtually to establish a constitutional monarchy in France—a monarchy remarkably similar to that which Talleyrand had envisioned during the idealistic days of the Assembly in 1789, with the difference that the principles of the Revolution had now an additional safeguard against encroachments by the executive: The sovereignty was no longer hereditary, but elective. After ten long years, the battle had been won. Talleyrand could now set to work in earnest to attain what he had always desired most and what France now desired with him: peace.

The years of the Consulate, from 1799 to 1804, were undoubtedly among the happiest of Talleyrand's life. Reinstated in the Ministry of Foreign Affairs, where he was to remain for seven years, his duty was the reconstruction of France and the pacification of Europe. For the first time, he could work openly for peace, with the support both of the people and of the government. The news of Bonaparte's ascension to power had been greeted everywhere in France with tremendous enthusiasm and relief—relief at the apparent end to ten years of disorder and uncertainty and enthusiasm for the man who seemed the harbinger of peace. A police report submitted by Fouché on November 12 states that "peace and Bonaparte's reestablishment of the Republic are viewed as a happy prospect," and the

Moniteur reports that Bonaparte, upon his return to Paris from St.-Cloud, was greeted by "long lines of people marching to cheers of 'Long live the Republic; long live peace!'" Thus supported by public opinion, Talleyrand first maneuvered himself into a position where he, and he alone, would have Bonaparte's ear regarding the establishment of peace.

> In order to render the power of the First Consul as effective as possible [he relates], on the very day of his installation, I made a proposal which was immediately accepted. It had already been decided that the three Consuls were to meet every day, and the ministers were to acquaint them with the affairs of their respective departments. I therefore pointed out to General Bonaparte the fact that since all matters connected with foreign affairs were essentially secret, they could not be discussed in council and that he alone should decide all questions of foreign policy. . . . He fully understood the value of that advice . . . and it was agreed, from the very first day, that I should work only with the First Consul.

The fruit of this intimate collaboration between Talleyrand and the First Consul was soon apparent. Bonaparte, at Talleyrand's prompting, in the first days of his regime, wrote to both the King of England and the Emperor of Austria "expressing his wish for a prompt reconciliation with the two countries." George of England did not deign to reply directly to Bonaparte. Instead, the Foreign Secretary, Lord Grenville, wrote to Talleyrand stating that if France truly wished peace, it must recall her legitimate dynasty forthwith. From Baron von Thugut, in Vienna, there came a reply less haughty in tone, but no less offensive in meaning. "These two measures," Talleyrand concludes, "led to no reconciliation and, indeed, could not have led to any. But they had a happy effect upon the internal peace of the country, since they revealed to the people that the great general who had become head of the government was also a skillful statesman." Actually, the attitudes of England and Austria—which believed France to be far weaker than it actually was—suited Bonaparte perfectly. He was convinced that peace was necessary in order to establish the new regime—but it must be a peace based on victory rather than on negotiation. Even Talleyrand, whose first and last hope was always for peace, realized that in this instance at least, "the only hope of altering the attitude of the hostile powers toward France now lay in fresh victories." The difference was that Talleyrand regarded war as the means to be employed, reluctantly, when all else had failed. But to Bonaparte, war was the indispensable means with which to bring his enemies to their knees before negotiations began.

This fundamental difference in approach to matters of foreign policy, though apparent from the beginnings of the relationship between Talleyrand and Bonaparte, was not yet so pronounced as to constitute a conflict in practice or even to disturb the harmony which was established between them in the early days of the Consulate. For Talleyrand and Bonaparte, from the beginning, achieved a functional working relationship which, given the disparity of temperament between the two men, was something of a wonder in itself. The First Consul was a demon for work, never happier than when dictating to several secretaries at once, keeping an eye on every detail and a finger in every pie. This enthusiasm for labor was one which Talleyrand hardly shared. He was lazy by nature, and he cultivated this natural quality so assiduously that his indolence was as famous as his intelligence. In his approach to his duties, he had a single inflexible principle: never to do anything himself that could possibly be delegated to another. Rarely did he ever write a letter, compose a dispatch, or dictate a memorandum. He would first set down on paper a few notes on any communication that he wished to issue from the ministry and then turn this formless outline over to one of his trusted subordinates—usually Desrenaudes, who, over the years, had learned to interpret Talleyrand's mind, as well as to decipher his handwriting. Desrenaudes would transform the letter or communication into an approximately final form and return it to the minister for comments. Even at this point, Talleyrand refused to exert himself. He would read the draft attentively and then usually reject it with the words, "No, that is not quite it," or "I think this needs more work," or simply "No." Then Desrenaudes or some other subordinate would set to work again and submit draft after draft until the final accolade would fall from Talleyrand's lips: *"Oui, c'est bien cela"*—"Yes, that's it." Then, painstakingly and in his own hand, he would change a word here and there and send the communication back to have a fair copy written. So adamant was he in his refusal to do one whit more than was absolutely necessary that he did not think it beneath his dignity, when protocol required that a letter be written in his own hand, to set down the necessary phrases at the dictation of one of his subordinates. The explanation offered by Talleyrand to the astonished D'Hauterive on one such occasion was: "It is really too much to expect one to write and compose simultaneously." One of his proudest boasts was that he expected no more of the most junior clerk in the ministry than of himself. In all seriousness, he described his staff as "loyal, intelligent, diligent, and punctual, but thanks to my example and training, they are not zealous. Except for the youngest among them—who, I must confess, seal their envelopes with unbecoming precipitation—everyone in this ministry works in the most perfect tranquillity, without haste or excitement."

This indolence remained forever a mystery to the frantically busy and bustling Bonaparte, for whom the days were never long enough. Yet he quickly discovered that Talleyrand, for all his lackadaisical approach to the responsibilities of his ministry, was not a man to be cowed or one who would hesitate to speak his mind. Bonaparte, Bourrienne recalls, "was always eager to see M. de Talleyrand. I have frequently been present at conferences between this great statesman and Napoleon, and I can state that I never once saw him flatter his ambitions or his dreams. To the contrary, he always was at pains to point out to him his true interests."

Of all the ministers, only Talleyrand and Fouché were formidable enough to express their own personalities in their work, and of the two, only Talleyrand was sufficiently courageous consistently to "point out to him his true interests." It was Talleyrand who persuaded Bonaparte to set aside his prejudices against Sieyès and, after the promulgation of the Constitution of the Year VII, to name the former Director a senator of the new regime and president of the Senate. It was also Talleyrand who abated Bonaparte's republican prejudices to the extent that he was able to establish contact between the First Consul and the Bourbon princes. This contact, however—at least so far as Bonaparte's intentions were concerned—was in no way a betrayal of the principles of the Revolution. In the days following the events of Brumaire, Europe and France itself had buzzed with speculation about whether Bonaparte had taken power for himself or merely to return it to France's former dynasty. Louis XVIII seems to have debated the question in his own mind, for shortly after the establishment of the Consulate, he composed a letter to Bonaparte: "Now that you have consolidated your power and demonstrated your abilities, it is time for me to explain myself. It is time for me to tell you of the hopes that I have founded on you. If I were writing to any man other than Bonaparte, I would offer rewards. A great man, however, has the right to decide his own destiny and that of his friends. Tell me, then, what it is that you wish for yourself and for them. Your wishes will be realized at the moment of my restoration." Through the incompetence of Louis' emissary, the Duke d'Avaray, the letter was never delivered. Yet the same message was conveyed orally by a representative of the Count d'Artois, the pretender's brother. This man, Hyde de Neuville, was an acquaintance of Talleyrand's from prerevolutionary days and had solicited his good offices in arranging an interview with the First Consul. Bonaparte consented to Talleyrand's request, not because he had the slightest intention of recalling the Bourbons, but because he wished to make it clear that the old things in France had passed away forever. The meeting was arranged with the greatest secrecy. Talleyrand met Hyde de Neuville and his companion, Count d'Andigné, on a street corner at night and drove them to the Luxembourg in his own carriage. While he went to great lengths to impress upon the royalist emissaries his sentiments of respectful friendship toward Artois, he was equally careful to quench any embers of hope that had been sparked by Bonaparte's willingness to meet with them. When the royalists attempted to persuade Talleyrand to give some hint of what the future might hold, they were asked: "Who can know the secrets of the future?" When questioned as to Bonaparte himself, Talleyrand responded, "If he lasts for a year, he will go far." To these fellow survivors of the *ancien régime*, Talleyrand confided that if he had not been forced into the church as the result of his lameness, he should have preferred a military career. Upon such things as a childhood accident, he observed, a man's destiny hinged. If it had not been for his crippled foot, who knew what path he might have followed. "I might be an émigré, like you," he told the startled Hyde de Neuville, "or even an emissary of the Bourbons."

With such comments, Hyde de Neuville had to be content, for he got little more from the First Consul, with whom he had two meetings. Shortly thereafter Bonaparte made his intentions clear in a brief but eloquent letter to Louis XVIII: "You must abandon all hope for returning to France, for you would then have to walk over the corpses of a hundred thousand men. Therefore, sacrifice your self-interest to the peace and happiness of France, and history will honor you for it." In private, he confided to Bourrienne, "If I recall the Bourbons, they will erect a statue to me—and then bury me under it."

The goodwill of the Bourbons, or at least their abandonment of a policy of open hostility, was desirable from two standpoints. One of these was that it would have been helpful in putting down the royalist insurgents in the Vendée; the other—and, in Talleyrand's eyes, this was the more important in the long run—was that it would have made possible a negotiated peace with England and Austria. The first objective Bonaparte was able to accomplish without the Bourbons, by lulling the militant royalists of the rebellious province by conciliatory words and then by enforcing the strictest measures against them. The second objective, now that London and Vienna had refused to negotiate or the Bourbons to accept reality, was not possible of realization. Therefore, only a peace based on victory remained. "Unavoidable wars," Bonaparte declared, "are always just wars." On May 5, he set out to take command of the armies once more. A few days later Talleyrand also left Paris and, in leisurely stages, drove to his favorite watering place at Bourbon-l'Archambault for a few days of rest.

On June 14, Bonaparte's army met that of the Austrians in Piedmont, near the town of Marengo, and a great battle was fought in which the Austrians were totally beaten. The next morning Austrian emissaries appeared at Bonaparte's tent to beg for an armistice. It was granted, on condition that the Austrian armies immediately be withdrawn from Mantua, Piedmont, and Lombardy. "I hope," Napoleon wrote from Milan, "that France will be pleased with its army." France was. In Paris, the *Moniteur* reports, "the cabarets were full until eleven o'clock at night, and not a single glass was drunk except in honor of the Republic, the First Consul, and the army." In the provinces—even in the Vendée—joy was no less universal than in Paris. This, of course, was precisely what the regime needed, and, more important, it was what Bonaparte needed. After the string of defeats which had characterized the last year of the Directory, Marengo appeared to the people as the symbol of change. In a few short months, Bonaparte had succeeded to a large extent in pacifying the country, in establishing some order in France's chaotic finances, and, now, in giving his people a taste of that military glory for which they had yearned. His hold upon the people was immeasurably strengthened, and the cheers which greeted him upon his return to Paris were, as he told Bourrienne, "as sweet to me as the sound of Josephine's voice."

It had probably occurred to Bonaparte that the Battle of Marengo, if it had been a disaster rather than a victory, might have meant the beginning of the end of the Consular regime. It had certainly occurred to others. For a day or so after Marengo, before Bonaparte's bulletins of victory had reached Paris, the city had buzzed with rumors of a great defeat and even of Bonaparte's death and capture—"which seems very probable," it was immediately reported to Louis XVIII. This, indeed, was a possibility which was never entirely absent from Talleyrand's mind or from Fouché's. What would become of France if Bonaparte, upon whom all hopes were founded, should be killed or defeated? There was much gossip to the effect that, while Bonaparte was in Italy, the two ministers—enemies at heart and competitors for Bonaparte's favor and attention—had joined forces and planned a *coup*, either to replace Bonaparte if he had been killed or to oust him if he had been defeated. Bonaparte's successor, according to various accounts, was to have been Louis XVIII, or the Duke d'Orléans, or a new Directorate. It does not seem likely that either Talleyrand or Fouché, even if they had in fact put aside their differences for the moment, could have agreed to a return of the Bourbons, from whom neither could expect gratitude or reward, or would have planned the reestablishment of a regime the incompetence and corruption of which they had so recently conspired to end. On the other hand, it seems highly probable, even though there is no concrete evidence for it, that Talleyrand, whose foresight was proverbial, had some plan in mind in the event that Bonaparte disappeared from the scene, either in battle or through assassination, by accident or by design.

Bonaparte, in any event, seemed convinced that there had been an active conspiracy afoot during his absence, abetted, if not actually organized, by Talleyrand and Fouché. "So," he roared at Bourrienne, "they thought I was dead! Do they think I am a Louis XVI? If so, they are seriously mistaken. For me, a battle lost is the same as a battle won. . . . I will save France in spite of the traitors and the incompetents!" But Bonaparte's rages went as easily as they came. The Minister of Foreign Affairs, along with the Minister of Police, was treated to a few sharp words on the subject of loyalty and gratitude, and the matter was forgotten. Bonaparte was well aware that whether or not Talleyrand and Fouché were conspirators or merely foresighted, he could afford to dispense with the services of neither. Fouché was the eye and ear of the government in France, and Talleyrand was its mind and mouth in Europe. A few days after Talleyrand's "disgrace," in fact, he was directed by Bonaparte to undertake the negotiation of the treaty of peace with Austria, a negotiation in which the Foreign Minister played the leading part and which he brought to a successful conclusion in February, 1801, at Lunéville. The terms of that treaty gave to France even greater gains than Bonaparte's victory at Marengo seemed to warrant: The left bank of the Rhine and some minor principalities beyond it were to be the new eastern frontier of the nation, while Luxembourg and Belgium were recognized as integral parts of France. In Italy, France received Piedmont, and the Cisalpine Republic and Liguria were placed under the protection of the Republic. The effect of the Treaty of Lunéville, in other words, was to give to France the largest territory in its history. The French, understandably, were dazzled, and Europe was cowed. Talleyrand, however, was neither. Rather than awe, submission, or even self-satisfaction, he experienced uneasiness over the meaning for the future of Bonaparte's policies toward defeated nations. "Two roads are open to him," he explained to Ouvrard. "There is the federal system, which would leave a defeated ruler as master in his own lands, but on terms favorable to the victor." The other path was that of annexation and the limitless expansion of France's boundaries. "If, on the other hand, he intends to unite and to incorporate, then he enters upon a road to which there can be no end."

Bonaparte's intentions would be demonstrated amply in the proximate future. For the moment, with Austria defeated and Britain isolated, the First Consul turned his attention to the task begun with his assumption of office: the conciliation of the various factions within France. Of these, the most important were the royalists and the Jacobins—the same conflicting forces which had plagued the Directory. Bonaparte, like Talleyrand, viewed Jacobins with undisguised contempt, but royalists with sympathy and a basic understanding. Neither man was insensitive to the attraction of the monarchical system; indeed, the Consulate itself, as Talleyrand had pointed out, was a limited monarchy of sorts. The only vice of the royalists, in Bonaparte's view, was their attachment to the lost cause of the Bourbons, and this he decided to attempt to remedy by securing, to the extent that he was able, the support of the old nobility—that is, of the most conservative and influential segment of the royalist party. As the first step in this direction and upon Talleyrand's urging, the First Consul issued a decree abolishing all penalties against the émigrés and inviting them to return to France. All but the most militant members of the Bourbon circle were included in this general absolution. And to those who availed themselves of it, the state offered to restore whatever property had been seized during the Revolution but which had not yet been sold. This lure, coupled with nostalgia for the homeland which some of the émigrés had not seen for twelve years, had an immediate and overwhelming effect: Some 40,000 émigré families promptly crossed the Channel and the Rhine to avail themselves of the Consul's offer.

The conciliatory policy of Bonaparte continued once the émigrés had returned, and since it represented a reasonable attempt to reconcile the old France with the new, it received from Talleyrand both approval and assistance. At sumptuous entertainments at the Hôtel Galliffet and at a property rented by Talleyrand at Neuilly, the First Consul met, for the first time, the bearers of some of the most glittering names of the *ancien régime,* intimates of the martyred Louis XVI, such as the Chevalier de Coigny and the Duke de La Rochefoucauld-Liancourt, as well as former diplomats and even recently reconstructed Vendéans. Not the least conspicuous of this group was Talleyrand's collection of noble ladies from the Faubourg St.-Germain—Madame de Custine, the Duchess d'Aiguillon, the Duchess de Fleury, the Countess de Noailles, among others, and even Madame de Flahaut. But out of regard for the feelings of the First Consul—who detested dinners, balls, and parties of any kind and who attended Talleyrand's entertainments only out of a sense of duty—Germaine de Staël's name was absent from Talleyrand's guest list. The lady might, and did, plead in vain for invitations, but Talleyrand was firm. These gatherings were "business," and he could not run the risk of a scene between the mercurial Madame de Staël and Bonaparte, whose initial aversion to the lady had been aggravated, rather than mitigated, by the passage of time.

The First Consul's efforts to conciliate the royalists were but one manifestation of his determination to restore order and a degree of normality in France. Another very important effort, toward the same end, was aimed at the regularizing of relations between the French government and the Roman Catholic Church. The virtual schism, provoked in 1792 by the Civil Constitution of the Clergy, had, by the time of the Consulate, largely disappeared in practice. The great majority of Frenchmen were Roman Catholics and had remained so—though sometimes after a brief fling with the *culte décadaire,* as the religion of the Revolution was known. By 1800 only those who were bound by duty to the official observance—that is, government employees—still refused allegiance to Rome. Bonaparte was aware that the alienation of the government of France from Rome was one of the chief and most justifiable criticisms leveled against it by the royalists and that if he could but reach an understanding with the church, in the person of Pope Pius VII, he not only would strengthen his hold on the loyalty of the ordinary Frenchman, but would also leave the extreme royalists high and dry, officers without an army, leaders without a cause. In this, with Talleyrand's help and active participation in negotiations, he was successful. A Concordat, signed in July, 1801, and promulgated early in 1802, recognized Roman Catholicism to be the religion "of the great majority of the French people," and its free exercise was permitted. The Pope agreed to reduce the number of bishoprics and also recognized the sale of church property which had occurred—upon Talleyrand's motion—during the Revolution. Henceforth, bishops were to be appointed by the First Consul and invested by the Pope and were to take an oath of loyalty to the head of the state. Both bishops and priests were to be paid by the French government. It was an ingenious solution, for it not only allowed Frenchmen to live at ease with their religious beliefs, but also permitted them to retain the church lands which they had purchased, at very low prices, in the days of the Assembly. Moreover, it turned the clergy into officials, therefore subordinates, of the state and thus weakened their ties to Rome in favor of those to Paris. "When Napoleon reestablished religion in France," Talleyrand wrote, "he performed an act not only of justice, but of great cleverness. The Napoleon of the Concordat is the truly great Napoleon, the man enlightened and guided by his genius." Talleyrand's opinion was that of the people as a whole. Everyone was delighted. France was once more the eldest daughter of the church—through the efforts of a deist First Consul and a former bishop.*

The *Mémoires* contain only a brief reference to the Concordat, and it ends with these words: "It was after this reconciliation with the church, in which I played a leading role, that Bonaparte obtained from the Pope a brief for my secularization." As an account of events, Talleyrand's words are true, but they are not the entire truth. The fact was that the decree of secularization, by which "Charles-Maurice de Talleyrand, Minister of Foreign Affairs of France, is authorized to reenter upon secular and lay life," was the result, not only of a series of conversations between Talleyrand and Bonaparte, but also, and especially, of the First Consul's determination that, come what might, his regime had to acquire an aura, or at least a

---

* The Concordat of 1802 was one of the most enduring of the results of the collaboration between Bonaparte and Talleyrand. It determined the relations between church and state in France for the whole of the nineteenth century and remained in effect until it was abrogated by the anticlerical forces of the Third Republic, in 1905.

veneer, of respectability. He had manifested this desire very openly on several occasions. Shortly after transferring his residence to the Tuileries, early in 1801, he had stood quietly staring for a while at a group of *merveilleuses* in their transparent gowns, and then he walked over to the fireplace and began throwing logs onto the fire. When someone asked what he was doing, Bonaparte replied, in a very loud voice, "We must have more heat! Don't you see that these ladies are naked?" And when Madame Tallien had appeared at the Opéra clad in nothing but a tiger skin, the First Consul announced to her that mythological fancy dress was no longer fashionable.

It was not that Bonaparte was a prude by nature, but that he was a puritan by policy. If France were to rejoin the family of European nations, it must be at least as respectable as its neighbors, and to achieve this, the sexual laxity which had characterized the Directory must be corrected. It was hardly surprising, therefore, that with the Church of Rome newly established in France, the First Consul experienced some embarrassment over the fact that his Foreign Minister, who was as close an adviser as Bonaparte ever tolerated, was a renegade priest and an excommunicated bishop; or that he was outraged, though perhaps not shocked, that Talleyrand was living openly "in sin" with a lady who, by all accounts, was no lady at all. The First Consul approached the problem with his customary bluntness and, after explaining his reasons for concern over a matter which seemed purely personal, suggested that Talleyrand abandon Catherine Grand and don once more the episcopal robes, which he had abandoned with such relief a decade before. This Talleyrand refused even to consider. He had been forced into the priesthood against his will, he pointed out, and the happiest day of his life had been that on which he had divested himself of his bishopric. He had no intention ever of taking up again a profession which he not only disliked, but also for which he was unsuited. Bonaparte, surprised not by the refusal but by the firmness exhibited, pressed on, offering Talleyrand a cardinal's hat. This handsome bribe was dismissed on the same grounds. Well, then, declared Bonaparte, if Talleyrand were determined to remain a layman, he must at least become a respectable layman, which meant that he must dismiss Madame Grand. Or if he did not wish to do so, he must marry her. To Talleyrand's argument that marriage for a bishop, even an excommunicated bishop, was unthinkable and that it would be a scandal even greater than that created by his cohabitation with his mistress, the First Consul answered, "Monsieur de Talleyrand, the Court of the Vatican can do anything."

Talleyrand knew better. Or at least he knew that even if Rome had the power to do as it wished, it seemed unwilling to use that power on his be-

half. Talleyrand speaks in the *Mémoires* of "the indulgence of Pius VII toward myself" and quotes the Pope as saying to a cardinal, "M. de Talleyrand! Ah! May God have his soul. As for me, I am very fond of him!" Yet,
there was no sign of that indulgence when Rome was asked to consider
Talleyrand's peculiar status. The truth was that even before Bonaparte had
spoken of Talleyrand's marriage, the Foreign Minister had queried Rome
regarding a release from his vow of celibacy. (Gossip had it that he wished
to marry—not Madame Grand, but another lady, unnamed, to whom he
was extremely attached.) Cardinal Caselli, the papal nuncio in Paris, was
eager to be of service in this matter, lest a disappointed Talleyrand prove a
stumbling block to the Concordat, which was then in the final stages of negotiation. "The Bishop of Autun," Caselli warned Rome, could be an
enemy "as implacable as he is powerful." Talleyrand himself wrote in more
diplomatic terms to Pope Pius, pointing out that "as France becomes once
more a Catholic nation, it is not fitting that a minister, especially one who
plays a major part in the stability of the government, be the object of uncertainty and controversy with respect to his former state in life." To support his bid for permission to marry, Talleyrand ransacked the lumber
rooms of history, producing precedent after precedent to show that Rome
indeed had the power, if only it would use it, to allow bishops to marry.
Even the case of Cesare Borgia was cited, and he, Talleyrand pointed out,
had been no mere bishop, but a cardinal. (He tactfully omitted any reference to the fact that Cesare had been also the son of the reigning Pope,
Alexander VI.) But Rome disallowed Talleyrand's precedents one by one.
Cesare Borgia, it was explained, who had been permitted to doff the red
hat and marry a French princess, had never been ordained a priest, let
alone consecrated a bishop, and therefore had never taken a vow of celibacy. In view of these circumstances, the Pope finally replied, it was mani-
festly impossible to offer any dispensation in Talleyrand's case, but as a
gesture of goodwill toward a repentant son, he allowed Talleyrand thenceforth "to wear the lay habit and to perform his duties on behalf of the
French Republic." This was the "brief for my secularization . . . which
Bonaparte obtained from the Pope," described in the *Mémoires*.

Bonaparte was not to be thwarted by a mere Roman Pope. Having decided that if he could not turn Talleyrand into a cardinal, he would make a
husband of him, he set about interpreting the papal brief in the sense that
he found most desirable. By an official decree, he announced that Talleyrand had not only been secularized, but also granted the right to contract
marriage. And while Pope Pius and the cardinals were still stupefied at this
felicitous misinterpretation of a brief which had been intentionally phrased
in the clearest possible terms, it was announced that Talleyrand and Ma-

dame Grand had been united in marriage in both civil and religious cere-monies.*

The satisfaction of the First Consul was equaled only by the astonish-ment of Paris. It seemed beyond belief that Talleyrand, of all people, could have acquiesced in such a misalliance, a match between a member of the highest and most ancient aristocracy and a woman of low origins and even lower reputation; and the journals of the time, like the salons, were filled with speculation on his reasons. Pasquier, who knew both Talleyrand and Catherine quite well, attributed the marriage to "weakness, which gave way to importunity and to the desire for a bit of peace, to the difficulty of overcoming habit, and, finally, to a total indifference to public opinion." The Duke de Fitz-James relates that Catherine's threats to expose certain of Talleyrand's peccadilloes were primarily responsible for the latter's de-cision. When Catherine had heard rumors that Talleyrand, at Bonaparte's insistence, might give her up rather than marry her, she said to Fitz-James, "Abandon! Abandon me indeed! If he thinks that he will be rid of me so easily, he is very wrong. Do you hear? Wrong! If that *piécourt* [short-foot] is not careful, I will make him shorter by another foot!" Talleyrand himself explained, years afterward, that there was, in fact, no explanation for his marriage to Catherine Grand. "It was done in a time of general disorder," he said. "One attached no great importance to anything—either to oneself or to others. One must have lived through it to realize how far one can go astray in times of social upheaval." This, however, was said in 1836—dec-ades after the marriage had run its course, and it is not altogether credible, since by 1802 the "social upheaval" of the Revolution and of the Directory had given way to the reconstructive efforts of Bonaparte and of Talleyrand himself. Perhaps the best reason that can be advanced is a combination of several motives: "the remains of love," as explained by General Thiébault, "and also perhaps by the wish not to irritate a woman whom it is impossi-ble to suppose he had not admitted into his confidence." These factors were certainly given new value by Bonaparte's insistence that Talleyrand either marry his mistress or abandon her. And this, added to his natural in-dolence and his lifelong contempt for public censure, made it difficult for him to resist pressure doubtless brought to bear by Catherine herself and by such friends of Catherine's as Josephine Bonaparte. Thus, he may well have consented, merely for the sake of peace and so as not to disturb a pat-

* The civil ceremony was celebrated on September 10, 1802, at the *Mairie* of the Tenth Arron-dissement of Paris, and the religious ceremony on the following day in the parish church of the vil-lage of Épernay. On September 9, Talleyrand and Catherine had drawn up a marriage contract in which Talleyrand transferred to his intended bride, among other things, jewelry worth 300,000 francs, securities and stocks in a Hamburg bank, a house in the rue d'Anjou-St.-Honoré, and the estate of Pont-de-Sains, which had originally belonged to the Duke d'Orléans. The witnesses to the contract were Bonaparte, Josephine, Talleyrand's two brothers, Archambault and Boson, and two notaries.

tern of life which he found agreeable enough, to a ceremony which, while it had no importance for him, seemed curiously important both to the First Consul, upon whom his career depended, and to Catherine herself, whose whim, if she were sufficiently aroused, might wreak havoc with the domestic tranquillity which he prized so highly. Catherine, in any case, was satisfied and a few days later wrote to the Minister of Foreign Affairs of Batavia that "as you will see, by the name which my union with M. de Talleyrand gives me the right to sign, how the tender and sincere affection of that amiable man has made me the happiest of women."

Bonaparte was less easy to please. The ambassadors who had formerly complained of having to pay formal calls on Talleyrand's mistress were now delighted to be received by the wife of the Minister of Foreign Affairs. But the First Consul had discovered that Catherine, of whose stupidity he had heard so much, was on occasion able to fire off a retort as effective as any conceived by her husband. The first time that she had been presented at the Tuileries, Bonaparte, in the spirit of despotic paternalism which was rapidly coming to the fore in his character, said to her, "I hope that the good conduct of the Citizeness Talleyrand will soon cause the indiscretions of Madame Grand to be forgotten." To which Citizeness Talleyrand promptly replied, her wide blue eyes innocently staring into Bonaparte's own, "In that respect, I surely cannot do better than follow the example of Citizeness Bonaparte." For this reproof, publicly administered, Bonaparte never forgave her, and ten years later he was still complaining, untruthfully, that Talleyrand "in spite of my objections, and to the great scandal of all Europe, married his shameless mistress, by whom he could not even hope to have children." Even now, after her retort—which, of course, was widely repeated and immediately entered into countless diaries and journals—he announced to Talleyrand that he would never again receive his wife. He had not, however, reckoned with that pride of family which was part of the Talleyrand heritage. Without a change in expression, the Foreign Minister informed the First Consul that since this was the case, he must regretfully resign his ministry. Bonaparte was adamant. But Talleyrand was even more adamant, and the matter was finally settled only when Bonaparte, with much grumbling, agreed to allow the lady to set foot in the Tuileries—provided that Talleyrand assured him that she would do so "as seldom as possible."

As these internal dramas, domestic and political, were being played out in France, the situation of the Republic vis-à-vis the other nations of Europe had begun to shift. After the signing of the Treaty of Lunéville with Austria and Britain's consequent isolation as the enemy of the Republic, the threat of France's armed might began to make itself felt on the Continent. One manifestation of this new development was the signing of an agreement by Prussia, Sweden, Denmark, and Russia which, under pretext of maintaining strict neutrality in the struggle between France and England, closed the ports of northern Europe to British shipping. This act was viewed with great satisfaction by the French, for it constituted a virtual alliance against England. It was indeed an advantage for France, but a precarious one, for it depended for its continuation on Russia, which had proposed it; and Russian constancy was based on nothing more stable than the whim of the half-mad Czar Paul, who, in the dim recesses of his confused mind and by virtue of an application of Napoleonic flattery, had conceived an overwhelming admiration for Bonaparte. The situation was drastically affected, therefore, in March, 1801, when Paul, in a palace *coup,* was dethroned and replaced by his son, Alexander I. Alexander did not share his father's admiration for Bonaparte or France; to the contrary, his personal preferences and the policies which he had in mind presupposed the creation of strong ties with Britain. Any hope that Talleyrand or Bonaparte might have had to persuade the new czar otherwise was destroyed when, only two weeks after Alexander's accession, the British, under Admiral Nelson, defeated and captured the Danish fleet off Copenhagen and thus made themselves masters of the Baltic—and of Russian shipping in that sea. When news reached Paris of the double tragedy of Paul's death and the Battle of Copenhagen, there was great consternation. The League of Neutrality, as the treaty among the northern nations was called, was dissolved *ipso facto,* and Bonaparte, who had planned to concentrate his forces against England, now found himself faced by two powerful enemies, one to the east and one to the west.

It was a difficult situation, both politically and militarily, and one with which Bonaparte was not yet prepared to deal. He therefore gave in to Talleyrand's repeated urgings and agreed to attempt a negotiated peace with England. Talleyrand, in fact, had not waited for the First Consul to come around to his way of thinking. Months before, in January, 1801, he had dispatched Montrond to England on a mission of reconnaissance; he was to discover whether public opinion in that country would be favorable to negotiation with the Republic. From Montrond—who spoke English well and was a popular figure in London—he learned that Henry Addington, the new prime minister (Pitt had died in the first weeks of the year), and Hawkesbury, who had replaced the intransigent Grenville in the Foreign Office, were eager to begin discussions. Now, with the First Consul's permission, negotiations were formally begun and continued over a period of almost six months, with Addington himself speaking for the British government and the French minister in London, Count de Mosloy, acting for Bonaparte. "England," Talleyrand wrote, "without allies abroad and experiencing some embarrassment internally [there was trouble in Ireland] felt the need of peace." This was something of an understatement. So intense was that need that Addington, after only token resistance, agreed to surrender virtually all that England had won since the beginning of hostilities in 1792: Martinique and Guadeloupe were returned to France; Surinam and the Cape of Good Hope to the Dutch; and Minorca to Spain. Of all its conquests, only Trinidad and Ceylon were retained. France, Talleyrand explains, "recovered all, without having to restore anything itself. Perhaps its dignity suffered from having left all the burden of compensation on Spain and Holland, its allies, who had been engaged in the war only for its sake and on its advice. But that is a consideration made by few people and one which never presents itself to the minds of the multitude, accustomed as it is to take the success of bad faith for cleverness."

The note of bitterness in this passage of the *Mémoires* is not gratuitous. The fact is that midway in the negotiations, Talleyrand had lost a large measure of control over events through Bonaparte's interference. Talleyrand was of the opinion, as always, that a strong Britain was essential to the well-being of Europe, and he was unwilling to strip it totally of all that it had won. Moreover, he wished the English to be satisfied with the peace, so that the time following its conclusion might be something more than an interval between wars. But Bonaparte was of the opposite view. Only when the English threatened to break off negotiations unless they were allowed to retain Trinidad, was Talleyrand able to persuade the First Consul to acquiesce on this point. As for Malta, which was restored to the Knights of St. John of Jerusalem, Talleyrand says that "I would willingly have left it to the English, provided the treaty had been signed by Mr. Pitt or by Mr. Fox, instead of by Mr. Addington." For he regarded Addington's government as transitory and Addington himself as a mediocrity whose concessions would immediately be resented, and sooner or later repudiated, by the English as a whole.

It seems that toward the end of the negotiations in London, the disagreement between Talleyrand and Bonaparte became rather heated. So much so that it was Bonaparte's eldest brother, Joseph, who was sent to England to sign the preliminary treaty, rather than Talleyrand, upon whom the task should naturally have devolved. The first inkling Talleyrand had that the preliminaries had been signed was the sound of the cannon salvos which conveyed the news to the rest of Paris in October, 1801. The couriers dispatched by Joseph Bonaparte had gone directly to the First Consul rather than to Talleyrand, and Bonaparte had not troubled to inform his Foreign Minister personally of the event. Talleyrand did not take kindly to such slights, which were public humiliations as well as breaches of protocol. But there were ways in which he could give as good as he got. In January, 1802, the final treaty of peace was signed at Amiens, with Lord Cornwallis acting for Britain and, again, Joseph Bonaparte for France. This time, however, Talleyrand had arranged matters to his own satisfaction. He was the first to be informed when the matter had been concluded, and he told Bonaparte nothing. The following morning he went to the First Consul's office with the business of the day and spent hours with him going over each item carefully. When the meeting had ended and Talleyrand was gathering up his papers, he picked up several sheets, stared at them for a moment, and then handed them casually to Bonaparte with the words, "Oh, incidentally, this is something that you may find interesting. It is the Treaty of Amiens, which has just been signed."

Bonaparte was flabbergasted. "Why didn't you tell me at once?" he demanded.

"Because," Talleyrand said, like a father to an irresponsible child, "I knew that, if I did, you would not have paid attention to any other business this morning." Then, taking his bundle of papers, he bowed and withdrew, leaving the First Consul to master his rage as best he could.

"Talleyrand," wrote General Macdonald, "wanted four things out of life: to be a bishop, a minister, a millionaire, and the husband of a fool. He succeeded in all four." If anyone in Europe had had any doubts concerning the last, the period immediately following the conclusion of the Peace of Amiens quickly dispelled them. For, one evening every week, Catherine insisted on displaying herself at a reception in the Hôtel Galliffet, to which every person of any distinction in the city was invited, and she also delighted in receiving guests at less formal entertainments at Neuilly. Now that peace had been made with Britain, prominent visiting Englishmen and their wives were among these guests. Charles James Fox came with his wife, the celebrated Bet Armistead, whose premarital career had been even more scandalous, and more professional, than that of Catherine Grand. So did Sir Elijah and Lady Impey, Lady Bessborough, and the Duchess of Cumberland. Thus, word of Catherine's beauty, and of her foolishness, spread beyond the Channel, for no one could resist the temptation to see, at first hand, the "fallen woman" whom Talleyrand had redeemed by marriage. "I will not *visit* Madame Cabarrús [Thérèse Tallien]," Lady Bessborough reported to Lord Granville, "though I hope to *see* her tomorrow. Your native sense of justice makes you place Madame de Talleyrand in the same line; but power and marriage make so great a difference here that not visiting the latter would be reckoned a ridicule. And in a later letter, she notes that "Madame de Talleyrand is like the

Duchess of Cumberland, and perfectly justifies the reason he gave for marrying her: *'Qu'elle emporte le prix de la bêtise'* [Because she is the silliest woman in the world]."

Talleyrand was content to sit and watch his wife's display and, occasionally, to intervene in an attempt to prevent a more than usually hilarious and repeatable *gaffe*. One of the most celebrated of the latter concerned Catherine's irreversible confusion between the adventures of Robinson Crusoe and those of a French explorer who was a guest at Talleyrand's table. Catherine had read Defoe's tale only a few days before, and somehow she had formed the opinion that this work of purest fiction was the true account of the explorer's voyages. It was said that she spent most of the evening raving to the unhappy man, and to the giggling company, over his good fortune in finding so fine a companion as Friday. Talleyrand, when he was asked about the story, years later, said only, "It did not happen in quite that way. But it would certainly have happened if I had not been there to prevent it." He never showed embarrassment over Catherine's foolishness. And he never pretended that she was other than what she was in fact: "Stupid," Talleyrand said, "as a rose." Sometimes he defended her indirectly, and himself less indirectly, by explaining that his wife, for all her faults, was preferable to more gifted ladies. "A clever woman," he said, "usually compromises her husband, but a foolish one compromises only herself." And comparing Catherine to Madame de Staël, he noted that "one must have loved a genius to appreciate the happiness of loving a fool." Catherine herself he treated with unfailing kindness and consideration so long as they lived together. No one was allowed in his house, no matter what his rank or dignity, who did not show her proper respect and deference. He seems to have enjoyed, in fact, the spectacle of great lords and ladies laughing in private at the vulgarity and stupidity of a woman to whom, in public and for the pleasure and distinction of his company, they paid the most assiduous homage.

Catherine's receptions, in addition to being a source of some amusement for Talleyrand, had a practical use. They enabled him to speak with and perhaps influence visiting statesmen. To Fox, Talleyrand confided that it was unfortunate that England had given way to all of Bonaparte's demands in the peace negotiations, for the First Consul "had declared repeatedly that he must have given up the chief points in dispute had they been persisted in." With Fox's assertion that "he could not conceive a worse [treaty of peace] than we had made" at Amiens, Talleyrand could readily agree. It was true that France, in 1802, through the efforts of Bonaparte and Talleyrand, had made incredible strides forward, both at home and abroad. The Jacobins had been muted, and the royalists, except for the most militant of them, reconciled by the recall of the émigrés and by the Concordat with Rome. The economy was flourishing, public services had been resumed, confidence in the government had never been greater, and France enjoyed a dominant position on the Continent such as had not been seen since the middle years of Louis XIV. "It can be said without exaggeration," Talleyrand wrote, "that at the time of the Peace of Amiens, France was, in its foreign relations, possessed of a power, a glory, and an influence as great as any which could have been desired for her by the most ambitious minds. And what rendered this situation even more astounding was the rapidity with which it had been accomplished. In less than two and a half years—that is, from the Eighteenth Brumaire (November 9, 1799) to March 25, 1802, the date of the Peace of Amiens—France had passed from the humiliating depths into which the Directory had plunged her, to the first rank of Europe."

Yet Talleyrand was not content. Proud though he might be of what had been accomplished, he was aware—and he seems to have been the only high government official who was—that what had been won so arduously might vanish in the twinkling of an eye unless the peace were preserved. Britain as a whole was dissatisfied with the Treaty of Amiens, he was certain, for the sentiments of Fox, only murmured in Talleyrand's drawing room in Paris, were preached from the rooftops in London by the Whigs. Only Addington and his Tory government seemed content, though perhaps not proud, of what had been done. In such circumstances, an extraordinary diplomatic agility on the part of France's Foreign Minister, as well as a pronounced degree of moderation on the part of the First Consul, must be exercised if the peace were to be preserved. Talleyrand was eminently capable of supplying the former. The latter, however, depended wholly upon Bonaparte, and Talleyrand, to his alarm, quickly discovered that Bonaparte, hailed everywhere as a conqueror and as the savior of France, was no longer receptive to counsels of moderation. Joseph Bonaparte's signature was hardly dry on the Treaty of Amiens when his consular brother in Paris began to rattle the sword—"to sow the seeds of new wars," Talleyrand said, "which were to overwhelm Europe and France and lead him to his doom."

The first steps in this direction were taken in September, 1802, when, over Talleyrand's vehement protests, the former kingdom of Piedmont* was formally annexed by France. Bonaparte, Talleyrand explains, "be-

---

* After Bonaparte's conquest of Piedmont in 1798, King Charles Emmanuel had renounced the throne and ordered his subjects to obey the French generals. In 1800, Bonaparte had offered to return Piedmont to its legitimate dynasty; but after the Battle of Marengo, he had become very elusive on the subject, and in the Treaty of Lunéville, he had refused to commit himself to anything in that respect. In April, 1801, Piedmont had been divided into *départements* and transformed into a military region of France. From there, it was a short step to annexation in 1802.

lieved that his personal interest required him to do so, his pride seemed to dictate that arbitrary step, and all my counsels of prudence failed to persuade him otherwise." There was a reason for this new, bold aggressiveness on the part of the First Consul. During the summer of 1802, by virtue of a plebiscite, Bonaparte had been declared Consul for life and given the authority to name his successor.* Earlier in the same year, upon the annexation of Piedmont, he had taken the title of President of the Italian Republic. He had, in other words, become a king, and greater than a king, in all but name, and there was no doubt, either in his mind or in that of others, that the life Consulate was but an intermediate step to grander things.

> In order to rule, and to rule hereditarily, [Talleyrand explains] as he aspired to do . . . and in order to justify his pretensions to the title of sovereign, he deemed it necessary to annex to France those countries which he alone had conquered . . . never understanding that he might be called to account for so monstrous a violation of what the law of nations considered to be most sacred. His illusion, however, was not destined to endure.

At that point, the troubles against which Talleyrand had warned Bonaparte began to manifest themselves. The British, claiming that Bonaparte's retention of Piedmont and his refusal to evacuate Holland as promised at Lunéville, voided certain of the terms of the Treaty of Amiens, announced their intention of retaining Malta. In February, 1803, in the presence of Talleyrand and the whole diplomatic corps, a terrible scene took place at the Tuileries, with Bonaparte shrieking wild threats of war at Lord Whitworth, the British ambassador. As the envoys of Europe listened, we are told, "mute with astonishment and fear," Bonaparte slammed out of the room with a final word for Whitworth: "We shall be fighting in two weeks. Malta—or war!"

The Consul's ultimatum was immediately communicated to London. "He must be mad!" Foreign Secretary Hawkesbury exclaimed. And then he set about formulating an ultimatum of his own. France must evacuate Holland immediately, in exchange for which Britain would agree to retain Malta for only ten years. To this proposal, Hawkesbury concluded, France must reply within seven days. Bonaparte, of course, was furious. The word "ultimatum," he told Talleyrand, implies war, and even worse, England's manner of negotiation "is that of a superior with an inferior." Talleyrand's efforts to settle matters, by proposing that Malta be turned over to one of the powers guaranteeing the Treaty of Amiens, were rejected by everyone

---

* Of the 3,500,000 Frenchmen who voted, fewer than 9,000 had opposed the life consulate. Even the strongly royalist province of the Vendée had expressed itself overwhelmingly in Bonaparte's favor: Only 6 citizens out of 17,000 who voted were unwilling to agree to the proposed extension of the Consul's term.

concerned. By then both Bonaparte and Britain were raging with the fever of war, and none of Talleyrand's strenuous efforts to preserve the peace had the slightest effect. On May 20, 1803, after only fourteen months of peace, France formally declared war on Great Britain.

Four days earlier, Bonaparte had explained to his ministers a plan which had left them speechless with surprise: "I intend to do something which will be the most difficult undertaking ever conceived in the realm of policy, but also the most effective so far as results are concerned. With some foggy weather and more or less favorable circumstances, I can land in England and, in three days' time, be master of London, Parliament, and the Bank." Immediately, he set the wheels into motion. The port of Boulogne, from which he had considered launching an invasion of England under the Directory, was reactivated, and he designed and ordered construction to begin on a fleet of flat-bottomed barges with which to transport his armies across the Channel and land them in England. There was no doubt that Bonaparte was in deadly earnest or that, over the continuing protests of Talleyrand, he was determined to pursue a policy of aggrandizement which Talleyrand foresaw must end in universal catastrophe. For the First Consul was indifferent to the opinions of those around him, as he was indifferent to their principles. When, in the summer of 1803, he set out on a tour of inspection of Belgium and northern France, to examine fortifications along the Channel, Talleyrand was ordered to accompany him—for no reason that is evident other than the wish to compel this overly independent Minister of Foreign Relations to seem to acquiesce in a policy of which he most strongly disapproved.

Traveling was never one of Talleyrand's favored pastimes. His lameness made it difficult for him to climb in and out of coaches without assistance, and his fastidiousness rendered the dusty roads and the lack of amenities —which Bonaparte seemed not to notice—intolerable. Yet on this occasion Bonaparte's spite produced an accidental result which, even from Talleyrand's viewpoint, made the tour worthwhile, for it was in Belgium that he met, and immediately was charmed by, a lady who was to become one of his most intimate and loyal friends: Claire de Vergennes, Countess de Rémusat, a member, both by birth and by marriage, of the ancient aristocracy of France. Talleyrand's enchantment with the lady was not immediately reciprocated. Madame de Rémusat had all the prejudices of her caste, and these had been reinforced by Talleyrand's reputation as a rake, gambler, and intriguer. She was wary at their meeting, even cool, yet she confesses that, like so many people of both sexes, she was unable to resist his charm:

> The elegance of his manner was a startling contrast to the rough ways of the soldiers by whom he was surrounded. In their midst, he was able some-

how always to retain the air of a *grand seigneur*. . . . His silence was impressive in its contempt, and although more artificial than anyone I had ever known, he was able, out of a thousand affectations, to construct a perfectly natural manner. In every situation, he retained these affectations as though they were quite natural to him. His method consistently of approaching serious subjects in the most frivolous possible manner was of great help to him. . . . It was only later, when I had overcome the shyness which seems to afflict everyone meeting him for the first time, that I was able to observe the curious mixture of which his character is composed.

Madame de Rémusat's shyness and her attachment to the old ways were not such as to prevent her from being persuaded to undertake the office which she was to hold for the next several years: lady-in-waiting to Josephine Bonaparte. Her acceptance was an indisputable feather in Talleyrand's cap, for it would have been impossible for the First Consul to command, or anyone else to persuade, a distinguished and reputable lady of the old nobility to consent to enter the service of Josephine, who, in addition to the burden of a questionable reputation which she bore so gracefully, was, after all, merely the wife of the First Consul and without an official position.

The surrender of Madame de Rémusat, and of so many of her noble friends, to the charm of Talleyrand or to the power of Bonaparte was a phenomenon repeated at every level of society. Yet it was not universal. There were still Jacobins who had clung to the belief that Bonaparte's rise would mark the realization of the ideals of the Revolution—until it became clear that Bonaparte aimed, not at a republic, but at an absolutism, with himself as master, greater than any of which even the most militant royalist dared dream. Then, when they voiced their dissatisfaction with the course which events had taken in France, they somehow disappeared from political life and occasionally, on one pretext or another, found themselves deported to the New World. Such punishments, however, were usually reserved for grave offenses against the dignity of the First Consul. Venial sins brought subtle but effective warnings of what might lie in store unless one's ways were speedily corrected. Benjamin Constant (Talleyrand's former colleague in the Constitutionalist Club and his successor as Germaine de Staël's lover) was the recipient of one such warning. Madame de Staël had invited a large number of people to a dinner party in Constant's honor when it happened that on the day before the party, Constant let fall a few words criticizing Bonaparte's absolutist tendencies. The next evening, at Germaine de Staël's dinner, only the hostess herself and the guest of honor were present. All the other guests, including Talleyrand, had suddenly developed colds or discovered business so pressing that it required their immediate attention. These warnings could not fail to be effective, and by

such methods, and others considerably less gentle, the forces of revolutionary republicanism in France were soon disarmed and disappeared from the
political scene. Republicanism, nonetheless, remained a bête noire of Bonaparte's, and occasionally, Fouché produced a few obscure Jacobins and
had them tried and condemned, so as to quiet his master's fears. In 1800,
when a serious attempt had been made on the First Consul's life, Bonaparte was absolutely certain that he had been the intended victim of a Jacobin plot and commanded Fouché to find the criminals. The Minister of
Police, knowing perfectly well that the attempt had been planned by the
royalists, obediently produced a list of more than a hundred Jacobin "conspirators," who were then sent to rot in Guiana. It was only when Talleyrand accused Fouché, a former Jacobin, of having been party to the plot,
that the Minister of Police was forced to produce the real criminals—who
were, as he had always claimed—royalists. In 1802, however, Talleyrand
was more successful in his attempt to eliminate his chief competitor as Bonaparte's minister par excellence. An embryonic military plot was discovered which, in the way of military men, was so clumsily organized and so
open as to be more of a farce than a serious threat. Somehow, Fouché's
name was implicated in this conspiracy, either because he had not acted to
suppress it or because, as was said, he had secretly encouraged General
Bernadotte, its nominal leader. In any event, Talleyrand was able to persuade Bonaparte to relieve Fouché of his office over this affair. But this
success was transitory, for Fouché's cleverness and effectiveness were
greatly valued by Bonaparte, and before long, he was reestablished in his
old position.

The fact was that Bonaparte needed Fouché to control his enemies, real
or imagined, within France; just as he needed Talleyrand to contend with
foreign powers, both friendly and hostile. His preoccupation with the waning forces of Jacobinism, and with the enemies which he had created
abroad, caused him to ignore the real danger to himself and his regime presented by royalist sentiment. The recall of the émigrés, the Concordat, and
Talleyrand's effort to reconcile the old aristocracy with the parvenus of the
new regime had gone a long way toward disarming such sentiments within
France itself, and this had been demonstrated by the overwhelming public
support given by the royalists to the extension of Bonaparte's term as Consul. The Duke de Laval, head of the powerful Montmorency family, a
former émigré who was bound to the Bourbons by tradition as well as by
conviction, expressed the thinking of intelligent royalists succinctly: "Who
the devil would we put in the place of that little scamp?"

The danger, however, was not from the likes of Laval and his friends, all
of whom had benefited from the studied benevolence which Talleyrand
had inspired in the First Consul. It was rather from the émigrés who had

been refused permission to return to France—the hard-core royalists who surrounded the persons of Louis XVIII and the Count d'Artois and who believed and preached to the sympathetic ears of Europe's "legitimate" sovereigns that Bonaparte, the usurper, was the enemy of legitimacy and of religion, the double foundation on which every throne of Europe was built. The English were particularly susceptible to this argument, perhaps because—as Talleyrand pointed out to the British Cabinet during the first round of the peace negotiations—their own "legitimate" sovereign, James II, was still living in Rome, while George III occupied his throne. Talleyrand, more aware of the danger from the Bourbon princes than Bonaparte, suggested several expedients for neutralizing their hostility. One such device was an offer from Bonaparte to Louis XVIII that the latter renounce forever, for himself and his heirs, all claim to the (then nonexistent) throne of France. In exchange the Bourbon princes would receive a very generous monetary settlement, which amounted to full value for the vast properties owned by the dynasty prior to the Revolution. Louis sent a reply so negative and so haughty that it could be regarded as nothing less than insulting.

On January 13, 1804, a conspiracy was discovered which brought home to Bonaparte, once and for all, that, for all of Talleyrand's efforts, the chasm between himself and the Bourbon princes was one that would never be bridged. The organizer of the plot was one Georges Cadoudal, a former émigré, who was sponsored, and whose pockets had been filled with gold, by the newly established government of Mr. Pitt. It is not really clear whether it was the abduction of Bonaparte or his assassination that Cadoudal planned. In either case, his executive agent was Charles Pichegru, the former leader of the Council of Five Hundred, who, after the Eighteenth Fructidor, had been deported to Cayenne for plotting with Louis XVIII.* Pichegru's illegal entry into France was immediately reported to Bonaparte, who ordered the immediate arrest of both Pichegru and Cadoudal, as well as that of General Moreau, who was reported to be one of the chief figures in the conspiracy. Thanks to the efficient police network organized by Fouché (who had now been reinstated as Minister of Police), the three men were soon in prison, where, with the fatalism of zealots, they told all. "I came to Paris," Cadoudal said, "to assassinate the First Consul. . . . I was not supposed to assassinate him until there was a prince in Paris, and so far none has arrived." When the interrogator asked whether or not the plot had been conceived and was to be executed "in cooperation with a French prince of the *ancien régime,*" Cadoudal answered simply, "Yes."

* Pichegru had escaped from Cayenne in 1797 and made his way to London, where he offered his services to the British government and to the Bourbons. He was engaged by both and given a pension by the former.

When the news of Cadoudal's confession was brought to Bonaparte, he was more angry than shocked. "Am I a dog to be killed in the streets, while my murderers are safe from punishment?"—the murderers obviously being the Bourbon princes. "The head of the guilty man will be my revenge." Somehow Bonaparte was convinced that the "guilty man" behind the plot was the Duke d'Enghien, a member of the Condé family and a prince of the blood, and that he was the "French prince" expected in Paris. Enghien, in fact, lived in Ettenheim, in the duchy of Baden, near the French frontier, and it was currently being rumored (falsely) that Enghien sometimes crossed the Rhine secretly into France. This was what Bonaparte seemed to have in mind when he swore that "the first of these princes who comes within reach will be shot without mercy."

On March 10 Bonaparte convened his Council in the Tuileries specifically to discuss the measures to be taken in response to this Bourbon-inspired, British-sponsored attempt on the life of the First Consul. Among the ministers present were Talleyrand and Fouché. Accounts differ on what took place during that session, but not on its result. That same night Bonaparte dispatched an order to General Louis-Alexandre Berthier, Minister of War: "You will order General Ordener to go to Strasbourg. . . . The aim of this mission is to advance to Ettenheim, surround that town, and remove the Duke d'Enghien. . . ." During the night of March 14 Bonaparte's order was carried out, and the duke was seized, on the neutral territory of the state of Baden and taken back across the frontier to Barrière de la Villette and then to Vincennes. There, after an interrogation which produced evidence so circumstantial that it was indicative of Enghien's naïveté, rather than of his guilt, and a trial presided over by General Pierre-Augustin Hulin, the duke was executed, on the night of March 20, in the moat of the chateau.

There is no doubt that Enghien was innocent of the specific crime imputed to him or that his innocence was generally accepted even at the time of his death. His abduction from neutral foreign territory, his trial by a hastily convened military court, and his even more hasty execution on the basis of the flimsiest evidence—all constituted a crime which even Bonaparte's staunchest supporters found difficult to explain and which the most assiduous cultivators of the Napoleonic legend are still hard put to justify. Josephine herself reprimanded the First Consul for the deed, and he felt called upon to explain in her salon that "I have caused blood to be shed because it was necessary for me to do so." And at table that night, he shouted angrily in reply to the silent accusations of his wife and his guests: "At least we have shown them what we are capable of! Perhaps now they will leave us in peace." Until the last days of his life he maintained that he had done only what was necessary. In this political testament, dictated less than two weeks before his death in 1821, he asserted that "I had the Duke d'Enghien arrested and tried because it was necessary for the security, tranquillity, and honor of the people of France. It was done at a time when the Count d'Artois, as he himself admitted, had sixty assassins in his pay in Paris. Under similar circumstances, I would do the same thing today."

Talleyrand maintains, in the *Mémoires*, that the assassination plot was merely Bonaparte's pretext for the seizure and execution of Enghien. The real motive, he says, was his determination to place himself among the ranks of those who had executed Louis XVI and thus irrevocably bind to himself the republicans. The duke's "assassination"—the term is Talleyrand's—therefore "can be neither excused nor forgiven; nor has it ever been forgiven. Bonaparte, therefore, is reduced to boasting of it."

Talleyrand's condemnation of Bonaparte, given his own part in this ignoble crime, is somewhat gratuitous. There is no evidence that in the Council meeting at which the fateful decision was taken, anyone other than Cambacérès, the ex-regicide, opposed Bonaparte—and was silenced with the remark "You've suddenly become very concerned about the blood of the Bourbons!" Talleyrand himself admits in the *Mémoires* that he prepared and signed the documents relating to the affair which it was necessary for his ministry to circulate—such as a dispatch to the French envoy in Baden explaining and justifying in the most disarmingly simple terms, the violation of that neutral state's territory: "The First Consul has thought it necessary to send two small detachments to Offenburg and to Ettenheim, in order to seize the instigators of a crime which, by its very nature, puts beyond the pale of international law those convicted of participating in it."

The memoirs of many of Talleyrand's contemporaries accuse him of suggesting to Bonaparte, and even insisting upon, the abduction and execution of the Duke d'Enghien. It is interesting to note that most of these accusers—Fouché, for example, and Savary, who stood behind General Hulin during Enghien's trial—were preoccupied solely with exculpating themselves of any responsibility for the deed. Or, as in the case of Chateaubriand, Molé, and (again) Savary, they were among Talleyrand's bitterest enemies in later years, at the time that their memoirs were composed. The most important piece of evidence was cited by Chateaubriand, who claims that on March 8, the day before the Council meeting, Talleyrand presented a memorandum to Bonaparte suggesting Enghien's arrest. Baron Méneval, who had replaced Bourrienne as the First Consul's secretary, states that this memorandum was but the written confirmation of an earlier conversation between Talleyrand and Bonaparte, in which the former had urged the latter to take whatever strong steps were necessary to convince the people that he had no intention ever of reinstating the Bourbons on the throne of France. And this seems confirmed by a remark of Bonaparte's, while on St. Helena, to the effect that:

> My ministers urged me to arrest the Duke d'Enghien, even though he was then residing in neutral territory. The Prince de Bénévent [Talleyrand] twice brought me the order for his arrest, and, with all the eloquence at his command, urged me to sign it. . . . It was repeated constantly to me that the new dynasty would never be secure so long as one Bourbon survived. This was Talleyrand's basic principle. It was the foundation, the corner-stone, of his political credo. . . . The result of my own observations led me to share this opinion of Talleyrand's.

The testimony of Talleyrand's enemies (among whom Bonaparte must be included, particularly in the bitter years of his final exile) is hardly proof that the Foreign Minister first inspired Bonaparte to the deed or even that he actively approved of the idea. It is certain, however, that he failed to react with the indignation which was habitual to him when Bonaparte, during the years of their association, committed an especially salient blun-der. D'Hauterive, Talleyrand's subordinate at the ministry and his good friend, related to Pasquier that he read the news of Enghien's death in the *Moniteur*, shortly before going into Talleyrand's office for his daily session of work. D'Hauterive's shock and horror were evident in his demeanor, for Talleyrand said to him sharply, "What is the matter with you? Your eyes are popping out of your head."

"What's wrong with me?" D'Hauterive replied. "You would feel the same if you had just read the *Moniteur*. What a terrible thing!"

"Come now," Talleyrand reprimanded him, "have you taken leave of your senses? What is so terrible? A conspirator was captured near the fron-tier, brought to Paris [*sic*], and shot. What is there to make such a fuss about?"

And we are told by several witnesses that Talleyrand's usual answer, to anyone who expressed outrage at the manner of Enghien's death, was: "After all, business is business."

On the other side of the ledger, there is only Talleyrand's denial of hav-ing advocated the arrest and death of the Bourbon prince or of having had any part in the affair beyond what was required of him as Minister of For-eign Affairs:

> It was neither through the Foreign Office nor, consequently, through me that the First Consul was informed about the plots, real or imaginary, that were being hatched at that time on the other side of the Rhine. Moreover, I had nothing to do with the whole business of the Duke d'Enghien. For me to have taken any part in this bloody drama, it must be supposed that I had done so voluntarily and that I had interfered for no reason other than

the love of bloodshed. Surely my character and my background place me above such an odious and infamous suspicion.

And in 1823 he wrote a strong letter to Louis XVIII, defending himself against the imputation of guilt in Enghien's death and explaining why his enemies were eager for it to be believed that he was guilty:

> I am not telling your majesty anything new when I say that I have many enemies, both near the throne and far removed from it. . . . All those libels, all those voluminous recollections from St. Helena in which, during the past two years, I have constantly been insulted by men . . . who have constituted themselves the testamentary executors of Napoleon Bonaparte's revenge.

It is certainly true that Talleyrand was not a cruel man or a bloodthirsty one. Quite the contrary. In normal circumstances, his forbearance was extraordinary, and his loathing of violence of any kind was well known. It has often been said that Talleyrand's opinion concerning the execution of Enghien was: "It was worse than a crime; it was a blunder." Talleyrand was not, in fact, the originator of that epigram. But he would have been if he had thought of it, for it expressed perfectly his own approach both to policy and to practical politics. In this instance, Talleyrand had nothing to gain from Enghien's execution and possibly had everything to lose. He had already taken pains not to burn his bridges behind him so far as the Bourbons were concerned, and it is difficult to believe that he actively would have forwarded a plan which would cut him off, once and for all, from any hope of mercy, let alone of power and influence, in the event of a restoration of the Bourbons. Within this context, it is possible to accept even Talleyrand's protest that he "tried, but in vain, to soften the wrath of the First Consul." Certainly, Talleyrand spoke the truth when he explained why it would have been illogical for him to have supported Bonaparte in his resolve:

> At this period, France, though again engaged in war with England, was at peace with the rest of the world. It was therefore the duty of the Minister of Foreign Affairs to do all that lay in his power, within the limits of right and justice, to preserve this peace. In this respect, it is almost impossible to describe the very complicated nature of such a duty. Standing between governments which were terrified, touchy, and uneasy as to their danger, though all more or less reconciled to each other, and a powerful sovereign, whose genius, character, and ambition gave just cause for unease and offense, the Minister of Foreign Affairs was required constantly to exercise an equal degree of vigilance with respect to the policies which he wanted to restrict and to those which he felt obliged to oppose. His negotiations with his own government were often much more difficult and much longer than those with governments which he wished to pacify. . . . The First Consul

had guarded himself against all such negotiations, and this fact of itself proves that I had done everything to prevent any occurrence which must inevitably lead my office into great and inextricable difficulties.

All these factors may justify one in concluding that Talleyrand's character, inclinations, ambitions, and responsibilities were such as to preclude his active participation in the planning and execution of the assassination of the Duke d'Enghien. Yet the fact remains that he did not protest strongly against the crime, that he publicly condoned it in his letter to the French minister in Baden, and that, after Enghien's death, he exhibited complete sangfroid in defending it. When Alexander of Russia demanded an explanation, Talleyrand did not hesitate to point out to the czar, in writing, that since France had not required an explanation for the mysterious death of Alexander's predecessor on the throne, it might be just as well for the czar not to set a dangerous precedent by asking for similar explanations from the First Consul.

This touch of bravura, even of insolence, on Talleyrand's part cannot obscure the fact that for all his denials, he was, at the very least, a passive accomplice in one of the most infamous public crimes of the Napoleonic era.

9

The Empire

THE DISCOVERY of the Cadoudal-Pichegru conspiracy against Bonaparte, and the execution of the Duke d'Enghien, marked the official end of the Consular period in France, just as it signaled the end of the hopes for peace in Europe. On April 30 the Tribunate voted the following resolution: "That Napoleon Bonaparte be named Emperor and that, in this capacity, he become responsible for the government of the French Republic; and that the title of Emperor and the imperial power be made hereditary in his family, from male to male, by primogeniture." On May 4 this resolution was officially communicated to the Senate. On May 10 the senators voted unanimously for Bonaparte's assumption of the title of Emperor, and, on May 19, Napoleon, Emperor of the French Republic (for such was the anomalous title which he first bore), replied: "I accept. I accept the title that you deem useful to the nation's glory."

Napoleon's proclamation as emperor and the subsequent creation of the Empire were not altogether spontaneous acts of the Tribunate and Senate. For more than a year, Bonaparte, as First Consul, had foreseen and planned just such a step. All that had been lacking was a favorable opportunity, and this had come early in 1804, with the discovery of the Cadoudal-Pichegru conspiracy which, when it was made public, had united France behind its leader as never before. So great was public sympathy and support that not even the scandal of Enghien's execution could diminish Bonaparte's popularity—except among the aristocrats of the Faubourg St.-Germain, who had never, in any case, been among the First Consul's most ardent admirers. So, Talleyrand says, "Bonaparte took advantage of the royalist plot . . . to wrench the title of Emperor from the Senate. It was a title which, with moderation and wisdom, he would have attained in any case, but not quite so soon. He therefore ascended the throne. But it was a throne smeared with innocent blood."

Among the new emperor's first acts was to constitute his court. Cambacérès was named Arch-Chancellor of the Empire; Lebrun, Arch-Treasurer; and Talleyrand, Grand Chamberlain of the Imperial Court, an honor which he accepted with becoming gratitude. It was in his capacity as Grand Chamberlain that he figured in the elaborate coronation rite celebrated at Notre Dame on December 2, 1804, in the course of which Napoleon took the crown—a circle of golden laurel leaves—from the trembling hands of Pius VII—who had been commanded to be present for the ceremony—and, facing the people, placed it firmly upon his head. David's epic painting of the ceremony depicts Talleyrand, standing among the new dignitaries of the Empire, with a slight smile upon his lips, an expression half of amusement, half of satisfaction. It is probable that these were indeed Talleyrand's sentiments during the lengthy ceremony—satisfaction that, after fourteen years of wandering, France had at last been brought safely into the secure haven of the monarchical system, and amusement at Bonaparte's temerity, at the most solemn moment of the ritual, in asserting symbolically that his crown and his power came, not from heaven through the hands of the Pope, but from the people and by virtue of his own deeds. These, at least, are the thoughts which he expressed in a circular letter sent to French emissaries abroad, explaining, for the benefit of foreign powers, the significance of Napoleon's coronation:

> The anointing and the coronation have, in effect, put an end to the revolution. They have placed France under a government which is both appropriate to the nation's power and in keeping with its traditions; traditions which France, after fourteen centuries, had abandoned only to lose herself in idealistic byways which had no link with the past and no guarantee for the future. The emperor . . . has saved the state, established internal peace, and fulfilled the hopes of all the people.

And, Talleyrand adds, the power by which Bonaparte wrought these wonders has now, by virtue of the coronation, been "rendered sacred."

At the time of the proclamation of the Emperor Napoleon, he and Talleyrand had collaborated for four and a half years. It had not always been an easy association, and as time had passed, Bonaparte had been transformed, by the exercise of power, from a willing student of the master into an increasingly stubborn and self-willed autocrat. Still, Talleyrand had served him loyally, offering good counsel whether or not Bonaparte had asked for it, excusing the First Consul's faults, defending his blunders, and putting the best face on his occasional tyrannies. It had been worth while, for while serving Bonaparte, Talleyrand was also serving France. In internal affairs, the reconciliation of the old order with the new had been his principal concern, and despite the flourishing of royalist conspiracies of varying degrees of seriousness, he had been largely successful. The aristocrats of the Faubourg St.-Germain, if not yet the bedfellows of the self-made men of Napoleonic France, at least no longer lived at sword's point with them. There had been a gradual resignation to the new regime, even an acceptance of it, and now old names began to appear alongside the new as officials of the newly established Empire. Bonaparte counted it as a great victory when the Countess de Montmorency, the Marquise de Mortemart, and the Duchess de Chevreuse consented to serve as ladies-in-waiting to the Empress Josephine, and he was aware that this visible reconciliation was due entirely to the good offices of his newly appointed Grand Chamberlain.

In the area of foreign affairs, Talleyrand had worked no less assiduously, as he describes it, "to establish such monarchical institutions in France which would guarantee the authority of the sovereign while maintaining it within its proper boundaries and to deal with the European powers in such a way as to induce them to forgive France for its good fortune and its glory." The most difficult of these objectives was not to design proper institutions for the exercise of authority or to pacify the countries of Europe, but to induce Napoleon to comport himself in such a way as to jeopardize neither the one nor the other achievement. It was a difficult task, almost an impossible one, for the success of Talleyrand's policies depended, as always, on prudence and moderation, and these were virtues foreign to Napoleon's temperament. Power was what he loved best; and, after power, glory. For both, he looked to conquest. Talleyrand, who had once declared, and always maintained, that the true power and glory of a nation lay in the mastery of its own territory, could not help foreseeing that the time was near when the ambitions of Bonaparte and the true interests of France would come into conflict. The rupture of the Peace of Amiens and the resumption of the war with England had been not the first but the surest indication of what was to come. Other signs, equally ominous, were quick to follow.

> The new war which Bonaparte had undertaken against England required all his resources [Talleyrand says], and it needed only the most common prudence to abstain from anything that might induce the powers on the Continent to make cause with his enemy. But vanity was his driving force. It was not enough that he had been proclaimed Emperor of the French. It was not enough that he had been consecrated by the Sovereign Pontiff. He wanted, in addition, to become King of Italy, so as to become the equal, as emperor and king, of the head of the House of Austria.

When Napoleon first signified this intention in 1804, Talleyrand tried every means in his power to dissuade him. There could never be peace in Europe, he knew, so long as one man ruled both France and Italy. Austria, who regarded Italy as its proper sphere of influence, would never accept such an arrangement, and behind Austria, there was mighty Russia, ruled by a czar sympathetic to England and openly hostile to Napoleon. When Talleyrand realized that Napoleon's grandiose ambitions could not be set aside by mere reasons of state, he attempted to mitigate the offense offered to Austria and Russia by suggesting that the emperor content himself with making a member of his family, rather than himself, sovereign of Italy. First, Joseph—now His Imperial Highness, Prince Joseph, Grand Elector of the Empire—was suggested, and Napoleon, who, for no good reason, thought highly of his eldest brother, seemed amenable. But Joseph did not want to be King of Italy. The name of Lucien Bonaparte was offered next, and Talleyrand reminded Napoleon that it was Lucien who, as president of the Council of Five Hundred, had worked so valiantly, even when the tide seemed to be running against him, to bring his brother to power. But Lucien was living in Rome, in disgrace. He had married beneath his station and had done so without Napoleon's permission. The emperor had therefore refused even to make him an imperial prince, like Joseph and Louis, and he could not be expected, he explained to Talleyrand, to place the crown of Italy upon the brow of so ungrateful a brother. Therefore, in May, 1805, Talleyrand records, Napoleon "had himself crowned at Milan, and instead of taking simply the title of King of Lombardy, he chose the more ambitious, and therefore the more alarming, title of King of Italy." As though this were not provocation enough, Genoa and Lucca, "where Napoleon's agents had been at work playing upon the fears of the people, sent deputations to ask, in the case of Genoa, for annexation to his empire and, in that of Lucca, to request a ruler from Napoleon's own family." In June the emperor granted both requests. Genoa was annexed to France, and Lucca received, as its sovereign, Napoleon's sister, Elisa Bonaparte, now Princess of Lucca and Piombino. When the news of Napoleon's coronation and his disposition of Genoa and Lucca reached the capitals of Europe, Talleyrand's worst fears were realized. "The man is insatiable!" Czar Alexander exclaimed. "His ambition knows no bounds. He is the scourge of the world. Well, since he wants war, he will get war. And the sooner, the better!"

Alexander's rage at the Italian ambitions of Napoleon was not, of itself, the worst of it. At the beginning of 1805, Napoleon had finally given in to Talleyrand's repeated arguments in favor of peace with England and had allowed him to make guarded overtures to London. The British, no less wary, had been evasive, replying that they must first consult with the other powers—especially with Czar Alexander. The Russians, meanwhile, as early as November, 1804, had taken the diplomatic initiative in attempting to form a third coalition against France, comprising Russia, Sweden, Prussia, Austria, and Britain. Of these, only Prussia had opted for neutrality, and then more out of fear than from a desire for peace. The first of the powers formally to join itself to Russia was Austria, which, in November, 1804, signed a secret convention promising to put almost a quarter million men into the field. Next came Britain, which, in April, 1805, when it had learned of Napoleon's plans to assume the crown of Italy, quickly signed a treaty of alliance with Alexander.

Napoleon, after his coronation in Italy, had gone to Boulogne, where his "armies of the coasts of the sea" had gathered, along with a great fleet of transports, for the invasion of England. He was there, ready to launch his forces across the Channel to a point about ten miles from Dover, waiting only for word from Talleyrand that negotiations had failed so as to give the order. "The English don't know what is in store for them," the emperor assured his staff. "If only we can retain control of the situation during the twelve hours of the crossing, it will be all over for them." Then there came a message from Talleyrand: The Austrians, with a force of 225,000 men, were moving toward the Inn River, with the apparent intention of invading the territory of Napoleon's ally, the Elector of Bavaria. At the same time, news reached Napoleon that the French fleet, under Admiral Villeneuve, needed to protect the invasion forces during the crossing and expected at Boulogne momentarily, had just put into port at Cádiz and abandoned the waters of the Channel to the superior naval forces of England. This last intelligence decided Napoleon. "As of this moment," he wrote to Talleyrand, "I have changed my plan of attack. I must gain twenty days and stop the Austrians from crossing the Inn while I myself cross the Rhine. They have no idea how rapidly I can make 200,000 men march. . . . When I have taught Austria a lesson, I shall get back to my original plans."

At this news, the Prussian ambassador reported to Berlin, "Monsieur de Talleyrand is in despair. If he had been able, or if he were able now, either to prevent the opening of hostilities or to halt them before ambition had been excited or honor compromised, he would consider this to be the most glorious accomplishment of his career." Talleyrand was to have his chance. In September, Napoleon reached the Rhine, where he made his headquarters at Strasbourg. Talleyrand, along with the other ministers and high officials of state, were ordered to join the emperor there, for Napoleon was chief of state, as well as sovereign and commander in chief, and where he was, there was the government of France. As pleased as Talleyrand may have been at the opportunity to exercise some measure of control over events by his presence at Napoleon's side, he did not relish the idea of travel, and he complained of it unceasingly and bitterly. Later, from Brünn, he wrote: "This is a ghastly place. There are four thousand wounded here right now, and every day there are a great many deaths. The smell yesterday was not to be believed. Today, however, it is freezing, which is just as well. Please be sure to send me some very dry Malaga, the driest possible."

On October 1, Napoleon and his men crossed the Rhine, leaving Talleyrand at Strasbourg. A few days later, a note arrived for Talleyrand from Stuttgart: "I am well. The Duke of Württemberg came to meet me outside the first gate of his palace. He is a sensible man." On the same day, there was another letter: "I am aware of Mack's movements, and they are everything I could wish. He will be caught in Ulm, like a fool!"

General Mack, the Austrian commander, was indeed in Ulm, and on October 15 he awoke, "like a fool," to find the city and his army surrounded by the French. He attempted a sortie, which was unsuccessful, and when the Austrian hussars withdrew into the city, Napoleon ordered Ulm to be bombarded. Whereupon General Mack agreed to an unconditional surrender.* "In announcing this victory to me," Talleyrand writes, "Napoleon explained the terms that he wished to impose upon Austria and what territories he wished to take from it. I immediately replied to him that his real interest was not to enfeeble Austria, but to remove it from the other side and place it on his own, so that it would become France's ally." In this memorandum to Napoleon, dated October 17, Talleyrand harped constantly on the theme that true victory in the struggle would be achieved only when France and Austria were united in a common front against a common enemy—that is, against Russia, whose expansionist tendencies westward into Europe could be checked only by the combined forces of the two empires. For Franco-Austrian friendship to be possible, however, it was necessary that obvious areas of friction be eliminated, and the most obvious of these areas was northern Italy. Austria must therefore be made to give up its possessions in that peninsula, and Venice should be set up as a buffer state between Austria and the French possessions in Italy. For this renunciation, Austria must be amply compensated in eastern Europe, with Moldavia, Bessarabia, Wallachia,† and part of Bulgaria. Thus, its power would be increased rather than diminished by its defeat at Napoleon's

---

* Vienna and the whole of Europe were filled with rumors that Napoleon had bribed Baron von Mack. There is not a shred of evidence to this effect, and the report was probably manufactured in Vienna in an effort to save face after a humiliating defeat. In any event, shortly after the capitulation of Ulm, on October 19, Mack was tried by court-martial in Vienna and sentenced to death for his "treasonable conduct." The sentence was commuted to five years' imprisonment by the Emperor Francis, who was probably more aware than anyone that under the circumstances Mack's surrender was the only possibility open to him.

† Roughly, the territory of the modern nation of Rumania.

hands, and this increment would serve a double purpose: first, to neutralize any resentment or hostility toward France and, second, to present Russia with a powerful enemy on its western frontier. Then Russia, knowing
that behind Austria there stood the French Empire, would be compelled to
seek an eastward, rather than a westward, expansion. In the East, however,
it must inevitably come into conflict with Britain, whose ambitions centered in the same area, and the two powers—which were France's only
dangerous enemies—would turn on each other, fight out their differences
in the Orient and, it was hoped, exhaust each other. The result would be
that Europe would be left in peace. Within this context, Talleyrand
pointed out, it was clear that only a solid and durable alliance between
France and Austria could assure the tranquillity of the Continent, both by
shattering the alliance between Russia and Great Britain and by removing
any cause of conflict between the French and the Austrian empires.

> The memorandum in which I set forth my reasoning made such an im-
> pression on him [Talleyrand says] that he placed the matter before the
> Council, which was held at Munich, for discussion. I had gone to meet him
> there, to induce him to follow the plan I had proposed. . . . But new ad-
> vantages, created by one of the divisions of his advance guard, fired his
> imagination and made him desire to march upon Vienna, to hurry on to
> new victories, and to be able to date his decrees from the Imperial Palace
> of Schönbrunn.

The "new advantages" to which Talleyrand referred were the Battle of
Austerlitz, one of Napoleon's most brilliant victories, in which the combined forces of Austria and Prussia were routed and the Czar Alexander
compelled to join his Hapsburg ally in flight before the irresistible armies
of the Corsican upstart. This was more than sufficient to induce Napoleon
to dismiss all of Talleyrand's arguments for prudence and moderation. But
the Foreign Minister was still not discouraged. Only two days after Austerlitz, when Europe was at the emperor's feet, he dared write another memorandum, insisting that the policies which he had outlined were the only
ones which would ensure the peace and prosperity of both France and of
Europe as a whole. He explained:

> The Austrian monarchy is composed of various states which differ
> among themselves in language, traditions, religion, and composition. They
> have a single thing in common: one and the same sovereign. The power of
> this monarch is therefore weak, yet it is a sufficient and a necessary obsta-
> cle to the barbarians. Austria is now defeated and humiliated. Its con-
> queror must now extend a generous hand and, by making it an ally, restore
> to it that confidence in itself of which it may be deprived by this series of
> defeats and disasters. I implore Your Majesty to read once more the mem-
> orandum which I had the honor to send from Strasbourg. Today, more

than ever, I daresay that it outlines the best and wisest policy to follow.
. . . It is now in the power of your majesty to destroy the Austrian monarchy or to raise it up. If you choose to destroy it, it will no longer be in
your power to make the pieces whole again, and the existence of this monarchy is necessary, indispensable, to the future security of civilization.

Talleyrand's letter had no effect on Bonaparte, and his insistence on the
preservation, even on the strengthening, of Austria was shrugged off. Still,
Talleyrand had done his duty, both to Napoleon and to France, in giving
wise counsel. That the emperor chose to ignore it was no surprise, for no
one, after Austerlitz, could have stifled Napoleon's ambition or caused him
to relinquish the satisfaction which his vanity derived from humiliating Europe's oldest and proudest dynasty. Talleyrand therefore resigned himself
to obeying Napoleon's instructions and negotiated the Peace of Pressburg
with the Austrian envoys, Prince Johann von Lichtenstein and General
Count Giulay, in accordance with the emperor's wishes. The treaty, which
was signed on December 27, deprived the Hapsburg dynasty of Venetia,
the Tyrol and Vorarlberg, and also its last foothold in Germany by recognizing Bavaria, Baden, and Württemberg as autonomous kingdoms. All in
all, Francis II lost 2,500,000 subjects and one-sixth of his revenue, and in
addition, he agreed to pay to France a war indemnity of 40,000,000 francs.
"Austria," Talleyrand remarks, "given the state to which it was now reduced, could do nothing other than accept the conditions imposed by its
conqueror, and those conditions were harsh indeed." In normal circumstances, Talleyrand, since he was Napoleon's negotiator, would have been
in a position to mitigate somewhat the severity of these terms. But on December 15 Napoleon had forced the King of Prussia's ambassador, Count
von Haugwitz, to sign a treaty giving Anspach and Neufchâtel to France,
in exchange for Hanover (a possession of the King of England), and recognizing the cessions which he required of Austria. Therefore, for Talleyrand
to attempt to circumvent his master's will with respect to these territories
would have voided, or at least made questionable, the Prussian treaty. He
had to be satisfied with "managing that the conditions imposed on Austria
should not be made even more severe through any possibility of fallacious
interpretation. Being responsible for the wording of the treaty, on which
Napoleon's influence was minimized by the distance between him and me,
I concentrated on making it as free as possible from any ambiguity." Even
this, however, was too much for Napoleon. When Talleyrand sent him the
draft of the treaty, he replied saying, "You have made, at Pressburg, a
treaty that annoys me a *great* deal," and accused Talleyrand of favoring
the Austrians to the detriment of the French. The Austrians saw it from a
different perspective, and Metternich noted later that it was to Talleyrand

that "we owe any more or less favorable *nuances* in the Treaty of Pressburg." Talleyrand himself was neither proud nor pleased with the result of his negotiations. After the signing of the treaty, he remarked to Napoleon, in a sibylline phrase, that "Never before has France dictated such a treaty, and never before has Austria signed one." But it was not until 1812, when Napoleon, at the zenith of his glory, decided to erect a monument to the Peace of Pressburg, that Talleyrand was able to make his resentment known in a public manner. He wrote to the emperor, refusing, in the most absolute terms, to have his name appear on the monument.

If it is possible to date a definitive break between Talleyrand and Napoleon, the most acceptable time is at the end of 1805, with the Treaty of Pressburg. By then, it was clear that there was an irreconcilable difference between the two men regarding not the end at which they both aimed—the peace and order of Europe—but the nature of the means to achieve that end. For Talleyrand, who had been raised in the school of international equilibrium, peace could be obtained only by diplomatic means supplemented, if absolutely necessary, by military might, and in the Europe of his day this meant, as he explained to Napoleon, that "Austria, which is the natural enemy of Russia, must have France as its natural ally." The basis for Napoleon's sovereignty and the sole justification for his military undertakings, Talleyrand once pointed out to Madame de Rémusat, were "to restore religion, morals and order in France; to encourage English civilization while restraining English political ambitions; to fortify France's frontiers by the Confederation of the Rhine; to make of Italy a kingdom independent both of Austria and of France; and to keep the czar at home. . . . There should have been the eternal designs of the emperor, and to these should have led every one of the treaties." To these practical methods of achieving peace, order, and prosperity, not only in France but in the whole of Europe, Napoleon opposed his own *modus agendi*. Even on St. Helena he had not yet learned his lesson, for he wrote that what he had intended was "order and peace for Europe," but it was to be a peace and an order imposed by force, by military conquest, and by cultural colonization—a new *pax Romana*, in other words, forced upon Europe, willy-nilly, by the man who regarded himself as the successor of Caesar. To this, Talleyrand knew, Europe would never consent, regardless of Napoleonic victories and dictated treaties of peace. He saw, stretching out into the future, not the blessings of peace, but endless years of war and bloodshed. He therefore began to prepare himself against the day when catastrophe must inevitably overwhelm France. Metternich, who was in a position to know whereof he spoke, recorded that in France there was no longer a single party, but two. One was composed of the militarists and the military men, whose fortunes were inextricably bound up with the Napoleonic idea of conquest and of a Europe ruled by France, and the other comprised those who foresaw that Napoleon's ambitions would end in ruin. Chief among the latter, he says, was Talleyrand, who, at the time of the campaign of 1805, "began to oppose, with all his strength and influence, the destructive projects of Napoleon."

Napoleon, as yet, was far from suspecting that his Foreign Minister no longer supported his policies, either foreign or domestic. In the new year of 1806,* he signified his approval of Talleyrand's services—"a marked proof of satisfaction," Talleyrand called it—by issuing a decree in his favor:

> Napoleon, by the Grace of God and the Constitution, Emperor of the French and King of Italy, to all those present and to come, greetings. Wishing to confer upon our Grand Chamberlain and Minister of Foreign Relations, Talleyrand, a sign of our gratitude for the services which he has rendered to us, we have resolved to transfer to him, and we do so transfer by these presents, the principality of Benevento, with the title of Prince and Duke of Benevento, which he is to hold in ownership and sovereignty as a direct fief of our crown.

Benevento was a small enclave in the kingdom of Naples which, along with the town of Pontecorvo, had been restored to its original proprietor, the Pope, in 1802. Now Napoleon again relieved His Holiness of the temporal sovereignty of these two places in order to confer one on Talleyrand and the other on Bernadotte. Though neither place was exactly princely in extent or wealth, Benevento was rather more grand than Pontecorvo, and Talleyrand undoubtedly got the better of the two. Thereafter, until the fall of the Empire in 1814, he was known as *Son Altesse Sérénissime, le Prince de Bénévent*—"His Most Serene Highness, the Prince of Benevento." As a sovereign prince, he ruled the Beneventese through an appointed deputy, and he ruled them with wisdom and prudence. To Talleyrand, his subjects were indebted for such blessings as decreased taxes and, most important of all, exemption from conscription into Napoleon's armies. But the new Prince de Bénévent never once set foot in his domain. And he never took his splendid new title very seriously. To one of his friends who insisted on calling him "Highness," he said wearily: "Please do not call me that. I am something less than a Highness—and perhaps something better. A simple 'Monsieur de Talleyrand' will do very nicely." Catherine Grand, however, was transported into the seventh heaven by Napoleon's decree, although she never mastered the intricacies of the correct usage of her new title and made Paris titter by signing herself, "Catherine, Sovereign Princess de Tal-

* On January 1, 1806, at Napoleon's command, France officially abandoned the revolutionary calendar and adopted once more the Gregorian.

leyrand," and even, when the spirit moved her, "Reigning Princess de Talleyrand."

Talleyrand was not the only one to benefit from Napoleon's generosity in 1806. In March, Joseph Bonaparte finally consented to accept a crown and was named King of Naples. The former sovereign, Ferdinand IV, a Bourbon, had had the temerity to side with Austria in the recent war, and for this he was deprived of his throne by a Napoleonic decree—dated, in accordance with the French emperor's ambition, from the Schönbrunn Palace—which stated simply that the King of the Two Sicilies (as Ferdinand was called) "has ceased to reign." At the same time, Joachim Murat, the son of an innkeeper, who had saved the day for Bonaparte at St.-Cloud in 1799, and who had married the emperor's sister Caroline, was created Grand Duke of Berg and Cleves. In June, Louis, younger brother of Napoleon, was named King of Holland. "Napoleon," Talleyrand explains, "since he had become an emperor, no longer wished for there to be any republics, especially in his vicinity." And Madame Reinhard, wife of Talleyrand's friend and successor-predecessor in the Ministry of Foreign Affairs, registered the effect of Napoleon's kingmaking abroad. "We wonder if we are dreaming," she wrote from Vienna, "and we ask ourselves if all this can really be happening on an earth inhabited by men and ruled by God in heaven. Here no one mentions it, or rather, everyone is silent about it, for everyone is overwhelmed by the consciousness of his own powerlessness." But Vienna thus far had had only a preview of what was to come. On July 12, Napoleon signed a compact with thirteen German princes* by the terms of which these princes separated themselves from the Holy Roman Empire, of which the Hapsburg emperor, Francis II, was the head, and constituted themselves into the Confederation of the Rhine, with Napoleon as their Protector. Simultaneously, the new confederation signed, with the Emperor of the French, a treaty of alliance both offensive and defensive. Francis of Austria, a realist, did the only thing he could do, abdicating his title of Holy Roman Emperor and taking that of Emperor of Austria. Talleyrand, also a realist, played the major role in Napoleon's reorganization of Germany, serving as arbiter in the countless frontier adjustments which took place among the principalities of the confederation. From the exercise of this responsibility, he realized a more than respectable sum in "gifts" from the princes, "demanding," one German envoy noted in astonishment, "not jewels, which are the customary gifts, but cash."

France was now at peace, albeit an uneasy peace, on the Continent.

* Mainz, Bavaria, Württemberg, Baden, the territories of the Prince-Primate of Germany (Aschaffenburg, Frankfurt, and Wetzlar), and Hesse were the most important of these principalities.

Prussia, in exchange for Hanover, had been forced, by Bonaparte's threats, to sign a treaty of alliance with France which established a state of war between the Prussians and the English. Austria, of course, was exhausted and humiliated and for the moment, it lacked the energy to rally its forces for further resistance to Bonaparte's tyranny. And Alexander of Russia, after the Battle of Austerlitz, had been compelled to withdraw his troops into his own territory. As before the Third Coalition, only England remained at sword's point with France. Early in 1806, however, there had occurred the death of Bonaparte's sworn enemy, Mr. Pitt, prime minister of His Britannic Majesty, George III. Pitt was succeeded, at least nominally, by Lord Grenville—Talleyrand's antagonist from the days of his London exile— but the true power in the government was Talleyrand's old friend Charles Fox, who had been named Foreign Secretary. Knowing Talleyrand's perennial disposition toward peace, Fox, who had always been an opponent of war with France, now watched for an opportunity to attempt negotiation. His chance came in February, with the discovery, in England, of a conspiracy to assassinate Napoleon. Fox immediately wrote to Talleyrand, informing him of the plot against the "leader of the French [chef des français]." By separate letter, he conveyed his personal regards to the French Foreign Minister and explained that no offense had been intended by the term used to designate Napoleon. Britain, he pointed out, had not yet recognized the Empire of the French, and therefore he could not, in official correspondence, refer to Bonaparte as empereur des français. Talleyrand brought the letter to Napoleon's attention, and the latter remarked: "I recognize in this letter the principles of honor and principle that have always characterized M. Fox." A week later, on March 2, the emperor declared to the legislature: "I desire to have peace with England, and I am ready to conclude it on the basis of the terms granted in the Peace of Amiens."

Thus encouraged, Talleyrand set to work with vigor. As intermediary between himself and Fox, he chose Lord Yarmouth, an Englishman living in Paris—or, more accurately, detained in Paris as an enemy alien—whom he trusted. "But," Talleyrand says, "after two or three conferences, Mr. Fox, to be agreeable to Lord Grenville, associated Lord Lauderdale to Lord Yarmouth." From that moment, nothing seemed to go well. The English declared that they would not continue negotiations unless the German possessions of George III—specifically, Hanover—were guaranteed. This was a matter of some embarrassment, since Napoleon had already given that state to his reluctant ally, Prussia. Nonetheless, at Talleyrand's urging, he agreed to this requirement, provided that some adequate compensation could be found for Prussia's loss. Then the discussions turned to Sicily, where the dispossessed Bourbon, King Ferdinand, still ruled under the protection of the English fleet. Even on this point, Napoleon was willing to be reasonable, and Talleyrand informed Lord Yarmouth that "since you have it, we shall not ask for it." But then Napoleon decided that he could not guarantee Sicily after all, and Talleyrand was obliged to retract his assurances to Yarmouth. Immediately, the hitherto trusting Fox, when he learned of this, was on his guard. It would seem, he told his government, that "they are playing a false game."

The most serious trouble, however, was over Hanover. "Peace between England and France," Talleyrand pointed out, "was morally impossible without the restitution of Hanover." This was the one point on which Fox would not budge. To make certain that there would be no imperial change of heart, as in the case of Sicily, Yarmouth took the precaution of informing the Prussian minister in Paris of Bonaparte's willingness to return the state to its legitimate proprietor, the King of England. Girolanio Lucchesini, the minister, immediately informed Berlin, and there was a great uproar. The Prussian king, Frederick William III, was furious at the perfidy of his French ally. The French were outraged at the duplicity of the English, for it seems that, somehow, Yarmouth had neglected to mention to Lucchesini that Napoleon had stipulated Prussia must receive compensation for the loss of Hanover. And Napoleon, naturally, believed that everyone but himself had been guilty of the most egregious bad faith.

Matters were further complicated at this moment by a misunderstanding—or rather, by too clear an understanding—with Russia. With the opening of negotiations between London and Paris, Czar Alexander, seeing his alliance with England about to dissolve, also sent an envoy to Paris to discuss peace. This man, Baron d'Oubril, negotiated with Talleyrand according to the instructions he had received before leaving St. Petersburg, and since there were few territorial conflicts between the two nations, agreement was quickly reached, and a preliminary treaty was signed in July. Napoleon was delighted. Given the contretemps with England and Prussia over Hanover, he foresaw the resumption of war, and the treaty with Russia would deprive those two powers of their most formidable ally. Fox, however, was at least as foresighted as the Emperor of the French, and the British government informed St. Petersburg that it considered the terms of the treaty signed by Oubril and Talleyrand "humiliating" to Russia. Czar Alexander, eager to avoid offense to the country which had so recently been his ally and so soon would be again, discovered, upon a careful reading of the text, that the English were perfectly correct. The agreement was clearly favorable to the French. With a great show of defiance, therefore, he informed Paris that he would not ratify the instrument.

At this point, Charles Fox died, and with him were buried any hopes of an understanding. Many years later, Napoleon would say: "The death of

Mr. Fox was one of the calamities of my life. If he had but lived, there would have been peace." It is possible that he was correct. In any case, the death of Fox was the signal for the renewal of hostilities. Frederick William of Prussia, with a great rattling of sabers, ordered his Paris envoy to return to Berlin and announced to Alexander: "Apparently, it is I who will be required to take the first step. My armies will march from all directions to hasten the moment." On October 7 a Prussian ultimatum was delivered to Napoleon, demanding that the French withdraw beyond the Rhine by October 8. By then the emperor and his troops were well on their way to Berlin, and Napoleon, always in the best of moods when marching to war at the head of his armies, answered:

> Your majesty has set an appointment for October 8 and, since I am a gentleman, I would not dream of disappointing you. I am already in the middle of Saxony. . . . Today your forces are intact, and you can still negotiate with me in a manner suitable to your rank. Within a month, however, you will be forced to negotiate in different circumstances.

Talleyrand noted that, despite this brave display, Napoleon felt a "secret uneasiness" about measuring his strength against that of Prussia. "The ancient glory of the Prussian army had made an impression upon him"— meaning that Prussian arms still enjoyed the reputation that they had gained under Frederick the Great. The Prussians themselves were confident that the spell of invincibility still held firm, and the Emperor of the French was not certain that it did not. Talleyrand, playing upon Napoleon's doubts, had done his best to persuade him not to allow hostilities to resume, to make a gesture of reconciliation toward both England and Prussia. But, as before, he was unheeded. Worse, he was commanded to follow the emperor's forces, and by the beginning of October he was on the road, following in the wake of the mighty army that was marching toward Berlin.

Talleyrand's first stop was at Mainz, on the Rhine, where he profited from a few days of leisure to take the waters at Wiesbaden, since the emperor's orders had deprived him of his customary sojourn at Bourbon-l'Archambault. Upon his return to Mainz, he busied himself with the purchase of books—a distraction which he enjoyed immensely—and with the cultivation of Hortense de Beauharnais, daughter of Josephine, wife of Louis Bonaparte, and recently created Queen of Holland. It was none of these qualities which attracted Talleyrand's interest, but rather the fact that Hortense was the mistress of young Charles de Flahaut, Talleyrand's son, now a strapping, handsome young officer attached (thanks to Talleyrand) to the staff of the emperor. There is no record of Talleyrand's impression of Hortense, but this daughter of Josephine could not resist the temptation to record in detail her impression of Talleyrand:

It was during this journey* that I became better acquainted with M. de Talleyrand. . . . I had observed him for years at Malmaison, limping into the salon, his coldness and nonchalance evident in his demeanor, leaning on a chair and scarcely bowing to me. He had seldom spoken to me, but at Mainz, he made a point of seeking me out and being very polite. I was surprised and even pleased. The attentions of a man who rarely confers them are always effective. I am certain that his reputation for great cleverness is due not so much to anything unusual that he does, but to the fact that he says so little, but says it so well. . . . The vanity of people is what makes Talleyrand so attractive to them. I was a victim of this myself. When he unbends to the extent of speaking to you, he seems utterly charming. And if he goes so far as to inquire about your health, you are prepared to love him forever.

As Talleyrand inspected rare editions, took the waters, and charmed the Queen of Holland, Napoleon met the Prussian army and, in a campaign lasting only three weeks, crushed it utterly at Jena and Auerstedt. More than 100,000 Prussians were taken, and 250 regimental flags. By the third week of October the emperor was in Berlin, ready to dictate the terms of peace to the Prussians, who, terrified, now forgot the glories of Frederick the Great and expended all their energies in an attempt to soften the heart of the conqueror. The hopes of the Prussians, in fact, centered on Talleyrand, whom Napoleon had commanded to present himself in Berlin immediately. They remembered the Foreign Minister's spirit of generosity while negotiating the Treaty of Pressburg, and they saw no reason why they should expect less than their Austrian cousins. Count von Haugwitz, who had had some experience with Talleyrand, told one of the Prussian negotiators:

> Since M. de Talleyrand is supposed to arrive shortly, I think that you may be able to count on hearing political ideas more sound than this terrible principle [of Napoleon's] which requires the destruction of Prussia as a guarantee of France's security. That enlightened Minister will surely see that if Prussia is so reduced as to be unable to restrain Russia or to neutralize Austria, these two powers will be in a stronger position to threaten the peace of France.

Haugwitz, however, had miscalculated. Napoleon's terms—the cession to France, by Prussia, of all the states between the Rhine and the Elbe—remained unchanged. Talleyrand had indeed arrived, at the end of October, to find Napoleon ensconced in the royal palace and in no mood to listen to arguments in favor of the Prussians. Nothing that Talleyrand said evoked

---

* Since it was feared that the English might attack Holland, Hortense had been ordered to the safety of Mainz for the duration of the campaign. The city was Napoleon's official headquarters, and Josephine, as well as the ministers and most of the imperial court, had taken up residence there.

the slightest reaction from the emperor other than one of mild impatience. If the Prussians wished to have peace, it was theirs for the asking. They had only to accept the terms which he had already dictated. The Prussians, he pointed out, were not being treated with undue harshness, given the magnitude of their offense—that is, the betrayal of the alliance which Napoleon had forced upon them in the first place. The Prussian dynasty, after all, was not being dispossessed—as had happened to the Bourbons of Naples and as was happening to Prussia's allies in northern Germany. With these latter, Napoleonic justice was swift and deadly. The Duke of Brunswick was deposed, and the Elector of Hesse-Kassel, who had remained neutral but had, nonetheless, mobilized his army, met the same fate. These territories and a few others were then formed into the kingdom of Westphalia, the crown of which was handed to Jérôme Bonaparte, Napoleon's youngest brother. Frederick Augustus of Saxony, however, had had the good sense to change sides in time, and he was rewarded by being promoted from simple Elector to King of Saxony.

These radically severe dispositions, Talleyrand knew—the unprecedented demolition and setting up of thrones at the conqueror's whim and especially the utterly humiliating peace imposed upon Prussia, which deprived that country of half its population and half its revenue, and, in addition, imposed an exorbitant indemnity*—were not the terms of a peace, but the prelude to a new war. Prussia, like Austria before it, might be crushed, and it might even be compelled—as it was by Napoleon's terms— to declare war on England. But it would never be more than a nominal ally if it were deprived by France of its pride and self-respect. Such a peace with Prussia must inevitably become merely a hostile truce, with the Prussians watching for the first opportunity to regain, not only their territories, but also and especially their place among the powers of Europe—an ancient and honorable place, which Napoleon was now determined to destroy forever. Therefore, the new alliance with Prussia, in Talleyrand's view, was no alliance at all, but rather a method of introducing into the bosom of the Empire a malevolent and dangerous enemy. That Napoleon could not, or would not, grasp these essential facts was a matter of utter astonishment and disgust to Talleyrand. "I was outraged at everything I saw and heard," he said, "but I was obliged to conceal my indignation." When, early in November, Bonaparte commanded him to prepare the text of a document declaring England to be in a state of blockade and closing all the ports of Europe to British shipping, he could do nothing but comply, even though he was bitterly opposed to such a step. The decree was pro-

---

* A total of 160,000,000 francs was exacted from Prussia and its German allies, with the former being required to pay most of that sum.

mulgated on November 21 and reproduced, almost verbatim, the draft
submitted by Talleyrand to Napoleon on the preceding day. It was an unprecedented act of tyranny. The emperor closed not only the ports of
France and of France's dependent states, but commanded even the neutral
nations of the Continent to do likewise. "I will conquer the sea by land
power," Napoleon proclaimed, and the threat was very clear: Any country
that refused to cooperate would face invasion by France's armies.

It was also at Berlin that occurred the incident which made Talleyrand
abandon, once and for all, any faint hope, which might have survived, of
leading Napoleon onto the path of reason. In 1806 the government of
Spain, which was then in the hands of Manuel de Godoy, a man who had
attained power and held it by the amazing, though not unprecedented, feat
of being simultaneously the lover of both Queen María Luisa and King
Carlos IV. Until that fateful year, Godoy had succeeded in maintaining
Spain's precarious neutrality, a success for which he received, from grateful Don Carlos, the title of Prince of the Peace. After the Peace of
Pressburg, however, Godoy had made the mistake of concluding that England, rather than France, was the stronger power, and he had issued a
proclamation ordering Spain to mobilize its forces, clearly with the intention either of participating actively on the side of England or of defending Spanish soil against French ambitions—which, in Napoleon's eyes,
amounted to the same thing. This proclamation reached Napoleon while
he was in Berlin, in the throes of his megalomaniac fury. His rage was terrible to witness. "He took an oath," Talleyrand says, "to destroy, at any
price, the Spanish branch of the House of Bourbon. And, at this, I—I, too,
took an oath: that I would cease, at any price, to be his Minister as soon as
we should have returned to France."

The Emperor Napoleon, having settled accounts with Prussia, now
turned his attention to the Russians. Czar Alexander, far from being willing to make peace after the defeat of Prussia, had tried vainly to revive the
coalition by urging Frederick William to resist Napoleon's demands and
by attempting to draw Austria back into the conflict. Although unsuccessful in either respect, he seemed determined to continue the war alone, with
whatever help he could obtain from his single remaining ally, Sweden. By
the end of 1806, it had become clear that since Russia would not make
peace, Napoleon would have to fight it in a winter campaign, in the snows
of East Prussia and Poland, with an army untrained and unequipped for
that kind of warfare.

In the last days of 1806, therefore, Napoleon left Berlin for Warsaw,
where he hoped to be able to obtain the active support of the Poles in the

conflict. Talleyrand was commanded to follow him, and he did so, in the greatest discomfort, over roads which were often nothing more than rivers of mud. In Warsaw he was somewhat compensated for the discomfort of the journey by being given, as his lodging, the princely palace of the Radzi-will family. He had reached the capital in time to greet Napoleon upon his return from the first part of the campaign, which ended in early January, 1807. A series of engagements between the French and the Russians had left most of Poland under Napoleon's control; but the Russian army was still intact, and it was obvious that when the weather improved, the final phase of the war would have to be fought out.

For several weeks, Napoleon remained in Warsaw, the lion of an unending round of feasts, receptions, and balls. In the course of these entertainments, Talleyrand presented to him a beautiful young Polish noblewoman, the Countess Marie Walewska, who subsequently bore him a son and who remained his faithful mistress for several years. Though the attachment between the emperor and Walewska seemed mutual and genuine, their meeting had been neither spontaneous nor without design. Marie had appeared before Napoleon as a sacrificial lamb upon the altar of Polish independence. A group of Polish nobles had noticed Bonaparte's initial attraction to her upon his arrival in Warsaw—an attraction to which, the lady says, she could never respond, lest she bring dishonor upon the name of her "fond and kind husband." Count Walewski, however, did not share her delicacy. A patriot, he thought Marie's virtue a small enough price to pay if it would ensure that for which every true Pole longed most: independence. In this, he was joined by a group of other nobles, headed by Prince Józef Poniatowski, who, according to Marie's own account, "raged, argued, pleaded, and even threatened" until she consented to the supreme sacrifice or, as she puts it, to "the final surrender." But Napoleon, who could never resist the temptation to boast of his conquests, assured one of his aides on St. Helena that "she did not struggle overmuch," and, he added, "It was Talleyrand who got her for me."

There is no reason to doubt that this was true; that Talleyrand took time out from composing memoranda on the Polish question to act as an unofficial procurer for his master, and that it was he who, in his capacity as Grand Chamberlain, presented the countess to Napoleon. Doubtless, he had rendered such services before, for, as Napoleon was to remark many years later, "Talleyrand always had a supply of women stashed away." In the case of Marie Walewska, however, Talleyrand's motives, though not pure, were not entirely unworthy. Hitherto Napoleon had shown himself immune to logic and reason in his relations with foreign powers; it was possible that he might be susceptible to appeals to more basic emotions

and that Walewska, a devoted patriot, might move him to do what statesmen such as Talleyrand could not—that is, to create an independent Polish state.

Talleyrand had always been a strong partisan of such a nation, and he
deplored the series of treaties by which Prussia, Russia, and Austria had
on three occasions partitioned Poland among themselves in such a way
that by 1806 nothing remained that was recognizable as a sovereign state.
The reasons behind this attitude were not altruistic, but practical. It was
his conviction that a strong, autonomous Poland was essential to the peace
of Europe and to the equilibrium of the Continent. He had argued, before
the Treaty of Pressburg, for the strengthening of Austria, so that it might
serve as a southern bulwark against Russian aggression in Europe, and
now he argued for an independent Poland, so that it might serve as a
northern barrier and as a buffer state between Russia and the West. But
Napoleon, as before, could never be persuaded of the necessity for such an
arrangement or even of its utility. To the petitions of the Polish patriots, as
to Talleyrand's arguments, he gave vaguely encouraging answers, and
nothing more. And Walewska was so overwhelmed by him that she could
not bring herself to plead the cause of her country. "Close up," she wrote,
"the man struck terror into my heart. What an extraordinary man! He was
like a volcano. The passion that dominated him was not love—which,
though violent, was transitory—but ambition."

It was ambition, in fact, which tore Napoleon from Walewska's arms in
early February, 1807, and sent him hurrying off into East Prussia, where
the Russian army had concentrated its forces. He met them at Eylau on
February 7 and won a clear but inconclusive victory. It was not until mid-
June, at Friedland, that the decisive battle was fought and the Russians
thoroughly routed. A truce was signed on June 21, and a meeting of the
two emperors was arranged for June 25, at Tilsit, on the Niemen River.

As Bonaparte had spent the latter part of the winter and all the spring of
1807 in pursuit of the Russian armies, Talleyrand, in Warsaw, had been
occupied by his duties as Foreign Minister. Much of his energy and time
was spent on a favorite project, the working out of an alliance between
France and Austria—an idea of the value of which he had yet to persuade
Napoleon. The Austrian government, having heard it rumored that the
emperor, if victorious against the Russians, would attempt to negotiate an
alliance with the czar, had become alarmed. Such an understanding, it was
obvious, would place Austria at the mercy of both emperors, and Austrian
territory would be theirs for the taking. To forestall this imminent possibility, an ambassador, Baron de Vincent, was sent to Warsaw, where Talleyrand quickly offered him a bargain. If Austria would agree to relinquish its
Polish possessions, it would be recompensed by the gift of Silesia—the

province which it had lost to Frederick the Great almost seventy years before, whose loss it had regretted ever since. It would then be feasible to set
up an alliance with Vienna and also to establish a viable Polish state—both
of which would preclude the possibility of an alliance between Napoleon
and Alexander. Talleyrand pressed Vincent for an immediate answer. He
knew that once Napoleon had obtained a decisive victory over the Russians, it would be impossible to persuade him of the value of an agreement
with Austria, whereas so long as the issue of the campaign was still in
doubt, he might be willing to accept such a bargain for the sake of the Austrian troops which an alliance would add to his own forces. But Vincent
hesitated. Since Napoleon had not yet defeated the Russians, there was
still a chance that the Russians might defeat Napoleon; and it would be a
tragic error to have chosen the wrong side at precisely the wrong moment.

It seems that in Talleyrand's negotiations with Austria, there was also
some discussion of what would happen should Napoleon be defeated and
captured or killed in battle, for upon this possibility hinged not only the
peace of Europe, but also its future. With Prussia crushed and Austria
powerless, the emperor's death or defeat would leave Western Europe
open to invasion by Russia or at least would leave the sovereigns of those
two countries in a position where they would be forced to acquiesce in any
territorial demands, however outrageous, that Alexander might choose to
make. This terrible possibility was one which concerned the Austrians as
much as it did Talleyrand, and there is evidence that a solution was agreed
upon by virtue of which, if Napoleon were to disappear from the scene, he
would be replaced by his eldest brother, Joseph Bonaparte, currently King
of Naples, and that an immediate peace would be signed.

As it happened, no such solution was needed. While Vincent was still
hesitating, the news of Napoleon's great victory at Friedland reached Warsaw, and all hope for an Austrian alliance vanished. The Austrian ambassador was despondent; he had gambled and lost. Talleyrand, however, had
played the game too long to feel any emotion other than resignation. With
a shrug, he read the emperor's command to proceed immediately to Tilsit,
where the terms of peace between France and Russia were to be discussed
by Napoleon and Alexander.

The idea of Tilsit had been Alexander's. "It was so romantically conceived," says Talleyrand, "and so magnificently arranged, that Napoleon,
who saw it as a brilliant episode in the romance of his life, accepted it." In
truth, Alexander, himself an incurable romantic, had outdone himself. The
first meeting between the two emperors took place aboard a large, richly
decorated raft, moored in the middle of the Niemen. The ruler of the West
and the ruler of the East talked alone, without attendants, and what was
said between them was never recorded. As they conferred, Frederick Wil-

liam, King of Prussia, waited on the riverbank, in the rain, to learn the decision of the two men who held his fate and that of his kingdom in their hands. "I was instructed," Talleyrand records, "not to negotiate with the Prussian plenipotentiaries, but simply to sign with them the treaty which contained the territorial cessions of Prussia, as though they had been agreed upon between the Emperor Napoleon and Czar Alexander." For Napoleon, out of contempt for Prussia, insisted that the terms he had already dictated to Prussia appear to have been decided upon by both himself and Alexander. It was Napoleon's way of making an ally of Alexander and, as Talleyrand notes, of making him "the enemy of his own former allies." And it worked well. At the end of this first meeting, which lasted for three hours, Napoleon allowed publicly that out of respect for the opinions of his friend the Czar Alexander, he had decided, instead of destroying Prussia, only to deprive it of half of its territory and population.

This was hardly what Frederick William had hoped for. Forgetting his dignity, he pleaded with Napoleon for mercy, but in vain. The Emperor of the French was capable of forgiving those who fought against him and even, occasionally, those who betrayed him, but he never learned to forgive weakness. Of Frederick William, he said: "He is a shallow and limited man, without character and without resources—a dunce, an idiot, and a bore." The King of Prussia, in despair, wrote to his wife, Queen Louisa: "The terms are frightful." He begged her to come to Tilsit personally to intercede with the emperor. She did so, only to be received with the brutal question: "How did you dare to make war against me, madame, with such feeble means at your disposal?" To which the Queen of Prussia answered, "Sire, we were blinded by the glory of the great Frederick. It misled us as to the true state of our power."

Talleyrand, who was present at the interview and recorded its failure, says that "The word 'glory,' so happily placed, and at Tilsit, in the very study of the Emperor Napoleon, seemed to me superbly fitting. I repeated this fine reply of the queen often enough for the emperor to say to me one day, 'I cannot imagine what you find so enchanting in that saying of the Queen of Prussia. I wish you would find something else to talk about.'"

When the disastrous meeting had been concluded, Talleyrand, as Grand Chamberlain, conducted the unhappy queen to her carriage. His sympathy for her was so obvious, he relates, "that the Queen of Prussia, who deserved to live in better days, was gracious enough to acknowledge it. If, in the recollections of my life, several things are necessarily painful, I remember at least with much sweetness the things that she had the goodness to say. . . . When I conducted her to her carriage, she said to me, 'Prince de Bénévent, there are only two persons who regret my having had to come here: I and you. You are not angry, I hope, that I believe this.' The tears of compassion and pride that filled my eyes were my only reply."

The treaties of Tilsit—those with Russia, signed on July 7, and that with Prussia, signed on July 9—were worked out in two weeks of meetings between Napoleon and Alexander. It was Talleyrand who, at the end of that time, affixed his signature to the documents, but he had had virtually no part in their formulation. All was done by the emperors themselves, in a spirit of intense mutual admiration and understanding. The two men, it appears, had fallen under each other's spell. "If Alexander were a woman," Napoleon wrote to Josephine after the first meeting on the Niemen, "I would make him my mistress." Alexander was no less taken with the Emperor of the French, and his letters to his mother, written from Tilsit, are more those of a young girl in love than of a defeated sovereign negotiating a peace with his conqueror: "Here I am spending my days with Bonaparte —hours at a time! I ask you, is it not like something out of a dream?"

As might be expected in this atmosphere of courtship, the terms of the treaty of peace with Russia were singularly generous. Alexander recognized the cessions of territory by Prussia and agreed to the creation of the grand duchy of Warsaw, which was to be ruled by Napoleon's friend and ally the new King of Saxony. In addition, Russian troops were to be withdrawn from such parts of Dalmatia as they occupied and from the Ionian Islands. Finally, Alexander was to act as mediator between France and England, and Napoleon was to assume the same role between Russia and Turkey—for he had, in 1806, incited the Turks to declare war on Russia in order to force Alexander to maintain a strong army in the Balkans.

The peace treaty, which was made public, was supplemented by a secret treaty of alliance. If England should refuse to make peace with France on terms favorable to the latter, Russia would declare war against it. The two emperors would then require their allies and client states—Austria, Denmark, and Sweden—to do likewise. If Napoleon's mediation between Constantinople and St. Petersburg failed, France would join Russia in a war against the sultan, and together they would strip him of his possessions— which they would then divide among themselves. Since the terms which were to be offered to England and Turkey were outrageous, the mediation of the two emperors was doomed to failure beforehand—as they knew very well. The treaty of alliance, therefore, was nothing less than a secret agreement between France and Russia to divide the world between themselves. But it did not remain a secret for long. Almost immediately, its terms were known in London, where everyone was aghast at the masterstroke by which Napoleon had turned his mightiest enemy, and Britain's ally, into his accomplice. There was little that England could do, but it did what it could and sent its fleet into the Baltic, where, after bombarding Copenhagen, it succeeded in capturing the sizable Danish fleet. These ships, at least, would not fall into Napoleon's hands.*

The campaigns of 1806–07 and the meeting of the emperors at Tilsit marked the turning point in Napoleon's career. There were years of glory still ahead of him, and to all appearances, the world was at his feet. Every state of any importance on the Continent was either his ally or his victim, or if any state was neither, it lived in such dread of invasion that it comported itself as though Napoleon were already its sovereign. Yet Napoleon, though surrounded by an aura of invincibility, had already determined to follow to the end the road that led, as Talleyrand pointed out, "from military dictatorship to universal monarchy and from universal monarchy to Moscow." For his part, Talleyrand, from the time of the treaties of Tilsit, determined that he must do everything in his power to save France from the impending catastrophe by frustrating the realization of the emperor's ambitions and, if possible, bringing about his downfall. "The emperor," he writes, "adhered for a long time to the views which I considered my duty to propose to him. But by 1807 he had already for some time, I must admit, strayed from the path on which I had done my best to keep him."

At Berlin, when informed of Napoleon's determination to take a final and fateful step away from that path by destroying the Spanish Bourbons, Talleyrand had sworn that he would resign his ministry. Upon his return to Paris from Tilsit, he did so, in August, 1807: "I served Bonaparte while he was emperor as I had served him when he was Consul—that is, with devotion, so long as I could believe that he himself was devoted to the interests of France. But as soon as I saw him beginning to undertake those radical enterprises which were to lead him to his doom, I resigned my ministry. For this, he never forgave me." Napoleon, on St. Helena, would claim that Talleyrand, far from resigning, had been dismissed as Minister of Foreign Affairs because of complaints received from the King of Bavaria and the King of Württemberg concerning his "extortions and his rapacious demands." Here, as in other instances, Bonaparte succumbed to the temptation common to retired conquerors and statesmen—Talleyrand was no ex-

* Fouché, in his *Mémoires*, maintains that it was Talleyrand who informed George Canning, the new Foreign Secretary, of the terms of the secret treaty of alliance. This is unsupported by any other source or by any evidence other than Fouché's word. It is not that Talleyrand was not capable of such an act, but that the risks involved in sending such a message from Tilsit to London were too great, particularly since the British could derive from such knowledge only a momentary and immediate advantage. The entire episode is cloaked in mystery and rumor, and nothing of it is known with any certainty whatever. Duff Cooper suggests that the informant may have been a member of Alexander's staff, and this seems very possible, for the Russian aristocracy, even after Tilsit, remained violently anti-French and pro-British.

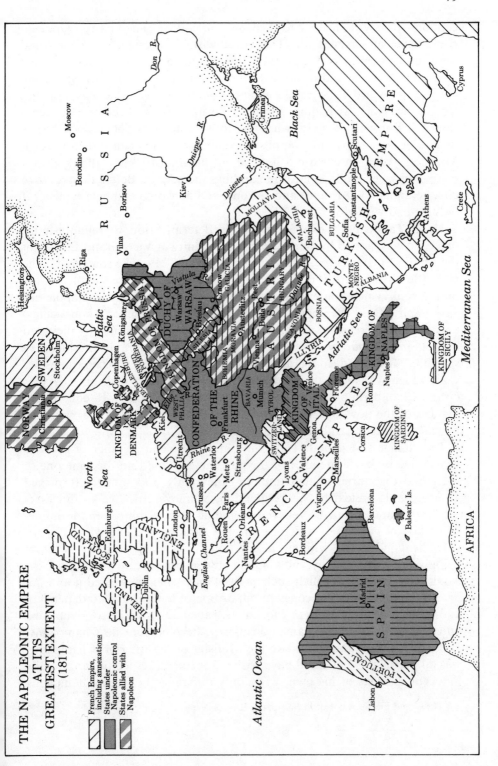

THE NAPOLEONIC EMPIRE
AT ITS
GREATEST EXTENT
(1811)

French Empire,
including annexations

States under
Napoleonic control

States allied with
Napoleon

ception—to rewrite history to their own advantage. The fact is, Napoleon could never understand why Talleyrand wished to resign, just as he could never understand why Talleyrand insisted upon arguing for policies which would bring peace and order to Europe rather than "glory" to Napoleon. He had not heard Talleyrand's explanation, in the privacy of his ministry, for his decision: "It is quite simple. I do not wish to become the executioner of Europe." In 1813, when the folly of his own policies was beginning to become apparent, Napoleon would ask Caulaincourt, then Foreign Minister, "Why on earth did he give up his ministry? My affairs always prospered when Talleyrand was handling them. . . . Better than anyone else, he understood France and Europe, and he would still be a minister if only he had wished it."

Upon Talleyrand's expression of his determination to relinquish his office, he was named by Bonaparte to the dignity of Vice-Grand Elector of the Empire* ("It was the only vice he had lacked," Fouché snickered). The new title hardly constituted a demotion, since it conferred upon Talleyrand a rank which made of him the third-highest dignitary in Napoleon's vast empire. Only the imperial family, the Arch-Chancellor (Cambacérès) and the Arch-Treasurer (Lebrun) took precedence over him. Talleyrand himself, in all modesty, described the office as an "honorable and lucrative sinecure." It was indeed lucrative, with a salary of some 330,000 francs per year, which was more than sufficient, when combined with his salary as Grand Chamberlain, to make it possible for him to face with equanimity the loss of the flow of "gifts" to which the Foreign Minister was, perhaps by custom and certainly by practice, entitled.

The change suited both Talleyrand and Napoleon in other respects as well. Since by law a member of the government could not become one of the grand dignitaries of the Empire, Talleyrand's appointment furnished an acceptable pretext for his resignation. Moreover, as Vice-Grand Elector, Talleyrand would be relieved of public responsibility for the implementation of policies of which he strongly disapproved and which, in private, he condemned without reservation. Napoleon, similarly, without being deprived of Talleyrand's advice and experience in foreign affairs, would now be able to solicit such counsel only when he wished it and not have to contend with the constant opposition of a minister as independent and strong-willed as himself. Indeed, as Talleyrand's successor, who took office on August 10, he named Jean-Baptiste Nompère de Champagny, Duke de Cadore, until that date the Minister of the Interior. Champagny was all that Napoleon could have wished: obedient, respectful, and totally innocent of ideas of his own. "The only difference between Champagny

* The Grand Elector was Joseph Bonaparte, King of Naples.

and myself," Talleyrand remarked, "is that if the emperor told him to have someone's head cut off, it would be done within the hour, whereas, it would have taken me a month, at the very least, to get around to it." So zealous was the new minister that Napoleon, who had been spoiled by Talleyrand's deliberate lack of haste, had to administer a mild reprimand: "You should always keep my letters on your desk for three or four days before sending them out." To this, Talleyrand added advice of his own: "You will find, after you have served the emperor for a while, that it is unwise to carry out his orders too quickly." Years later he was to note: "The emperor compromised himself on the very day that it became possible for him to do fifteen minutes early that which I had always insisted he do fifteen minutes later." For it was zeal and haste, characteristics which Talleyrand always deplored, that led Napoleon, almost as soon as Talleyrand resigned, to the double calamity which marked the beginning of the road to ruin: the Spanish affair and the Erfurt interview.

10

Erfurt and Beyond

"THE SPANISH affair," Napoleon admitted when it was too late, "was the greatest mistake I made." It was actually a series of mistakes and misjudgments, which eventually drained the strength of the Empire, reduced its military and political efficiency, and contributed largely to Napoleon's eventual downfall.

The first of these errors in judgment had taken place at Berlin, late in 1806, when Napoleon, in response to Manuel de Godoy's mobilization proclamation, had sworn to destroy the Spanish Bourbons and thus finally brought Talleyrand to the realization that he could not continue in office. The reason for Godoy's proclamation, Talleyrand explains, was not so much that Godoy was planning to attack France, but that he, as the favorite of both King Carlos and Queen María Luisa and as their omnipotent minister, was the rival in power of the heir to the Spanish throne, Ferdinand, Prince of the Asturias. Godoy suspected Ferdinand of attempting to persuade King Carlos to dismiss his minister and then of assuming power himself by forcing Carlos to abdicate. His suspicions were correct. Ferdinand, for his part, believed that Godoy was intriguing to obtain a crown for himself—either that of Spain or of a kingdom that might be carved out in the Iberian Peninsula. He, too, was justified in his suspicions. In this situation, Spain was divided between the supporters of the throne—that is, of Carlos and María Luisa, in the person of Godoy—and those of the Prince of the Asturias. Seen from across the Pyrenees, the country seemed a plum ripe for the picking, and Napoleon could not resist it.

Spain held a certain strategic importance for France because it was the road to Portugal. And Portugal was, as always, an ally of England. As such, it had refused to implement the blockade of English shipping ordered by Napoleon in 1806 and thus incurred the emperor's wrath. This was a plausible pretext for a secret agreement concluded between Napoleon and Godoy, in October, 1807, after Talleyrand's retirement from office, which provided for the partition of Portugal between France and Spain or, rather, between France and Godoy, who was to have his "kingdom" in the south of Portugal. In this way, it was possible for the French army to enter Spain without opposition. "To conquer Spain without striking a blow," Talleyrand explains, "there existed but one means. It was, to introduce, under the shadow of friendship, sufficient men to prevent or to suppress whatever resistance would be offered."

As the French forces, under Marshal Andoche Junot, approached Lisbon, the regent of Portugal and his court boarded ship and set sail across the Atlantic, toward Portugal's colony of Brazil, leaving their country to the invader. This disconcerted Napoleon somewhat, for it deprived him of any reason for maintaining a large army on Spanish soil. But it did not stop him. Under General René-Antoine Dupont, 40,000 French troops took up strategic positions in northern and western Spain, where they were welcomed as liberators by the people, who believed that Dupont had come to overthrow Godoy and set up the Prince of the Asturias. Before long, however, it had been recognized, even by the imbecilic Carlos IV and his queen, that their kingdom had fallen, almost inadvertently, into the hands of the Emperor of the French. When the royal couple asked Godoy for advice, he gave it: their Catholic Majesties should follow the example set by their cousins of Portugal and take refuge in the New World.

Carlos and María Luisa blindly accepted this counsel. Or rather, they attempted to follow it and set out, in great state, for their port of Cádiz. Before they could reach that city, they were accosted by an infuriated mob, howling for Godoy's head. "They accused him loudly," Talleyrand recounts, "of having counseled the king to abandon Madrid. And this advice, they said, could come only from a man who has sought to fill the soul of the king with personal fears. The moment had come, they said, to deliver the country from its oppressor." Carlos, frightened out of his wits, promised that Godoy would be brought to trial immediately. Then he submitted one of his periodic abdications.

As soon as he was safe from the mob, the abdication was withdrawn—as was Carlos' habit. The situation now suited Napoleon's designs. There were two kings in Spain; Carlos IV, whom almost everyone mistrusted because he was known to be the puppet of the hated Godoy, and Ferdinand VII, whom almost everyone supported for no reason other than that he was the only alternative to Godoy, and whom his own mother, in a rare burst of good judgment, described as having "the heart of a tiger and the head of a mule." Neither king was fit to rule a country as important to Napoleon as Spain. "I have but two choices open to me," the emperor said. "One is to take over all Spain and give it to a ruler of my own family, under the pretext of avenging the rebellion of a son against his father [Ferdinand VII had refused to recognize his father's withdrawal of his abdication]. The other is to take and annex to France the northern province of Spain, by negotiating with Ferdinand VII and recognizing him as King of Spain."

At this point, Talleyrand, knowing that Napoleon was determined upon taking one or the other alternative, argued mightily for the occupation of Catalonia as the lesser of the two evils. He had always been opposed to the exaggerated extension of the territory of France, and although an unjust occupation is hardly better than an unjust annexation, it had the virtue at least of being temporary and perhaps even justifiable as a military expedient. But Napoleon had already made up his mind. He offered the crown of Spain to his brother, Louis, King of Holland, since, he wrote, "the climate of Holland does not agree with you." Louis, however, had come to regard himself as a Hollander, and he refused. Therefore, Joseph Bonaparte, King of Naples, was ordered to pack his bags and become King of Spain.

The next problem was to give the appearance of legality to the installation of Don José I (as Joseph would insist upon calling himself) on the throne of Spain. The solution Napoleon devised was one worthy of Talleyrand's genius—to whom, however, Napoleon did not communicate it. First, he announced a plan to pay a personal visit to Madrid and, at the same time, to confer upon Ferdinand the hand of a Bonaparte princess. Simultaneously, he sent word to King Carlos and Queen María Luisa that he was displeased by the retraction of Carlos' abdication, that he did not understand how Spain could have two kings, but that he would be willing to listen to Carlos' explanation and, if he found it satisfactory, recognize him once more as true King of Spain. Carlos and his queen, full of innocent hope, set out to confer with the Emperor of the French at Bayonne. Once there, on May 5, 1808, they were met with threats which so terrified them that Carlos once more abdicated—this time, in favor of whomever Napoleon might choose to nominate for the throne of Spain. Ferdinand, when he arrived, received approximately the same treatment and thus was persuaded to put his signature to an instrument by virtue of which he renounced his rights to the throne in favor of his father. It was not until he had signed that he was told that his father's rights were now vested in the Emperor Napoleon. *"Yo estoy traido"* ["I have been betrayed!"], Ferdinand shrieked. Then, with his younger brothers and his uncle, the Duke of

San Carlos, he was led off into captivity in France. Carlos and María Luisa, less dangerous, were given Compiègne and Chambord and a pension of 6,000,000 francs. On June 7, Napoleon, still at Bayonne, received, with great pomp, his brother, "Don José I, by the Grace of God, King of Castile, Aragón, the Two Sicilies, Jerusalem and Navarre." By the time the new king reached his capital of Madrid, a month later, Spain had risen in revolt against him, and after a stay of eleven harrowing days he had to flee the city. The insurgents were to continue their resistance for several years, draining resources desperately needed by Napoleon in eastern Europe. The battle eventually would be taken up by a British army under Wellington, and Spain finally cleared of the French by the Battle of Vittoria, in 1813.

Talleyrand, throughout his life, maintained that he had opposed Napoleon's Spanish adventure from the very beginning and that as Napoleon had taken step after step in this enterprise, it had been either without Talleyrand's knowledge or against his advice. Napoleon, however, charged that Talleyrand had been aware of what was being done from the very beginning and had approved and encouraged it and that he had withdrawn his approval only when it became obvious that the Spanish affair was leading toward disaster. Talleyrand says that the Treaty of Fontainebleau was negotiated secretly "unknown to M. de Champagny, Foreign Minister, and also unknown to me, although at that time I was chief Councillor of State* and was at Fontainebleau." Napoleon claimed that it was Talleyrand who actually negotiated the treaty, but if so, he offers no explanation of why Talleyrand was not the signatory for France. Moreover, it is hardly likely that Talleyrand would have consented to, to say nothing of having advised, the installation of a Bonaparte on the Spanish throne. Under the Consulate and in the early days of the Empire, he had opposed vigorously every inclination of Napoleon to destroy the legitimate dynasties of Europe or even to weaken them. So true was this that both the Austrians and the Prussians, after their defeat by Napoleon, had placed their hope for survival in Talleyrand. Before embarking on the Spanish affair, Napoleon had warned the Portuguese ambassador openly: "If Portugal does not do as I say, within two months the House of Braganza will cease to reign." And it was to Talleyrand that Portugal had turned for protection. His resignation from office, shortly afterward, was perceived as nothing less than a tragedy by the Portuguese, whose ambassador told Champagny: "I must, in good conscience, and in accordance with my duties, tell your Excellency that the resignation of His Serene Highness, the Prince de Bénévent, is a cause of the utmost regret to us."

* One of the duties of the chief Councillor of State was to sign all treaties on France's behalf.

Finally, there remains the fact that it was not years after Fontainebleau and Bayonne that Talleyrand publicly denounced Napoleon's Spanish ambitions (as Napoleon himself claimed), but a few months. He also took great pains, long before it had become evident that Napoleon's Spanish designs had miscarried, to explain to Napoleon precisely why the whole undertaking must ineluctably do serious harm both to France and to the emperor himself. "If a gentleman does foolish things," he explained, "if he has mistresses or treats his wife and friends shabbily, he will certainly be blamed; but, if he is rich, powerful and clever, society will treat him with indulgence. But if that same man cheats at cards, he will forthwith be banished from decent society, and he will never be forgiven." When Napoleon heard this, Talleyrand says, "he turned pale, seemed confused, and spoke to me no more that day. But I can say that from that moment dated the more or less open break between him and me. Never after did he pronounce the name of Spain or mine without adding some injurious epithet supplied by his temper." It was not until much later that Napoleon seems to have grasped the meaning of Talleyrand's parable. On St. Helena, he admitted that "I embarked very badly on the Spanish affair. I confess that the immorality of it was too shocking, the injustice too cynical." He had indeed committed the sin which European society would never forgive, by depriving the Spanish Bourbons of their throne, not by force—for which he might have been absolved—but by deceit. He had, in other words, cheated at cards.

Since he had been caught at it, his first concern was to implicate as many other players as possible in his crime. For this reason, Talleyrand was appointed official jailer of the Spanish princes, and as though this were not enough, it was on Talleyrand's own property, in his own house, that these victims of Napoleonic duplicity were detained during the years of their imprisonment.

In 1803, Napoleon had instructed Talleyrand to "buy a handsome property. I want you to be able to entertain the diplomatic corps and distinguished foreigners as brilliantly as possible. People must enjoy being there, and an invitation from you must come to be regarded as a mark of distinction for the ambassadors of those sovereigns with whom I am pleased." There was such an estate, called Valençay, in the *département* of Indre, about 200 kilometers south of Paris. There was more to Valençay than a magnificent chateau. It was surrounded by almost 40,000 acres of forests and fields, and it included twenty-three villages, over which the lord of Valençay ruled in almost feudal state. The chateau itself, containing twenty-five master suites, was enclosed by a carefully maintained park of 350 acres. Valençay was, in a word, one of the great estates of France. Having somehow survived intact the storms of the Revolution, it had passed into the hands of one of Bonaparte's officials, M. de Luçay. And it happened to be on the market. It was precisely what Bonaparte had ordered, but the price, Talleyrand had complained, was "beyond my modest means." Bonaparte had answered, "Nonetheless, you must buy it," and had offered to pay whatever amount Talleyrand lacked. Thus, in May, 1803, the chateau and princely domain of Valençay had become Talleyrand's and was to remain his until his death.

It was to Valençay that Napoleon, in May, 1808, sent the Spanish princes and their entourage. Talleyrand was informed of this by a note from the emperor, telling him that the prisoners would arrive "at Valençay on Tuesday. Please be there Monday evening, at the latest. I want the princes to be received rather simply, without too much fuss, but you must do whatever is possible to provide for their amusement. . . . You might ask Madame de Talleyrand to join you, with four or five of her ladies. No harm will be done if the Prince of the Asturias forms an attachment for some pretty woman, so long as there is no scandal; this will provide yet another means of keeping him under surveillance. So far as you yourself are concerned, your mission is an honorable one. To receive and entertain three illustrious personages is in keeping both with the traditions of France and with your own rank. Besides, the eight or ten days that you will be there with them will give you some insight into their minds and will help me decide what must be done."

There can be little doubt that Talleyrand was made the keeper of the Spanish princes in order to implicate him in the crime of their captivity, and so it was generally believed at the time. Moreover, the designation of Valençay as the place of detention was Bonaparte's way of reminding Talleyrand that regardless of the latter's disapproval of the Spanish policy which he had adopted, he was still the servant of the emperor and, as such, at his disposal.

Talleyrand, in any event, carried out Napoleon's orders with exemplary thoroughness:

> I had been at Valençay for several days when the princes arrived. This moment left an impression which will never be forgotten. The princes were young, and around them—in their clothing, the liveries of their servants— was the aura of bygone centuries. The coach from which I saw them alight might have been taken for a carriage of Philip V. This air of antiquity, by recalling their grandeur, added to the interest of their position. They were the first Bourbons that I had seen after so many years of storms and disasters. It was not they who were embarrassed; it was I, and I am pleased to admit it.

He treated them with no less courtesy than he would have shown to them had their situations been reversed, and he would permit no one to do otherwise. One of Napoleon's police agents, Colonel Henri, who accompanied them, was disposed to handle the princes with severity, but this Talleyrand would not allow. "I adopted with this man the tone of a master," Talleyrand relates, "in order to make him understand that it was not Napoleon who ruled here, in the chateau and park of Valençay."

For six years, the princes and their uncle, the Duke of San Carlos, remained at Valençay, living in luxury, doing the things that Spanish princes enjoyed most: hunting, dancing, and attending religious services. "Every day," Talleyrand says, "closed with a public prayer, which I required all visitors to the chateau, as well as the officers of the guard and even the gendarmes, to attend."

Napoleon's hopes for an affair between the Prince of the Asturias and one of Catherine Grand's ladies were never realized. It was a cause of considerable comment, however, when the Duke of San Carlos succumbed to the now-overripe charms of the lady of the house herself. Talleyrand was not particularly disturbed by this unexpected turn, since he had by now grown as weary as everyone else of Catherine's stupidity. He was not unwilling that she find some distraction other than himself. His only condition, as always, was that her amusements not be a cause of embarrassment either to herself or to him. But Catherine did not know the meaning of discretion, and before long, news of the affair between herself and San Carlos was brought to the emperor. One day, at court, before a crowd of officials, Napoleon asked Talleyrand, "Why didn't you tell me that the Duke of San Carlos is your wife's lover?"

"Because," replied Talleyrand, "I did not think it compatible with either my own honor or that of your majesty to do so."

Yet Talleyrand, while urging prudence on his wife and her lover, did not resent San Carlos' amorous attachment to Catherine, which was to endure for two decades. Indeed, he seemed almost pleased that Catherine had been able to attract so sensible and distinguished a man. Years later, in 1828, when he heard that the duke had died, he was quite disturbed by the news and explained to a solicitous friend: "You see, the Duke of San Carlos was my wife's lover. He was a fine and honorable man, and he gave her much good advice—which she needed very badly. God only knows into whose hands she will now fall."

Talleyrand remained at Valençay until August, when he was summoned to Nantes and then to Paris by Napoleon. At the time of the meeting between the emperor and Czar Alexander at Tilsit, a second encounter had been planned, at Erfurt. Talleyrand, though he was no longer Foreign Minister or even in Napoleon's good graces, was ordered to be present to perform the double function of Grand Chamberlain of the Imperial Court and adviser to the emperor. The departure from Valençay was a sad one. "As I was leaving," Talleyrand says, "the princes came to take leave of me in my apartment, with tears in their eyes. They asked me what they could do to give me some mark of their friendship and gratitude (it is in these words that they expressed themselves). Each of them offered me the old prayer book which he used at church. I received these with respect and with an emotion I shall not try to express. I have dared recall the word 'gratitude,' of which they made use on that occasion, because that term is so rare with princes that it honors them who employ it." At the end of the month, when he was already in Paris, Talleyrand received a touching note of farewell from the princes, signed by "your affectionate cousins and friends." On the road to Erfurt, he recalled, "my mind, my heart, and my memories were filled with the princes of Spain."

He would never meet them again.* And it would be eight eventful years before he set foot once more in his domain of Valençay.

As Napoleon and Talleyrand made their way westward toward Saxony and the city of Erfurt, Alexander was moving eastward from St. Petersburg. The Autocrat of All the Russias was troubled. Shortly before leaving, he had received a letter from his mother, the empress dowager, expressing, in the strongest terms, her disapproval of both his new friendship and his alliance with the Emperor of the French. She also wrote of her great alarm at the proposed meeting with Napoleon, pointing out that it was on just such an occasion that the royal family of Spain had entrusted themselves to Napoleon's hands, in a city controlled, like Erfurt, by French troops. The sentiments of his mother, Alexander knew, were shared by most of the nobles and all the merchants of his empire. Napoleon's vaunted Continental System, specifically the ban on trade with Britain, had destroyed a great market for Russian wheat and raw materials, and the value of the ruble was beginning to reflect that loss. Nonetheless, he had put a brave face on it and replied to his mother that the security of his empire required peace with Bonaparte and that he could not refuse a meeting with the Emperor of the French if it were possible to ensure peace by that meeting. But his answer satisfied neither Alexander himself nor his mother when she received it. The czar had had time to reflect since Tilsit, and changeable as he was by nature, he had largely recovered from his infatuation with Napoleon. After two defeats and a treaty of peace which he had described privately as "shameful," he was going to Erfurt as a beggar to a feast, with nothing more to offer than his acquiescence in whatever schemes Bona-

---

* Ferdinand and his younger brothers, Carlos and Antonio, remained at Valençay until March 3, 1814, when they were released under the terms of the Treaty of Valençay and returned to Spain.

parte would propose. He dared not do otherwise, for to contradict the Emperor of the French, as had been amply demonstrated, would probably mean war and, quite likely, another defeat, and then there would be terms of peace as crushing as those imposed upon Austria and Prussia. Opposition was therefore impossible, yet cooperation with Napoleon would be equivalent to sacrificing the interests of his own people to those of the French. It was in this somber frame of mind that Alexander reached Erfurt late in September, 1808.

Napoleon had, in the months since Tilsit, somehow sensed the cooling of Alexander's ardor for the French alliance, and one of his objectives at Erfurt was to revive a friendship that gave evidence of flagging, or, if that could not be done, to treat Alexander to such a display of power and glory that the czar would be led to admit that resistance was futile. He would then be compelled, willing or not, to give whatever Napoleon required of him. "I want Alexander to be dazzled by the spectacle of my power!" Such had been Napoleon's instruction to Talleyrand on the eve of Erfurt. And the Grand Chamberlain, at his master's bidding, had assembled, in the small city, the kings of Saxony, Württemberg, and Baden and an innumerable flock of sovereign princelings, all allies of Napoleon, with which to overawe the czar.

In truth, this crowd of subordinate rulers, clustered around Napoleon's throne, was wholly superfluous. No one, other than Napoleon himself, was more aware than Alexander of France's might in 1808. The Emperor of the French, in addition to ruling over an imperial domain of some 130 *départements*, was King of Italy and Protector of the Confederation of the Rhine —which, by then, included all Germany except Prussia and Austria and, with the addition of Westphalia, Saxony, and the grand duchy of Warsaw, extended to the Russian frontier. Napoleon's brother Joseph was King of Spain; Jérôme Bonaparte was King of Westphalia; Louis Bonaparte was King of Holland; Joachim Murat, the emperor's brother-in-law, had recently been installed on Joseph's abandoned throne in Naples. And Prussia and Austria, the two powers nearest Russian territory, were Napoleon's allies, however reluctantly.

This much Alexander knew for certain. What he sensed only vaguely were Napoleon's objectives at Erfurt. The first of these was to ensure a final victory over Britain by a total enforcement of the blockade. But this could not be achieved so long as Spain and Portugal had not been totally conquered and forced to close their ports to English shipping. Napoleon had sufficient strength to do this. But what troubled the Emperor of the French was that he dared not concentrate more than a portion of his forces in the Iberian Peninsula. For Austria, encouraged by reports of Napoleon's difficulties in Spain, had now begun to show unmistakable signs of restlessness. Talleyrand had been right at Pressburg. Napoleon, instead of turning Austria into an ally, had created a bitter enemy watching for the first opportunity to avenge itself for the humiliation it had suffered. It was therefore Napoleon's secondary aim at Erfurt to secure Alexander's agreement that if war should be declared between Austria and France, Alexander would come to his assistance against Austria and thus allow him a free hand in the Iberian Peninsula.

To both of Napoleon's objectives at Erfurt, Talleyrand was utterly opposed, and he was determined to do everything in his power to frustrate his sovereign's plans. Europe, without a strong Austria in the East and a strong Britain in the West, was unthinkable. The former was necessary as a bulwark against Russia and as a buffer between the empire of the czar and that of Napoleon. If Austria were destroyed—and Napoleon was capable of wiping it off the map altogether—France and Russia would be in constant contact and, inevitably, at war constantly. And just as Austria was necessary to the political and military balance of the Continent, England was necessary to its social and cultural equilibrium. "If the English Constitution is destroyed," Talleyrand told Madame de Rémusat, "you may be certain that the earth will be shaken to its very foundations."

Yet it was Talleyrand upon whom Napoleon relied to sway Alexander's thinking. "My dear Talleyrand," he had told him, "I should like you to arrive at Erfurt a day or so before I do. You know Czar Alexander well, and you and he speak the same language." It seems highly unlikely, after Pressburg and Tilsit and in the wake of the Spanish affair, that Napoleon was unaware of Talleyrand's convictions concerning England and Austria, or of his consequent opposition to his own plans for Erfurt. Yet, before leaving France for the meeting with Alexander, he had ordered Champagny to turn over to Talleyrand all data on Russia, so that the former Foreign Minister might be in a position to act as his negotiator with the Russian czar. Such complacency can be attributed only to Napoleon's belief that he was so completely master of Europe and of every man in it that no individual was capable of doing him harm. But a mind subtler than Napoleon's had taken a more accurate measure of Talleyrand. Prince Metternich, who was now Austrian ambassador in Paris, reported back to Vienna: "Men such as Talleyrand are like swords honed to a sharp edge. It is extremely dangerous to toy with them."

Yet Napoleon insisted upon toying. He instructed Talleyrand to prepare the draft of a treaty with Alexander, defining what he expected from the Russians: intervention in the event of a hostile move on the part of Austria and an assurance of Alexander's solidarity with Napoleon in the war against England. In return for these considerations, Napoleon was willing to give Russia the provinces of Moldavia and Walachia and perhaps even some territory to be carved out of the Ottoman Empire. The main thrust of the treaty, however, must be to establish a unity of purpose and action between France and Russia against Britain. When Talleyrand presented the draft, Napoleon noticed that he had omitted any reference to Austria—the country which, Napoleon said, "is my true enemy."

"Perhaps she is your enemy at present, sire, but at heart, her policy is not in opposition to that of France. She is not aggressive, but conservative."

"I know that is your opinion," the emperor replied. "We will speak of it when the Spanish business is over. . . . But this is the essential article. How could you have left it out? Are you still an Austrian?"

"Perhaps, sire. But it would be more accurate to say that I am never a Russian and always a Frenchman."

It was in this spirit, with the full and open intention of frustrating Napoleon's ambitions, that Talleyrand approached the Erfurt conference, which began, with Alexander's arrival, on September 28. The first meeting between Napoleon and the czar, with Talleyrand in attendance, was cordial. As Alexander returned to his carriage, accompanied by the Grand Chamberlain, he repeated several times to Talleyrand, in a low voice: *"Nous nous verrons"* ["We will see each other"]. When Talleyrand reached his own apartment, he found a note waiting for him, from the Princess of Thurn and Taxis, a sister of the Queen of Prussia, informing him of her arrival. "I immediately went to her," Talleyrand reports, "and I was not with her a quarter of an hour when the czar was announced. He was most amiable and communicative and asked the princess for some tea, telling her that she ought to give us some every day." And so it was arranged that they would meet every evening in the lady's drawing room, after the round of daily conferences and entertainments were done. At one of the earliest of these meetings, Talleyrand laid his cards on the table. "Sire," he said to Alexander, "what are you doing here? It is in your power to save Europe, but you can do so only by standing up to Napoleon. The French people are civilized, but their sovereign is not. The sovereign of Russia is civilized, but his people are not. What could be more fitting than that the sovereign of Russia be the ally of the people of France? The Rhine, the Alps, and the Pyrennees are acquisitions of France. The rest are acquisitions of the emperor. France has no wish to keep them." All Frenchmen, Talleyrand went on, desired nothing more than peace, but unless Alexander opposed Napoleon's designs, they all would "be dragged as victims to their destruction." These themes were repeated evening after evening in the drawing room of the Princess of Thurn and Taxis, by Talleyrand and by others of the group, until eventually the czar was persuaded that they were indeed the opinions "of all sensible people in France."

While Talleyrand was busy deceiving Napoleon, Napoleon was busy, less successfully, in attempting to deceive Talleyrand. He believed that the old understanding of Tilsit, the affectionate and open exchange of views between himself and Alexander, directly and without intermediaries, could be revived and that he could charm Alexander at Erfurt as he had aboard the imperial raft in the Niemen River. Napoleon therefore drafted a treaty which he regarded as a vast improvement over that presented to him earlier by Talleyrand. And this, he told Alexander, "was a convention drawn up for their mutual advantage." Talleyrand notes that "he gave it to the czar after having made him swear not to show it to anyone, not even to one of his ministers. It was an affair, he added, which must be treated between themselves. And to prove the importance that he attached to its being kept a secret, he said, he had written out some of the articles himself, so that no one else would see them."

Later that night, in the drawing room of the princess, Alexander pulled the document from his pocket and handed it to Talleyrand, who remarked that "Napoleon had taken the trouble to copy, as well as he could, nearly all the draft I had given him." One or two articles had been changed slightly, and one added, stipulating that the czar, under pretext of fortifying the frontier between Russia and the Ottoman Empire, station an army corps near the Austrian frontier. "Russian secrets seem to be rather badly kept," Talleyrand adds, "for, early the next morning, Baron de Vincent [the Austrian ambassador] came to me and told me that he knew negotiations had already begun, and that a draft treaty had been drawn up. I assured him . . . that I was opposed to any measures that would be detrimental to the security or dignity of Austria."

It soon became the custom for Alexander and Talleyrand every evening to discuss the "secret" negotiations which had taken place earlier in the day between the czar and the emperor. The proposals, arguments, and counterarguments of the two sovereigns were discussed in detail, and Talleyrand would suggest fresh proposals and arguments for the meeting on the following day. On more than one occasion, the Czar of All the Russias made notes while Talleyrand dictated.

From the very outset of the talks between the two emperors, Napoleon noticed that the czar was a different man from that of Tilsit. "He has grown wary," he sighed to Caulaincourt. And to Talleyrand he complained, "I have been able to do nothing with the Czar Alexander. . . . He is simply acting a part. If he cares so much for me, why does he not sign?"

He did not sign, Talleyrand offered, because being noble and pure at heart, he did not understand the need for complicated treaties between men of honor. "He believes that his word and his affection for you are more binding than treaties."

"Shit!" cried the Emperor of the French.

There can be no doubt that by any usual standard, Talleyrand's behavior at Erfurt constituted treason to France and treachery to Napoleon. His victims were the two emperors who ruled the civilized world. Of Alexander, he made a spy, who reported to him on the most secret thoughts of his sovereign; and of Napoleon, he made a dupe. It was an intricate game, and a dangerous one, but the stakes were vast: the future of France and of Europe. Talleyrand was aware, as he played Alexander against Napoleon, that at any moment he risked exposure and disgrace. Then everything that he possessed—his position, his great wealth, his honor, and perhaps even his life—would be forfeit to Napoleon, who had hitherto destroyed ruthlessly all opposition to his imperial will. It is difficult, in retrospect, to qualify as "treason," as so many have, the efforts of Talleyrand to preserve Europe from continuous bloodshed and chaos and to frustrate the will of Napoleon at the zenith of his power, for no reason other than the unshakable conviction that Napoleon's policies were contrary to the best interests of France. Talleyrand himself felt nothing but pride in his role at Erfurt. He describes it at length and with obvious delight. In the *Mémoires* and in later life, he often justified his conduct with a quotation from Corneille: *"La Perfidie est noble envers la tyrannie."* * And to Madame de Rémusat he confided that his part in the Erfurt negotiations was "the final service that I was able to render to Europe during Napoleon's reign."

As the days went on, negotiations between Napoleon and Alexander, understandably, became more and more difficult. There were sharp words and even an occasional scene. On one occasion, Napoleon lost control of himself and threw his hat to the floor. "You are violent," Alexander said calmly, "but I am stubborn. Your rage will get you nowhere. Either we talk like reasonable men, or we shall not talk at all."

Finally, both Alexander and Napoleon gave in on a few points, and a treaty was signed. The czar agreed that if Austria attacked France, he and Napoleon would join forces against it. This would leave Napoleon free to conquer Spain and Portugal. In exchange for his acquiescence, Alexander was to be allowed to invade Finland and to annex the Danubian provinces that he had always coveted. That night Napoleon wrote to Josephine: "I am very well pleased with the czar, and he should be equally pleased with me."

Napoleon would have been less pleased had he known that Alexander accepted the proposal for Russian intervention against Austria only upon Talleyrand's advice and that, following that advice, he had not the slightest intention of keeping his word. Indeed, the next morning the czar wrote to

---

* "Perfidy is noble when tyranny is its target."

the Emperor Francis assuring him of this. "The Emperor Francis," Talley-rand remarked, "is in great need of consolation, and I have no doubt that your majesty's letter will provide it."

A few days before the Erfurt meeting was adjourned, Talleyrand relates, he was with Napoleon late one night. "He was very pleased with the day, and he had me stay with him a long time after he had retired. His agitation was singular. He asked me questions without waiting for my answer. He tried to speak to me; he wanted to say something other than what he actu-ally said. And then he announced the word: *divorce*. 'My destiny requires it,' he said, 'and the tranquillity of France demands it. I have no successor. Joseph is nothing, and he has only daughters. It is I who must found a dy-nasty, but I can do so only by marrying a princess from one of the reigning houses of Europe. The Emperor Alexander has sisters, and there is one whose age is suitable.' " Talleyrand said that he would speak to the czar on the subject. "Good," Napoleon said. "But remember that it must not sound as though it is coming from me."

The next morning Talleyrand put the question to Alexander. "At the first word he understood me," he says, "and he understood me precisely as I wished him to." The czar replied that he would willingly agree to such a match, but that his approval was not what was needed. The destiny of his sisters was entirely in the hands of their mother, the empress dowager, and it would be necessary to have her consent. And the empress dowager, as all Europe knew, would sooner have seen one of her daughters on the street than married to Bonaparte, whom she regarded as a "Corsican adven-turer" and the devil incarnate. Talleyrand, immensely pleased, then ar-ranged that the next morning Alexander himself would suggest to Napo-leon the idea of a marriage between him and the Grand Duchess Catherine of Russia. He even suggested the words that the czar should use so as to make the proposal as vague as possible. "That will be my text," Alexander replied. "It is a fertile field." Napoleon, delighted with the idea that he would have to reply to the offer of the grand duchess' hand, rather than ask for it, scarcely noticed that the offer was so hedged with conditions and stipulations that it was meaningless.

Shortly afterward Napoleon set out for Paris, and Alexander for St. Petersburg, both well pleased with themselves. But more pleased than ei-ther was the true victor of the Erfurt meeting, who had found the instru-ment by means of which Napoleon's stranglehold on Europe could be bro-ken. "I had done everything in my power to win the confidence of the Czar Alexander," he said, "and I succeeded." As proof of this achievement, Alexander thenceforth maintained two ambassadors in Paris. One was officially accredited to the Imperial Court. This was Prince Kurakin, an ec-centric who caused a great deal of hilarity by his idiosyncrasies. The other was Count Nesselrode, ostensibly a counselor to Kurakin, but actually Alexander's personal ambassador to Talleyrand. The first meeting between the two men took place shortly after the return from Erfurt, when Nesselrode presented himself before Talleyrand with the words: "I have just come from St. Petersburg. I hold an official position with Prince Kurakin, but it is to you that I am really accredited. I am responsible for maintaining a private correspondence with the czar, and I bring you now one of his letters."

The intimacy between Alexander and Talleyrand brought benefits at the domestic as well as at the diplomatic level. Talleyrand had long been concerned over the fact that having no legitimate children, he had no direct heir. All that he had accumulated—which was a great deal and would be much more—would go, in the natural course of events, to Count Edmond de Périgord, second son of his brother Archambaud.* Edmond was now twenty-one, the age for marriage, and Talleyrand, with almost paternal solicitude, was determined that he should make as splendid a marriage as possible. The difficulty was in finding a suitable bride. In France, there was no one whom Talleyrand would consider except a daughter of a royal or imperial house, and these princesses were jealously guarded by Napoleon and portioned out as wives to his own newly created nobles and aides. It was possible that Napoleon might make an exception in the case of Talleyrand's nephew, but the Grand Chamberlain did not dare ask. In 1803, Bonaparte, then First Consul, had sought a young lady of the Talleyrand-Périgord line for Josephine's son, Eugène de Beauharnais, and though Talleyrand had not dared refuse outright, the lady in question had been married off so suddenly to a member of the ancient Noailles family that all Paris had buzzed with the scandal of it. Napoleon had never once referred to the incident; but he was a man who nursed his grudges lovingly, and Talleyrand would not condescend to expose himself to an embarrassing refusal by asking that an exception be made for his nephew. He had therefore had a search conducted abroad by two friends, Dalberg and a man named Batowski, whom he had come to know in Warsaw. It was Batowski who discovered what Talleyrand sought. The widowed Duchess of Courland, he reported, had four daughters, of whom the youngest, Dorothea of Courland, was singularly rich, intelligent, and nubile. An ancient and honorable dynasty of sovereign princes, the House of Courland was as distinguished as that of Talleyrand and, as attested by the dowager duchess, notably prolific. All in all, it seemed a perfect match for Edmond de Périgord and a brilliant alliance for the House of Talleyrand.

* Louis, Archambaud's eldest son, had died in Berlin in 1808.

Since the duchy of Courland was an appanage of the Russian crown, it was to Alexander that Talleyrand addressed himself on the subject of the marriage, asking "as a favor . . . the hand of the Princess Dorothea of Courland, who will fulfill the dreams of my nephew." Alexander, knowing Talleyrand's reputation for soliciting "gifts," was delighted to grant a request which cost him nothing, yet which would serve to bind Talleyrand to him more closely. He even consented to approach the Duchess of Courland himself with the request for Dorothea's hand. The proposal was accepted avidly by the widowed duchess. Her daughter, extremely wealthy in her own right, was surrounded by German suitors, but none of these pleased the mother, for she had set her sights higher. It was her ambition to live in Paris, the capital of Europe and the center of all that was lively and gay in the world. The prospect of Dorothea's marriage to Edmond de Périgord, nephew and heir to the Grand Chamberlain of the Imperial Court of France, seemed to provide a perfect opportunity.

Dorothea's consent, however, was not as easy to obtain. Though only fifteen, she was strongly attached—and had been, since her earliest childhood—to one of the heroes of Polish independence, the handsome and dashing Prince Adam Czartoryski. Romantically, she declared that it was Czartoryski whom she would marry, and no one else. Czar Alexander pointed out to her that there was a strong physical resemblance between Edmond de Périgord and the Polish prince, but Dorothea replied that, if so, she failed to see it. At this point, the Duchess of Courland intervened. "You know," she told her daughter, "that in Russia everything depends upon the whim of the sovereign, and it is therefore of the greatest importance to me that we retain his goodwill. I have promised him that I would do my best to obtain your consent to this marriage, so please do not decide until you have weighed carefully all the advantages that may accrue to our family from such a match."

Dorothea therefore put aside her dream of marriage to Prince Czartoryski and submitted to the will of the Russian czar. Yet she felt obliged to dispel any illusions that Edmond may have had. "I hope," she told him, "that you will find happiness in the marriage that has been arranged for us. But I should tell you, as you may already know, that I have consented only to please my mother. I have done so without repugnance, but with the most complete indifference to you. It may be that I shall be happy. I would like to think so. I hope that you will not object to my reluctance to leave my home and my friends and that you will not be offended if, at least in the beginning, I seem to be sad." And Edmond, to his credit, replied with equal candor: "I should tell you that I, too, will marry only because my uncle wills it. At my age, you know, the life of a bachelor is much more pleasant." With this understanding, the young couple was married on

April 22, 1809, in Frankfurt. At the end of April, the new Countess Edmond de Périgord, accompanied by her mother and her governess, moved
into Talleyrand's new house, the great Hôtel de Monaco, on the rue de
Varenne. Talleyrand, at first sight, was disappointed. He found Dorothea
thin and undeveloped, affected and pedantic. The truth was, he preferred
the full-blown charms of mature women, and the Duchess of Courland,
who was still young and handsome, pleased him much more than his new
niece.

It was not only the beauty of the duchess which won Talleyrand's admiration. "The mother," he confided to Caulaincourt, "is delightful." And
delight, in Talleyrand's understanding of the term, could emanate only
from a combination of qualities. Jean-Jacques Coulmann, who knew her
well at this time, tells us that Anne-Charlotte-Dorothea of Courland
"shone with a brilliance equaled only by her natural grace and dignity."
The lady, moreover, was immensely rich and enjoyed a reputation for extraordinary intelligence and a ready tongue. In a word, she was everything
that Talleyrand's wife was not, and as it happened, she came upon the
scene at a time when Talleyrand had grown utterly bored with Catherine's
invincible stupidity and the perennial embarrassment of her social blunders. Publicly, he still treated her with perfect courtesy; but privately, they
lived as individuals who shared nothing more than a name and a house.
The advent of the Duchess of Courland, therefore, was as felicitous as it
was accidental. She and Talleyrand became friends instantly and, almost
as instantly, lovers. By the spring of 1810, their liaison was a feature of Parisian society. "The degree of admiration with which her ageing lover
gazed upon the duchess," Countess Potocka assures us, "was such as to
make his entire seraglio *perish* of jealousy."

After Erfurt, Talleyrand claims, he "settled into the insignificant life of a
Grand Dignitary of the Empire." His meaning was that since he no longer
had any official responsibility in the government, he was free to do and say
what he pleased. In fact, having taken the first steps toward the destruction
of Napoleon, he went out of his way to let Paris know that he was thoroughly in opposition to Napoleon's policies. He also went to great lengths
to convince the public that there was afoot a vast and active conspiracy
which aimed at the curtailment of the imperial regime by forcing it to moderate its ambitions. At every opportunity, in public and in private, in his
own house or in those of others, Talleyrand criticized the government in
the severest terms and encouraged others to do the same. Since the emperor was not in Paris—he had left for Spain shortly after returning from
Erfurt—there were many who found the courage to express in public the

criticisms and resentments which, until now, they had spoken only in the presence of trusted friends.

If anyone else had had the temerity so openly to attack Napoleon, it would have been ascribed to foolish indiscretion. But Talleyrand was famous for the ability to conceal his thoughts, and the fact that he now went everywhere speaking his mind so freely was interpreted as a stratagem of some kind. In all probability, it was. The only reasonable explanation was that it was Talleyrand's intention to gather around himself the disparate elements of opposition which had hitherto remained disorganized and more or less hidden. If this opposition presented a strong front, he reasoned, public opinion—which Talleyrand was certain favored peace and opposed war—would force the emperor to moderate his ambitions.

The masterstroke in this policy of Talleyrand's was an at least apparent reconciliation with his old enemy and antagonist, Joseph Fouché, the Minister of Police. The antipathy between the two men was one of the facts of political life in Europe. It was universally acknowledged and universally commented upon. Both Talleyrand and Fouché had periodically and publicly attacked each other's veracity and integrity in the bitterest terms. To speak of a reconciliation between Talleyrand and Fouché, therefore, seemed as ridiculous as the thought of a reconciliation between the Bourbons and the Bonapartes. Yet they were reconciled. It is not known who made the first move or in what circumstances. But the news was announced to Paris with a characteristically dramatic flourish in the fall of 1808, at one of Talleyrand's receptions in the rue de Varenne. Late in the evening, after all the other guests had arrived, Talleyrand's majordomo, in a very loud voice, announced the Minister of Police. An instant silence fell upon the room, and every head turned toward the entrance of the salon. There stood Fouché, badly dressed as usual, his unprepossessing visage twisted into a semblance of amiability. The only sound was that of Talleyrand limping across the room, a smile upon his face, to greet the new arrival. Then, linking arms, the two men moved through the rooms, their heads together, elaborately absorbed in a lengthy whispered conversation. From that time, they were seen together frequently, always conversing in the softest of voices, the very picture of men who were plotting to overthrow the government.

The *coup* of reconciliation gave to Talleyrand's conspiratorial posture the credibility that it needed and, as intended, had an impact upon public opinion. Metternich reported to Vienna: "In order to be able to judge the true position of M. de Talleyrand, it is necessary for one to be in Paris, and to be here for a long period. In him, the moral man cannot be separated from the political man. If he were moral, it would not be possible for him to have been, or to be, what he is. On the other hand, he is a politician, a superb one, and a master of methods. . . . There are now two parties in France, which are as much opposed to one another as the interests of Europe are opposed to the ideas of Napoleon. The leader of one of these parties is the emperor. . . . The other party is made up of the great mass of the people. It is an inert and unwieldy mass; but, at its head are the most eminent persons of the state, M. de Talleyrand and the Minister of Police." The joining of forces between the two men was also duly reported: "There are two men who hold the first rank in opinion and influence in France, and they are M. de Talleyrand and M. Fouché. Although in the past they were opposed in opinions and interests, they have now been drawn together by circumstances. I do not hesitate to report that at present their aims and their means of realizing those aims are identical." The general opinion, Metternich goes on to explain, was that Talleyrand and Fouché were working, not for the overthrow of the emperor, but for the consolidation of his regime through the establishment of peace and by the founding of a dynasty; and this latter implied a new marriage for Napoleon, since the Empress Josephine had borne the emperor no children and indeed was past the age when she could be expected to do so.

It is possible that what Metternich cites as the general opinion was correct. Certainly, both Talleyrand and Fouché had always been advocates of an imperial divorce, for both regarded it as essential to the stability of the regime that Napoleon both marry into one of Europe's legitimate dynasties and produce an heir. And they both had more to gain from a reformed Napoleonic regime than from restoration of the Bourbons, let alone from any form of republican government.

In any event, the apparent collusion between Talleyrand and Fouché was immediately reported in every capital in Europe. And news of it was carried no less speedily to Napoleon in Spain, for the emperor's mother, Madame Mère, as she was called, had been present at one of Talleyrand's receptions and had witnessed one of his conversations with Fouché—a fact which, that very night, she included in a long letter to her son. Upon receipt of the letter, Napoleon announced his departure for Paris. There was much that needed his attention there. He had learned that Austria was rearming at an alarming rate, and the cordiality of the czar had diminished to such an extent that there was grave doubt he could be counted upon to fulfill the terms of the Erfurt treaty if war should break out with Austria. But most disturbing of all was the news of Talleyrand and Fouché, who, if they were acting in concert, now presented a threat more formidable than the mere mobilization of Austria.

On January 27, 1809, the day after his arrival in the capital, Napoleon summoned Fouché to the Tuileries, where he subjected him to a lengthy and bitter tongue-lashing. The Minister of Police accepted it with becoming humility. The following day it was Talleyrand's turn. A special meeting of the Council was convened, at which the Grand Dignitaries of the Empire and the ministers all were present. The emperor opened the session with a lecture to the effect that his officials "must cease giving free rein to their private thoughts." Ministers, he pointed out, and even Grand Dignitaries of the Empire existed by his will alone, and they were nothing more than reflections of the one who had created them. To doubt the emperor, Napoleon pointed out, was to betray the emperor, and to differ with the emperor was treason.

Having whipped himself into a fury, Napoleon began pacing back and forth between the fireplace and the table against which Talleyrand was leaning. For an hour, a flood of abuse and invective poured from the imperial lips. There was not a crime of which Talleyrand was not accused, not a blunder of Bonaparte's for which he was not blamed. "You say you were not involved in the murder of the Duke d'Enghien," he roared. "Have you forgotten that it was you who advised me, in writing, to have him killed? You say you are not involved in the Spanish war? Have you forgotten that it was you who insisted that I adopt the policies of Louis XIV? Have you forgotten that you were the negotiator in the business that resulted in the present [Spanish] war?" Talleyrand was called an ingrate, a thief, a traitor, a liar, a coward, an atheist. Even Méréval, Napoleon's secretary and greatest admirer, admits that the emperor completely abandoned his dignity.

Through it all, Talleyrand did not move a single muscle or indicate by a change of expression that he was aware of being addressed. He leaned against his table, staring straight ahead. Napoleon, irritated beyond endurance by Talleyrand's impassivity, lost all control and taunted him with his lameness, his wife's stupidity, and her infidelity. Finally, at the point of apoplexy, he howled, "Answer me! What are your schemes? What is it that you want? Do you dare tell me? I could break you into a thousand pieces, and I have the power to do it! But I hold you in too much contempt to take the trouble!" Then, reverting to the language of the camp, he informed the Prince de Bénévent, Vice-Grand Elector of the Empire, Grand Chamberlain of the Imperial Court, that he was "shit in a silk stocking."

Everyone sat in stunned silence, not daring to intervene. But the emperor had now exhausted his repertory and stamped to the door, where he fired a last warning at Talleyrand and Fouché: "Remember this: if there is a revolution, you will be the first to be crushed by it!" Then he was gone. It was not until then that Talleyrand came to life, and only, after a grave bow to his embarrassed colleagues, to limp to the door and into the corridor. To one of the ministers who followed him, he said, "What a pity that so great a man should be so ill bred." But that night, to his friends of the old nobility, he carefully related the whole scandalous scene, omitting nothing and sparing himself nothing. Their indignation was far greater than his, as he knew it would be. And, as he had once pointed out, "More men are destroyed by the tongues of the Faubourg St.-Germain than by the cannons of the emperor."

Madame de Laval, one of the last representatives of the great Montmorency family and a dear friend, was beside herself with rage when Talleyrand, lounging on a sofa in her drawing room, related the story to her and her guests. Finally, she could contain herself no longer and interrupted him to ask indignantly: "You listened to that? You did not snatch up a chair, a poker, or the fire tongs and smash it over his head?"

"Ah, well," Talleyrand drawled, "I confess that the idea occurred to me, but I was too lazy."

Anyone who did not know Napoleon or Talleyrand would have concluded that the disgrace was final and irrevocable, and that Talleyrand must now fade into insignificance under the impact of imperial displeasure. Nothing could have been further from the truth. The scene in Council had taken place on a Saturday. On Sundays, it was Napoleon's custom to hold a reception at the Tuileries, at which he desired as many ministers and dignitaries as possible to be present. One of the earliest arrivals was the Minister of Finance, the Duke of Gaeta, who had been present at the Council meeting of the previous day. He was astounded to see Talleyrand, leaning against the fireplace, totally at ease. Gaeta noted carefully the treatment Talleyrand received from Napoleon, who spoke to the men on both sides of him but pretended not to have noticed the presence of his Vice-Grand Elector. The following Sunday, Talleyrand was once more at the emperor's reception. Gaeta reported that when Napoleon reached the man next to Talleyrand, he asked him a question which the man could not answer concerning some detail of administration. Talleyrand immediately supplied the information, as though the emperor had spoken to him personally. The ice had been broken. To the casual observer, it appeared that Talleyrand had responded to a query from the emperor addressed to himself; the emperor had the satisfaction of knowing that Talleyrand had been the first to speak, and Talleyrand had the undoubted consolation of knowing that even if Napoleon had not spoken to him, he had at least been allowed to speak to Napoleon. Thereafter, the situation was relieved somewhat. In all likelihood, the emperor was acutely embarrassed by his extraordinary display of temper and was as pleased as Talleyrand that a way had been found to extricate him from the uncomfortable position of not being on speaking terms with the third-highest dignitary of the Empire. In any event, he contented himself, as punishment for the crimes of which he had accused Talleyrand, with depriving him of his office of Grand Chamberlain—but allowed him to retain that of Vice-Grand Elector.

The fact was that Napoleon often treated his courtiers and even foreign sovereigns (as in the case of Alexander at Erfurt) to displays of temper. Sometimes these tantrums were genuine, and sometimes they were carefully calculated for the effect they would produce. In either case, he expected that they would be forgotten and forgiven by others as quickly as by himself. Often they were, for the emperor, being constitutionally unable to brook opposition in any form, had surrounded himself with ministers and military men who saw nothing untoward in the Napoleonic doctrine that to differ with the emperor was treason. But Napoleon should have known Talleyrand well enough to realize that the insults he had directed at him, before an audience, were of the kind that no aristocrat worthy of the name would ever forgive. As in the Spanish affair, Napoleon was cheating at cards. The Spanish royal family had been unable to defend themselves. But Talleyrand was no degenerate Bourbon. The day following the stormy Council session, he had presented himself at Metternich's embassy and announced, "The time has come. It is my duty to enter into direct contact with Vienna."

On April 12, 1809, a report came to Napoleon from Marshal Berthier announcing that the Austrians had once more crossed the Inn River and were invading Bavaria. "The war has begun," Napoleon said, "and I am off to Vienna with nothing more than my little draftees,* my big boots, and my name." In truth, he had little more, and it was only the mobility of Napoleon's forces and the masterful disposal of his troops in the field that saved him from disaster. Vienna fell on May 13; but the bridges were cut, and the bulk of the Austrian army was camped on the northern bank of the Danube. Napoleon, in attempting to engage them, was forced back at Essling and lost 20,000 men.† It was his first major defeat, and the news spread throughout Europe like a thunderclap. England began making plans to invade the Continent, and even the timid King of Prussia swore to his Minister of War: "If there is one more Austrian victory, I shall join in."

If Russia had been willing to keep the promises made by Alexander at Erfurt, there would have been no danger to Napoleon. Instead, the czar, following the course of action suggested to him by Talleyrand, had diligently moved his forces from one place to another along the frontier, while carefully avoiding any possibility of giving offense to Austria. "This is not

---

* The army of 250,000 which Napoleon had assembled were, most of them, raw conscripts. The few experienced units in the army had had to be withdrawn from Germany and, as Napoleon had feared, from Spain.

† The encounter is sometimes known as the Battle of Aspern.

much of an alliance," Napoleon remarked. "They are all expecting to have a rendezvous on my grave, but I shall disappoint them."

As Napoleon was brooding in his captured Hapsburg palace in Vienna, Paris was in an uproar. The news had reached the capital that in an attempt to storm the town of Ratisbon, Napoleon had been wounded. The report was true. The wound had been slight, and its only effect had been to make walking uncomfortable—a round had grazed the emperor's Achilles' tendon. But it brought home to everyone that the emperor was not, after all, immortal; and he had no heir. In 1809, Louis XVIII had narrowly escaped assassination, but he had been unperturbed. "The only difference it would have made," the Bourbon pretender had remarked, "would have been that the King of France would be called Charles X instead of Louis XVIII." In the case of Napoleon, it was impossible, for either the emperor or his people, to show such equanimity. A single accident, a stray bullet, and the structure of the Empire would come crashing down into chaos. The wound at Ratisbon therefore focused public attention on the fragility of the imperial regime and its total dependence upon Napoleon's personal survival; and there was much alarm and many questions were asked.

The encounter at Essling was of even greater concern, for it had produced an immediate effect. Napoleon had issued bulletins minimizing the battle, and it is true that it had little effect upon the campaign as a whole. Yet it had become obvious, for the first time, that Napoleon was not invincible and that, in fact, he had been beaten by the Austrian army, which was hardly the most feared in Europe, under the command of a mere archduke.

The news of Essling reached Paris at the same time as reports that the British were preparing to invade the Continent by way of the Netherlands. This meant, in effect, that if they were successful in landing, France would lie open before them, for the emperor and the army were at the other end of Europe. In this critical situation, the true value of the sycophants with whom Napoleon had surrounded himself was made evident. The minister of war, who was responsible for the defense of France in Napoleon's absence, rather than consider measures to resist the British, preferred to ignore the danger and pretend that he could do nothing without instructions from the emperor himself (which was true). The only one of the ministers who was sufficiently independent to take action was Fouché, who, in addition to being Minister of Police, was also acting Minister of the Interior.

Fouché realized how serious the danger was and was determined to find a way to meet it. All his ministerial colleagues were terrified of acting in so delicate a matter without the express consent of the emperor; and of the Grand Dignitaries of the Empire, only one supported Fouché's decision: Talleyrand. But Talleyrand's fall from favor had mitigated his influence, and the timid could no longer follow him with full confidence of the emperor's blessing. With Talleyrand's backing and counsel, therefore, Fouché decided that the only way to meet the emergency was mobilize the National Guard. To this, the Minister of War was violently opposed, but Fouché ignored him, issued the necessary instructions, and, within a short space of time, had collected and provisioned an army of 60,000 men and dispatched them to the frontier. In command was the controversial Marshal Bernadotte, who had once been involved in a plot against Napoleon and whose services were now available only because Napoleon had sent him home from Austria in disgrace.

As it happened, Fouché's action, though successful, was unnecessary. The weather was so bad that the British transports were unable to land and had to return to their home ports. Shortly thereafter word was received that Napoleon had inflicted a decisive defeat upon the Austrians, at Wagram, on July 6. It was to be the last of Napoleon's great victories, but this was not yet apparent. The British canceled their plans for an invasion of the Continent, the Prussian king heaved a sigh of relief at having so narrowly avoided choosing the wrong side again, and Czar Alexander's courtiers noted that their master spent long hours brooding in his Winter Palace at St. Petersburg.

Napoleon returned to Paris in triumph, and the court waited for Fouché's head to fall and perhaps that of Talleyrand to follow it. But no such thing happened. The true nature of Fouché's accomplishment seems to have escaped the emperor. What the minister had proved was not that France could be defended even while Napoleon was absent, but that a mere Minister of Police, with the backing only of a semidisgraced Talleyrand, could take effective control of the machinery of government, override all of Napoleon's functionaries, and call a new army into being. The lesson was lost on Napoleon, who still refused to believe that any man could offer him serious injury. Instead of punishing Fouché for daring to take the reins of power into his hands, he lauded him publicly and made him Duke d'Otrante. Of Talleyrand's shadowy role in the affair, nothing was said by Fouché, by Napoleon, or by Talleyrand.

The years from 1809 to 1814 were strange ones for Talleyrand. He was a personage of the imperial court, but one in a difficult and unusual position. He was out of favor with the emperor, and he remained so, for, during this period, Napoleon was constantly receiving evidence—since Talleyrand made no effort to conceal it—of Talleyrand's betrayal. But he remained Vice-Grand Elector of the Empire and, as such, continued to be employed by Napoleon in various ceremonial capacities. Napoleon explained on St. Helena that he had allowed Talleyrand to retain his office because he did not believe that he had sufficient influence to harm him and because he had retained something of his old affection for the man who had been with him since the days of Brumaire. Neither reason is entirely false. Napoleon's secret police were highly organized, and he could feel confident that he was kept fully informed of Talleyrand's every plan and plot. Moreover, he did not seem really to believe that Talleyrand had sufficient influence or even sufficient understanding to present a real danger. On one occasion, Napoleon told Count Molé: "I swear to you, I cannot honestly say that Talleyrand was ever of much help to me. I don't even believe, as you do, that he is a very intelligent man. You have only to take a close look at his life to see that. He was, to begin with, one of the most eminent personages of the nobility and the clergy—and what did he do? He moved heaven and earth to bring about their downfall. Then, when he came back from exile in America, he degraded himself by becoming publicly attached to a stupid old whore. I tried to get him out of that mess, at the time of the Concordat, by asking the Pope to grant him a cardinal's hat, and I nearly got it for him. But he wouldn't hear of it. Instead, and over my objections, he married that disreputable woman, who could not even give him children and scandalized all Europe. As you know, he has stolen more money than anyone in the world, and yet he hasn't a franc to his name. I support him, you know, and I pay his debts."

"Your majesty must admit," Molé replied, "that Talleyrand's conversation has elegance and charm."

"I admit it," said Napoleon. "That is his triumph—and he well knows it."

This seems to have been Napoleon's lasting impression of Talleyrand, or at least it was the opinion of which Napoleon persuaded himself when he wished to be rid of Talleyrand's constant opposition as Minister of Foreign Affairs and, later, as chief negotiator. In any case, he was convinced that Talleyrand, the former revolutionary, would never be able to make peace with the Bourbons and that he would have nothing to gain from the overthrow of the Empire and the restoration of the old dynasty. He could therefore be ignored and left to enjoy his Vice-Grand Electorate in comparative peace.

Talleyrand's public role in the last years of the Empire was small, but he was, nonetheless, constantly busy and still exercised much influence behind the scenes of power. The great question of the year 1810 was that of Napoleon's divorce from Josephine—to which the emperor had finally consented, with great reluctance, at the end of November, 1809—and of his marriage to a princess of one of Europe's legitimate dynasties.* Talley-

* Though the dissolution of the imperial marriage is usually referred to as a "divorce," it was, in fact, an annulment, which was granted by a docile synod of French bishops after the Pope had re-

rand had always strongly supported the divorce, not because he was impervious to Josephine's charm, but because he realized that until the imperial succession was settled, the Empire could endure no longer than Napoleon himself; and this was one of the points on which he and Fouché were in perfect agreement. When it came to the choice of a new empress, however, the two men parted company. A special meeting of the Council was held in January, 1810, at which each of the ministers and Grand Dignitaries of the Empire was asked to give his opinion on the matter. (Napoleon himself was realistically neutral on who the lady would be, since he had agreed to separate from Josephine, whom he loved, solely in order to produce an heir. "I am going to marry a womb" is how he expressed it to Cambacérès.)

The choice lay chiefly among three princesses: the sister of Czar Alexander, whom the latter had promised in such vague terms at Erfurt; a daughter of the King of Saxony; and a daughter of the House of Hapsburg. Cambacérès spoke first, and expressed himself as favoring the Grand Duchess Catherine of Russia, since this would preserve the rapidly disintegrating Russian alliance. In this, he was supported by Fouché. Lebrun, however, for reasons known only to himself, opted for the Saxon princess. When Talleyrand's turn came, he spoke eloquently and at length in favor of an Austrian marriage, pointing out that such a match would serve, in the eyes of legitimist Europe, to expiate the crimes of the Revolution, especially the execution of Marie-Antoinette, and thus would reconcile the powers of Europe to the Empire. He did not say, though he surely thought, that an Austrian wife might very well persuade Napoleon to permit the existence of a reasonably strong Austrian state. He also did not mention, since it would have been superfluous, that Austrian archduchesses were famous for their ability to bear great numbers of children. His argument carried the day, and, on April 2, the Emperor of the French and the Archduchess Marie-Louise of Austria were married in a religious ceremony in the Tuileries. As a token of appreciation of Talleyrand's efforts on behalf of Marie-Louise, the new Empress of the French appointed Dorothea de Périgord, Edmond's wife, one of her twelve ladies-in-waiting.

As visible as Talleyrand remained at the Tuileries, in court dress, at receptions, balls, and other festivities and as often as he entertained both in Paris and at Valençay, he was careful always openly to criticize Napoleon's policies, sometimes in the most biting terms. These remarks, of course, were reported directly to Napoleon, as Talleyrand knew they would. And the emperor would shake his head at the ingratitude of his Vice-Grand

---

fused to do so. The fact that Napoleon had sent French troops into Rome during the Austrian campaign was widely believed to have had some influence on the papal decision.

Elector, make disparaging remarks to his aides, and then dismiss the matter from his mind, confident that so long as he knew what Talleyrand was doing, Talleyrand could do nothing. What he seemed never to have suspected was that Talleyrand's open disapproval was mere camouflage, carefully designed to persuade the emperor and his spies that they saw all that was to be seen. Meanwhile, in total secrecy, he was pursuing a course of action intended to make both Austria and Russia aware of Napoleon's plans. Metternich's dispatches from Paris to Vienna are filled with information obtained from "X"—the somewhat melodramatic *nom d'espion* assigned to Talleyrand. The reports of Nesselrode, from the Russian embassy, which were equally copious, also made use of a code name: Henri.

The information contained in these documents was obtained partly by Talleyrand himself and partly by Fouché, for Talleyrand, no longer a minister or even a trusted adviser, had no access to matters of state comparable to that of Fouché. The system worked very well for a while. But then, in 1810, a problem arose which seriously impaired Talleyrand's intelligence-gathering activities. Fouché, in the wake of his success during Napoleon's absence in Austria, seems to have had his head turned. Having discovered that he could make war or threaten to make war on his own initiative, he now decided to try his hand at making peace. It was discovered that he had secretly and without the slightest authority opened negotiations with England. Napoleon instantly dismissed him from office and ordered him to leave France.

This was a cruel blow to Talleyrand, and Fouché's departure was immediately reflected in the quality of the information which he was able to communicate to Nesselrode regarding Napoleon's designs on Russia and to Metternich concerning Austria. The situation was soon corrected, however, when Talleyrand succeeded in finding less highly placed and less ambitious sources of information.

His relations with Czar Alexander were therefore good. It was perhaps this consideration which led Talleyrand to an act which was so indelicate as to be surprising, though not unique, in his career. By 1810 Napoleon's Continental System was causing economic distress not only to Russia, but in all parts of Europe where the blockade was in effect. Among the banking houses ruined at this time was that of Simons,* in Belgium, in which Talleyrand had a great deal of money. The failure of this firm was totally unexpected, and it found Talleyrand with very little cash, so little that he was unable to pay his debts. He sold his library, but the proceeds were not sufficient to meet even his most pressing needs. In these straits, he ap-

---

* M. Simons was the husband of the lady—the former Mademoiselle Lange of the Parisian stage—who had entertained Talleyrand and his friends on the night of the Nineteenth Brumaire.

pealed to the Emperor of Russia for help—an appeal which shocked the sensitive Alexander, who, after all, was a foreign sovereign with whom Talleyrand, although a high official in his own country, was in secret and treasonable communication. The czar therefore replied, courteously but firmly, that he could not oblige his friend, for to do so would place both lender and borrower in an extremely embarrassing position.

Talleyrand's difficulty was finally solved by Napoleon himself, who, in order to accommodate the Vice-Grand Elector, purchased his house for a sum far beyond the building's actual value. Given Talleyrand's machinations with Austria and Russia, his acceptance of Napoleon's money was no more defensible than his plea to Alexander. But then his conduct with regard to money was always difficult to justify. He had only one principle so far as his personal finances were concerned. He had enunciated it in his youth, and he clung to it at every stage of his life: *Il ne faut jamais être pauvre diable*—"One must never be counted among the wretched poor."

Most of Talleyrand's activities, between the time of his loss of Napoleon's favor and the fall of the Empire, took place in the houses of his friends or in his own in the presence of his friends. These activities are recorded, not in the archives of state, but in the journals of those friends and acquaintances, most of whom were copious scribblers. And some are contained in the diaries of his enemies. One of the latter was the Countess Kielmannsegge, a Saxon lady who was an intimate friend of the Duchess of Courland. Since the duchess was Talleyrand's mistress, Kielmannsegge had no difficulty in obtaining admission to his circle. But her purpose there was not to admire so much as to observe, for she was the mistress of Savary, the Duke de Rovigo, who had replaced Fouché in the Ministry of Police. And Rovigo was no friend of Talleyrand's. From this perspective, the countess recorded her impressions upon first meeting Talleyrand in 1811: "He approached me with his limp, his heavy body, his brilliant eyes, his serpentine mouth and jaw, his paralyzing smile, and his affected compliments. It was as though nature had given him the choice between a snake and a tiger, and he chose to be the former." But even this lady, police spy though she was, could not withhold some degree of admiration from Talleyrand:

> Before I knew him better, I tried not to be alone with him, for he caused me to feel a certain discomfort. When I came to know him better, however, I must admit that I found him easy to be with, both from natural disposition and from laziness. He is indolent from habit and inclination, but powerful in eloquence and intellect, clever and tireless in charming anyone who can be of use to him and who is weak enough to allow himself to be enslaved.

The countess' duties on behalf of her lover were exhausting, for she found much to observe and report. During the summer of 1811, the Duchess of Courland took a small chateau at St.-Germain, where Talleyrand seems to have been a more or less permanent guest. The chateau, Kielmannsegge noted, was a veritable nest of anti-Napoleonic intrigue and conspiracy. Nesselrode was a frequent visitor, and there were long conversations between Talleyrand and him. But these, unfortunately, took place behind closed doors. The Duchess of Courland herself was in regular correspondence with the Czar of Russia, but her letters were written by Talleyrand in draft form, then copied out by Madame de Laval, and finally read and signed by the duchess. Even the duchess, Kielmannsegge complained to the Minister of Police, would not tell her what was in the letters.

The Duke de Rovigo's reports to Napoleon doubtless contained all of Kielmannsegge's observations, yet the emperor continued to make use of Talleyrand's services in various capacities. Early in 1812, for example, he was appointed to the commission of inquiry investigating the propriety of General Dupont's behavior in surrendering his army to the Spanish insurgents at Beylen, in 1808. Talleyrand was much impressed by Dupont's defense and persuaded the commission to report that Dupont's surrender had been, at worst, not an act of treason, but only an error in judgment. Despite this recommendation, the emperor insisted on sentencing the general to imprisonment for life. (Dupont was still serving this sentence two years later, when Talleyrand procured first his release and then his appointment as Minister of War to the restored Bourbon monarch, Louis XVIII.)

Although Napoleon had disagreed with Talleyrand's recommended verdict, he did not necessarily disapprove of the sense of justice which had moved him to make that recommendation. His attitude toward Talleyrand, though never so cordial as it had been, thawed to the extent that at court functions he occasionally nodded a greeting and, less frequently, smiled. Gossip had it that the Vice-Grand Elector was working his way back into the imperial favor. There may have been some substance to this rumor, for later in the same year, Napoleon decided once more to entrust a delicate and important diplomatic mission to his former Minister of Foreign Affairs. The emperor foresaw, as did the rest of Europe, that he would shortly be marching to battle again, and this time against his faithless ally, the Czar of Russia. Although, in 1812 as in earlier years, he refused to commit himself definitely to the establishment of a truly independent Polish state, he was aware that to a large extent his success against Russia would depend on the support he would be able to obtain from the Poles. The post of ambassador at Warsaw would therefore be one of great responsibility, requiring vast diplomatic experience and consummate skill.

There was only one man who possessed the necessary qualifications, and so Napoleon, despite the suspicion that Talleyrand was conspiring with Czar Alexander, appears to have made up his mind to offer him the appointment. Somehow, he never did so. The Duke de Rovigo explains that Napoleon changed his mind when it was reported to him that Talleyrand was speculating in international exchanges, but, Rovigo adds, Talleyrand actually was doing nothing more than obtaining the Polish currency that was necessary for him to take up his post in Warsaw. Countess Kielmannsegge, however, relates that the emperor was indignant that some of Talleyrand's friends from the Faubourg St.-Germain—the Viscountess de Laval and the Duchess de Luynes, specifically—began gossiping about the appointment before it was confirmed, and he therefore retracted his offer to Talleyrand. Whatever the case, it is certain that Talleyrand was on the verge of being reinstated in the active diplomatic service, in an important and honorable post, when the emperor changed his mind.

This disappointment was felt more acutely by Talleyrand's friends than by Talleyrand himself. To console himself for the loss of the ambassadorship and for that of the house which he had sold to Napoleon, Talleyrand purchased a new residence in Paris, in the rue St.-Florentin.* The house, before the Revolution, had been inhabited by a Spanish grandee, the Duke de Infantado, and was truly a princely edifice, more than sufficiently grand and spacious for the lavish entertainments in which Talleyrand delighted. Before the year was out, he was established there, in company with his niece, the Countess Edmond de Périgord. Count Edmond himself had been called to his regiment, away from Paris. And the Duchess of Courland, alarmed by the imminence of hostilities between France and Russia, had hurried off to her estates in Germany to assure that her possessions were amply protected from the ravages of war. She left not a moment too soon, for Napoleon, outraged at reports that Alexander of Russia was massing troops on the Polish frontier and seeking allies in Austria, Sweden, Prussia, and Poland, ordered full mobilization. On May 9, 1812, the *Moniteur* announced: "The Emperor left today on an inspection tour of the Grand Army, now camped on the Vistula." By June 23 Napoleon's army of more than 400,000 men, speaking a dozen languages, was ready to cross the Niemen into Russian territory.

With the Duchess of Courland absent and Count Edmond de Périgord marching with the emperor into Russia, Talleyrand had the opportunity to become better acquainted with Edmond's wife, Dorothea, his niece. She was now a young lady of nineteen, and the last traces of the immature

---

* The house, located at the corner of the rue St.-Florentin and the rue de Rivoli, still stands and presently houses the United States embassy.

child had vanished. She was not pretty, for her rather haughty features and her great dark eyes—"gaslight eyes," Lady Granville said—were too unusual for such a conventional term. She would, in the years to come, be called beautiful; certainly, Talleyrand believed that she was and frequently said so. But in fact, she was more striking than beautiful and more imposing than handsome. More important, in Talleyrand's eyes, were her keen intelligence and her eagerness to learn. She also possessed qualities which Talleyrand prized highly: a sense of decorum, of what was fitting and just for a member of society, and a profound mistrust of drastic change and innovation. These were factors which had conditioned Talleyrand's own life, and he was delighted to find them reproduced now in this lady whom he had so recently, it seemed, found "undeveloped, affected, and pedantic." It also helped that Dorothea showed great deference for her distinguished uncle and a genuine interest in his ideas and beliefs. There was not a trace of benign hypocrisy in this attitude. Talleyrand, with his vast experience, wisdom, and knowledge of men and of the world, held the key to a universe which was strange to Dorothea, but which fascinated her. From the very beginning, it seemed that two kindred spirits had met and recognized each other across the gulf of age and experience which separated them. In the winter months of 1812, the foundations of the relationship between Talleyrand and Dorothea were laid.

When Napoleon had marched off to make war on Russia in the summer of 1812, Talleyrand had remarked to his friends that the emperor was now "at the beginning of the end." The next few months proved him correct. As summer turned into autumn and autumn into winter, the news from Russia grew more and more disturbing. The Grand Army had moved into Russia unopposed, finding neither Russian armies, Russian shelter, nor Russian food. Rather than fight the French, the czar had decided to let the vastness of Russia and the approaching winter do the job. Napoleon, undaunted, continued to move forward, determined to engage the Russian army, to show his power, to winter in Moscow, the Holy City of Russia, in the palace of the czars. And so he marched. By the time he reached Smolensk, halfway to Moscow, of the 400,000 men of the Grand Army, only 160,000 remained. The rest either had died from exhaustion and disease or had deserted. On September 14, Moscow was reached. It was empty and in flames. There were no provisions in the city for the 100,000 men of the Grand Army who remained. For a month, Napoleon had tried to negotiate peace with the czar, who was at St. Petersburg, 300 miles away, but without success. Winter was at hand, and Alexander knew that the peace would be won without negotiation. In November, Napoleon ordered the Grand Army to decamp. They were going home. But it was too late. The first snows began to fall before the army reached Smolensk. From then on, temperatures remained below freezing, and thousands died from exposure. Thousands were murdered by peasants. And thousands were ambushed and killed by Cossacks. In December, Napoleon's troops began to straggle across the Niemen—a mere 30,000 men out of the 400,000 who had crossed only a few months before. There was no longer a Grand Army of the Empire.

On December 18, Napoleon's Bulletin XXIX reached Paris, informing the people of the Russian disaster. On the night of December 19, Dorothea was on duty as lady-in-waiting in the apartments of the Empress Marie-Louise when she heard someone outside the door, demanding to be let in. She rushed into the antechamber, and saw there two men, bundled in furs. One was Caulaincourt, and the other was the Emperor Napoleon, home from Russia.

Almost immediately upon his return, the emperor convened his Council to hear their advice. When it was Talleyrand's turn to speak, he urged that peace be made immediately. "Negotiate," he told Napoleon. "Today you have something with which to bargain. Tomorrow you may have nothing, and you will then be able to offer nothing."

Napoleon in defeat was more reasonable than Napoleon triumphant. He saw the wisdom in Talleyrand's proposal, and he did not wince when Talleyrand explained that, in his opinion, France must offer to withdraw its forces to the boundaries established at the Treaty of Lunéville. Instead, he asked Talleyrand to remain after the others had gone. When they were alone, he bluntly invited him to return to the Ministry of Foreign Affairs.

"I cannot," Talleyrand replied. "I am no longer acquainted with the affairs of your majesty."

"You know them well enough," Napoleon cried, furious, "but you are planning to betray me!"

"No, sire. I cannot assume office because in my opinion your policies are contrary to my own conception of the glory and happiness of my country."

Napoleon was home in Paris, but the war with Russia had not ended. In February, 1814, Prussia, overjoyed at the disintegration of the Grand Army, signed an alliance with Russia and declared war on France. The Confederation of the Rhine was declared dissolved. Saxony withdrew from the French alliance. Austria was hesitating between prudence and greed. And England was offering subsidies to any country that would fight against Napoleon.

With Austria undecided, Napoleon resolved to strike quickly in order to dispose of his other major opponents, Russia and Prussia. In April, he returned to Germany to undertake a campaign aimed at the capture of Leipzig. He was victorious in a few minor skirmishes, and the King of Saxony returned to the fold. But his forces were too weak to exploit these successes, and he had to agree to an armistice in June. When hostilities resumed in August, Austria had joined the Russians and Prussians, as had Sweden. Although outnumbered, the French won a brilliant victory at Dresden, but in October, Napoleon's forces, weakened by the desertion of Bavaria and Saxony from the alliance, were decisively defeated at Leipzig. The emperor and his army narrowly escaped being surrounded but succeeded in breaking through at Hanau and in retreating across the Rhine into France, with the Russians, Austrians, and Prussians upon their heels. The battle for France had begun.

In November, a few days after the crossing of the Rhine, an old acquaintance of Talleyrand's, Madame de la Tour du Pin, was passing through Paris on her way home to Amiens. Eager for news to take back to her husband, she called on Talleyrand. "He received me, as always, with that charming and pleasant familiarity which he has always shown me. He has been much abused, and he has probably deserved even more than he has received; but in spite of everything, he possessed more charm than any other man I have ever known." When she asked for news, Talleyrand replied that the emperor was said to be on the way to Paris and that he was expected to arrive the following day. He therefore suggested that Madame de la Tour remain in the city overnight and return to his house the next evening, after he had had the opportunity to see Napoleon.

During the afternoon of the next day, she heard the booming of the cannon which announced the emperor's arrival in his capital. Late that evening, she drove to Talleyrand's house, only to be told that he had not yet returned from the Tuileries. She waited for an hour, until eleven o'clock, but when Talleyrand finally arrived, he brushed off her impatient questions.

"Come now," he said. "Surely you don't intend to leave tonight. It is madness to travel in such cold weather."

But Madame de la Tour refused to be put off. "Have you seen the emperor?" she insisted. "Is he well? What does he intend to do? What does he say about his defeat?"

"Oh," Talleyrand said, "let's not talk about the emperor. He is finished."

"Finished? What do you mean?"

"I mean that he is a man ready to crawl into a hole."

To Madame de la Tour's persistent questioning, Talleyrand would reply only, "He has lost everything. He is through. Do you understand?" Then he pulled an English newspaper out of his pocket and handed it to the lady. "Here," he said, "since you know English, read me this article."

"The article," Madame de la Tour noted in her *Journal*, "was an account

of a dinner party given by the prince regent in honor of the Duchess d'Angoulême, the daughter of Louis XVI. When I had read it, I stopped and
looked at him in amazement. He took the paper, folded it carefully, and
put it back into his huge pocket. Then, with that sly, exquisite smile that he
alone possessed, he said, 'Oh, how silly you are! Now be off, and don't
catch cold.' He rang and told the footman to call my carriage."

It was not until Madame de la Tour had reached Amiens that she
grasped Talleyrand's meaning. She explained it carefully to her husband,
who was prefect of that city. But neither of them, she says, could bring
themselves to believe that they were shortly to witness the end of the Empire and the restoration of the Bourbons.

Yet Talleyrand had been correct, and this was precisely what was about
to happen. During the winter of 1813-14 and well into the spring, the line
of battle shifted between Paris and the frontier. The emperor's military
genius had not deserted him, and the campaign that he fought on French
soil was the most brilliant of his career. But the political situation had
changed profoundly. Germany, Spain, and Italy were irrevocably lost. The
armies of Prussia were marching on Paris, while, in the south, Wellington
was carrying all before him. From a military standpoint, the situation was
hopeless. Yet so long as the allied nations could not agree on precisely
what their aims were with respect to France, there was an opportunity to
maneuver and to strike a bargain with the highest bidder. If Napoleon had
been a diplomat, he would have taken advantage of that opportunity. Metternich, for example, who mistrusted Russian ambitions, insisted on offering France a generous peace based upon the "natural boundaries" of the
latter: the Rhine, the Alps, the Pyrenees. But as Napoleon hesitated, unable to decide whether to accept the offer, the British Foreign Secretary,
Lord Castlereagh, arrived at the allied headquarters and insisted that neither the Low Countries nor the Rhineland be left in France's possession.
Metternich's offer—the "Frankfurt proposals," as they were called—was
withdrawn, and instead, the allies demanded that France accept its 1792
boundaries. "If only Talleyrand were here," Napoleon said wearily, "he
would get me out of this."

In fairness to Bonaparte, it must be said that no minister, however able,
could have saved him. Caulaincourt, then Minister of Foreign Affairs, did
precisely what Talleyrand would have done and insisted that Napoleon accept the latest proposal of the allies. But the French had just won an unimportant battle, and Napoleon refused to listen to Caulaincourt. So confident was he of eventual victory that he refused even to discuss an
armistice offered by the allies. In the face of such blind obstinacy, the British, Russians, Austrians, and Prussians could conclude only that it was impossible to negotiate with Napoleon and that they must therefore rid Eu-

rope of him, once and for all. On March 9, at Chaumont, the four powers formally committed themselves to a twenty-year pact aimed solely at the defeat of Napoleon, with each nation promising to put 150,000 men into the field if ever the peace of Europe were threatened by the reappearance of a Bonaparte in France.

The Treaty of Chaumont was signed at the insistence of Castlereagh, who held the purse strings of the alliance and who had refused to disburse a single shilling unless the powers agreed to do as England wished. But what England wished was not a mere alliance against Bonaparte. It was determined that once Napoleon had been evicted from the throne of France, the Bourbons would be restored. And it was waiting only for a favorable response from Napoleon's enemies in Paris to impose that condition also upon its allies.

That response was not easy to obtain. In Paris, Napoleon's popularity had vanished utterly, and gradually the conviction grew that his rule was over forever. "There was no conspiracy against the emperor in Paris," Talleyrand says, "but there reigned a general and very marked anxiety about the consequences that his recklessness and his determination not to conclude peace were likely to produce. It was of the greatest importance to know what view the allied powers would take when the power of Napoleon was overthrown. Would they continue to treat with him? Would another government be imposed upon France? Or would the allies leave France at liberty to choose a government for itself—and thus deliver it up to an anarchy, of which it was impossible to foresee the results?" In the face of this uncertainty, opinion in the city was divided. Some wished for Napoleon's son by Marie-Louise, the King of Rome, to succeed to the throne by virtue of Napoleon's abdication. Others demanded a republic. But Talleyrand had already decided, though not without much reflection, that only the restoration of the Bourbons could save France from chaos. Napoleon's son was still an infant, and his regime would never survive the unrest and disorder that must necessarily follow the defeat of France by the allies. A republic—this had already been tried, and Talleyrand knew, from his own experience, to what excesses it would lead. There remained only the Bourbons.

> France [Talleyrand reasoned] in the midst of the horror of invasion, wished to be free and respected. This was equivalent to wishing for the return of the House of Bourbon, in the order prescribed by legitimacy. Europe, uneasy, wished France to disarm and resume its former boundaries, so that peace should no longer need constantly to be guarded. For this, it required guarantees. And this, too, was to wish for the return of the Bourbons. . . . The House of Bourbon alone could veil from the eyes of the French nation, so jealous of its military glory, the reverses which had just

befallen its flag. The House of Bourbon alone could, in a moment and without danger to Europe, cause to be withdrawn the foreign armies that covered the soil of France. . . . It alone could avert the vengeance that twenty years of violence had stored up against it.

Talleyrand, having concluded that the Bourbon dynasty presented the only alternative to the destruction of France, now set about the task of signifying France's willingness, and his own, to welcome the Bourbons before they actually returned to France in the trail of the allied armies. This was not easy. A message to the exiled princes, even with Napoleon's power so obviously waning, could still cost a man his head. A resourceful messenger would then have to be found, who could carry safely to the allied representatives and even to the Bourbon princes themselves a report on the increased support which the Bourbon cause, preached by Talleyrand and his friends, was enjoying in Paris. Fortuitously, such a man was at hand: the Baron de Vitrolles, an ardent royalist, utterly and completely devoted to the Bourbon cause. To him, Talleyrand entrusted his message, which Vitrolles, after many adventures and narrow escapes, succeeded in carrying to the headquarters of the allies. There, however, he encountered skepticism. Talleyrand, out of prudence, had given Vitrolles no written word or any other kind of proof that the young baron was truly his representative and spokesman. It was Vitrolles' obvious sincerity which finally persuaded Metternich, Castlereagh, Nesselrode, and Hardenberg (the Prussian representative) of the authenticity of his mission. His sincerity, and also his naïveté; for one of the first questions asked concerned Talleyrand's attitude toward the Bourbons. "You can consider M. de Talleyrand wholly attached to the cause," Vitrolles answered, his voice throbbing with conviction, "at least in his heart." Whereupon the statesmen burst into laughter. Vitrolles, blushing violently, amended his statement: "Well, then, in his mind, if you prefer."

Vitrolles records that, when he discussed with the Count d'Artois the question of the government to be established in France in the interval between Napoleon's disappearance and the reappearance of the Bourbons, "the name of M. de Talleyrand was the first, and indeed the only one, that was mentioned. The prince seemed to enjoy speaking of M. de Talleyrand, whom he still called the Bishop of Autun."

As Talleyrand's envoy was discussing the future of France with the Bourbons, the armies of the allied nations were advancing rapidly on Paris, and Napoleon's position appeared hopeless. Marie-Louise, who had been appointed regent in Napoleon's absence, on March 28 convoked a meeting of the Council of the Regency to discuss whether, given the circumstances, she and her son should leave Paris for a safe place or remain in the city until the end. Talleyrand argued strongly that the empress and the King of Rome remain, for if the regent fled, the government had to follow her. If this happened, the city would inevitably capitulate. Such, it happened, was the prevalent opinion in the Council, and it was suggeested further that the empress issue a call to arms to all citizens and then, with her son in her arms, go to the Hôtel de Ville and then to every quarter of the city. But Joseph Bonaparte, ex-King of Naples, ex-King of Spain, Grand Elector of the Empire, argued otherwise, pointing out that Napoleon himself, only a month before, had given instructions that if Paris were threatened, the empress must leave. This proved the decisive argument, and it was determined that Marie-Louise would depart the following morning for Blois. As the Council adjourned, Talleyrand told the Duke de Rovigo, "This is nonsense. It is like throwing away the game with good cards still in one's hand."

As a member of the Council, it was Talleyrand's duty to follow the empress. By March 30, however, the allies were at the gates of Paris, and if one were to leave, it would have to be done quickly. Indeed, the Emperor's brothers, Joseph and Jérôme, when they saw that the defense of the city was hopeless, rode off to join Marie-Louise. But Talleyrand had no intention of following their example. Napoleon, who had brought France to the brink of chaos, was virtually defeated and in full retreat. And the Czar of Russia, with whom Talleyrand was on amicable terms and who could be instrumental in the necessary restoration of the Bourbons, was in the outskirts of the capital. It was in Paris that the fate of France would be decided, and Talleyrand must therefore remain in Paris. Still, he must not seem to neglect his duty to the empress.

With the help of Madame de Rémusat, a solution was devised. As it happened, the Count de Rémusat was in command of one of the gates of Paris, and it was at this gate that Talleyrand presented himself late in the evening of March 30. With exquisite courtesy, M. de Rémusat expressed to the Prince de Bénévent his regret at his inability to allow him to proceed. Talleyrand was determined to play his role for all it was worth. In a voice loud enough to be heard by the soldiers and citizens standing around, he protested that duty required him to join the Empress Marie-Louise, that the commander of the gate had no right to deny him passage, and that the commander had not heard the last of this "abuse of authority." Then Talleyrand returned immediately to his own house. He could now say that he had tried to join the empress, but that he had been prevented by force from doing so. Moreover, he had witnesses to prove it.

Six weeks earlier, Napoleon had written a letter to Joseph Bonaparte: "If our forces should have to evacuate Paris, and Talleyrand attempts to persuade the empress to remain in the city, then you will know that he is plotting treachery. Beware of that man. He is, beyond a doubt, the greatest enemy of our house." The emperor, now that luck had forsaken him, possessed an insight which he had lacked in happier days.

Part Four

THE RECONSTRUCTION OF EUROPE

(1814–1815)

I had not seen Talleyrand since 1806, but I was struck once more by the intellectual sublimity of the look, the imperturbable calm of the features, the demeanor of the preeminent man whom I, along with everyone gathered in Vienna, considered the foremost diplomat of his time. He seemed to dominate that illustrious assembly by the charm of his mind and the ascendancy of his genius.

—COUNT DE LA GARDE-CHAMBONAS,
Souvenir du Congrès de Vienne, Vol. I, 143

11

The Treaty of Paris and the First Restoration

TWO HOURS after his amicable encounter with M. de Rémusat, Talleyrand appeared at the house of Marshal Marmont, commander of the imperial forces in the capital. It was midnight, but Marmont's drawing room was filled with people—senators, generals, grave statesmen, all come to offer their advice. With them was Count Orloff, aide-de-camp to Czar Alexander, who had been sent to discuss the possibility of an armistice and its terms. Bourrienne, who was there, says that the dominant tone was one of hostility to Napoleon and to the Empire and that "the name of the Bourbons was mentioned for the first time."

Leaving his guests to their discussions, Marmont received Talleyrand privately, in the dining room. It is not known what passed between the two men, since neither has left any record of their conversation; but it is perhaps significant that almost everyone in Paris—including the men in Marmont's drawing room—came to believe that the marshal's subsequent surrender of the city to the allies was undertaken on Talleyrand's advice. In any event, from the dining room Talleyrand went into the drawing room, where his appearance was the occasion of great surprise, for everyone believed that he, along with the rest of the imperial government and court, had followed Marie-Louise to Blois. Pretending not to notice this reaction, Talleyrand went directly to Count Orloff and, in a voice loud enough to be heard by the others, asked the Russian to convey "the Prince of Benevento's expression of deepest respect to His Majesty the Czar of Russia." Then he bowed to the company and limped from the room. A few hours later—

at 4 A.M.—Marmont's representatives signed the capitulation, commending "the city of Paris to the generosity of the allied powers."

On the morning of the same day, at 11 A.M., the armies of the allies entered Paris through the Barrière de Pantin. At their head rode Alexander, Autocrat of All the Russias, dressed in a white uniform, his considerable waist girdled into a semblance of military leanness by a vast black belt and his narrow shoulders disguised by glistening epaulettes of gold. The pusillanimous Frederick William, King of Prussia, followed in his wake, unnoticed. It was for Alexander alone that the Parisians had eyes. No mere German prince could compete with the Agamemnon of kings for public attention. Surrounded by the giant Cossacks of the Imperial Guard, trailed by ministers, generals, representatives of the allied powers, and a cluster of subordinate sovereigns, Alexander seemed that day of March 31, 1814, the arbiter of the destinies of Europe, the conqueror of the mighty armies of Napoleon, the man who had brought crashing down the greatest empire seen since Rome had ruled the world. Some citizens of the city were sufficiently awed to doff their hats at the czar's approach. To these, Alexander responded with a bow and a wave of his plump, dimpled hand. "How handsome he is," the Parisians whispered, "and how gracefully he bows!"

That morning, contrary to his usual custom, Talleyrand had risen early. He had hardly finished his elaborate toilette when Nesselrode, an old acquaintance, arrived at the rue St.-Florentin. "He received me with great cordiality," Nesselrode noted, "and being in the act of combing his hair, he covered me with powder from head to foot." Later, while the allies were making their victorious entry into Paris, Talleyrand and Nesselrode were busily drafting a proclamation to the people of France. They had barely finished when Czar Alexander, having reviewed his troops in the Champs-Élysées, appeared in the courtyard. Talleyrand met him at the entryway. "Monsieur de Talleyrand," Alexander said, "I have decided to stay in your house because you have my confidence and that of my allies. We will settle nothing until we have heard your views. You know France, its needs and its desires. Say what we ought to do, and we will do it." *

Czar Alexander was a man capable of rhetorical excesses, as his career proved, yet he was also sincere and well intentioned. He was genuinely

---

* Talleyrand's explanation for the emperor's visit was that "it had been arranged that the Czar Alexander should reside at the Élysée Palace, but on someone's advice—I do not know whose—he preferred to stay at my house" (*Mémoires*, Vol. II, p. 122). Count Nesselrode gives a somewhat different account: "On the morning of the thirty-first, the emperor sent me to Paris. . . . I reported at once to M. de Talleyrand's *hôtel* on the rue St.-Florentin . . . while I was at M. de Talleyrand's house, the Czar Alexander sent word that he had received a report to the effect that the Élysée Palace, where he was supposed to stay, had been undermined and that he would not be able to reside there. M. de Talleyrand said that he did not believe the report, but that if the czar preferred to stay elsewhere, he would place his own house at his disposal. The czar accepted, and it is in this way that he came to stay in the rue St.-Florentin." (*Ibid.*, n.3)

eager to ascertain the wishes of the French people, and he was convinced that only Talleyrand was in a position to enlighten him in that respect. All depended upon Alexander as the most powerful of the allied sovereigns, the monarch whose people had most suffered from the Napoleonic storm, and as commander of the allied armies. At this critical moment Alexander looked to Talleyrand for guidance. There is no doubt that the decisions at which he was to arrive and to which, in spite of other influences, he was to adhere were due mainly to the advice of Talleyrand. This advice was not so much offered to Alexander as pressed upon him. There had been times in Talleyrand's life when he had experienced doubts and hesitations, but this was not one of those occasions. At this critical moment in his own life and in the history of France, his mind was made up, and Alexander was able to find in him the spirit of determination which that vacillating prince lacked in himself.

The first matter brought up by Talleyrand, once the amenities had been observed, concerned the future government of France. It was no secret to him that Alexander was not kindly disposed to the exiled Bourbons, whom the czar regarded as hopelessly behind the times, vainglorious, and incompetent. Moreover, Alexander had discussed, with anyone who would listen, the possibility of excluding the Bourbons entirely and allowing the young King of Rome to succeed as Napoleon II, under the regency of Marie-Louise, or of offering the crown to Bernadotte, Crown Prince of Sweden, or to Eugène de Beauharnais. At times, he had spoken also of giving the throne to the Duke d'Orléans, head of the cadet branch of the Bourbons. But it had never been reported that Alexander inclined toward, or even was disposed to accept, however reluctantly, the pretender, who, from the safety of his English haven, for twenty years had been calling himself Louis XVIII, King of France by the grace of God.* Talleyrand therefore began by disabusing the czar of his pipedreams concerning the royal succession in France. "Neither you, sire," he said, "nor I, whom you believe to have some influence—neither of us could impose a king upon France.

---

* Some eminent historians (among them Sir Charles Webster in *The Congress of Vienna*, p. 58, n.1) maintain that a letter from Castlereagh to Lord Liverpool, dated April 4, 1814 (F.O. Continent Archives 2), demonstrates the reinstatement of the Bourbons to have been a foregone conclusion among the allied sovereigns, including Alexander. This opinion, however, ignores two considerations: first, the likelihood that Castlereagh believed Talleyrand entirely capable of persuading Alexander to accept Louis XVIII and, second, the certainty that Castlereagh's political and diplomatic judgment, so far as the Continent was concerned, was only infrequently influenced by reality—as will be amply demonstrated by Castlereagh's performance at the Congress of Vienna. (See also Webster's *The Foreign Policy of Castlereagh*, Vol. I, p. 243, where it is stated that "the fate of the Bourbons was decided" by Castlereagh, Metternich, and the Austrian emperor—as though Alexander, the strongest by far of the allies and the one whose people had most suffered from French ambition, would blandly acquiesce in whatever arrangements those three gentlemen, who were sipping burgundy at Dijon while Alexander was meeting with Talleyrand in Paris, might choose to make.)

France is a conquered country, and you are its conqueror; even so, you have not that power. . . . In order to establish a durable state of affairs, one which can be accepted without protest, one must act upon a principle. With a principle, we are strong, there will be no resistance, and whatever opposition now exists will soon vanish. And there is only one principle. Louis XVIII is that principle. He is the legitimate King of France."

Then, having enunciated the principle of legitimacy which was to become the cornerstone of the peace, Talleyrand went on to explain that the restoration of the former royal dynasty was "the choice both of those who dreamed of the old monarchy . . . and of those who desired a new monarchy."

Alexander asked, "How can I know for certain that France desires to recall the House of Bourbon?"

Talleyrand had the answer ready: "It is the wish expressed by the only body that can speak in the name of the people. . . . I will take it upon myself to have a declaration made by the Senate, and your majesty will see its effect immediately."

"You are sure of it?"

"I will guarantee it."

That afternoon of March 31, 1814, marked the zenith of Talleyrand's career. He found himself in a position more powerful and more responsible than any that he had occupied before or that he was ever to occupy again. The Bonapartes had departed, the Bourbons had not yet arrived, and there was only one man to whom the allies, in the person of Alexander, looked for guidance and decision. At this time, Talleyrand was sixty years old. The preceding forty years of misfortune, humiliation, and sorrow, with its alternating periods of activity and meditation, danger and ridiculous adventure, terrible confusion and skillful planning, good luck and bad luck— all had pointed toward this encounter between Talleyrand and the mightiest sovereign on earth. The discussion that took place that afternoon was to decide the fate, not only of France, but of a large portion of mankind. Unfortunately, we know very little of what was actually said. All that history records are the results of that momentous conversation.

The most immediate consequence of Talleyrand's position was the issuance, on the morning of April 1, of the proclamation that he and Nesselrode had composed the day before and that Alexander had signed after revising it in favor of the French people. In every public place, Parisians read:

> The armies of the allied powers have occupied the capital of France. The allied sovereigns are prepared to accept the wishes of the French nation. They declare:

That although the conditions of peace must carry the strongest guarantees in order to restrain the ambition of Bonaparte, they will become more lenient when France, by returning to a wiser government, will itself offer security for peace. The allied sovereigns therefore proclaim:

That they will make no treaty with Napoleon Bonaparte or with any member of his family;

That they will respect the integrity of French territory as it was under its legitimate kings. They can do even more than that, for they recognize the principle that it is necessary to the welfare of Europe that France remain large and strong;

That they will recognize and uphold the constitution which the French nation decides upon. They therefore invite the Senate to appoint a provisional government which can carry on the administration and draw up a constitution acceptable to the people of France.

The aims that I have just expressed are those of all the allied powers.

ALEXANDER

On the morning of the same day, Talleyrand dispatched a message to the Count d'Artois, by an emissary of the latter who had been waiting in Paris. This communication contained an expression of his sincere hope that Artois and those who followed him would adopt the national colors of France, the tricolor, which, for twenty years, French soldiers had covered with glory. The tricolor, however, was too bitter a pill for the émigrés. It represented to them, not a record of victory, but the symbol of revolution, and they rejected, with great indignation, this first effort of Talleyrand's to reconcile the return of the old order with the continuance of the new. In the afternoon, Talleyrand was to be more successful. As Vice-Grand Elector of the Empire (virtually the only dignitary of the Empire who was not in hiding), he convened the Senate under his own chairmanship. Of 140 senators, only 64 were present. The remainder had either fled Paris at the approach of the allies or were too timid to appear publicly as functionaries of the extinct imperial government. Talleyrand was able, without difficulty, to persuade his colleagues to appoint a provisional government consisting of himself, as president, and of the Duke de Dalberg, the Count de Jaucourt, General Beurnonville, and the Abbé de Montesquieu.* On the following day the Senate, at Talleyrand's request, proclaimed the deposition of Napoleon, freed the people and the Army from their oath of allegiance to him, and formally invited Louis XVIII to return to France. This done, the obedient senators were formally presented to Alexander. "I must say

* Chateaubriand, the most articulate and certainly one of the most resentful of the royalist émigrés, contemptuously described these men as "Talleyrand's whist four" (*Mémoires d'Outre-Tombe*, Vol. III, p. 5). Certainly, all effective power remained in Talleyrand's hands, and the function of Dalberg, Jaucourt, Beurnonville, and Montesquieu was to confer the semblance of popularity on the provisional government rather than actually to govern.

that the Czar Alexander was amazed," Talleyrand noted, "when he saw, among the senators who asked for the return of the House of Bourbon, the names of several of the very men who had voted for the death of Louis XVI." Despite Talleyrand's tone of self-satisfaction, his purpose was more to persuade Alexander than to gloat over the confusion of the erstwhile regicides. In pointing out that the solemn senators who bowed so low before the czar had themselves voted to send their last king to the guillotine, Talleyrand's intention was to impress upon Alexander the importance of having obtained the support of the regicides for the restoration of their victim's brother. If these men had represented France in pulling down the throne of the Bourbons, they were now representing France in restoring it.

The respect paid by Talleyrand and Alexander to the Senate and their careful regard for the prerogatives of that body, seemed, to such émigrés as the Baron de Vitrolles, to be signs of deplorable weakness, if not of outright treachery. They believed that the battle had already been won; that nothing remained but for Louis XVIII, the rightful King of France, to mount the throne of his ancestors; that the people of France, far from accepting any concessions, might consider themselves fortunate if their misdeeds of the past quarter century were overlooked. Artois' party did not know, as Talleyrand did, that while the civil population might be indifferent, the army was suspicious and that some placatory gesture was necessary in order to reassure so powerful a body and to gain active public support for the Bourbons. By the third day of April that intermediate objective was achieved. The legislative body, following the lead of the Senate, voted deposition, and Talleyrand, with much fanfare, gathered a score of prominent men at his house to discuss the Constitution requested in Alexander's manifesto and promised by the Senate. All this encouraged the royalists to come out into the open. During the afternoon of the third and the morning of the fourth, the Cour de Cassation, Cour des Comptes and the Paris *mairies,* as well as many officers of the National Guard, openly proclaimed support of the decree of deposition, and many of them expressed their hopes for the restoration of the Bourbons. By the evening of the fourth Talleyrand was writing to Dorothea: "I have good news for you, my dear. Marshal Marmont has just come over to us with his army corps. For that, we can thank our proclamations and papers. He no longer wishes to serve Napoleon against the country." Thus, Alexander, who had entered the city opposed to the idea of a Bourbon restoration and convinced that the Bourbon cause was without support, found there a vigorous and active Bourbon party which Talleyrand, the most astute head in Europe, was leading.

Talleyrand, with Alexander's blessing, now turned his attention to the promised Constitution. Charles Lebrun, Duke de Plaisance, former Arch-

TALLEYRAND AT THE AGE OF SIXTEEN

GIRAUDON

CATHERINE GRAND, PRINCESS DE TALLEYRAND

METROPOLITAN MUSEUM OF ART

DOROTHEA OF COURLAND, DUCHESS DE DINO

BULLOZ

Baron Vincent   *Talleyrand*   *Napoleon*   *Alexander of Russia*

NAPOLEON AT ERFURT

BULLOZ

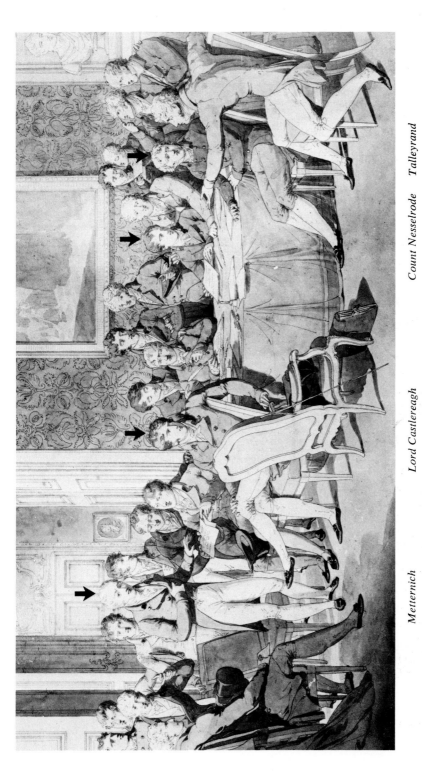

Metternich   *Lord Castlereagh*   *Count Nesselrode*   *Talleyrand*

SIGNING OF THE FINAL ACT OF THE CONGRESS OF VIENNA

BULLOZ

TALLEYRAND, BY GÉRARD

RÉALITÉS-PÉTREMAND

CHATEAU OF VALENÇAY

GIRAUDON

HÔTEL TALLEYRAND, IN THE RUE ST.-FLORENTIN
(U.S. EMBASSY BUILDING)

ETEVE, PARIS

TALLEYRAND (TERRA-COTTA)

PHOTO SCHNAPP

Treasurer of the Empire, former Third Consul, was instructed to prepare a draft. What he produced was practically the Constitution of 1791, which Talleyrand handed over to the Senate for improvement and revision, insisting only upon the substitution of two chambers for one. At the same time, he reminded them that the new king would probably prove as good a judge of constitutions as any of them; that, in the old days of the Constituent Assembly, Louis had been noted for his liberal sentiments, and that his long exile in England had no doubt provided him with the opportunity for a profound study of democratic institutions. On April 5, the plan of the new Constitution—baptized by Talleyrand as the *Charte Constitutionelle*, or Constitutional Charter—was unanimously approved by the Senate. Two of its articles were of particular significance:

> *Article 2*: The people of France, freely and without restraint, do call to the throne of France, Louis-Stanislas-Xavier of France, brother of the last king, and after him the other members of the House of Bourbon, in accordance with the ancient law of succession.

> *Article 29*: The present Constitution shall be submitted to the will of the people of France in the shape decided upon. Louis-Stanislas-Xavier shall be proclaimed King of the French as soon as he shall have sworn to and signed an act stating, "I do accept the Constitution. . . ."

Alexander, persuaded that he had no alternative but to bring back to the French throne the Bourbons whom he despised, had the comfort at least of knowing that the exiled Louis would not return as an absolute monarch. In this respect, he and the head of the new provisional government had been of one mind. Talleyrand explains his own position as follows:

> By the political relationships I had maintained and by those which I had newly established, I had the advantage of being able to tell the foreign sovereigns what they could do, and by my long acquaintance with politics, I had been able to fathom and fully understand the needs and wishes of my country. . . . The decree of the Senate being passed, the House of Bourbon could consider itself as seated, almost peaceably, not on the throne of Louis XIV, but on a more solid throne, one resting on really monarchical and constitutional foundations, which should render it not only steady, but even unassailable.

Thus were dashed the hopes of Artois' party for the restoration of the old regime *in toto,* with its ancient prerogatives intact, as though there had never been a Revolution and as though there had never been an interruption in the rule of the Bourbons. Baron de Vitrolles himself was in Paris at this moment, and he was given a dramatic opportunity to ascertain the true significance of events. The baron was to be the bearer of dispatches from the provisional government—that is, from Talleyrand—to the Count d'Artois, and at ten o'clock on the morning of April 4 he presented himself at the rue St.-Florentin to receive his instructions. He found Talleyrand still in bed, in the bedroom on the ground floor in which all the affairs of the provisional government were conducted. Sitting by the bedside, Vitrolles proceeded to draw up the complete program of Artois' entry into Paris. Once this had been done, he was eager to leave, but Talleyrand asked him to delay his departure until later in the day, as he would then have a private letter to give him.

Vitrolles found Talleyrand unexpectedly easy to deal with:

> There was this advantage with him, that no question surprised him and that the most unexpected ones were those that pleased him most. . . . The whole policy of the provisional government was the *laisser-aller* and *laisser-faire* of Monsieur de Talleyrand, and his genius presided over all the intrigues and lurked behind all the business. . . . I overcame my awe of this famous statesman, for his reputation was more imposing than his personality. He was easy to get along with. Phantoms disappear when one is close to them. It was in the simplest conversation that Monsieur de Talleyrand let fall the remarks to which he attached the greatest importance, and they always had a purpose. He sowed them carelessly, like the seed that nature scatters, and, as in nature, the majority perished without issue . . . it was in this way that he told me, with apparent indifference, of his last dealings with the Count d'Artois, in 1789. He spoke in a tone that made me take note of his words, but with a smile that robbed them of all importance.

Talleyrand then recounted the facts and the circumstances of that interview on the occasion of Artois' flight—an account which was, as Vitrolles himself realized, "the complete justification, in a few words, of his conduct during the Revolution."

All that day Vitrolles waited for Talleyrand's "personal letters." He was prepared to start out in the afternoon but then was put off again until evening. At eight o'clock, he was sitting with Talleyrand, who was about to put the letter into his hands that would invite the Count d'Artois to make a formal entry into Paris. Their conversation was interrupted by the sound of spurs upon the parquet flooring, and an aide-de-camp entered to inform Talleyrand that Napoleon's envoys had arrived with new proposals and were discussing them with the czar on the floor above. Talleyrand quickly replaced the letter to Artois in his pocket. "This is an incident," he said to Vitrolles—stressing the noun to emphasize its importance—"and we must see how it turns out. For the moment, you must not leave. The Emperor Alexander is capable of doing the unexpected. It is not for nothing that one is the son of Paul I."

Vitrolles waited until midnight and then went home to bed. But Talleyrand stayed up all that night, and when Vitrolles returned early the next morning, he was told that the prince had just retired and that he must postpone his return to Artois until later. While Vitrolles had slept, the last card had been played on behalf of Napoleon, and owing to Talleyrand's vigilance, it had been played in vain.

Napoleon, as soon as he heard of the Senate's decree of deposition of April 2, had called an advisory council composed of Berthier, Macdonald, Ney, Lefebvre, and Oudinot. To these marshals of France he proposed a last, desperate plan: With Marmont's 20,000 men at his disposal, he would march on Paris, drive the allies from the city, link up with the armies of the south, and reestablish the situation. The marshals sat in embarrassed silence throughout Napoleon's exposition—a silence which conveyed more than adequately their opposition to any renewal of the campaign. Napoleon, crestfallen, had then formulated another tactic, or rather, he had decided on a final gamble. The following day he dispatched the faithful Caulaincourt, along with Marshal Macdonald and Marshal Ney, to Paris with a written offer of his abdication in favor of his son, the King of Rome. On their way, at Essonnes, they met Marmont, who confessed that he had agreed to desert Napoleon and place his 20,000 men at the disposal of the allies. Upon learning of the abdication offer, however, he agreed that the situation had now taken on a new color and agreed to accompany Caulaincourt to Paris. The imperial emissaries had reached the rue St.-Florentin early on April 5 and were received at once by the Czar Alexander.

Talleyrand was justified in his apprehensions concerning Alexander's instability. At the interview, which Caulaincourt, Macdonald, and Ney had with the czar, Alexander showed signs of being ready to accept Napoleon's proposals. He was touched by the plight of his great friend of Tilsit days. He was eager to avoid further bloodshed. Above all, he was conscious that the military position of the allies was not impregnable. At that moment, however, an imperial aide entered and spoke to the czar in Russian. Caulaincourt understood every word: Marmont's entire corps had just appeared at the allied headquarters at Versailles, after marching from Essonnes, and had placed themselves at the disposal of the allied sovereigns. "We are lost," Caulaincourt whispered to Macdonald, "he knows everything." Making some excuse, Alexander left the room and hurried downstairs to confer with Talleyrand. The latter, with icy force, denounced Napoleon's offer as a transparent ruse. Whatever form of regency might be established for the young King of Rome, he argued, Napoleon would still remain dominant, decisive, and sinister. Within a year, he would be openly in control, and the army would once more be in the field. The only hope for the recovery of France and for the peace of Europe was the restoration of the Bourbon dynasty.

Alexander, thus fortified, returned to Caulaincourt and informed him that Napoleon must abdicate without conditions. "We shall not deprive him of all hope of existence," he said. "We shall give him a kingdom of his own."

"What sort of kingdom," asked Caulaincourt, "and where?"

Corsica, Sardinia, and Corfu were in turn suggested and rejected. Then Elba was mentioned, and thus, between noon and 2 P.M. on April 5, they decided on that island. Caulaincourt returned dejectedly to Napoleon at Fontainebleau, arriving shortly past midnight on April 6. The emperor was asleep, and Caulaincourt roused him by shaking him deferentially by the shoulder. He gave him the news. Napoleon received it with calm bitterness. The defection of Marmont, he said, had robbed him of a great victory. At 6 A.M., Napoleon sent for Caulaincourt and Ney. Would Marie-Louise be allowed to join him immediately? Would she be able to persuade her father, the Austrian emperor, to give him Tuscany rather than Elba? And why Elba, of all places? But Caulaincourt had none of the answers. Sighing, Napoleon sat down at his table and signed his final abdication: "The Emperor Napoleon, remaining faithful to his oath, declares that he renounces for himself and his heirs the thrones of France and Italy. . . ." With his customary attention to detail, Napoleon dated this unconditional abdication from "*the* palace of Fontainebleau," whereas the first, conditional abdication had been dated from "*our* palace of Fontainebleau." It was on the same day, April 6, that the Senate, under Talleyrand's direction, passed the new Constitution, or Charter. The fate of the House of Bonaparte was sealed.

Again Caulaincourt returned to Paris, and again he saw Czar Alexander. The latter, as always, was gentle and considerate, but this time he remained firm. It would be impossible to give Tuscany to Napoleon; as it was, it would be difficult to induce Austria and Britain to endorse the promise of Elba. The empress would be amply provided for. And all reasonable consideration would be shown to the emperor personally and to his family. Caulaincourt then spent the rest of the night drafting the final terms of the arrangement. Throughout April 8 and 9 he remained in constant and amicable negotiation with Alexander and Nesselrode. His single meeting with Talleyrand, however, was less agreeable: He found the Prince "obdurate," and there were objections to Elba and objections to Napoleon's proposed annuity being paid out of the French treasury.

The next day Lord Castlereagh and Prince Metternich arrived in Paris, and both seconded Talleyrand's objections with regard to Elba. Castlereagh would have preferred "some less objectionable station" and even went so far as to suggest that Napoleon might find asylum in Great Britain itself.* Fouché, for his part, thought the United States of America—"the land of the Franklins, the Washingtons, and the Jeffersons," as he called it —an appropriate place of exile. And Metternich contended that to send Napoleon to Elba would be to invite another war within two years. At 3 P.M. a final meeting took place in Alexander's rooms, and the terms of the treaty were finally agreed to. They then descended to the lower floor, where Talleyrand gave his consent to the treaty (subsequently called the Treaty of Fontainebleau), and Caulaincourt, in turn, handed him Napoleon's act of abdication.† Talleyrand then took the occasion to suggest to Caulaincourt and Macdonald that they might now take office under the Bourbon dynasty, but they refused this offer abruptly. "The Prince of Benevento," records Caulaincourt, "was incapable of changing color or of turning pale, but his face swelled out, as if stuffed with rage and about to explode."

A further delay was caused by the difficulty of determining the order in which the several plenipotentiaries should affix their names; in the end, it was decided that separate documents should be prepared for each of the signatories. It was not until the early morning of April 12, that the treaty, although dated April 11, was finally signed. Caulaincourt returned with it that afternoon, to Fontainebleau, in order to obtain Napoleon's ratification. There, he found the emperor in despair. That night Napoleon attempted to commit suicide by poison. By the next morning, however, he had recovered, and encouraged by a letter from Marie-Louise promising to

---

* Castlereagh, as usual, understood poorly the temper of the people whom he represented. An indication of the true feelings of the English toward Napoleon at this time may be gathered from the *Times*, April 14, 1814, when it was thought that Gibraltar might be used as a place of internment for the fallen emperor: "We should be really sorry if any British possession were polluted by such a wretch. He would be a disgrace to Botany Bay."

† The Treaty of Fontainebleau, officially known as "A Treaty between the Allied Powers and His Majesty the Emperor Napoleon," was surprisingly generous to the Bonapartes and, as Talleyrand noted (*Mémoires*, Vol. II, p. 125), "even respected their dignity by the very terms employed in the wording." Its chief provisions were as follows: Article I, Napoleon renounced all claim to the throne of France, Italy, and any other country. Article II, Napoleon and Marie-Louise were to retain their imperial rank and titles during their lifetimes, and Napoleon's family—his mother, brothers, sisters, nephews, and nieces—were to be addressed as Imperial Highnesses and to hold princely rank. Article III, the island of Elba was to belong to Napoleon "in full sovereignty and property," and he was to have an annual revenue of 2,000,000 francs from French funds. Article IV, the Italian duchy of Parma and Guastalla was to be granted to Marie-Louise, with reversion to the King of Rome. Article V bound the allies to induce the Barbary pirates to respect the flag of Elba. Articles VI and VII provided for annuities to be paid to members of Napoleon's family— including an annual pension of 1,000,000 francs for the Empress Josephine. Article VIII promised Eugène de Beauharnais, viceroy of Italy, "a suitable establishment out of France." The remaining articles dealt with debts, pensions, the return of the state diamonds, and the number of French soldiers that Napoleon might take with him to Elba. The treaty was signed by Metternich, Stadion, Rzaoumovski, Nesselrode, and Hardenberg for the allies, and Ney and Caulaincourt for the emperor. (Castlereagh did not sign the treaty, for he had serious objections to the chivalrous terms granted by Alexander to his fallen foe. He merely acceded, on April 27, to those parts which concerned the grant of sovereignty over Elba and the duchy of Parma.)

join him on Elba, he signed and ratified the Treaty of Fontainebleau. Not quite two weeks later, he boarded the HMS *Undaunted*, an English frigate, and set sail for Elba. A French warship had been set aside for Napoleon's voyage, but he had refused to board it for fear that he would be exposed to insult at the hands of the people who had so lately been willing to die for him on the battlefields of Europe.

As Napoleon had agonized over his unconditional abdication at Fontainebleau, the Count d'Artois, in response to Talleyrand's invitation (which had finally been dispatched through the patient Baron de Vitrolles), was on the road to Paris in company with Vitrolles. At one of their rest stops, a messenger arrived from Paris, bringing a copy of the charter. Vitrolles, no less than Artois, considered the document a calamity of the first order. Leaving his august companion, he hurried on to Paris alone in order, if possible, to undo the work that had been accomplished in his absence. Talleyrand received him with his usual urbanity and lightheartedly assented to the suggestion that the Senate register letters patent appointing Artois Lieutenant General of the Realm. Vitrolles breathed again, believing he had gained a great victory for the principle of absolute monarchy. A few moments later, however, Talleyrand, who had in the meantime been talking to another visitor, returned to Vitrolles with the remark "Oh, by the way, his highness' letters patent cannot be recognized by the Senate." He went on to explain that the king must first accept and take the oath to the Constitution. What then, objected Vitrolles, was to be Artois' position? The king would not arrive for two weeks, and meanwhile, it was unthinkable that his brother should occupy any subordinate post. Talleyrand solved the problem by the suggestion that he should himself resign as president of the provisional government and that Artois should take his place. With this, Vitrolles had to content himself, and he returned once more to his master.

April 10 was Easter, and at the command of the Czar Alexander, a solemn *Te Deum* was celebrated in the former Place de la Révolution, according to the rites of the Orthodox Church. Talleyrand could see the ceremony from his window. That day, the czar dined with him, together with the Duchess of Courland and her daughter, Dorothea de Périgord. On April 12, the Count d'Artois made his entry into Paris after twenty-five years of exile, and Talleyrand was one of those who greeted him on the outskirts of the city. No one knew for sure whether Artois had come as an official representative of Louis XVIII or as a private individual. Yet Paris greeted him as the authentic representative of the legitimate king, and enthusiasm for the Bourbons ran high—sincere enthusiasm and mercenary enthusiasm, which are always found together during civil upheavals for the victor of the moment. The marshals, the magistrates, the administration, the various academies—all rallied to the monarchy in a few days, as if they had been awaiting it eagerly for twenty years. Statues of Napoleon were pulled down, and former Bonapartist noblemen rode about the city with the once-precious *Légion d'honneur* tied to their horses' tails. Even the old guard of the Revolution—Barras, Carnot, the Abbé Grégoire—emerged from the obscure retreat to which it had been driven, in order to applaud. Taking advantage of this display of public support, Talleyrand immediately prevailed upon the Senate to confer the government of France on Artois, who was given the title of Lieutenant General of the Realm, "until Louis of France, summoned to the throne of France, will have accepted the constitutional bill." On April 14, Artois, with none too good a grace, formally accepted his new title, and declared:

> I have taken cognizance of the constitutional act which summons the king, my august brother, to the throne of France. He has not given me the authority to accept the Constitution; but I know his sentiments and his principles, and I do not fear to be disclaimed when I assure you, in his name, that he will accept its basic facts.

Talleyrand was properly grateful for this tactful, albeit somewhat evasive statement and seems to have been received cordially by Artois. "I found in him the same kindness as on the night of July 17, 1789," he wrote, "when we separated, he to emigrate, and I to fling myself into the exciting events which were to end by making me head of the provisional government. Strange destinies!" *

Artois' somewhat reluctant apotheosis was followed, on April 16, by the official organization of his new government, in the form of a Grand Council of State comprising the five members of the former provisional government, with the addition of Marshal Moncey, Marshal Oudinot, and General Dessoles. France now had a government with which to treat with the allies. It was just in time, for Francis I, Emperor of Austria, had arrived in Paris the preceding day, while Metternich and Castlereagh, as already noted, had been there for several days. Frederick William of Prussia, of course, had been present, albeit invisibly and in Alexander's shadow, since April 1. With Napoleon and his family disposed of and a Bourbon at the head of the state, it remained for these principals of the allied powers to conclude peace with France. Almost immediately, the sovereigns and their representatives began to squabble. A report sent by Count Münster, minis-

---

* *Mémoires*, Vol. II, p. 127. Lady Elizabeth Holland, whose judgment of persons was obscured neither by political considerations nor by charity, has summed up Artois' character more accurately: "The Comte d'Artois is a man of slender abilities with violent passions. Before the Revolution, he was weak and volatile; he is now weak and revengeful." (*Lady Holland to Her Son*, p. 117.)

ter from Hanover, to the prince regent, describes the attitude of the English, Austrian, and Prussian governments: "I am tempted to think that if the English, Austrian, and Prussian ministers had been in Paris when the capital was taken, they would not have sanctioned the proclamation of March 31, made by the Emperor Alexander in the name of the allies. This manifesto, drawn up by Talleyrand, is a veritable Pandora's box." It mattered little that the Pandora's box had assured the peace and safety of Europe in twenty-four hours by opening the way for developments that had deprived Napoleon of his last army corps. It mattered less that the Austrians and the English had entered Paris to find the city, not an armed camp, but a banquet hall all decked in white, and the Parisians, not sullen and resentful, but infatuated with Alexander, the Bourbons, the Count d'Artois, and Louis XVIII—whom nobody knew and who was still in England. They witnessed royalty and Revolution embracing each other at every street corner. And they saw the Emperor of Russia strutting about as the liberator of mankind and reaping the congratulations and homage of everybody, from the grandest nobles to the meanest citizens.

The basis of the disagreement among the allies, however, was not really political or diplomatic in nature. It was a conflict in personalities. Metternich, Castlereagh, and Alexander were an explosive or at least a bizarre combination of bedfellows.

Metternich, on arriving in Paris, had found the city in a frenzy of joyful expectation. Then he saw Alexander, in the guise of a demigod, riding the crest of this blissful wave—Alexander, the fanatic, with whom he had nothing in common and whom he considered frivolous, not overly bright, and rather dangerous. The Austrian minister and the Russian czar had done nothing but disagree during the war: about the command of the allied armies, for instance, and about the invasion of Switzerland. Then, immediately upon Metternich's arrival in Paris, they had set to again with respect to the Treaty of Fontainebleau which had sent Napoleon to Elba. "This treaty . . . will bring us back to the field of battle in less than two years," Metternich had protested. Alexander had replied loftily, "One cannot doubt the word of a soldier and a sovereign without insulting him." Metternich, who would have had no qualms in offering this insult to Napoleon, had signed the treaty only because he had arrived too late to have it annulled.

The incompatibility, not to say the antipathy, between Metternich and the Russian czar was one of intellect and temperament. The atmosphere of Paris, brought to a pitch by Alexander's contagious idealism and the universal acclaim he received, had very little appeal for the temperament of the young Austrian chancellor. Like Talleyrand, Metternich was an aristocrat from head to foot, but of another stamp. He was a refined and humane *grand seigneur,* prudent and moderate, preferring whenever possible to yield to force rather than fight it, precisely because, although it was repugnant to his innate delicacy, he was convinced that force always has the best chance of winning. In short, he was neither enough of a thinker nor daring enough to be guided by a principle, not even the principle of monarchy, and, like Talleyrand, to entrust it with his fate and that of the state he governed. But though unlike Talleyrand he was not a constructive genius, his loathing for the spirit of adventure was even greater than Talleyrand's. He was far too civilized, far too cautious for that. Too weak to have principles, he became the victim of circumstances. Until the very end, except for an occasional prophetic gleam, he had thought Napoleon invincible, and he had never believed in the restoration of the Bourbons. He admired Talleyrand but was too much afraid of public opinion to ignore the enmity of the church and the nobility for the ex-bishop and therefore doubted the permanence of the latter's achievements, the new France of Louis XVIII. He was suspicious of everything and everyone: Napoleon and the Bourbons, Talleyrand and Alexander, the Revolution and the Restoration.

Castlereagh's case is simpler. With his political views crystallized in and by the narrow, insular policy of his government, he was completely unable to understand the exalted frenzy and ideological transformation taking place in Europe. In the great drama of his age, he saw only a balance of power that was injurious to England and must therefore be changed by forcing France to stay within its former boundaries—neither more nor less than that. In his opinion, Alexander was too magnanimous and trusting toward France. He distrusted both Talleyrand and his ideas, understanding the latter only up to a certain point and smelling a trap. His outlook was clear and uncomplicated so far as it went, but it did not go far enough and was too narrow.

The men with whom Talleyrand had to negotiate the terms of peace, therefore, were these: Castlereagh, an insular empiricist; Alexander, a brilliant fanatic; and Metternich, a *grand seigneur* with a streak of Hamlet in him. Fortunately, Paris in April, 1814, was carried away by a joyful excitement that inspired everyone with courage, and Talleyrand resolutely began to set the stage for the negotiations. On April 16, the Count d'Artois had organized his government, and peace negotiations were begun immediately afterward. But until there was a king in France—that is, until Louis XVIII had returned and accepted the Charter—Artois' Council of State was no more than a shadow. It might later acquire substance, but it might also disappear. It seemed unlikely that one could negotiate peace with a shadow. And yet the allies not only opened negotiations through Talleyrand, but, on April 23, signed a preliminary treaty or convention. Under its terms,

France undertook to evacuate the fortresses still occupied by French troops outside the boundaries of 1792, and the allies, "in order to make definite the reconciliation between the allied powers and France and to allow the latter to enjoy the advantages of peace," volunteered to withdraw their armies beyond the same boundaries. It was a splendid feather in the cap of the Council—that is, of Talleyrand, who, despite the presence of Artois, continued to act as France's chief negotiator. It was a momentous decision in view of the circumstances, since France still had only a phantom government, since no one knew for sure whether the adherence of Napoleon's armies to the monarchy was sincere, and since everything in France (as in all Europe) was in a state of uncertainty. Yet the allies agreed to evacuate French territory before making peace. An extraordinary arrangement, perhaps, but one that was expedient, if not a logical necessity, in view of the spirit of the proclamation of April 1. Alexander, at Talleyrand's dictation, had promised that the allied powers "will become more lenient when France, by returning to a wiser government, will itself offer security for peace." Napoleon was now in exile, the Bourbons—or at least a Bourbon—were once more at the head of the state, and the conditions of the proclamation had been fulfilled. The allies, therefore, with the idealistically honorable Alexander at their head, felt bound to carry out their part of the bargain and to "respect the integrity of French territory as it was under its legitimate kings."

The convention, for all its significance, provided only the circumstances in which a genuine and permanent peace might be concluded. For the peace itself, the consent of France was needed, and for diplomatic purposes, France had become Louis XVIII. Everything depended on him, and still he delayed his arrival. The reason was nothing more serious than an attack of gout. By April 20 he had been well enough to travel and had left Hartwell. On the twenty-first, he had made a stately entrance into London. He then proceeded, by way of Dover, to the Continent, arriving at Compiègne on April 29. There he held court for three days, receiving the Council of State, a deputation from the legislature, and a great many people of high rank from Paris. The most prominent visitor, of course, was Talleyrand himself: "I saw him [Louis] for the first time at Compiègne. He was in his study. M. de Duras escorted me there. The king, on seeing me, held out his hand, and, in the kindest and most cordial manner, said, 'I am exceedingly pleased to see you. Our houses date from the same epoch. My ancestors were the cleverest. If yours had been more so than mine, you would have said to me today, Take a chair, draw near, and let us speak of our affairs. But today it is I who say it to you. Let us sit down and talk.' " The king's reference to Talleyrand's ancient lineage pleased the prince no end.

"Soon after, I had the pleasure of repeating these words of the king's to my uncle, the Archbishop of Rheims, so complimentary to all our family. I also repeated them the same evening to the Czar of Russia, who was at Compiègne, and who, greatly interested, asked me 'if I had been pleased with the king' [*si j'avais été content du roi*]. I employ the terms that he used. I have not been so weak as to speak of the opening of this interview with other people." Then, Talleyrand concludes, "I gave the king an account of the state in which he would find things. That first conversation was a very long one." In the course of it, Louis charged Talleyrand with drawing up a proclamation on the subject of the Constitutional Charter, to be promulgated before his entry into Paris. The Czar Alexander also came to Compiègne, on May 1, for a day's visit. The pretext of his visit was to congratulate the French dynasty on its happy return to the throne, of which he flattered himself on having been the chief instrument; the purpose of it, however, was to insist upon King Louis' acceptance of the Constitution approved by the Senate. Alexander returned to Paris in a rage after dinner that night, complaining loudly that the Bourbons were less affable than the Bonapartes had been. Louis had given him a tiny suite, and at dinner, the king had been served first, seated in a comfortable armchair, while Alexander had been seated in an ordinary chair, like the other guests. As for the czar's advice concerning the Constitution, Louis had been polite, but cold, and had promptly dropped the subject. The next day Louis proclaimed his own version of the constitutional declaration, and this version was different from the one drawn up by Talleyrand with Alexander's help:

> After having read carefully the Constitution proposed by the Senate in the session of April 6, we acknowledge that its fundamental principles are good, but that a great many articles, bearing signs of the haste with which they were drawn up, cannot, in their present form, become the basic law of the state. Being resolved therefore to adopt a liberal constitution which shall be wisely drawn up and being unable to accept one which must inevitably be corrected, we hereby convoke, for June 10 of this year, the Senate and the Legislature, undertaking to put before them the work which we shall have accomplished, assisted by a commission chosen from those two bodies, and to base that constitution on the following guarantees. . . .

The Senate's Constitution—that is, Talleyrand's—had, in effect, been vetoed. Nonetheless, the guarantees that Louis promised were virtually the same as those embodied in that Constitution, and the new Constitution that Louis had in mind would differ only in minor details from the one already approved by the Senate.* For a century and a half, historians have

---

* These modifications were concessions to Bourbon pride rather than changes in substance: The Charter was dated "in the nineteenth year of our reign" (the son of Louis XVI, the putative Louis XVII, had died in 1795); it was "presented" to the people by the free will of the king; and the

wondered how Louis could have been so maladroit and why he had risked angering the men and the institution to whom he owed his restoration to the throne: Talleyrand, Alexander, and the Senate. And they were indeed angry. Talleyrand explains Louis' actions as follows: "The king decided, before arriving at Paris, to issue a proclamation in which his dispositions should be announced. He drafted it himself. . . . During the night, which he passed at St.-Ouen, the intriguers who surrounded the king caused several changes to be added to that declaration—changes of which I did not approve." Talleyrand's displeasure was expressed on the eve of King Louis' entry into Paris:

> The address that I read him in presenting the Senate to him the evening before his entrance into Paris, will show more than all I could say what was my opinion and what was that which I sought to give him. Here is the address:
>
> Sire . . . scourges without number have made desolate the kingdom of your fathers. Our glory has taken refuge in the camps; the armies have saved the honor of the French. In ascending the throne, you succeed to twenty years of ruin and misfortune. . . . The more difficult the situation, the more need of power and of reverence toward the king. In speaking to the imagination by the brilliant past it recalls, royal authority will know how to conciliate all the desires of modern reason by borrowing from the wisest political theories. A Constitutional Charter will link all interests to those of the crown and strengthen the prince's will by backing it with the will of the nation. You know better than we, sire, how well such institutions, as has been proved lately by a neighboring people, give support, not obstacles, to monarchs who are friends of the law and fathers of their people.
>
> Yes, sire, the nation and the Senate, full of confidence in the great enlightenment and magnanimous sentiments of your majesty, desire with you that France be free and the king be powerful.

Talleyrand, though he had forgotten nothing of the joys of life under the *ancien régime,* had learned a great deal since 1791. His suggestion that the tricolor of the Revolution be adopted by the Bourbon party, his careful respect for the Senate's prerogatives, his insistence that first Artois and then Louis accept the Charter at least in principle demonstrate Talleyrand's wish to incorporate into the restored monarchy the best and most viable contributions of the Empire and the Revolution. As always, moderation and conciliation were Talleyrand's principles. They were not principles for which he was prepared to die or even perhaps to suffer grave inconvenience. But he held to them with singular tenacity, and he was faithful to

---

areas of responsibility of the various ministers were deliberately left vague. For the rest—that is, in every important respect—Louis XVIII came to occupy precisely the place in the government of France that Talleyrand had intended.

them—in his fashion—and he was determined to work for them when circumstances permitted. These principles were what had enabled Talleyrand to formulate a policy and to adhere to it when the Czar Alexander had been inspired by nothing more than a vague desire to "do good" and to make that policy prevail in the vacuum created by the fall of Napoleon.

Louis, however, was also a man with principles, and his were not those of Talleyrand. It was not that he was basically opposed to constitutional government. In fact, he was considerably more liberal in that respect than most of the royalists. He was determined, however, that if a constitution should be granted, it must come as an act of grace from the throne, not as a condition imposed by the people upon his return to that throne. This attitude is perhaps easier to understand if one recalls that, in 1814, the great drama of legitimacy was being played out. Louis XVIII, this fat, pompous old man who had come back to France at the age of fifty-nine, after twenty-five years of exile, was more than a prince whose palaces, wealth, and crown were now being restored. He symbolized the ancient principle of legitimate monarchy. Now he found himself King of France, recalled by the nobles, acclaimed by the populace, and awaited with eager impatience by the repentant former revolutionaries as the only man who could make peace. For he was the king, by virtue of an ancient law still recognized by the majority of the people—a law that Talleyrand himself had invoked to win Alexander's approval of Louis' return. And Louis XVIII returned to the throne convinced that he owed that event not to Talleyrand's intervention, but only to his own right. In his first meeting with Talleyrand at Compiègne, he had held a conversation with the prince that has come down to us in two different versions, but of which the general sense was crystal clear: "You and France have far more need of me than I have of you." In a word, Louis did not want to return to the throne as the choice of Talleyrand and Alexander or even as the choice of the people of France, but as the legitimate and indisputable successor of Louis XVII. He wished to grant representative institutions to France, not as the executor of a deceased revolution, but as a sovereign entrusted by God with the welfare of his people. During their quarter century of exile, the Bourbons had forgotten nothing, and they had learned nothing.*

It was in this frame of mind that Louis, at three o'clock in the afternoon

---

* J. Lucas-Dubreton, in his *Louis-Philippe*, transcribes an anecdote that illustrates, on however mundane a level, the attachment of Louis XVIII to the ways and ideals of his ancestors. It seems that one day Louis slipped and fell heavily to the floor. Fat as he was, he lay helpless and unable to raise himself. A certain Monsieur de Nogent, an officer of the guard, rushed forward to help the king, but Louis, horrified and angered by this presumption, cried out, "*Non, o non*, Monsieur de Nogent!" Then he lay patiently on the floor, surrounded by several nervous courtiers, until the arrival of an official (in this case, the captain of the guard) whose rank was sufficiently high to permit him to help the king to rise.

of May 3, made his state entry into the capital. It was a splendid day, and Paris had prepared a welcome beneath its sun and blue sky. The city seemed bathed in white—white cockades, white dresses, white wreaths, white flags. The bells sounded and the cannon boomed as Louis, riding in a carriage drawn by eight white horses with swaying white plumes on their heads and ignoring his still-throbbing toes, smiled and acknowledged the clamor of the delirious crowd. "On all sides," Talleyrand assures us, "he was shown that France saw in him the guarantor of its peace, the preserver of its glory, and the restorer of its liberty. There was gratitude on every face. . . . The courts of the Tuileries, the public squares, the theaters were filled with people. There was a crowd everywhere, but an orderly crowd, and not a soldier was to be seen." At Louis' side rode the figure, stiff and morose, of Marie-Thérèse, Duchess d'Angoulême, daughter of Louis XVI and Marie-Antoinette, who had heard this same crowd, then a mob, twenty-two years earlier, howling their hatred in the streets of the city. Even the Parisians, however, were not without a memory or a conscience, and "when madame, the Duchess d'Angoulême, fell upon her knees in the Church of Notre Dame—a sublime sight—every eye was filled with tears." King Louis himself, though not a prepossessing man, was a more sympathetic and less tragic figure. A contemporary's description of the king at the time of the Restoration is as accurate as it is brief: "He is small, fat, and holds himself badly on his legs, but he has a handsome head and sparkling eyes. He takes snuff incessantly and is sloppy in his dress. One forgets all this, however, because of the charm and dignity of his manners. He is witty and, at the same time, deep and cultured. . . ."

As workmen filled the Tuileries, removing the imperial eagles and bees from every ceiling and corner of the palace and replacing them with the fleur-de-lis of the Bourbon kings, the incumbent set to work at a task that required all his wit and much of his charm: the replacement of Artois' shadow government with a definitive one. The chief problem, obviously, was what to do with the man who, up till then, had been, in effect, France's chief of state. It was no secret that Talleyrand aspired to become president of the Council and, as such, the acting counterpart of the king. To Louis, however, with his stern remembrance of things past, such ambitions were absurd. A degraded nobleman, an apostate and married bishop, a former minister of the Directory, the Consulate, and the Empire, could not become premier minister of a King of France by the grace of God. Still, the apostate bishop had a great deal of experience, a formidable political reputation, and great influence with the allied sovereigns; and he could be useful during the peace negotiations. So, on May 8, Talleyrand was named Minister of Foreign Affairs, while Louis, perhaps to soften the blow, kept for himself the chair of president of the Council.* This virtual exclusion of Talleyrand from the domestic affairs of the kingdom was the occasion for a rare bitterness in the *Mémoires*:

> Very soon, it was necessary to begin work on the [second, revised] draft of the Charter which had been announced. And then intriguing and incapable persons beset the king and induced him to entrust to them the drawing up of this important document. I had no part in it. The king did not even designate me to be a member of the commission to which it had been entrusted. . . . I knew the Charter only because M. Dambray, the chancellor, read it in a council of ministers on the evening before the opening of the chamber, and I was ignorant of the names of those persons who were to compose the Chamber of Peers, until the royal sitting, when the chancellor announced them.

Be that as it may, on May 13, Talleyrand was once more Foreign Minister of France, and once more he entered as master the *hôtel* in the rue du Bac from which he had directed foreign affairs for the Republic and for the Empire. He records this appointment in a cursory fashion, almost as an afterthought: "The king had appointed me Minister of Foreign Affairs, and I was supposed, in that capacity, to occupy myself with the treaties of peace." That is, to negotiate with the coalition made up of England, Austria, Prussia, Russia, Sweden, Portugal, and Spain—the representatives of which were now growing impatient. Castlereagh complained to the Foreign Office that Paris was "a bad place for business," and he was referring particularly to the round of balls, dinners, reviews, and festivals that consumed so much time and distracted the sovereigns and their ministers from more serious work.

To make peace, however, was a question of reorganizing the European system, and that reorganization had to begin by giving half of Europe, still without governments, institutions that were capable of governing it. Given the magnitude of the task, it would have been reasonable to foresee long, tedious, and difficult negotiations, complicated at each stage by the hatreds and fears of an inexpiable war and by the vengeance of the victors. Talleyrand himself, who knew France's situation better than anyone, fully appreciated his country's, and his own, position vis-à-vis the allied representatives:

> . . . It is necessary to take into consideration the condition to which the faults of Napoleon had reduced France. It was drained of money, men,

---

* Joseph de Maistre, a contemporary observer and a stalwart defender of monarchical absolutism, noted realistically that "there is a touch of Talleyrand in everything that is done here. Such a man at the side of a King of France is a bizarre spectacle, but it seems clear that he had rendered great services to the good cause. The king will, then, make use of the man and the minister—while leaving the bishop to God's judgment."

and resources. It had been invaded on all its frontiers at the same time, through the Pyrenees, the Alps, the Rhine, and Belgium, by innumerable armies composed, as a rule, not of mercenary soldiers, but of a people completely animated by the spirit of hate and revenge. Over a period of twenty years, these people had seen their own countries occupied and ravaged by the armies of France. They had been oppressed by every means, insulted, and treated with the most profound contempt. There was no outrage that one can mention for which they could not seek revenge. And if they determined to take that revenge, how could France oppose them? Surely not by the scattered remnants of its armies, dispersed as they were throughout the country and disunited and commanded by rival chiefs who had not always been obedient even under Napoleon's iron rule. . . . It was under such circumstances that the French plenipotentiaries had to negotiate with those united powers, and that, in the very capital of France.

Certainly, Castlereagh seemed scandalously optimistic when he expressed the hope that a general settlement might be reached by May 15. Yet, as it turned out, Castlereagh was not far wrong. By the end of May one of the most difficult peace treaties in history, known as the First Peace of Paris, was drawn up and signed. Moreover, the negotiations were so uncomplicated that there is scarcely any record of them, and one would be hard put to give a day-by-day account of the discussions. The whole thing was only slightly less than a miracle. Even Metternich, even Francis I were carried along. And even Castlereagh, who had come to Paris full of suspicion and full of determination to avoid responsibility for anything that might go wrong in the peace settlement, was now writing to London that he was "inclined to a liberal line upon subordinate questions, having secured the Continent, the ancient family, and the leading features of our own peace." The two men who achieved this marvel of cooperation and goodwill were Czar Alexander and Talleyrand. Alexander's contribution was his infectious enthusiasm. With his slightly out-of-focus but undiminished exaltation, he kept the fires of confidence and goodwill burning bright in French and allied circles, fires which had been kindled by the sudden end of the war and by the general reaction against the abuse of force by which Europe had been victimized for a quarter of a century. And Talleyrand, working with Alexander and sure in his principles and in his panoramic vision of present and future, formulated and coordinated the benevolent forces concealed beneath the general high spirits of the moment—spirits which he knew were destined to die with the passing of time.

Under the effect of Talleyrand's partnership with Alexander, any thoughts of partition or mutilation were abandoned. Indeed, France, under the terms of the final treaty, received territorial gains beyond its boundaries of 1792: Mulhouse, Landau, and Chambéry, among other lands. King Louis, at one point, had almost disrupted the negotiations by an ill-advised insistence upon obtaining also a large part of Belgium. This Castlereagh opposed vehemently, and a lively exchange had ensued, with Castlereagh declaring that no lasting peace could be achieved unless the French gave up "this false notion of Flanders being necessary to France." Thanks to Talleyrand's intervention, Louis declined to press the matter further, and the difference was settled amicably. Thereafter Castlereagh adhered to the "liberal line upon subordinate questions" to which he was now inclined. Britain promised to restore the colonies, fisheries, factories, and other establishments that France had owned before January 1, 1792, in America, Africa, and Asia—with the exception of the islands of Tobago and St. Lucia, Île de France and its dependencies, and that part of Santo Domingo ceded to France by the Treaty of Basel. Here again, King Louis' marshals and generals persuaded him to ask for more favorable terms and to refuse to acquiesce in the suppression of the slave trade—a suppression upon which Castlereagh and his chief, Lord Liverpool, under the pressure of almost-fanatical public opinion in England, insisted. Talleyrand, mindful of the justice of Castlereagh's retort that England, having spent 600,000,000 pounds in resisting French aggression, was not being overly harsh in demanding three small islands from France, once again smoothed matters over. The islands were formally ceded, and France agreed that the slave trade should be abolished by 1819; moreover, it promised to support the principle of abolition at the forthcoming general peace conference to be held at Vienna later that year.

Great Britain, for its 600,000,000 pounds, and Prussia and Russia, for the incredible humiliations to which they had been subjected, were in an excellent position to demand not only restitution of annexed territories, but enormous indemnities. Yet they renounced any indemnity. They even agreed, at Talleyrand's request, not to reclaim the innumerable works of art which Napoleon had collected, *manu militari,* throughout Europe, especially in Italy. These things, however, were the elements of the allies' peace with France. There remained the most difficult problem of all—that of determining what was to become of the immense territory which had been a part of the French Empire.

Throughout the May discussions in Paris, the allies and the French met on the common ground of belief in the complex of political and diplomatic principles known as the law of nations.* One of the basic rules of that law

* The law of nations, articulated by eighteenth-century political theorists, is not to be confused with international law, which became a particular special branch of university studies in the nineteenth century and which derives from the law of nations of the *ancien régime.* International law is a system of more or less fixed juridical principles; the law of nations was a body of humane rules designed to prevent the abuse of force. Montesquieu clearly stated the basic precept of this law: in peace, men should do each other the greatest possible good; in war, they should do each other the least possible harm. Despite the importance of the law of nations to an understanding of European

of nations was that possession by conquest could never confer legitimate sovereignty, even though the invader might occupy a territory for centuries. Consequently, it was necessary for the negotiators to differentiate among the various annexations of the Revolution and the Empire, the acquisitons effected by conquest, and the acquisitions which were legitimate because they were based upon formal cessions of territory to France. According to the law of nations, those territories which had been annexed by force had never ceased to belong to their former sovereigns, and these had to be returned to the latter, for the coalition had no right to dispose of them. Next came the territories over which revolutionary France was the legitimate sovereign, since they had been ceded to it by treaty. France, however, had now agreed to withdraw within its boundaries of 1792, and therefore, these regions, forming almost half of Europe, were left without rulers. It was from this enormous and inchoate mass of lands and peoples that the new Europe was to be molded. Since France alone possessed legitimate sovereignty, France alone could transfer that sovereignty to rulers who would then become themselves legitimate. Thus, the Pope received back the lands that Napoleon had taken from him in 1808, but not the part which he had formally ceded to France in 1797, by the Treaty of Tolentino. To the King of Sardinia was returned that portion of his kingdom annexed, without treaty, by Napoleon in 1803, but he did not get back Nice or Savoy, both of which had been ceded to France by the Treaty of 1797.

During the month of May the allies had discussed various plans for the disposal of the territories legitimately acquired by France. It was a difficult question, and one to which the allies, during the war, had adverted by stating their intention to establish a balance of power that would ensure peace in Europe. They had touched on several concrete plans, such as the substitution of a German Confederation for the now defunct Holy Roman Empire. But they had never considered the matter thoroughly. It was a complex problem, particularly because there were several claimants for even the smallest principality, and it was not long before the allied sovereigns and their ministers were in agreement with Talleyrand that all the solutions presented were too hastily conceived to do justice to the problem. A great deal of time would be needed if everyone were to be satisfied and if there were to be a just and equitable transfer of the territories involved to the proper claimant. It was therefore proposed, and accepted, that the difficulties could best be met and solved by a process of elimination. First, peace would be made with France, during the present conference, and the

---

diplomatic and political history during the periods of the Revolution and the Restoration, it has been almost universally ignored by scholars and even by many of the great modern authorities on the negotiations which followed the Napoleonic era. Indeed, the most recent and competent work on the subject (Emmerich de Vattel, *The Law of Nations*) was published in 1883.

question of its boundaries settled. Then, at the same conference, France would pave the way for later discussions by the formal renunciation of its sovereignty over all the territories in question. The question of their disposal was to be settled later in the year, at a congress that would be held in Vienna. Somehow, Talleyrand was also able to secure certain commitments from the allies, commitments which were of enormous importance for the security of France and for the final results of the forthcoming Congress of Vienna. These concessions were, in fact, concrete guarantees that Great Britain, Prussia, Russia, and Austria, once their representatives had gathered in Vienna, would adopt the same spirit of benevolence toward France that they had shown in Paris. As befitting formal guarantees, they were incorporated into the treaty itself. Article 6, for example, reads:

> Holland, placed under the sovereignty of the House of Orange, will receive an increase of territory. The title and sovereignty of it, however, will not be conferred upon any prince who wears or is called upon to wear a foreign crown. The German states will be independent and will be united into a federation. Independent Switzerland will continue to be self-governing. Italy, except for those territories restored to Austria, will be composed of sovereign states.

The meaning of the article is clear: The allies, by promising to respect the independence of Germany, Switzerland, and non-Austrian Italy, were offering a guarantee to France that they would not expand in those areas, to France's disadvantage, by establishing protectorates, either outright or disguised.

Talleyrand's pleasure and pride in his achievements were undisguised. On May 31, the day after the signing of the treaty, he wrote to the Duchess of Courland:

> I have concluded peace with the four great powers. The three accessions* are only trivial. At four o'clock the peace was signed, and it is very good— nay, even noble—being based as it is on the standard of the most complete equality, even though France is still covered with foreigners. My friends, and you at their head, ought to be content with me.

The *Mémoires* are even more explicit:

> When I think of the date of these treaties of 1814, of the difficulties of every kind that I experienced, and of the spirit of vengeance that I encountered in some of the representatives with whom I had to deal and whom I had to defeat, I await with confidence the judgment of posterity. I shall simply call attention to the fact that six weeks after the king's entrance into Paris, France's territory was secure, foreign soldiers had left French soil

---

* *I.e.,* of the lesser powers: Spain, Portugal, and Sweden.

and, by the return of the garrisons of foreign fortresses abroad and of the prisoners, it possessed a superb army, and, finally, that we had preserved all the admirable works of art carried off by our armies from nearly all the museums of Europe.

Beyond doubt, the First Peace of Paris was a masterpiece of constructive diplomacy, not only in its terms, but also in its implications for the future of France. For dismemberment or crushing indemnities had not been the only dangers confronting the French nation. Even by permitting France to retain what it had possessed before 1792, the allies, in aggrandizing themselves, could have made it a second-rate power. Europe was theirs for the taking. England might have claimed Belgium and Holland. Austria, which had been pursuing its imperialistic ambitions in Italy with success for centuries, openly lusted after Piedmont and the papal legations. The German states, not only without power but also without rulers, were ripe for an equal division between Austria and Prussia. What Europe might have been like if Napoleon's conquerors had not resisted the temptation to imitate him is anyone's guess. All that is certain is that there was nothing that France could have done in May, 1814, if they had succumbed to that temptation. That they did not, is due principally to Alexander, who inspired them with momentary generosity, and to Talleyrand, who maneuvered them into expressing that generosity on paper and thereby perpetuating it.

Czar Alexander's powers of persuasion stemmed from the military forces at his command, the risks he had run, the manifesto of April 1, his youthful enthusiasm, his idealistic humanitarianism—all of which had made him not only the leader of the allied representatives, but also the idol of the masses of Europe. His name was on everyone's lips, and in the meanest hovel he was regarded with reverence, as the man who would fulfill the hopes of the people and bring them the happiness which they had not known for so long. This tremendous popularity gave him authority, even though it provoked jealousy, for all the allies were still, as before, very conscious of changes in public opinion—changes which they themselves had used to good effect against Napoleon. Talleyrand, however, enjoyed no such popularity, and he had no military forces at his disposal. He was merely Foreign Minister to a new and not entirely secure king. Yet he had been able to wring phenomenal concessions from the victorious allies. The explanation must probably combine two major factors: the personal position of Talleyrand and the political position of the allied governments.

With respect to the first factor, there is no doubt that Talleyrand's "betrayal" of Napoleon at Erfurt had much to do with his success in the Peace of Paris. While the French Empire and Talleyrand himself had still been strong, Talleyrand had begun calling for justice. Now he was in a position where he could remind the allies that he, when Napoleon had been master of Europe and at great peril to himself, had protested against that abuse of force of which the allies were then the victims. At the hour of Bonaparte's fall, Talleyrand could therefore present himself as the first champion of the allied cause in France, and his opposition to Napoleon after Austerlitz now became a credit upon which France, in the person of Talleyrand, could draw when dealing with its conquerors. Before preaching moderation and justice, Talleyrand had practiced those virtues himself.

The leniency of the allies, however, was based on political as well as sentimental considerations. What the allied governments and their peoples desired above all else was security and tranquillity. They were aware that the loss of the Napoleonic conquests would in itself be a severe shock to French public opinion. Any further dismemberment could only weaken the position of the Bourbons, aggravate resentment among the French, and perhaps lead to a resurgence of Bonapartism. Moreover, imperialism in those days had only just begun to be inspired by economics. When the allies gave up any claim to reparations, it was because they preferred to cut their losses than to run the risk of another war. When Castlereagh so amicably surrendered any claim to the Indies, it was because he was either unaware of or indifferent to the raw materials and markets represented by those lands. His eyes were turned toward the past rather than the future, and his only concern was to secure naval stations for sailing ships rather than economic footholds in Asia and in the New World for England.

Europe, therefore, with one eye on its own future security and the other on Talleyrand's services in the past, had set out the main lines of the great work of reconstruction. Three of the principal allies—Prussia, England, and Austria—had put their cards on the table and stated their principal claims. In view of twenty years of warfare, these claims were characterized by an amazing leniency. But there was still one sovereign who had not yet been heard from in this respect. Alexander, while preaching goodness and justice to everyone else, had not committed herself to those virtues in the Peace of Paris. France and Talleyrand now knew the maximum demands of the three other powers, but what about Russia? Alexander had been silent on that score. He had read carefully the secret article of the peace providing that "The relations whence a system of real and permanent balance of power is to be derived shall be regulated at the congress, upon principles determined by the allied powers among themselves." And he had decided to bide his time, until the congress assembled at Vienna later in the year.

That decision was to become the thorn in Talleyrand's side, and the occasion of Alexander's tragedy, at the Congress of Vienna.

12

London Interlude

THE TREATIES of Paris were signed not only by the four great powers, but by some of the smaller allies as well—Spain, Sweden, and Portugal. It was clear from the very first, however, that the English, the Austrians, the Prussians, and especially the Russians never intended anyone other than themselves to have a share in decisions. And France had already recognized that the ultimate reorganization of Europe lay exclusively in the hands of the allies, by virtue of the secret articles of the Paris treaty:

> The disposition of the territories which His Most Christian Majesty forgoes, by Article III of the open treaty of this date, and the future relations of the various states from which there is to result a system of real and durable equilibrium in Europe, shall be regulated at a congress, on a basis agreed upon *between the allied powers*. . . .

It was obvious, therefore, that the future Congress of Vienna was intended to be no more than an assembly convoked to ratify the decisions of the four major allied powers.* If these powers could arrive at some preliminary agreement among themselves before the congress, they felt certain that Talleyrand would have no choice in Vienna but to affix his signature with a minimum of argument. For this purpose, the Prince Regent of England invited the Czar of Russia, the Emperor of Austria, the King of Prus-

---

* Castlereagh was quite candid about this: ". . . Our conferences might be continued in London, and all essential points arranged for the ratification of the Congress." Letter to Lord Liverpool, May 5, 1814 (*Correspondence*, Vol. IX, p. 460).

sia, and their ministers to London. Alexander and Frederick William accepted, while Austria was represented by the emperor's minister, Prince Metternich. There everyone's hopes—except those of Talleyrand, who had, of course, not been invited—were doomed to disappointment. The London Conference was destined to be a fiasco.

The fault was partly that of Castlereagh, who, as usual, had misjudged the situation. In Paris, he had been wary of Alexander and had relied on Austria and Metternich. As it happened, the British Cabinet, the prime minister, and the prince regent were of precisely the opposite sentiments. They shared Europe's adulatory attitude toward the Czar of Russia, and they had little confidence in Austria and even less in its Foreign Minister.

Had Alexander been astute enough to take advantage of the situation, he might have succeeded in discrediting Castlereagh and winning British support for his schemes at the forthcoming congress. Instead, through a series of diplomatic and social *faux pas,* he managed not only to lose the friendship of the Tory Cabinet and of the prince regent, but also to alienate Talleyrand and thereby to drive England, France, and Austria into a virtual alliance against Russia.

Talleyrand had been the first to feel the effects of Alexander's emotional instability. The czar, never enchanted with the Bourbons or with the prospect of their return to the throne of France, had acquiesced in the Restoration only at Talleyrand's insistence. Now he was not pleased with the way that Louis XVIII was conducting himself. On June 4, Louis had gone before the legislature and presented his Charter. Fundamentally, this document was not unlike the Constitution favored by Talleyrand, but it was more precise and more detailed. Its inspiration had been Montesquieu, and its model had been the Constitution of the United States. The legislative power was divided between the king and the two assemblies, as it had been in the Constitution; now, however, the initiation of laws was mainly the function of the throne, while the two houses had the right only to ask the king to initiate legislation. Among the other differences was the stipulation that to be eligible for membership in either the Chamber of Deputies or the Chamber of Peers, one must have attained the age of forty and pay a direct tax of 1,000 francs and that, to be able to vote, a citizen must be thirty years of age and pay a tax of 300 francs. This, then, was a constitution, but a constitution under which only the wealthy might enjoy the right of opposition. Both the Constitution and the Charter, however, provided that no law could be promulgated and no tax levied without the consent of both chambers, and both documents provided for freedom of the press, freedom of assembly, and so forth.

On the face of it, there was little in this new charter that might upset Alexander. Yet on June 3, the night before the Charter was presented, he left Paris in a rage, with Frederick William of Prussia following, bound for London. He refused to see or to receive any communication from Prince Talleyrand, and he loudly declared to everyone that Talleyrand had betrayed him by allowing the Charter of Louis XVIII to be presented. The reason for his fury was not to be found in the contents of Louis' Charter, but in its origin. The Constitution of the Senate, drawn up under Talleyrand's guidance and with Alexander's blessing, had been, in the latter's eyes, a pact. Under it, Louis would have become King of France by the will of the people, and only after the Constitution had been accepted by both king and people. A plebiscite was therefore called for, the nature of which—in the words of the Constitution—"would be determined." The Charter, on the other hand, was a concession from the throne, made by Louis XVIII, King of France since the death of Louis XVII and successor to the throne in a long and unbroken line of French kings, in "the nineteenth year of his reign." The king stated as much in his Charter, with a vigor and clarity that left no doubt of his meaning.

Talleyrand waited a few days for the imperial temper to cool, and then, on June 13, he wrote a soothing letter to his erstwhile friend:

SIRE:

I did not see your majesty before your departure, and I take the liberty of reproaching you for it, with all the sincere respect of my most affectionate attachment.

Sire, important exchanges between us disclosed to you my most secret sentiments a long time ago. Your esteem was the result of such disclosure. It comforted me for many years and enabled me to bear painful ordeals. I foresaw your destiny and felt that I, Frenchman though I am, could associate myself some day with your projects, because they would never cease to be magnanimous. You have now completely attained that grand destiny. Seeing that I have followed you in your noble career, do not deprive me of my reward. I ask it from the hero of my daydreams and, dare I add, of my heart.

You have saved France. Your entry into Paris was the signal for the end of despotism. Whatever may be your secret observations, if you were again called there, what you have already done you would do again. You could not fail in your glory, even if you were to believe the monarchy disposed to assume a little more authority than you think necessary and the French people careless of their freedom. After all, what are we yet? And who can flatter himself, after such a catastrophe, that he understands in a short time the character of the French? Do not doubt it, sire: The king, whom you have brought back to us, shall be obliged, if he intends to give us useful institutions, to take certain precautions, and to seek in his faithful memory what we were formerly, in order to judge what will really suit us. Because we abandoned our national customs during a period of gloomy oppression, we shall, for a long time, seem foreign to the government that shall be given us.

The French, in general, have been and will be somewhat fickle in their impressions. They will always be ready to make these impressions known, because they know, by a secret instinct, that they are not to last long. This versatility will lead them very soon to place an unlimited confidence in their sovereign, and our king will not abuse that confidence. . . .

The king has long studied our history. He knows us, he knows how to give a royal character to all that proceeds from him, and when we shall have become ourselves again, we shall resume that truly French custom of adapting to ourselves the actions and qualities of our king. Besides, liberal principles are in keeping with the spirit of the age. We cannot fail to do the same, and, if your majesty will have confidence in my word, I will promise you that we shall have a monarchy blended with liberty, that you shall witness men of merit welcomed and honored in France. And it will be your glory to have made the happiness of our country. . . .

Your majesty will pardon the length of my letter. It was indispensable in order to reply to the greatest portion of your generous anxieties; it will replace the spoken explanation that I should so much like to have given you. General Pozzo, whom I see every day and whom I cannot thank you enough, sire, for having left with us, shall look to our interests and warn us, for we sometimes need to be warned. I shall discuss with him our national interests, and, if, as I hope, your majesty honors France with a short visit, upon his return, he will tell you, and you will yourself see, that I have not deceived you.

Another confidant, one only, has received the secret of my grief, I mean the Duchess of Courland, whom you honor with your kindness and who so well understands my anxiety. When we shall have the happiness of seeing you again, I shall leave it to her to tell you how grieved I have been, and she will also tell you that I did not deserve to be so.

May, sire, your generous soul have a little patience! Allow a good Frenchman, as I am, to ask of you, in the old French language, to permit us to resume the former *accoutumance** of love for our kings; it is certainly not yours to refuse to understand the influence of that sentiment on a great nation.

Please deign to accept, sire, with your usual kindness, the homage of the profound respect with which I am, sire, your majesty's most humble and obedient servant.

Prince of Benevento

Alexander, in short, had almost come to blows with the French king and with Talleyrand because Louis XVIII had refused to accept his crown from the hands of his people. This the czar regarded as nothing less than a betrayal of principle—but of Alexander's principles, not Louis'. For Alexander was perfectly sincere in his infatuation with democratic ideals. Because he was sincere, he was always irritated when he encountered opposition. Because he was a fanatic, he always interpreted opposition as deception and betrayal. And not all of Talleyrand's eloquent reasoning

---

* An old French expression, now obsolete, meaning what one is wont to do.

could make him swerve a hairsbreadth from his chosen path of righteous indignation.

The Czar of All the Russias arrived in London on June 7, three days after the proclamation of Louis' Charter, in a mood to complete the work of alienation that he had begun in Paris. Alexander, Frederick William, and their retinues were hailed by huge and enthusiastic crowds. In London in June, as in Paris in April, Alexander could well believe himself the liberator of Europe, the *restitutor orbis,* the hope of the nations, admired, loved, and applauded by high and low. On the one hand, he daily traversed crowded London and received frenzied ovations in sections where the prince regent dared not show his face for fear of being jeered. On the other, he received a doctorate from Oxford as "the defender of the rights of Europe." After so much effort, anguish, and sorrow, Alexander was now intoxicated by adulation, and throwing caution to the winds, he determined to relax and enjoy his laurels.

Had matters remained there and had Alexander been content to ride through the streets of the English capital, to show himself at the innumerable receptions and banquets that had been planned in his honor, and to leave social initiatives to his hosts and political negotiations to Nesselrode, his capable minister, all might have been well. But this was not to be. At the social level, Alexander committed the grave error of allowing his sister, the Grand Duchess Catherine, to join him in London.* There, despite the entreaties and protests of the Russian ambassador, Count (later Prince) Lieven, and his wife, she proceeded to offend, at once and irreparably, everyone in sight. Between her and the prince regent there was an instant antipathy. At their first meeting the prince had muttered to Countess Lieven, "Your grand duchess is not good-looking." (As indeed she was not.) And Catherine, on her side, had whispered to the countess, "Your prince is ill-bred." (The prince regent was famed for his elegance of dress and manner and was known as "the First Gentleman of Europe.") An official dinner at the prince's residence, Carlton House, was even more inauspicious. The grand duchess threw an initial chill over the party by insisting that the band be sent away "because music always makes me vomit." The prince regent sought to brighten things by asking Catherine why she still was in mourning for her late husband and suggesting that a woman of her obvious charms must not prolong widowhood unduly. "She answered," records

---

* Catherine was reputedly Alexander's mistress, as well as his sister, and the widow of Prince George of Oldenburg. She had always had great influence over her imperial brother, by means of a talent for satisfying both his lusts and his ego. The Russian ambassadress in London, Princess (then Countess) Lieven, describes her thus: "She had an excessive thirst for authority and a very high opinion of herself, which perhaps exceeded her desserts. . . . Her mind was cultivated, brilliant, and daring; her character, resolute and imperious. She startled and astonished the English more than she pleased them. . . . She is greedy of everything, especially people."

Lieven, "by an astonished silence and looks full of haughtiness." Then the grand duchess undertook to upbraid the prince regent for his strictness with his daughter, the Princess Charlotte, and, incidentally, to reprove the prince for his estrangement from his own wife, the Princess of Wales. "This is intolerable," the prince gasped to Lieven, and, that lady assures us, he turned "quite purple." She concludes: "From that evening, she and the regent hated each other mutually, and the feeling remained to the end."

Catherine's *gaffes* were bad enough, but to make matters worse, her strange behavior was thoroughly approved of and closely imitated by the enthralled czar. Alexander, to the prince regent's dismay, had insisted on staying at a private hostelry, the Pulteney Hotel, rather than at St. James's Palace, and it happened that the Pulteney Hotel was in a section of the city particularly hostile to "Prinny" (as the regent was known, affectionately to his friends and contemptuously to his enemies). Upon Alexander's arrival, on June 7, the regent sent a message to Alexander announcing his intention to visit him "immediately." The czar and the Grand Duchess Catherine had then waited for several hours, while Alexander grew increasingly irritated at the delay, and Catherine did her best to inflame his resentment at being kept waiting. "This is exactly what the man is like," she hissed to her imperial and very sensitive brother. Finally, another message arrived: "His royal highness has been threatened with annoyance in the street if he shows himself; it is therefore impossible for him to come and see the emperor." Alexander had no choice but to go to Carlton House, where he found an understandably embarrassed and angry prince regent. "A poor prince, indeed," was Alexander's comment after his first and only private interview with England's ruler. The antipathy between czar and regent did not diminish as the days passed. Rather, it degenerated into an exchange of thinly veiled insults. On one occasion, the regent kept his guest waiting for an hour in Hyde Park, and the czar retaliated by arriving for dinner at Carlton House four hours late.

There was bizarre political, as well as social, comportment on the part of Alexander and his sister. Catherine, in the days since her arrival, had assiduously cultivated the opposition—the Whigs—rather than the Tories, who were then in power. Not caring a whit that an insult to the ruler of a nation was, in those days, regarded as an insult to the nation as a whole, she became the intimate friend and adviser of Princess Charlotte, the rebellious and therefore disgraced daughter of the regent. It was commonly believed —and it may have been true—that it was because of Catherine's influence that Charlotte defied the wishes of her father and refused to marry the Prince of Orange. She also threatened to visit the unhappy Princess of Wales, with whom the prince regent had now publicly broken off all relations, and she was only prevented from carrying out her threat by Lieven's counterthreat to resign instantly if she did.

The climax of this chilling visit to England came on June 18, on the occasion of a Guildhall banquet. The Emperor Alexander, resplendent in scarlet and gold, drove to the City in the prince regent's carriage—accompanied by Catherine, whose attendance had been discouraged in the strongest terms and who had been warned that it was not customary for ladies to be present on such occasions.* As the royal party—the regent, the emperor, the King of Prussia, the grand duchess, the Duchess of York, and Countess Lieven—passed up the aisle among the guests, Alexander caught sight of the two most articulate leaders of the opposition, Lord Grey and Lord Holland, who were the regent's bitterest enemies, and he stopped to chat with them—while the regent, red in the face, had to pause and wait. During the banquet which followed, the regent spoke not a word to Alexander and his sister. "All agree," one observer wrote, "that Prinny will either die or go mad. He is worn out with fuss, fatigue, and *rage*." It did not mitigate Prinny's rage that the Italian singers who had been hired to entertain his guests could not perform because the grand duchess loudly complained, when they began, that she was about to vomit. The lady's nausea was such that she could barely bring herself to agree, and then sulkily, to allow "God Save the King" to be played after the royal toast. Alexander, during this insulting display of bad manners, sat mute, while everyone around him was muttering indignantly.† Even Lord Liverpool, the mildest of men, said to Lieven: "When folks don't know how to behave, they would do better to stay at home, and your duchess has chosen against all usage to go to men's dinners."

The members of the government were not the only ones shocked by the impertinence of the grand duchess and her brother. The leaders of the opposition were understandably embarrassed by the favor that Alexander went out of his way to show them. Lord Grey, whom Alexander had cultivated with particular fervor, described the czar as "a vain, silly fellow." It was natural for British politicians to show contempt for the prince regent, he felt, but it was quite something else for a foreigner to insult him publicly. This feeling seems to have infected the public as a whole. As Alexander's visit drew to a close, London crowds no longer greeted Alexander with their former enthusiasm. Their applause was now reserved for Blücher, the Prussian general, and Platov, a flamboyant Cossack in Alexander's retinue.

* When it was seen that Catherine, despite the best efforts of Countess Lieven, was determined to attend the banquet, invited or uninvited, an invitation was issued. Then, so that she might not be the only woman present, a few other ladies were invited—to the disgust of everyone concerned.

† In fairness to Alexander, it should be noted that he was becoming increasingly deaf at this time.

No one—certainly not Talleyrand and least of all Castlereagh—had imagined, when in Paris, what havoc Alexander's mischievous ill temper, aggravated by his erratic sister, would wreak among the allied sovereigns. Now, however, they all were delighted. Talleyrand, because he knew that any rift among the allies could only benefit France; Castlereagh, because the Cabinet and the regent and the British people as a whole were now united with him in his distrust of Alexander; and Metternich, because he suspected that Alexander had exaggerated designs on Polish territory and that only a firm and united stand against Russia by the other allies, at the forthcoming congress, could frustrate a plan so dangerous to Austrian security. Indeed, Metternich had done all that he could in London to widen the breach between the British government and the Russian czar, by making fun of Alexander when talking to the prince regent and ridiculing the regent when speaking to the czar. Meanwhile, he carefully avoided all contact with the opposition, paid assiduous court to the regent, and behaved with the utmost tact with respect to the Tory ministry.

In such an atmosphere, it was out of the question for the English, Prussian, Austrian, and Russian representatives to transact any important business, let alone to reach an agreement that, as Castlereagh had hoped, would result in "All essential points [being] arranged for the ratification of the Congress." Two important questions—that of Prussian claims upon the territory of Saxony and that of Alexander's demands for sections of Poland—were indeed discussed. But in both respects Alexander showed himself wholly intractable, and since Russian troops were occupying almost the whole of Poland and Saxony, both questions had then to be postponed until the congress met in Vienna. The inference was overwhelming that Alexander desired not only peace and justice, as he had proclaimed so loudly and so long, but most of Poland as well.

The four powers were now faced with the fact that they would have to convene the congress without having first reached a decision on the two most difficult questions on the agenda. But since they were determined to settle these matters themselves and without interference from Talleyrand, they resolved officially that the organization of the congress must be "according to a plan which will have been determined by the four Courts." For this purpose, the ministers of the four powers were to meet at Vienna a short time before the rest of the congress assembled. Alexander agreed, however, only when the other powers promised to decide nothing until he himself had arrived in Vienna. It was also agreed that no action should be taken with respect to occupied countries until their fate had been decided by formal treaty and that each of the four powers would maintain a force of at least 75,000 troops at combat readiness until the reorganization of Europe had been carried out. The one specific territorial settlement reached, and that of minor importance, ratified the incorporation of the Low Countries into Holland,* although recognition of the new state was deferred until the congress.

Then, on June 27, Alexander sailed from Dover for the Continent, and everyone breathed a sigh of relief. The next day a message arrived from him, addressed to Castlereagh. Alexander now realized that the congress was likely to last longer than he had thought, and he wished to visit Russia before going to Vienna. The opening of the congress was therefore postponed from the beginning of August until the end of September.

Meanwhile, in Paris, Prince Talleyrand had been watching developments in London with keen interest. The rift between Alexander and the British government and Metternich's diplomatic jockeying for position fitted very nicely into his plans for the forthcoming congress. France, he knew, would be virtually helpless in Vienna if confronted by four allied sovereigns acting in unison. With the Russians isolated, however, and with Great Britain, Austria, and Prussia united against them, France might well find itself in a key position. It could become the catalyst of a European settlement, rather than its victim—but only if it were extremely careful in the way it played the game. For despite the auspicious events in London, Talleyrand had no illusions about France's position:

> In such a state of affairs, the part France had to play was singularly difficult. It was very tempting and very easy for cabinets, embittered for so long a period, to refuse to admit it to a council assembled to discuss the important interests of Europe. By the Treaty of Paris, France had escaped destruction, but it had not resumed its rightful rank in the system of general politics. Moreover, experienced eyes could easily see, in several of the principal plenipotentiaries, a secret desire to reduce it to a secondary role. . . . If, therefore, France herself did not demand, at the very beginning of the Congress, the place it deserved by virtue both of its power and of the transitory generosity of some of the allied sovereigns, it would have to accept the alternative of remaining, for a long time to come, an outsider in the affairs of Europe, and it would have to submit to becoming the victim of alliances created by its own past successes—successes which it had so much abused—which might be renewed through jealousy. In short, France would lose the hope of being able to establish a line of demarcation between the Napoleonic Empire and the Restoration which would prevent the governments of Europe from requiring it to pay for the violence and excesses of revolutionary France.

If Restoration France were to avoid becoming Europe's expiatory "victim" and "demand . . . the place it deserved," the voice articulating this

---

* The question of the Dutch colonies was finally settled by a Convention of August 13, 1814, between the Netherlands and Great Britain. The latter retained the Cape of Good Hope and some smaller territories, but returned the Dutch East Indies to their former owners.

demand would have to be one strong enough to speak with authority and familiar enough in the courts of Europe to command respectful attention. Moreover, this negotiator must be a man "fully convinced of the importance of the situation, thoroughly familiar with the circumstances that had contributed to the changes brought about in France, and so situated as to speak firmly and truly to the cabinets." The French plenipotentiary, above all, must wholly believe and be able to impress others with the fact that "France desired only what it possessed; that it had frankly repudiated the heritage of conquest; that it thought itself strong enough in its old boundaries; that it had no intention of extending them; and that, finally, it gloried only in its moderation and that, if it wished its voice to be heard in the councils of Europe, it was solely in order to defend the rights of others against violations of any sort."

Such men, as described by Talleyrand, were not easy to find in the Paris of the early Restoration. "The émigrés who had returned with the king had remained strangers to general politics, and the men who had been supporters of the former regime could not yet grasp the interests and position of the newly revived monarchy . . . [whereas] it was, in fact, the duty of the plenipotentiary to complete the work of the restoration by ensuring the solidity of the edifice that Providence had permitted to be constructed." There was therefore a single qualified candidate for the post of France's ambassador to the Congress of Vienna. And Talleyrand, who knew the credentials of France's diplomats to such an extent that modesty on his part would have been ridiculous, regarded it not only as his right, but as his duty, to claim that post. "The king did not allow me to finish the request [for the post] that I was about to put to him. He interrupted me by saying, 'Draw me up a project for your instructions.' "

The prince needed no urging. "Within a few days, I was able to place before the king the project of instructions that he had asked me for. He approved of it, and I believe that when the instructions . . . are known, France will take pride in the sovereign who signed them."

This brilliant and deservedly famous document was so conceived, in practice, as to ensure the achievement, to the extent that was possible, of France's chief goals in the organization of postwar Europe. Talleyrand spelled out these aims candidly, in their order of importance:

1. To prevent Austria from placing a Hapsburg prince on the throne of Sardinia;
2. To eject Murat from the Neapolitan throne and restore that kingdom to its former (Bourbon) ruler;
3. To prevent Russia from annexing the whole of Poland;
4. To frustrate Prussian plans for acquiring the whole of the kingdom of Saxony.

The Instructions enunciated three principles designed both to accomplish these aims and to reduce chaos in Europe by replacing disorder with order. The most celebrated of these was the first, the principle of legitimacy, which Talleyrand had already used with great success in persuading Czar Alexander to allow the restoration of the Bourbons in France: "Sovereignty cannot be acquired by the simple act of conquest or be transfered to the conqueror unless the sovereign cedes it willingly. . . . A sovereign whose dominions are conquered does not lose his sovereignty unless he cedes his right to the throne or abdicates; he loses only the actual possession through conquest and consequently preserves the right to do everything not implied by possession."

What Talleyrand was saying, in effect, was that the countries annexed to France by the unilateral action of the regimes preceding the Restoration— whether revolutionary or Napoleonic—had never really been lost to their legitimate sovereigns. Those countries must therefore be restored to such sovereigns in fact as well as in principle. In practice, this had already been done. But it still remained to dispose of those countries whose "legitimate sovereigns" either had disappeared (as in the case of the Republic of Genoa) or had renounced their sovereignty, but without ceding it to anyone else. In this latter category were all the countries annexed to France by the Revolution and the Empire after regular treaties of cession, for France had surrendered the sovereignty of these countries by the Treaty of Paris without ceding them specifically to anyone else. It was an unprecedented situation: Half the countries of Europe were without legitimate regimes.

But who possessed the transcendent power to create such a miracle of legitimacy? Not the allied powers, surely, for they had merely "conquered" these states in conquering the French Empire, and they, not possessing legitimate sovereignty, could not transfer it to another. To solve this problem, Talleyrand introduced a second principle, which may perhaps be called the principle of reality: "No title of sovereignty—and consequently no law which is based upon that title—has any reality for other states unless they recognize it." In other words, if the sovereignty of a regime is to be *real* as well as *legitimate,* its legitimacy must be agreed upon and recognized by the other states of Europe. The only way to attain that agreement and recognition is for *all* Europe, not only the victorious allies, to decide upon the legitimacy of a regime: "This can be done only by the sanction of Europe."

Talleyrand's position, however shrouded in diplomatic circumlocution, was perfectly clear: The fate of the countries lacking a legitimate sovereign since the Peace of Paris must be decided by the whole of Europe met in congress. In the Instructions, Europe was made into what it had never been before, an almost metaphysical union of states which had the power, when acting together, to create and recognize the right of sovereignty. This was a new law, or rather, it was the logical extension, based upon expediency, of the old law of nations.

There is no doubt that Talleyrand, under cover of the law of nations, was mounting a flank attack upon the first of the secret articles of the Treaty of Paris, according to which France had yielded its sovereignty and possession of all its conquered territories and promised to accept "the decisions made in Vienna, according to principles agreed upon by the powers among themselves." He was the first to see that according to the letter of the law, this arrangement was self-contradictory. France, by renouncing its rights of sovereignty, had surrendered the power to transfer that sovereignty. And the allied powers, in their turn, could not bestow sovereignty, since it had never been transferred to them by France. By the first secret article, therefore, a legal vacuum had been created, and Talleyrand was now taking advantage of that vacuum to unify the whole of Europe into a superior authority empowered to decide the fate of the countries in question. Not coincidentally, this arrangement would effectively wrest from the allies the power to decide on the distribution of these countries and justify France's intervention in the common and legitimate interests of Europe.

Talleyrand's plan of operations for the congress was both a noble vision of European unity and an adroit maneuver for French influence. But both vision and maneuver were vulnerable unless the new law evolved by Talleyrand alone had a chance of being recognized and accepted at the congress. The prince therefore set about finding allies among the powers. Russia was considered, but rejected. It is true that Alexander had alienated the English and the Austrians during the London negotiations and that he was attempting to repair his relations with France by negotiating a marriage between his sister, the Grand Duchess Anne, and the Duke de Berry. He failed, however, to conciliate King Louis XVIII, and his matrimonial project came to nothing. Austria, too, had been sounded out, and Prince Metternich, at Talleyrand's invitation, had visited Paris before returning to Vienna after the London conferences. Metternich, however, had displayed an attitude of such wariness toward Talleyrand and of such caution concerning the principles articulated in the Instructions that both Talleyrand and King Louis had concluded that nothing could be expected from Austria. And Prussia, still bound by the subservience of King Frederick William to Czar Alexander, would no doubt follow Russia's lead in the Vienna convocation.

Only England was left, and it was to England that Talleyrand now looked for support. Castlereagh, of course, was never unconscious of the fact that France was a possible ally, should all other resources fail to settle the difficulties between England and Russia. When, therefore, Castlereagh took the precaution of communicating the convention of June 29 to Talleyrand and explaining the reasons for the postponement of the congress' opening, he was answered by an eager request that France and England should act together in Vienna as the only two disinterested powers. Talleyrand, moreover, advanced several points regarding the settlement of the Polish and Italian questions, in which he was convinced that Castlereagh's views coincided with his own. The exchange culminated with an urgent request for Castlereagh to visit Paris on his way to Vienna. Rumors, meanwhile, had been circulating in London of Alexander's attempt to effect repairs, via a dynastic alliance, on his relations with the French government, and Castlereagh recognized that France, if Talleyrand's overtures were rejected, might well throw its weight on Russia's side. He therefore decided to accept Talleyrand's invitation. But before committing himself, he sought the advice of the Duke of Wellington, who replied with his usual—if somewhat lapidary—good sense: "The situation of affairs will naturally constitute England and France as arbitrators at the Congress, if these Powers *understand* each other."

It was obvious that Great Britain and France, having, for very different reasons, no special territorial demands of their own to make to the congress and both desiring a general balance of power on the Continent, would be in a position together to act as mediators among the other powers, whose ambitions were bound to conflict. It was equally evident that if Great Britain were to make common cause with France too openly, it would not only violate the secret clause of the Peace of Paris, but also might provoke a countercombination among its former allies. Castlereagh therefore replied cordially, but cautiously, to Talleyrand's overture, making it clear that he would consent to meet with him in Paris only on condition that nothing would be proposed that might compromise the alliance of the four powers. He reached Paris on August 24, 1814, en route to Vienna for the preliminary meetings with the three other powers. Talleyrand received him twice, both times in the presence of Louis XVIII, and, during these two lengthy interviews, asked for and received Castlereagh's assurance that nothing to France's detriment would be undertaken during these meetings. In return, he authorized the Englishman to express the views of the French government until he himself arrived in Vienna in late September and offered France's support in frustrating Russian designs on Poland. When Castlereagh left Paris a few days later, a special relationship had been formed between France and England, a commonality of interests established, of which Talleyrand was to make advantageous use in the next few months and which was to become a decisive factor in the resolution of the supreme crisis of the Congress of Vienna.

With the Instructions in their final form and approved by King Louis and with a powerful ally secured for French interests at the congress, Talleyrand could now turn his attention to the organization of the embassy which he was to head. This was in his view a matter of no little importance.

> It appeared to me necessary to shake off the hostile prejudice which imperial France had inspired in the high and influential society of Vienna. . . . It was necessary also that the dignity that it should display should be expressed with nobility and even with brilliancy.

Talleyrand's appointments, therefore, were made with one eye on the prestige of his embassy and the other upon the usefulness of his appointees. The Duke de Dalberg, a man famous for his many indiscretions, was made his second plenipotentiary, because, says the *Mémoires*, "I wished to distinguish him, and I was bound to him by ties of friendship. Moreover, by his birth, his family connections in Germany, and his ability, he would be for me a useful collaborator." With the Duchess of Courland, however, he was more candid: Dalberg was chosen so that he might "broadcast those of my secrets that I want everyone to know." As a representative of the extreme royalist party, he selected a former aide-de-camp to the Count d'Artois, the Count Alexis de Noailles. "If one must be spied on," he wrote Courland, "at least it is better to choose the spy oneself." For his distinguished lineage and social graces, the Marquis de la Tour du Pin-Gouvernet was chosen. ("He will do to sign passports.") For the real work of the congress, he chose the Count de La Besnardière, "whom I regard as the most distinguished man who has appeared in the Ministry of Foreign Affairs for a great many years." The Count de Jaucourt, a friend from prerevolutionary days and a member of émigré society at Juniper Hall, was to be left in Paris as acting Minister of Foreign Affairs. Jaucourt, Talleyrand knew, could be relied upon both to carry out his policies and to keep him informed of all developments in the French capital.

There was still one very important position to be filled. If there was one thing of which all Europe was certain, it was that the social life of Vienna would be brilliant and onerous and that, according to the custom of the day, as many major decisions would be made in the drawing rooms and ballrooms as at the conference table. The French embassy would therefore require a capable hostess, one, moreover, whose beauty, breeding, and intelligence would facilitate Talleyrand's mission.

Propriety, no doubt, decreed that Talleyrand take his wife, Catherine, with him to Vienna. But here propriety was at variance with both political expediency and personal inclination. No one was more aware than Talleyrand himself that Catherine would have made a pitiful ambassadress. By 1814 all that she had had of youthful exuberance had gone. The Princess

Talleyrand was now a blowsy, overdressed, and gossipy old woman, who spent her time boasting of her former beauty. The charm that had once excused, or at least obscured, the total absence of wit and intelligence had now deserted her completely, although, according to the Countess de Boigne, "the remains of her great beauty still adorned her stupidity with a certain amount of dignity." At this time, her absurdities were so well known and her social sins so public that nothing less than total disaster might be expected if this lady were suddenly thrust into the midst of Europe's most snobbish and arrogant society or became involved in the web of political intrigue that was to underlie the social life of the congress. As an illustration of her invincible gaucherie, De Boigne tells the following story:

> In 1814, this same Édouard,* on his return from exile, was driving with me to call on the Princess de Talleyrand. . . . She received him wonderfully well and in a very simple way. . . . Madame de Talleyrand did not keep her naïve remarks solely for her own use. She had more than enough to spare some for M. de Talleyrand. For instance, she never failed to remark that such and such a person (another of my uncles, for example, Arthur Dillon) had been a fellow student of the prince's at the seminary. Then she would call to him [Talleyrand] from the other side of the drawing room, asking him to affirm that the ornament he liked best was a bishop's cross of diamonds that she was wearing. Someone remarked that she should have larger pendants made for her pearl earrings; she answered loudly, "Do you think that I have married the Pope instead of a mere bishop?"
>
> There are too many such absurdities to quote. M. de Talleyrand met them all with his imperturbable calm, but I am convinced that he must have often wondered how he could have married this woman.

If the Princess de Talleyrand was obviously unsuitable as her husband's consort in Vienna, there was another lady of his family who was as well equipped for the work of the congress as the princess was inadequate. Dorothea de Périgord had been gifted with an intellect that made her the equal of the statesmen with whom the French emissary would have to deal. In beauty, she compared favorably with any flower of the European aristocracy. By birth, she was entitled to a place of honor in the most exalted circles; indeed, a vast number of the personages designated to represent their countries in Vienna were her blood relatives. The Prussian royal family were her oldest friends. The Russian czar was an intimate of her mother's. And each of her sisters would be strategically placed in Vienna for the transmittal of information: Wilhelmina, Duchess of Sagan, was a lover of

* Édouard Dillon, the Countess de Boigne's uncle, who had been one of Catherine's lovers before her marriage to Talleyrand.

Prince Metternich's and aspired to the position of his exclusive mistress; Pauline, Princess of Hohenzollern-Hechingen, had a husband among the sovereign princes and a lover among the leading negotiators; and Jeanne, Duchess of Acerenza, was a determined candidate for the bed of Baron Friedrich von Gentz, secretary-general to the congress and an unerring source of well-informed gossip. Such qualifications, added to the fondness that Talleyrand had always felt for his nephew's wife, made the choice inevitable. "I asked my niece, the Countess de Périgord, to accompany me," Talleyrand recorded in all simplicity. "By her superior intellect and tact, she knew how to attract and to please."

Dorothea accepted her uncle's suggestion without hesitation. Dissatisfaction with her marriage and irritation with life in Parisian society made her eager for a change. It was, nonetheless, a drastic decision, for it signaled to the world the breakup of her union with Count Edmond de Périgord. And to much of this same world—in which Talleyrand was notorious as a libertine—it implied a surrender to the importunities of her uncle. To Parisian society, the news that Talleyrand and Dorothea were going together to Vienna and that both the Count de Périgord and the Princess de Talleyrand were being left behind could mean only one thing, and the denizens of that society did not hesitate to announce it at the tops of their voices.

There is not a shred of evidence to indicate that at the time of the arrangements for the congress, Talleyrand regarded Dorothea in any light other than as a relative to whom he was genuinely attached and who was admirably qualified to help him in his difficult Viennese assignment. Even so, as experienced as he was in the ways of the world, he could not fail to realize that the gossips of Paris would be quick, even eager, to link him and his niece in unholy alliance. In an attempt to quiet the gossip, he therefore arranged to meet Dorothea discreetly in a country house near Paris and then continue on to Vienna together.

If Talleyrand's choice was, for Parisian society, the occasion for malicious gossip, it was a source of tragedy for his wife. The Countess de Boigne was visiting Catherine's house in Paris when an eager talebearer burst in to inform Catherine of Talleyrand's selection of Dorothea to accompany him and of the arrangements he had made to meet her en route to Vienna. "Madame de Talleyrand made no mistake about the importance of this meeting," she recalls, "and she could neither conceal her anxiety nor recover from it. She was not mistaken in her apprehensions, for, from that day forward, she never again laid eyes on M. de Talleyrand, and she was soon banished from his house." *

---

* Madame de Talleyrand, however, still retained some of her spirit. She toyed for a while with the idea of going to Vienna, unannounced, and claiming her rightful place as mistress of the

Then, on September 16, having ended, for all practical purposes, a marriage imposed upon him by the tyranny of Napoleon and having begun a relationship which was to endure to the end of his days, Talleyrand left Paris for Vienna and the great work that awaited him there.

prince's house. At the last moment, however, she lost her nerve. "I shall always regret that I gave way to a moment of false pride. I knew what airs Mme. Edmond was giving herself in M. Talleyrand's house in Vienna, and I had no wish to see it for myself. This susceptibility prevented me from going to join him as I should have done. . . . If I had been in Vienna, M. de Talleyrand would have been forced to receive me. I know him well enough to say that he would have done it with perfect grace and that the more irritated he might have been, the less he would have shown it."

13

The Congress of Vienna

TALLEYRAND and his household arrived in Vienna on September 23 and immediately took up residence in the splendid Hotel Kaunitz. Already in the city was an assembly of statesmen, soldiers, nobles, and sovereigns that was, in the opinion of the day, the most brilliant that Europe had ever seen. The home of the Austrian emperor, the Hofburg, had been virtually transformed into a princely lodging house sheltering two emperors, two empresses, four kings, one queen, two crown princes, two grand duchesses, and three reigning princes. Minor royalties and the innumerable princelings of the German states were scattered throughout the city like autumn leaves, and around them clustered their crowds of officers and servants. Everything that was most noble in Europe, all the wealthiest and most distinguished men, all the most beautiful women, all who either played or aspired to play a role in the political or social world were there. Most of them had no work at the congress, and most of them never intended to work, for the eighteenth-century tradition of leisure and pleasure lingered in their hearts. The glitter of decorations and uniforms, the mobs of imperial, royal, and serene highnesses, and the diligence with which these great lords and ladies pursued their amusements naturally created an atmosphere in which work, at least superficially, appeared secondary. The Prince de Linge, the embodiment of the eighteenth century, summed it up nicely in a famous dictum: *"Le Congrès ne marche pas; il danse."* *

* "The congress does not walk [*i.e.*, work]; it dances."

The imperial court of Vienna had manifested its solicitude for the visiting dignitaries in two ways. First, it had planned a display of luxurious hospitality and entertainment unequaled since the days of the Roman emperors. This was to satisfy the visitors' thirst for amusement. Second, it had provided for a surveillance designed to keep track of the most innocuous comings and goings of the sovereigns and delegates. Baron Francis Hager, chief of police, was to receive daily reports from his agents on what each illustrious representative said or did, and he was to receive, from the imperial postal service, daily reports on all their correspondence. Talleyrand's delegation, in particular, was subject to a surveillance worthy of its importance, numbers, and elegance. The police, for instance, lost no time in discovering a highly suspect individual in the prince's retinue, an Austrian named Sigismund von Neukomm. Metternich took fright at Neukomm's presence at the French embassy and ordered an especially strict watch on the man. It was soon discovered that Neukomm was a pianist and composer from Salzburg, that he had been living in Talleyrand's house and on his bounty since 1809, and that he served as a sort of musician in residence. But this made no difference. Metternich was certain that a plot was brewing, and Neukomm's most innocent words and acts were recorded in a police dossier that was soon filled to overflowing.

In short, Vienna in 1814 constituted a world apart, a world that had consigned to oblivion, and now assembled to rectify, the excesses of the preceding quarter century. It was, moreover, a world in which Talleyrand felt himself perfectly at home.* The impression that his exquisite *ancien régime* manners and comportment created on the society of the congress is reflected in the description left by the Count de la Garde-Chambonas, one of Vienna's innumerable pleasure seekers, who visited the Hotel Kaunitz shortly after Talleyrand's arrival:

> I reached the embassy early. There was no one there except M. de Talleyrand, the Duke de Dalberg, and Madame Edmond de Périgord. The prince made me welcome with the perfect grace that was second nature to him. Taking hold of my hand with the kindliness reminiscent of a bygone period, he said, "Monsieur, I have come to Vienna in order to have the pleasure of receiving you in my house."
> I had not seen him since 1806, but I was struck once more by the intel-

---

* In reconstructionist Vienna, a Prince of Benevento would have been regarded as a son of the Revolution. After the signing of the Peace of Paris, therefore, Talleyrand never again used or allowed others to use in addressing him the title that Napoleon had conferred upon him. The chief negotiators of the allied powers were all noblemen of the *ancien régime,* and it was imperative that the representative of France be no less. Talleyrand's calling cards in Vienna now carried the style, "Prince de Talleyrand"—a title that was considerably more respectable, in the eyes of legitimist Europe, than that of "Prince of Benevento." The principality of Benevento, in any case, now meant little to him, since its revenues had been in Murat's hands since the fall of the Empire.

lectual sublimity of his look, the imperturbable calm of his features, the demeanor of this preeminent man, whom I, along with everyone in Vienna, considered the foremost statesman of his time. There was also the same grave and deep tone of voice, the same easy and natural manners, the same ingrained familiarity with the usages of the best society—a reflection, so to speak, of an era that existed no longer and of which he was one of the last representatives. He seemed to dominate that illustrious assembly by the charm of his mind and the ascendancy of his genius. . . .

A short time later, the count was a guest at dinner and wrote that "at table, M. de Talleyrand not only showed his natural grace and urbanity, but was in reality even more amiable than in his reception rooms. It was no longer the habitual silence which, as has been said, he had transformed into a kind of divination. Though less profound, his talk was perhaps all the more charming. It came straight from the heart and flowed without restraint."

Talleyrand, however, was not in Vienna to exhibit his charm or to allow himself to be amused, although he did a good deal of both. If he needed any reminder of the seriousness of the task at hand, it greeted him upon the very day of his arrival in Vienna, in the form of a report that the plenipotentiaries of Austria (Prince Metternich), Prussia (Prince Hardenberg and Baron Humboldt), Great Britain (Lord Castlereagh), and Russia (Count Nesselrode) had arrived at two ominous decisions on the preceding day:

> 1. Great Britain, Austria, Prussia and Russia were to sign an agreement, or protocol, reserving to themselves the final decision on all territorial questions;
>
> 2. France and Spain and all other nations represented at the congress would not be consulted on these questions until the four allied powers had arrived at a "perfect agreement" regarding the disposition of the duchy of Warsaw and the vacant territories of Germany and Italy.

These decisions were justified, in the protocol of the conference, by citing the necessity of avoiding "the whole business of intrigues and cabals which, in large part, is responsible for the tragedy of the last few years." For if France participates in the preliminary discussions, "it will take sides on each separate question, whether it touches its own interests or not. It will oppose this or that prince according to its own point of view, and the little rulers will take that as their cue." Moreover, "the disposition of the conquered provinces falls naturally to the powers whose efforts have effected their conquest."

The decisions and the reasoning offered to support them were obviously contradictory to what had been done earlier at Paris and London. In Paris, during May, the allies had been content with a promise from Talleyrand that France would accept the "principles agreed upon" by them for the reconstruction of Europe. Spain, Portugal, and Sweden were each to have a share in this determination. In London, the following month, the four powers had agreed to establish a preliminary plan for the distribution of territories and then to communicate this plan to France, Spain, and Sweden (Portugal now being excluded from participation), whereupon these three would join the allies in preparing the actual scheme of adjustment for Europe.

The agreements of Paris and London had left France an important part to play. The resolutions of September 22, however, eliminated Sweden and allowed Spain to discuss only those matters that directly affected its own interests. And Talleyrand was not to be. allowed to present France's views until after the four great powers had reached an agreement among themselves. During the three months' interlude, France and the allies had taken different paths. Talleyrand's policy, as reflected in the Instructions, was to turn France toward Europe in order to identify its interests with those of the Continent as a whole. The allies had turned away from Europe to form an exclusive club of conquerors. To Talleyrand's idea of a superior law for all of Europe, the allies were now opposing a law of *force majeure*.

The reason for this setback was not hard to find. It lay, above all, in Czar Alexander's lust for Polish territory. "The duchy of Warsaw," he wrote to Nesselrode, "is mine by right of conquest. . . . Now that victory has enabled the principal states of Europe to be reconstituted as they were before the last wars of Bonaparte and even enabled some of them to obtain important gains, it is only fair that my subjects be indemnified for so many sacrifices and that a buffer state guard them forever from the danger of a new invasion." Thus, Alexander was affirming the right of might as a basis for sovereignty. Since he had conquered and was in possession of Poland, his allies were in no position to contest his claim too vigorously. It was not surprising, therefore, that Nesselrode, seeing his master in such a frame of mind, voted for the resolution of September 22 or that, over the protests of Castlereagh, he dragged Metternich (who had plans of his own for Italy), and Hardenberg and Humboldt (whose king wanted the whole of Saxony) along with him.

In short, Talleyrand found in Vienna a secret hostility to the spirit of conciliation which, in Paris, had seemed triumphant. On September 25, he wrote to King Louis: "In Vienna, the language of reason and moderation is no longer to be heard from the lips of the plenipotentiaries." He was convinced, however, that it was Metternich, not Alexander, who was responsible for this situation, and on September 29, he wrote: "Unfortunately, the man who has charge of things in Austria and who pretends to

control them in Europe considers the surest sign of genius to be an instability that, on the one hand, borders on the ridiculous and, on the other,
becomes, in the minister of a great state and under such circumstances, a
calamity."

This conviction—and the bitterness with which it was expressed—was
based on something more than a clash of personalities or of interests. What
happened was that on September 25, Alexander of Russia had made his
entry into Vienna, still trailed by the obedient King of Prussia, and had
sent for Talleyrand immediately upon his arrival. A private audience was
arranged for October 1. Talleyrand was looking forward to October 1 more
on account of his audience than of the opening of the congress, which at
that time seemed to have been postponed indefinitely. Then, on the morning of September 30, he received a brief note from Metternich—in Metternich's name alone—asking him to attend a preliminary conference that
same afternoon at the latter's house. There, the note said, Talleyrand
would find not only Metternich, but also the ministers of Prussia, England,
and Russia. Metternich added that he was sending a similar invitation to
M. de Labrador, the minister of Spain.* Talleyrand replied that he would
be "very pleased to meet the ministers of Russia, England, Spain and Prussia at his house." At this point, Count de Labrador arrived at the Hotel
Kaunitz to show Talleyrand his invitation. It "was in the same terms as the
one I received," Talleyrand noted,† "except that it was written in the third
person and was in the name of Prince Metternich *and his colleagues*." Talleyrand then showed Labrador what he had written in answer and advised
him to reply in identical terms—but naming France before the other powers. "Thus Count de Labrador and myself intentionally united what the
others seemed so eager to divide, and we divided what they seemed especially anxious to unite.

"I was at Prince Metternich's before two o'clock," Talleyrand continues.
"The ministers of the four courts were already sitting in conference around
a long table. At one end was Lord Castlereagh, apparently presiding. At
the other was a gentleman whom Prince Metternich introduced to me as
filling the office of secretary at their conferences. It was Herr von Gentz. I
was then shown to a vacant chair between Lord Castlereagh and Prince
Metternich. I immediately asked why I, alone of your majesty's embassy,
had been invited."

* According to Friedrich von Gentz, secretary-general of the congress, the purpose of this conference was to make France and Spain accept the resolutions of September 22 (*Dépêches inédites
aux Hospodars de Valachie*, Vol. I, p. 108).

† The circumstances of this first meeting between Talleyrand and the ministers of the four allied
powers are described in a letter to King Louis, dated October 4, 1814, which is reproduced in the
Mémoires, II, p. 234 ff., and in the *Correspondance inédite*, p. 17 ff. Talleyrand's account of the conference is confirmed by, and corresponds in every detail to, that of Gentz (*op. cit.*, Vol. I, pp. 107–
18).

"It was wished to bring together only the heads of the Cabinets at the preliminary conferences," Castlereagh explained.

"But Count de Labrador is not a head of Cabinet, and he has also been invited."

"That is because the Secretary of State of Spain is not in Vienna," Metternich said.

"Even so," Talleyrand continued, "I see that Herr von Humboldt is here, in addition to Prince von Hardenberg, and he is not a Secretary of State."

"This is an exception to the rule, made necessary by the infirmity with which, as you know, Prince Hardenberg is afflicted." *

"Well then," Talleyrand replied mildly, "if it is a question of infirmities, each of us has one of his own, and we can all claim an exception on that basis." Then, having already put the allied ministers on the defensive, Talleyrand "thought it useless to insist further" on this point.

Next, Lord Castlereagh read a very strong letter from the Portuguese ambassador, Count de Palmella, protesting Portugal's exclusion from the preliminary conferences and citing the agreements of May 30. Talleyrand and Labrador seconded Palmella's sentiments, and the other ministers—Castlereagh, particularly—seemed disposed to allow not only Portugal, but also Spain and Sweden, to attend. But Metternich insisted that a decision be deferred until the next conference.

Castlereagh, from the chair, now opened the agenda. "The object of to-day's conference," he said, "is to acquaint you with what the four courts have done since we have been here." Then, turning to Prince Metternich, he added, "You have the protocol." Metternich handed to Talleyrand a document signed by Metternich himself, Nesselrode, Castlereagh, and Hardenberg.

"In this document," Talleyrand noted, "the word 'allies' occurred in every paragraph. I objected to that expression. I said it had become necessary for me to ask where we were. Were we still at Chaumont? Or at Laon? † If we had not made peace, then had there been a declaration of war? And, if so, against whom?"

Everyone hastened to assure Talleyrand that they attached no importance to the word "allies" and that it had been used "only for the sake of brevity."

"However important it may be to be brief," Talleyrand remarked icily, "that importance cannot be such as to justify inaccuracy."

Then he began reading the protocol. "It was but a tissue of metaphysical

* Hardenberg was almost completely deaf.

† On March 25, 1814, the allied sovereigns, after the breaking off of negotiations at Châtillon, had signed a declaration at Laon agreeing anew to the provisions of the Treaty of Chaumont.

deductions, intended to justify pretensions based on treaties unknown to us. To discuss these arguments and pretensions would have opened up an area of endless dispute. I therefore felt it necessary to meet the whole thing with one peremptory argument."

After reading several paragraphs, Talleyrand looked up with a puzzled expression and said, "I do not understand." Then he read a few more paragraphs. "I do not understand any better. To me, there are but two dates: that of May 30, when the formation of a congress was agreed to, and that of October 1, when this congress was to meet. Between those two dates, there is only a vacuum. Nothing that has been done in that interval exists, so far as I am concerned, and I will ignore it."

At this the allied plenipotentiaries seemed much embarrassed and replied that the document actually meant nothing and that they would be happy to withdraw it.

"If it means so little," Count de Labrador interjected, "why did you sign it?"

No one had an answer. Prince Metternich withdrew the offending protocol and put it aside. "And there was no longer any question of it," Talleyrand noted with satisfaction.

Metternich, however, was not so easily conquered. No sooner was the protocol out of sight than he produced another document, which he proposed that Talleyrand and Labrador sign, along with the four other ministers. This declaration, after a long preamble on the necessity of simplifying the work of the congress and after many assurances that there was no intention of encroaching on the rights of any nation, proposed that the various problems to be settled by the congress be divided into two series and that a committee be appointed for each series. The countries that had an interest in any particular problem could then address themselves to the proper committee, and the committee, after sifting the pros and cons of a question, would present their findings to the congress as a whole. The congress, moreover, was not to assemble until the two committees had completed their work.

Talleyrand was instantly on his guard. "This plan was obviously intended to render the four powers, who call themselves 'allies,' absolute masters of all the deliberations of the congress. If the six major powers constituted themselves judges of the questions relating to the composition of the congress, the matters that it should settle, and the order in which they should be settled, and if they should, alone and without control, appoint the committees and prepare all the work, then France and Spain, even if they always agreed on all questions, would still be only two votes against four."

Talleyrand played for time, declaring that it was impossible to arrive at a decision on the spot. It would be necessary to determine whether or not this new proposal was compatible with the rights that the congress had assembled to protect. "We have assembled to consecrate and secure the rights of each of the powers," he said, "and how unfortunate it would be if we started out by violating them." Moreover, "The idea of arranging everything before the congress assembles is quite new to me. You are proposing that we begin by doing what, in my opinion, we should finish by doing."

Here Lord Castlereagh said that Talleyrand's objections had occurred to him also and that he fully appreciated their cogency. "But," he added, "what other way can we find to avoid involving ourselves in inextricable and dilatory proceedings?"

Again Talleyrand resorted to a frontal attack. "Why is the congress not assembled here and now?" he demanded. A general discussion followed, with each minister giving the reasons why it was impossible to convene the delegates at this stage of the proceedings. In the midst of it all, someone mentioned the intricacy of the problem posed by the disposal of the Neapolitan throne—or, as Talleyrand expressed it, "the question of him who reigns at Naples," for he could not bring himself to speak Murat's name. On this point, Labrador expressed himself "without reserve," while Talleyrand sat in stony silence. When the Spaniard had finished and Metternich attempted to reply to him, Talleyrand interrupted: "Of what King of Naples are you speaking? We do not know who he is."

To Humboldt's comment that the powers had recognized Murat's sovereignty and had guaranteed his kingdom, Talleyrand replied: "Those who gave him such a guarantee had no right, and therefore no power, to do so." But then he turned the discussion back to the organization of the congress, saying that the difficulties might be less than they all anticipated and that it was surely possible to find some way of resolving them. The Prussian minister declared that he did not favor one expedient more than any other, but that some way must be found to keep the princes of Leiden and Liechtenstein,* for instance, from interfering in the general arrangements of Europe. The other ministers murmured agreement and adjourned until the next day.

Thus, at the very first meeting between Talleyrand and the allied ministers, there had been a clash and a victory for Talleyrand. The most striking thing, however, was not Talleyrand's strength, but the weakness of the allies. They were the conquerors of France, and their armies occupied the whole of Europe. Yet at the first strong objection from Talleyrand they

---

* Two of the smallest and weakest principalities of Europe. Liechtenstein, for example, had only 7,000 inhabitants at the time and an area of some 65 square miles.

had withdrawn their proposal to keep all power of decision in their own hands and introduced a second and milder plan. Then, the latter having been also challenged, they hastily put everything off till a later date and agreed to start all over again with Talleyrand's assistance. "The intervention of Talleyrand," the awestruck Gentz wrote, "hopelessly upset our plans. It was a scene I shall never forget." And Talleyrand noted, not without complacency, "So, France, by the sheer force of reason and the power of principles, shattered an alliance that was directed against it. . . . I was able to write to Paris that the House of Bourbon, which had only returned to France five months ago, and France itself, which had been conquered five months previously, found themselves already reestablished in their proper place in Europe and exercising the influence that was their due in the most important deliberations of the congress."

Talleyrand, having broken through the allied front on a relatively weak sector, moved quickly to exploit his tactical advantage. On October 1, rather than wait for the meeting fixed for the following day, he sent a formal memorandum to the ministers of Austria, Great Britain, Prussia, Russia, and Spain in which he argued that only the congress had the right to make decisions and that the eight powers* that had signed the Peace of Paris were qualified only to act as a committee delegated to prepare the agenda of the congress and to propose the formation of such committees as appeared necessary. Then he left for his interview with the Czar of Russia.

Talleyrand found Alexander courteous, but "not at all as affectionate as he once had been." His speech was brusque, his manner serious and even a bit solemn. "I saw clearly that he was determined to play a part," Talleyrand noted.

After inquiring after Talleyrand's own position in France and the stability of the Bourbon government, Alexander said suddenly, "Very well. Now let us get down to business. We must settle matters here."

"That depends upon your majesty," Talleyrand replied. "If your majesty displays the same nobility and generosity as he did when dealing with France, everything shall be concluded promptly and happily."

"But it is important that each of us obtain what suits him best."

"It is important rather that each of us obtains his rights."

"I shall keep what I have."

"Surely your majesty would keep only what belongs to him."

"I have an agreement with the great powers."

"I do not know whether your majesty reckons France as one of the great powers."

* That is, the five recipients of the memorandum, along with France, Portugal, and Sweden.

"Yes, certainly I do. But if you do not admit that each of us is to get what suits him best, what do you mean?"

"I place right first and interest after."

"The interests of Europe constitute rights."

"This language, sire, is not yours. It is foreign to your feelings, and your heart must disapprove it."

"No, I shall repeat it," Alexander said firmly. "The interests of Europe constitute rights."

The czar was not the only one capable of playing a part. Upon hearing Alexander's reaffirmation of the primacy of self-interest, Talleyrand records that, "I turned toward the wainscot closest to me, and putting my head against it, I struck it with my forehead, exclaiming, 'Europe, O Europe! Unhappy Europe!' " Then, turning to Alexander, he said in solemn tones, "Shall it be said, then, that you have brought about Europe's ruin?"

"I prefer to go to war rather than to renounce what I already possess," the czar answered.

Talleyrand said nothing but let his arms fall in a gesture of despair. Alexander, after a few moments of apparent reflection, murmured: "Yes, I prefer war." Then he suddenly shouted that the Emperor of Austria was expecting him and that he must go. But having opened the door to leave, he rushed back to Talleyrand, clasped him in his arms, and said "in a voice that was no longer his own, 'Adieu, adieu! We shall meet again!' " With a great crashing of doors, he was gone, leaving the astounded Talleyrand alone with his thoughts. Expediency, Alexander had said in effect, makes right. The unbalanced prince of whom Talleyrand had been able to make such good use in the treaty of peace was now in the opposite camp. It was a tragic defection, and Talleyrand concluded his report of the interview to King Louis on a pessimistic note: "Your Majesty must see that our position here is a difficult one, and it may grow even more difficult from day to day."

Talleyrand was right. It was impossible to count on Alexander. The czar had arrived in Vienna furious with Metternich, alienated from Great Britain, distrustful of Talleyrand, and friendly only with Frederick William of Prussia, who was more devoted and submissive than ever. He had arrived, moreover, in a kind of erotic frenzy which obscured a mind that, even in the best of circumstances, was never very stable. This frenzy was also to have its repercussions. Vienna had become the headquarters for the loveliest women of the European aristocracy, and now a huge carnival, celebrating the peace, was swelling the ranks of those who had come to attend the congress. Alexander at this time was thirty-seven, and he fully intended to take advantage of the freedom of action which the carnival granted even to the most august crowned heads of Europe. Indeed, he wasted no time in that respect. On October 2, the police were already informing Baron Hager that the czar had visited Princess Bagration* the night of the thirtieth and that she had "received him alone, in her bedroom, *en negligée.*" The police report concludes with the remark *Honi soit qui mal y pense.*†

With Alexander hostile and occupied with other matters, there was nothing Talleyrand could do now but wait for his note to the other powers to take effect. He had not long to wait. All the allied ministers were angry with him for having embodied in an official communication the results of a private discussion. Prussia and Russia were so indignant that they publicly accused France of wanting to provoke a war so that it might recover the left bank of the Rhine. Castlereagh, equally miffed but more prudent, contented himself with complaining to Lord Liverpool that Talleyrand's note had given an official and public character to a purely informal and confidential meeting—which, of course, was precisely what it had been intended to do. The allies must now either justify, before the whole of Europe, their determination to keep all decision-making power in the hands of the six ministers who had attended the conference or else abandon their plan to do so.

The four delegates met on the morning of October 2 to consider their reply. They decided to give up the idea of the six powers altogether, since it had no foundation in the Peace of Paris, and to accept Talleyrand's demand that all eight signatories of the peace constitute a formal directing committee. They still insisted, however, that the full congress not be convened until the eight powers had agreed upon the agenda and the order of business. It was also decided that this reply be submitted to Talleyrand orally and that the written answer simply be filed with the other papers of the conference.

Accordingly, Talleyrand was told by Castlereagh of the powers' decision on the evening of October 4, at a social gathering in the drawing room of the fair Duchess of Sagan, and was handed a revised declaration drawn up by Castlereagh himself, which said, in essence, that the proposals now made by the allies were the direct result of the first secret article of the Treaty of Paris.** Talleyrand, though delighted that the allied powers had

* This lady was famous in Vienna for both her beauty and her outrageous décolletage, and it was generally conceded that she was a morsel fit for a king. The czar, however, was allowed only a taste of this delicacy. Earlier, in Dresden, the princess had been the mistress of Metternich, who had abandoned her for the equally beautiful Duchess of Sagan (Dorothea de Périgord's sister). The duchess was now also in Vienna, moving in the midst of a veritable army of lovers, among whom Prince Metternich seemed the only permanent fixture. The antipathy between Metternich and Alexander, already serious, was considerably aggravated by the harebrained jealousies of the two beauties.

† A dictum immortalized as the motto of the British royal family—"Shame on him who thinks ill of it."

**Castlereagh's declaration began, in fact, by quoting the article in question: "After an interval of two months, all the powers that have been engaged, on one side or another, in the present war, given in on this important point, was still wary. "A reading of the declaration," he wrote to the Count de Jaucourt in Paris, "confirms us in our opinion that the four great allied powers will continue to act as though Bonaparte were still on the throne of France and will refuse to take into account the reestablishment of the House of Bourbon. . . . At first glance, it is plain that great danger must result from this attitude and that a real and durable balance becomes impossible." Talleyrand's pessimism was not that of a man without hope. He still had several cards in his hand. The first one he played immediately, calling a conference of smaller German powers and, by some rhetorical miracle, persuading them that France, so recently the devourer of small nations, was now their protector. The delegates of these duchies and principalities gave him their ardent support, convinced that they must present a common front with Talleyrand against the dictatorship of the four powers.

Thus fortified, the next day Talleyrand replied to the declaration with a long letter to Lord Castlereagh, in which he formally rejected the new proposals and again insisted that the congress be convened immediately. He then proposed that three committees be established: "one for Italy; another for distributing territories in Germany; and a third for the latter's federal constitution. I still insist, however, that these committees be chosen with the consent of the congress. The reason that law and order are so much admired and respected in England is that they are homegrown products."

On the same day, October 5, the six plenipotentiaries assembled once more. Castlereagh read the letter to the conference. The indignant allied delegates asked Talleyrand, in the strongest possible terms, to withdraw it. He refused peremptorily. A lengthy debate followed, the theme of which was that unless some agreement could be reached, the opening of the congress would have to be postponed indefinitely. In the end, Talleyrand declared that, in view of the difficulties, he would not object to a postponement of two or three weeks—but only on condition that a date be fixed for the opening and that the notice of convocation establish the rule for admission, which rule must be announced at once. This rule, Talleyrand insisted, must be of his own composition, and he was so determined on this point that he wrote it out for the delegates. It was not, of course, made on the spur of the moment, but drawn from the Instructions:

> Any prince may send plenipotentiaries to the congress who had universally recognized sovereignty over a state that took part in the recent war, who has not ceded that sovereignty, and whose sovereignty is uncontested.

shall send plenipotentiaries to Vienna to settle, at a general congress, the arrangements which are to complete the provisions of the present treaty."

The same holds true for any state which was independent before the recent war and which, having participated in the war, is now independent again. No prince or state other than these may send plenipotentiaries.

The purpose of Talleyrand's rule was obvious. It would have excluded Murat, whose sovereignty was not "uncontested" and whose Neapolitan throne Talleyrand wished to see restored to its former Bourbon occupants. And it would have admitted the King of Saxony, who had had the bad judgment to side with Napoleon in the final struggle against the allies, but whose kingdom Talleyrand wished to preserve so as to block the aggrandizement of Prussia. In both instances, it was a question of legitimate sovereignty versus sovereignty by usurpation, either actual or proposed. "I ask for nothing," Talleyrand informed the frustrated ministers, "but I give you something of great importance: the sacred principle of legitimacy."

The only hope in dealing with so logical and determined an antagonist was for the four allied ministers to retreat and regroup in a rear area, and the conference, Talleyrand says, "evaporated rather than adjourned." On the way out, Castlereagh made a last attempt to win over Talleyrand to his own opinions, arguing that "certain matters that were of great interest to France would be arranged to its satisfaction." Talleyrand was indignant. "It is not a question of individual 'matters'," he replied, "but of the law which must govern such matters."

"Eh," Castlereagh muttered. "There are difficulties of which you are unaware."

"Yes, I am unaware of them," Talleyrand said. He added in his report to Paris that he had spoken "in a tone of voice which implied I had no desire to be enlightened in that respect."

The next two days went by without a conference. On the first, everyone was invited to a great banquet. The second was spent in hunting. A little entertainment was not amiss. On October 8, however, Talleyrand received a note from Metternich, announcing a conference at eight o'clock that evening and asking him to come a little earlier, because there were "some extremely important matters" he wanted to discuss. Talleyrand accordingly arrived at seven o'clock and was immediately shown in. Metternich greeted him warmly and began speaking of a declaration that he had had drawn up which "differed a little" from Talleyrand's, but which was on the whole "very similar." Talleyrand asked to see the document, but Metternich said that he did not have a copy in the house. "Probably it is being communicated to the allies," Talleyrand remarked.

"Come, speak no more of allies," Metternich said. "There are no longer any."

Talleyrand immediately came to the core of his differences with Metternich. "How can you have the courage to place Russia as a belt around your principal and most important possessions, Hungary and Bohemia? And how can you allow the patrimony of an old and good neighbor [King Frederick Augustus of Saxony], into whose family an archduchess has married, to be given to your natural enemy? How strange it is that it is we who object to this and you who support it!"

"Ah, you have no confidence in me then?"

"How can I have confidence in a man whose affairs are all a mystery, even to those who are most willing to arrive at some accommodation? I myself make no mystery, and I have no need to do so. That is the advantage of negotiating only from principles. Here are pens and paper. Write down that France asks for nothing and will accept nothing—and I will sign it."

"But there is the question of Naples," Metternich said, "which is something that concerns you."

"No more me than anyone else. For me, it is only a question of principle. I ask only that he who has a right to Naples, have Naples. Nothing more. . . . If principles are observed, you will find me easy to deal with. But let me tell you what I never can, and never shall, consent to. I believe that the King of Saxony, in his present position, may be obliged to make a sacrifice, and I believe that he will be disposed to make one, because he is a wise man. But if they mean to deprive him of all his states and give the kingdom of Saxony to Prussia, I shall never consent to that. Nor shall I ever consent to Prussia having Luxembourg or Mainz. Nor to Russia crossing the Vistula and having forty-four million subjects in Europe and its frontiers on the Oder. But I shall not object if Luxembourg be given to Holland and Mainz to Bavaria, or if the kingdom of Saxony is preserved, and if Russia does not cross the Vistula."

Metternich listened to this without a change in expression. Then he took Talleyrand's hand and said, "Our views are not so opposed as you seem to think. I can promise you that Prussia shall have neither Luxembourg nor Mainz. As for Russia, we desire no more than you that it be increased beyond measure. And with respect to Saxony, we shall do our best to preserve at least a portion of it." Then, reverting to the convocation of the congress, Metternich insisted on the importance of not publishing immediately the rule of admission that Talleyrand had proposed. "It would scare everyone," he argued. "As for myself, it would place me in a difficult position. Murat, once he sees his plenipotentiary denied admission, will have us at a disadvantage, because of his violent temper and because he is already established in Italy and we are not."

At this point, the ministers of Russia, Prussia, Great Britain, Spain, Portugal, and Sweden were announced, and the conference was formally opened by Prince Metternich, who began by reading two projects for the organization of the congress, that of Talleyrand and his own. The Prussians immediately declared themselves for Metternich's, saying that the Austrian proposal prejudged nothing, while Talleyrand's prejudged a great deal. Count Nesselrode expressed the same opinion. Gustavus von Löwenhielm, the newly arrived Swedish minister, said that it was important that nothing be prejudged. All the ministers were correct, of course; Metternich's proposal prejudged nothing—for the simple reason that, as Talleyrand remarked, it "merely set the opening of the congress for November 1, and said nothing more."

A stormy discussion followed. Talleyrand, finally, "because the old pretensions had now been abandoned and it was no longer a question of everything being controlled by the eight powers and of leaving to the congress only the faculty of approving, and because the plenipotentiaries were now speaking only of preparing, by free and confidential discussions with the ministers of the other powers, the questions to be put before the congress," said that he would consent to the adoption of Metternich's proposal. As an absolute condition of approval, however, he insisted that a phrase be added signifying that all discussions, actions, and procedure "shall be made according to the principles of public law."

There was an immediate uproar. Hardenberg jumped up and shouted, "No, no! The term 'public law' is useless. Why should we say that we will act only according to public law? That goes without saying!"

"If it goes without saying," Talleyrand answered quietly, "it would go even better by being said."

Baron von Humboldt exclaimed: "What has public law to do with our business here?"

And Talleyrand answered: "It has this to do with it, that the public law is the only reason for our being here at all."

Here Lord Castlereagh drew Talleyrand to one side and asked, in a low voice whether, if the other ministers yielded on this point, he would show himself easier to deal with on other matters. Talleyrand, in answer, asked whether Castlereagh would be cooperative on the question of Naples if he, Talleyrand, would no longer insist on using the term "public law."

Castlereagh replied that he would. "I shall speak of it to Metternich," he added. "I have the right to advise him on this question."

"Do you give me your word that you will do so?"

"I do."

"And I," Talleyrand retorted, "give you mine that I will be difficult only on such principles as I cannot abandon."

In the meantime, however, Gentz had pointed out to Metternich that the powers could hardly refuse to speak of public law in a proposal dealing

with the distribution of the lands and peoples of a continent. When Talleyrand and Castlereagh returned to the conference table, therefore, they
found the other ministers prepared, albeit reluctantly, to consent to the addition of Talleyrand's phrase. Gentz was therefore instructed to prepare a
communiqué in the name, not of the four, or even of the six, but of the
eight powers signatory to the Peace of Paris. The communiqué, which was
signed and issued on October 12, reads as follows:

> The plenipotentiaries of the courts that signed the peace treaty of Paris
> on May 30, 1814, having considered the provisions of Article 32 of this
> treaty, which states that all the powers engaged, on either side, during the
> recent war will send plenipotentiaries to Vienna in order that in a general
> congress they may settle the terms which are to complete the dispositions
> of the said treaty; and having considered the situation in which they now
> find themselves and the duties which devolve upon them, they have real-
> ized that they cannot better fulfill those duties than by first establishing
> free and confidential communications among the plenipotentiaries of all
> the powers.
> At the same time, however, they are convinced that it is in the general in-
> terest of all concerned parties to delay the general assembly of the plenipo-
> tentiaries until such time as the questions on which pronouncements must
> be made will have reached a point where the result is *in harmony with public
> law, the provisions of the recent peace, and the expectations of the age.*
> Therefore, the formal opening of the congress will be postponed until
> November 1, and the aforesaid plenipotentiaries feel certain that the work
> to which this delay will be consecrated, by defining ideas and conciliating
> opinions, will essentially advance the great work which is the purpose of
> their mission.

Talleyrand reported to Count de Jaucourt, a few days later: "It is claimed
that we have gained a victory by having forced the introduction of the expression 'public law.' This opinion will give you an indication of the spirit
which pervades the congress."

Actually, Talleyrand's victory was more important than possibly even he
realized or was willing to admit. The discussion, which had lasted for all of
eight days, had been a battle between self-interest and principle, the like of
which had never before been seen in the history of diplomatic congresses.*
And principle, in the person of Talleyrand, had won the victory. The representatives of Russia, Prussia, Austria, and England, who in Paris had
seemed in agreement on the principles of reconstruction, now disagreed on
three points of vital importance: Poland, Saxony, and Naples. The czar

---

* The perceptive Friedrich von Gentz, for one, saw immediately what had been accomplished.
At the adjournment of the conference of October 8, he said to the ministers: "Gentlemen, this
belongs to the history of the congress. It is not I who shall divulge it, because my duty forbids me
to do so; but it will be found there, certainly" (letter to King Louis XVIII, dated October 9, 1814.
Mémoires, Vol. II, p. 249).

wanted the duchy of Warsaw, and as the price for Prussian acquiescence, he was willing to let King Frederick William grab Saxony. Prussia wanted Saxony and therefore was willing to let Alexander have whatever he wanted in Poland. Austria wanted neither Russia on the Vistula nor Prussia in Dresden, but it did want Murat in Naples in order to deprive the Bourbons of that kingdom and to exclude French influence from Italy. England—or at least Castlereagh—was willing to let Prussia have Saxony but regarded a Russian annexation of Warsaw as a catastrophe. As for the fate of Naples, he was indifferent. All these were primarily questions of self-interest. In Paris, the allied plenipotentiaries had been willing to accept Talleyrand's principle of legitimacy, based on public law. In Vienna, however, they were afraid that the same law might militate to their disadvantage in individual questions, and they were therefore willing, even eager, to reject it. It was Talleyrand's accomplishment that by his stubborn insistence on principle, he forced the other ministers to accept public law and legitimate sovereignty as the bases for the settlement of all questions before the congress. Having thus secured the victory of philosophy over politics, or rather of political philosophy over expediency, and having won for France, at least in theory, an undisputed place among the policy-makers of the congress, it now remained for him to exploit his advantage in the course of the "confidential communications among the plenipotentiaries of all the powers." For the triumph of principle was not enough. It was necessary to ensure that the principle consented to in theory not be violated in its application.

14

The Confidential Approach

T HE IDEA of proceeding to the business of the congress by means of "confidential communications among the plenipotentiaries of all the powers" seems to have originated in Metternich's fertile mind. It was essentially a compromise between the exclusive control of the congress by the four allied powers and the official organization of the legislative congress. The three weeks from October 8 to the proposed opening date of the congress, therefore, constituted a sort of preliminary and unofficial congress, during which the plenipotentiaries of "all the powers" were to come to agreement on the principal questions by means of off-the-record discussion—that is, through discreet, *sotto voce* conversations. These exchanges took place, not around the conference tables of Vienna—for that would have given them an official character—but in its salons and ballrooms, to the sound of violins and in waltz time.

The great balls of Viennese society—or of European society, for that matter—were by no means so strange a place for diplomacy as it may seem to later ages. In the view of the aristocracy, balls, banquets and parties were not private amusements, but sumptuous and semiofficial ornaments of society, supported by state and church alike. Their splendor and magnificence were necessarily proportionate to the eminence of the political power or the religious authority of the host, and it was required, too, that they be worthy of the rank of the guests and of the significance of the events which occasioned them.

The general host of the Congress of Vienna was the Emperor of Austria. In his palace were the crowned heads of Europe; and in his capital city, the

political elite and the social cream of Europe. The occasion was the determination of these guests to put an end to twenty years of revolution and
warfare. Given the eminence of his guests and the importance of the occasion, the Austrian emperor was obliged to give evidence of both inexhaustible imagination and inexhaustible wealth—neither of which he possessed
in fact. (The expenses of the imperial table alone, at the beginning of the
congress, never ran less than 50,000 florins a day—which was roughly what
was budgeted for the daily expenses of the Austrian Ministry of Foreign
Affairs.) To aid him, the emperor had appointed a committee. This committee's responsibility was to devise entertainments and amusements for
the delegates, their wives and retinues. The committee did its work well.
Not a day passed that there was not something new offered for the delecta-
tion of the visitors: banquets, concerts, masked and unmasked balls, hunting parties, tournaments, carousels, military reviews, theatrical comedies
and tragedies. The emperor's example was imitated—at his urging, in
order to avoid depletion of his own funds—by the princes of the imperial
house, by the great Austrian and Hungarian aristocrats, by the nobility
that had come to Vienna from every corner of Europe, and by the delega-
tions of the various powers. All Europe gathered together in the salons and
ballrooms of the Countess Dorothea de Périgord, Lady Castlereagh, the
Duchess of Sagan, Countess Zichy, Madame Fuchs, Princess Esterházy,
Princess Liechtenstein, Princess Fürstenberg, Princess Thurn and Taxis,
and, of course, the amorous Princess Bagration. There all Europe flirted,
gossiped, ate, and danced. And there all the ministers plenipotentiary
talked, negotiated, fought, and, on occasion, reached agreements and compromises. A French nobleman of the period, the Count de la Garde, gave
an account of the first masked ball given by the imperial court, in September, which explains the mechanics of these informal diplomatic tête-à-
têtes. The ball, La Garde tells us, was "a brilliant human tapestry," in
which the initiates could recognize, in the crowd of dominos, the giant
figure of the Russian emperor, Frederick William of Prussia, the King of
Württemberg, the fat King of Bavaria, and Eugène de Beauharnais. Leading off from the main ballroom were small salons, in which kings and ministers—in costume, but with their masks removed—continued the negotiations that they had begun at an earlier ball. Here ambassadors could
approach sovereigns to discuss business without the formality of asking for
an audience. Indeed, the art of approaching a sovereign in a ballroom, engaging his attention, and luring him into one of the salons assumed the
proportions of an art form during the congress and was an important factor in its diplomacy.

Such was Metternich's plan, as witnessed in operation. As the Austrian
minister had foreseen and as Talleyrand had feared, it resulted almost im-

mediately in the total exclusion of France and the smaller powers from any share in these "confidential communications." Talleyrand, obviously, had no control over, and no pretext to join, a whispered conversation between, say, Castlereagh and Nesselrode, carried on in a salon, on the subject of Poland, or one between Baron von Humboldt and Metternich regarding Saxony. Talleyrand's isolation was so complete and so public that the Spanish ambassador, Count de Labrador, was accused of "desertion" when it was noted that he paid frequent visits at the French embassy. And the King of Bavaria confided to his circle that even he dared not speak to Talleyrand as often as he would like.

Metternich's plot to deprive France of a voice in the organization of the affairs of the congress, and especially to circumvent the principle of public law that Talleyrand had introduced, was clever and cautious, like Metternich himself. The Austrian, however, had forgotten to take into account two important factors. One was Talleyrand's subtlety and ingenuity, and the other was the Czar Alexander's inflexible determination to have his own way, at any cost and no matter what the obstacles. By the end of October, after three weeks' of the "confidential approach" to European affairs, it transpired that Metternich's carelessness in this regard had brought his scheme to the point of ruin, the congress to the verge of dissolution before it was even convened, and Europe to the edge of war.

The seeds of dissension had been sown several days before the conference of October 8. On October 4, Castlereagh had sent a memorandum to Metternich, Hardenberg, and Nesselrode, unequivocally rejecting the czar's Polish claims as "contrary to treaties," "preposterous," and "dangerous" to peace in Europe. The treaty signed on June 27, 1813, between Austria, Prussia, and Russia had stipulated that the duchy of Warsaw be partitioned among the three powers. How then, he asked, could Alexander, after signing such a treaty, dare to claim the whole duchy? Castlereagh himself gave the answer: The czar had not seriously studied the matter and had acted impetuously. Moreover, "so long as His Majesty adheres to that unfortunate plan, it will be impossible for any plan of adjustment for the reconstruction of Europe to be arrived at by the plenipotentiaries of the Allied Powers, or for the present Congress to assemble formally to discuss and sanction any such plan."

So real was Castlereagh's fear of Russian expansion into Western Europe that it had infected even Prince Hardenberg. On October 9 the latter wrote to Metternich that "Prussia . . . is ready to concur in all measures which the two courts [Vienna and London] might consider appropriate in persuading Russia . . . to modify its claims with regard to Poland." Still, as a condition of its concurrence, Hardenberg went on, Prussia must have guarantees that it would receive both the whole of Saxony and Mainz.

"Has not Prussia," he reasoned, "which made the greatest efforts and the greatest sacrifices in the common cause, the right to claim acquisitions proportionate to those of its neighbors?" He sent a copy of this note to Castlereagh, who joined with Metternich in assuring Hardenberg that he was willing to sacrifice Saxony "for the future tranquillity of Europe"—but only on condition that Prussia oppose the annexation of the duchy of Warsaw by Russia. As a token of his good faith, he gave his consent in principle to the occupation of Saxony by Prussian troops, which was one of the "guarantees" that Hardenberg had demanded. Prussia had now joined, hesitantly, with England and Austria in opposing Alexander—a situation that enraged the never even-tempered autocrat of Russia. The most incredible scenes followed, first between Alexander and Talleyrand—who Alexander mistakenly believed had united his former allies against him—and then between Alexander and Metternich. "I have two hundred thousand men in the duchy of Warsaw," he shouted at Talleyrand. "Let them drive me out—if they can. . . . And if the King of Saxony refuses to abdicate, he shall be taken to Russia, where he will die. One King of Poland has already died there.* Why not a King of Saxony?"

"Words failed me," Talleyrand wrote to King Louis, "and I scarcely knew how to restrain my indignation."

Metternich, when his turn came the following day (October 24), fared even worse. After taking much the same line as Talleyrand, he was told by the czar that his words were "indecent" and that he was the only man in Austria who dared take on such a "tone of revolt." All this was delivered by Alexander in what can only be described as a bellow of rage. Metternich at this point stormed out furiously, swearing that he would never again see the Emperor of Russia in private.

The breach now seemed complete between England and Austria—and perhaps Prussia—on the one hand and Russia on the other. On October 31, however, the Western powers made a final, if somewhat melodramatic, attempt to win over Alexander, by making use of Princess Bagration. They pinned their hopes on a visit to her which the czar had arranged for the night of October 31. The visit took place and, according to the police report on the meeting, lasted from ten thirty until two o'clock in the morning. There had been more than enough time to discuss politics. Later in the morning, however, the princess confessed to a police agent that her boudoir had been no more conducive to success than had her salons and ballroom.

> He will not listen to reason on this subject. He considers it a question of honor and says he has given his word to the Poles and that he must keep it.

---

* Stanislas II Poniatowski, who was king at the time of the last partition of Poland. He abdicated in 1795 and died two years later in St. Petersburg.

He says that even if the whole world unites against him, he will not yield. He intends to go to Munich, then to Berlin, and then to Warsaw to be proclaimed King of Poland. And if anyone wants to oppose him, he says, he will be ready.

The failure of Princess Bagration's undoubted charms to elicit a favorable political response from Alexander served merely to confirm rumors that were already rampant in Vienna. On October 20, a secret report to Baron Hager drew the following conclusions regarding the atmosphere in the city:

There is more and more talk about the imminent dissolution of the congress and the departure of the sovereigns and their ministers. Fear of war is strong, and no one can see how peace can be preserved, and everyone satisfied, in view of . . . the claims of Russia on Poland and by the appetite of Prussia. The King of Bavaria wishes to leave, and he has declared publicly that the partition of Saxony would be an infamous crime. Hardenberg also believes that a general departure is at hand. And finally, it is being said everywhere that Metternich is striving to increase the confusion.

Three days later, another secret report stated:

No one knows any longer whom or what to believe. One day, it is said that Russia is giving in; the next, it is we who are surrendering; and the next, we are being firm, Europe is on our side, the King of Saxony is saved, and Poland will be only partly Russian. At one moment we are told that Murat has been sentenced to death and, at the next, that his throne is more secure than ever. The truth is that no one knows anything.

Talleyrand himself had no need of police reports to apprize him of the perilous situation. On October 17, only ten days after Metternich's "confidential approach" had been adopted, he was writing to King Louis that Austria would probably go to war against Russia and Prussia if Metternich thought that he could count on French support:

I believe it not only possible, but probable, that if Czar Alexander's attitude should destroy all hope that he may yield to persuasion, Prince Metternich will ask me whether and to what extent Austria may count upon our cooperation. The Instructions which your majesty has issued state that if Russian designs on Poland threaten Europe and that if that threat can be removed only by force of arms, then we must resort to arms without hesitation. This, in my opinion, authorizes me to promise, in general terms, and in this case only, the help of your majesty's troops. But in order to reply positively to a definite request and to promise specific help, I will need special authorization and instructions, which I take the liberty of begging your majesty to send me. . . .

As Alexander was rattling his saber and Austria was preparing to un-
sheath its own, Talleyrand was doing more than reporting on the situation
to Paris. According to an astute observer, the papal legate, Cardinal Consalvi, the French plenipotentiary spent the whole of his time in October
mounting a vigorous campaign of opposition, among the other powers,
against the allies, particularly on their plans to destroy Saxony and Poland—plans which he consistently referred to as "intrigues." So effective
was this campaign and so persuasively did Talleyrand present France as
the champion of peace, of justice, and of the smaller nations that by the
end of the month he had completely won over an ally more powerful than
either Castlereagh or Metternich: public opinion. A secret report prepared
for Baron Hager paints the situation in brilliant colors:

> Opinion with regard to the congress is still bad. Everyone says that there
> is no agreement; that no one talks any more about reestablishing order and
> justice but of each one taking what he can; that all indications are that a
> general war is imminent. . . . It is said openly that Alexander cannot bear
> Metternich; that Talleyrand is the only one talking sense now; that the
> Gospel, even if preached by the devil himself, would still be the Gospel. It
> is said that Talleyrand truly asks for nothing for France and that he wants
> only justice, stability, moderation, and peace, erected on the sacred princi-
> ples of right and reason. . . .
> This attitude places the French in a superior position in the opinion of
> the upper and middle classes, while the Russians, the Prussians, and our
> own minister have lost favor in the public eye.

The English, for their part, had made themselves so despised for Castlereagh's apparent inability to take a firm stand on anything and for his
lack of tact that their plenipotentiary was now treated with thinly concealed contempt in the salons of Vienna:

> Last Friday, the twenty-eighth, the English ambassador visited Madame
> de Sagan during the evening. All of a sudden, this eccentric turned to her
> and said, "What do you think of Alexander? I myself consider him to be
> an ambitious lunatic and a charlatan. That is my opinion. What is yours?"
> The duchess, startled and embarrassed by this disclosure, made in the
> presence of ten other persons, smiled and said: "My opinion, my lord, is
> that you are taking the bit in your teeth, like the horse which you gave my
> sister Dorothea this morning and which came within an inch of breaking
> her neck on the Prater." Whereupon, she got up and went to talk with
> someone else.

Such was the situation at the end of October, only a few days before the
full congress was to be convened. Britain and Austria were united against
Russia, with Prussia still hesitating over the choice of sides, and with
France, in the person of Talleyrand, standing firmly on the same principles

which he had enunciated at the beginning of October and supported, just as firmly, by the smaller powers and by public opinion. At this point, it was necessary that something be done to break the deadlock. The four powers realized, finally, that they would have to abandon the "confidential approach"—at least in its current form—that had helped bring them all to such a pass and from which only France, though excluded from all participation, had derived any profit. The first step in that direction was once more to convene a conference of the eight signatories to the Peace of Paris. This was done on October 30, and at that meeting, Talleyrand was asked to submit a procedural plan to the other delegates. He did so the next day. His plan called for the establishment of a directing committee (*une commission générale*), to be composed of representatives of all the sovereign heads, including the Pope. Four subcommittees would then be nominated by this general committee, to discuss the questions of Italy, Switzerland, Poland, and Saxony. The subcommittees would report to the general committee and the general committee to the congress. By way of concession, he proposed that representatives of sovereigns whose positions were under challenge (Murat and King Augustus of Saxony) might be present at discussions but would have no vote. While the various committees were working on the questions that concerned them, the credentials of all plenipotentiaries were to be examined, by still another committee, so that, once the work of the general commission had been completed, the full congress might be convened at once.

This was too much, even for the hard-pressed Allies. There was still too wide a gap between Talleyrand's position and that of the other ministers—a gap which Löwenhielm, the Swedish minister, described with perfect accuracy:

> The French plenipotentiary understands the word "Congress" in its usual sense. . . . The ministers of the other great powers, however, will not accept that interpretation and consider the congress to be nothing more than a gathering of all the powers in one spot for the purpose of putting into execution whatever arrangements they [the allied powers] may choose to make.

The only decisions reached, therefore, were to postpone the plenary sessions of the congress,* to establish a credentials committee of three powers (drawn by lot), and formally to elect Metternich to preside over the committee of eight.

* In fact, as Gentz later remarked, there never was a Congress of Vienna. At a conference on November 18, the opening date was postponed "indefinitely" (*British and Foreign State Papers*, Vol. II, p. 570). As it happened, the "opening date" and "closing date" were to be the same—June 9, 1815—when it gathered to sign the appropriately named Final Act, which had been drafted, almost in its entirety, by the great powers.

To these decisions, Talleyrand could, and did, agree with good humor. His proposal had been rejected—he did not expect otherwise—but he had made his point. The "confidential approach" was still in use (of necessity, since no agreement could be reached on any other *modus agendi*), but henceforth Talleyrand could no longer be shut out with the ministers of the small states. His opposition, as he had already proved, would be too dangerous.

On November 5, Talleyrand was invited by Metternich to visit him at four o'clock. With Metternich, he found both Castlereagh and Nesselrode. Metternich began by stating that the Congress had reached an impasse and asked Talleyrand, in his own name and in that of Castlereagh and Nesselrode, to lay aside all personal feelings and help them arrive at a solution. Talleyrand replied that if the congress was at an impasse, it was because the congress had never been convened. "It will be necessary, in any case, to convene it sooner or later," he added. "The longer we delay to do so, the more it will appear that we are trying to hide something."

Castlereagh said he agreed with Talleyrand, but that "the very mention of the congress seems to terrify the Prussian delegates" and that "Hardenberg, in particular, is obsessed with fear." Metternich also agreed in principle, but said it would still be better to wait "until some agreement has been reached, at least on the important questions." He then informed Talleyrand that they had every intention of settling the affairs of Switzerland with Talleyrand's help, and he proposed to begin immediately, with Talleyrand, the discussion of Italy's affairs.

The question of Italy appeared relatively simple. In the Italian peninsula, the armies of the Revolution had destroyed the *ancien régime* and imposed, by force, French military dictatorships in the guise of autonomous republics. The problem now was to fill the void created by the downfall of the French Empire. The obvious solution was to restore the *ancien régime*. Both the King of Piedmont and the Pope had returned to their states and had been enthusiastically welcomed by their people. Genoa wished to revive its republic, as it had been before the Revolution, and had sent a delegate to Vienna to ask the congress to perform this miracle. All Italy, in fact, seemed with one voice to demand the restoration of the old order. Led by the church, the upper and middle classes in Italy were united in their hatred for the Revolution. They wanted no more talk of constitutions or of liberty and equality.

Despite this unanimity of sentiment, there were intricate problems. One was presented by the grand duchy of Tuscany. In 1801, Napoleon had forced the Duke of Parma and the Grand Duke of Tuscany formally to cede their states to him. Parma had been annexed to France outright, and the Duke of Parma, in recompense, had been given Tuscany and the title of King of Etruria. The former Grand Duke of Tuscany, Ferdinand, had received, in his turn, the German duchy of Würzburg. In 1807, however, Napoleon had annexed Etruria to France, promising the Queen Regent of Etruria to give her a hypothetical kingdom of Lusitania that he intended to create in Portugal. Then, in May, 1814, France had ceded to the allies the *départements* created out of the former duchy of Parma and the former grand duchy of Tuscany.

The case of Parma was simple enough. It had been formally ceded, first to France and then by France to the allies. It was therefore vacant territory, and the congress could legally dispose of it. The Tuscan problem was more complicated. Grand Duke Ferdinand had ceded it to Napoleon, who had ceded it to the former Duke of Parma, who became King of Etruria. Then the widow and heir of the King of Etruria had ceded Tuscany back to Napoleon, against the promise of a future kingdom of Lusitania. But since the imperial promise had not been kept, the cession was null and void. Therefore, the Queen of Etruria had never ceased being the legitimate sovereign of the former grand duchy of Tuscany, and the congress, according to public law, had only to recognize that sovereignty. Such, in fact, was the thesis of Talleyrand's Instructions. But here another factor intruded. The former Grand Duke of Tuscany, Ferdinand, had, in September, 1814, forsaken his bleak duchy of Würzburg and, completely on his own, had returned to his Tuscan garden, taken up residence in the Pitti Palace, and resumed the government of Tuscany with the warm approval of the Tuscans. So Ferdinand was the legitimate sovereign of Tuscany by virtue of the "ancient law of possession"—a law which Talleyrand himself recognized to be one of the foundations of legitimacy. Moreover, Ferdinand was the brother of the Emperor of Austria, and if the congress decided in favor of the Queen of Etruria and asked Ferdinand to leave Tuscany, it would have been an intolerable insult to the House of Hapsburg.

Various solutions were proposed to the dilemma. Talleyrand had thought of recompensing the Queen of Etruria with Parma, Piacenza, and Guastalla, which were vacant territories. But the treaty signed between Napoleon and the allies (April 11, 1814) had promised these lands to the Empress Marie-Louise. Then it was proposed to give the queen part of the Papal States, as the Pope had ceded some of his provinces (or legations, as they were called), to France by the Treaty of Tolentino. The Queen of Etruria, however, was a pious woman, and she refused to accept them, particularly since Cardinal Consalvi was threatening with hellfire any sovereign who dared touch one clod of the former pontifical territory.

A final aggravation of the Italian problem was the presence of King Joachim Murat in Naples. At the beginning of 1814, Austria, terrified of Napoleon, had accepted Murat's offer of help and had signed a treaty of alliance with him (January 11). Now, in October, with Napoleon in exile, Austria found this treaty very troublesome. It was difficult to fit Murat, a vestige of the Revolution and erstwhile creature-king of Napoleon's, into a European order established "in harmony with public law." Yet to repudiate Murat would have been a breach of the Austrian emperor's pledged word. Even more disastrous, Murat might be provoked to such an extent that he would put himself at the head of all those who had supported the revolutionary regime in Italy and attempt to establish a separate and independent kingdom of Italy. This latter possibility was Metternich's chief concern, and it was the reason why, on November 5, in the course of the first discussion of Italian affairs in which Talleyrand participated, the Austrian minister suggested that the question of Naples be deleted from the congress' agenda and be postponed to some future date. "The natural course of events," he explained to Talleyrand, "will inevitably bring about the return of the Bourbons to the throne of Naples."

"The natural course of events," Talleyrand answered, "seems to me most propitious at this very moment. The congress must settle this question. From a geographical standpoint, it would come up as the last of the Italian problems, and I am willing that we should follow a geographical order. Further than that, I am unable to go."

Metternich then spoke of Murat's supporters in Italy, but Talleyrand interrupted. "If you organize Italy, Murat will have no supporters. Establish the succession in Sardinia; send an archduke to administer Milan; recognize the claims of the Queen of Etruria; and restore to the Pope what belongs to him—lands that your own troops are occupying. Then Murat will have no more hold over the people, and Italy will consider him nothing more than a brigand." In answer, Metternich said that it was not so simple as Talleyrand seemed to think and that there were "complications" of which he was unaware. Then, after everyone had agreed to take up the Italian questions as Talleyrand had suggested, in their geographical order, from north to south, beginning with Sardinia, the conference adjourned. "The word 'complication,'" Talleyrand wrote to King Louis, "is one which M. de Metternich uses constantly in order to cling to the vagueness required by his weak policies."

News of Talleyrand's *de facto* inclusion among the ministers directing the congress reached Czar Alexander immediately and left him troubled. With Austria and England firmly and openly opposed to Russian expansion in Poland, and with Prussia wavering, France's new status as a full partner with the allied powers might well force the czar either to abandon his plans to crown himself King of Poland or to go to war and win the Polish throne by force of arms. He therefore decided upon a bizarre stratagem to win back the loyalty of the vacillating King of Prussia. He invited Frederick William to dinner and used all his considerable powers of persuasion to convince him that his own interests required an open declaration in favor of the Russian czar. Then, at the end of the dinner, Alexander summoned Prince Hardenberg, who was chancellor of Prussia, as well as Frederick William's plenipotentiary at the congress. The unhappy Hardenberg was informed by Alexander, in the strongest possible language, that Russia and Prussia, in the persons of their respective monarchs, had arrived at a "definite and unshakable" agreement with respect to Poland. Alexander then commanded Hardenberg to say outright, without evasion, whether or not he was going to obey Frederick William's commands on this subject. Hardenberg now had either to acquiesce or resign, and he acquiesced. Later Hardenberg remarked to Gentz that he had never been in such a position in his whole life. It was, in fact, a position that left the Prussian chancellor no choice but to follow the orders of the Russian emperor. Accordingly, on November 7, he handed Castlereagh a confidential memorandum declaring that all resistance to Alexander's plans must be abandoned and that all future discussion on the question of Poland must be confined to the subject of the boundaries of Alexander's new kingdom of Poland. "Unless the Emperor of Russia can be brought to a more moderate and sound course of public conduct," Castlereagh reported to London, "the peace which we have so dearly purchased will be of short duration."

Metternich, of course, was outraged at Frederick William's capitulation. He assured Talleyrand that he had been stripped of all his illusions regarding Prussia and that Austria would "never again abandon Saxony." "As for Poland," Talleyrand wrote to Louis, "he gave me to understand that he would be willing to yield a large part of it—which means that he is prepared to yield everything." He added: "I was still with him when a report was brought in describing the condition of the Austrian army. He showed it to me. The present strength of this army is 374,000 men, including 52,000 cavalry and 800 guns. Yet, with all these forces, he still believes the Austrian crown has no choice other than to submit to everything and to resign itself to the inevitable."

Metternich's weakness was a mystery that eluded even the subtle Frenchman. Yet Talleyrand was not wholly displeased with Austria's new policy. If Metternich remained firm on Saxony, he would alienate Prussia, and if he were indeed "willing to yield a large part" of Poland, he would offend England. In either case, the allied coalition would be divided, even more seriously than was already the case, on the two most serious questions confronting the congress, and it would be a breach which France could easily turn to its own advantage. In order to bring this about, however, it was essential that Talleyrand avoid giving Austria and England the slightest basis for believing that France might still be drawn into the Russian camp. For this reason, he began deliberately avoiding Alexander, and replied evasively to an invitation from the czar to visit him. Alexander, who apparently believed that a reconciliation with Talleyrand was possible, then began seeking him out in the various salons of Vienna. On November 12, there was a large reception at the house of Count Zichy, which Talleyrand was required to attend even though he knew the czar would also be a guest. Talleyrand spent almost the whole evening in the game room in order not to encounter the czar, and when the guests began to sit down to dinner, he took advantage of the confusion to make his escape. Just as he reached the door of the anteroom, he felt a hand on his shoulder. It was Alexander. After reproaching Talleyrand for his inacessibility, the czar asked him to visit him on Monday, November 14, "in ordinary clothes rather than court dress, as a friend." This time there was no way out, and Talleyrand had to accept. "I was careful, however, to inform Prince Metternich and Lord Castlereagh of what had happened, so as to remove any hint of mystery and to prevent all suspicion on their part."

As it happened, the dreaded interview with Alexander went smoothly, even cordially. There was a candid statement of respective viewpoints with regard to Poland and Saxony, with Talleyrand not giving way an inch. Finally, Alexander proposed a bargain: "Give way to me on the question of Saxony, and I will do the same for you on that of Naples. I have given no promise there."

"Your majesty knows that such a bargain is impossible. The two questions are wholly dissimilar. It is not possible for your majesty to differ from us with respect to Naples."

Throughout the interview and despite their differences of opinion, Talleyrand reported to Louis, "his tone has changed since my last audience with him. Throughout the whole interview, he gave not a sign of irritation or bad humor. All was calm and pleasant." The purpose of the interview, he felt, was to discover France's military situation and to sound out Talleyrand on the possibility of a Franco-Russian alliance if the necessity for it should arise. Alexander had now abandoned his self-created role of imperial knight-errant of Europe and was assuming that of a political gambler. And, Talleyrand suspected, he was playing his diplomatic cards with incontestable skill. It was evident that Alexander no longer counted on obtaining what he wanted through the support of his former allies and that, like Austria, he was beginning to lean toward France.

During his conversation with the czar, Talleyrand had declared that France would consent to give up even a part of Saxony to Prussia "only with the most profound regret . . . but it is a sacrifice that we are willing to make for the sake of peace." Upon returning to the Hotel Kaunitz, he discovered that Europe, and France—whether or not it were willing to consent to the disappearance of Saxony—had been presented with a *fait accompli.* In his antechamber he found the Saxon plenipotentiary, bearing a note of protest from King Frederick Augustus of Saxony, along with a grave piece of news: Prince Repnin, the Russian governor-general of Saxony, had just proclaimed that as a consequence of an agreement between Russia and Prussia, he was turning over the administration of Saxony to representatives of the Prussian king. The agreement to which Repnin alluded was dated September 28 and explained that the Emperor of Russia, in disposing of the Saxon throne, was "acting in concert with England and Austria." Castlereagh and Metternich protested immediately and violently that Alexander had abused their consent, by making it absolute when they had intended it to be purely conditional. Talleyrand was willing to believe them, but he could not help noting, with a sense of self-satisfaction, that the whole affair "shows how little agreement there is among these closely united allies—and this after protesting so loudly that France wanted to divide them."

The day after this bombshell Lord Castlereagh came to call on Talleyrand. "Deceived in the hopes he had built on Prussia," Talleyrand noted, "and seeing the whole basis of his policy crumbling, he has fallen into a kind of depression. He came to consult me as to the means of giving an impetus to affairs, to make them advance more rapidly. I told him . . . that they [England and Austria] had subordinated the question of Poland to that of Saxony and that this arrangement had not succeeded; that it was now necessary to separate the two questions and finish that of Poland first. Then Austria, at ease in this respect and no longer obliged to deal with both matters at once, would turn its whole attention to the question of Saxony—which all the Austrian generals consider by far the more important of the two. Russia, once satisfied on the question that interested it directly, would probably trouble itself very little about the other; Prussia would then find itself alone, facing England, Austria, France, and Spain, and the affair would be easily and quickly arranged."

Talleyrand's insistence on the priority of the Polish question seems to have borne fruit. A week later he was reporting that "the progress of affairs is being hindered by the great issues of Poland and Saxony." And indeed, although the eight powers met in conference had discussed the affairs of the Queen of Etruria, all attention was focused on the crisis created by Prussia's intrusion into Saxony. Prince Metternich and Lord Castlereagh both sent firm letters of protest to Berlin, declaring that the assumption of the Saxon crown by Frederick William would be admitted only conditionally and that if Prussia would not cooperate in settling the Polish question to their satisfaction, their concessions with respect to Saxony would become null and void. Privately, Talleyrand believed, Metternich and Castlereagh were prepared to go beyond formal protests:

> They are persuaded that if the Emperor of Russia and the King of Prussia refuse these overtures [*i.e.,* their notes of protest], it will become necessary to make preparations for imposing moderation on them by force. We are, in fact, assured that military preparations have been concerted, and a plan of campaign discussed between the governments of Austria and Bavaria. The cooperation of France is considered necessary for this."

Talleyrand's suspicions were well founded. So bellicose had Castlereagh's attitude become that the British Cabinet thought it wise to issue a formal instruction on the subject. "It is unnecessary for me to point out to you," Lord Bathurst wrote from London, "the impossibility of His Royal Highness consenting to involve this country in hostilities at this time for any of the objects which have been hitherto under discussion at Vienna." King Louis, however, aware of the menace to France from Prussian expansion, took a different attitude. "I am going to give orders for the army to be held in readiness to take the field," he had written a few weeks before, when Talleyrand had pointed out the possibility of a new outbreak of hostilities. Bavaria and Austria, as has been noted, were already conferring on a plan of military operations. Meanwhile, Alexander was announcing regularly that he intended to have his way with Poland and Saxony even if it meant war. "It is not yet possible to foresee the final move of the Emperor of Russia," Talleyrand wrote, "who, alone, by his presumption and impossible ideas, is on the verge of lighting the torch of war."

15

Crisis and Solution: The Triple Alliance

ALEXANDER'S "impossible ideas," as Talleyrand described them, were the result, not of a disordered mind or even of unbridled ambition, but of a congenital quirk. He was, by nature, a rebel, a compulsive oppositionist. If he supported an idea or a cause and that idea or cause triumphed, he became immediately and violently opposed to it. After having been for years a sincere liberal and a supporter of the Revolution and of Napoleon, he had suddenly converted to legitimacy and conservatism and had begun supporting the reestablishment of the *ancien régime.* Then, as soon as Europe, under the impact of Talleyrand's pertinacious rhetoric, had agreed to reorganize the Continent in conformity with the principle of legitimacy and public law, Alexander underwent another metamorphosis and became once more the champion of revolutionary principles. He could—and did—protest that his Polish schemes were motivated solely by a "moral duty" to see Poland free and independent. And he wished Prussia to have all, rather than a part, of Saxony, because the Saxons themselves, he said, wished it: "If there were any possibility of counting the votes, they [the people of Saxony] would almost unanimously be against dismemberment." To legitimacy and the old regime, Alexander, who had so recently made war against the tyranny of the Revolution, was now proposing *liberté, égalité,* and *fraternité* for Poland and a hypothetically popular plebiscite for the Saxons. He had come full circle. Now, if a general war were to be averted, someone would have somehow to lead him either to reacceptance of the public law or at least to realization of the impossibility of his Polish ambitions.

Lord Castlereagh was the first to try his hand at it. His scheme, from the very beginning, had been to present a united front of the Western opposition—British, Austrian, and Prussian—to Alexander's assumption of the Polish crown.* In its first phase, this plan had failed because of the defection of the Prussian king and the czar's browbeating of Prince Hardenberg. The second phase, which now was undertaken, was no more successful. Castlereagh's hopes centered on a visit to Budapest which the Emperor of Austria, the Czar of Russia, and the King of Prussia were to undertake. There the Austrian monarch, aghast at the idea either of a Prussian Saxony or a Russian Poland, and Frederick William of Prussia, who had been given massive infusions of courage by Hardenberg and Metternich, were to announce to Alexander their unqualified opposition to his Polish scheme. At the critical moment, however, the Prussian king defected. Alexander, as soon as the subject was broached, launched into an attack of unparalleled bitterness on Metternich and Hardenberg, in the presence of their masters, and Frederick William, thoroughly cowed, immediately gave way. No one was surprised, except Castlereagh, who wrote petulantly to London that the King of Prussia had spoiled his whole plan and announced that he was withdrawing from the negotiations. His failure to take into account the Prussian king's well-known weakness of character had, indeed, been the cause of his failure. But the effects of his blindness were not limited to a stabilization of the status quo. Metternich, outraged at Frederick William's retreat, intimated to Hardenberg that any further joint action against Russia was out of the question. Nesselrode, who had cooperated at least passively in Castlereagh's plan and who had been on good terms with Russia's former allies, now lost Alexander's confidence to the extent that he was expected momentarily to be superseded as Russian plenipotentiary. The total effect of Castlereagh's attempt to play the mediator, therefore, had been to chase a hesitant Prussia into the Russian camp, to alienate Austria from Prussia, and to reduce to impotence the West's strongest friend in Alexander's entourage.

Prince Hardenberg was the next to try leading Alexander to the path of reason. He proposed what amounted to a partition of Poland, with Alexander getting the largest share, Prussia getting the fortress of Thurn and the line of the Warta River, and Austria getting Cracow and the line of the Nida River. Then, he added, there would be no objection if Alexander wanted to make himself sovereign of this truncated kingdom of Poland. Alexander's answer was delivered by Prince Adam Czartoryski and Baron

* Castlereagh's instructions for the congress have never been discovered, but it seems certain that his intention was not to establish an independent Poland, but to effect a new partition of that country among Russia, Prussia, and Austria. *C.f.* letter to Lord Liverpool, dated October 24, 1814 (F.O. Continent 7).

Heinrich Friedrich vom und zum Stein, who along with Count Capo d'Istria and Frédéric de La Harpe had unofficially replaced the unhappy Nesselrode as Alexander's advisers.* His only concession was an expression of willingness to make Thurn and Cracow free cities—on condition that Saxony be given to Prussia. Metternich, of course, could not even consider such a proposal. His willingness, and Castlereagh's, to sacrifice Saxony to Prussia had been conditioned upon Prussia's active cooperation against Russia. Since Prussia now sided with the czar, Austria was determined that it should not have Saxony. If Prussia were denied Saxony, and if it could not, because of Alexander, seek territorial gains to the east, in Poland, it would either have to content itself with its actual frontiers or seek compensation among the minor German states other than Saxony. Hardenberg's intervention therefore had completed the work that Castlereagh's clumsiness had begun: The failure to check Russia had made Austria and Prussia irreconcilable rivals in Germany, and Prussia now joined Russia in talking openly of war.

Alexander was sufficiently astute to see that this breach might drive Austria and England into the arms of France. He therefore sent Prince Czartoryski to Talleyrand with a message, saying that he no longer desired the complete destruction of Saxony but would accept the existence of a small, independent kingdom. At the same time, he asked Talleyrand to tell him frankly whether France had made any commitment to Austria. When Talleyrand answered in the negative, Czartoryski asked whether, in case no agreement could be reached on Saxony—that is, in case of war—France would make any such commitment. Talleyrand's answer was: "I should be very sorry if it came to that."

Alexander, dissatisfied with Talleyrand's answers, arranged an interview with Metternich. It was, predictably, a stormy session, with Alexander being "cold, sharp, and severe." Apparently, Metternich was equally cold, sharp, and severe. After the interview, the Russian czar announced to the Emperor Francis of Austria that Metternich had insulted him and that he was going to challenge him to a duel. All that unhappy Europe needed was a duel, fought before the whole congress, between the Emperor of Russia and the chancellor of Austria, to settle the question of Saxony. Fortunately, nothing more was heard of Alexander's threat. He may have been a little mad, but like a Shakespearean hero, he was mad only north-northwest. Where his own interests were concerned, he could be eminently sane. He therefore contented himself with denouncing Metternich to the other plenipotentiaries as the chief disturber of the peace of Europe. By the mid-

* It is interesting that, at this period, Alexander's most influential ministers were all foreigners. Czartoryski was a Polish nobleman; Stein, a Prussian; Capo d'Istria, a native of Corfu; and La Harpe, a Swiss.

dle of December public opinion concerning the congress was extremely pessimistic: No agreement would be reached, either on Saxony or on Poland; on all sides, the powers were arming; and war would begin in a few days.

Talleyrand was in a better position than the public to judge, and he was far from sharing its pessimism. In a letter to King Louis, dated December 15, he remarked that things were going along satisfactorily. The reason for this relative optimism was that, early in December, Castlereagh had received orders from London to join France and Austria in their opposition to the annexation of Saxony. The Duke of Wellington, who was then ambassador in Paris, had been blunt as ever in his choice of words: "The instructions given to Lord Castlereagh, and with which he [Wellington] was well acquainted, were absolutely opposed to the designs of the Emperor Alexander on Poland, and consequently on Saxony, since the fate of Saxony depends entirely on the determination arrived at with regard to Poland." Castlereagh, going against these instructions, had "thought he was in a position to bend the Emperor of Russia, and succeeded only in irritating him." London called him to task and issued supplementary instructions, written in very plain language, which reached Vienna on December 7. The very next morning Castlereagh had written to Metternich, informing him that England now stood firmly with Austria on the question of Saxony. Even so, Talleyrand concluded, "we can reasonably expect England and Austria to make real and sincere overtures to us only in a case of the most urgent necessity."

Another cause of encouragement to Talleyrand had been Metternich's behavior during this critical period. On December 10, the Austrian chancellor had sent Hardenberg a note stating that Austria would be willing to let Alexander have his way on the Polish question, but that it could never consent to the total suppression of Saxony. In the latter respect, however, it would not object if Prussia took part of the country—say Lower Lusatia, part of Upper Lusatia, and the Elba circle on both sides of the river. Since everyone wanted an agreement to be reached, Metternich's note should have been well received. Instead, it caused a storm. The Prussians wanted the whole of Saxony, and Metternich had offered them only one-fifth of it. Hardenberg protested bitterly to the czar, who passed the complaint on to the Emperor Francis. Austria's offer was rejected, almost with disdain, and all Saxony was claimed in the harshest terms.

On December 14, the day before writing to King Louis that all was well in Vienna, Talleyrand had gone to see Metternich, who offered to show him the much-discussed note to Prussia. Talleyrand replied that he knew the contents and wanted only official confirmation. "My precise motive for insisting on a formal disclosure," he reported to Paris, "was the fact that this would mark the true date of the repudiation of the coalition [of Austria, England, Prussia, and Russia against France]." After a slight hesitation, Metternich produced the note and handed it to Talleyrand; accompanying it was a personal message which concluded with this sentiment: "I am happy to find myself in agreement with your Cabinet on a point which is so nobly defensible."

As the congress was being reduced to chaos, and Europe to war, Talleyrand had been waiting quietly, though not idly, for his chance to strike. Now Castlereagh's maladroit planning, Alexander's obstinacy, Frederick William's weakness, Hardenberg's temper, and Metternich's vacillation had created the "case of the most urgent necessity" that Talleyrand had been watching for. The moment had arrived to catalyze that necessity and give England and Austria the slight push that was required to send them in the direction of France and of Talleyrand.

In two notes, dated December 19 and December 26, Talleyrand set about supplying that push. He announced to Metternich and to the world that the dethronement of the King of Saxony and the rape of his kingdom would constitute an outrageous violation of justice and of the principle of legitimacy. Frederick Augustus might, if he wished, give away parts of his kingdom, but he could do so only as the legitimate sovereign of Saxony— that is, only if he were universally recognized as such. At the same time, Talleyrand intimated that he had arranged with all the minor German powers to address a collective protest to the congress against the absorption of Saxony by Prussia. The contents of this note, when it became known, so infuriated the Prussians that Hardenberg was moved to announce that any further opposition to Prussia's annexation of Saxony would be regarded as a declaration of war.

This reaction was precisely what Talleyrand had intended to evoke. Now that Metternich had come out against the annihilation of Saxony, it remained only for Castlereagh to follow his instructions from London and declare himself. Then France, Austria, and England together could present a united front against Russia and Prussia and, Talleyrand hoped, force them to back down without having to resort to war. In fact, a few days later Lord Castlereagh presented himself at Talleyrand's house. Talleyrand immediately showed him a copy of his note to Metternich. "He read it very calmly," King Louis was told. "He read it completely. And then he returned it without a word, either of approval or disapproval." The fact was, the phlegmatic Englishman had come not to discuss political philosophy, but to suggest the formation of a statistical committee to verify the estimates of the population of Saxony. Single-minded as he was, he was unwilling to discuss or comment upon any other subject at that moment. Still, Talleyrand was determined to push Castlereagh as far as possible. While agreeing to Castlereagh's suggestion regarding the committee, he remarked pointedly that "before verifying accounts, it was altogether necessary to acknowledge the rights of the King of Saxony, and that, on this subject, we might—Prince Metternich and myself—come to some agreement."

"An agreement?" Castlereagh replied in astonishment. "Is it an alliance then that you are proposing?"

"This agreement may well take place without an alliance," Talleyrand said, "but, if you prefer, it can be an alliance. I have no objection."

"But an alliance presupposes war or may lead to war. And we should do everything in our power to avoid war."

"That is also my opinion," Talleyrand declared. "Every sacrifice must be made to prevent war. Every sacrifice, that is, except that of honor, justice, and the future of Europe." And when Castlereagh replied that a new war would not be easily accepted by the people of Europe, Talleyrand countered: "A war would be popular in your country if its aim were sufficiently exalted, if its purpose were the good of Europe."

"What, then, would be its purpose?"

"The reestablishment of Poland."

Castlereagh sat silent for a moment. When he spoke, it was in a low voice. "Not yet," he said. "Not yet."

The seed had been planted and was already germinating. British resistance was weakening.

Talleyrand's well-devised plan for a formal rupture among the allies and the formation of a new coalition that would include France was brought to fruition almost immediately—but by Alexander rather than by Talleyrand. The Russian czar, who had foreseen Talleyrand's stratagem, launched a surprise counterattack late in December by making a final, supreme effort to restore harmony among the allies. At his invitation, the allied plenipotentiaries (except the disgraced Nesselrode, who was replaced by Prince Razoumoffsky on this occasion) met on December 29 in order to arrive at a solution, without the participation of France or the congress, of two apparently insoluble problems: Poland and Saxony. At the first meeting, nothing was decided. At the second session, on December 30, Razoumoffsky decided to lay his cards on the table by revealing Alexander's exact plans. Russia, he said, wanted the whole of the duchy of Warsaw, excepting Gnesen, Posen, and the former provinces of western Prussia. These latter territories would be given to Prussia. Austria might have a small bit of land on the right bank of the Vistula, including the salt mines of Wieliczka. Thurn and Cracow were to be free cities. With regard to Saxony, Alexander's stand remained unchanged: The whole of the kingdom must be given to the Prussian king. King Frederick Augustus of Saxony, however, was to be indemnified with a state of some 700,000 inhabitants on the left bank of the Rhine (the duchy of Luxembourg, parts of the archbishoprics of Trier and Cologne, Bonn, and the lands of a few ecclesiastical fiefs).

This time trouble came from an unexpected quarter. The Prussians were delighted with Alexander's proposal. The Austrians were willing to acquiesce so far as Poland was concerned, but objected to the Saxon solution. It was Castlereagh who brought things to a head by flying into a rage. No one knows what the immediate provocation was. It seems likely that Prince Razoumoffsky had had the bad judgment to present Alexander's proposal as an ultimatum thinly disguised as a compromise and that this act of effrontery wounded the British plenipotentiary in his most—indeed, his only—sensitive spot: his Britannic pride. Or it may be that Alexander's unrelenting obstinacy had finally exhausted even Castlereagh's heretofore-unlimited patience. In any case, Castlereagh called on Talleyrand the next day, complaining in the most violent terms about Russia, protesting that the czar was behaving in a tyrannical manner and trying to lay down the law for the whole of Europe, and declaring that England would not allow itself to be dictated to. Talleyrand took advantage of Castlereagh's indignation to bring up, once more, the subject of an alliance among England, France, and Austria. Castlereagh, who only a few days before had thought the time had "not yet" come, now showed enthusiasm for the idea, even suggesting that he himself draw up a draft of the proposed alliance in black and white. "The day after this conversation," Talleyrand recorded, "he called on me again, and I was astonished to discover that he had already drawn up his ideas in the form of articles." Talleyrand accepted the document, along with Castlereagh's suggestion that he show it immediately to Metternich. That same evening Metternich and Talleyrand, after making a few changes in the wording, adopted Castlereagh's treaty draft in the form of a convention. "When dealing with weak characters," Talleyrand remarked to King Louis, "the important thing is to press on to the end. And so we signed it tonight." * The three powers pledged themselves "to act in concert, with the most complete impartiality and good faith, to assure that the measures designed to fulfill the stipulations of the Treaty of Paris are carried out in such a manner as to conform as closely as possible to the true spirit of the treaty." To do this, they agreed to furnish mutual support in the event that any one of them was attacked "on account of the proposals to which they had mutually agreed for the fulfillment of the Treaty of Paris" (Article I). At the practical level, Austria and France promised each to provide 15,000 men, and Great Britain to furnish an equivalent number of men or a proportionate subsidy (Article II). Hanover, Sardinia, Bavaria,

---

* The letter, though dated January 4, was apparently written on the night of January 3—the date of the treaty itself.

and Hesse-Darmstadt would be invited to sign the treaty (Article IV). Finally, a military commission was to be established to prepare joint plans in the event of an advance of Russian armies into Western Europe (Article V).

Talleyrand did not attempt to conceal his jubilation at this spectacular triumph. "The coalition is destroyed," he wrote to his royal master in Paris, "and destroyed forever. Not only is France no longer isolated in Europe, but your majesty now has a treaty system such as fifty years of negotiation could hardly hope to produce. It is acting in concert with two of the greatest powers, three states of the second rank, and soon with all the states that follow principles other than those of revolution. France will, in reality, be the chief and soul of this alliance, formed for the defense of principles which it has been the first to preach." Then he added diplomatically or perhaps ironically: "A change so great and so fortunate can be attributed only to the protection of that Providence which has been so plainly visible in the restoration of your majesty."

The uncharacteristic modesty with which Talleyrand attributes the alliance to the intervention of Providence is probably unfounded. The alliance with England and Austria was no mere expedient concocted in order to have his way with Saxony and Poland. It was a goal for which he had worked almost all his life. He had preached it before the Revolution. He had worked for it during the Revolution. He had pursued it while in office during the Feuillant and Girondin regimes. He had advocated it from his American exile. Under the Directory and the Consulate, he had attempted to return to it. He had been mindful of it at Erfurt. When Bonaparte was supreme in Europe, he had more than once risked his political neck to support it. At Vienna, finally, he had triumphed.

Since Castlereagh's ambitions and accomplishments were more modest, he could afford to be less enthusiastic than Talleyrand. "The alarm of war," he wrote to London, "is over." He was right. Even so, it took a few hours for that fact to become obvious to the rest of the world, for it was not until January 4 that news of the "secret" treaty constituting the Triple Alliance (as it came to be called) was circulated through the salons of the Austrian capital. Indeed, on January 3, Hardenberg and Capo d'Istria had come to a meeting of the four powers without an inkling of what had happened. They were astonished when the Austrian chancellor began suddenly to insist that Talleyrand be admitted to their deliberations. Otherwise, Metternich declared, Austria would not negotiate on Saxony. By the time, a few days later, that Castlereagh presented a memorandum saying that, "In my opinion, the minister of France should be invited to attend the deliberations," news of the Triple Alliance had penetrated every level of Viennese society, and Prussia and Russia realized that further resistance on this point was useless. Talleyrand was thenceforth invited to all meetings, and the Committee of Four, which was to transact all the real business of the Congress of Vienna, now became the Committee of Five.

The newly constituted committee held its inaugural session on January 12, and the first subject on the agenda was Poland. Vienna held its breath, expecting a mighty clash between the great powers. They were disappointed. Castlereagh pointed out that Austria, on January 3, had stated that it was prepared to discuss the proposals of the czar and that since this was so, England would abandon its opposition to those proposals, on the condition that Austria, Prussia, and Russia guarantee Poland "a system of administration whose form would be both conciliatory and in harmony with the character of the people." This step had been discussed with Talleyrand a few days before, and Talleyrand, whose position on Poland was moderate enough, being only that the whole of Poland should not be given to Russia, had consented to it.

Alexander, now having every hope of obtaining what he wanted, was at pains to be conciliatory about what he did not want. Poland was his chief aim. Saxony was secondary, for its annihilation would benefit not himself, but Frederick William of Prussia. Therefore, he indicated that after all was said and done, he would not reject a compromise on Saxony. Prussia did not give up so easily. At the meeting of the Committee of Five on January 12, it once more demanded all of Saxony. This time Talleyrand, Metternich, and Castlereagh opposed this demand en bloc and worked for two weeks attempting to prepare a suitable compromise plan. They could reach no agreement. Talleyrand, whose policy regarding Saxony was that "Prussia shall not acquire the kingdom of Saxony, at least not in its totality," was perfectly willing to sacrifice part of Frederick Augustus' kingdom, and in this, he was seconded by Metternich. Castlereagh, however, seemed willing to give almost the whole of it to Prussia. After much discussion, agreement was reached, and on January 29 the plan was presented. It offered Prussia some 800,000 of the King of Saxony's subjects and, in addition, 1,400,000 on the Rhine. This, in addition to what it already had, would make Prussia a country of 10,000,000 inhabitants. But Hardenberg was not satisfied. He—or rather, his king—demanded Leipzig as well, and the bargaining began again, more bitter than ever.

Finally, Providence, in the guise of English politics, intervened to dispel the clouds surrounding the Saxon problem. This intervention took the form of Castlereagh's recall to London and the announcement of his replacement in Vienna by the Duke of Wellington. The British government was not completely satisfied with its plenipotentiary in Vienna, and the opposition had been attacking him unmercifully. His policies were generally considered weak, irresolute, and uncertain—a fact which public opinion in England had been as quick to ascertain as Castlereagh's own (Tory) party, and the (Whig) opposition, had been. The recall was therefore justified on the grounds that Parliament was sitting and that Castlereagh, as minister, should be present to defend the government against the attacks that were sure to be launched against it. Still, Castlereagh was unwilling to leave Vienna without having accomplished something. He had been there five months, and he had precious little to show for it. In an uncharacteristic burst of energy, he set about a last attempt to find an answer to the Saxon question. Working day and night with Talleyrand and Metternich on the one side and with Hardenberg, Frederick William, and Alexander on the other, he finally arrived at a new proposal—the third. On February 9, it was formally submitted to Prussia and, somewhat reluctantly, accepted. Saxony was to be divided in half. The more populous and prosperous half, comprising 1,200,000 subjects, was to be left to King Frederick Augustus; it included the city of Leipzig, which Prussia had been demanding so loudly. The half which Prussia was to receive was neither so wealthy nor important as that retained by the King of Saxony, and to console Frederick William for the loss of Leipzig, Alexander agreed to let him have Thurn (which had been hitherto included in the projected kingdom of Poland). This solution had not been easy to arrive at, but the difficulties were due more to Castlereagh than to the Prussians. The Englishman insisted, up to the very last, that Prussia must be given most, and the best parts, of Saxony. Talleyrand, on the other hand, was determined that Prussia should receive as little as possible of that country, and in this, he was supported—albeit "very badly"—by Metternich. Talleyrand explains precisely what the problems were during the discussions:

> Lord Castlereagh, even if he should now be willing (in spite of his former leaning toward Prussia, and the fear he has of compromising what he calls his *character*) to allow only a very small share to be given to Prussia, has such imperfect notions—not to call it outright ignorance—on even the simplest notions of Continental geography, that it is extremely difficult to persuade him of anything. It is said that an Englishman who was here in Prince Kaunitz's time* retailed a number of absurdities respecting the German states and that Prince Kaunitz, instead of amusing himself by refuting them, exclaimed in a tone of the greatest astonishment, "How ignorant the English are!"
> How often have I had occasion to make the same comment, in my own mind, during my conferences with Lord Castlereagh!

On February 1, Talleyrand wrote to King Louis to announce that he had

---

* Prince Wenzel Anton von Kaunitz, an aristocrat not unlike Talleyrand in either temperament or accomplishment, was chancellor of Austria during the reign of the Empress Maria Theresa.

prevailed over Castlereagh's insistence on giving most of Saxony's people to Prussia. "I must say," he added wearily, "that I am even now surprised by my success."

So the five powers were finally in agreement. But the end was not yet. In his notes of December 19 and December 29, Talleyrand had insisted that Saxon territory could not be touched without the consent of Frederick Augustus, legitimate sovereign of that land. On this point, too, he had been victorious against Castlereagh's principle that the king's consent would not be necessary to any disposition made of his territory. Now, in order to preserve the principle of legitimacy for which Talleyrand had fought so hard, the consent of Frederick Augustus to the division of Saxony had to be obtained. It was therefore decided that Talleyrand, Wellington,* and Metternich should journey, early in March, to Pressburg as representatives of Europe. There they were to lay before the King of Saxony the earnest plea of the congress that he agree to make certain sacrifices for the general peace.

By the middle of February the five great powers had settled the two critical problems of Poland and Saxony. In both instances, the solutions had been very much those which Talleyrand had envisaged and of which he approved. Something, at last, had been accomplished, and the congress as a whole, as though encouraged by the strenuous efforts of the Committee of Five, had witnessed increased activity on other fronts. Other committees were formed to discuss specific problems, until there were ten of them.† Secondary but important questions—the abolition of slavery, the policing of rivers and streams, etc.—occupied the attention of the congress more and more. Even a Committee on Diplomatic Precedence had been established to codify the rituals that had been one of the victims of the Revolution. Many meetings were held; hours were spent in debate; reams of reports were submitted. But very little was settled, particularly on important matters. Between November 14 and January 16, for instance, the Swiss Committee had met ten times, but no conclusion on the reconstruction of Switzerland had yet been reached.

Nor had the congress come to any decision on a point close to Talleyrand's heart: the expulsion of Joachim Murat from the kingdom of Naples. The fate of smaller Italian territories was likewise in doubt. No one knew whether to restore Parma to the Bourbons or to give it to Marie-Louise,

---

* Wellington had arrived in Vienna on February 3, but Castlereagh remained at the congress until February 14, in order to complete the agreement on Saxony and to introduce his successor.

† The German Committee; the Slave Trade Committee; the Swiss Committee; the Committee on Tuscany; the Committee on Sardinia and Genoa; the Committee on the Duchy of Bouillon; the Committee on International Rivers; the Committee on Diplomatic Precedence; the Statistical Committee; and the Drafting Committee.

former Empress of the French. Grand Duke Ferdinand, that resilient sprig of the Hapsburg tree, was still in Tuscany, and no one could say if he should be left there or, if not, how to go about getting him out. Cardinal Consalvi, the papal legate, was making a career of alternately cajoling and threatening the delegates of the great powers, but without obtaining anything from anyone. The same was true of the other representatives, official and otherwise, of the Italian princes and states: Neri Corsini, representing the Grand Duke of Tuscany; Ferdinando Marescaldi, who had been retained by Marie-Louise to look after her interests; Antonio Aldini, who filled the same office on behalf of Elisa Bonaparte Bacciochi with respect to her duchy of Lucca. The plenipotentiary of Piedmont was meeting with everyone who could help him, and with a good many who could not, in his efforts to obtain the territorial expansion desired by his sovereign.

In short, the delegates continued to banquet, to dance, to court beautiful women, to whisper among themselves in the salons, and even to meet in the conference chambers of Vienna. Then, abruptly, all the gaiety, frivolity, lovemaking, and business was interrupted—by a funeral mass. Talleyrand had conceived the idea of the mass for the repose of the soul of King Louis XVI, to be held on January 21—the twenty-second anniversary of the execution of that unhappy monarch. At the invitation of the French ambassador, all the sovereigns and nobles of Europe who were in Vienna flocked to the Church of St. Stephen to pray to God for the soul of their brother and cousin, to thank God for having escaped his fate themselves and to weep over the Abbé de Zaignelins' moving sermon. The only notable absentee was Czar Alexander, who denounced the mass as an antirevolutionary provocation. Talleyrand was enormously pleased with the result. "Nothing was wanting in the ceremony," he wrote to King Louis, "neither the pomp due to the object, nor the choice of spectators, nor the grief that the event it recalled must ever excite." The funeral mass, however, was not uniquely moral in intent. It had also a political purpose, as Talleyrand was the first to admit, which was to offer a "solemn lesson" to the assembled sovereigns and ambassadors. Louis XVI had been the victim of the guillotine, but before that, he had been the victim of the weakening of respect for law and of the panic that seizes a nation when it senses that its rulers are incapable of dealing firmly and successfully with crises. Now Louis' brother monarchs, praying in Vienna for the repose of his soul, might still wear their crowns; but woe to them if their subjects once again became aware that the fabric of law was being shredded and the authority of sovereigns arbitrarily being circumscribed during the Viennesse deliberations. Everything about the ceremony—the sermon, the solemnly lugubrious liturgy of the dead, and even Neukomm's music—was designed to expound that lesson. It was altogether a magnificent bit of staging, and Talleyrand

was certain that its moral had not been lost even on the frivolous spectators. Or, at least, he reported, "the heads of the great embassies and the
people of the highest rank who dined with me today persuaded me that
this end had been attained."

Talleyrand may have been correct in his appraisal of the immediate
effect of the funeral mass. It was not, however, an effect that was to endure. Having been conjured up by a sort of liturgical legerdemain, it dissipated quickly once the sovereigns, plenipotentiaries, and nobles returned
to their customary amusements, and much remained to be decided as the
congress dragged on into late February and then into March. It is true that
the settlement of the Saxon and Polish problems had resolved the most explosive issues facing the delegates. There remained, nonetheless, the question of how to reorganize and reapportion the minor states of Germany.
And there remained especially, so far as Talleyrand was concerned, the
problem of Naples. His chief goal in Italy had been summarized in the Instructions very simply: "That Naples be restored to Ferdinand IV." He
would have been content if the congress had moved to expel "him who
reigns at Naples" (as he insisted on calling Murat) and to recognize the
sovereignty of Ferdinand, the Bourbon monarch who had been so uncere-
moniously dethroned by Napoleon. This goal, however, was made difficult
by a treaty (January 6, 1814) in which Austria had guaranteed Murat his
throne and even promised him an increase of territory at the expense of the
states of the church, in return for 30,000 Neapolitan troops. The treaty,
moreover, had been recognized by England (January 11, 1814).* This al-
ready-complicated situation was rendered even more delicate by the fact
that Metternich had been (and possibly still was) the lover of Murat's wife,
Caroline Bonaparte—a predicament which led the usually placid Louis
XVIII to make an unfavorable comparison between the Austrian emperor
and Marc Antony. The latter, Louis remarked, had at least had the honesty to claim Cleopatra for himself and not to allow his policies to be dictated by the amatory adventures of a mere minister. Even so, after the Triple Alliance of January 3, the Austrian government found it increasingly
difficult to support Murat against France and began to drift away from its
Italian ally. By February the breach was so open that Austria began to col-
lect an army of 100,000 men in the Po Valley, to be used in case of trouble
with Murat. The truth of the matter was that Metternich, whatever his relations with Queen Caroline, was sick of King Joachim Murat, whom he
suspected of fomenting unrest in northern—that is, Austrian—Italy. He
now realized that Murat, as a Napoleonic relic, would always be a threat

---

* There is not the slightest documentary evidence to support the belief of many historians that
England and Austria had signed a secret treaty at Prague, in 1813, regarding a postwar settlement
in Italy.

to the peace of Europe and, more important, to Austrian domination in the peninsula. In this, he was supported by England, which feared Murat as a threat to its control of the Mediterranean. Both Metternich and Castlereagh, in fact, by the end of 1814 had made up their minds that Murat must go, and Metternich, with characteristic deviousness, had begun writing directly to Paris, to the Count de Blacas, King Louis' favorite, to that effect. Castlereagh, of course, was kept fully informed and lent his support to Metternich's machinations. Indeed, early in February, after being replaced by Wellington in Vienna, he had stopped over in Paris on his way to London, had a long interview with King Louis, and succeeded in persuading the French king to support some of the Austrian designs on northern Italy, in return for the abandonment of Murat by England and Austria.* Talleyrand, of course, was kept informed of what was happening† and not without foreboding, concurred in this arrangement. His reluctance in this respect was based upon the fact that the bargain on northern Italy, in some of its aspects, violated the precious principle of legitimacy. (The duchies of Parma, Piacenza, and Guastalla, for example, were to be taken from the Queen of Etruria and given to Marie-Louise, former Empress of the French.) And the English, he remarked acidly, given their policy in India, were obviously incapable of understanding what was meant by "legitimacy."

Metternich's deviousness, Castlereagh's bargaining, Louis' acquiescence, and even Talleyrand's vexation—all proved wasted in the final analysis. Murat was indeed to lose his throne, but he was to be deprived of it, not by the Congress of Vienna, but by an astonishing turn of fortune's wheel: the resumption of his imperial crown by Napoleon I, Emperor of the French.

---

* A copy of the instructions drawn up by King Louis after Castlereagh's visit is contained in the Foreign Office archives (F.O. Continent 8). The entire, tortuous story of the Neapolitan negotiations and counternegotiations is contained, in exhaustive detail, in M. H. Weil's *Joachim Murat, roi de Naples, la dernière Année de Règne,* 5 vols., Paris, 1910. On Castlereagh's visit to Louis, see particularly Vol. III, p. 12 ff.

† Some eminent British historians, among them Sir Charles Webster, claim that Talleyrand was "ignorant of the game that was being played." What Webster should say is that the English *thought* him ignorant. In fact, King Louis told Talleyrand more than enough for him to be aware of what was happening (see, for example, Louis' letter of January 28, 1815, *Mémoires,* Vol. III, p. 27), and Metternich himself was constantly throwing out the broadest hints to Talleyrand (see, for instance, Talleyrand's report of February 15, *ibid.,* p. 41ff.).

16

Italy and the Hundred Days

O N THE MORNING of March 7, before Talleyrand had risen, his
niece, Dorothea, was sitting by his bed discussing the rehearsal that
day of an amateur theatrical presentation in which she had a part.
A servant interrupted their conversation to hand Talleyrand a note from
Metternich. Thinking that it was simply a message informing him of a
meeting of the Committee of Five, Talleyrand asked Dorothea to read it to
him. She opened it, and exclaimed, "Napoleon has left Elba! Oh, Uncle,
my rehearsal!"

"Your rehearsal, madame, will take place nonetheless," Talleyrand replied, and then set about preparing for the intricate toilette with which he
began every day. When he was ready, he set out for Metternich's house.
He was the first of the plenipotentiaries to arrive. Metternich immediately
read him a message he had received at six that morning, from the Austrian
consul general at Genoa. It contained only a few lines:

> The English commissioner Campbell has just entered the harbor, inquir-
> ing whether anyone had seen Napoleon at Genoa, in view of that fact that
> he had disappeared from the island of Elba. The answer being in the nega-
> tive, the English frigate immediately put out to sea again.

Talleyrand showed not a flicker of surprise. He asked simply, "Do you
know where Napoleon is making for?"

"The report makes no mention of it."

"He will land on some part of the Italian coast and then make for Switzerland."

"No," Metternich replied. "He will make straight for Paris."

At this point, the other plenipotentiaries—Hardenberg, Nesselrode, Wellington—arrived, and were read the same message. The reaction of all five men was immediate and unanimous. "In less than an hour," Metternich recorded, "we decided on war."

"The results of this occurrence cannot yet be foreseen," Talleyrand wrote to King Louis that night. Yet the business of the congress had to continue. Therefore, Talleyrand explained, on March 9, he, Wellington, and Metternich would go to Pressburg, as planned, to communicate to King Frederick Augustus of Saxony the congress' decision regarding the partition of his kingdom. The ministers were in Pressburg on the appointed day. But before seeing the King of Saxony, Talleyrand had a personal matter to take care of. In the city was Madame de Brionne, the lady who had loved Talleyrand when he was young and who had tried to obtain a cardinal's hat for him when he was still a fledgling cleric. With the advent of the Revolution, she had severed all connection with Talleyrand and, even under the Empire, had been cool to him, so strongly did she disapprove of his politics. Now Madame de Brionne was old and, as Talleyrand had learned, was dying, and she had sent word that as he was now in the service of a legitimate King of France, she was willing to forget the past. Therefore, the King of Saxony, the Duke of Wellington, and Prince Metternich were allowed to wait, forgotten, as Talleyrand knelt before the woman he had once loved and begged her forgiveness for having offended her. He saw tears on her cheeks, and he heard her voice: "So, you are here with me once more. I have always known that I would see you again. As deeply as I have disapproved of you, I have never, for a single moment, ceased to love you."

Talleyrand, the man whose impassivity was a legend in the courts of Europe, was so overcome that he was unable to speak and was obliged to retire to Madame de Brionne's garden until he could recover his composure. When he returned, the two old friends spoke of things past and present and then parted, knowing that they would never again see each other. A few days later Madame de Brionne was dead.

The visit to the king, the following day, was a difficult one. Frederick Augustus "took the protocol which M. de Metternich gave him and handed it, unopened, to his minister . . . and then, turning to us, he spoke a few civil words, but in a very cold and distant manner. . . . We exhausted all the reasons we could to induce the king to consent to the arrangements agreed upon by the powers for the benefit of Prussia. The king and his minister overwhelmed us with objections. They seemed to nourish the hope that all that had been settled could once more be subject to negotiation."

Wellington was less diplomatic in choosing the words for his report to London: "He treated with contempt, and a good deal of vivacity, the recommendation which I gave him not to allow himself to delay his decision from any hopes he might entertain of the success of Bonaparte's plans."

There was nothing to do but declare, however brutally, that Frederick Augustus' protests notwithstanding, the partition of Saxony would proceed according to plan. This Talleyrand, Metternich, and Wellington did, in the form of a positive declaration, just before leaving Pressburg. And, a few days later in Vienna, the areas in question were formally handed over to Prussia.

The chief concern of Europe at this moment was not the spoliation of Saxony or the protests of the Saxon king, but the progress of Napoleon. At Pressburg, Talleyrand, Wellington, and Metternich had learned that on March 1 Bonaparte had disembarked in Juan Gulf and that he had been repulsed at Antibes by a determined commandant. On March 10, the news flashed like lightning throughout the Continent that the city of Lyons had not only opened its gates to the Emperor, but also had accorded him a liberator's welcome. On the thirteenth, the congress issued a declaration "offering to the King of France and the French nation" whatever assistance they might require to repulse the tyrant, and proclaiming that "Napoleon Buonaparte has placed himself beyond the pale of civil and social relations and that, as the disturber of world peace, he has exposed himself to public indictment." On March 16, Louis XVIII consented, for the first time, to wear the ribbon of the Legion of Honor and declared to the Chamber of Deputies, "How can I, at the age of sixty, better end my career than by dying in defense of my country?" On March 17, news reached Louis that Marshal Ney, on whose troops everyone had counted to arrest Bonaparte, had gone over, with all his men, to his former commander in chief. On March 18, Louis XVIII, wearing bedroom slippers, shuffled out of the Tuileries, climbed into his carriage, and was driven away to wait out the Napoleonic hurricane in the safety of Ghent. On the night of March 20 a carriage escorted by a troop of cavalry galloped into the capital. It was instantly surrounded by an immense crowd of cheering citizens, who tore open the carriage doors, hoisted the occupant upon their shoulders, and bore him, in the rain, to the Tuileries, where all Paris had gathered to shout *Vive l'empereur.* By midnight Napoleon I, Emperor of the French, was asleep in his old bed in the palace so hurriedly vacated by the Bourbon king. "A thousand candles," remarked the Count de la Garde-Chambonas, "seemed to have been extinguished in a single instant." And Lord Clancarty, who had replaced Wellington as British plenipotentiary in Vienna,*

---

* Wellington, as soon as he had heard of the turn of events and caught the smell of war in the

wrote: "It was not difficult to perceive that fear was predominant in all the Imperial and Royal personages."

Fear can paralyze, but it can also catalyze. In the case of the Congress of Vienna, it had, somewhat unexpectedly, the latter effect. The fetes and balls continued, of course, but Bonaparte's thunder was sufficient to stir the delegates from their lethargy. Switzerland was the first to benefit from this newfound energy. On March 19 the delegates of the signatories to the Peace of Paris adopted the resolutions reached earlier by the committee on Swiss affairs, and at Talleyrand's suggestion, these resolutions, in the form of a declaration, would be "confidentially and officially" communicated to the Swiss Diet only after it had unofficially, and even more confidentially, accepted them.* Talleyrand was confident that the Diet would do so. "The Swiss plenipotentiaries," he explained to King Louis, "do not think it will completely satisfy one party or completely dissatisfy the other party; thus, the stipulations it contains will, they believe, be generally adopted."

The affairs of Germany were handled no less expeditiously. On March 22, after four months of inactivity—the Committee on German Affairs had not met since November 16—the plenipotentiaries of the sovereign princes and free cities of Germany delivered a note to the Austrian and Prussian delegates demanding, in explicit terms, "a free and permanent union" among the states of Germany and that "the citizens of Germany be assured a liberal constitution and accorded political rights." It was made perfectly clear that, if the great powers wished Germany's help against Napoleon, they would have to agree. Agree they did, responding to the German note in identical terms.†

Both these solutions pleased Talleyrand enormously. The declared neutrality of Switzerland "is especially favorable to France, which, surrounded by fortresses on all other points of its frontiers, is deprived of any on those

---

air, had left Vienna with a hurried explanation to London: "I am going into the Low Countries to take command of the army."

* In these resolutions, the twenty-two cantons were acknowledged, and it was strongly recommended that all the cantons adhere to a federal pact; Vienne and the bishopric of Basel were integrated into Berne; the boundary of Neuchâtel was adjusted; a route between Switzerland and the seaport of Genoa was assured by way of Versoix; and compromises were suggested to resolve the various disputes between cantons over certain territories. Finally, the declaration added that all the powers would recognize "the permanent neutrality of Switzerland within her new boundaries." Thus, Swiss neutrality ceased to be a variable factor and became a principle of international law.

† The dream of a liberal German Confederation was not to be realized. After months of discussion, it was finally decided (June 9, 1815) that a federal Diet should be constituted at Frankfurt, under the presidency of Austria, which would become the central organ of all thirty-eight German states. It would be the role of the Diet to draft the laws of the German Confederation; but, according to Article XIII of this federal act, it would be up to each individual sovereign to grant a constitution to his subjects. Thus, both nationalism and liberalism were rejected in practice, and it would be left to a later age, and to a later statesman, to forge German unity out of blood and iron.

bordering on Switzerland. The neutrality of that country thus gives it a perfectly secure frontier on the only point where it is weak and unarmed." The embryonic German Confederation promised "to be one of the most important elements in the equilibrium of Europe." Still, there remained the problem of Italy, especially of Naples, and to Talleyrand, this was of much more importance than the settlement of German and Swiss affairs. Two of the three "points of the utmost importance to France" that he had set down in the Instructions centered on Italy:

"1. That no opportunity be left to Austria to obtain possession, for the princes of her house, or rather for herself, of the estates of the King of Sardinia.
"2. That Naples be restored to Ferdinand IV."

Now the solution to the Italian problem was coming to a head almost of its own accord. On March 5, Murat had written to the Austrian and British governments that come what might and regardless of Bonaparte's fate, he would remain loyal to his treaties with those governments. But only ten days later, when it seemed clear, at least to Murat, that there was no real obstacle to Napoleon's resumption of power in France, he had made a fatal move and launched an invasion of the Papal States with a force of 40,000 men. Talleyrand was delighted. He had spent months trying to engineer Murat's downfall. Now, he exulted, "Murat himself came to my aid. He was in a state of continual agitation, writing letters upon letters, making declarations, ordering his troops to make marches and counter-marches, and furnishing me with a thousand opportunities for exposing his bad faith."

He had reason to rejoice. Napoleon's success in France, coupled with the threat from Murat in Italy, united the five great powers of Europe as no argument of Talleyrand's would have been able to do. On March 25, England, Prussia, Austria, and Russia concluded a new alliance (called the Quadruple Alliance) which renewed the Treaty of Chaumont and, on the same day, invited France to join it. On March 27, Talleyrand accepted. France, by some trick of fate, was now one of the allies, and along with its co-signatories, it bound itself not to lay down its arms until Napoleon had been utterly crushed, once and for all.

Murat, meanwhile, had continued to advance toward the Po without meeting any resistance. On March 30, however, he had reached the Papal States, which were occupied by Austria. The Austrian outposts had retreated after a token battle, and on April 2 the Neapolitan army entered Bologna. The clash with Austria's troops and the seizure of Bologna had been an overt act of war, and Murat knew it. Yet he was determined to leave a road open for himself in case Napoleon should fail. On April 8 his representative in Vienna presented a note to Metternich, complaining of the "unfriendly attitude" of the Austrian court and declaring that although he had every intention of remaining faithful to his alliance with Austria, he intended, as a "precautionary measure," to occupy the bank of the Po so as to "guarantee order in central and southern Italy." It was a foolish move, Talleyrand noted gleefully, and one "which was regarded as an aggression, and that aggression became the signal of his ruin." Metternich was of precisely the same view. On April 10 he replied to Murat's representative—with a formal declaration of war. The Austrian army immediately went into action by taking the offensive, and Murat beat a hasty retreat down the peninsula. Meanwhile, the court of Vienna was busily signing a new treaty with Naples, but this one was with the former Bourbon monarch, Ferdinand IV. By May 20 Murat, having been beaten at Tolentino and Mignano, signed the Treaty of Casalanza and formally relinquished his crown. Three days later Austrian troops entered Naples, and Ferdinand IV was loudly proclaimed King, not only of Naples, but of the Two Sicilies.*

This final solution was to everyone's liking, except Murat's. Metternich was happy because Ferdinand IV, in return for Austrian support, had pledged himself not to grant a constitution to his Neapolitans and Sicilians, and Austrian Italy was therefore saved from the danger of liberalizing winds from the south. Talleyrand was also content, but for a different reason: "The restitution of the realm of Naples to Ferdinand IV," he wrote, "consecrates anew, by a striking example, the principle of legitimacy. And besides, it was useful to France, because it gave it, as an ally in Italy, the most powerful state of that country."

There was, no doubt, a touch of vinegar in Talleyrand's cup of joy. Ferdinand, after all, had been restored to his kingdom by Austria rather than by France, and it was Austria that imposed its will on northern Italy. But satisfied with having had his way with Naples, Talleyrand yielded willingly on the rest. Marie-Louise obtained the duchies of Parma, Piacenza, and Guastalla for her lifetime. The Archduke Ferdinand of Austria was reestablished in Tuscany, with his old title of Grand Duke. The Queen of Etruria received for herself and her descendants the city of Lucca. And the Archduke Francesco d'Este was acknowledged Duke of Modena, Reggio, and Mirandola. All in all, it was a small price to pay for a large success, and Talleyrand was inclined to be philosophical about it. "Your majesty will perceive that the arrangements to be settled by the congress are being

* October, 1815, Murat made a final attempt to win back his throne, but he was quickly captured by Ferdinand's troops and put to death by a firing squad composed of his former subjects.

carried out before they have been decided," he wrote to King Louis. "But this is of no great importance, and besides, we have not the power to prevent it."

The Italian settlement marked, for all practical purposes, the end of the business of the congress. On June 9 the Final Act was signed, promulgating all that had been decided and done earlier, and the greatest diplomatic convocation that Europe had ever seen was officially over. Its accomplishment had been to give to the Continent the shape that it was to retain, substantially, for the next hundred years and to do so by means of a system of checks and balances so effective that, during this span and for the first time since the *pax Romana* of the Caesars, there was to be only one war of major proportions. The credit for this achievement is primarily Talleyrand's. It was he, who, by his insistence upon the precious principle of legitimacy, by his devotion to the public law, and by his skill in the conference chambers and salons of Vienna, compelled, first the allied plenipotentiaries and then all Europe to accept the principles that were to generate peace and security for the future.

Before the solutions of the congress could be imposed upon Europe, however, a great battle had to be fought. It was reported that the armies of the allies were gathering in Belgium and the Netherlands, and it was there, everyone believed, that the final confrontation would take place between the forces of legitimacy and those of the man whom Talleyrand had branded as "the usurper." No one dallied in Vienna after the closing of the congress. The smell of war was like thunder in the air, and it dissipated utterly the spirit of irrepressible gaiety that had dominated the city for the better part of a year. Trunks were hurriedly packed, and coaches, emblazoned with the arms of their owners, streamed from the Austrian capital as though Bonaparte were at the very gates of the Hofburg. In one of the coaches Prince Talleyrand rode, hurrying to Ghent to join his sovereign. "I long greatly to have you near me," Louis had written. And Talleyrand had replied: "I start at once to lay at your majesty's feet my most respectful homage and devotion." Neither man suspected yet that Talleyrand, having just affixed his name to the greatest achievement of his life, was riding to receive, not his reward, but his dismissal from the king's service.

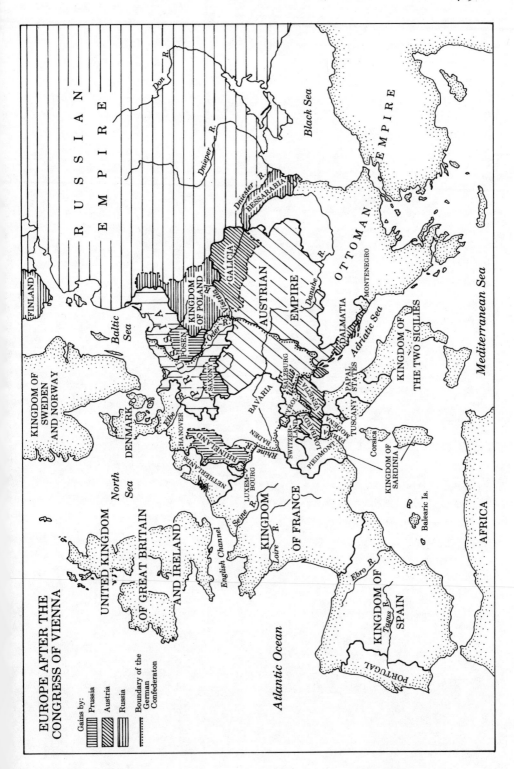

EUROPE AFTER THE
CONGRESS OF VIENNA

Gains by:
Prussia
Austria
Russia
Boundary of the
German
Confederaton

RUSSIAN EMPIRE

OTTOMAN EMPIRE

AUSTRIAN EMPIRE

KINGDOM OF POLAND

GALICIA

BESSARABIA

Don R.

Dnieper R.

Dniester R.

Black Sea

FINLAND

KINGDOM OF SWEDEN AND NORWAY

Baltic Sea

DENMARK

POSEN

SAXONY

Oder R.

Vistula

Danube R.

Danube

DALMATIA

MONTENEGRO

Adriatic Sea

KINGDOM OF THE TWO SICILIES

Mediterranean Sea

PAPAL STATES

TUSCANY

MODENA

PARMA

VENETIA

LOMBARDY

SALZBURG

TYROL

SWITZER-LAND

BAVARIA

BADEN

WÜRTTEMBERG

HANOVER

RHINELAND

NETHERLANDS

LUXEM-BOURG

Elbe R.

Rhine R.

North Sea

UNITED KINGDOM OF GREAT BRITAIN AND IRELAND

English Channel

KINGDOM OF FRANCE

Seine R.

Loire R.

Atlantic Ocean

PIEDMONT

KINGDOM OF SARDINIA

Corsica

Balearic Is.

Ebro R.

KINGDOM OF SPAIN

Tagus R.

PORTUGAL

AFRICA

Part Five

RESTORATION, RETIREMENT, AND REVOLUTION

(1815–1830)

I agree with you that Talleyrand cannot be relied on, and yet I know not on whom His Majesty can better depend. The fact is, France is a den of thieves and brigands, and they can only be governed by criminals like themselves.

—Lord Castlereagh

17

Talleyrand's Hundred Days

A S PRINCE TALLEYRAND proceeded from Vienna at his customary—that is, leisurely—pace to join his sovereign, the Emperor Napoleon was fighting desperately, if not for his life, then at least for his throne. With his usual energy, he had spent the interval since his entry into Paris, on March 20, in reorganizing his government and raising armies. Overcoming, almost miraculously, shortages in supplies, war weariness, and royalist opposition, he succeeded in putting some 284,000 men under arms. The major part of this army—128,000 troops—he formed into a single striking force that he planned to lead into Belgium.

No less energetic on the diplomatic front, he had inaugurated various overtures designed to divide his enemies. The most promising, and to be the most fateful so far as Talleyrand was concerned, was Napoleon's delivery to the Czar Alexander of a copy of the secret anti-Russian treaty signed by Talleyrand, Metternich, and Castlereagh in Vienna. Alexander, as Napoleon had foreseen, was indeed furious, but for the moment, he feared Napoleon even more than the possibility of a coalition among the English, Austrians, and royalist French and, in a burst of good sense, refused to be diverted from the objective of crushing Napoleonic ambitions once and for all.

The prospects of the French emperor were therefore bleak. Facing his army of fewer than 300,000 men were 600,000 Allied troops: 92,000 English, Dutch, and German units under Wellington's command near Brussels; 121,000 Prussians, led by Blücher, on Wellington's left flank; Schwarzenberg's 225,000 Austrian troops, moving westward toward Al-

423

sace; and 168,000 Russians, commanded by the redoubtable Alexander himself, following on the heels of Schwarzenberg's force. But Napoleon was never a man to be daunted by unfavorable odds. He determined to launch a lightning attack into Belgium and there to defeat Wellington and Blücher, the most famous and the most fearsome of the Allied commanders. The psychological impact of such a victory so early in the war would be, he knew, incalculable, both in France and abroad. By June 14 he had grouped his forces. On the fifteenth, he was at Charleroi, and, on the sixteenth, he roundly defeated the Prussians at Ligny. Early in the morning of the eighteenth, a Sunday, the people of Paris were awakened by the cannon of the Invalides booming out the news of Ligny, and the *Moniteur* published the following, decidedly inaccurate, communiqué from the front: "The emperor has just won a sweeping victory over the English and Prussian armies under the command of Lord Wellington and Marshal Blücher. The army is now entering the village of Ligny, beyond Fleurus, in hot pursuit of the enemy."

Imperial Paris then knew its final hours of happy triumph. Mobs of people, beside themselves with joy, surged through the streets and into the squares to hear details of the victory. And as they listened, the final act of the Napoleonic drama was being played out many miles to the north, near an obscure place called Waterloo. At dusk, as the capital of France was illuminated to celebrate the defeat of the allies, the emperor was launching his final attack. Eight battalions of the Old Guard, covered by a heavy artillery barrage, charged Wellington's lines. But the British stood firm and then, despite heavy losses, delivered a volley that shattered simultaneously Napoleon's attack and his last hope of victory. The conqueror of Europe had expended his last reserves and now had no choice but to retreat. With Wellington and Blücher in full pursuit, the retreat degenerated into a rout. Units of the Guard fought with superhuman courage to cover the withdrawal and perished in the attempt. As the confident Parisians were putting out their lights before retiring for the night, their emperor was riding sadly away from the last remnant of his faithful grenadiers. Fearing the effect upon public opinion of the news of Waterloo, he had decided to make a dash to his capital in a final effort to save whatever could be saved.

It was on the day following Waterloo, July 19, at Aachen, that Talleyrand learned of these tremendous events. The bearer of the news was Condé, a prince of the blood and the grandfather of the unfortunate Duke d'Enghien. At the same time, Condé congratulated Talleyrand upon his achievement in Vienna "with a grace," Talleyrand reported to Dorothea, "that I shall never forget."

It is not curious that Talleyrand was more gratified by Condé's courtesy than by Bonaparte's downfall. A royalist of the extreme right, Condé, like the rest of the royal family and their friends, had never ceased to regard Talleyrand with the gravest suspicion. That Condé would now seek out the renegade bishop, ex-revolutionary, and former Bonapartist to offer his congratulations might be a sign of a promising shift in France's political winds. Napoleon's defeat, on the other hand, was, so far as Talleyrand was concerned, an utterly predictable and completely inevitable happening. He had seen the allied sovereigns in Vienna. He knew that given their inflexible determination to resist any form of Napoleonic rule and their numerical superiority, they would sooner or later trap and defeat the emperor. He realized what Napoleon had not: that even an initial French victory over Wellington and Blücher would have changed nothing either in the allies' resolve or in their ability ultimately to triumph.

Thus encouraged and vindicated, Talleyrand drove on to Brussels. There, learning that King Louis, determined to set foot on French soil and repossess his kingdom as soon as humanly possible, had moved his headquarters to Mons, he set out immediately for that town. He arrived on June 24, almost two weeks after leaving Vienna: fourteen days for a trip that normally required seven. The prince had assured King Louis that he was "hastening" to his side, but haste was foreign to Talleyrand's nature. Even when he had reached Mons and it was suggested that he present himself to the king without delay, the prince could not bring himself to accept the inconvenience even of necessary haste. "I am never in a hurry," he yawned, "and there will be time enough tomorrow for that sort of thing."

This reply, of course, was reported to the king within the hour, and the monarch reddened with indignation. However, at the insistence of Chateaubriand—a good friend to Louis and no supporter of Talleyrand—he allowed the courtier to go to Talleyrand and ask him to reconsider. The prince refused. It was late. He was tired. He had been "traveling for weeks." He wished time to meditate before reporting to his majesty. Chateaubriand had to return to his sovereign without the elusive ambassador.

Louis' rage was now truly royal. If M. de Talleyrand did not wish to see him tonight, then he would not see him on the morrow. Orders were given for horses and carriages to be readied. The king would leave Mons the next morning—no, that very night, as soon as the carriages were ready.

A friend, alarmed by the dimensions of the wrath of the usually phlegmatic Louis, fled to Talleyrand's house and announced the king's imminent departure, whereupon the prince leaped out of bed and, after the most hurried toilet of his long life, had himself driven at full speed to the royal lodging. In the courtyard, he found Louis already in his carriage, ready to leave. A courtier dared approach the fuming monarch to whisper, "Sire, it is M. de Talleyrand."

"Impossible," Louis replied loftily. "No doubt M. de Talleyrand is sleeping."

Finally, after Louis had allowed himself to be persuaded that the prince was indeed awake and waiting to see him, he consented, with every sign of reluctance, to receive him in his apartment.

Talleyrand assures us, in his *Mémoires*, that his purpose in seeking an interview at this strange hour was not simply to avoid a royal snub; he wished to save not only Louis, but the Bourbon monarchy, by preventing Louis from showing himself in France as part of the baggage of the allies:

> He was following the English army, and it was this that I wished to prevent. . . . I did not conceal from him how grieved I was to see the manner in which he intended returning to France, that I felt he ought not to appear there in the ranks of foreigners, that he was ruining his own cause, that he should proceed with some kind of escort—or, better still, without any at all—to some part of the French frontier which the foreigners had not yet reached and there establish the seat of his government. . . . I insisted that the king not return there [to Paris] until he could reign as undisputed sovereign and until Paris should be rid of factions and of all foreign troops.

To all this, Louis listened patiently and coldly. When Talleyrand had finished and had handed him a lengthy memorandum setting out his thoughts in detail, Louis spoke: "Prince, we understand that you are about to leave us. The waters will do you good. You will write and give us news of yourself." He then nodded, in an imperious and unmistakable sign of dismissal, and the prince had no choice but to follow the king to the courtyard and stand in respectful silence as Louis entered his carriage and gave the order for the royal procession to set out on the road to Le Cateau.

Talleyrand was left there, pale with anger and humiliation. Turning to the Duke de Lévis-Mirepois, one of the king's friends, he spat out: "Go, M. le Duc. Go and tell all Europe how I have been treated by the king—I, who set the crown of France upon his head!" His only other recorded comment upon this scene was written to Dorothea the next day, when he had regained his composure: "I was not very pleased by my first interview with the king."

The following evening Talleyrand dined with the mayor of Mons and astonished everyone by his good humor and equanimity. "He was in a charming mood," wrote Count Beugnot, one of the guests, "and displayed his wit in amusing stories and telling phrases. I have never before seen him so open and pleasant. Anyone seeing or hearing him would have never believed that he was a minister who had been disgraced only a few hours before. Was he pleased at the prospect of being freed from the burden of affairs when France was in a position more precarious and difficult than ever before? Or was he perhaps disguising, by a show of high spirits, the regret and anger by which he was secretly consumed?"

The likely answer to these questions is that Talleyrand felt both relief and anger, but that neither of these sentiments was the dominant one. Deeper than any such superficial emotions there ran a certainty, a deep and abiding conviction, that, come what might, disgrace or decorations, congratulation or blame, King Louis could not survive without Prince Talleyrand. This Louis knew, and Talleyrand knew that he knew it. More important, Talleyrand was aware that the rest of Europe knew it, too. He was therefore content to sit back and wait for matters to take their expected course.

Almost at once, a desperate group of people set to work to effect a reconciliation. Chateaubriand, according to his own account, turned his talents and his not inconsiderable influence to the task, as did Count Beugnot. "At Mons," Talleyrand noted, "the king's friends harassed me by representing the dangers he was exposed to. . . . At last, pestered and pursued by those who described to me the absolute desolation to which the king would be reduced by his mania for returning to the Tuileries and by the fears that the strangers among whom he would be alone would take advantage of his position to the detriment of France, I surrendered my own convictions." He adds, "I consented to follow the king to Cambrai and to become, like him, part of the English army's baggage."

There was a factor other than the solicitation of King Louis' friends that no doubt contributed to Talleyrand's willingness to "become part of the English army's baggage." This was the assurance of the allies that he, Talleyrand, was correct and that King Louis was wrong. Metternich, for one, urged Talleyrand to "remain firm to *your* idea. Make the king go to France; to the south; to the north; to the west—provided only that it is in his own country, surrounded by Frenchmen, and away from foreign bayonets and foreign support." Vitrolles tells us that there was a letter from Wellington, too, strongly advising Talleyrand to surrender not only his convictions, but his pride as well, for the sake of France and the monarchy.

The astute English duke had sized up the situation as capably as Talleyrand himself. "Notwithstanding the respect and regard I feel for the King [Louis]," he confided to Castlereagh, "I cannot help feeling that the conduct of his family and his government during the late occurrences, whatever may have been his own conduct, must and will affect his own character, and has lowered them much in the public estimation."

Wellington and indeed the English government were very apprehensive over the future of the Bourbon dynasty, and for good reason. It was by no means a foregone conclusion that after Napoleon's final defeat, King Louis would be restored once more to the throne of his ancestors. Among the allies and in France itself, there were many who favored a republic. Others believed that tranquillity would be restored only if Napoleon's son, the King of Rome, were allowed to mount the throne under the aegis of a dependable regency.* And a large party—among whom the Russian czar was preeminent—was agitating openly for the replacement of the elder branch of the Bourbons with the cadet branch, the House of Orléans, in the person of the Duke d'Orléans.

Talleyrand was naturally informed of the Orléanist pretensions, and he recognized the danger to the Bourbon dynasty that they represented. The greatest danger, however, was not from the House of Orléans, but from the Bourbons themselves. Louis' prestige had been drastically weakened during the first Restoration, and the memorandum handed to the king by Talleyrand during the unhappy interview at Mons was largely devoted to a catalogue of the sins of Louis' government during the Congress of Vienna:

> The principle of legitimacy suffered . . . from the faults of the defenders of legitimate power, for they confused two completely different things— *i.e.,* the source of power and the exercise of power. They persuaded themselves, or at least acted as though they were persuaded, that if power is legitimate, it must necessarily be absolute.

These faults, Talleyrand insisted respectfully, had deprived the throne of public support, and in order to regain that support, Louis would have to make certain concessions—"guarantees," Talleyrand called them diplomatically. He would have to recognize and allow liberty of the individual, liberty of the press, an independent judicial system, and the responsibility of the ministers of state for public policy. These were the points on which Talleyrand had insisted in his memorandum. They were the points he had emphasized, when still a bishop, in 1789. And they were the points that he had every intention of pressing upon King Louis in Cambrai, with all the firmness of which he was capable.

King Louis, in fact, now awaiting Talleyrand at Cambrai, was in considerable need of good counsel. Despite the remonstrances of Talleyrand, Chateaubriand, and others, he was more determined than ever to head straight for Paris at the earliest opportunity. This project had been furthered on June 29, when Napoleon had abandoned Paris for Malmaison. At this point, Louis, encouraged by the ultraroyalists in his entourage, particularly by his brother, the Count d'Artois, had decided to smooth the road to Paris by issuing a proclamation to the French people:

---

* On June 22, four days after Waterloo, Napoleon, by then in Paris, had signed an act of abdication in favor of the King of Rome. It was his hope that at least the throne might be salvaged for his son from the wreck of the Empire.

Frenchmen!

When the most wicked of enterprises, supported by the most inconceivable defection, obliged us to leave our kingdom, we warned you of the dangers which threatened you if you did not hasten to throw off the yoke of the tyrant usurper.

We did not wish to join our arms or those of our family to those of the instruments used by Providence to punish this treason. But now that the power of our allies has dispersed the tyrant's followers, we hasten to reenter our country in order to reestablish the Constitution we gave to France, to correct by every means in our power the evils that are the necessary consequence of war and revolt, to reward the good, to enforce the law against the guilty, and, finally, to gather around our ancestral throne that mass of Frenchmen whose fidelity and devotion have comforted and consoled our hearts.

Chateau Cambresis, June 25, 1815.

LOUIS

What France did not need at that particular moment was a statement by its king in exile, threatening Bonaparte's supporters with his royal vengeance and pretending that the royal family, alone among the citizens of *la patrie*, were without blame for the hurricane of Napoleon's Hundred Days. Louis' ill-conceived proclamation offended everyone, the people of France as well as the allies—everyone, that is, except the ultraroyalists headed by the Count d'Artois.

When Talleyrand reached Cambrai on June 26, Louis' credit in Europe had reached its nadir. The people of France, not yet totally disenchanted with Bonaparte, were wavering between indifference and outrage. The allies were disgusted, and Wellington declared that he had been put in an impossible position in his efforts to negotiate terms with the remnants of the imperial government in Paris. Talleyrand, of course, was also disgusted at Louis' lack of judgment. No sooner had he reached the royal headquarters than a Council meeting was called to discuss how to retrieve the situation. With the help of Count Beugnot, the prince had already drafted another proclamation for Louis' signature—one that was "designed to allay, if not to do away with, the evil efforts of the unfortunate one which had been issued at Chateau Cambresis." In it, Louis was to acknowledge that his government had erred during the Restoration and to promise to correct his ways. In other respects, the new proclamation was to be a paraphrase of Talleyrand's memorandum to the king at Mons:

Learning that one of the gates of my kingdom is open to me, I hasten to present myself. I do so in order to recall my misguided subjects; to mitigate those evils I had hoped to prevent; to place myself a second time between the allied armies and the French people. . . . In this way only have I thought fit to take part in this war. I have not allowed any prince of my family to appear in the ranks of the foreigners. . . .

My government may have made mistakes and probably has done so, for there are times when even the purest of motives are unable to guide one and may even occasionally mislead one. Experience alone can teach us, and it will not have done so in vain. . . .

I intend to exclude from my presence only those men whose reputation is a source of grief to France and of terror to the rest of Europe. In the conspiracy hatched by these men, I see many of my subjects who have been misled and a few who are guilty. I who, as all Europe knows, have never made any promise without fulfilling it now promise, as regards those Frenchmen who have been misled, to pardon all. . . . Nevertheless, I owe it to the dignity of my throne, in the interest of my people, and to the peace of Europe, to exempt from pardon the authors and agents of this detestable conspiracy. They will be handed over to be dealt with by the two Chambers which I propose to summon at once.

Frenchmen, these are the sentiments with which I again appear among you. I, whose sentiments time cannot change, nor misfortune erode, nor injustice corrupt; I, your king, whose fathers reigned over your fathers for more than eight hundred years, now return to devote the rest of my days to your defense and comfort.

It was Beugnot's duty to read the draft of Talleyrand's proclamation to the royal Council. When he had finished, there was a moment of silence, and then Louis, his voice not quite steady, asked Beugnot to read it again. After he had done so, the Count d'Artois launched into an impassioned denunciation of the document. It was more a confession and a promise of amendment than a proclamation, he shouted, and such words were unworthy of a king.

"Monsieur will allow me to differ with him," Talleyrand responded quietly. "The use of such words is necessary and, for that matter, appropriate. The king has indeed made mistakes. And he has indeed allowed his affections to mislead him. That is a simple matter of fact."

"Is it to me that you are indirectly referring?" Artois demanded.

"Yes. Since Monsieur has chosen to ask the question, I may answer that Monsieur has done a great deal of harm."

"Prince Talleyrand goes too far!" protested Artois.

"Ah, perhaps that is so," Talleyrand answered quietly. "But then it is the truth that carries me away."

At this point, the Duke de Berry, Artois' son, began a violent attack on the wording of the proclamation and on Talleyrand as well, but he was silenced, to everyone's amazement and to his own great embarrassment, by King Louis: "That is enough, Nephew. I alone decide what may be said in my presence and in my Council." Whereupon the Council, over the objections of Artois and Berry, accepted the proclamation. It was signed by

Louis, countersigned by Talleyrand, and issued from Cambrai on June 28.

The allies were appeased, and the people of France were encouraged. Wellington, in Paris, was delighted; Talleyrand's proclamation would facilitate his task enormously. But Talleyrand himself was not entirely satisfied. Louis had acquiesced, in principle, to the necessity for conciliation, yet he had been impervious to Talleyrand's arguments against an immediate return to Paris. What this meant, in Talleyrand's view, was that Louis, in a capital occupied by the allies, would be unable to give to France the kind of constitutional monarchy that the country must have if the throne were to survive:

> I was convinced that France could find peace and freedom only under a constitutional monarchy. . . . Yet how was a true constitution to be framed in Paris in the presence of sovereigns who were either absolute or aspired to become absolute* and who had no wish to see a great country set an example that they had no intention of following? Far from being able to hope that they would be favorable to the constitutional system in France, there was only too much reason to fear that those who still held the principles of the émigrés [*i.e.,* the ultraroyalists, led by Artois] would make use of them, if not for the immediate accomplishment of their purposes, at any rate as a preparation for future triumphs.

Whether or not Talleyrand was correct on this point was to be demonstrated in the years to come. But for the moment, there was nothing for him to do but to join Louis and his court in the baggage train of the English army on the road to Paris.

The procession halted at Roye on July 3, and Talleyrand took advantage of the layover to relay the latest reports to Dorothea: "Bonaparte is in Cherbourg, looking for a ship. I hope that the English capture him. He has taken a great deal of money with him, and it is said that he intends to go to America."

Actually, the intelligence received by King Louis and his government was garbled, and the truth of Napoleon's situation was somewhat more dramatic. The emperor had arrived in Paris on June 21, after the disaster at Waterloo. His brother Lucien had suggested that he go immediately to the Chamber of Deputies and attempt to salvage what he could by proclaiming a dictatorship. Instead, Napoleon, depressed and in agony with an infected bladder, went straight to Caulaincourt's house and immersed himself in a hot bath. Fouché, the Minister of Police, who was already in touch with Wellington, busied himself with a series of visits—to the Bonapartists among the peers and deputies, whom he told that Napoleon must

---

* The "sovereigns" Talleyrand had in mind were no doubt Alexander of Russia and Frederick William of Prussia, both the embodiment of autocracy in their own domains.

abdicate in favor of the King of Rome, and to the liberals, such as Lafayette, whom he told that Bonaparte must be prevented by any means from establishing a dictatorship.

Napoleon, in fact, was not adverse to assuming the powers of a dictator, but he was curiously unwilling to accept them without the cover of legality. "In the public interest," he explained, "I could seize such power, but it would be preferable for it to be given me by the chambers." But it was too late to expect anything from the chambers, for both legislative bodies had been informed by the tireless Fouché that the emperor intended to dissolve them permanently. On the motion of Lafayette, therefore, the Assembly declared itself in permanent session and decreed that anyone endeavoring to dissolve it would be guilty of treason. Then the chambers voted to send a commission, with Fouché at its head, to the allies, to negotiate the terms of peace; and they did so without consulting the emperor or even advising him of their decision. It was an open rebellion against the imperial authority, and Napoleon was quick to see the implications. He considered a *coup d'état* but, unsure of popular support, could not bring himself to attempt it. He now had a choice: He could abdicate, or he would be deposed. "If I abdicate today," he told Benjamin Constant, "two days from now you will no longer have an army. Those poor fellows do not understand your subtleties. Can you possibly believe that metaphysical axioms, declarations of rights, or harangues from a podium will hold an army together? I could have understood it if I had been rejected when I landed at Cannes, but to abandon me now—that is what I cannot understand. A government cannot be overthrown with impunity when the enemy is only twenty-five leagues away. Does anyone imagine that the foreign powers will be won over by fine approaches?"

The chambers, however, with Fouché and Lafayette at their head, were now willing to try fine speeches, since the force of arms obviously could not prevail. Napoleon, therefore, on June 22, in despair, signed an act of abdication in favor of the King of Rome, while outside, all Paris milled about, shouting *"Vive l'empereur!"* Then, on the twenty-fifth, he left Paris for Malmaison and, from there, made his way first to Noirot and then to Rochefort, where, Fouché had promised, there would be two ships waiting to take him to a neutral country. What Fouché had not told the emperor was that British ships would be patrolling the harbor, and since this was so, Napoleon was unable to board either ship. He was there, on July 3, while Talleyrand was reporting to Dorothea that he was in Cherbourg, trying to get passage to America.*

* The basis of the rumor was that Napoleon's elder brother, Joseph, former King of Spain, had chartered an American vessel at Bordeaux for his own escape. Joseph proposed to Napoleon that they change places and that the emperor sail for America in his stead. Napoleon refused the offer

On July 9, Napoleon indeed opened negotiations with the British, and on the fifteenth, he surrendered to the master of the *Bellerophon*, a Captain Maitland. The arrangement was that the emperor would be granted asylum in England, a short distance from London—an arrangement in which Maitland considerably overstepped the bounds of his authority. The British government was enormously embarrassed. It did not know what to do with the ex-emperor, but it did know that it did not want him in England. Lord Liverpool even suggested to Castlereagh that the best solution might be to turn Napoleon over to Louis XVIII to have him shot. In any case, he explained, it was impossible for him to take up residence in the British Isles, where he was apt to become "an object of popular compassion." Finally, on July 28, after much discussion and agitation, it was decided to send Napoleon into exile on the island of St. Helena.

The important thing, on July 3 so far as Talleyrand was concerned, was that Napoleon was no longer in Paris, that he had been replaced in power by a provisional government, and that the way was open for a second restoration of the Bourbon dynasty. Open, that is, unless Czar Alexander could have his way and put the Duke d'Orléans on the throne; or unless the Bonapartists could compel the chambers to honor Napoleon's abdication and recognize the King of Rome as Napoleon II; or unless the republican party was successful in abolishing the throne altogether. The key to success, as always in French affairs, lay in Paris. Whoever controlled the capital was in a position virtually to do as he wished, or at least to see that what he wished was done. And the man who controlled Paris after Napoleon's departure was Bonaparte's longtime Minister of Police and Talleyrand's perennial associate collaborator and antagonist, Joseph Fouché, Duke d'Otrante. Fouché would have to be won over, somehow, to the Bourbon cause.

The chief problem in this undertaking was not Fouché himself, but King Louis and his extremist entourage. Fouché, despite his fine ducal title, was a regicide, pure and simple; as a member of the Assembly in 1793, he had voted for the death of King Louis XVI. Louis XVIII was prepared to go far in forgiving and forgetting the past, but he was not quite prepared to parley with one of his martyred brother's murderers, let alone accept the implications that such negotiation would necessarily entail—that is, a prominent place for the regicide in the new government.

Talleyrand, while deploring the necessity of making use of a man such as Fouché, whom he regarded as a man who thought only of making capital of a power he no longer possessed and only of giving such advice as

---

and said that he intended to throw himself on the mercy of the English. Joseph therefore boarded his ship alone, on July 4, and sailed for the United States on the same day.

tended to free himself from personal blame, was ever practical. If it was necessary to flatter and bribe Fouché in order to preserve the Bourbon throne, then by all means, Fouché must be flattered and bribed. Moreover, King Louis must be made to accept the situation. Talleyrand's first step was to bring up the matter, in a veiled manner, at a Council meeting on July 3, at Roye. He proposed to the king that the posts in the new government be open to "anyone who is capable of filling them"—even those who had voted for the death of Louis XVI. The effect of his words was unexpected. King Louis, ordinarily the very soul of equanimity, jumped forward in his chair, slammed his hands down upon the armrests, and shouted, "Never! Never, so long as I live!" And there the matter remained, at least for the moment. The idea had been planted in Louis' mind, and knowing Louis, Talleyrand knew also that the seed, if tended carefully, could be brought to germination at the proper time.

Wellington, like Talleyrand, was an eminently practical man, quick to sum up any situation and quicker yet to take any necessary steps. From his own vantage point as commander of the allied armies, he saw that Paris could be occupied peacefully only with Fouché's cooperation, and he was already in communication with the Minister of Police. In the course of several meetings at Neuilly, Fouché had taken great pains to persuade Wellington of what the English duke and Talleyrand already knew very well: that the reestablishment of the Bourbons obliged King Louis to make use of men of the Revolution and even of the regicides of 1793. Wellington now shared Talleyrand's determination to bring Fouché to the king's notice.* When the royal entourage had progressed as far as St.-Denis, where Louis was to spend a few days while Paris was being prepared for his state entry, it was arranged that on July 5, Wellington would invite to dinner, at Neuilly, Talleyrand, Pozzo di Borgo (the czar's eyes and ears)—and Fouché. Louis, under pressure from Talleyrand and Wellington, did not forbid the interview. Indeed, though he could not bring himself to give it his blessing, he did acquiesce in it, albeit sadly. After instructing Talleyrand that he and Wellington were to do whatever was most useful for the royal cause, Louis reported to Vitrolles, he added this line: "I asked them to be gentle with me, and I reminded them that it was my virginity." Vitrolles, who was much more a royalist than the king, stormed out in disgust.

---

* Talleyrand remarks in the *Mémoires* (Vol. III, pp. 161–62) that "Fouché, during the Hundred Days, had engaged in secret correspondence, first with M. de Metternich and then with the court at Ghent, and finally with the Duke of Wellington, persuading them all that he was indispensable to the restoration of the monarchy, because he held the threads of all the intrigues that had overthrown it." Talleyrand's observation is accurate, and a detailed description of Fouché's elaborate intrigues with Metternich, as well as his negotiations with Wellington, is given in a number of contemporary works, among them Thiers, Vol. XVIII, p. 488 ff., and the *Mémoires* of Fleury de Chaboulon, Vol. II, pp. 1–42.

Meanwhile, at Neuilly, Talleyrand, Wellington, and Pozzo di Borgo sat at dinner, listening to Fouché describe the difficulties of the situation in Paris. He exaggerated considerably, as Talleyrand and Wellington knew, the strength of the Orléanist and republican parties in the city, and he did so in order to magnify the importance of the services he was prepared to render King Louis. This was the kind of language which Talleyrand understood better than anyone in the world. From Fouché's rambling account, the prince extracted these facts: An uprising was being prepared in Paris, an armed contest among republicans, Orléanists, and royalists that might break out at the slightest provocation. Fouché was in a position to head off that provocation—or to supply it, depending on where his own advantage lay. Talleyrand therefore cut off Fouché in mid-sentence with a realistic offer: a complete amnesty for his friends and the Ministry of Police for himself in the new government. The price was right. Fouché accepted with alacrity. Everyone shook hands and went home. Since it was very late, as soon as he reached his house Talleyrand began to prepare himself for bed. While his two valets were undressing him—this was at 4 A.M.—there was a commotion in the corridor outside his chamber, and the Baron de Vitrolles burst into the room, in a state of great excitement. Talleyrand took no notice of Vitrolles' agitation but greeted him politely and continued to prepare for bed. To the ultraroyalist's insistent questioning regarding the interview with Fouché, he replied, after an elaborate yawn: "Well, now, M. de Vitrolles. Your Duke d'Otrante told us nothing at all. What do you think of that?"

And poor Vitrolles, flabbergasted—and not knowing that Fouché had accepted the Ministry of Police in Louis' government—could only reply: "He is not *my* Duke d'Otrante. He is *your* Duke d'Otrante." Then, at the crack of dawn, Vitrolles hurried off to Fouché and demanded to know why he had "said nothing to the king's emissaries." Fouché, taking a page from Talleyrand's book, replied, "What would you have had me say to people who said nothing to me?"

Everyone's protestations that nothing had been said did not prevent Talleyrand from escorting Fouché, the very next day—July 7—to Louis at St.-Denis, in order to allow the king to meet his new minister and to allow Fouché to swear allegiance to the king. Chateaubriand has left a vivid portrait of the scene, at which he was present. With his fine eye for the ironies of history, he would not for the world have missed the opportunity of seeing one of Louis XVI's murderers swear loyalty to his victim's brother: "All at once, the door opened, and there entered, in total silence, Vice, supported by Crime—that is, M. de Talleyrand on the arm of M. Fouché. This infernal vision passed slowly before me [in the royal antechamber], entered the king's cabinet, and was lost to view. Fouché had come to swear faith and homage to his lord. The confirmed regicide, on his knees, placed his hands—hands that had caused the head of Louis XVI to fall—between the hands of the martyr-king's brother. The apostate bishop bore witness to the oath." Another witness, Pozzo di Borgo, was more human, if somewhat less dramatic, in his comments. As he watched the ex-bishop and the ex-terrorist leave the king's presence, he muttered to a neighbor, "I'd give anything to hear what those two are saying."

With Fouché safely in the royal stable, as it were, King Louis could now return to his capital, and he did so the day after Fouché's visit, on July 8. The Parisians received him calmly, without counterdemonstrations, but also without noticeable enthusiasm, as he entered the city following the traditional route of the kings of France, by way of the rue St.-Denis. The pomp and splendor of his entry could not obscure the fact that he was returning publicly to the royal city in the wake of foreign armies. Talleyrand was determined that the same would not be said of him. He had chosen to enter Paris at the same time as Louis, but alone, in a borrowed carriage, through the Faubourg St.-Honoré. From there, he drove straight to the rue St.-Florentin. Upon arriving, he found his entire household staff, with his faithful valet, Courtiade, waiting on the doorstep. The house was in perfect order, as though its master had been absent for only a day.

For all practical purposes, the situation of French politics had changed as little as that of Talleyrand's house in the rue St.-Florentin. The day after Louis' official entry into Paris, a royal proclamation announced the formation of the new government, "to the head of which," Talleyrand records, "I was called as president of the Council, [i.e., prime minister] and Minister for Foreign Affairs." With the exception of Fouché, Talleyrand's ministers were, predictably, moderate men all of whom had served under the first Restoration and, before that, under the Empire: Baron Pasquier as Minister of Justice; Baron Louis, Finance; Marshal Bouvion, War; Count de Jaucourt, Marine. There were two major considerations in Talleyrand's mind when these appointments were made, other than the new appointees' undoubted abilities. The first was the necessity of establishing a continuity between the regime of the First Restoration and that of the Second. Never for a moment must it appear to the public that the Hundred Days had been anything more than a temporary suspension of legitimate government. The second was that it was essential "to counterbalance the unhappy choice of the Duke d'Otrante." Fouché may have been necessary to the peaceful reestablishment of the Bourbons, but no one, Talleyrand least of all, was under any illusion concerning the Minister of Police's gift for loyalty to any regime.

The new government was accepted by the king and by the public for what it was: a well-balanced group of men who could, if anyone could,

heal the wounds of the recent upheaval. Only the ultraroyalists were outraged, and their indignation was founded upon the very quality for which
the new ministers had been chosen: moderation. Their exclusion, however,
had been their own rather than Talleyrand's doing. A noted ultra (as the
supermonarchists were called), the Duke de Richelieu, had been offered an
honorable and influential post as Master of the Royal Household, but he
had declined on the grounds that "I have been absent from France for
twenty-four years . . . and I am a stranger there, both to men and to institutions, and I am ignorant of how public affairs are managed." * Richelieu's protestations of ignorance had the appearance of truth to them. But
the real reason, as everyone knew, was that the duke, devoted as he was to
the cause of monarchical absolutism, would have died before consenting to
be in the same room—let alone serve in the same government—with the
likes of Fouché. Talleyrand's disappointment at Richelieu's refusal was
genuine, for he sincerely desired, and believed in the necessity of, a government where all shades of opinion would be represented. Moreover, he
knew that the ultras were safer in the government, where he could keep an
eye on them, than outside it. After failing to persuade the duke to change
his mind, however, he made the best of a bad situation and persuaded
Louis to accept, as Master of the Royal Household, young Alexis de
Noailles, who had been Talleyrand's associate in Vienna and who remained "the prince's man."

The first task of this new, moderate, and nonetheless somewhat disap-
pointing government of Talleyrand's was to restore order to France and to
begin by reorganizing the legislative branch. On July 13, only five days
after his entry into Paris, King Louis issued a proclamation announcing
the dissolution of the Chamber of Deputies and convoking the electoral
colleges for August 25.†

The election of the deputies was, by its nature, largely out of the government's hands, and once given impetus by Louis' proclamation, it went forward almost of its own momentum. But the upper chamber was another
matter. The peers, constitutionally, held the preponderance of legislative
power in the government, and peerages were created by the crown, coun-

---

* Richelieu had entered the service of the Russian czar in 1791, during the Revolution, and had
achieved considerable success, and fame, as governor of the Crimea. His letter to Talleyrand is reproduced in the *Mémoires*, Vol. III, p. 163.

† Each district of France had its own electoral college. This body submitted a list of candidates
to the electoral college of their *département,* and the latter selected the deputies from among the
candidates proposed by the districts. There was a wide margin of choice, for each district's list of
names contained a number of candidates equal to the total number of deputies to which the *de-
partement* was entitled. The departmental college, moreover, could—and often did—name deputies who had not been nominated by the districts. In this instance, King Louis' proclamation stipulated that the departmental colleges must choose at least one-half of their deputies from the
district lists.

seled by the government. Talleyrand therefore held in his hands the key to the upper chamber, and he was determined to use it judiciously. Nonetheless, the opening skirmish ended in a minor defeat for him. In order to preserve the dignity and integrity of the upper chamber, he attempted to persuade King Louis to amnesty all peers for political crimes committed during the Hundred Days, excepting those who had belonged to the chamber of 1814 and who had consented to continue to serve under Napoleon. The latter were to be punished only by the forfeiture of their seats. "I believed," Talleyrand explained, "that by striking in this way at the highest persons in the state, enough of an example would be made to punish those who cooperated in the revolution of March 20 and to emphasize the sanctity of the oath betrayed by those who had abandoned the royal cause." The ultras, however, would have none of Talleyrand's willingness to forget and forgive. They demanded prosecution and prescriptions. Talleyrand then proposed that a decision be postponed until the chambers had been convoked, "to whom, if it became necessary, might be left the responsibility of pointing out the guilty. I hoped that by delaying the decision, time might serve to soften it, if not eliminate it altogether." But Fouché, under pressure from the extreme royalist party, countered by laying before the Council a list of more than a hundred persons whom he accused of treason and who, he demanded, must be either proscribed or tried by courts-martial. "In all fairness," Talleyrand quipped, "it should be noted that Fouché has omitted none of his friends." In the *Mémoires*, he remarks that "after a painful struggle, it was necessary for me to yield, but the list was reduced to fifty-seven persons." Of these, nineteen—almost all military men—were to be brought before a military court or the Court of Assizes, and the other thirty-eight were to leave Paris within twenty-four hours and withdraw to places designated by the police. Talleyrand was able to secure a rather bizarre mitigation: The nineteen men subject to prosecution were to be warned in good time, so that they might escape if they thought proper. "Nonetheless," he observed, "the measure was an act of blundering folly, calculated only to create difficulties and dangers for the government."

This list was compiled by Fouché, and prominent among the names written down was that of Carnot, a sincere revolutionary and republican who had abetted Napoleon's return in March because he believed (as did most old Jacobins) that Bonaparte, for all his faults, was a lesser evil than a Bourbon, however virtuous. Fouché, who had sat with Carnot on a number of committees during the Revolution, took it upon himself to announce to his old associate that he would be permanently exiled from Paris. Carnot, in answer, shouted, "Where would you have me go, traitor?"

It was then left to Talleyrand, as president of the Council, to draw up the list of peers who, having sat in the chamber during the Hundred Days, could no longer be part of the new chamber. Some thirty Bonapartist noblemen were thus deprived of their legislative dignity by a proclamation dated July 24. A more pleasant task was the obverse one, to draw up a list of new peers. This was one that he had approached with some trepidation. King Louis wished to adopt a system of lifetime peerages, so that when a peer died, the title and the seat in the upper chamber would expire with him. The obvious advantage to the throne in this arrangement was that King Louis (and his successors), having the power to create new peers, would be in a position to exercise some measure of control over the policies and votes of the upper chamber. To this, Talleyrand was categorically opposed, and he argued that a hereditary peerage would compensate by its stability and prestige for what it might lack in submissiveness to the royal wish. When Louis finally agreed, "much against his will," Talleyrand set about drawing up a list of new peers for the king's approval. And he did so with an insouciance, not to say a flippancy, that amazed all but those who knew him best.

The eternally astonished Vitrolles records:

> I arrived one morning at the house of M. de Talleyrand and found him there, alone with M. Pasquier [the new Minister of Justice]. He was walking up and down while M. Pasquier sat with pen in hand. "You see," Talleyrand said, "we are busy manufacturing peers. The chambers will meet soon, and since we do not know how much influence we shall have with the deputies, we must be certain of the support of the Chamber of Peers."
>
> Then, continuing to pace back and forth, the prince began mentioning names as they occurred to him—in precisely the way that he might have done it if he had been drawing up a list of guests for a ball or a dinner.

As other members of the government dropped in, Talleyrand asked them all to suggest names, and Vitrolles, although indignant at this offhand—although typical—method of Talleyrand's, could not resist the temptation to make a few suggestions of his own, one of them being the name of a well-known naval commander. Talleyrand, we are assured, was delighted and remarked, "Excellent! That should please the Navy."

The list of new peers was submitted to, and signed by, the king with one objection. He took exception to the name of Count Louis-Mathieu Molé, scion of an ancient and distinguished family, on the grounds that Molé had served—though without noticeable enthusiasm—during the Hundred Days. To Talleyrand's consternation, he erased the name with his own royal hand. But the prince persisted: "Sire, be pleased to restore this name. It is Mathieu Molé * who asks it of you." And Louis, with only a pause,

---

* Count Molé was the direct descendant of Mathieu Molé, first president of the Parlement of Paris.

wrote in Molé's name again and, affixing his signature, approved the list.

That evening Talleyrand, in his drawing room, offhandedly mentioned to the company that the list would be published in the *Moniteur* the next morning, and for the rest of the evening, no other subject was discussed. No one knew but that in a few hours he might find himself, or his father or son, a peer of France. Molé himself was there that evening, and he writes that "tense expectation was on every face. But that of M. de Talleyrand seemed to me more of a mask than ever. It was as though he felt genuinely sorry for people who were capable of so much excitement over such trifles. 'Good Lord,' he answered those who questioned him, 'you'll read the list in the paper. I really don't remember myself who's on it. I believe there is a Monsieur so-and-so.' " And then, Molé says, "He named myself and three others who were present. . . . I was never more amazed in my life."

That was not the end of it. Later that evening, as Talleyrand later told Vitrolles, perhaps spitefully, it was discovered that two important names had been omitted: the Count de Blacas and M. de la Châtre. "And who do you imagine finally reminded me of them?" he asked Vitrolles, with great glee. "No one but Madame de Jaucourt herself, who happened to be dining with me." This Madame de Jaucourt had been, in the days of Juniper Hall, Madame de la Châtre. She had since divorced La Châtre and married Jaucourt, who had been her lover. But apparently she felt constrained in all fairness to plead the cause of her present, as well as her former, husband. And "M. de Talleyrand was vastly amused by this incident," Vitrolles reports. To make matters worse, in Vitrolles' eyes, since the king was already asleep at the hour when Mme. de Jaucourt was busy pleading her husbands' cause, Talleyrand inserted the two names on his own authority and the amended list of ninety-two names was then dispatched to the printer. (King Louis, when he was told of the change, good-naturedly gave his royal approval to it.)

Talleyrand's apparently frivolous approach to the creation of a hereditary peerage disguised—as did his notorious laziness—a deep and well-concealed determination to achieve what he wished. If people chose to think him careless, *léger,* then so much the better; there would be less difficulty in winning approval for his candidates for the peerage. In fact, the ninety-two names submitted to King Louis had been selected only after considerable forethought and with an eye toward the political exigencies of post-Napoleonic France and Europe. The Bonapartists were well represented—by Marshals Berthier and Bessières, for example—as were the ultras, in the persons of Boissy d'Anglas, the Count d'Aboville, and the Count de Canclaux. As in all of Talleyrand's dispositions, there was something for everyone, but not too much for anyone. The concept of the balance of power was as applicable to France as it was to Europe at large.

So far as the Chamber of Deputies was concerned, he was less success-ful. Or rather, he was much too successful. The prince had wished to peo-ple the lower chamber, as he had filled the upper, with a fair representation of public opinion: a working majority of government supporters, of course, but liberally sprinkled with republicans, Jacobins, and Bonapartists. Tal-leyrand, with his profound admiration for the British parliamentary sys-tem, visualized a strong royalist party counterbalanced by an articulate, and perhaps loyal, opposition. But the results of the elections in August were an unpleasant surprise. The Bonapartists, the republicans, the Jaco-bins and, worst of all, the constitutional monarchists—all were virtually wiped out. The large majority of the deputies elected were indeed royalists, but extreme royalists and reactionaries, all of whom regarded the govern-ment in general and Talleyrand in particular with thinly disguised suspi-cion and hostility. Who would have thought that revolutionary France, the scourge of absolutism and the terror of the autocrats, would have been willing to resume the yoke that it had so lately and with so much bloodshed succeeded in shedding? Talleyrand was not the only one in France to be shocked and astonished. The pundits and opinion makers (who had not succeeded very well in this instance in making opinions) promptly christened these amazing deputies *les introuvables*—"the unfind-ables," or, rather, "the impossibles."

The government—that is, Talleyrand's Cabinet—as a result of this unex-pected and wholly unpredictable turn of events, was placed in a difficult position. Several of Talleyrand's ministers—notably Fouché and even Tal-leyrand himself—had been more or less forced upon King Louis by the ex-igencies of the political situation of France and Europe at the conclusion of the Hundred Days. All Europe, including Talleyrand, had thought it necessary for the monarchy's survival to gain popular support by concilia-ting the Bonapartists, placating the republicans, wooing the old Jacobins, and, insofar as might be possible, neutralizing the ultras. The government itself had been formed on the basis of those assumptions, and its ministers were, to a man, moderates and conciliators. Now that middle-of-the-road government was immediately put into the position of having to look for support to a chamber of extremists. And Talleyrand and his ministers were caught between a coldly unsympathetic monarch and a decidedly hostile lower chamber.

Something, obviously, had to be done if the government were to survive, indeed, if it were going to be able to govern. Talleyrand quickly hit upon an expedient; a sacrificial offering to the ultraroyalists: Fouché.

Joseph Fouché was a logical victim. He had been a leader in the Revolu-tion, one of the principal personages of the Empire, and—purely by acci-dent—he had neglected to offer his services to the Bourbons during the

First Restoration. Moreover, his current performance as Minister of Police happily left much to be desired. His harsh measures had awakened great resentment and unrest throughout France, so much so that riots and demonstrations broke out in the south. Fouché's answer was not to soften his methods, but to react with greater severity than before. The people, encouraged as well as outraged by the sight of blood, took to massacring anyone they could lay their hands on who had, actually or fictively, been responsible for any personal or public injustices during the Revolution or the Empire. The government made every attempt to reestablish order, and King Louis issued a proclamation lamenting the fact that "under pretense of making themselves the instruments of public vengeance, Frenchmen have shed the blood of Frenchmen, to gratify their private hatred and revenge," and warning that "all social order will be overthrown if men are allowed to act as both judges and executioners, either as regards the injuries they have sustained or the outrages committed against our own person."

As mild as this proclamation may seem (Talleyrand called it "perfectly normal under the circumstances"), the ultraroyalists—that is, the Chamber of Deputies—took it as a reason, or at least as a pretext, to vote to censure the government. Fouché's obstinate clumsiness had had the effect not only of throwing all France into an uproar, but also, as Talleyrand pointed out, of weakening the government. And now, as though Fouché were not already in a sufficiently precarious position, he brought himself to the edge of the cliff by a surprisingly maladroit attempt at self-exculpation. Or, as Talleyrand expresses it, "Fouché, alarmed at the mischief that he had done . . . wished to retrace his steps and get out of the difficulty by an act of perfidy calculated, as he thought, to bias public opinion in his favor." The "act of perfidy" was to make two confidential reports to the king. In one of them, he depicted the deplorable condition to which the conduct of the allied armies was reducing the people of the occupied provinces and, in the most vivid terms, the consequences that must necessarily be expected. In the second report, he described in great detail the disorder in the south and the violence of partisan emotions in every part of the country. So far as the content of these reports was concerned, Talleyrand admits, "there was nothing to find fault with. M. Fouché had only done his duty, and we are quite ready to admit that what he said in his reports was not far from the truth." The perfidy came when both reports, which were destined for the king's eyes only, were "leaked" to the public press—and especially when Fouché loudly complained that copies had been stolen from him by a person or persons unknown. No one in Paris was unaware that the putatively "unknown" person could be only Fouché himself. Clearly, as Talleyrand said, "it was no longer possible to have anything to do with a man who could have recourse to such measures." He adds, "I asked the king for his dismissal from the ministry. It was not long before he was removed."

The actual removal of Fouché was witnessed and recorded by the ubiquitous Baron de Vitrolles. It occurred late one evening in August, as a Council meeting, held in the rue St.-Florentin, was coming to an end. The ministers were gathering up their papers, and Talleyrand, half sitting on his desk with his bad leg dangling and the other supporting him on the floor, began to speak, apparently at random, of the adventure of travel to distant lands, of France's embassies in far-off places, and particularly of the United States of America. "America! What a splendid country! I know it well, for I have lived there. It is superb."

Some of the ministers—those who had never witnessed one of Talleyrand's characteristic scenes—began taking their leave. But those who knew that the prince rarely rambled without purpose, remained, silent and fascinated, to learn where this apparently pointless discourse on the charms of the New World would lead. Fouché was one of those who remained, making a great show of arranging his papers but listening to every word.

"Ah! The rivers of America," Talleyrand went on, "are rivers such as Europeans have never seen. There is nothing more beautiful than the Potomac. And the trees! There are towering forests of—what do you call them, M. de Vitrolles—we grow them only in boxes here."

"Daturas," supplied Vitrolles.

Talleyrand then abruptly switched subjects and began speaking of the difficulties of being a minister in France and of the thorny questions that the government was soon to settle with the occupying allies. Then the ax fell. "Gentlemen, there is still one country, and only one country, where a minister of the king can retain the advantages of his rank and exercise real influence. And that minister is he who shall represent France in the United States. Gentlemen, I have at my disposal that particular appointment—the best that the king can confer."

An absolute silence fell upon the room. Everyone understood immediately. And Fouché understood. A look of utter hatred blazed in his eyes for an instant, and then he was gone from the rue St.-Florentin, from the government of France, and from the stage of history.*

Scarcely was the disgraced minister out of earshot when Talleyrand turned to Vitrolles and said in a pleasant voice, "I think that this time I've finally managed to wring his neck."

* Talleyrand relented in his determination to be rid of Fouché to the extent that the ex-minister was offered the Dresden, rather than the Washington, embassy. He accepted, and served for a few months, until he was banished for intriguing against the best interests of France. Only Austria, of all the governments to which he applied, would grant him refuge and then only with the somewhat ironic stipulation that Fouché must consent to constant police surveillance of his comings and goings. He died at Trieste in 1820. A mot current in Europe at that time might well serve as his epitaph: "He lacked nothing in ability or in intelligence, but everything in virtue."

But Fouché's neck was not enough to satisfy either public opinion or the ultraroyalists. To both, Talleyrand and Fouché were a team; more, they were and had always been accomplices. They were both defrocked priests. They had both been leaders of the Revolution, ministers under the Directory and under the Empire. Napoleon had regarded them highly, rewarded them richly, and been betrayed by them simultaneously. After Talleyrand himself, Fouché had been the best mind and the most capable servant in the emperor's service. And Napoleon had known it. Indeed, he seldom spoke of one without mentioning the other. Even in his saddest hour, immediately after his final abdication, his sole regret, as he expressed it, was that he had not had enough time to order that both Talleyrand and Fouché be hanged. "But," he had added, "I am willing to leave that chore to the Bourbons."

It was impossible that two men, who had been associated so publicly and for so long a time, could now be separated one from the other in the mind of the people. In fact, the people of France seemed to regard Fouché's dismissal as the prelude to Talleyrand's own. It was rumored in Paris, then throughout the whole of Europe, that Talleyrand's days were numbered; that his government could not survive without the support of the king and the deputies; and that what would seal his fate was the open hostility of an old enemy and even older friend, that most imperious of allied sovereigns, the Autocrat of All the Russias, who had neither forgotten nor forgiven Talleyrand's performance in Vienna.

Talleyrand certainly was not unaware of the precariousness of his position; but he was curiously unmoved by it, and even more strangely, he did nothing to neutralize it. Two of the statesmen who were most closely associated with the prince at this time, Molé and Pasquier, both noted that he seemed to be indifferent to his political circumstance and that he seemed afflicted by a state of intellectual torpor. On one occasion, for example, the prince had considered attempting to mend his bridges with Alexander of Russia but could not bring himself to make the effort. "I feel I should write to the Emperor of Russia," he told Madame de Rémusat, "but it would be a bore, and I would much rather go and play whist with Madame de Laval. You must write the letter for me." She did so, but apparently she did a bad job of it, for Alexander never bothered to acknowledge this indirect overture.

It is possible that Prince Talleyrand simply was tired, that he was beginning to feel the effects of approaching old age—he was sixty-one at the time—or that he had seen too many enemies go down in defeat to believe that a group of fanatics and zealots from the provinces could bring down the man who had vanquished the Russian emperor and the Prussian king at Vienna. It appears more likely that the reason for this lassitude was the one cited by both Molé and Pasquier: an affair of the heart.

> As for M. de Talleyrand, [Pasquier writes] if one had not seen it for one-self, one could hardly believe that, at this moment of all others, when he should be occupied exclusively with business whose weight and responsi-bility would have terrified the most skillful and confident of statesmen, and though more than sixty years old, he should have chosen to indulge himself in a passion so intense as completely to deprive him of his presence of mind.

Something very strange had happened to bring Talleyrand to this pass. And it had happened in Vienna. Dorothea, in the midst of her duties as official hostess of the French embassy during the congress and despite the demands upon her time made by the whirl of amateur theatricals, balls, re-ceptions, and salons, had found the time to take a lover, an Austrian officer, Count Clam-Martinitz. Clam, the offspring of an ancient dynasty, was handsome, young, brilliant, amusing—everything that a young woman might find desirable in a suitor. Moreover, he seemed head over heels in love with Dorothea. By January, 1815, their affair was an accepted feature of Viennese society and an accepted fact in the Hotel Kaunitz. Talleyrand, far from playing the indignant guardian of reluctant virtue, had been calm about the whole matter. His relationship with Dorothea, based as it was at this time exclusively upon familial ties and a social and intellectual com-munity of interests, did not entitle him to interfere. Moreover, he suspected that, once the congress was over and Dorothea and Clam were separated— she to return to Paris, he to pursue his military career as Marshal Schwartzenberg's aide—distance and time would finish what proximity and opportunity had allowed to begin. (Dorothea's husband, Count Ed-mond de Périgord, was almost as phlegmatic as Talleyrand. When he heard of the affair, he proclaimed loudly his intention of challenging his rival to a duel. Then he proceeded to seek forgetfulness in his customary pastimes: whores and gambling.)

Following Talleyrand's appointment as president of the Council, Doro-thea had returned to Paris from Vienna, after a visit to her German proper-ties, and rejoined Talleyrand. But the prince had been wrong in his esti-mate of the situation. Instead of settling down into the routine of domestic life, Dorothea had seemed restless, discontent. Her original indifference to Edmond de Périgord had now, possibly by virtue of comparison with Count Clam-Martinitz, deepened into aversion, and rather than return to his house, she had installed herself on the first floor of the house in the rue St.-Florentin. Parisian society was large enough and loose enough for the husband and wife to go where they wished, each one independently of the other, without risking the embarrassment of an encounter.

And then Count Clam materialized in Paris, his passion for Dorothea intact after months of separation. Talleyrand was alarmed, for the city soon buzzed with the public scandal, and even Edmond, pricked by the needle of public opnion, took notice. Honor demanded satisfaction, and a challenge was issued. An anonymous Austrian spy in the French capital reported, on August 14, to his Viennese master:

> An Austrian major has fought a duel with the Count de Périgord, who is the nephew of Talleyrand and the husband of the youngest of the princesses of Courland. . . . Périgord was wounded by a great saber slash across his face, and the Courland family—Périgord's wife included—are delighted. She is known to have been seeking a separation from him before this event.*

From that point, Dorothea's life in Paris steadily deteriorated. Her loyalties were torn between her children and her lover, her existence made miserable by the presence of an increasingly hostile and bitter husband, her friends estranged by the scandal of it all. By the end of October her situation had become intolerable, and Talleyrand, against his better judgment, consented to her leaving Paris and returning to Vienna. In the first days of November, she and Count Clam left Paris for the Austrian capital, with a detour through Italy. "Madame de Périgord is journeying to Italy," the Austrian spy reported, "where the Duchess of Sagan is already. She will arrive in Vienna with her other sister, the Princess Hohenzollern, and then continue on her way. She is still Talleyrand's favorite."

The report was an understatement. Dorothea's flight from Paris had the effect of revealing to Talleyrand, for the first time, the depth of his feeling for his niece. He realized how intensely and how passionately he loved her. And this long-delayed revelation alarmed him and threw him into consternation, to such an extent that this master of the immobile countenance, this diplomat whose mask was a legend, could no longer conceal his feelings. Chancellor Pasquier, who had already noted that Dorothea's journey to Vienna had completely deprived Talleyrand of his presence of mind, now concluded: "When he realized that the lady, whose presence is so precious to him, had left him in order to go and live in Vienna, he fell into a state of moral and physical prostration that it would be simply impossible to describe."

Everyone who knew Talleyrand—indeed, all Paris—seemed aware of Talleyrand's predicament. Charles de Rémusat remarked that "it was his regret at her absence, the torments of desire and jealousy, the need to see

---

* The Paris police files have no record of this duel—which is not strange, considering that, at this time (early August), Talleyrand was the king's first minister, and Fouché was still Minister of Police.

her once more, that caused M. de Talleyrand to seem so much off his usual form during the last few months." Madame de Boigne (who, it should be remembered, was a friend of Talleyrand's wife) wrote, not without a hint of satisfaction, that "Dorothea's departure drove M. de Talleyrand out of his mind." Molé, a more sympathetic observer, describes Talleyrand as withering away, languishing, "eaten away by the slow fever induced by the loss of the one he loved, and, in a word, dying of a broken heart."

It is possible that Talleyrand was as deeply affected as everyone thought he was. It is also possible that he, who seemed never to act on impulse or without prior reflection, knew Dorothea well enough to realize that only by appealing to her conscience, to her sense of obligation and familial responsibility, could he draw her once more to his side and away from her lover. Whatever the case, this much is certain: Prince Talleyrand, who was famed for the façade of icy impassivity which he presented to the world, was so upset by Dorothea's desertion that he abandoned many of his normal patterns of behavior.

Many, but not all. He was still the consummate diplomat, the intriguer par excellence, and with the skill of the first and the subtlety of the second, he set to work to repair the damage that Dorothea's precipitate departure had wreaked in his personal life. He wrote to Dorothea herself, to the Duchess of Sagan, and to Friedrich von Gentz. The latter (with whom, Talleyrand says, he was "on perfect terms"), was enlisted to represent the prince in Vienna to negotiate for Dorothea's return. Gentz aquitted himself of this mission with his customary assiduity.* He arranged his affairs in such a way as to see a great deal of Dorothea and her lover and, finally, on January 21, entertained them at tea and then at dinner. To all outward appearances, the diligent Gentz was making little progress. Dorothea never received him unless Clam was present, and in Clam's presence, Gentz dared not play his part of Talleyrand's proxy with too great enthusiasm. Yet Gentz knew something that Vienna did not. On January 22, Count Clam paid a formal call upon him—in order to make his adieux. The Austrian officer was leaving that very night, upon orders to rejoin Schwarzenberg's headquarters in Milan.

After his departure, Gentz waited patiently for four days; four days were

---

* Friedrich von Gentz's relationship of respectful familiarity with Talleyrand dated from the Congress of Vienna, where Gentz, as secretary-general of the congress, had ample opportunity to observe and admire the master diplomat in his natural element. Gentz, although himself a statesman of no mean acumen and judgment, was at the same time admirably suited for this sort of quasi-amorous, quasi-familial intrigue. His own sexual irregularities were at once the scandal and the amusement of Viennese society, and his perfect willingness to accept gold as payment for political preference was an open secret in the chancelleries of Europe. Yet for all that, his competence as Metternich's collaborator afforded him both social and political security until his death in 1832. He was, as Harold Nicholson described him, "one of those rare men who are universally mistrusted and yet esteemed."

no doubt sufficient to dull the agony of separation for a lady as resilient as Dorothea. Then, on January 26, he once more called upon Talleyrand's niece and this time was received by her alone. "I spent two hours conversing with Madame de Périgord about her family affairs," he noted in his diary. A similar entry was made under the date of January 30, and a final conversation took place on February 18. On February 19, Dorothea gave a farewell ball to take leave of her Viennese friends, and three days later she entered her coach for the return trip to Paris, under the gratified eyes of Friedrich von Gentz, who duly noted in his journal that night that Dorothea was "a woman remarkable both for the subtlety of her mind as for the depravity of her heart. She has been for me an object of much study and of much amusement."

Many people other than Baron von Gentz speculated on the reason for Dorothea's abandonment of Vienna, and their puzzlement was bequeathed to generations of historians and biographers. The most widely accepted explanation during Dorothea's lifetime, as in later years, was that offered by Count Molé, to the effect that it was in Dorothea's nature and that it was her overriding ambition "to govern some famous and very powerful man." He adds, "It was a role that she had been brilliantly equipped by nature to play." On this occasion, she was "willing to sacrifice love to ambition." This explanation, although it is the one usually accepted,* seems too simple and does justice neither to the uncle nor to the niece. That Dorothea was ambitious, no one could deny; but to state that ambition was the sole reason for her return to Paris and to Prince Talleyrand ignores the complexity of human, especially feminine, nature. For one thing, Talleyrand, as all Europe knew, far from being "very powerful" in February, 1816, was in complete disfavor with the king and at sword's point with both chambers. It seemed hardly likely that so long as the present dynasty retained the crown, there was any chance of a return to real power. And, far from intending to "govern" her uncle, Dorothea seems to have spent her life in a perpetual act of acquiescence. Years after Talleyrand's death, she was to write, "The thing I have least forgotten from my past life is my capacity for submission." And an observer, Sosthène de Rochefoucauld, noted: "In her role as an old man's right hand, she was always able, while he lived, to disguise her own importance and conceal her personal ambitions."

It seems likely that several factors—or rather, several aspects of a single factor—eventually drove Dorothea away from Vienna and Clam and back

---

* See Duff Cooper's *Talleyrand*, p. 230. Talleyrand's most recent biographer, Jean Orieux, ignores the question altogether and speaks vaguely of the mutual "admiration" of uncle and niece. Dorothea's current biographers, on the other hand, adopt a reasoned and comprehensive approach to the problem of Dorothea's motives. (See *Talleyrand's Last Duchess*, by Françoise de Bernardy, pp. 123–31; and *The Duchess of Dino*, by Philip Ziegler, pp. 131–37.)

to Paris and Talleyrand. Clam was, after all, nothing more than a handsome young officer, albeit a promising one, whose head and mouth were filled with the glories of battle and the delights of balls. He may well have bored Dorothea into leaving him. She later complained that her exposure to "M. de Talleyrand's expressive powers have made me difficult to please where the rest of the world is concerned. The minds I now encounter seem to me slow, imprecise, easily distracted by unimportant things." Moreover, Talleyrand, though now aging and increasingly debilitated, still exercised a strong influence on women of all ages, and various ladies of Paris at this time duly noted the prince's "great attractiveness" (Marquise de la Tour du Pin) and his "inexpressible charm" (Aimée de Coigny).

All these things, certainly, played some part in Dorothea's decision to return to Paris. Yet beneath it all there was another, more mysterious element that may well have been the decisive factor in that decision. And this was the unfathomable link that bound together uncle and niece almost from the beginning of their relationship—the mutual knowledge, almost the intuition, that enabled them to arrive almost instantaneously at perfect mutual understanding. "It is very rare," Talleyrand said to her on one occasion, "to have someone who is entirely one's own, without mental reservations, without secrets, without conflicting interests." At about the time of her flight to Vienna, he pointed out to her that "it would certainly be very wrong of us to deprive ourselves of each other, since I should then be compelled to give up my agility, and you, in turn, would be deprived of your peace of mind." It was this almost mystical bond that drew Dorothea to Paris, away from Vienna; to Talleyrand, away from Clam. It was this same bond that was to unite them, once and for all, in that relationship of complete understanding and perfect empathy that was to endure until death intervened twenty-four years later.*

Dorothea's return, to whatever extent it settled the personal affairs of Prince Talleyrand, did little to improve those of France. Talleyrand's enemies and friends might complain of his inattention to affairs of state; but the fact remained that those affairs were controlled, not by Talleyrand's government, or by the chambers, or by the throne, but by the allies. The government of France was in the peculiar position, technically, of being

---

* There is a curious historical tradition, unsupported by evidence, that Dorothea's sister, the Duchess of Sagan, upon her arrival in Vienna shortly after Clam's departure, informed Dorothea of some infidelity on Clam's part and that it was Clam, not Dorothea, who terminated the affair. It is not impossible, in fact, that Clam was already in love with the woman whom he was later to marry, Lady Selina Meade, daughter of an Irish peer. Yet the fact remains that a few weeks after Dorothea had left Vienna, Count Clam was back in the Austrian capital telling all his friends of his deep disappointment and heartbreak over Dorothea's desertion and that he wrote a series of letters to his lost love, pleading for her return. These considerations, coupled with the absence of documentary evidence for the contrary tradition, seems to compel the acceptance of the story that it was Clam, not Dorothea, who was the rejected lover.

still at war with the countries whose armies were occupying its territory: England, Prussia, Austria, and, of course, Russia. Moreover, the government—that is, Talleyrand himself—now faced a Herculean task: the negotiation of a peace honorable to France.

The task was virtually impossible because France simply had no cards left to play. The goodwill that had seemed miraculously to envelop the allied conquerors—particularly the Czar Alexander—in 1814 had now vanished, along with Alexander's friendship and respect for Talleyrand. There was no more talk of fairness or even of principles. There was talk only of the spoils of war. The Prussians wanted, and were demanding, Alsace-Lorraine, the Saar Valley, Luxembourg, Savoy, an indemnity of 1,200,000 francs, and the destruction of the Pont d'Iena. They were also bent on revenge for the humiliations inflicted upon them by Bonaparte, and their army of occupation behaved with such brutality that the Duke of Wellington seriously considered limiting the troops of occupation to British, Austrian, and Russian soldiers. Castlereagh—who had come to Paris to lend Wellington a hand in the negotiations—wrote home that "there is a temper in the Prussian Army little less alarming to the peace of Europe, and little less menacing to the authority of their own Sovereign, than what prevails in the Army of France."

The British government, urged by Wellington and Castlereagh, refused to listen to the schemes of the Prussians and, backed by Russia, put forward more moderate proposals: The northern fortresses of France were to be occupied by an allied army; other French fortresses were to be dismantled, and several frontier districts were to be ceded. Reparation and restitution were to take the form of an indemnity and of the return of the works of art of which Napoleonic France had systematically plundered Europe since 1804 (and which France had been allowed to retain by the First Peace of Paris).

Czar Alexander thought even these proposals too severe; but he found them far preferable to the impossible terms advanced by the Prussian generals, and declaring that he bore France no ill will, he consented to them. Prussia, therefore, standing alone against Britain, Austria, and Russia, was forced to acquiesce, and these were the terms that were presented to Talleyrand, in their final form, in the middle of September, 1815. Talleyrand reacted violently, denouncing both the allied claims and the words in which they were phrased as "insolent." "There was only one opinion in the Council as to the reply that I proposed to make to it, and the king fully shared this opinion." The opinion, set out in two notes dated September 9 and 21, denied, in effect, any and all allied claims to French territory, French money, or works of art then in French museums and asserted in the strongest terms that since the war of the Hundred Days had been against a man (Napoleon), not against a nation, France should be free of any such claims and that the terms of the First Peace of Paris were still in effect and binding upon the allies. Even so, the note went on, the King of France was willing to admit "the cession of any territory which did not form part of ancient France; the payment of an indemnity; and a provisional occupation by a certain number of troops, and for a certain period to be determined later"—all within reasonable limits, of course. Talleyrand, in fact, despite the vagueness of the terms he used in describing the concessions that France might be willing to make, in private was specific about them: "By clinging with energy and decision to the principles and ideas developed in this note, we would have triumphed over the demands of the plenipotentiaries of some of our allies and maintained our position, conceding only: (1) an insignificant cession of territory under pretext of rectifying our frontier; (2) a contribution of at most three or four millions of francs; (3) a temporary occupation by foreign troops of a few fortresses."

The answer of the allied plenipotentiaries was predictable in its indignant refusal to believe that Talleyrand was serious in wishing "to insinuate, in these present negotiations, the doctrine of the *pretended inviolability of the territory of France*" (the emphasis is Talleyrand's) or in putting forward the counterproposals that he had. When Talleyrand presented this note of September 22, expressing the allies' "astonishment" at France's attitude, to Louis XVIII, he found the king "much alarmed as to the results it might have. The *emigrant faction* [*i.e.*, the ultras], who, above all, dreaded being abandoned to their own resources, had so thoroughly persuaded the king that to irritate the allies by any peremptory refusals would compromise both himself and the kingdom of France that his courage at last gave way. He informed me that negotiations must continue, that various temperaments must be appraised and taken into account, and that our present position must be given up only when it appeared that it would be absolutely necessary to do so. Yet, he said, when that necessity was reached, then we must be prepared to make full concessions."

Louis' fear of offending the allies beyond the possibility of reconciliation and thereby of losing allied support for his regime may or may not have been well founded. Talleyrand did not think so. He recognized immediately the implications of Louis' command: "To discuss a demand for cessions was virtually to admit that such cessions were legitimate. It meant reducing the discussions merely to the amount that would be ceded. In short, it rendered us powerless to do anything but concede."

In the face of such a denial of the principles for which Talleyrand had, with Louis' support, fought so long and hard at Vienna, the prince was faced with a difficult decision. He must either obey King Louis and, ultimately, concede everything that the allies demanded or resign from office. The position of Louis—that is, of the monarchy in France—was also in the balance. "The king found himself caught between the allies, who were reiterating their demands, and the courtiers, who pretended to an anxiety about the safety of his person that they did not really feel—and also a chief minister whose views were inflexible and who did not fear to set himself in opposition to the princes of the Council." It was, as Talleyrand himself was the first to appreciate, "a hopeless and cruel dilemma." Yet it was impossible for him to act on the king's instructions. "I was irreversibly determined never, under any pretext whatsoever, to recognize a right that the allies could not possibly have or to affix my signature to any document treating of the concession of any portion of our territory."

On September 24, in a chilling interview with King Louis, Talleyrand put his cards on the table. If the king were unable to give the government his unconditional and complete support, then the president of the council and his ministers would have no choice but to resign immediately. Louis, with an air of total indifference that would have done credit to Talleyrand himself, stared at the ceiling for a moment and then replied casually, "Well, then, I suppose I shall have to find new ministers." Whereupon Talleyrand submitted his resignation, which the king "accepted with the air of a man greatly relieved."

Louis' relief, apparently, was not shared by certain of the allies he had hoped to please. Metternich, Castlereagh, and Lord Stewart (Castlereagh's brother) came together to call on Talleyrand and ask him to reconsider his resignation. "Why do you refuse to become minister of *Europe* with us?" Castlereagh asked.

"Because," Talleyrand replied, "I wish to be minister only of *France*."

The Czar of Russia, on the other hand, not only was pleased at Talleyrand's disappearance from the active political scene, but quite possibly had had a major role in that event. "My retirement," Talleyrand says, "was also a relief to the Emperor of Russia, who did me the honor to hate me not, as he claimed, because I was the friend of the English . . . but because I was the man who, having observed him closely in many different situations, in good and bad fortune, knew precisely how far to count on his generosity of character, on his former liberalism, and on his recent devotion. What he required was a dupe, and this I could never be."

What Talleyrand only hints at was said openly by others. Alexander, through Pozzo di Borgo, his ambassador in Paris, had worked openly and unceasingly for the ruin of Talleyrand's government. Sir Henry Bulwer, who was on terms of friendship with Wellington and Castlereagh, as well as with Metternich, assures us that the situation which forced Talleyrand's resignation was deliberately and directly contrived by Alexander. The czar, he says, had bluntly informed King Louis that France could expect nothing from him so long as Talleyrand was in office but that if the king replaced Talleyrand with the Duke de Richelieu, then France might "expect everything"—that is, the czar would use his influence among the allies to obtain a peace favorable to the interests of France. This was shortly after Waterloo, when Paris and much of France were occupied by allied armies and at a moment when Blücher and his Prussians were demanding, as it were, their pound of flesh.

Bulwer's explanation is supported and clarified by Count de Rochechouart, an intimate of Alexander and of the Duke de Richelieu at this time. Rochechouart explains that the reason for the czar's now frank hatred of Talleyrand was the discovery by the Russian monarch of a copy of the secret treaty signed in Vienna, on January 3, 1815, by Talleyrand, Metternich, and Castlereagh in which France, Austria, and Britain had pledged themselves to resist Alexander's Polish ambitions, if necessary, by war.* Thereafter, Rochechouart says, the czar could hardly bring himself to behave civilly in Talleyrand's presence and was vehemently opposed to the idea that a man who had "conspired" against Russian interests could remain at the head of the affairs of France.

What pleased Alexander most, Talleyrand adds, was not his resignation on September 24, but the appointment, as his successor, both as president of the Council and as Minister of Foreign Affairs, of the Duke de Richelieu. The very same Duke de Richelieu who, three months earlier, had refused a post in Talleyrand's government on the grounds that "I have been absent from France for twenty-four years . . . and I am a stranger there, both to men and to institutions." The very same Duke de Richelieu who held a commission as lieutenant general in the Russian army, who had served long (and well) as governor of the czar's important province of the Crimea, and who, in Talleyrand's somewhat hyperbolic words, was "fully persuaded that, among the images of the divinity on earth, there was none nobler than the Emperor Alexander of Russia."

In the final analysis, Alexander's machinations and his glee were relatively minor considerations in Talleyrand's decision to retire to private life:

> I withdrew from office without very great regret. Truth to say, the honor of governing France should be the aim of the noblest ambition, but circumstances at that time were such that the gratification of this ambition would have been purchased at too high a price. In addition to the sacrifices

* Louis XVIII, in his haste to flee his capital as Napoleon began his Hundred Days, had left a signed copy of the document in his desk drawer, where it was found by Napoleon. Napoleon immediately sent it to Czar Alexander, in the hope of alienating Russia from Austria, Britain, and France. Capo d'Istria was present when Alexander received the treaty and relates that the emperor's "ears turned red with rage."

demanded by our allies (who were now our enemies), I should have encountered difficulties that affected me personally and that would have
made the exercise of power almost impossible for me. Louis XVIII, even
while granting the Charter, was very reluctant to admit the independence
of the ministers as stipulated in that document. Moreover, he bore, with
scarcely concealed revulsion, the burden of gratitude he felt he owed me.

His courtiers, encouraged by the elections, which had resulted in a
Chamber of Deputies eager for reaction, would have constantly tried to
undermine the cabinet over which I presided. And the chamber itself, supported by the king's secret opposition [to Talleyrand's policies], would
have exhibited an ever-increasing animosity and violence. . . . My age,
too, and the fatigue I had undergone because of past events required the
retirement for which I yearned.

I can say, therefore, that it was without regret that I withdrew from public affairs, fully determined never again to assume a position of leadership
in them.

All these remarks of Talleyrand's are, no doubt, in conformity with the
facts of the matter. Yet they are not the whole truth. The various problems
and difficulties cited in the *Mémoires* and even the determination of Alexander to bring about the downfall of his enemy would have been neither
insuperable nor insoluble if Talleyrand had possessed, or had had any
hope of obtaining, the support of the king. Louis' final decision to withhold
that support had little to do with Talleyrand's policies and everything to do
with Talleyrand himself. No one knew that better than the fallen minister.

Louis made his decision out of fear. He was old, he was ill, and he was
immobilized by gout. He had been twice exiled and twice imposed upon
France by foreign armies. Now, in his old age, he wanted nothing more
than to be left in peace and to be allowed to die a king in his royal palace.
If the allies withdrew and left France to its own devices ("abandoned to
their own resources," Talleyrand had said), there would be no peace for
him or, indeed, for France. There was still talk of a republic, of a regency,
of an Orléanist monarchy. Even worse, if the Russian emperor withdrew in
a huff, there was the possibility of France, and Louis, being left to the dubious mercies of the Prussian barbarians. If the inflexible Talleyrand must
go in order to spare his king and his country these horrors, then go he
must. What Louis needed, simply, was Talleyrand's policies, without Talleyrand. And this, despite Talleyrand's reservations with respect to his successor, the Duke de Richelieu, was approximately what he got.

Talleyrand, upon hearing of Richelieu's appointment, had remarked:
"What a perfect choice! He knows the Crimea better than any man in
France." It is true that compared to Talleyrand, Richelieu was hopelessly
inexperienced. Yet he was not without intelligence and good sense, and he
had a streak of stubbornness that had often stood him in good stead. In

addition, he possessed the one quality that Talleyrand, at this critical juncture of history, wholly lacked: the confidence of his king and, more important, the support of the Czar of Russia. With Louis' backing and Alexander's blessing, he was able to grasp firmly what had eluded Talleyrand's
nimble fingers: a peace with which Frenchmen could live. He was forced
to retreat somewhat from the firm line drawn by Talleyrand, but not so far
as to compromise either the strength of France or its honor. The final
treaty, signed on November 20, 1815,* and known as the Second Peace of
Paris, gave to the Netherlands a small strip of France's frontier and, to
Prussia, the Saar. Piedmont received a part of Savoy; Switzerland, a strip
of frontier territory. An indemnity of 700,000,000 francs was imposed, in
addition to which France was required to pay an additional sum to settle
the claims of private citizens for losses sustained during the various Napoleonic invasions.† An army of 150,000 allied soldiers was to occupy the
northern departments of France for five years, with the understanding that
this period might be reduced later to three years.** This army was to be
commanded by the Duke of Wellington, and its relations with the government of France were to be determined by agreement among the ambassadors of the four powers in Paris. The expenses of occupation (estimated at
150,000,000 francs annually) were, of course, to be borne by the French.‡

The single point on which Richelieu had had to acquiesce completely
was that regarding the restoration of the works of art appropriated by
France's imperial armies.§ In fact, he had little choice in the matter. The

* On the same date, the Allied plenipotentiaries signed another document, a treaty in which a
new alliance—the Quadruple Alliance—was formed. The purpose of this coalition was generally
to guarantee the peace of Europe and specifically to guarantee the immediate invasion of France
in the event of the accession of Napoleon "or of that of any of his race" to power in France (Castlereagh to Liverpool, July 17, 1815. F.O. Continent 21).

† The amount of the claims filed by individuals totaled 1.2 billion francs, a sum which Richelieu
regarded as ridiculous and refused to pay. The matter was finally settled in 1818, after torturous
negotiations, for 240,000,000 francs.

** The allies, in their note of September 15, had demanded a seven-year period of occupation.
The occupation, in fact, lasted only three years, and the last allied troops were withdrawn after the
Conference of Aix-la-Chapelle in October, 1818.

‡ At first glance, the sums of money which Richelieu agreed that France must pay seem exorbitant. But it must be recalled that the Napoleonic Wars, which had cost France so dearly in man-
power, had cost it nothing in money. Napoleon, astute Corsican that he was, had made a practice
of compelling the rest of Europe to pay for France's conquests. Upon the emperor's final abdication in 1815, the government of France owed not a franc to anyone and, therefore, had no difficulty in raising the funds necessary to meet its obligations under the Second Peace of Paris. Indeed, France was better off, economically, than any of the occupying powers, with the exception
of Great Britain, and even the British government must have envied the solvency of the French
state, for the English, almost single-handedly, had borne the cost of the anti-Napoleonic campaigns over a ten-year period.

§ Castlereagh and Alexander were as opposed as Talleyrand to the stripping of France's museums in order to make restoration of such works to their original owners. Talleyrand was opposed
because, as he argued, some of these treasures were unclaimed and others had been formally relinquished by treaty. The resistance of Castlereagh and Alexander to the claims of Prussia, Austria,

Prussians, without awaiting the sanction of any treaty or the agreement of their allies, had already begun hauling the objects that they had owned (and some that they had not) to Berlin. Thus encouraged, some of the lesser powers, acting with equal insolence, recovered many of the works that they had deeded to France in past years, either as part of the price of peace or as a token of their affection for its warlike emperor. While Paris looked on in rage and dismay, the King of the Netherlands repossessed those Flemish masterpieces that Napoleon had so proudly displayed in the Louvre. The Florentines took back their Venus of the Medici. The great horses of St. Mark's were taken down from the arch of the Carrousel and restored to their pedestals in Venice. And, perhaps most insulting of all, the Pope, whose predecessor had been as lavish with presents of paintings and statuary to Napoleon as he had been eager to attract the imperial favor, sent a representative, the sculptor Antonio Canova, to make a list of the "stolen goods." To someone who referred to this man as "the Ambassador of the Holy See," Talleyrand replied: "Call him rather the Holy Father's shipping clerk."

Talleyrand's pique was not limited to Richelieu's concessions or to the despoilers of Paris' treasures. That Louis should accept his resignation with alacrity was understandable under the circumstances. But that he should do so peremptorily, without so much as an expression of regret, was a source of particular irritation to the man who, above all, insisted that all things should be done in a fitting manner. The day after his resignation, he was writing to the Duchess of Courland that "we left office without so much as a compliment from the king. The official announcement [of the new government] was cut and dried, and no mention was made of us. It was as though we had never existed."

Louis, however, was as sensitive to good form as Talleyrand. On September 28, he named Talleyrand his Grand Chamberlain—the same office in which the prince had served Napoleon. It was a sinecure, of course, but a dignified one, which gave the recipient entrée to the royal apartments and a place of honor at functions of state. Best of all, it carried with it the not inconsiderable annual stipend of 100,000 francs. Talleyrand was duly notified of the appointment by a royal letter, delivered by a royal herald, and the letter was followed by an official visit of felicitation by the Duke de Richelieu. Talleyrand was mollified. "This has all been done in the proper way," he noted with satisfaction.

Talleyrand's concern with the details of propriety and his apparent lack of concern over the acceptance of his resignation betray a certain rather

---

and many of the Italian states may have been based upon a sincere desire to counteract Prussian vindictiveness, or it may have had its origin in the fact that neither Great Britain nor Russia had been so despoiled.

surprising naïveté. He may well have believed that King Louis, like Napoleon before him, could not do without him and that he would shortly be recalled to office. It is also likely that it never occurred to him that the elder branch of the Bourbon family, the dynasty on whom he had, on two separate occasions, virtually conferred the crown of France, would prove so ungrateful as never to offer him employment again. On both counts, he was wrong. So long as a Bourbon reigned in France, Prince Talleyrand would be left to his own devices and amusements.

18

The Years of Retirement

TALLEYRAND'S fall from power was not entirely a bitter pill or one that he necessarily found difficult to swallow. There was no disgrace attached to it, as proved by his almost simultaneous appointment as Grand Chamberlain. Moreover, the income from this honorable sinecure, added to the considerable wealth that he had accumulated, in one way or another, over the years, made it possible for him to continue to live and to entertain upon the scale that he considered indispensable to his position in the world. Talleyrand's position and his wealth would have been sufficient to ensure his peace of mind. To this, however, were added other things, which, if they did not cause his cup to overflow, at least filled it to the brim. For one thing, he knew, despite his public barbs to the contrary and though his government had fallen, that his policy of moderation would be continued under the Duke de Richelieu and the duke's powerful Minister of Police, Élie Decazes (whom Talleyrand, still smarting from the circumstances of his resignation, described as "a good-looking young barber's apprentice").

More important than policies or politics, however, and possibly even more important than wealth, Talleyrand had finally reached the moment of his existence in which both the women in his life, Dorothea and his wife, were precisely where he wished them to be: Dorothea, at his side, and Catherine, anywhere but in his house.

Dorothea's reappearance in Paris after the Clam-Martinitz *affaire* naturally did not pass unnoticed, nor was Parisian society especially kind in its appraisal of the situation. There was no denying the fact that the Countess

Edmond de Périgord was living, not under the roof of Count Edmond de Périgord* but under that of Prince Talleyrand. In addition, it was well known that the count and countess had obtained no official separation, either civil or ecclesiastical—a point of some importance in legitimist, Catholic France. It was equally common knowledge, or at least common belief, that the relationship between Prince Talleyrand and his niece was something more than platonic. As one visiting English lady, Mary Berry, wrote home, "I went to Prince Talleyrand's; that is to say, *chez la Comtesse Edmond de Périgord*, his niece, whom he has separated from his nephew and whom he has taken to live with himself *dans tout l'étendue du terme à ce qu'on dit* [in every sense that one usually attaches to that term]."

Talleyrand knew better than Miss Berry the utter importance of appearances in Restoration France, and he knew that so long as appearances—that is, the sensibilities of others—were respected, there would be no public scandal. He was extremely careful, therefore, to arrange his household in such a way as to permit society, if it wished, to gloss over his familial irregularities, and, fortunately, the house in the rue St.-Florentin was spacious enough to permit such an arrangement. The prince's suite, consisting of six rooms, was on the mezzanine floor, in the right wing opening onto the rue de Rivoli. On the floor above were the drawing rooms, facing the Tuileries. On the opposite side of the courtyard, literally as far away as possible from Talleyrand's apartments, was Dorothea's suite. But Talleyrand's concessions to public opinion went beyond that. He carefully created and maintained the fiction that his niece was but one member of a large family group, each individual of which was housed, apparently on equal terms, in the prince's house. In addition to the innumerable transient relatives and friends, there were permanent guests in abundance: Alexandre de Talleyrand and his wife, Charlotte, with their four children; Perrey, Talleyrand's secretary; Neukomm, the musician in residence; Bertrand, onetime lover of Madame de Souza, who had left that lady's bed and board for a more secure berth in Talleyrand's household; and the Countess Tyszkiewicz. The latter became Talleyrand and Dorothea's more or less permanent chaperone, accompanied them on all their journeys, and had apartments permanently at her disposal in all the houses belonging to her two charges. Talleyrand's tact and his understanding of human nature thus kept to a minimum both public resentment of and personal pique at his unorthodox ménage. After the initial flurry of gossip, as relayed by the easily shocked Miss Berry (who was a maiden lady), the situation was quickly accepted by European society, at the court of Louis XVIII, and even by the Duchess of Courland—from whom one might have expected a bitter reaction when she was replaced by her daughter in Talleyrand's affections.

* Count Edmond was still living in the rue de la Grange-Batelière.

If Dorothea's permanent presence at Talleyrand's side was a large factor in the tranquil contentment of his years of retirement, the permanent absence of the Princess de Talleyrand played an equally important role. Catherine, at the beginning of the Hundred Days, had fled to England, intending to return to Paris after Napoleon's final destruction. This, however, Talleyrand absolutely forbade. The last thing in the world he wanted was his wife in Paris, let alone, as she undoubtedly wished, in the *hôtel* Talleyrand. Time had not been kind to the once-lovely woman. She had grown fat, red-faced, and ill-tempered. Her lack of taste and of tact, although hardly outstanding in the parvenu society of the Empire, would be nothing less than a scandal among the legitimist nobles who now flocked around the throne of France. Most important of all, Talleyrand was passionately in love with the lady who now, with infinite grace and discretion, did the honors of the rue St.-Florentin.

Once Talleyrand had decided, he lost no time in using every plausible argument, and a few less plausible ones, to persuade the princess to keep the Channel firmly between them. He even wrote to the Marquis d'Osmond, the French ambassador in London (who had been appointed through Talleyrand's influence), asking him to make Catherine "see reason." Osmond did his best—he dared not do otherwise—but it was a difficult task, for Catherine was as ingenious in devising reasons to leave as the prince was in finding pretexts for her to remain. She could not afford the London prices. Her sense of duty required that she be at her husband's side. The English climate was killing her, and her health required absolutely that she return to the sweet air of France. Finally, swearing that she would never consent to remain in England, she consented. "I submit," she told the Marquise d'Osmond. "M. de Talleyrand will find me perfectly ready to avoid any action that might increase the scandal." Then she promptly left England, landed in France, and proceeded to establish herself not far from Paris, at Pont-de-Sains, a property made over to her by Talleyrand at the time of their marriage. It was her intention, she said, to remain at Pont-de-Sains during the summer and to winter in Brussels. Talleyrand, fearing to push her too far, protested, but feebly.

Dorothea, however, was not so easily cowed:

> I have thought a good deal about Madame de Talleyrand's answer [she informed the prince] and I have the feeling that one fine day she will walk into your room. At first, she will say that she intends to stay only an hour, but wants a personal explanation from you—all in the hope of getting more money.
>
> The only proper thing for both yourself and her, since Europe is fated to possess this treasure, is that she reside in England. Looking as she does, she can hardly dare talk of the bad effects of the climate, which she had borne very well, not once but several times. It is perfectly clear that what she wants is to live in France. . . .

Since money is the chief reason for anything that Madame de Talley-rand does, one should always deal with her from that standpoint. So let me presume to give you some advice intended to spare you a distasteful public exchange: Send Monsieur Perrey with a sort of letter of credit and have him tell Madame de Talleyrand for you that she will not receive a farthing of the income from it until she is back in England and that elsewhere she will not get a halfpenny. Then have Monsieur Perrey go with her to Calais or Ostend and stay there with her until he himself has seen her embark.

This, I assure you, is good advice, and you will not do wrong if you fol-low it.

The letter does Dorothea no credit. Its logic may be flawless, and its conclusions may have been sound; but its reflections on the princess' ap-pearance and personality are cruel and vindictive. It may be that it even stirred Talleyrand to pity the woman who, years before, had so charmed him by her beauty and vitality. In any event, he could not bring himself to act with the ruthlessness suggested by Dorothea. Instead, he continued to pay Catherine an annual allowance of 30,000 francs* but commanded that she not stir from Pont-de-Sains.

A few days after Talleyrand had completed arranging his affairs with re-spect to his wife, in mid-June, 1816, he was visited by Charles de Rémusat, who noted that his host, for some reason, was in a mood of sustained exu-berance. "He is at once delighted and delightful. He laughs at everything. He is enchanted with everything. He has not a harsh word to say about anyone or anything."

Catherine's mood, predictably, was quite the contrary. Bitterly unhappy, crushed by her rejection, she remained at Pont-de-Sains, complaining to her friends of "this little cottage, for it is actually that and not a chateau at all," and of the state to which she was reduced. "It is a real privation for me," she wrote to the Chevalier Millin, "which I must simply add to those with which Providence has chosen to overwhelm me. . . . I have sold some of my jewels to buy furniture, china, and table napkins, and I have nothing before me for my peace of soul but the virtue of patience. Amen."

She was constantly begging for news of the great world, and she particu-larly insisted that her correspondents keep her fully informed of the com-ings and goings of Talleyrand and his household. Was M. le prince well? How did he look? Was he in Paris or at Valençay? "If you should have any enchanting details of the pleasures of Valençay, then you should recall, Monsieur le Chevalier, that Valençay is still as much my home as my present house," she wrote imploringly and rather movingly to Millin.

In truth, Pont-de-Sains was not a kind exile for a woman of the princess'

* The amount was doubled in 1826, when Catherine signed over to Talleyrand the property of Pont-de-Sains.

tastes and habits. It was, as she herself said, little more than a cottage, though scarcely a modest one. It was relatively isolated, with no close neighbors, and it attracted few visitors. It was a perfect spot for a recluse—or for a statesman who placed a high value on the solitary pleasures of contemplation, study, and reading. But Catherine, who shared her husband's enthusiasm for people, life, and gaiety, had never known the joys of solitude and had no interest in developing a taste for them. Pont-de-Sains, in a word, bored her to the point of madness. Then, late in 1817, when at last she could bear it no longer, she risked her husband's wrath—to say nothing of her 30,000 francs a year—and, in a mood of near despair, appeared suddenly in Paris.

Prince Talleyrand, who had existed in self-imposed ignorance of his wife's moods, was immediately informed that the princess had been seen in the city. Puzzled but above all indignant that she should thus expose him to public scandal and perhaps to equally public ridicule, he pretended to be completely indifferent to the lady's whereabouts. To anyone who referred to her reported presence in the capital, he replied with calculated and icy contempt. Even the King of France was not spared when he ventured to speak of Talleyrand's embarrassment. One morning, at the levee, in the presence of a crowd of nobles, Louis essayed a jibe at his Grand Chamberlain's expense: "Is it true, Monsieur le Prince, that Madame la Princesse is back? If so, it is a situation to which you can hardly pretend indifference."

"Sire," Talleyrand riposted, "it is indeed true. It seems that I, too, have my March 20"—March 20 being the day of Napoleon's triumphant reoccupation of the Tuileries and of Louis' headlong flight up the road to Ghent. The king paled with anger, then blushed with shame, but could think of no suitable reply. The assembled courtiers exchanged shocked glances and edged away from Talleyrand, who stood in their midst, his face expressionless, a study in tranquillity. But their caution was vain, for from that day, no one at court, least of all the king, dared mention the Princess de Talleyrand's name in the presence of her husband.

Despite the embarrassment of Catherine's presence in Paris, Talleyrand could not bring himself to punish her disobedience, as he threatened to do, by depriving her of funds. Perhaps he was touched by Catherine's apparent desperation, and perhaps he had no wish to risk aggravating the scandal. Whatever the reason, he continued to pretend that he was oblivious to her very existence. And Catherine, with the good sense of which she was often capable, respected the limits of her husband's forbearance. She never ventured to present herself in the rue St.-Florentin, and she never presumed to question either the fact, or the propriety of the fact, that Dorothea—

"Madame Edmond," as she called her—was now and forever more the undoubted mistress both of Talleyrand's heart and of his house.

With resignation in her heart and a substantial income in her purse, she rented a house in the suburb of Auteuil, and there she settled to make what she could of the rest of her years, alone, lonely, slightly ridiculous, comforted only by the occasional company of a few loyal friends.

Never once, in the eighteen years that were left to her, was she to see Prince Talleyrand.

In the several volumes of Talleyrand's *Mémoires*, the interval between 1815 and 1830 is hardly mentioned.* It is as though the prince, having been one of the chief actors in the great drama of the Revolution, the Empire, and the Restoration, found little in those years that merited his attention or at least his own and posterity's consideration. His judgment was correct, to the extent that for the feeble Restoration comedy that was being played out, actors of less brilliance than Talleyrand were certainly adequate and perhaps essential. Still, it was difficult for the prince to reconcile himself to a less prominent position in the conduct of affairs than he had always occupied. Never, so far as is known, did he express openly any desire for a return to power. To do so would have been foreign to his nature. His restiveness, however, was apparent in the concentrated bitterness with which he attacked Richelieu, his works, and his partisans. His letters were capsules of political venom. To Madame de Bauffremont he wrote: "The Richelieu ministry is everywhere despised. Nothing that it does escapes public contempt. And M. de Richelieu himself is the most despised of all, but only because he is the one most in the public eye. No one knows any of the others." In the Chamber of Peers, when the first of Fouché's "criminals," Marshal Ney, was tried, Talleyrand loudly declined to sit in judgment on him. "How sad a day this is for those who signed the Treaty of Pressburg!" he exclaimed. "What an ignominious age we live in!"

King Louis had great esteem for Richelieu and was deeply devoted to his new and powerful Minister of Police, Decazes. Talleyrand's public attacks on the ministers and his private comments as well quickly reached the royal ears. (Decazes had inherited Fouché's highly efficient police agents, and he made constant use of them in keeping his enemies under surveillance.) Louis knew his Grand Chamberlain. "It is wounded vanity and disappointed ambition," he said. Hoping to heal the one and to satisfy the other, he and Richelieu devised a gift for Christmas of 1815. By royal order, Prince Talleyrand, being without male issue, was authorized to be-

* There is only an appendix of some two dozen pages, devoted to his own defense against charges that were brought against him by his enemies during this period. Even those pages are no more than a justification for certain actions during the Napoleonic period.

queath his hereditary peerage and his title of Prince to his brother, Archambaud. Thereafter both peerage and title were to descend in the male line to Archambaud's posterity. Talleyrand was no less delighted than his brother at this dispensation and could scarcely conceal his satisfaction. But "wounded vanity and disappointed ambition" could not be bought off so cheaply, and the antigovernment barbs continued without noticeable abatement.

Early in 1816, Talleyrand decided to visit Valençay. He had not seen his property there since 1808, at the time when the Spanish princes had been his unwilling guests. Dorothea, of course, went with him. She had always preferred the country to Paris, and she delighted in the almost feudal relations which still existed between chateau and village in that remote part of Berry in which Valençay was located.* For her uncle's sake, therefore, she gave up any idea of living on her own estate at Rosny or on any of her properties in Prussia and promptly fell in love with the property, with its immense Renaissance chateau and its great covered avenue.

Talleyrand and his niece quickly set to work removing the traces, or rather repairing the damages, of the princes. The Spaniards had proved to be less than ideal tenants. They had been devoted gardeners, and their experiments in indoor horticulture, with the concomitant need for irrigating their crops, had ruined many of the chateau's exquisite parquet floors. One of the princes, no doubt out of boredom, had been seized with a passion for the building of wolf traps, and, with a truly royal disregard for the property of others, had nailed specimens of his handiwork to the fine paneling of the house. On one occasion, Talleyrand's prisoner-guests had narrowly missed burning down the whole chateau as the result of a Spanish-style auto-da-fé, the victims of this pious exercise being the works of two prominent heretics: Voltaire and Rousseau. Yet, despite the condition of the house and grounds and despite Dorothea's impression that the chateau was *unheimlich*—"not homelike"—they liked everything about the estate from the very first. True, everything would have to be restored and refurbished, yet, Talleyrand wrote to Besnardière, "With a little trouble, Valençay can be made into one of the finest places that one could ask to live in."

One of the first parts of the house to be restored was the apartment that had been assigned to the Duchess of Courland. "I am personally going to concern myself with your room," he wrote to her, "have the carpet taken up, clean everything, and make sure that you will be comfortable here in October. It gives me the greatest pain to see you setting out on so long a journey,† but I hope that you will be able to arrange things so that it will

---

* Valençay lay at a twenty-four-hour carriage ride from Paris and was quite far from any stage-coach or posthorse route.

† The duchess was on the point of leaving Paris on a trip to her estates in Germany.

not be necessary in the years to come and that, my dearest friend, we may pass our lives in the same places, the same enjoyments, and in the same manner as we have in the past. I can think of nothing comparable to the happiness of passing my life with you."

The duchess did not wait for October. In the course of the summer, the prefect of Indre and his secretary paid a courtesy call on the newly established lord of the manor and found the prince busily arranging books in his library,* aided by two "beautiful and elegant women," Dorothea and her mother. It was a reassuring tableau, and the prefect hastened to report to Paris that the prince and his household seemed to have settled down for a long stay at Valençay.

The prefect's visit was not entirely a social one. He came to take the prince's political temperature. Someone from Valençay, who apparently was a frequent guest at the chateau, had reported that Talleyrand was in the midst of an intrigue to restore the Bonaparte dynasty in the person of Napoleon II, the former King of Rome and present Duke of Reichstadt.† For himself, the informant explained, the prince coveted the post of regent of France. In order to foment unrest in the country, he had spread the story that Napoleon was not at St. Helena, but in hiding nearby. All these things, the report continued, had been heard from the prince's own lips. Nothing more was heard of this alleged intrigue, and one may assume that the curious prefect of Indre had been disarmed as much by the sight of Talleyrand's domestic bliss as by the prince's own reassurances.

The prefect was not entirely mistaken in his estimate of the situation. Free from the burden of public office, constantly in the company of the two women whom he most esteemed, he seemed to thrive in the comparatively relaxed atmosphere of the country. Since the post from Paris arrived only twice a week, it was easy to forget the crises and problems of Europe and, as the prince had told his friends, to cultivate his garden. But Talleyrand did nothing on a small scale. In this case, the "garden" was the whole of the surrounding countryside. He took as keen an interest in local affairs at Valençay as he had in European affairs in Vienna. He was now determined to make up for so many years of absentee landlordship, and the little town quickly felt the effects of his benevolence. A new belfry was built for the parish church. A pharmacy and clinic were established, where the poor could obtain medication free of charge. A poorhouse was set up, and

---

* These were the books that Talleyrand had chosen to keep from his library in Paris. The other books were disposed of at auction in London in three series. The third sale had just been completed (May, 1816), and it was by far the most lucrative one, bringing in over 200,000 francs.

† The *Aiglon*, as he was known to the Bonapartists, was a virtual prisoner in Austria, a pathetic youth, abandoned by his mother and left to the care of tutors, who were, in fact, jailers. He contracted tuberculosis, perhaps as the result of neglect, and died in 1832, forgotten by everyone, at the age of twenty-one.

a girls' school was organized. The villagers, in recognition of the efforts of their *seigneur*, elected him mayor—an office which Talleyrand retained for six years.

The prince, for all his attention to his responsibilities as lord of Valençay, was not a country squire. Nor did he pretend to be. Life in the chateau was lived on a scale only slightly less lavish than in the rue St.-Florentin. Talleyrand seldom rose until late in the morning and usually spent several hours preparing himself for the day. His table in the country was equal to that in Paris; the latter, presided over by the celebrated Carême, was reputed to be the finest in all Europe. For Talleyrand was France's reigning gourmet, as well as its most illustrious statesman. Food, like official pronouncements, was not meant to be swallowed in one gulp, but to be savored by means of analysis and debate. Lady Shelley gives the following account of a meal at the prince's table: "During the whole repast, the general conversation was upon eating. Every dish was discussed, and the antiquity of the wine supplied the most eloquent annotations. Talleyrand himself analyzed the dinner with as much interest and seriousness as if he had been discussing some political question of importance."

After dinner, which was served early in the afternoon, Talleyrand customarily went for a drive on his estate, during which he occupied himself with such matters as planting, landscaping, and stocking his fields, forests, and streams with game for his sporting friends. Upon his return to the chateau, some form of entertainment was usually available. Whist and piquet were favorite pastimes, and hardly a day passed that the prince did not play. To a young woman who declared that she did not like cards, Talleyrand said, "My dear, what a sad old age you are preparing for yourself!"

Charades and private theatricals were also popular, and books of all kinds were read by the dozens, both aloud and privately. The supreme entertainment for Talleyrand, however, was what it had always been: conversation. Decades before, in another world, he had been able, as a young man, to enchant the sophisticates of Versailles. Now his words, in addition to their natural charm were able to provide exclusive and authentic information on almost every major event of the past half century, and the prince had no trouble finding a willing audience. There was a constant stream of carriages from Paris to remote Valençay. Old friends came, of course—Countess Tyszkiewicz, Baron de Vitrolles—but new ones also, and some unexpected ones. One of these was Pierre-Paul Royer-Collard, a fervent Catholic and a devout royalist, who once stated that the very sight of a married priest made him want to vomit. Royer-Collard, however, was no self-righteous prig. In an era of political and religious cynicism, no one, not even the few enemies he had, thought even to question the quality of his loyalty to the throne or the sincerity of his religious faith. Royer-Collard happened to be a neighbor of Talleyrand's in the country and by far the most prominent of the personalities in the area. As such, it was to be expected that in the normal course of events, Royer-Collard and his wife would come to pay their respects at Valençay. As the weeks passed and nothing of the kind happened, Talleyrand sent a message to the Royer house, asking if M. le prince might come to call on Monsieur and Madame Royer-Collard. The answer was formal and cold: Monsieur regretted to inform M. le Prince de Talleyrand that the health of Madame Royer-Collard was such that she was unable either to receive or to return visits. But Talleyrand was not to be put off. He had himself driven the twelve miles to Royer-Collard's estate, and as he descended from his carriage and was met by the reluctant host, he said gently: *"Monsieur, vous avez des abords bien sévères"*—"Sir, you are a rather difficult man to approach." Almost immediately, a strong and lasting friendship sprang up between the renegade bishop and the eminent Catholic, between the prince who was living in sin with his niece and the paragon of domestic virtue, a friendship that was to last until Talleyrand's death. Fifteen years after their first meeting, Royer-Collard wrote to Talleyrand: "You know the place that you have had in my life for so many years, a place that no one else can ever fill. You are the only survivor of a race of giants."

Another new friend was a young man by the name of Adolphe Thiers who, fifty years later, was to become President of a French Republic which he helped found. Thiers and Talleyrand were a study in contrasts and not only by reason of the disparity in their ages. Thiers was as bourgeois as Talleyrand was aristocratic, as open and enthusiastic as the prince was reserved, as much a chatterbox as the latter was a conversationalist. Talleyrand was the eighteenth century; Thiers, the nineteenth. Thiers was zeal personified, and Talleyrand had always had a horror of too much zeal. Yet each was attracted to the other by the differences of temperament and outlook that they represented—even though Talleyrand's preoccupation with life, rather than with events, presented an enigma that Thiers was never able to solve. On one occasion, the younger man complained to the older that whenever he wished to talk politics, the prince always found a way to turn the conversation to the subject of women. "But," Talleyrand answered with a smile, "what are politics, if not women?"

Thus, the years of retirement passed, agreeably enough, in the midst of good friends, good food, and good conversation, with summers at Valençay and winters in Paris. In between times, there were vacations in the mountains or at various watering places. Many years before, Talleyrand had formed the habit of visiting Bourbon-l'Archambault, a spa in the central region of France. He had always been happy there, and his servants had noted that he had seemed to throw off the cares of office as soon as he arrived and become the most indulgent of masters and the most pleasant of holiday companions to the humblest of them. Now he returned to Bourbon frequently, and as of old, he seemed always in an almost jocular mood. His letters from there are free even of venomous stories about Richelieu's administration and are designed to amuse and entertain his correspondents rather than to proselytize them. In one letter, he complains that he is out of touch with the world because "nobody sends letters to Bourbon. However, I should say that we have just received a new batch of paralytics recently. So far this year there is not a single rheumatism of our acquaintance." Although Talleyrand always retained his affection for Bourbon, he frequently experimented with new places. For three years in succession, from 1817, he visited the Pyrenees. One summer he went to Switzerland, and, in the fall, to Marseilles. The following year, he was at Hyères. In the last year of his retirement (1829), he visited Aix-la-Chapelle.

Needless to say, the prince did not travel alone. He was always accompanied by Dorothea and (so long as she lived) by the faithful Countess Tyszkiewicz. On such occasions, Talleyrand, his niece, and the countess always traveled separately, each one jolting and lurching across the roads of France in the midst of a separate convoy of coaches and baggage wagons, with maids, grooms, footmen, doctors and secretaries. Dorothea and sometimes Countess Tyszkiewicz usually traveled ahead of Talleyrand in order to make certain that proper accommodations would be ready for him when he arrived. The presence of the Polish countess, the separate travel arrangements—all were part of the patina of respectability which the prince was determined to impart to his household. A new spirit seemed to have taken hold in society; one of morality, almost of puritanism, which, in the way of such things, was most often translated into an exaggerated care for appearances. Before the Revolution, the Abbé Périgord would have amused himself as he saw fit, and so long as he was well mannered about it, no one would have objected. In the days of the Directory and the Consulate, the Minister of Foreign Affairs had lived quite publicly with his mistress and sometimes consorted with other men's mistresses. No one had been shocked—except the prudish Bonaparte. Now the winds of public opinion were blowing in the opposite direction. A rather homely young princess named Victoria was growing up in England, and already the spirit to which she was to give her name was gaining strength. Immorality, or at least the appearance of immorality, was frowned upon by the best society. Talleyrand, always sensitive to the opinions of the great world, was now as careful of appearances as he had been lax in this respect when the existence of a King of France was nothing more than a memory. As Grand Chamberlain to the Most Christian King of France, as a peer of the realm, the prince could not be too careful.

The king apparently agreed. His chamberlain was indeed an ex-bishop, and a married one at that, who treated his wife shabbily and who, it was said, was cohabiting with his nephew's wife. So be it. At least he had had the delicacy not to offend others by making a spectacle of his delinquencies. Louis, therefore, had no qualms in pretending to know nothing of Talleyrand's affairs. And, in June, 1816, he commanded the prince to return to Paris from Valençay for the wedding of the Duke de Berry* to Caroline, Princess of the Two Sicilies.

In fact, he could do no less. Protocol required the presence of the Grand Chamberlain. Moreover, the match had been, to a certain extent, Talleyrand's doing. The first choice for Berry had been the Grand Duchess Anna of Russia, Czar Alexander's sister. The prince had strongly opposed this marriage, ostensibly because of the difference in religion and because he regarded it as a misalliance. A daughter of the parvenu House of Holstein-Romanov was hardly a match for a descendant of Hugues Capet. This was the kind of reasoning that the Bourbons understood, and, when Talleyrand suggested Princess Caroline—who was, after all, also a Bourbon—the royal family had readily agreed to the choice. His real motivation, obviously, was his fear of seeing his enemy's sister seated one day on the throne of France and his unwillingness to see Alexander's influence over the royal family extended by any means whatever.

The wedding, therefore, was something of a personal triumph for the retired minister. He was invited to ride in the king's carriage from Paris to Fontainebleau to meet the bride at a certain crossroads in the forest. (As it happened, it was the very same crossroads where, in 1806, he had stood with Napoleon to greet Pope Pius VII, who was coming to crown an Emperor of the French.) Talleyrand was delighted, of course, and the drive to Fontainebleau passed as agreeably as though the two men were the closest friends. It was one of Louis' chief delights in life to retail gossip and anecdotes about members of his court, a malicious exercise in which, as an accomplished raconteur, he was eminently successful. Talleyrand, who prized clever conversation so highly, was enchanted by the king's affability. "His conversation," he observed, "never flags and is always interesting."

He was no less delighted with the nuptial celebrations at the Tuileries, over which presided the royal chaplain, Monseigneur de Talleyrand-Périgord, the prince's uncle. The prince himself was the center of attention and astonished everyone by his good humor. "He was," Charles de Rémusat

---

* The Count d'Artois' second son, who was next, after the Duke d'Angoulême, in the line of succession. Angoulême had married Marie of France, daughter of Louis XVI, but they were childless and seemed fated to remain so. The sole hope for continuing the direct Bourbon line, therefore, lay with Berry and his bride.

reported to his mother, "as charming as only he can be, constantly laughing, entertaining the king, telling a thousand stories. He was perfectly at ease, with absolutely nothing of the minister—and especially nothing of the dismissed minister—in his demeanor." Talleyrand spent his idle moments in communicating his own observations to Dorothea:* The bride was "charming, gay, alert, and clever," but her neck was not particularly well formed, and she had not yet acquired the poise that was necessary to a Duchess de Berry.

The wedding festivities seemed to indicate to Europe that Talleyrand, despite his more or less forced resignation, was in high favor with the king. Nothing could have been further from the truth. Louis was never a man to confuse affability with approval. He could be, and often was, perfectly charming to his worst enemies. Occasionally, he succeeded in converting critics into friends by this simple stratagem, for few men of the Restoration could resist the warmth of a royal smile or despise the camaraderie implied by Louis' trick of communicating a fact "in strictest confidence" to someone whom he wished to disarm. Prince Talleyrand, however, was one such man. The king might be as brilliant a storyteller and as indefatigable a gossip as he wished; he would not cause the prince to change his politics by an iota. In this case, Talleyrand's politics were one of opposition, and of violent opposition, to the government. So much so that he not only put himself beyond the reach of the king's favor, but shocked and scandalized even his friends. There were even those who, hearing the torrent of abuse issuing from the lips of one who was famed for his prudence and discrimination, concluded that the great statesman's faculties were beginning to fail. "He has completely gone to pieces," the Prussian minister wrote to Berlin. Even Wellington, who was ordinarily well disposed to Talleyrand, told London that "there is absolutely nothing more to be done with him."

The climax came at a dinner party at the British embassy, on November 18, 1816. At this time, the prince was on a rather bizarre diet, according to which he fasted completely until evening. It was noted that in consequence, he ate and especially drank more than was proper at the one meal that he was allowed. By the end of dinner each evening, so long as this regimen lasted, he gave signs of being slightly drunk—and was often overly

* This was their first separation since Dorothea's return from Vienna and the establishment of their relationship upon a permanent basis. It was the beginning of a correspondence, voluminous even by the standards of a letter-writing age, since they were constantly exchanging notes and letters even when occupying the same house. Most of this correspondence—perhaps as many as 3,000 pieces—eventually found its way to the archives of Sagan after Talleyrand's death, where it remained intact, but inaccessible to scholars. In 1945, the archives were removed from the chateau by two men, one apparently a French officer and the other an American, and nothing has been heard of them since. Neither the French nor the American government have any official record of the requisitioned archives.

and indiscriminately loquacious. "Like a woman," Molé notes, "he was unable to resist saying anything that was on his mind. Since the fall of his government, he habitually devoted the time after dinner to diatribes against Decazes and M. de Richelieu." On this occasion, after dinner was over and the other guests had left the dining room, the prince led a group of guests into an alcove, where he began to inveigh against the government. His voice rose, and more people gathered around him. He accused Decazes, probably with some justification, of having set spies upon him at Valençay and Bourbon-l'Archambault. He stopped barely short of accusing the government of treason for having agreed to the terms of the Second Peace of Paris.

Pasquier, who had been Minister of Justice and was now President of the Chamber, was present. He overheard enough of Talleyrand's remarks to make him eager to be gone. When some new guests entered the room, he thought to escape, but Talleyrand noticed his maneuver and shouted after him, in a voice loud enough for everyone to hear, that his criticism of the government was directed only against the Minister of Police, Decazes, the king's favorite, and that Decazes was a *maquereau*—a pimp—with whom "the Chamber cannot have any dealings without degrading itself."

The insult was too gross even for the timorous Pasquier to ignore. Turning to Talleyrand, he replied (according to his own account of the incident) that "M. de Talleyrand may think as he likes, but so long as the king has a Minister of Police, no one has the right to refer to him in such language." Thereupon he fled from the room, as Talleyrand shouted after him, "And the Chamber of Deputies allows itself to be run by the Minister of Police!" This was a direct and mortal insult to Pasquier, who presided over the deputies, but since he was already through the doorway when it was spoken, he pretended not to have heard and continued his headlong flight out of the house. Needless to say, the party was quickly over. The guests could not wait to leave so as to spread the scandal.

Since the evening was still young, Talleyrand himself went to Madame de Laval's house. He now realized that he had acted foolishly. He knew that his enemies would know how to take advantage of his lapse in judgment. He knew, too, the necessity of spreading his own version of the incident. It was in Madame de Laval's salon that, in 1809, he had told the story of his famous scene with the emperor. But in 1809 it was Talleyrand who had been the victim of Napoleon's bad manners. Now it was a minister of the king who had been grossly insulted by Talleyrand, and that under the roof of a foreign ambassador. And, although Madame de Laval and her friends dutifully repeated the prince's highly amusing, but wholly fictitious, account of his evening at the British embassy, no one believed it. There had been too many witnesses to the actual events, and the truth had spread too rapidly throughout Paris. As though the truth were not bad enough, every new telling of it added some detail and put some new expression into the prince's mouth, so that, finally, all Paris believed that the prince had behaved like a maniac and that Decazes had been criminally libeled, if not actually assaulted.

The story spread beyond France, and versions of it appeared in the English press. This even Talleyrand could not ignore, and he wrote—for publication—a letter to Lord Castlereagh, phrased in flawless English, minimizing the incident and appealing to an English guest at the disastrous dinner, a Mr. Tierney, to confirm the accuracy of his account. Unfortunately, Mr. Tierney could not bring himself to do so, and the prince's protestations served only to confirm everyone's belief that he had spoken and acted irresponsibly and even irrationally.

In the face of a scandal of such proportions, the Council of Ministers had no choice but to take some corrective action. A high dignitary of the royal court could not be allowed to insult the king's ministers, or at least he could not be allowed to do so with impunity. The Council met to discuss the case. Molé (Pasquier tells us) insisted that the prince must be deprived of his office of Grand Chamberlain. Most of the ministers—and Pasquier includes himself in this number—felt that a reprimand, to be administered privately by the king himself, would be sufficient. Richelieu and Decazes, however, who had been the chief victims of Talleyrand's rage, adopted a middle course. Perhaps they wished to spare Louis the painful scene, and probably the sharp words, that such an interview might entail. In any event, they argued for, and the Council approved, a decision to banish the Grand Chamberlain from court for an indefinite period. M. de la Châtre, First Gentleman of the Bedchamber, was dispatched with a letter from the king, commanding Talleyrand to refrain from entering the Tuileries until His Majesty specifically should permit him to do so. The prince replied to Louis, in writing, that he submitted himself to the Council's judgment, even though he knew himself to be innocent of any wrongdoing. But he was not so submissive that he could resist the opportunity for a bit of subtle insolence. The letter ended with this phrase: "I would ask your majesty's pardon for my bad handwriting if I did not know that he has long been accustomed to it and that he reads it very easily indeed." To the Duchess of Courland he wrote, "I complained about one of the ministers, and you see where it has gotten me."

The exile from court was not of long duration. After three months, in February, 1817, the prince received another letter from the king, informing him that "at the request of M. le duc de Richelieu," the sentence had been lifted and inviting him to resume his functions at court. Louis' reference to Richelieu's magnanimity could only have been an essay at revenge for the closing sentence of Talleyrand's letter of November. But for the moment, the prince was content to let Louis have the last word. "Let us leave well enough alone," he wrote to the Duchess of Courland. "Let us behave as though we are satisfied and hold our tongues."

A few days later Pozzo di Borgo, Talleyrand's old adversary in Vienna and presently Russian minister in Paris, wrote a curious note to Count Nesselrode: "As I informed your excellency, the Duke de Richelieu very thoughtfully asked the king to allow the Prince de Talleyrand to reappear at court. . . . A new intrigue has been the result of that kindness."

"Intrigue" was too strong a word. What had happened was that Talleyrand had indeed returned to court and had been well received by the king. Both men pretended that nothing had happened, that there had been no "incident," that Talleyrand's recall had not been motivated by Richelieu's belated realization that to keep the prince away from the court was to make the rue St.-Florentin the unofficial center of opposition. In the same spirit of oblivion, Talleyrand had presented a request directly to the king— over the Council's head—asking that he be created Duke de Valençay. Louis, thinking the request harmless enough and since it cost nothing to erect a dukedom, immediately sat down and signed the letters patent that Talleyrand had prepared. But the Council, when it heard of the king's action, was thrown into an uproar. Valençay, it was explained to Louis, was the place where Napoleon had held part of the Spanish royal family captive. If the village and chateau were made a duchy, it would seem that the Bourbons were approving retroactively of the emperor's perfidious treatment of Louis' relatives. Actually, the point was well taken. The King of Spain at the moment was none other than Ferdinand VII—the Spanish prince who had nailed wolftraps onto Valençay's splendid paneling. Louis withdrew his signature, and Talleyrand was compelled, at least for the moment, to submit once more.*

If Louis was required to be firm about erecting Valençay into a duchy, he was disposed to be more accommodating about the principle of creating a dukedom. Sensing Talleyrand's disappointment and sensing too that a disappointed Talleyrand would probably be more dangerous than a ducal Talleyrand, the king determined to do what he could to satisfy him. If he wished to be a duke, then a duke he would be. On August 31, Louis conferred the title of duke—not Duke de Valençay, but Duke de Talleyrand— and peer of the realm on his former premier. But it transpired that it had

* Talleyrand was to obtain his wish in 1829, when, on the occasion of the marriage of his nephew Louis to Alix de Montmorency, King Charles X conferred the title of Duke de Valençay on the happy bridegroom. Talleyrand was only slightly less generous than the king and made over the property of Valençay to his nephew, but he reserved to himself the use of the chateau and the income from the land for the rest of his life.

not been for himself that Talleyrand had sought the ducal coronet. Titles he had aplenty, and he preferred to retain the princely style that he had made illustrious, and feared, throughout Europe. It was, he explained to his majesty, for his brother, Archambaud. So, in October, Louis wearily set his seal to another decree, this one permitting the prince to transfer the title and the peerage* to his brother Archambaud and to his male descendants in the direct line.†

Talleyrand was happy, but not entirely. As fond as he may have been of Archambaud, it was not wholly in a spirit of fraternal benevolence that he had cajoled Louis into making him a duke. He wanted the honor for Archambaud's heirs, or more accurately, he wanted Dorothea to be a duchess. But the proprieties had to be observed. It would have been unseemly to make the son a duke when the father remained a simple marquis. Moreover, there was precious little in the son's career that could warrant such a splendid title. Dorothea would therefore have to remain Countess de Talleyrand until, in the natural course of events, Archambaud's coronet descended to his heirs. Since the new duke was eight years younger than his brother, the event did not seem imminent.

But very shortly, Providence, and another king, intervened. On December 2 a letter arrived in Paris, by royal courier, from Ferdinand, King of the Two Sicilies. Ferdinand had already, late in 1815, conferred the title of duke on Talleyrand, as a token of royal gratitude for the prince's surrender of his sovereign principality of Benevento.** It had been, however, merely a titular and personal honor: a dukedom without a duchy, but with an income—which Talleyrand valued more than land—of 60,000 francs. Now Ferdinand added a territorial title, the duchy of Dino. Since Archambaud was already outfitted with a French dukedom, Talleyrand felt free to pass this new title on to Edmond, though he was careful to keep the income for himself. Thus, Dorothea was transformed from the Countess de Talleyrand into the Duchess de Dino—the style by which she is best known in history.

Talleyrand was ecstatic. "Today," he wrote to the Duchess of Courland, "Dorothea enters into the enjoyment of all those advantages at court pertaining to the title of duchess.‡ . . . The King of Naples has just granted to

---

* A title of nobility and a peerage were not synonymous in France. A peerage gave the right to sit in the upper chamber and conferred a position at court. The great majority of French nobles, even when their titles were authentic (and many were not), were not peers of the realm.

† Archambaud thus founded the ducal line of the Talleyrand family, which continued into the twentieth century and was not extinguished until the mid-1960's, with the death in New York of the fifth duke's widow, Anna Gould, heiress to one of America's great robber-baron fortunes.

** Talleyrand's efforts at Vienna to oust Murat from the Neapolitan throne had already been rewarded with a gift of 6,000,000 francs.

‡ "All those advantages," in the final reckoning, were comparatively few and only slightly more ridiculous than those that later generations were to prize so highly. The most cherished of these was the right of a duchess to sit, in the royal presence, on a taboret (a backless and armless stool),

Edmond and Dorothea the title given me to go with my Neapolitan duchy. They are to be called the Duke and Duchess of Dino. Dino is the name of a royal estate located in Calabria." The truth was that Dino was hardly "royal" or even ducal. It was a bleak and tiny island in the Gulf of Poli-castro, known only for the abundance of rabbits on its barren shores and of anchovies in its waters. But Dorothea was as pleased as her uncle, both for his sake and for her own. It was true that to a Princess of Courland, a wretched little stretch of Mediterranean rock may not have seemed very grand and that rabbits, even in huge numbers, were not the stuff of which splendid titles were ordinarily made. But a duchy was a duchy, and there were many such in Germany and even in France that were hardly more magnificent than the island of Dino. Moreover, the title had a fine ring to it, and the prestige and precedence that it gave at court were most accept-able.

Despite this veritable shower of honors on the House of Talleyrand, the year 1817 was not entirely a happy one. It signaled the beginning of the end of the friends and intimates who belonged to Talleyrand's own genera-tion and initiated a string of personal losses which were to continue until the prince's own demise. The first death was that of the earliest of Talley-rand's friends, Choiseul, whose friendship had survived a half century of differences in opinion. "He was the last of the people with whom I was raised," Talleyrand wrote, "and I am almost the only survivor of that gen-eration. How sad it is." In the same year, Madame de Staël and Du Pont de Nemours also died. The prince had always been fond of the latter, and he seemed deeply moved by this new loss: "I was associated with him from my early youth. The losses that now befall me every day serve to attach me even more to those whom I love." Of Germaine de Staël, however, he had as little good to say when she was dead as he had when she was alive. He was too old to feel the need for hypocrisy. "Paris talks of nothing but the death of Madame de Staël," he wrote to Courland, "and especially of her marriage—which we learned of only when she was dead. For years, it seems, she had been Madame Rocca, but had not had the courage to let it be known.* This was not as it should have been. And it was even less so that she gave birth to a little Rocca, who has suddenly appeared to claim a third of her estate and whose existence she forgot to mention during the negotiations for the marriage of Madame de Broglie.† You must admit

---

while less distinguished ladies were required to stand. So seriously were such privileges taken in the kingdom of France that the right to the taboret had been the cause of a violent and lengthy al-tercation, during the reigns of Louis XIV and Louis XV, between the nonroyal dukes and the princes of the blood.

* In a final excess of folly, Madame de Staël had married her lover of long standing, a slightly unsavory Italian of unknown antecedents.

† Madame de Staël's daughter, whose dowry to the Duke de Broglie had been arranged on the supposition that she would be the sole heir to her mother's immense fortune.

that I was right in saying, as I always did, that she was an insensitive woman."

The greatest blows came in 1821, which saw the deaths of Madame de Rémusat, whose friendship Talleyrand had treasured, half-amorously, since the carefree days of the Consulate, and of the gentle and beloved Cardinal de Talleyrand, the prince's uncle. The hardest to bear, however, was the death, in August of that year, of the Duchess of Courland, whom he had loved for many years and whose intimate friendship he had retained once passion had cooled. Dorothea's mother, in addition to her uncontested beauty, had been gifted with wit, intelligence, and judgment, and it was these qualities that had endeared her to the discriminating man who had been her lover for so long. It had undoubtedly been difficult for her when she was displaced in Talleyrand's heart by her own daughter, but she seems never to have given any outward sign of bitterness, let alone indulged herself in recriminations and accusations of infidelity.* "I shall mourn for her until the day of my death," Talleyrand wrote, "a day which I am now able to face without regret." These were not empty words, uttered in a moment of intense sorrow and then forgotten as the pain of loss lessened with the passage of time. Many years later Dorothea found him in tears over a portrait of the duchess. Greatly embarrassed, he wiped away the tears and said softly, "I do not believe that there was ever a woman on earth more worthy of being adored."

It was this same year, 1821, that another death occurred, but one which resounded far beyond the narrow confine of Parisian society. On July 14, Talleyrand was dining at the house of Madame Crawford—the center, for the moment, of the *beau monde*—when the news was received that, on May 5, Napoleon had died on St. Helena. Everyone in the room was stunned, unable to speak, until Madame Crawford broke the silence with a cry: "Oh, good God! What an event!" She was answered by the prince's quiet, deep voice, from a corner of the room: "No, madame. It is no longer an event. It is only a bit of news." Then he went on to speak of the man who had been his master and then his enemy in words that are perhaps the sole adequate summing up of the most remarkable man of modern history:

> That he was a genius is undeniable. He had no equal in energy, in imagination, in intellect, in his capacity for work, in his extraordinary productivity. And he was a sagacious man. He was not equally gifted in judgment, but even here, when he was willing to take the necessary time for it, he knew how to make use of the judgment of others. Thus, he acted only rarely on the basis of his own unsound judgments, and he did so only when

---

* The Countess de Boigne refers in her *Mémoires* to the Duchess of Courland's "despair" at being "thrown over" by Prince Talleyrand. But despair is a condition that the countess seems to attribute to anyone and everyone in any circumstance that was less than happy.

he was unwilling to pause long enough to ask the advice of others. He had a keen understanding of what was great, but not of what was fitting or beautiful.

His career was the most astonishing one in a thousand years of history. But he made three serious mistakes, and it was these mistakes that caused his fall—a fall that was hardly less amazing than his rise to power. These were: Spain, Russia, and the Pope. Aside from these three, he made few political errors—surprisingly few, when one considers the number and extent of his commitments and the importance and rapidity of the events of which he was a part.

He was, beyond doubt, a great man, an extraordinary man, almost as extraordinary by virtue of his talents as by his accomplishments. He was, in my own opinion, the most extraordinary man to appear in our time or in many hundreds of years.

By the end of his first year in retirement it had become clear to Talleyrand that his chances of being recalled to office were very small indeed. His excessive language in criticizing the government, his particular and vocal antipathy toward Decazes (who was, after all, not only one of the most able of the ministers, but also the king's favorite), and his stubborn refusal to see any good in Richelieu (whose policies of moderation and sanity were precisely those established by Talleyrand himself and approved by King Louis), and, finally, his public disgrace over the scandal at the British embassy had put him beyond the political pale so far as the government was concerned.

So, freed not only of the burdens and restrictions of office, but also of the immediate possibility of their recurrence, he undertook two projects, both of which, apparently, he had considered for some time. The first of these was the composition of the *Mémoires*, or at least of that section of them—Part I to Part IX—covering the period up to August, 1816. The second project does him less credit than the first. It was, in essence (and in truth), to sell certain state documents of France to the Austrian government.* On January 12, 1817, Talleyrand wrote, to Prince Metternich in Vienna, a letter which was delivered by a Portuguese courier (through the good offices of Madame de Souza). The letter is remarkable for the majestic tranquillity with which the prince proposes to strike a not very reputable bargain with the Austrian premier:

> It is my intention to suggest something to you today which, in my opinion, will not be without interest for you. A certain Russian gentleman has recently inquired at the Ministry of Foreign Affairs whether or not the cor-

---

* The whole affair of the French papers remained totally unknown until 1933, when, through the efforts of M. Lacour-Gayet, the pertinent documentation was published in *Revue de Paris*, issue of December 15, 1933. It was therefore too late for this incident to be included in Lacour-Gayet's biography or in that of Duff Cooper.

respondence exchanged between Bonaparte and myself is in the archives of
the ministry and whether or not the minister might be willing to present
these papers to Russia. This material, however, was not to be found, and
the gentleman was told that it was probably in my possession. I was then
approached and asked if I would turn the letters over to the czar.

The tone of this inquiry, together with the fact of strong Russian influence in this country, has made me apprehensive that the day might come
when the correspondence will be simply taken away from me. I have therefore decided simply to rid myself of it, and I hereby offer it to you.

These papers are undoubtedly the most desirable material of the archives. In addition to Bonaparte's correspondence with me, beginning in
the Year VII [1799] . . . there is the 1807 and 1808 correspondence between Bonaparte and M. de Champagny* and between Bonaparte and
Maret† in 1813.

These are, of course, the originals of the correspondence, bearing the signature of Bonaparte himself, and make up twelve large bundles. England
and Prussia, no doubt, would be delighted to have them and would be willing to pay generously for them. (I mention England and Prussia because I
would never, under any circumstances, allow them to fall into Russian
hands.)

I should be grateful, my dear prince, if you would mention my offer to
the emperor. . . . You know that although I am a Frenchman first, I am an
Austrian second, and I want nothing more than that this precious and
sometimes compromising documentation of contemporary history find its
way safely into your hands.

One could probably make a case for the legality of Talleyrand's offer to
sell the correspondence between himself and Bonaparte. The matter becomes highly suspect, however, when it is a question of correspondence exchanged between the emperor on the one hand and Champagny and
Maret on the other. It was not (and is not) unheard of for high government
officials, upon retirement, to "take" (Talleyrand himself uses the word *em-
porter*—"remove") documents pertaining to their administration. But to
take documents pertaining to other administrations is something else
again—something that seems hardly distinguishable from theft, and to
offer such documents to a foreign power may easily be construed as treason.

The price that Talleyrand set upon his honor, one must admit, was high:
half a million francs. But then, the risks were also high. If he were apprehended, he might well be prosecuted and disgraced. He had thought of
this, too, and one of the conditions of the sale was that the Emperor of
Austria must grant him asylum "at Vienna, or in some other part of his

* Jean-Baptiste Nompère, Count de Champagny and Duke de Cadore, had been Talleyrand's
successor as Napoleon's Minister of Foreign Affairs (1807–11).

† Hugues Maret—better known as the Duke de Bassano, one of Napoleon's most devoted supporters and most trusted diplomats—was Foreign Minister from 1811 to 1813.

states if circumstances in France made his [Talleyrand's] departure seem desirable." *

To Metternich, the price and the conditions seemed reasonable, and the exchange was made. Some 832 documents arrived in Vienna, and a message was sent to Talleyrand assuring him that the merchandise had been received in good order.

What happened next is not clear. There is no record (nor would there necessarily be one, given the nature of the transaction) that Talleyrand's 500,000 francs were ever sent or received. What is certain is that more than a year later, in June, 1818, the documents were sent back to Talleyrand, with Metternich's assurance that they had been properly "examined." The Viennese examination had proved thorough indeed. Metternich had had copies made of all the material before returning it. It seems very possible that he took advantage of Talleyrand's delicate position to refuse payment, on the grounds that the documents were less important than the prince had pretended. If so, the entire transaction had been a double double cross. For, of the 832 pieces sent to Vienna, only 73 were the "originals," signed by Napoleon, that Talleyrand had promised. The rest were merely routine letters of no interest to anyone but a historian. Whatever the case, Prince Metternich apparently had the last laugh. Not all the 73 original autographed letters were returned. Some of them are still in the Vienna archives.† In any event, after 1818, there existed a marked lack of cordiality in relations between Prince Talleyrand and Prince Metternich.

If, at this time, Talleyrand's love of money was alienating his friends in Austria, his love of Dorothea was causing him considerable worry about money in Paris. Edmond, the new Duke de Dino, suddenly found himself on the verge of ruin. Indeed, his dukedom seems to have arrived at the same time as his virtual bankruptcy. From his mother, he had inherited 3,000,000 francs and the magnificent house and estate of Rosny. By the end of 1817 the 3,000,000 had been dissipated on gambling and riotous living, and Edmond had begun to make inroads into Dorothea's own fortune as well. To make matters worse, the Duke de Dino had debts in almost incredible quantity, and his creditors had lost all patience with his promises to pay. At this juncture, Talleyrand suggested—or rather, insisted—that

* Decazes' spies, in fact, reported that Talleyrand had secretly received a visit from one of Metternich's agents, to whom the prince handed over "a bundle of papers." The papers were then carried to the Austrian embassy and from there sent, by diplomatic courier, to Vienna. There is no indication, however, despite this report, that any action was ever contemplated by the government against Talleyrand. Perhaps the documents purloined by the prince were too "compromising" for the king to be willing to risk an international scandal.

† Most of the material that was left was stolen from Talleyrand in 1827, probably by Perrey, his secretary, and taken to London, where it was sold to private collectors. Whatever remained in the prince's possession was taken by Dorothea to Sagan after her uncle's death, and remained there until 1945, when the chateau was burned during the Russian invasion of eastern Germany.

Dorothea ask the courts for a legal separation of her property from that of her husband. It was granted in March, 1818, after a full court hearing, and none too soon, for Edmond was soon forced to sell Rosny in order to satisfy his creditors.* Once their financial affairs had been settled—and Dorothea's fortune put beyond the spendthrift duke's reach—the couple seem to have reached an amicable understanding regarding the conduct of their respective lives; and, although they continued to live apart (as they had for several years), they saw each other frequently.† But appearances notwithstanding, the gossips said, their marriage undeniably had moved one step closer to dissolution.

As though to give the lie to this tale of the drawing room, Edmond, in the spring of 1820, gave up his own house and moved into the rue St.-Florentin. To all appearances, he had been reconciled with Dorothea, and the Duke and Duchess de Dino were once more united in conjugal bliss. Paris was astounded, almost scandalized. They were suspicious, too, for it soon became known that, as though by some miracle, simultaneous with the transfer of the duke's belongings, all his debts had been paid. Had Talleyrand arrived at some settlement with his nephew? If so, why should he have invited Edmond, whom he had always despised and whose wife he loved, to share his house? All these were mysteries hotly debated in the salons of the Faubourg St.-Germain, and in lesser establishments as well, during the summer months of 1820. The gossip took on new vigor on December 29 of the same year, when Dorothea gave birth to a daughter, who was christened Pauline. Society did not hesitate to assume that Talleyrand was the father of the child and that he had paid Edmond a vast sum to join Dorothea in the rue St.-Florentin and thus to confer a spurious legitimacy on the birth of Pauline. Madame de Souza (who, as Madame de Flahaut, had been something of an authority on paternity) wrote to her son that "Madame Dorothea has become a true mystic, and poor Edmond is a pitiable witness to this magical pregnancy conferred by the grace of God. . . . He sees their [Dorothea's and Talleyrand's] minds so disposed to believe in miracles that for all he knows, he may be asked to suckle the infant."

Talleyrand himself did not bother to try to stop the gossip. He was unwilling even to take notice of it. Pauline was and remained his absolute favorite among the children who lived in his house. He made no attempt to

* The estate then passed into the hands of the Duchess of Berry, to the horror and disgust of the villagers, who had regarded Edmond's dissipation as the privilege of a gentleman, but who could never accustom themselves to the sight of the new lady of the manor returning from the hunt with a string of bleeding rabbits' ears dangling from her neck.

† Polite society, however, had always chosen to believe that Dorothea and her husband still resided under one roof, in the rue d'Aguesseau. The *Almanach des 25,000 Adresses*, a sort of early *Social Register*, gives that address for Dorothea as well as for the duke, even in the years following the property separation.

disguise his love for her, and although it may be difficult to distinguish between grandfatherly and fatherly affection, the fact remains that in his will Pauline was remembered with far more generosity than any of Dorothea's other children. All this, Paris noted carefully, and it was always believed that the prince was, beyond a doubt, Pauline's true father. Any inclination that anyone may have felt to give Dorothea the benefit of the doubt was dissipated a few months later, when the Duke and Duchess of Dino separated once more, this time for good.

Once all the evidence has been examined and weighed, it is very possible, even likely, that the gossips were right; that Talleyrand was Pauline's father. It seems equally probable that the liaison began after Dorothea's return from Vienna and her final break with Count Clam-Martinitz, and that it ended, so far as sexual relations were concerned, with the birth of Pauline. This, however, is conjectural and based solely on circumstantial evidence; *viz.,* that it was highly improbable that the Duke de Dino was the father of the duchess' child, given the history of the couple's relationship; that, so far as can possibly be known, Dorothea's name was not seriously associated at this time with that of any man, other than Prince Talleyrand, who could have been responsible for her pregnancy; that, as has already been noted, Talleyrand, to the end of his life, had a marked and overriding affection for Pauline; and that, although the whole of Europe firmly believed Talleyrand to be the child's father, neither the prince nor Dorothea ever made the slightest effort to correct that impression.

In addition to these circumstances, it is worth noting that Talleyrand, even at the age of sixty-six, was notoriously attractive to women and enjoyed a great reputation as a lover. It hardly seems probable that his passion for Dorothea would have been restrained by considerations of sexual morality which, even as a churchman, he had always ignored. The duchess was, after all, only his niece by marriage, and if Edmond could not hold his wife, then he must run the same risks as any other husband in a similar position.

So far as Dorothea herself was concerned, her *Souvenirs*—which she began several years after Pauline's birth—offer a key to her attitude and perhaps a justification of her conduct:

> If, in the course of my life, people have expressed surprise that a great difference in age seemed to me only a minor consideration in the various relationships which my life has had to offer, they should remember the time when, on the threshold of womanhood, I accustomed myself to the idea of marrying a man twenty-five years older than myself. In fact, I not only accustomed myself to the idea, but positively welcomed it, because my self-esteem made me believe that I was the better for behaving so exceptionally.

But even though Talleyrand was eager and Dorothea willing, there must still remain some element of doubt. It is by no means certain that the prince, given his age and poor health, was capable of giving his niece a child. Moreover, much of the circumstantial evidence adduced by contemporaries is less than convincing. Rémusat's observation, for example, that Pauline resembled her mother, but had "a turned-up nose that was sufficient to lend credibility to the possibility of Talleyrand's paternity" ignores the fact that the Duke de Dino, Pauline's putative (and legal) father, was perfectly capable, genetically, of passing on this family characteristic. Similarly, Edmond's statement in 1824, when he and the duchess were in the process of obtaining a legal separation, that "he must return an absolute and formal refusal to receive madame la duchesse, his wife, into his house, or to go to live with her, for serious reasons that he believed it his duty not to reveal" was generally interpreted as a reference to Dorothea's pregnancy by Talleyrand. Yet Edmond, who was certainly no model of domestic affection, always treated Pauline with at least as much consideration as he did the children of whom he was the undoubted father and in no way gave any sign that he regarded her as anything less than his own flesh and blood.

The entire truth of Pauline's paternity will probably never be known. The weight of evidence, such as it is, leads one to believe that she was indeed the daughter of the prince. But anyone who prefers to believe that Dorothea's relations with her uncle were free of any sexual involvement can muster a fairly strong argument to support that point of view.

Dorothea's legal separation from Edmond, particularly when coupled with the circumstances of Pauline's birth, was viewed in a very dim light at the Tuileries and consequently among the nobility of the *ancien régime* in the fashionable *faubourgs* of Paris. The spirit of the court had changed from one of revolutionary tolerance to one of legitimist austerity. The reason was perhaps that Louis knew his seat upon the throne to be precarious, and shaky regimes have a tendency to appeal to law, order, and "public morality" as a means of muzzling the opposition. Or it may simply have been that certain of Talleyrand's influential relatives at court—the Countess Juste de Noailles,* for example—had sided with Edmond in the separation proceedings and had used their influence with the royal family to cast Dorothea in the role of the fallen woman.† Whatever the cause, Dorothea

---

* Talleyrand's niece Mélanie, daughter of Archambaud.

† Dorothea, in fact was never *persona grata* with the various members of Talleyrand's family, and they viewed her influence over the prince with great consternation. It was not Talleyrand's life, domestic or political, that concerned them, but his death. He was reputed to be one of the wealthiest men in Europe, and his relatives were terrified that this vast inheritance would pass out of their own hands and into those of the Duchess de Dino. As later events show, this fear was not wholly unfounded.

found little opportunity to exercise her ducal prerogatives at the court of Louis XVIII. She was invited to the palace only when not to have done so would have been an intolerable public insult, and she accepted royal invitations only when it would have been unthinkable to do otherwise.

The attitude of the Tuileries quickly infected that part of Parisian society which prided itself upon its virtue or at least upon its respectability. The "outcry from the Tuileries," as Dorothea described it, caused certain of France's noblest doors to be closed to her and certain others to be left only slightly ajar. It mattered little that many of the ancient noble houses that pretended outrage at Dorothea's domestic situation sheltered ladies whose own morals could not bear close scrutiny. Years later this rejection by society still rankled, and Dorothea's bitterness overflowed into her *Souvenirs*: "During the Restoration, Madame de Castellane cut me. Without thinking of the harm it was in my power to do her,* she broke off her friendship with me. I was cut to the quick, because I loved her dearly." Indeed, this censure on the part of society was a source of deep pain to Dorothea, and she adverted to it frequently for the rest of her life, often referring to "all the little wounds that one person or another inflicted upon me" and to "my very bitter memories." So keenly did she feel the slights of the king and the court nobility that her resentment became apparent even to those who did not know her very well. The Duchess de Broglie saw her in 1822, at the house of the Duke d'Orléans, and commented upon the change in her appearance: "She has beautiful features, but one senses that she is being consumed by some inner anxiety. Her eyes have a piercing blaze to them, and the expression on her face of that of a person much older than her years."

The reputation thus created for her by the king and his court was to remain for the rest of the duchess' life and reached such proportions that France came to take it for granted that she was a loose and wicked woman. Thomas Creevey confided to his *Papers*, ten years later, that "As for D[ino], villain as she is, I never saw anyone more striking and imposing. . . . And yet, to think of this devil living as mistress with old T, the uncle of her husband, and having three or four children by him. Was there ever . . . ?" Certainly, not everyone had as active an imagination as Mr. Creevey, but the sort of gossip that he retailed was common in both Paris and London. Until Dorothea's death, it was enough for her to be seen in the company of a man for him to be declared her "latest" lover, and if she spoke kindly of anyone, the word went out quickly that the duchess was launched on another of her affairs. (The truth was that in the years to come, Dorothea was to have several affairs, but no more than many other

* The allusion is to the Countess de Castellane's long-standing affair with Count Molé, of which Dorothea was perfectly aware.

ladies of comparable rank and considerably fewer than some of those who delighted in slandering her.)

Eventually, the duchess developed an immunity to the stings of the tale-bearers. In 1835 she was to write to a friend that "I used to be deeply wounded, very much upset, and very unhappy. . . . However, as it would be absurd to allow one's peace of mind to be at the mercy of persons whom one despises, I have made up my mind to ignore the evil that people think or say or write about me and my friends." In 1821, however, Dorothea was far from developing this measure of self-protection. Too proud to protest against the malicious gossip and too self-confident to be willing to change her ways, she chose to defy court society and to regard its lies and rumors as proof of its wickedness. The king and his nobles might have absolved her eventually from blame for her marital peccadilloes, but they could never forgive her for the contempt and indifference with which she met their attacks on her. She, in her turn, never forgave the court for its calumnies. It was all she could do, twice a year, to bring herself to make a brief curtsy before the king's armchair.

This was not an unheard-of situation. Many ladies of the highest nobility never deigned to appear at the court of King Louis. Some of them were bored by the unending ceremony; some despised either the king himself, his family, or his ministers; and some were kept away by the king's displeasure. Dorothea's case, however, held a significance which that of the other ladies did not. The day was to come when the Bourbons might have cause to regret their coldness toward the Duchess de Dino and the consequent insult, however indirect, to Europe's most eminent statesman.

Talleyrand himself, except for the brief period of his official disgrace, was always an honored guest at court, and his office of Grand Chamberlain required that he be there frequently. The mere act of presence was a cold consolation to him for the fact that, however courteously he might be received and listened to, his counsels were ignored and he was made to feel—as indeed he was—an outsider in the government of France. Even more difficult for Talleyrand to bear was that the royal court had become the center of the dullest—that is, the most conservative—people in Paris. While Dorothea resented the cold courtesy with which her uncle was received at the Tuileries, it is typical of Talleyrand that what he himself found most irritating was the lack of congenial company.

The stupefying boredom of life at the court of Louis XVIII was compensated for by the vivacity of another royal household in Paris, that of Louis-Philippe, Duke d'Orléans, at the Palais Royal. There the prince and his niece found better company, better conversation, and better treatment. They went to the Palais Royal not out of a sense of duty, but for their own pleasure, and there were many, including Decazes' spies, who noted that the Prince de Talleyrand and the Duchess de Dino were seen much more frequently at the house of the Duke d'Orléans than at the Tuileries.

The Palais Royal was at this time the gathering place for the smartest and gayest society of Paris. The Duke d'Orléans may have been the son of a regicide, but he was still first prince of the blood and the wealthiest man in France and perhaps in Europe. His house was open to all, whatever their political opinions, and a reception or ball at this house was an infinitely more agreeable affair than its counterpart at the Tuileries. Formality was kept to a minimum, the atmosphere was relaxed, and it was possible positively to enjoy oneself in the house of the duke. Yet Louis-Philippe never let it be forgotten that he was head of a branch of the royal family which, though junior to the Bourbons, was no less noble, no less distinguished, and no less legitimately possessed of the ancient blood of France.

Talleyrand, of course, had known the Duke d'Orléans for many years and had known his father, the Red Prince, very well. Moreover, Adélaïde, the duke's sister, and the prince were both eager to renew the friendship begun in London in 1792. Talleyrand had always had an attachment to the House of Orléans, and its representatives had always manifested an openness and a liberalism of sentiment which he found much more sympathetic than the political opportunism of the elder branch of the Bourbons. He had demonstrated his affection for Louis-Philippe's family in 1816, when, over the objections of King Louis XVIII, he had insisted that the throne restore to the House of Orléans its vast possessions, which had been confiscated during the Revolution. It was hardly extraordinary, therefore, that Orléans and Talleyrand should find one another's company congenial.

In addition to his respectful affection for Talleyrand, the duke now exerted himself to charm Dorothea, and the pair became constant and no doubt sincere friends. Yet it is likely that for Orléans, Dorothea's chief attraction lay in the power and influence of her uncle. Orléans, whenever he reflected on the single step that separated him from the throne of France, could not but realize that, of all men, only Talleyrand possessed the wisdom, experience, and skill that he would require if ever his royal ambition were to be satisfied.

The new ties between the rue St.-Florentin and the Palais Royal were not ignored at the Tuileries, and there was whispered talk of an "Orléanist faction" and even of an "Orléanist plot." The whispers grew so loud that Madame de Rémusat screwed up her courage one night and, in the midst of a conversation about politics, asked the prince whether it might not be best to replace the Bourbons with the Orléans branch. The question, she explains, was intended to draw Talleyrand out, and Talleyrand, obviously, knew precisely what the lady was about. "He categorically rejected the whole idea," Madame de Rémusat confided to her journal, "and he did so with such emphasis and tenacity that I had the impression, in spite of myself, that he was going out of his way to dispel the current rumors on that subject."

The rumors persisted, however, and they did not rise solely from Talleyrand's social relations with the Orléans family. In 1816, not long after the prince's resignation from office, a man named Didier had been executed at Grenoble for organizing a revolt against the government. Before his death, he was reported to have said: "Tell the king to keep the Duke d'Orléans and Monsieur de Talleyrand as far from the throne and as far from France as possible." The only evidence in this instance was the word of the general who put down the futile uprising—a man who was later discovered to have been guilty of such incredible exaggeration in *all* his reports on the incident that he became something of a legend and a joke in France. Even so, no one who knew Talleyrand could doubt that he must have looked ahead and noted that if and when the follies of the Bourbons became intolerable to the people of France, a substitute—and a sympathetic one—would be available in the person of the Duke d'Orléans. He had even gone so far as to warn the Bourbons, in the person of their obedient servant, the Baron de Vitrolles: "They must take care, Monsieur de Vitrolles, the Duke d'Orléans is treading on their heels." Despite this display of prudence, it must be said that Talleyrand's political conduct, in the years between his retirement and the events of July, 1830, is often difficult to follow and occasionally even more difficult to justify. King Louis, upon Talleyrand's resignation, had not turned, as he might have been logically expected to do, to the extreme right—that is, to the ultraroyalists—to form a government. He knew, as his brother, Artois, and his followers did not, that too much had happened in the previous quarter century for Frenchmen ever again to submit to absolutism, even absolutism by divine right. Louis was therefore determined not to be ruled by the extremists who had been the immediate cause of Talleyrand's fall. His appointment of Richelieu, a convinced moderate, as president of the Council, and of Decazes, always an advocate of conciliation, as minister of police, reflected that determination. Yet during the years of Louis' reign, Europe was treated to the spectacle of a king and his ministers defending the cause of liberalism against France's royalists— that is, against the most rabid supporters of the crown, who were determined not only to revive as much of the *ancien régime* as they could, but to avenge the king, whether or not he was willing, for the wrongs that his family had suffered at the hands of the Revolution and the Empire.

It might be expected that Talleyrand, whose own principles of liberalism in government were shared by the king and by his ministers, after his initial pique at the circumstances of his resignation, would give his support to a regime that accepted his own political ideology and that, in a very real sense, he himself had created. But this was not to be the case. The prince's open hostility to Richelieu and his successors began at the moment of Richelieu's appointment, and it was to continue unabated until the final fall of the House of Bourbon. Talleyrand himself protested that "I can honestly say that I never ceased to desire the continuance of the Restoration. . . . I did nothing to disturb it, and utterly repudiate all connection with those who boast that they helped in its downfall." Yet his initial determination to bring down Richelieu's government at any cost showed itself not only in his vitriolic attacks on Richelieu himself and on Decazes, but by the astonishing political alliances that he formed in order to bring this about. The first such occasion was in 1817, when the government sponsored a bill in the chamber extending the franchise to anyone in France who paid at least 300 francs in annual taxes. The bill was heatedly opposed by the ultras, led by the Count d'Artois and his sons—Talleyrand's old enemies. Talleyrand, who had always favored liberalization of the voting law, on the one hand, and who had, on the other, always opposed most vehemently Artois' party of reactionaries,* now did a complete turnabout. Fully aware that defeat of the bill could only weaken the government, undermine the prestige of the throne and spread discontent among the people, he placed himself at the head of the opposition to it and succeeded in defeating it by arguing that the proposed law was contrary to the best interests of legitimacy. As Europe watched this strange comedy in puzzled amazement, Pozzo di Borgo wrote the explanation to Czar Alexander: "This intrigue, M. de Talleyrand hopes, will result in success [*i.e.,* of his efforts to overthrow Richelieu's government]. He pretends to share the

---

* It is somewhat misleading to refer to "political parties" in Restoration France in the sense that that term was understood in the United States or in Great Britain at the time—that is, as disciplined and well-defined ideological groups. There were, however, groups united by common political ideals and ambitions; and it was the actions of these groups—or "parties," for lack of a better word—that guided the politics of the Restoration. Chief among them were:

The *ultras,* or royalists of the extreme right. Their purpose was simple: to abolish entirely the gains of the Revolution and the Empire and to reestablish the *ancien régime* in its entirety. The Count d'Artois, brother of Louis XVIII, an heir to the throne, was the inspiration of this group, which included most of the families of the old nobility and the higher clergy. A religious organization directed by the Jesuits and known as the Congregation (*Congregation de la Vierge*), comprising militant reactionary laymen, was established uniquely to exert political pressure on the government.

The *liberals* (or independents) were the party of the left and included a wide range of opinions, from the republican convictions of the Marquis de Lafayette to the constitutional monarchism of Benjamin Constant and the Bonapartism of Jacques-Antoine Manuel. Their general aim was to replace the regime of Louis XVIII and then of Charles X with a more liberal form of government.

The *center* was composed of the moderates who generally supported the liberal reforms of the Revolution and the Empire but who wished them to be exercised within the framework of the Restoration monarchy.

The *doctrinaires,* led by Talleyrand's friend, Pierre-Paul Royer-Collard, and by François Guizot, were close to both the liberals and the center in many respects and regarded the Charter as the best assurance against both revolution and radical reaction.

anxiety of the princes [Artois and his family] and declares himself to be the zealous protector of legitimacy—which will be endangered by the possibility of an irresponsible choice of deputies. In this posture, he appears in the Chamber of Peers in the company of MM. Polignac, Mathieu de Montmorency, Chateaubriand, and others who, it is thought, act only upon the instructions of the princes."

The key to the interpretation of Talleyrand's sudden jump into the camp of the ultras is difficult, but not impossible, to find. Richelieu, in his eyes, was nothing more than a puppet of Talleyrand's mortal enemy, the Czar of Russia. (This, of course, explains Pozzo di Borgo's cynicism regarding Talleyrand's motives.) And the Czar of Russia, in turn, was the chief of the forces of reaction and absolutism in Europe.* Since the liberalism in France was now represented by the creature of Czar Alexander (that is, Richelieu), Talleyrand had been placed squarely between Scylla and Charybdis. If he supported Richelieu, he would, in effect, be supporting the spread of Russian influence in France and in Western Europe—an influence which, for all its liberal veneer in Richelieu's government, was essentially and ultimately vowed to repression, absolutism, and royal government by divine right. If he sided with the only other possible party, the ultras, he might indeed destroy Richelieu and Alexander's influence along with him. The issue was never really in doubt. Between a party whose reactionism he might come to control and a foreign autocrat whose intentions were, in his opinion, detrimental, if not fatal, to the real interests of France, he had no difficulty in choosing. Already, from Vienna, he had warned King Louis of the Russian intention to "meddle in every matter and to take a tone of authority and to dictate to everyone else."

Even the British were now becoming alarmed by Alexander's open ambition. Creevey, who had once (as had Talleyrand) shared the confidence of the British government in Alexander's liberalism and magnanimity, was writing that there was "a fixed intention on the part of Russia to make Constantinople the seat of her power and to reestablish the Greek Church upon the ruins of Mohammedanism. A new crusade, in short, by a new and enormous Power, and brought into the field by our own selves, and one that may put our existence at stake to drive out again." On the Continent, the alarm was even greater, and Metternich, the imperturbable Metternich, was on the verge of panic over Russian ambitions in Germany and was proposing an anti-Russian front among Austria, Great Britain, and France. The Quadruple Alliance, created at Chaumont, preserved dur-

* As early as April, 1816, Alexander was making no secret of his plans for the Holy Alliance. It was intended, he wrote to Princess Lieven, "to confirm the contracting sovereigns in the principles of political and social conservation." In the same letter, he gave his definition of the forces of liberalism in Europe, calling it "the genius of evil."

ing the Congress of Vienna, and revived after the Second Peace of Paris, seemed already in danger of disintegration.

Talleyrand, obviously, was not alone in his mistrust of Alexander's ambitions—ambitions which, in France, were represented by the man who had been the czar's candidate and virtually his appointee: the Duke de Richelieu. It is not surprising that he should have been alarmed by the weakness or at least by the sense of expediency of a king who apparently had yielded to Russian pressure and made such a man his chief minister. "In 1814 and 1815," he wrote, "I believed, and I still do, that France could have no solid and durable institutions except those that were based on legitimacy and on liberal and sagacious principles. . . . Such will always be my opinion and my political *credo*. But from the moment that legitimacy itself betrayed its own principles by breaking its vows, it became necessary to look to the safety of France at all costs." He had abandoned the Revolution when it had turned from Liberty, Equality, and Fraternity to the Terror; he had abandoned and determined to destroy the Empire when Napoleon had forsaken "those liberal and wise principles of which the Revolution of 1789 had shown the practical possibility." He was now abandoning the king and the government when they, like their predecessors, had abandoned those same principles and, along with them, had abandoned "us"—the people of France.*

Talleyrand's struggle, from 1817 to 1819, against Richelieu's "liberal" government was, in fact, merely a continuation of the stratagem that he had outlined, several years before, to Czar Alexander. It was his intention to side with the ultras, despite his contrary convictions, and thereby to eliminate the influence of Alexander in the person of Richelieu. In the Chamber of Peers he made common cause with Artois' party against Richelieu's voting bill and in other matters as well. So enthusiastic was his opposition that the rue St.-Florentin became the acknowledged center of antigovernment sentiment in Paris, and never, not even at the height of his power, had the prince's drawing rooms been so crowded. There were his usual friends, of course; but there were now also his old enemies who had

---

* Historians and biographers have often failed to take into account that Talleyrand's opposition to Richelieu's government and his eventual abandonment of the Bourbons, far from constituting a "betrayal" of his principles, were, in fact, a logical application of those principles. To have supported a man whom Talleyrand regarded as a Russian puppet and to have defended a regime that became increasingly blind to the needs of the people of France would have been impossible for the statesman who had forsaken the revolutionaries of 1789 and had brought down Napoleon—both at the risk of his own neck—for precisely the same sort of blindness. Yet even Duff Cooper, certainly the most sympathetic of biographers, states: "At no time was Talleyrand so open to the charge of being false to his political principles as when he sought to curry favor with the Ultras at the expense of Louis XVIII's more moderate Ministers. That he did attempt to do so in order to return to power is undeniable . . ." (p. 251). Tarlé, Talleyrand's Russian biographer, speaks (understandably, given Russian interests at the time) of the prince's "treason" (p. 291).

become his new friends, and the ultras, with whom he had been at sword's point since the early days of the Restoration, now hailed him as their champion. As their champion—but still not as one of them. Talleyrand was asked one day if it were true that he had become an ultra, and he replied: "If you mean, am I against the government, then I must say yes. I am indeed against the government in general, and against M. Decazes in particular."

So far did his animus against the Minister of Police carry him that he deliberately chose Wednesday as his day "at home," knowing that Wednesday was also Decazes' day to receive his friends and hoping that the minister would find himself with an empty salon. On at least one occasion, Talleyrand invited every minister—except Decazes, of course—to an elaborate dinner the same night that Decazes had previously invited them. The poor ministers, not daring to refuse either host in favor of the other, all pleaded illness or pressing business and remained at home that night.

Such behavior naturally pleased the ultras enormously, for they were as determined as Talleyrand to be rid of Richelieu and his government in one way or another, and until they could do so, they were constantly hatching plots and intrigues to embarrass the ministers and generally to make their lives so unbearable that they would resign. At one point, the Count d'Artois had the preposterous idea of asking the Czar Alexander himself to demand that Richelieu resign and the even more preposterous idea that Prince Talleyrand might be persuaded to approach Alexander on the subject.* The task of enlisting Talleyrand's aid was entrusted to M. de Vitrolles, who, in addition to being Artois' trusted friend, was an intimate friend of Dorothea's.† He therefore approached the duchess with the suggestion that Talleyrand sign a secret memorandum which he, Vitrolles, had written at the instruction of the Count d'Artois. This note, complaining of the situation in France and placing its onus squarely on Richelieu's shoulders, was to be handed to Alexander. So far were both Artois and Vitrolles unaware of the true relations between the czar and Talleyrand that they believed that the memorandum would carry more weight if the prince's signature were on it. Dorothea, who knew the true situation, was understandably cool to the idea. She made it clear to Vitrolles that

---

* The czar was then (the fall of 1818) at Aix-la-Chapelle, attending a conference of the great powers which was to arrange for the evacuation of French territory by allied troops and to settle the question of the reparations to be paid by France.

† Although Vitrolles was passionately in love with the Duchess de Dino, and common gossip to the contrary, she never consented to become his mistress. The pair remained the closest of friends until 1829, when they quarreled over a matter the nature of which is unknown. The break, in any event, seems to have been final and not without bitterness, for, even after Talleyrand's death, when Dorothea wrote to her closest friends asking that her letters be returned to her, she could not bring herself to approach Vitrolles. Her correspondence with the baron was therefore preserved for future generations.

while she would consent to present the plan to her uncle, she would not try to persuade him to accept it if, as she suspected, he seemed unwilling. Dorothea's intuition was perfectly correct. The prince, while he did not refuse to cooperate, managed to find one pretext after another for delaying the memorandum. Meanwhile, he saw to it, with great discretion, that word reached Artois of his reservations regarding the plan, and at that moment, the intrigue was abandoned.

Abandoned, but not forgotten. Talleyrand's judgment in choosing his conspiracies was, as always, impeccable. Shortly afterward the memorandum fell, or was leaked by the government, into the hands of the press, and Vitrolles was proclaimed its author. He was forced to resign as minister of state, and the *Moniteur* announced his disgrace to the world.

The various conspiracies and intrigues against the Duke de Richelieu could not have been directed against a less likely target or one less tenacious of power. Though a devoted royalist and once a friend of the ultras, he combined a sense of political moderation with considerable ability and a total lack of personal ambition. He had, in fact, accepted office with the greatest reluctance and only after the combined pleas and commands of King Louis and Czar Alexander. From the time of his appointment, Richelieu had longed, as vehemently as Talleyrand, for the moment of his release from office. Frequently, he threatened resignation. On those occasions, only the counterthreat that, in the event of his resignation, the king would be forced to send for Talleyrand compelled him to remain. "Ah, M. le Duc," Louis sighed on one occasion, "you will reduce me to the deplorable extremity of having to call for M. de Talleyrand, whom I neither like nor respect." So the duke remained. In truth, there was no one else. The ultras, as demonstrated by the silliness of their conspiracies, could produce no man of superior ability in politics—no one, that is, except the pseudo-ultra, Talleyrand. Among the moderates, Richelieu's own followers, the situation was the same. Who had always been the champion of moderation in France except Talleyrand? It seemed therefore inevitable that if a change of government became necessary, it was Talleyrand, whose competence, experience, and prestige were unparalleled, who should be called to head it. Talleyrand himself shared this opinion, for not even his bitterest enemies would have thought of accusing him of sharing Richelieu's dislike of public office. He regarded his return to power as certain, and he spared no effort to ensure that it should take place at the earliest possible moment. It was his intention—as it had been in 1816—to form a government composed of representatives of all parties, and to this end, he continued in his efforts to win over the ultras. He even made peace, of a sort, with his bête noire, Decazes. Madame de Rémusat records her surprise in March, 1819, upon finding Dorothea paying a friendly call upon Madame Decazes and her near-fatal astonishment a few days later when Talleyrand "spoke of M. Decazes in a very complimentary way, saying that he was the only man in the government and that he was very capable."

What Madame de Rémusat did not know was that Decazes had sided with Talleyrand in the bitter debate over Richelieu's voting law and had shown himself willing to pretend that the prince had never uttered a word against him either in the salon or in the chamber. It is possible that Talleyrand was genuinely impressed by the sincerity of Decazes' liberal convictions and by his generosity of character. It is also possible that his rapprochement with the Minister of Police was simply a matter of expediency: An alliance between the prince and the minister against Richelieu was a formidable combination indeed.

Richelieu himself was acutely aware of this, and he was determined that the defeat of the voting bill would be the last humiliation that he would suffer as president of the Council. Since there was no hope of reconciliation between the chambers and the government, his conscience at last permitted him to do what his personal preferences had long ago urged. He submitted his resignation and, with a sigh of inexpressible relief, retired into private life, taking a somewhat less willing Molé with him. Decazes was now the only one of Louis' friends who had the monarch's complete confidence, and it was generally expected that he would advise the king to ask M. de Talleyrand to form a new government. It may have been that Louis himself refused to call upon the man whom he "neither liked nor respected." Or, as Molé reports, Decazes may have recalled that Talleyrand, as president of the Council, would, in all probability, prove to be a force that a mere minister of police, however close to the throne, could never hope to control, let alone to master. Or Louis may have felt that his regime, unsteady as it was, would not survive "the shame and humiliation of recalling M. de Talleyrand," as the Count d'Artois put it. For Artois, like Decazes, seems to have been frightened by the strength of the man with whom he had so lately been content to ally himself and his ultra followers. Whatever the case, Richelieu was finally replaced (December, 1818) not by Talleyrand, but by Augustin Dessoles, a political mediocrity who was too obscure to have made many enemies. Dessoles, though well intentioned, was too inexperienced to perceive clearly either the depth of the emotions or the distinctions of ideology that separated the various parties. Himself a general of the Empire, he sought to rally the Bonapartists around his government, and by retaining (indeed, he had little choice) Decazes in the ministry, he thought to reconcile the ultras, the liberals, the moderates, and even Talleyrand to his government. He was mistaken on all counts. By consenting to serve the Bourbons, he discredited himself in the eyes of the Bonapartists; by being a Bonapartist, he alienated the extreme royalists.

Because he had too little support in the two chambers, he disappointed and finally disgusted the liberals and moderates. And, simply because he was president of the Council, he forfeited the support of Talleyrand, who had expected to occupy that position himself. Things went so badly that even Molé was moved to express to Richelieu his (belated) regret that Dessoles, rather than Talleyrand, had succeeded the duke in office. Indeed, it was universally accepted that at any moment Dessoles would attempt to buttress his tottering government by inviting Talleyrand to join it as Minister of Foreign Affairs; but the call never came, because Dessoles suspected that Talleyrand and the "Orléanists" were plotting his downfall.

Dessoles' government, predictably, was of short duration and of less accomplishment. He resigned late in 1819. Again, Talleyrand's hopes rose, and, again, he was disappointed. Decazes, who had been the power behind Dessoles' ministerial throne, now decided openly to exercise the office that he had only informally controlled. Having the complete confidence of the throne, he thought it no longer necessary to have the support of the prince, and he not only omitted Talleyrand's name from his list of ministers, but avoided consulting him on matters either of appointment or of policy. To the dismay of everyone concerned, for guidance Decazes turned instead to the one man whom circumstances had proved least capable of giving it: the Duke de Richelieu.

Decazes, for all his ability, fared no better than his predecessors in office. Under Richelieu's tutelage and with the king's support, he put together a government of exclusively liberal ministers. He saw no need, as Talleyrand did, of a cabinet truly representative of the various political parties, and he therefore not only inherited the enmities created by the policies of Richelieu and Dessoles, but exacerbated them by the skill with which he waged open warfare against the ultraroyalists. Resentment was brought to a tragic climax on February 13, 1820, when the Duke de Berry, second son of the Count d'Artois and third in line to the throne of France, was assassinated at the Opéra. The Duchess de Berry, who was there when the assassin, a man named Louvel, struck the fatal blow, pointed at Decazes and, in a voice loud enough to be heard over the ensuing din, screamed: "There! There is the man who is the real murderer!"

There is absolutely no evidence that Decazes was even remotely connected with the deed. On the other hand, there is no denying that his violent anti-ultra diatribes had whipped up great emotion among the people of France and that the murder of the duke was very likely a consequence of that emotion. To that extent, the Duchess de Berry seemed justified in her dramatic accusation. Moreover, her sentiment was shared by the people of Paris, who sent up such a howl of resentment against Decazes that he had no choice but to offer, or King Louis but to accept, the minister's resignation. So violent was the continued reaction against Decazes that Louis hastily thrust upon him the title of duke and the office of ambassador and bundled him off to London, where, presumably, he would be beyond the reach of his enemies. The same public sentiment now encouraged the ultraroyalists to speak openly of imposing a minister of their own choosing on the king. Their choice for the position was Talleyrand. The prince, however, was noncommittal, and the intrigue never went beyond the drawing rooms of the Faubourg St.-Germain.

King Louis, meanwhile, was considering a list of men whom he might ask to form a new government: Richelieu, Molé, Pasquier, and the Count de Villèle, who was one of the leaders of the ultraroyalists. Then it was announced, to the dismay of everyone—most of all of Richelieu himself—that the king had named Richelieu to the presidency of the Council. The duke, who was ill in bed at the time, accepted with the greatest reluctance and only after the Count d'Artois had sworn, "on his honor, as a prince and a gentleman," that he and his followers would support the new government. Richelieu shared with Louis XVIII an inability to learn from experience, for Artois' word "as a prince and a gentleman" was usually broken as soon as it was given, and this was to be no exception. Almost immediately, the ultras combined once more with the liberals to block the government at every turn and to render impossible Richelieu's intention of governing along the lines of moderation and constitutionality. The duke, despite his declining health, struggled manfully for a time, but it was obvious to everyone that the days of his government were numbered.

It would have been impossible, under the circumstances, for anyone, perhaps even for Talleyrand, to have governed France effectively during the decade following Berry's death. The act of assassination, like others before and after it in history, gave rise to, or at least furnished the pretext for, a veritable hurricane of reactionary sentiment. It also marked the virtual withdrawal of liberal and moderate ministers from the government. One did not have to have the experience of a Talleyrand to realize that the liberalism of the bourgeoisie and the reactionary convictions of the upper classes were now in direct confrontation and that this confrontation would increase in bitterness and destructiveness until France must either be transformed into a truly constitutional monarchy or undergo a revolution. Yet Talleyrand still had hope for the monarchy of the Restoration. "His latest feeling," records Madame de Rémusat, "is that if Madame the Duchess de Berry's* child is a boy, this will strike a responsive chord

---

* The duchess was two months pregnant when the duke was assassinated. Since Louis XVIII was childless, his heir was his brother, the Count d'Artois. Artois had two sons, the Duke d'Angoulême, who was also childless, and the Duke de Berry. Unless Berry had a male heir, the ancient Bourbon line would end, and the Orléans family would accede to the throne.

in the hearts of all Frenchmen. But if the child is a girl, then her birth will signal the end of the ties [to the Bourbons]." Talleyrand's prediction seemed well founded. At two o'clock in the morning of September 29, 1820, the Duchess de Berry gave birth. It all happened so quickly that there was no time to call in official witnesses to the birth, and the duchess had to lie unattended, with the child still held in her arms, while her ladies ran madly about looking for witnesses competent to certify that she had given birth to a son. King Louis, as soon as he heard the news, went practically mad with joy and, on the spot, named thirty-five new knights of the various royal orders in honor of the newborn Duke de Bordeaux, as the child was called. Among these was Prince Talleyrand, who was invested with the blue silk cordon of France's noblest order, the St.-Esprit.

Louis' joy was shared by his subjects. Strangers kissed each other in the streets, and poets, serious and otherwise, sat down to write verses on this infant who was a marvel, a miracle, a child of France who would perpetuate the dynasty and thus ensure the peace of the realm. One family, however, did not celebrate. The House of Orléans, by the birth of the young prince, had been pushed a decisive step farther from the throne, and their chagrin and disappointment were only too obvious to everyone. On the day that the Orléans family went to pay their mandatory visit to the infant Duke de Bordeaux and his mother, Orléans' sister, Adélaïde, remarked sourly to the Duchess de Berry: "After all, madame, there were no witnesses."

"I beg to differ," the duchess replied. "Marshal Suchet was present." * Thereupon Orléans himself turned to one of the duchess' ladies, who was holding the child, and made such offensive comments about the young prince's appearance that the lady burst into tears. The next day the duke called upon Marshal Suchet and questioned him closely, demanding to hear from his own lips whether he was indeed a witness at the confinement of the Duchess de Berry and whether she was truly the mother of a prince. The old marshal answered: "She is truly so, Monseigneur. As truly as you are the father of the Duke de Chartres."

Thus frustrated, Orléans sent Madame Adélaïde to apologize to the duchess for her family's behavior. "Don't be angry with my brother," she pleaded. "After all, one cannot lose a crown for one's children without some regret."

Talleyrand had hoped that the birth of the Duke de Bordeaux might

---

* Suchet had arrived about a half hour after the actual birth. In the meantime, two national guardsmen, a private and a sergeant, red-faced and painfully embarrassed, had been practically dragged into the duchess' bedroom to bear witness to the fact that the infant was no changeling, but the true and undoubted son of the Duke and Duchess de Berry and therefore heir to the crown of France.

unite the country once more behind the Bourbon throne. For a time, a short time, it did so. But before a year had passed, the spirit of contradiction manifested itself as strongly as ever on the part of the ultraroyalists. Artois and his followers, believing the birth of the heir had placed the throne out of danger of revolution, now wished to place it also beyond attack. Under pressure from them, Richelieu consented in 1821 to allow his government to sponsor a censorship bill that would have drastically curtailed the liberty of the press. To oppose such a measure at such a time was to open oneself to violent attack from the right. Yet Talleyrand chose precisely this moment to expose himself to such an onslaught from the ultras whom he had courted so assiduously in recent years and thereby to bring about a definitive and this time an irrevocable break with the reactionaries. He remained in Paris expressly to speak and to vote against this bill. "After all," he explained to Dorothea, "one must be true to the principles that one has professed all of one's life." In his speech on this occasion, he emphasized the necessity of acting in harmony with the spirit of the age, declaring that the freedom of the press was necessary at that time and place and that the government, in denying that necessity, was placing itself in grave danger. "For," he said, "without freedom of the press, there can be no representative government."

As the peers sat in shocked silence, he went on, in the presence of the ministers of the ultra-dominated government, to praise the accomplishments of the Revolution of 1789, maintaining that the principles of that Revolution were in accord with the spirit of the age to the extent that they proclaimed freedom of conscience, equality before the law, liberty of the individual, the right of trial by jury, and freedom of the press. Then, as in 1821, Talleyrand said, it was the people ultimately who judged what was necessary for their time and what was not. He concluded with a thinly veiled warning to the government: "in this day and age, it is difficult to deceive the people for long. . . . For there is someone who is more clever than Voltaire, more intelligent than Bonaparte, than any of the Directors, than any past, present or future government; and that person is the people [*tout le monde*]."

What Talleyrand was saying, in effect, was that no government, no regime, can possibly govern against the wishes of the people and that the present government and the present regime were attempting to do precisely that. The measures of repression undertaken by Richelieu's ministry were clearly in contravention of the "spirit of the age." As such, they were doomed to failure. The government, if it continued along the reactionary path that it had chosen, must necessarily fall. And the Bourbon monarchy itself, if its intentions and convictions were truly reflected in such measures, must disappear, for it had become an anachronism and was no longer capable of responding to the needs of France. Talleyrand understood this perfectly. There can be little doubt that Louis XVIII also understood it. But the king was the prisoner of the opinions of his family, of his advisers. He was too tired, too ill, to cut himself free from the political apron strings of the Count d'Artois and his party, too weak to make the turn to the left that Talleyrand insisted he must if the government and his dynasty were to survive.

Talleyrand's own brusque thrust toward the left came at the worst possible moment so far as his immediate political prospects were concerned. Richelieu's government was limping toward its end, and the ultras now had the ear of the king and were apparently in full control of the government. It would be the ultras, therefore, who would decide on Richelieu's successor as chief minister of France. It was at that precise moment, when he seemed on the verge of attaining the office that he had coveted for the past five years, that the prince stepped forward to defend the principles of liberalism that had been rejected and were so despised by the ultras. He had courted the extremists assiduously for several years, and when it seemed necessary, he had allied himself with them. But now, when France stood at a crossroads that must lead either to absolutism or to revolution, he could no longer act on the principle of expediency. If the government and even the Bourbon monarchy must be sacrificed for the preservation of *liberté, egalité, fraternité*, then he had no choice. He was faced with the moment of decision, and he decided in accordance with the principles he had always professed. It was not, in truth, Talleyrand who abandoned the king, but the king who abandoned France. From the time of the prince's defense of the freedom of the press before the Chamber of Peers, he would never again subordinate his principles or the long-range interests of the people of France to immediate political advantage.

Richelieu's long-anticipated resignation was announced. His successor, not unexpectedly, was the Count de Villèle, one of the spokesmen of the ultraroyalist party. King Louis had once again bowed to the arguments of the Count d'Artois, and the Bourbon monarchy moved one step closer to the precipice. Talleyrand expressed the situation to perfection: "The Count d'Artois holds his royalty cheap." He happened to be at the Tuileries on the day when Richelieu came to take his leave of the king and, simultaneously, when Villèle came to receive his formal appointment. Standing at the foot of the stairs, he saw Richelieu going up and Villèle coming down, and he could not resist a mot that was widely repeated throughout Paris: "How extraordinary! Richelieu, who is coming down, is going up, and Villèle, who is going up, is coming down."

Villèle's first act in office bore out the truth of Talleyrand's observation. He abandoned the bill circumscribing freedom of the press—largely as the result of the public outcry whipped up by Talleyrand's speech—but introduced a new measure transferring all offenses connected with the press from a jury hearing to royal courts, where there were no juries and in which (government-appointed) judges decided the guilt or innocence of the accused. The government, in other words, was to be simultaneously the prosecutor and the judge in any action against the press. On July 24, 1822, Talleyrand once more came to the defense of the press, arguing that the bill went against the spirit of the Charter, that it was therefore contrary to the king's promise to uphold the Charter, and, once more, that it contradicted the spirit of the age. Then, speaking of Lamoignon de Malesherbes, who, before the Revolution, had defended freedom of the press against the pretensions of the king and then, during the Revolution, had been guillotined for defending the king against the pretensions of the Assembly, he concluded: "My lords, I vote with M. de Malesherbes, and against the proposed law." There was a buzz of astonishment that Talleyrand would dare to hold up as an example a man who had both disgraced himself in the eyes of a Bourbon king and been punished as a traitor by the Revolution— until it was realized that it was not of Malesherbes, but of himself, that the prince was speaking. A profound silence followed that realization. Only one speaker, the Duke de Fitz-James, dared rise to speak for the bill, and his words were not so much a defense of the government as a violent attack on Talleyrand's principles, his career under the Revolution and the Empire, and on his personal life. The chamber was transfixed, and Talleyrand, who had seldom in his life been subjected to such a vehement public attack, betrayed not by the flicker of an eyelash that he understood a word that the duke was speaking. When Fitz-James had finished, Talleyrand turned to a neighbor and said pleasantly, "The duke is certainly a talented man. Except for its rather bitter overtones, it was a remarkably good speech."

The measure was defeated. But that was not the end of it. A few months later Villèle proposed a new censorship law, which he named "the law of justice and love." Chateaubriand called it rather "the law of the Vandals." And Talleyrand appraised it as "so silly that it cannot possibly be French."

At this most unpropitious juncture in French history, when the country, from the villages to the capital, was torn between the policies of the liberals and those of the reactionaries, the government of Villèle chose to commit the nation's resources and its men to intervention in the affairs of a foreign nation and, worst of all, on the side of absolutism. King Ferdinand of Spain, a Bourbon, had been forced in 1820 to grant a constitution to his subjects which provided, as a means to limit royal power, for an upper and a lower parliamentary establishment (the Cortes). Even this rudimentary form of democracy, however, was too much for the Spanish absolutists—

that is, the great nobles of both church and state—and in 1822, an uprising took place, the purpose of which was to abolish the constitution and to dissolve the Cortes.

The ultraroyalists in France, with Artois at their head, immediately demanded that France send an army to fight alongside the Spanish insurgents and to reestablish King Ferdinand's power on its former absolutist and autocratic basis. Everyone was opposed to intervention, Talleyrand most of all. Everyone, that is, except the ultras, and the ultras were in power. On October 20, representatives of the Holy Alliance met in Verona to decide the question of intervention. The French ambassadors on that occasion were two of the most rabid interventionists in France: Montmorency and Chateaubriand. Both were determined that France would be the champion of this "new crusade" against forces that sought to overthrow both throne and altar in one of Christendom's most ancient monarchies. When the congress adjourned on December 14, they had had their way. The decision was announced in Louis' address from the throne on January 28, 1823, and the army was ordered to mobilize immediately. Even worse, it was announced, at the same time, that Montmorency had resigned as Villèle's foreign minister and that the most ultra of all the ultraroyalists, Chateaubriand, had been appointed to replace him.

Talleyrand immediately became the center of opposition to the Spanish war (a fact which Chateaubriand took as a personal affront and which caused him henceforth to regard Talleyrand as his bitterest enemy) and mounted a campaign which combined oratory with invective in equal proportions. His sayings were, as always, eagerly repeated throughout Paris, and he was at pains to give both his admirers and his detractors something to repeat. On one occasion, in the midst of France's campaign of intervention, it was reported that the king had just concluded a three-hour secret session with his Council. One of the peers asked Talleyrand anxiously, "Imagine, three hours! What could they have been discussing?"

"How to while away three hours," Talleyrand replied.

Of Blacas, Decazes' replacement as the king's favorite, the prince remarked, in tones of profound admiration: "He is truly amazing. Out of an income of 150,000 francs, he manages to save 8,000,000 francs a year."

One day, in the chamber, the prince watched the aged Count Ferrand enter, supported by two footmen. Turning to his neighbors, he said: "Look at Ferrand, he is exactly in the same situation as the government. He thinks that he is moving under his own power, whereas in fact he is being carried along."

Not everything that was repeated with such avidity had to be coated with venom for it to be effective. Nothing that Talleyrand said to anyone remained private for long, and the prince did not intend that it should. He knew that his conversations found their way, in one form or another, to the ears of the government and the king, and he relied upon this social and political grapevine "to give such warnings as I was able, sometimes in the Chamber of Peers and sometimes in private conversation. I did not hesitate to point out the perils of the domestic and foreign policy that had been adopted by the government or rather had been imposed by the government." One such "private" conversation took place between Talleyrand and his good friend Adolphe Thiers,* who supported the Spanish intervention. "What we are getting involved in," Talleyrand argued, "is an internal insurrection, which is the worst kind of war possible. We are in precisely the same kind of situation as formerly, when I advised Napoleon not to involve himself in the affairs of Spain. Napoleon ignored my advice, and stirred up a hornet's nest. . . . Well, if we persist in our Spanish adventure, history will repeat itself, and we will fall flat on our faces."

Talleyrand's most effective or at least his most formal opposition was intended to be voiced in the Chamber of Peers in January, 1823, immediately following Louis' address from the throne. His words adhered closely to the theme that he had expounded to Thiers:

> Sixteen years ago, I was asked by him who then ruled the world to speak my mind on the question of a Spanish war. I was unfortunate enough to displease him by foretelling the future and revealing to him all the perils resulting from an aggression as unjust as it was uncalled for. . . . How strange that fate, after so long a time, requires that once again I undertake the same task, and offer the same advice, to a legitimate sovereign. . . . The sole wish of France, as everyone knows, is for peace. France has had enough of military glory. It had thought that, under the leadership of its king, it would be able to heal, by an interval of peace, the wounds of thirty years of war."

Then, recalling something of his earlier career under the early Restoration, the speech concluded with an oath to the effect that the prince would work, with all the force of which he was capable, "to prevent that the work of wisdom and justice which was begun be now compromised by insane and unbridled passion." †

* Future minister, president of the Council, and, after the Franco-Prussian War of 1870, first President of the Third Republic.

†Chateaubriand tells us that as Talleyrand "came down from the tribune and returned impassively to his seat, my eyes followed him, and my mind was torn between a kind of horror and a kind of admiration. To think that this man had received such a degree of authority from nature that it was in his power so to distort the truth, or even to destroy it entirely!" One may question the sincerity of Chateaubriand's moral indignation. The fact is that Talleyrand's speech was never delivered, and Chateaubriand's description of the scene is wholly fictitious. The government—that is, Chateaubriand himself—had ordered all debate on the Spanish war to be suspended long before it was Talleyrand's turn to speak. According to the custom of the time, undelivered speeches were printed in the records of the upper chamber, and it was in this way that Chateaubriand and the public learned of the text.

Chateaubriand's "insane and unbridled passion" did serve, in fact, eventually to contribute to the discredit of the Bourbon regime, although it did not end in the military fiasco that Napoleon's venture had known. In two months, the Duke d'Angoulême, elder son of the Count d'Artois and commander in chief of the French forces, was in Madrid, and, with the fall of Cádiz in September, 1823, the war was over. On October 12, a solemn *Te Deum* was chanted in Notre Dame to celebrate the victory of French arms. The Prince de Talleyrand, to the vast amusement of the court, was required, as Grand Chamberlain, to attend this celebration of a war that he had condemned. It was not the impassive Talleyrand, however, who was the center of attention, but the king. It was remarked that during the lengthy ceremony, Louis XVIII kept fumbling with his prayerbook, dropped it several times, and, on several occasions, looked around with a vague and puzzled expression on his face. Those who were close to him realized that they were watching the beginning of the end of a reign.

Talleyrand's spirited opposition to the Spanish war, particularly the publication of the speech prepared for delivery in the Chamber of Peers, had stirred up great admiration throughout Europe, and the prince was now the hero of liberals everywhere. Stendhal wrote in one of the London papers that the speech, "memorable as it is from the political standpoint, must also take first rank in literature. Public opinion states: 'Nothing equal to it has been seen since the palmy days of Mirabeau.'" Unfortunately, it also served to stir up his enemies and to provoke an attack on one of the prince's least defensible fronts. On October 9, 1823, René Savary, Duke de Rovigo and a former minister of police under the Empire, published an article, consisting largely of extracts from his memoirs, in which he formally accused Talleyrand of having proposed and urged upon Napoleon the arrest of the Duke d'Enghien in 1804 and of having insisted upon the duke's execution.

Talleyrand, who was at Valençay when Rovigo's article appeared, hurried back to Paris to meet the storm head on, leaving Dorothea to follow him later with their baggage. "The winter is off to a bad start," she wrote to her friend Prosper Barante. It was indeed. Public opinion, always mindful of the glory that France had known under Napoleon, was and remained extraordinarily sensitive to any revelation concerning the secrets of that time of imperial grandeur. Rovigo's disclosures, if not refuted immediately, might well discredit Talleyrand personally and ruin him politically. The problem was how to go about the refutation. Dorothea, backed by Royer-Collard, urged her uncle to "go to the top"—that is, to appeal to the king himself for vindication. Talleyrand did so on November 8, calling to Louis' attention that he had enemies "both near the throne and also far removed from it" and protesting that it was his contribution "to the restoration of your august throne and the triumph of legitimacy" that "this former minister of the emperor, whose name I dare not even pronounce before your majesty," could never forgive. After pointing out that not even the Condé family, of which Enghien was a member, had "felt itself entitled to demand from me the blood" of the fallen Duke d'Enghien, Talleyrand informed King Louis of his intentions in the matter: "Sire, my name, my age, my character, the high rank I owe to your goodness, do not permit me to submit to such an outrage without seeking satisfaction. . . . I shall therefore indict my accuser before the Chamber of Peers, from which I shall obtain an inquiry and a judgment. The calumny will then be confounded, and its impotent rage will expire before the great light of truth."

King Louis, in truth, wanted nothing less than a public debate on the Duke d'Enghien's death. There was tumult enough in France without resurrecting the controversies of twenty years before. Moreover, a public airing of the circumstances of Enghien's death would undoubtedly lead to demonstrations and counterdemonstrations, the final outcome of which would inevitably profit only the Bonapartists. If Talleyrand were indeed guilty, then Napoleon would be exculpated, and if, as Talleyrand intended to prove, Rovigo were guilty, then, again, the onus would be lifted from Napoleon. The loser in any such debate must ultimately be, not Talleyrand or Rovigo, but the Bourbon throne. Louis, therefore, determined to squelch the entire affair immediately. On November 15, the following letter from the Count de Villèle, was delivered to the rue St.-Florentin:

> PRINCE,
>
> The King has read your letter of November 8 with great attention.
> His majesty desires me to say that he notes with astonishment your intention to call for a special investigation by the Chamber of Peers of the article just published by M. le Duc de Rovigo. His majesty wishes that the past should be buried in oblivion, excepting always as regards the services rendered to France and to himself.
> The king cannot therefore approve such a needless and extraordinary procedure, which would give rise to vexatious debates and revive the most painful recollections.
> The exalted place that you continue to hold at court, Prince, is a convincing proof that the accusations, which have so disturbed you, have made not the slightest impression on his majesty.

A few days after the receipt of this letter, a curt announcement appeared in the *Moniteur* of November 17: "The king has forbidden the Duke de Rovigo to enter the palace of the Tuileries." When Talleyrand next went to pay his respects to the king, Louis assured him that "you and your family are free to come here without fear of any unpleasant encounters." Absolution from the king was the best possible vindication, and even Talleyrand was satisfied. "One must not attach much importance to the Duke de Rovigo's attack," he wrote to Dalberg. "The people have granted me justice, and complete justice. Judgment has been rendered, and it is this: No one wants to hear another word about this affair." The Duchess de Broglie noted that "M. de Talleyrand has emerged from his affair as white as snow. He seems to thrive on being slandered."

What is certain is that such attacks and the king's expressions of confidence did nothing to diminish the ardor with which Talleyrand continued his attacks on the repressionist tendencies of the government. Villèle's measures were now aimed both at individuals and at the country as a whole. When Jean-Jacques de Cambacérès, one of the compilers of Napoleon's Civil Code and the former Arch-Chancellor of the Empire, died in March, 1824, the government ordered the police to impound every scrap of paper found in his belongings. "I see," remarked Talleyrand, "that the Tuileries has issued a warning to the rue St.-Florentin."

At the national level, Villèle was no less diligent in attempting to protect his regime. In the fall of 1824 he reintroduced Richelieu's old bill calling for a widening of the electorate, hoping—so little did he understand the temper of the country—that the petit bourgeoisie would return to the Chamber of Deputies representatives who would support his government. It was a serious miscalculation. Talleyrand succeeded in putting together a majority in the upper chamber by the extraordinary method of combining the votes of his own liberal followers, of the ultras, and of the clergy. And the latter were enlisted by a personal appeal from Monseigneur de Quelen, Archbishop of Paris, as the result of a visit from the Duchess de Dino to the archiepiscopal palace.* Even Chateaubriand, Villèle's own foreign minister and Talleyrand's sworn enemy, so far forgot himself as to side with the prince.

Villèle, of course, was furious, and since there was nothing that he could do to revenge himself against Talleyrand, he was compelled to vent his anger on a less satisfactory target. Chateaubriand was called in, roundly reprimanded, and dismissed from his ministry—"fired like a servant," he tells us. But again Chateaubriand exaggerated. As a consolation for the loss of Foreign Affairs, he was given the ambassadorship to Genoa, a post which he retained only a short while before disappearing forever from the political scene.† A few months later someone told Talleyrand that the Vis-

---

* The Countess de Boigne asserts that Dorothea accomplished her purpose by "throwing herself" at the venerable prelate and thereby causing him to fall madly in love with her. In this respect, two things should be noted: First, Dorothea and the archbishop had been close friends for years and would remain so until the latter's death in 1839; second, Madame de Boigne, in addition to being the most malicious and the most amusing gossip in Paris, was an admirer of Talleyrand's wife and, consequently, one of Dorothea's bitterest enemies.

† Chateaubriand managed to attain more success in literary and theological circles than he had in politics. After his "retirement" from public affairs, he devoted himself to writing, and produced,

count de Chateaubriand had become almost completely deaf. "Ah, no," Talleyrand replied. "He only thinks that he is deaf because he cannot hear anyone talking about him."

The year 1824, however, was a time of events of greater significance than Chateaubriand's disgrace. Early in August, Louis XVIII collapsed at the dinner table and had to be put to bed. Throughout the month, his strength ebbed until, by the beginning of September, he was so weak that he was unable to sit up or even to hold up his head without assistance. He was incredibly thin; his sight was almost entirely gone, and his voice barely audible. By then the Grand Chamberlain of France had cut short his stay at Bourbon-l'Archambault and returned to Paris to assist, as etiquette required, at the death of his sovereign. Talleyrand himself was not in the best of health—he was in his seventieth year—and Dorothea was genuinely alarmed that if the king's agony went on for many more days, the prince would be unable to bear the strain. Protocol required that the Grand Chamberlain remain standing in the king's chamber for many hours each day and that, as Dorothea noted, he render services which were "the most painful and disgusting ones possible for a man of the age and infirmities of M. de Talleyrand."

By September 12 the Abbé Rocher, the king's confessor, presented himself at the bedside, hesitantly, protesting that he had never before dared approach his majesty unsummoned. The king, seeing him, expressed astonishment, saying that he was not so ill as to require a priest.

On September 15, at three o'clock in the morning, Talleyrand, along with the princes of the blood and other high functionaries of the court, received a brief message: "The king is dying." He rushed to the Tuileries, to find that Louis had somehow revived and that his pulse was now strong. The following day the summons came again, and this time there was no mistake. At four o'clock in the afternoon, Louis XVIII drew his last breath. The physicians tried to revive him, but without success, and formally pronounced him dead. A nobleman approached him who, a moment before, had been the Count d'Artois and made the ritual announcement, "Sire, the king is dead." A *De profundis* was recited. Then the doors of the bedchamber were thrown open and the Duke de Blacas proclaimed to those waiting in the anteroom, "Gentlemen, the king!" And King Charles X, closely followed by the Grand Chamberlain, passed through the room.

Charles X was crowned on May 29, 1825, although his reign had begun at the instant of his predecessor's death. The transformation from Count d'Artois into King of France had no permanent effect upon his principles

---

among other works, the famous *Génie du christianisme*, and his *Mémoires d'Outre-tombe*—both of which demonstrate not only his intellectual gifts and stylistic brilliance, but also his reliance upon imagination at the expense of accuracy.

or policies. He began auspiciously enough, it is true, by ordering the government to abandon its censorship bill, but then, as soon as the government was attacked by the press, he lapsed into the open ultraroyalism that had been his chief characteristic under Louis XVIII and set about, with blind determination, on a course designed to deprive the peasantry and the bourgeoisie of the advantages they had gained during the Revolution and the Empire.

King Louis, long before his death, had taken his brother's measure and expressed his findings succinctly and prophetically: "He conspired against Louis XVI. He has conspired against me. And, finally, he will conspire against himself." It would be more accurate to say that King Charles, a prince of much less substance and intelligence than Louis XVIII, allowed himself to be persuaded to conspire against himself. Villèle, realizing that this indolent king, whose sympathies lay with the extremists, would not oppose him, began to introduce measures which first surprised France and then made it anxious and finally enraged it. His first move was to insult the Army by arbitrarily retiring 150 Napoleonic generals—by far the most experienced commanders in the service. This action was regarded, as indeed it was, as nothing less than a purge of officers whose loyalties not to France but to the regime were questionable. Next, he threw the peasants and the bourgeoisie into a fury by imposing the controversial *milliard des émigrés*— an indemnity to be paid, out of public monies, to the émigrés who, upon returning to France during the Restoration, found that their estates had been confiscated and sold. Talleyrand, who had gained considerably more than he had lost since the Revolution, remarked in the chamber how revolting it was to see those who had fought against liberty, equality, and fraternity, and indeed against France itself, thus rewarded. The Duke of Orléans also protested, but not before pocketing the 16,000,000 francs that he and his sister, Adélaïde, received as their share of the *milliard.*

Having successfully alienated most of France, the government now proceeded to finish the job by enacting a law—the famous *Loi de sacrilège*— imposing the death penalty for the profanation of churches. This enactment, the Duke de Broglie wrote, was accomplished "not in 1204, on the eve of the Crusade urged by Pope Innocent III against the Albigensians, or in 1572, on the eve of the Massacre of St. Bartholomew; but in the nineteenth century, in a free country, where freedom of worship is universally acknowledged." Broglie was not alone in his indignation. Rage swept through the ranks of the liberals, the republicans, the atheists, the anticlericals—that is, through almost everyone except the nobility of the *ancien régime* and the clergy. The public outcry was so loud that it was necessary to do something, and the most effective suggestion that the government could make was that the king show himself in public and thus regain the confidence of the people. Accordingly, Charles X rode in procession to the Champ de Mars, where a review of the National Guard had been arranged. Along the way, all went well. The king's appearance seemed to have the desired effect, and his party was greeted with loud shouts of *Vive le roi!* At the parade ground itself, however, it was a different story. The guard received their sovereign with cries of "Down with the ministers!" and "Down with the Jesuits!" * The uproar continued throughout the inspection, relieved only by infrequent shouts of *Vive le roi!* King Charles, to his credit, continued the review to the end and, with a sangfroid worthy of Talleyrand himself, acknowledged the loyal cries and wholly ignored everything else. The following day the National Guard was disbanded. A short time later it was reported that the government was once again attempting to formulate a censorship law that would effectively stifle all criticism of itself or its policies. Talleyrand, who was at Bourbon-l'Archambault during that eventful summer, wrote:

> I have never before left Paris with such a feeling of impending disaster in public affairs. Without knowing what the future holds, I fear that, whether we are willing or not, if the government succumbs to the temptation offered by censorship, then we will find ourselves standing at the threshold of revolution. This [censorship] is the first link in the chain of events that will drag us all over the cliff.

Meanwhile, "incidents" were multiplying in the streets, and every new event, whether government-inspired or not, seemed the occasion for a new outbreak of demonstrations against the regime. The death of the famed actor Talma was one such occasion. Talma had died outside the church, having absolutely refused, on his deathbed, to receive the sacraments or even to speak to a priest. The church therefore refused to allow the corpse to be buried in consecrated ground, and interment took place in a "civil" cemetery. The hearse was followed by a vast and ominously silent crowd, and following the eulogy, there was a heated demonstration aimed, ostensibly, at the church and the Congregation. The throne and the altar, however, were so closely allied in conservatism and absolutism at this time that it was difficult to establish where the acts of one began and those of the other left off. Indeed, the people made no great effort to distinguish, and it was obvious that the king was as much the target of the demonstration as the priests.

Another incident occurred early in 1828, and since this one directly involved the government's principal and most active opponent, Talleyrand, it was to have repercussions on the regime. In January, a service was held

---

* The Jesuits were widely regarded as being responsible for the Law of Sacrilege through pressure by their powerful religious confraternity, the Congregation.

at the Abbey of St.-Denis to commemorate the death of King Louis XVI. After the service, Talleyrand was standing at the entrance to the abbey as the king, the dauphin, and the Duke and Duchess d'Angoulême passed through the gate. There was a sudden commotion. A man thrust himself through the rank of guards, rushed at the prince, and, with all the strength of a comparatively young and robust man, struck him several times on the head and face with his open hand. Talleyrand fell to the ground. The man kicked him several times before the guards were able to intervene. It had all happened in the space of a few seconds, so quickly that no one knew quite what had happened. At first, it was thought that the Grand Chamberlain had been assassinated. When it was seen that he was not wounded, but only stunned, he was carried to his carriage and, followed by a great crowd of people, driven quickly to the rue St.-Florentin and put to bed. The house was, as usual, full of people, and the word spread instantly through Paris that France's most eminent statesman had been the victim of a public assault.

The assailant, who readily identified himself, was Marie-Armand Guerri de Maubreuil, Marquis d'Oravault. He belonged to an ancient, but impecunious, Breton family which had emigrated to England during the Revolution. His fervent royalism had not prevented him from serving in Napoleon's army, where he had been disgraced for some breach of trust. Thereafter he had been arrested and jailed on several occasions under both the Empire and the Restoration.* On the occasion of his first arrest for highway robbery in 1814, he had claimed to be in the employ of Talleyrand, who was then head of the provisional government, and at his trial he had maintained that he had been hired by the prince to assassinate the Emperor Napoleon. The charges were so fantastic, and the list of other personalities against whom he leveled equally incredible accusations was so long (including Czar Alexander, among many others), that Maubreuil had been regarded as mad and was sent to prison for being dangerously so. Now, in the hands of the police for assaulting one of the king's highest officers, he repeated his charges, adding that he hated Talleyrand because the prince had ruined the ancient families of France, including his own, and because he was an "unfrocked priest." The first charge Talleyrand disproves effectively in the Mémoires, adding that it "could have been invented only by a fool or a madman." † As for the second and third

---

* The adventures of this man, who was also known as the Count de Maubreuil, are not sufficiently documented—or at least the documents have not been discovered—to know the precise nature of his offenses. The only certain point is the reason for his first arrest in 1814; while serving as equerry to Jérôme Bonaparte, King of Westphalia, he decided to embark on an additional career as a highwayman, but had the singular lack of judgment to choose, as his first victim, Catherine of Württemburg—who happened to be King Jérôme's wife.

† Talleyrand's refutation is in the Addendum in Part IX, and was written in 1824 in response to Maubreuil's accusations in 1814. The fact that anyone as sensitive about loyalty as Talleyrand

charges, they could hardly be denied, for Talleyrand's role in the revolutionary overthrow of the *ancien régime,* in both church and state in France, had always been a matter of intense pride to him. His sentiments apparently were shared by the people of Paris, for Maubreuil's insistence and emphasis upon those two points—especially his repetition, on every possible occasion, of the term "unfrocked priest"—not only awakened great sympathy for the prince, but actually identified Maubreuil, in the public mind, with the party of clerical and civil reactionaries—that is, with the government of Villèle.*

This was a situation that Talleyrand was equipped to handle. Although, to a man of his years, any physical assault is something of a shock, he had suffered no real injury beyond a few bruises. Nonetheless, when *tout Paris* called to express sympathy and gather material for gossip, it found the prince stretched out on a couch, surrounded by pillows, his head swathed in voluminous bandages, and doctors and nurses in constant attendance. To everyone who came, Talleyrand argued that Maubreuil's assault had been nothing less than an attempt at assassination; and he was careful, even in his official report to the police, to explain that Maubreuil had struck him "with his closed fists"—for while anyone may be assaulted, no gentleman can have his face slapped and retain his honor intact. "He felled me like an ox," the prince insisted, as he clenched his fist and demonstrated the blow for the benefit of his audience. Even Charles X was not suffered to labor under any misunderstanding on this point. When, a few days later, the king inquired after his Grand Chamberlain's health and expressed the hope that the culprit would be suitably punished,† Talleyrand answered very firmly: "Sire, it was a blow with his fist."

Talleyrand's humiliation at having been publicly slapped, even by one who was mad, as well as the tedium of his convalescence, was relieved somewhat by his reconciliation with Chancellor Pasquier, who had not called in the rue St.-Florentin or even spoken to Talleyrand since the terrible scene at the British embassy ten years before. Now Pasquier called to inquire after the prince's health, and Talleyrand, profoundly moved, embraced his old friend and associate.

---

could have waited ten years to answer such a charge—and then do so only in a footnote, as it were, to his refutation of the Duke de Rovigo's more serious allegations—is an indication of the degree of seriousness with which the prince and the public regarded them, both in 1814 and in 1824.

* There is not the slightest evidentiary indication that Maubreuil had any contact with any government official. On the contrary, there is every reason to believe that his charges, like his act of violence, were the acts of a madman—as Talleyrand said.

† In February, 1828, Maubreuil was sentenced to five years in prison and a fine of 500 francs. Upon appeal, however, the sentence was reduced to two years of confinement and a fine of 200 francs. It is known that he served the sentence and was released in 1830. Thereafter, his madness was channeled into less hazardous pursuits, and he lived in unrelieved obscurity until his death in 1855.

Pasquier's visit may well have been inspired by sympathy for the plight of a man whom he had known so long and so well. Yet, as a member of the government, it was also his business to keep abreast of what the opposition was about. And there was no spot on the body politic where the pulse of that opposition could be taken with more accuracy than in the rue St.-Florentin.

Talleyrand, after the death of Louis XVIII and the accession of Charles X, had begun openly to ally himself with the liberal opposition to the government, not only by his speeches in the chamber against governmental policies, but also by drawing closer to the leaders of that opposition with whom he already had personal ties: Royer-Collard, Thiers, and François Mignet, the historian. Talleyrand and his friends met often, usually at the Palais Royal, which, under the benevolent hand of the Duke d'Orléans, had quickly become the meeting place of the malcontents. The (then secret) police records of the time are full of warnings concerning the habitués of the duke's house; Talleyrand and his friends, of course, but also Dupin, Laffitte, Sebastiani, Périer, the Duc de Broglie, the Marquis de Lafayette—all of whom were collectively identified in the reports as "the Orléanist camp." One report, curiously enough, after reporting in detail on a meeting at the Palais Royal and naming those who attended, concluded with this remark: "The King need have no fear with respect to His Royal Highness the Duke d'Orléans, his good and most devoted cousin." The fact was that the duke, knowing himself to be the one most open to suspicion and accusation, had decided that for the moment the most reasonable course was one of personal inaction. Indeed, he had little need of direct intervention, for his sister, Adélaïde, was sufficiently active for both of them. She had all the boldness that her brother lacked and none of the caution that tempered his ambition. She exulted in intrigue, lived for conspiracy, and was never happier than when presiding over the deliberations of some secret committee. She cherished the notion, not entirely an illusion, that she was the *éminence grise* of the House of Orléans, the true leader of the Orléanist circle.

Talleyrand, always prudent, hesitated openly to become a party to the conspiratorial environment that Madame Adélaïde had created around her brother in the Palais Royal. Yet he was in constant communication with the duke's sister and with the Orléanists, both through his old friend Montrond (who acted as a go-between) and through their common friends: Thiers, Mignet, Sebastiani, General Foy, Laffitte, Royer-Collard. He was preparing for the storm that he knew was to come. The king, in his determination to govern, as had his ancestors, by divine right, had discredited himself with the people and aligned the middle classes against the crown and the ancient nobility. And the government, presided over by Villèle, had reached the point where it was unable any longer to govern. Villèle's Cabinet, although composed exclusively of ultraroyalists, was never reactionary enough for the more rabid members of their own party, and the opposition of the ultras to the government was as strong as that of the liberals. In this they felt, not wrongly, that they had the support of the crown itself.

The government therefore found itself standing alone. Its measures were constantly and bitterly attacked by every party represented in either chamber, not only by the ultras and the liberals, but by the Bonapartists, under the leadership of Marshal Jourdan, by the republican party of the perennial Marquis de Lafayette, and by the Protestants, presided over by that fervent Orléanist, the Duke de Broglie. With both chambers and all parties united against him, Villèle could do nothing but resign. Instead, in 1827, he dissolved the Chamber of Deputies and called for a new election. Completely misunderstanding the temper of France, he hoped the people would return more tractable representatives to Paris. When it became clear that the new chamber was, if anything, more irreversibly liberal than its predecessor, he submitted himself to the inevitable and tendered his resignation to the king.

For a few days, France breathed easier. It was accepted as a foregone conclusion that the king would now be forced to look to the left for a new government and that Talleyrand would be given the opportunity, for the third time within living memory, to preserve the Bourbon crown. Instead, Charles X, having forgotten all and learned nothing, appointed to the presidency of the Council the Viscount de Martignac, who, other than an ancient and honorable name and a fine presence, had little either to commend him to the chambers and the people or to enable him to heal the breach caused by the Villèle government's insensitivity to the public need. Even the king was disappointed in him. Instead of forming a government of the extreme right, as Charles X wished, Martignac insisted upon following the policies established by his hapless predecessor. Whereupon the king withdrew his support, the chambers and the parties united solidly against the new ministry, and, after a month in office, Martignac was compelled to submit his resignation.

Now Charles X was openly determined to choose a first minister to his own liking. In August, 1829, the news broke that the new president of the Council and Minister of Foreign Affairs was to be Prince Jules de Polignac, the king's dearest friend and confidant and the acknowledged leader of the extremist faction among the ultraroyalists. He was also the son of that Princess de Polignac who had been the intimate of Marie-Antoinette and on whom that unhappy queen had showered every gift in her power. This friendship had brought universal odium upon Marie-Antoinette, and the Princess de Polignac had been accused by the revolutionaries of every conceivable vice and of the most sordid corruption. Of the queen's friends, it was commonly believed that she alone had been her majesty's evil genius, and it was publicly said and generally believed at the time that the Princess de Polignac and the queen were not friends, but lovers. The Princess de Polignac's death under the guillotine had not expiated her faults, real or imagined, and the very name of Polignac stood, in the mind of almost every Frenchman, for all the errors and vices of the *ancien régime*.

Whether or not Polignac deserved this ill fame is a matter of conjecture. Guizot, who was himself to become a minister under the successor of Charles X, described Polignac's situation pithily and, to all appearances, accurately:

> M. de Polignac was sincerely astonished at not being acknowledged as a minister devoted to constitutional rule, for the public, without bothering to inquire into his sincerity, had determined to regard him as the champion of the *ancien régime* and the standard-bearer of the reactionaries. Disturbed by this reputation and fearing to confirm it by his acts, M. de Polignac therefore did nothing.*

Whatever the truth of the matter, the fact remained that the king had committed a great and perhaps fatal error in appointing his friend to head the government. Throughout the kingdom, the news of Polignac's appointment was heard as the thunderclap of doom for the regime. A visitor to the Chateau d'Eu, where the Orléans family was staying at the time, describes the scene there: "On entering the drawing room, I perceived that everyone was greatly disturbed. Madame de Montjoie handed me the *Moniteur*, and I read the words, '*Polignac Minister.*' Madame de Montjoie was groaning aloud, and Princess Adélaïde, who was already ill, had collapsed entirely." In the rue St.-Florentin, the news was received with less hysteria, but with perhaps a better understanding of its implications for France: "Charles X took the foolish step of changing his government and summoning the most unpopular men to his Council, men whose only virtue was that of obedience, and an obedience that was as blind as was the stubbornness of the unfortunate king himself. It was now impossible to conceal from ourselves that we were rushing toward destruction."

Henceforth Talleyrand knew what he must do. "From the moment that legitimacy itself betrayed its own principles by breaking its vows, it became necessary at all costs to look to the safety of France and to rescue, if

* Guizot, ironically, although a gifted historian as well as a statesman, proved unable to learn from the lessons of history. As chief minister of King Louis-Philippe from 1839 to 1848, he was to forget the liberalism of his earlier years and adopt an attitude of such conservatism that he was the Polignac, as it were, of Louis-Philippe. His policies were to become the occasion for the downfall of that monarch.

it were still possible, the principle of monarchy, independent of the principle of legitimacy, in the great storm that arose." In the fall of that year, at Rochecotte—a small estate in Touraine that he had given to Dorothea in 1825—Talleyrand received a visit from Adolphe Thiers and a brilliantly promising young writer and politician named Armand Carrel.* Thiers and Carrel were determined to fight the government through the press. But already Polignac's policies had intimidated the press whose freedom Talleyrand had fought so vigorously to preserve under earlier governments. They had therefore decided to publish a newspaper of their own, one that was bold enough to suit their tastes. Talent they had aplenty; what they lacked was funds. They had come to one of France's wealthiest and most alarmed citizens for money. They did not have to argue long to achieve their purpose. A month later, in January, 1830, the first issue of the new organ appeared and was duly noted by a man who prided himself on knowing all, Stendhal. "Messieurs Thiers, Mignet, Stapfer—the translator of Goethe— and Carrel have founded the *National*," he wrote to an English friend. "They have put all that they have into it, and Monsieur de Talleyrand has provided the rest. The beautiful eyes of the Duchess de Dino are no doubt M. Thiers' inspiration. As for old Talleyrand, he has said in public that he recalled the Bourbons in order to have peace and that it is now necessary to drive them out again in order to restore peace."

The notion of preserving the monarchy by sacrificing the principle of legitimacy—that is, of replacing the House of Bourbon, if it became necessary, by that of Orléans—hardly originated with Talleyrand: "The idea of substituting the younger for the older branch of the royal family, as had been done in England in 1688, had, as it were, become a common subject of conversation ever since the formation of Charles X's last ministry [*i.e.*, that of Polignac]." The newspapers, both those that were friendly and those that were inimical to this ministry, discussed it openly, and it was in everyone's thoughts. Indeed, for Talleyrand, there was no acceptable alternative, other than Orléans, to the Bourbon dynasty. The only other possibility was one that could not even be considered: "I saw nothing before us but another republic and the terrible consequences it would entail: anarchy, a revolutionary war, and all the other evils from which France had been rescued with so much difficulty in 1815." The "terrible consequences" of republican government, as difficult as it may be for later generations to accept, were very real to France in the third decade of the nineteenth century. The middle classes, the bourgeoisie and the landed peasantry alike, remembered the revolutionary Republic only for its excesses, its wars, its

* Carrel's promise was cut short in 1836, when he was killed in a duel with another famous journalist of the era, Émile de Girardin.

ruinous effect upon the economy of France. The very word "Republic" signified to the most solid and industrious of Frenchmen nothing more than anarchy and ruin. This very large and influential segment of the people was therefore rabidly opposed to the idea, and in this at least, they concurred with the upper classes, who depended upon the continuation of the monarchy, in one form or another, for the survival of their own privileged social and economic position in society. Yet, as everyone seemed to realize, by 1829 the Bourbon monarchy had irreversibly entered upon its final agony and would shortly have to be replaced—either by another dynasty or by another form of government.

Everyone realized it, that is, except Charles X and his government. Jules de Polignac made no secret of his desire to restore to the Bourbons the plenitude of political and economic power—in other words, to restore the *ancien régime* in all its glory and in all its misery. One newspaper described the situation boldly and accurately:

> Here again is the court, with its old prejudices, the émigrés with their grudges, the clergy with its hatred of liberty, all come to place themselves between France and its king. All that was overcome by forty years of hard work and misery is now once again being imposed on France. Unhappy France! And unhappy king!

The king, meanwhile, was oblivious to the true sentiments of the people. Indeed, he felt that the common people were with him and that it was only Talleyrand and his friends and followers of "the Orléanist party" who were in opposition. So incensed was he at the vehemence of this clique, as he called it, that at a court reception he did not hesitate to address a thinly disguised threat to Talleyrand. In a voice loud enough to be heard by those around him, he said: "When a king is threatened, he has no choice but to climb onto his horse [*i.e.*, to fight]; either that or he will find himself in a tumbril [like Louis XVI, on the way to the guillotine]." Talleyrand, whose tongue had not spared monarchs more to be feared than Charles X, replied—also loudly: "Sire, may I suggest that your Majesty has forgotten another means of conveyance: the stagecoach."

A coach to the frontier was no doubt what Talleyrand had in mind for the Bourbons by 1830. The *National*, operated by Thiers and Mignet and financed by the prince and Jacques Laffitte, the banker, was the organ of the Orléanist opposition, and as soon as it appeared, it was gobbled up by the liberal bourgeoisie. The ideas that it disseminated and that were widely discussed and embroidered upon were not designed to render the Bourbon throne secure. There were constant references to the parallel between the Bourbons and the Stuarts: execution, restoration, succession by a brother of the king. Everyone was reminded that Charles X and James II were alike in their policies. They did not have to be reminded that James, after a bloodless revolution, had been deposed and succeeded by a member of his own family, for it was obvious that there was a royal cousin waiting, with great discretion and with evident ambition, in the Palais Royal; a Duke d'Orléans, who embodied the liberal principles that the Bourbons had forsaken; a prince, it was repeated, who had the support of M. de Talleyrand himself. For it was acknowledged that the prince's house had become the gathering place for many of the most prominent Orléanists. Late in 1829, after Talleyrand had returned from Valençay, Vitrolles came to visit in the rue St.-Florentin one evening. He was stupefied at the number and especially at the politics of the people assembled there and asked Pasquier for an explanation. "He had only to tell me the names of these people," Vitrolles commented, "for everything to become immediately clear. I recognized once more the wise man who is prepared for all events."

It was obvious to some of King Charles' devoted followers that the time had come for conciliation. Villèle, for one, when Charles was preparing his address from the throne, to be delivered on March 2, 1830, earnestly advised the king to make use of the opportunity thus presented to make a conciliatory gesture. Instead, Charles chose to speak in harsh, almost threatening tones to the combined chambers: "If nefarious plots create obstacles for my government that I cannot foresee, I shall find the strength to crush them in my determination to maintain public order." At the moment that he spoke these words, he threw back his head in a gesture of defiance. His hat fell off and rolled down the steps of the throne. An omen. Everyone watched in fascinated silence to see whether the king would know how to turn the portent to best account. Then the Duke d'Orléans walked over, picked up the king's hat, and held it until the address was over.

The chambers replied respectfully, but firmly: Let the king assure the peace and well-being of France by dismissing the Prince de Polignac and his ministers. Charles' response, after wavering for a moment, was to yield to Polignac's insistence and declare the chambers dissolved. New elections were announced for June 23 and July 3, with the convocation of the new chambers to be held on August 3.

It was madness on Polignac's part to believe that an election could result in anything but an overwhelming victory for the liberals, and folly on that of the king to listen to Polignac. France was astounded by the blind obstinacy of its king, and it was aware of where it would all lead: "The government," it was said openly, "is paving the way to the throne for the Duke d'Orléans." Talleyrand was hardly more circumspect. "Nothing," he wrote to the Princess de Vaudémont, "can now prevent a disaster." Those who knew Talleyrand recalled that he, "the wise man who is prepared for all events," had never once, in his inordinately checkered career, backed the wrong side.

If, as Talleyrand had written, disaster was inevitable, there was nothing more to be done, either for the cause of Charles X—even if the prince had been so inclined—or against it. He was openly allied with the Orléanist party. He had contributed both his prestige and his money to the further-ance of their cause. He and Dorothea were on excellent terms with the Duke of Orléans and with his strong-minded and ambitious sister, Adé-laïde. He had, in other words, written off the House of Bourbon and estab-lished himself with the House of Orléans. Now there was nothing more to be done but to see if events once more proved him right. Early in April, therefore, weeks before the usual time, Talleyrand and Dorothea left Paris for Valençay to wait out the storm that was rising in Paris. From the coun-try, he wrote to Barante: "We are speeding through unknown waters, with-out a rudder and without a pilot. Only one thing is certain: We will end up being shipwrecked."

There were signs enough in the sky to enable Charles X, if he had been wiser, to steer a safer course. One of his contemporaries describes him as being "so addicted to the pursuit of pleasure that he had neglected the claims of art and science, and he was quite uneducated. . . . He could not converse on intellectual or political subjects. Indeed, he could hardly even read the newspapers." But Charles' difficulties went deeper than a lack of education or intellectual curiosity. He had inherited both the fatal Bour-bon talent for ignoring what was unpleasant and the lack of energy to un-derstand what was real. There was no lack of warnings of the "shipwreck" that lay ahead, and a wise man would have read those signs—indeed, many already had—and steered a course accordingly. But Charles ignored all. On May 31, he attended a ball in honor of the King and Queen of Na-ples at the Palais Royal, despite the warning of the Baron d'Haussey that "At the Palais Royal, one meets only the enemies of your majesty." All evening long, the streets around the house echoed with the shouts of a mob gathered in the gardens and courtyards of the Palais: "*Vive le Duc d'Or-léans!*" But when the king appeared on a terrace and bowed to the mob, an instant silence fell. There was not a cheer, not a single *Vive le roi*. Charles remained for a few moments, waving his hand, then turned on his heel and, shortly afterward, left the Palais. Thereupon the mob stacked benches and chairs in the garden and set fire to them, while women shrieked and men were trampled underfoot. Finally, troops had to be called in to restore order. This was the first riot of 1830, the first distant thunderclap of the tempest. One of the guests at the Palais Royal, a Monsieur de Salvandy, expressed the general opinion perfectly. "This is truly a Neapolitan ball," he said. "We are dancing on a live volcano." Even the Countess de Boigne, who was as naïve politically as she was socially perceptive, saw the handwriting on the wall: "For the first time," she confided to her diary, "I could not help believing that the Duke d'Orléans had certain intentions which terrified me."

Throughout his disastrous evening at the Palais Royal, King Charles had maintained a perfect serenity; the serenity of a man who believes that, all appearances to the contrary, he would yet survive, and his government with him. On the very same day, a military expedition had been dispatched to Algiers, ostensibly to exact vengeance for an insult to a French consul, but actually to present the people of France with a conquest that would turn their attention from internal affairs. Many a shaky regime, before and since, has been buttressed by such accomplishments. On June 10, news reached Paris—by means of that marvel of the age, the telegraph—that the expedition had been successful and that the way was now open to the establishment of a splendid colony in North Africa. The people of France, who had not tasted of glory for a decade and a half, danced in the streets. But there were a few heads who foresaw that, colonial empires or not, France could not now be satisfied with anything less than what the government was obviously unwilling to give: a radical change of policy at home. To Barante, Talleyrand wrote, almost sadly, that it was too late for such "distractions" as Algiers, that it would have been far wiser for the government, "rather than squander money for conquest, to reduce taxes at home."

Talleyrand's appreciation of what was important to France was not shared by Charles or his ministers. The king, his confidence bolstered by the news from Africa and by the joyful popular demonstrations that followed it, determined to take the unprecedented step of appealing directly to the people to return conservative deputies in the forthcoming election. On June 13, he issued a royal proclamation declaring that "the last Chamber of Deputies misconstrued my intentions. I had the right to count on its support in order to accomplish the good that I contemplated. It refused. . . . Do not allow yourselves to be misled by the voices of our insidious enemies. Reject unfounded suspicions and fictitious fears, which would only undermine public confidence and may well stir up serious disorders. . . . Be reassured concerning your rights. I unite them with mine, and I will protect them with equal solicitude."

The electors recalled, however, that this king who spoke of protecting their liberties was the same one who had, by royal ordinance, abrogated the freedom of the press guaranteed in the Charter and had promulgated the infamous "law of justice and love" that punished with death crimes against the church in France. Their votes reflected this recollection. When the last ballot had been counted on July 19, it was announced that, far from responding to the king's plea for reactionary deputies, the electors had chosen to fill the seats of the Chamber with 274 liberal deputies and 142 conservatives. It was an unequivocal defeat for King Charles, for Jules de Polignac, and for the cause of ultraroyalism in France.

The eyes of the king were now opened, though he still could not see clearly enough to distinguish between moderation and republicanism. "The spirit of revolution now exists in the fullest sense in the men of the left," he announced to his Council. "It is the monarchical system that they wish to overthrow. Unhappily, I have more experience on this point than you, gentlemen, who are not old enough to have seen the Revolution. I remember what happened then. The first time that my brother made concessions was the beginning of the end for him. . . . If I give in to them this time, they will end up by treating us as they treated my brother." Genuinely alarmed, he acted quickly. What he intended was nothing less than a royal *coup d'état* which, he was advised, was the only certain way of making his people see the error of their ways. On Sunday, July 25, invoking Article 14 of the Charter, which empowered the king to "establish regulations and ordinances necessary to the implementation of the laws and the security of the state," he signed a series of four ordinances.

The first suspended freedom of the press and stipulated that "all works published without authorization shall be seized immediately." The second dissolved the newly elected Chamber of Deputies (which had not yet been convened) because "of the maneuvers which have been practiced in many places in our realm in order to deceive and mislead electors during the recent operations of the electoral colleges." The third ordinance, in order "to prevent a recurrence of the maneuvers which exercised so pernicious an influence during the recent proceedings of the electoral colleges," reduced the number of deputies and narrowed the franchise to "one-fourth of the electors of the department who are most heavily taxed." * And the fourth implemented and supplemented the third by calling for new elections early in September and convoking the chambers late in the same month.

Talleyrand, who had heard rumors of the ordinances and had hurriedly returned to Paris on July 24, sat quietly at home, awaiting the inevitable. No intervention on his part was required, no advice was to be given to anyone at this moment. The time would come, but it was not yet. Meanwhile, he ordered his broker to sell his government bonds and wrote to his friends that "everyone is disturbed; everyone, at every level of society."

---

* In other words, the right to vote was limited to 25 percent of the electors who had just returned an overwhelmingly liberal Chamber of Deputies. Now, instead of having between 30,000,000 and 33,000,000 represented by a mere 100,000 of their wealthier compatriots, Charles intended that no more than 25,000 electors—the richest and presumably the most conservative .0083 percent of the population—would have a voice in future elections.

This was perhaps an understatement. The household of the Duke d'Or-léans, at Neuilly, for one, was something more than simply "disturbed." On the morning of July 26, after one look at the *Moniteur*, the duke screamed, "They are insane! They will be thrown out again!" Madame Adélaïde ran into the room, disheveled, to see what had happened. The duke handed her the newspaper without comment. She glanced at it, im-mediately knew the worst—or the best—and calmly instructed the ladies of the household: "Quickly. Let us begin making cockades." She then went directly to her apartment and brought back to the drawing room every stitch she owned that was red, white, or blue. In a few hours, the room was strewn with the tricolor cockades of the Revolution. Through the long day and most of the night, the duke himself sat there, watching, listening to the ladies talk, but saying very little himself.

In Paris, everything was in an uproar. Forty-five journalists, representing a dozen of the country's most influential journals, had signed and pub-lished a direct challenge to the government:

> The rule of law has ended, and that of force has begun. . . . The govern-ment has acted illegally, and we are therefore absolved from the obligation of obedience. We intend to publish our papers without asking for the au-thorization imposed by the ordinances. . . . The government has now for-feited the right to be obeyed, and we intend to defy it in those matters that concern us. As for France itself, it must decide to what lengths its own re-sistance is to go.

On the following day, the recently elected deputies of Paris, not to be outdone, threw down the gauntlet with a resounding clash:

> The undersigned . . . consider themselves absolutely bound by their duty and their honor to protest the measures that the councillors of the crown have recently enacted. . . .
>
> These measures, as contained in the ordinances of July 25, are, in the opinion of the undersigned, directly contrary to the constitutional rights of the Chamber of Peers, to the public law of France, to the prerogatives and decrees of the courts. . . .
>
> Accordingly, the undersigned, in accordance with the spirit of their oath, do protest with one accord, against these measures and against all acts that may emanate from them. . . . Seeing, on the one hand, that the Chamber of Deputies cannot legally be dissolved because it has never been convened and, on the other, that the attempt to form another Chamber of Deputies, by new and arbitrary means, is in direct contradiction to the Charter and the rights of the electors, the undersigned declare that they still consider themselves to have been legally elected by the district and departmental colleges. . . .
>
> If the undersigned do not effectively exercise the rights and perform the duties of the office to which they have been legally elected, it will be only because they shall have been prevented by physical violence from doing so.

The cause of the Bourbons was still not entirely beyond hope. King Charles might have rescinded the incendiary ordinances; he might have dismissed Polignac and asked someone—Talleyrand was perhaps the only acceptable possibility at this juncture—to form a new government. Instead, Charles, from his chateau of St.-Cloud, ordered the Minister of Police to smash the printing presses of the journals that had defied the ordinances and published these treasonable declarations. On the day this became known, Paris became, once more, the city of revolution. People poured into the streets, marching up and down the boulevards, shouting, shaking clenched fists. Then they set to work erecting barricades in the streets. By early evening the crowds were so dense in the boulevards that no one could pass. The Garde Royale and the Gendarmerie, as well as several battalions of infantry, were called out—to be greeted by a hail of stones, furniture, tiles, pots, and pans and by a chorus of jeers. The soldiers fired into the air, hoping to frighten the demonstrators, but instead, this only increased their fury and they began tearing up the cobblestones from the streets to hurl at the king's men. Order was finally restored, not by the royal troops, but by exhaustion, which drove the people to their homes after darkness had fallen. Thus ended the first of the *Trois Glorieuses*, as they were known—the Three Glorious Days of the Revolution of 1830.

In the rue St.-Florentin, perfect tranquillity reigned throughout the day. Occasionally, a courier arrived bearing information on events in the city, but Talleyrand, though he listened with interest to such reports and to the excited conversation of his guests, was content to interject an occasional observation of no great consequence. He was waiting. The issue between the Parisians and the government was still in doubt, and as a prudent statesman he did not act until he was able to read the signs of victory.

The second Glorious Day, Wednesday, July 28, dawned bright and hot. A mob gathered immediately before the Hôtel de Ville. By eight o'clock the building had been occupied by the people, and two government arsenals, as well as several gunsmiths' shops, had been looted. An hour later, Marshal Marmont, the Duke de Ragusa, who had been made commandant of Paris, declared the city in a state of siege and stationed his battalions throughout the city. By noon the streets were filled with angry Parisians, many of whom were armed, and the battle began in earnest. The king's troops were lured from the boulevards into the narrow side streets, where they were exposed to murderous fire from the housetops. As they were engaged in defending themselves, barricades were erected behind them, cutting off the possibility of retreat. By midafternoon the streets in the heart of the city were littered with corpses, the doorsteps spattered with blood. Marmont was compelled to call out the artillery, and as darkness fell, the boom of the cannon, the sinister toll of the tocsin from Notre

Dame, the rumble of the drums calling all citizens to arms combined to demonstrate, if anyone still doubted it, that a revolution was in progress and that it must end either in the subjugation of the people or in the downfall of the Bourbons.

The sound of the tocsin was heard in the rue St.-Florentin. "Listen!" the prince exclaimed. "The tocsin! We are winning!"

"We?" a guest asked. "Who are 'we'?"

"Shush! Not a word! I will tell you tomorrow."

King Charles, still at St.-Cloud, seemed hardly better informed than Talleyrand's guest. He had been assured by his ministers that there was no danger, that Marmont was in full control of the situation. Late in the evening, Baron de Nevas, a military aide, burst into the king's presence, dusty and out of breath. He told of the butchery in the capital, of the lack of food and ammunition for the royal troops, and especially of the utter determination of the people to fight on to the end.

"My dear baron," Charles said, "surely you exaggerate the situation."

"So little do I exaggerate, sire, that, unless you agree to negotiate within three hours, the crown that your Majesty wears will have fallen from your head."

The king was silent for a moment. Then he sat down to play a game of whist.

The Baron de Nevas had indeed exaggerated, but only by not being sufficiently generous in counting the hours left for Charles X to wear the crown of France. For the rest, he was accurate. By the afternoon of the following day, July 29, Marmont realized that the situation was hopeless. Many of his regiments had deserted to the people, and those that remained to him were tired, hungry, and demoralized. He had no alternative but to order them to withdraw from the city toward St.-Cloud. With their departure, all traces of royal authority in Paris vanished, and the people were victorious. The deputies acted quickly to avoid anarchy. A municipal commission was appointed to administer the city, and the National Guard was reestablished—under the command of the man more experienced than any other in the art of revolution, the Marquis de Lafayette.

King Charles, meanwhile, had been assured by Polignac that there had been no incidents in the city during the previous night, that the insurgents were without arms and ammunition, that the great majority of the Parisians were loyal to his majesty, and that the rabble in the streets was eager to negotiate. He was therefore astonished by the arrival of his ministers in an unmarked, dirty carriage during the afternoon, and astonished, above all, that they had been forced to flee Paris to avoid being torn to pieces by a threatening mob. The ministers were shortly followed by an ultra peer, the Marquis de Sémonville, who implored the king immediately to revoke the ordinances of July 25 and to dismiss Polignac and his ministers. "Unless your majesty does so at once, everything will be lost, and tomorrow your majesty will no longer be King of France." Charles answered sadly, "I now find myself in the same position as my unfortunate brother in 1792. In three days, the monarchy will be a thing of the past."

Still he hesitated to act. It was not until late afternoon of the twenty-ninth, when a series of messages had arrived informing him that the insurgents were indisputably victorious, that he could bring himself to grasp at a straw of hope. With a stroke of his pen, he dismissed his government and replaced Polignac with the Duke de Mortemart.

It was too late. In Paris, at midday, Talleyrand, looking out of his window and seeing the people in command of the streets, glanced at his watch and told the assembled company, "My friends, today, July 29, at five minutes past noon, the elder branch of the House of Bourbon ceased to reign in France." Then, withdrawing to his study, he wrote a few words on a sheet of paper, summoned his secretary, Colmache, and dispatched the man and the message to Madame Adélaïde, sister of the Duke d'Orléans at Neuilly. The written message was nothing more than a note establishing Colmache's credentials. The secretary's oral message, however, was as direct as it was brief: The Prince de Talleyrand, in the strongest possible terms, urged the Duke d'Orléans to come to Paris immediately and place himself at the head of the insurgents. Louis-Philippe, Duke d'Orléans, was hesitant, undecided. Who knew how all this might end? What if the revolution failed? And what if it succeeded and the people refused to accept him? But Adélaïde entertained no such doubts; she had only ambition, confidence—and gratitude. "Ah, the good prince," she explained. "I knew that he would not forget us." To Louis-Philippe she said sharply, *Marche en avant!*—"Be the leader."

Thus summoned by Talleyrand and prodded by Adélaïde, the duke returned to Paris on the following day, July 30, to find the city engaged in a tug of war between the Orléanists and the republicans. For many hours, the outcome was uncertain, but Talleyrand's friends—Thiers, especially, and Laffitte—had not been idle. The walls of the buildings in the capital had been hurriedly covered with giant posters:

"The Duke d'Orléans is a prince devoted to the cause of the Revolution."

"The Duke d'Orléans has borne the tricolor in battle. Only he can bear it again. We will accept no other."

"The Duke d'Orléans has spoken. He will accept the Charter as we have always demanded it."

"It is from the people that the Duke d'Orléans will accept his crown."

The duke was encouraged, but he was uncertain of what should be done next. Madame Adélaïde was not. Power was now in the hands of the people; therefore, if her brother was to accept power, it would necessarily be from the representatives of the people. "First of all," she told Thiers, "the deputies must act. Once this has been done, my brother will no longer hesitate. If necessary, I myself will accept power in his name." Thiers—whom Orléans himself had been unwilling to receive—was overwhelmed by the lady's strength of mind. "Madame," he blurted out, "you bestow a crown upon your house."

M. Thiers' words were hyperbolic. He knew perfectly well that it was not Madame Adélaïde who was in the habit of bestowing or withholding crowns in France. Nevertheless, the script had been written, and it must be acted out. Early in the morning of July 31, a group of deputies arrived at the Palais Royal to ask Orléans, "in the name of France," to accept from the people the title of lieutenant general of the kingdom. The duke, troubled and still uncertain, asked for an hour in which to meditate on his decision. A messenger was quickly dispatched to the rue St.-Florentin asking for Talleyrand's advice. It was forthcoming, and it was unequivocal: "Let him accept." Shortly after the messenger had reentered the Palais Royal, Orléans presented himself before the deputies and announced his decision: He would accept. The representatives of the people bowed with great reverence and withdrew, knowing that they had seen Louis-Philippe plant his foot firmly on the steps to the throne.

His ascent, however, was not yet certain. In the course of the morning, news reached Paris that King Charles X, fearing for his safety, had left St.-Cloud and withdrawn with his family to Rambouillet, about 50 kilometers west of Paris. "You see," Talleyrand announced, "it is not I who have abandoned the king. It is the king who abandons us."

The rest of Paris received the news in much the same spirit. Rambouillet was to Charles X what Varennes had been to Louis XVI. By seeming to flee from his people, he had relinquished the last hold that he may have had upon their loyalty and their trust. Power was now within the grasp of any man who was strong enough to seize it. Lafayette, as head of the newly reconstituted National Guard and as one of the most popular figures in France, was urged to proclaim a republic with himself as its head. But the marquis was now seventy-three and ailing; moreover, he feared that the establishment of a republic would lead to the same radical abuses in 1830 as it had in 1792. He declined, and the republicans, deprived of a rallying point, were thrown into confusion.

It was now the turn of the Orléanists. At two o'clock in the afternoon, accompanied by a large group of deputies, Louis-Philippe, wearing one of Madame Adélaïde's cockades in his hat, rode to the Hôtel de Ville, about a mile distant from the Palais Royal. It was a calculated risk. Many of the people in the mob watching him were strongly republican, and there were a few cries of "No more Bourbons!" and other expressions even less complimentary. Yet the mood of the crowd as a whole seemed to be more friendly than hostile. As the duke reached the Hôtel de Ville and was received by Lafayette* and the municipal commission, the crowds began cheering, *"Vive le Duc d'Orléans! Vive la liberté!"* And when Orléans and Lafayette appeared together on a balcony a short while later, with Orléans carrying the tricolor of the Revolution, "the cheers and the applause," records one witness, "became frantic, and never has a prince been greeted with such joy by an armed crowd."

It was literally all over but the shouting. Louis-Philippe was not yet king; he was still only Lieutenant General of France. But this was quickly rectified. On August 2, Charles X confirmed Orléans' appointment as Lieutenant General and abdicated (both for himself and for his son) in favor of his grandson, the Duke de Bordeaux, son of the Duke de Berry. Then, abandoned by everyone but his family and a handful of loyal troops, the former king entered his coach and was driven to Cherbourg, where he embarked for England and exile.†

The document of abdication represented perhaps the single stroke of political genius of Charles' life. In it, he appointed the Duke d'Orléans to be regent during the minority of his grandson.** Charles had hoped to tie the hands of Orléans with the rope of honor and prevent him from placing the crown upon his own head, but the hope was vain, for the disposition of the crown did not depend solely, or even largely, upon Orléans. In any event, the lieutenant general of the realm, now that he had been blessed by Talleyrand, acclaimed by the people, and kissed by Lafayette,‡ had no intention of accepting second place. He dutifully proclaimed the abdication— but neglected to mention the accession of King Charles' grandson.

That night, very late, a meeting took place between Prince Talleyrand and Louis-Philippe, at the Palais Royal, which continued on until dawn. No one knows precisely what was discussed, other than that the Charter, which had been the stumbling block of the Bourbon Restoration, was discussed at great length and revised in a very liberal sense. All that is certain is that, for the next few days, things moved with great rapidity and preci-

---

* Orléans' arrival seems to have taken Lafayette and his republicans by surprise. Yet, says General de Rumigny, who was present, Lafayette "put a good face on it and showed himself to be a good citizen."

† Charles remained in England only briefly and then moved his household to Austria, where he died in 1836.

** The Duke de Bordeaux was, officially at least and in the eyes of the legitimists, King of France for a few days, under the style of Henri V.

‡ The crowd had been delighted by this osculatory display, for Lafayette was famous for his love of kissing. The people referred to him fondly as *Père baiseur*—"Kissing Daddy."

sion. On August 7, the chambers, convoked by Louis-Philippe, declared the throne to be vacant since "Charles X and His Royal Highness Louis-Antoine, the dauphin, and all members of the elder branch of the royal house are presently leaving French territory" and proclaimed that "the general and urgent interest of the French people summons to the throne his royal highness Louis-Philippe of Orléans, Duke d'Orléans, Lieutenant General of the Realm, and his descendants in perpetuity." At the same time, the chambers voted to accept the revised Constitutional Charter offered by Orléans and prepared by Talleyrand.*

On August 9, 1830, the Duke d'Orléans was officially proclaimed Louis-Philippe I, King of the French, and his faithful aide-de-camp, General de Rumigny, noted in his diary that "it is like the rainbow at the end of the storm."

Talleyrand's assessment of the situation was less poetic: "Here we are, in power once again."

* The revision of the Charter had evidently been worked out in detail by Talleyrand before his meeting with Orléans, for it carefully exorcised those parts that had furnished Charles X with the pretext for acting as an absolute monarch. The first such element to be suppressed was the stipulation, imposed by Louis XVIII in 1814, that the king was granting the Charter of his own free will, as a concession. By this simple omission, the Charter was, in effect, placed above the crown and acquired an existence independent of the monarch's goodwill. Among the other significant revisions was the abolition of Roman Catholicism as the religion of state; a formal guarantee that freedom of the press would never be violated; the suppression of the power to the crown to govern by decree in times of emergency and to suspend laws. In addition, the new Charter declared that "all new appointments and creations of peers made during the reign of Charles are null and void" and provided for new legislation, "within the shortest possible time," on trial by jury, on the organization of the National Guard, on freedom of instruction in the schools, and on the qualification of voters, among other reforms. (B. Duvergier, *Collection complète des lois, décrets, ordonnances, reglements* . . . Vol. 30, p. 177 ff.)

Part Six

THE LONDON EMBASSY

(1830–1834)

I have no hesitation in saying that, in every one of the great transactions that took place at the Congress of Vienna, and in every transaction in which I have been engaged with Prince Talleyrand since, from the first to the last of them, no man could have conducted himself with more uprightness and honour in all his communications.

—DUKE OF WELLINGTON

I T WAS evident to everyone, from the first days of the new regime, that the July Revolution represented the final and decisive victory of the bourgeoisie in France: a victory begun forty-one years before with the storming of the Bastille; a victory over absolutism and nonrepresentative government; and therefore a victory over the spirit of aristocracy. But for all that, it was not necessarily a victory over the aristocrats themselves, at least not over one particular aristocrat of ancient lineage and blood of undoubted blue, whose services the bourgeoisie and the new bourgeois King of the French could not forgo. The Prince de Talleyrand, at the age of seventy-six, a decade and a half after having reached, in his own words, "the end of my political career . . . this perhaps too protracted career," now suddenly found himself once more in the foreground of public affairs.

It was not only because, with his usual clairvoyance, he had, long before July 1830, thrown his support to the future victors—Louis-Philippe d'Orléans, Madame Adélaïde, and Thiers—but also, and especially, because his particular talents were as indispensable to Louis-Philippe as they had been to the Assembly, the Directory, the Consulate, the Empire, and the Bourbons. Talleyrand knew it. Louis-Philippe knew it. And each knew that the other knew. There seemed to be no reason, therefore, for the two men to play the usual game of false reticence on the one side or of condescending indifference on the other. A meeting took place almost as soon as the chambers had assigned the crown to the new king and was the occasion for a very candid exchange. The situation of Louis-Philippe, as both men knew very well, was far from secure, particularly with respect to the foreign powers. The Czar of Russia, Nicholas I, who in 1825 had succeeded his brother, Alexander I,* both on the throne of Russia and in the leadership of the conservative forces of Europe, was openly preaching a crusade to overthrow "the barricade king," as he called Louis-Philippe, and to re-establish the Bourbons. Nicholas, in fact, had already sent one of his generals to Berlin to solicit Prussian cooperation in an invasion of France. And it might be expected that the other conservative monarchies of the Continent—Prussia and Austria—although stopping short of armed intervention, would have little enthusiasm for a monarch who, in their eyes, was nothing more than a usurper. In view of France's isolation, therefore, it was of overwhelming importance for Louis-Philippe to assure himself first of Great Britain's diplomatic recognition and then of its diplomatic support.

"The first subject we touched on," Talleyrand recalls, "was naturally the impression that this new revolution would produce in Europe. We both realized that the first thing to be done was to procure the recognition of the principle of this revolution by the foreign governments and obtain, if not their goodwill, then at least their absolute noninterference with the internal affairs of France. We naturally looked first to England, our nearest neighbor, who, by its institutions and its past revolutions, ought to be the power best disposed to us."

Louis-Philippe, acting on this principle, at once dispatched his aide-de-camp, General Count Baudrand,† to England. Baudrand returned a few days later, bringing with him assurance from the British government that it would shortly extend recognition.** This pleased both the king and Talleyrand immensely; the king, because he felt that England's example would soon be followed by the other powers; and Talleyrand, because England's assurances of support demonstrated the soundness of a principle that he had held since the beginning of his public life: that France's true strength lay in a close association with Britain rather than with the powers of central and eastern Europe. He had preached this principle to Mirabeau, he had urged it, more discreetly, on Napoleon, and now he did all that he could to impress it on Louis-Philippe. "It is in London," he told the king, "that the new government must seek directions as to its foreign policy."

* Alexander's death is as controversial as his life. Officially, he died on December 1, 1825. There is a recurrent story—which has never been disproved—that he did not die, but left Russia aboard a ship belonging to the Earl of Cathcart and returned later, in disguise, to spend the remainder of his life as a monk. It is believed by some that a Siberian hermit named Feodor Kuzmich, who was famous for his austerity and saintliness and who died in 1864, was actually the Czar Alexander. The story gains credibility from the fact that, when the Soviet government ordered Alexander's tomb opened in 1926, it was found to be empty.

† Baudrand, as a reward for his services in this matter, was made lieutenant general and a peer of France.

** Recognition was forthcoming at the end of August, 1830.

Louis-Philippe was willing to accept this advice from France's elder statesman. But advice was not enough. He needed, in addition, a man who was capable of representing France in London in such a way as to implement the policy that it established. "It was indispensable," Talleyrand tells us, "that an experienced ambassador should be sent there, one who was already well known in Europe." France actually had only one such man, Talleyrand himself—as Talleyrand well knew. He was the only one who was well acquainted with the most important figures in the British government (with Wellington, for example, who was Prime Minister at this time, and Lord Aberdeen,* Foreign Secretary; the only one whose reputation alone was almost sufficient to ensure the success of his mission, and the only one who, to vast experience and great prestige, added an aristocratic heritage so authentic that even the conservative Tory government must regard him as one of themselves—an advantage greatly prized in England at that time and later.

"The king at once offered me this somewhat difficult post," the prince continues, "but I declined on account of my great age, the activity that such a mission would require, and the endless difficulties that were necessarily connected with it." For a time, it seemed that the old man would stand firm. By the first week in September he had still not accepted the king's offer, while Louis-Philippe and his ministers alternately pleaded, cajoled, and, to the extent that they dared, insisted.

To the exhortations of the Palais Royal were added the arguments of someone whose pleasure in this matter meant more to the prince than Louis-Philippe's wish. On September 1, Dorothea had returned to Paris from Rochecotte to pay her respects to the new King of the French. She had found her uncle undecided, the king increasingly insistent, and Molé, the new foreign minister†—though not wholly enthusiastic about the prospect of such an overwhelming ambassador—doing his best to please the king by persuading the prince. At this point, she intervened. Talleyrand had to accept. She was convinced that the London embassy was the perfect position for her uncle, the one best suited both to his tastes and his talents. Moreover, if the prince went to London, she would accompany him, and that city presented a social vista that she properly regarded as the only one in which she could feel truly happy and at home: an aristocratic society unhampered either by the dreariness of a Restoration or the bonhommie of

---

* George Gordon, Earl of Aberdeen, had represented England at Vienna in 1814.

† The new ministry had been formed on August 11 and comprised, in addition to Count Molé, François Guizot as Minister of the Interior; the Duke de Broglie, President of the Council and Minister of Public Instruction and Religion; Baron Louis, Minister of Finance; General Gérard, Minister of War; General Sebastiani, Minister of Marine. In addition, a number of ministers without portfolio were named, among whom were Laffitte, Talleyrand's collaborator in the Orléanist cause, and Casimir Périer.

a victorious bourgeoisie. Finally, such an appointment would satisfy her ambition to play a role for which, at Vienna, she had been too young, too inexperienced. It is also possible, as the Countess de Boigne states, that Dorothea was eager to be free of a troublesome love affair with an unsavory character named Piscatory or that, as the countess charged in a more benign mood, she was simply tired of what passed at the time as "a quiet life." In any event, Dorothea used all her powers of persuasion to convince her uncle that he must accept.

Finally, on September 3, the prince received a note from Molé, transmitting what was nothing less than a command:

> It is half past six. I have just returned from the Palais Royal, dead with fatigue and with a bad headache. The king is determined, *insists* on it more strongly than I can say. . . . Were I less exhausted and in less pain, I would come and tell you about it.

Talleyrand was, as he described, "compelled to give in to the solicitations of the king and of his ministers. . . . I thought the next government could only gain stability by the maintenance of peace, and . . . I felt assured that my name, the services I had rendered Europe in former days, and all my efforts would perhaps succeed in averting that most terrible of all evils, a revolutionary and general war."

By Sunday, September 5, Talleyrand had signified his acquiescence, and Louis-Philippe was writing a note to express his "gratification" and "delight" at the prince's decision. The official appointment was announced the following day in the *Moniteur*, and news of it spread rapidly throughout Europe, reaching even distant St. Petersburg within a few days. Czar Nicholas had not been very fortunate thus far in his attempts to intervene against the man who, in Nicholas' words, had "usurped" the throne of the grandson of Charles X. Neither Prussia, under Frederick William III, nor Austria, guided by the prudent Metternich, had responded favorably to the czar's plan to invade France. Nonetheless, the Autocrat of All the Russias seemed determined to stand fast, even if it meant standing alone. But when the news of Talleyrand's nomination reached him, the czar reacted curiously. His exact words, according to one of Molé's informants in the Winter Palace, were: "Since M. de Talleyrand has associated himself to the new government of France, this government must necessarily have a good chance of survival." It is not known whether Nicholas was attempting sarcasm or was genuinely impressed. What is certain, however, is that, six weeks later, Russia recognized the Orléans monarchy, while Austria, Prussia, Spain, and the smaller powers all followed her lead. It is also known that Europe generally believed Talleyrand's appointment caused

Nicholas to do his about-face. Sir Henry Bulwer, an intimate of Palmerston and of Lord Charles Grey, assures us that Talleyrand's support of the new dynasty "exercised considerable influence on the other courts; and we can say, more accurately, that it weighed in their decision in favor of recognition." Even Nicholas' ambassador in Paris, Pozzo di Borgo, who was no friend to Talleyrand, saw that, with Talleyrand's appointment, a rapprochement between England and France was imminent and that his imperial master must now face the situation realistically. And the Countess de Boigne, whose father, the Marquis d'Osmond, had been ambassador to London during the Restoration and who was perfectly at home in that England, reported: "The appointment to London of M. de Talleyrand immediately placed the new throne on a very high level on the diplomatic scale."

Reaction in France itself was mixed. Talleyrand's friends, of course, were delighted, but many did not share their sentiments. The radicals and even many of the liberals were convinced that Talleyrand, in order to accomplish his mission of conciliation with the British, was prepared to surrender more than was consonant with the honor of France. It was said that the prince was determined to place the question of Belgian independence* entirely in the hands of the British so as to facilitate a solution and even, if Wellington required it, to renounce the Algerian conquest. Talleyrand was, of course, aware of the rumors. "Everyone was against me," he wrote. But he was unconcerned. He knew what had to be done, and he knew how to go about it. So, on September 24, he sailed from Calais, "filled with hope," he confessed, for all the world like a junior diplomat embarking on his first mission. Dorothea was to follow him a week later.

"As I heard the booming of the cannon from the fortress announcing the arrival of the French ambassador [at Dover]," Talleyrand wrote later, "I could not help remembering the time when, thirty-six years before, I had sailed from these same English shores, exiled from my country by revolutionary upheavals and chased from British soil by the intrigues of the émigrés."

It was not, however, with resentment that Talleyrand recalled England's treatment of him almost four decades before. Indeed, he seemed never to bear resentment against the English for anything they did. They might chase him from their territory, make war upon his country, occupy his be-

* Belgium, then a province of the Netherlands, in the wake of the events of July, 1830, in France, was demanding that it be separated from the Netherlands, to which it had been joined by the Congress of Vienna. The French radicals and most liberals—along with many Belgians—favored union of their country with France, but Britain was firmly opposed to this political and economic enlargement.

loved Paris, oppose him at Vienna. Nothing altered the basic affection and admiration he felt throughout his life for the customs, institutions, and people of the island kingdom. Even in the midst of the Napoleonic adventure, when to speak well of England was little short of treason, Talleyrand had never ceased to speak, even to Napoleon himself, of the virtues of the English. A German officer, Ferdinand von Funck, observed in 1806 that "Talleyrand liked the English people. . . . He spoke of them without mincing his words, for in general he was not as careful in what he said as one might expect of so skilled a statesman. Whenever he had the chance to speak well of the English, he took advantage of it. He loved to talk about his sojourn in that country, and he always spoke with great candor and cordiality."

However constant Talleyrand's love of England may have been, the fact was that the object of his affection had changed considerably since he had been "chased from British soil by the intrigues of the émigrés." In 1794, it had been the England of Pitt, whom Talleyrand had respected as "the most astute and also the most logical" statesman of English history, and now it was the England of Wellington, Palmerston, and Lord Grey. It had been the England of George III, "mad George," of a charming and profligate Prince of Wales, of powdered wigs and minuets. Now it was an England on the threshold of the Victorian era, a land of top hats and frock coats, where the waltz had replaced the more stately dances of yesteryear and even the strictest parents had grown accustomed to seeing their daughters embraced on the dance floor by perfect strangers.

The signs of the times could be read in the political arena, as well as in society. In June, 1830, George IV had died and been replaced by his rather simpleminded brother, William IV. The new king was popularly supposed to have liberal ideas. The truth was that he had no ideas at all; but even that was liberalism in a sense, for it guaranteed that the crown would no longer oppose liberal reforms. The demand for such reforms was growing louder every year, not only in Parliament but among the people. The general election that had accompanied William's succession had cost the conservative Tory government fifty seats in the House of Commons, and the Duke of Wellington, rather than place himself at the head of the reform movement and thereby be enabled to moderate it, had categorically refused not only to introduce any bill of reform, but "to resist such measures when proposed by others." His government, therefore, and conservatism with it, was dying simultaneously of old age and self-inflicted wounds. England, in a word, was going through a revolution of its own. But, unlike its counterpart in France, it was a revolution not of the middle, but of the upper, classes. The revolutionaries were as wellborn and as wealthy as the pillars of the *ancien régime,* and Lord Grey would shortly boast that his own liberal, reforming government was composed of the richest men that had ever formed a British Cabinet.

The England to which Talleyrand was returning was therefore an enigma and a paradox, a country in which new ideas and radical reforms were being disseminated by members of an aristocracy reputed to be the most rigid and exclusive in the world. Foreigners were mystified by this unprecedented method of reform. They had never before seen a hierarchy, based on caste and antique values, in the process of dismantling itself voluntarily and then regrouping and renovating itself in keeping with the spirit of the times. Even Dorothea, who by now had learned a great deal from fifteen years of life with Talleyrand, was blind to the real genius of reform in England and complained of the apparent hopelessness of the situation. "When I see to which heights of power and glory London has risen," she wrote, "I ask myself if it can ever change." Drawing upon her own experience of revolutions, she concluded that abuse, by its very intensification, must inevitably bring about a reaction: "It is only when I am revolted by the excess of misery that I see existing alongside an excess of luxury, that I can answer 'Yes.'"

The puzzlement of foreigners with respect to the English was equaled by the reserve of the English vis-à-vis foreigners and, in this instance, particularly so far as the new French ambassador and his entourage were concerned. The people, like the government, were not hostile toward the new regime in France, but they were uneasy. The first French Revolution had plunged the whole of Europe into a seemingly endless cycle of wars. Would the second do the same? The Bourbons, it is true—and especially Charles X—had not enjoyed great esteem in England, but at least they had been "legitimate" and therefore a known quantity. Louis-Philippe, on the other hand, was not only little known, but had taken the throne in circumstances that, to say the least, were unusual. This counted for a great deal in a country that had been lavish in the spilling of blood over the principle of legitimacy, that had thought so highly of that principle as a bulwark of internal peace that it had gone to Scotland, on one occasion, for a legitimate king and, later, to the German state of Hanover for an entire dynasty. The reigning monarch of that dynasty, in fact, was the present King of England, William IV, and as might be expected, he was the staunchest supporter of legitimacy. He considered Louis-Philippe an "infamous scoundrel," and he said so on every possible occasion, public and private, until the Duke of Wellington, at wit's end, was compelled to inform his majesty that the exercise of a truly royal reserve would be more in keeping with his position.

The ambassador of Louis-Philippe, the representative of this highly suspect revolution, could hardly expect to be greeted, at least initially, with universal approbation. Yet he was determined to do what he could, from the very beginning, to assure himself—and therefore France—of public favor. His official entry into the British capital, on September 25, was calculated to further that intention. His carriage was decked in tricolor streamers, and he and his grooms wore gigantic cockades in their hats. The message was clear to the meanest subject of his Britannic majesty: The Prince de Talleyrand was in London as the representative of a popular and even a revolutionary government. The July Revolution had come to London. The crowds were amused and vastly pleased and applauded wildly. If they had seen this ambassador of the people at the Duke of Wellington's table that evening, decked out in silks, covered with diamonds, his hair scrupulously powdered in the style of the *ancien régime,* they might have become suspicious, for they could not know that the former Bishop of Autun had always observed diligently at least one of the Pauline precepts: Be all things to all men. With the crowds, he was the revolutionary, but in the houses of England's noble lords and fair ladies, especially in that of its conservative prime minister, he must be nothing less than the *grand seigneur,* a representative of the most ancient and authentic aristocratic traditions of Europe. This versatility, however, did not always succeed in charming his audience. Lady Granville, who saw him at Wellington's dinner, reported that "he crawled past me like a lizard along the wall." And Dorothea, whose reputation had preceded her in a highly romanticized form, was also viewed with some suspicion. "The Queen," Mr. Creevey reported gleefully, "would have no time for any private meeting with the Dino."

With respect to such gossip, transmitted in private, Talleyrand was defenseless and probably indifferent. Publicly, however, it soon became known that one did not question the new regime with impunity, at least in Talleyrand's presence. Princess Lieven, wife of the czar's ambassador in London, who resented not so much Talleyrand's politics as the social preeminence of the French embassy, went to great lengths to manufacture mots that would be repeated to Talleyrand's discredit. Occasionally, she succeeded, as when she remarked: "The Duke of Wellington is completely under M. de Talleyrand's spell. You would hardly believe your ears if you could hear him arguing that he [Talleyrand] is the most honorable man in the world and that anything that has been said to the contrary is pure calumny. It seems to me that the honesty of M. de Talleyrand is about on a par with the intelligence of M. de Polignac.* The Duke of Wellington is not very good at judging character." The comparison between Talleyrand's

* Prince Jules de Polignac, former prime minister of Charles X, enjoyed a wide reputation not only as an honest ultraconservative, but also as a dunce.

probity and Polignac's acuity was too good not to repeat, and Lieven's thrust was received everywhere with great hilarity. This, Talleyrand was content to ignore. But one night, at a diplomatic reception, the princess dared to refer to the July Revolution as "a usurpation," and this was too much for even Talleyrand's limitless forbearance. "Madame," he replied icily, "you are quite correct. The only thing to be regretted is that this usurpation did not occur sixteen years earlier—as the czar, your master, wished and desired." * It was noted that no Russian diplomat thereafter spoke of Louis-Philippe as a usurper.

It did not make Talleyrand's position any less difficult that the former King of France, Charles X, and most of his family were living in Britain, at Holyrood Palace. Charles, of course, never missed an opportunity to point out that France had but one legitimate dynasty and one true king and that he was that king. The British government was as embarrassed as Talleyrand at this state of affairs, but with its long tradition of offering hospitality to foreign exiles, there was little they could do except hope for the best and wish secretly that Charles and all his kin might decide—as eventually they did—to seek refuge in a more pleasant climate. In the meantime, there were contretemps enough to keep the Foreign Office, the diplomatic community, and even the royal family off-balance. Adelaide, the Queen of England, for instance, felt constrained to apologize to Dorothea for having accepted a small contribution from Charles' household for a charity bazaar that she was organizing—as she had no doubt apologized to the exiled Charles for receiving Louis-Philippe's ambassador. On another occasion, Princess Esterházy, niece of the Austrian emperor and wife of that sovereign's ambassador to England, came to Dorothea and explained to her, in confidence, that she felt duty-bound to pay a call on the Duchess de Berry, Charles' daughter-in-law. She hoped, she said, that M. de Talleyrand and his government would not take it amiss. This time, however, the awkwardness of Charles' presence in England was turned to the advantage of France. Dorothea suggested that it might be soothing to ruffled feathers if, upon her next visit to Vienna, the princess arranged her itinerary so as to pay a call at the Palais Royal in Paris. It proved to be an ingenious suggestion. The Duchess de Berry, knowing Princess Esterházy to be a friend of Dorothea's, received her coldly, spoke only a few words, and then dismissed her abruptly. In Paris, however, at a hint from Talleyrand, Louis-Philippe and Madame Adélaïde outdid themselves in providing the most extravagant welcome possible for their visitor and entertaining her with a royal disregard for expense. Thenceforth the Orléans dynasty had an unwavering advocate in the imperial house of Austria.

* At the time of the allied occupation of Paris in 1814, Czar Alexander II had seriously supported a movement to call the Duke d'Orléans to France's throne, rather than Louis XVIII.

Talleyrand, in recording in his *Mémoires* that he had asked the Duchess de Dino to accompany him to London, had explained that he would then have available to him "all the resources of her capable and fascinating mind, not only to supply me with valuable support, but also win for us both the goodwill of that English society which is so well known for its exclusiveness." In many ways, Dorothea proved that her uncle's estimate of her abilities was, if anything, pessimistic. Less than a month after her arrival, she had already begun to win, by her intelligence and charm, the "goodwill" of which the prince had spoken. Wellington found her fascinating and took great pleasure in her company. But her competence did not extend only to Talleyrand's friends. In a single evening at Wellington's house, she managed not only to charm Prince Paul Esterházy, the Austrian ambassador, but even to thaw the Prussian representative, Baron von Bülow, whose family she had known as a child. This was no small victory, considering that Prussia and Austria, along with Russia, were resolute opponents of the new regime in France. The only awkward moment of the evening came when Lord Burghersh, in a possibly well-intentioned but thoroughly misdirected attempt to engage Dorothea in conversation, inquired after the health of her husband. Dorothea, with complete self-possession, replied evenly, "I know nothing of him, sir." * So far as is known, this was the last time that the name of Edmond de Périgord was mentioned to Dorothea in London.

Dorothea's usefulness, however, was more than strictly social, and it was greatly to her liking to function not only as Talleyrand's hostess but also as his confidant, counselor, and private secretary. Her ability in such capacities came to the fore quite by accident, on the occasion of the official presentation by Talleyrand to King William. The interview between the monarch and the French ambassador, arranged for October 6, was viewed by Wellington with no little apprehension. The king had not been overly pru-

---

* Dorothea's reply to Lord Burghersh was quite truthful, so far as it went. She had indeed heard nothing of or from her husband for several months, nor was she eager for news to pass on to Edmond's English friends. For her husband was not unknown in London. In the fall of 1829, with his creditors at his heels, he had fled to that city. On the strength of his connections with Talleyrand, he had borrowed 300,000 francs there, on the pretext of settling his debts. Instead, he used the money to gamble and promptly lost 60,000 francs at cards. When this became known, his English creditors insisted upon immediate repayment of the entire 300,000 francs, and when he could not meet their demands, Edmond was thrown into debtors' prison. He was released only when the Duke de Laval, then ambassador in London, paid the sums due. Thereupon Edmond fled to Brussels, penniless, and appealed to Talleyrand for aid. "All the brains of all the business agents put together seem capable of coming up with only one answer," Talleyrand wrote to M. de Vaudémont, "and that is that everything will be all right because, in the end, M. de Talleyrand will pay up. The trouble is, M. de Talleyrand cannot." Nor did he. Edmond, unable to return to France for fear of spending the rest of his life in St.-Pelagie (the debtors' prison), moved on to Florence, where he remained for the next four decades, living as best he could on an annual allowance paid to him first by Dorothea and then by his children. The flight to Italy, in May, 1830, marked his final disappearance from Dorothea's life.

dent in making known his feelings about the Orléans dynasty, and it was feared that William might, despite Wellington's repeated reprimands, lapse into the strong language for which he had earned a just reputation. Talleyrand was aware of Wellington's unease, but he did not share it. He had charmed men of sterner stuff than William of England, and William, in turn, had been beguiled by men of much less talent than Talleyrand. On the day of the meeting, as his orders were being pinned to his coat, Talleyrand turned toward Dorothea and observed casually that under the former dynasty of France, ambassadors had been permitted to make a short address to the sovereign upon presenting their credentials. It might be an excellent idea, he said, to revive the custom. "Now then, madame, would you sit down and think up two or three sentences for me to recite to the king? Write them down in your biggest writing." Talleyrand glanced at what Dorothea had written, made a few changes, and then left for the audience.

At the palace, as William sat glowering at him, the prince spoke Dorothea's lines: a simple reference to "the descendant of the most illustrious House of Brunswick." The allusion was an obvious compliment, but at the same time, it was an open reminder to William that the ascent of his ancestors to the English throne, in 1688, had taken place in circumstances remarkably similar to those surrounding the elevation of Louis-Philippe to that of France. The king grasped Talleyrand's meaning immediately, and always an admirer of courage and unvarnished truth, he was enormously pleased. The audience then continued in a friendly atmosphere as Talleyrand went on to explain that his master had been called to the throne "by the unanimous voice of a great people." * William was to understand, therefore, that the Orléans dynasty was firmly established and that, since it had been anointed, as it were, by the people, there was little use in opposing it. "I spoke of the king," Talleyrand reported to Madame Adélaïde, "as I had spoken so long before in the Constituent Assembly." This, too, William understood and approved, and the interview concluded with a mutual exchange of compliments—to the immense relief of the Duke of Wellington. The key to this success, Talleyrand felt, had been the happy reference, devised by Dorothea, to the House of Brunswick, and thereafter he sought her opinion on most matters of importance that came before him.

Dorothea's good disposition, as well as her intellectual and social gifts, served quickly to thaw the reserve of London's aristocrats. The fact was that English society, once it had had the opportunity to observe for itself the legendary Talleyrand and his niece, was content to accept them and their relationship at face value and almost without comment. Lady Grey,

* The statement was, to put it kindly, hyperbolic. Louis-Philippe had been elected by a vote of the combined chambers, which were representative only of the upper classes in France. Even then, he had received a total of only 308 votes out of 542.

as famous for the austerity of her morals as for the brilliance of her soirees, expressed not only her own sentiments, but those of her class, when she explained that, "I am very fond of Madame de Dino. She is always very good-humored and is very agreeable company. Since she never says anything to offend me, I have nothing to do with the lovers that she is supposed to have had. I take no credit for being different from her; mine is a very lucky case." Even King William eventually came around—but not until Wellington had reminded him that the Emperor and Empress of Austria, those incarnations of moral probity, had readily accepted Dorothea as ambassadress in Vienna. Among those who had known the prince and his niece in France, their relationship was accepted out of habit. The sour-tongued Countess de Boigne, who could be depended upon to rake up any scandalous tidbit that might serve to discredit the woman who had replaced her old friend Catherine de Talleyrand in the prince's household, did no more than observe that the ambassador "kept a very large house in which the Duchess de Dino did the honors perfectly."

But mere acceptance of himself and Dorothea was not enough for Talleyrand. The principal aim of his diplomacy, as he never tired of preaching, was to bind together France and England with ties of closest friendship. "England's feelings in our regard will decide those of Europe," he wrote to the Princess de Vaudémont, "and it would be a serious mistake for us to look for support elsewhere." In order to win England's friendship, he had first to win that of the men who governed England. He himself had everything needed to gain their respect and attention, but it was now necessary to create an atmosphere in which he could expect also to benefit from their sympathy and goodwill. This, specifically, was a task that he assigned to Dorothea from the very beginning. It was one for which she was admirably equipped both by nature and preference and which she approached with great energy and imagination. Though dissatisfied with the old embassy at 50 Portland Place, she quickly transformed it into the kind of house that would simultaneously attract Englishmen and enhance France's prestige. Prince Adam Czartoryski, one of the great magnates of Poland, expressed astonished admiration "at the magnificent receptions in the French Embassy. . . . The rooms were decorated with all the splendor of the great salons of the French aristocracy in the eighteenth century. The cuisine was perfection itself, while the inexhaustible wit of the host and the charm of the hostess made their receptions the most brilliant and the most eagerly frequented in London." Visiting French dignitaries were equally impressed and somewhat relieved. "The July Revolution is sometimes a bit bourgeois," one of them remarked, "but thanks to M. de Talleyrand, it has taken on a very grand style in London." Occasionally, their admiration was mixed with sympathy for what their ambassador was suffering for the glory of France. "I did not think it was possible," said the Duke de Broglie after attending one of the prince's receptions, "for any official function to be simultaneously so magnificent and so tedious." Even the Countess de Boigne, who never quite forgave Talleyrand and Dorothea for outshining her father in the embassy, confessed that "they succeeded in establishing themselves as the leaders of everything that was most fashionable at the moment." The countess might have found it easier to forgive the newcomers their success if she had known the price of it. By the end of her first month in England Dorothea was writing home to Prosper Barante that "our dinners are earning us much success here, and they will no doubt go down as landmarks in the gastronomic history of London; but they are ruinously costly, and M. de Talleyrand is greatly alarmed at the expense." To Thiers, she confided that Talleyrand hoped not to prolong his mission in England, "for he has no wish either to exhaust himself or to go into bankruptcy. He could hardly fail to do the latter, for you would never believe how much we are spending here, or how stingy the Ministry of Foreign Affairs has been."

The prince's visions of impending ruin apparently receded to some extent, for during his four years in the British capital there was no evident reduction in the opulence that marked the beginning of his embassy and no obvious diminution of his fortune. Indeed, after a while he and Dorothea came to feel that the house in Portland Place was too small to be suitable for their entertainments, and they leased a larger and more magnificent establishment in Hanover Square. The new embassy surpassed by far the "splendor" so admired by Adam Czartoryski, and became the setting for the most sumptuous dinners and the most lavish balls in Europe. Invitations were eagerly sought and more eagerly displayed to one's friends. No other house enjoyed such popularity among the English aristocracy and the diplomatic corps, or so great a vogue. Within a few months of his arrival, no other foreigner in England enjoyed so much influence at all levels of society as Talleyrand. Prosper Mérimée, who was in London at the time, summed it up nicely: "No matter where he goes, he creates a court around himself and dictates the law."

Talleyrand had only one serious competitor in London society, but since it was not himself, but France, that he and Dorothea were striving to make respectable, this was a formidable competitor indeed: Russia, in the persons of its ambassador and his wife, Prince and Princess Lieven. Princess Lieven was one of those diplomatic wives who fully earned and exercised the title of ambassadress, for it was she, rather than her usually invisible husband, who, in all but name, represented Czar Nicholas at the Court of St. James's, just as she had earlier represented Alexander II, of happy memory. "Madame de Lieven," Dorothea noted with her customary realism, "is the woman to be most feared, respected, cultivated, and courted. Her political importance, which was founded on her intelligence and her experience, was accompanied by an authority which no one dared question. Her house was the most exclusive in London. It was inevitable that the two embassies—that is, the two women who reigned over them—would enter into competition with each other, and the contest was highly publicized and a favorite diversion of London society. "The female Lieven and the Dino," wrote Creevey, "were the people for sport. They are both professional talkers—artists, in that department. We had them both quite at ease, and perpetually at work with each other."

The "sport" to which Creevey referred, however, was more than that. Dorothea did not exaggerate the extent of Lieven's political importance and authority. The princess had lived in England since 1812. She knew everyone in the government, as well as anyone who was likely, at some time in the future, to be in it. She was particularly intimate with Lord Grey, who was shortly to replace Wellington as prime minister; and it was with this devoted friend of the Russian ambassadress that Talleyrand would have to deal in his negotiations with England. Yet, for all the seriousness of their competition, neither hostess seemed to bring personal animus to the contest. Indeed, Lieven was to become a friend and guest of Talleyrand and Dorothea in later years. It was a friendship based upon a mutual appreciation of the talents that they shared, although Lieven's appreciation was often expressed in the snappish manner that was known as her style. Of Talleyrand's statesmanship she said in grudging admiration: "A man who has spent the first seventy-five years of his life in intrigue does not forget the art in his seventy-sixth." Which was her way of paying homage to the prince's undiminished vigor of mind. Dorothea was treated more conventionally: "I esteem her as a most excellent and good-natured person, whatever anyone may say to the contrary, and in addition, she has many brilliant social qualities."

Society's estimate of the French ambassador and his niece was shared by the British government or at least by those who were at the head of it. The Duke of Wellington, as Princess Lieven had said, was captivated by Talleyrand and, in his usual forthright way, defended him against any and all gossip. Indeed, the two had enough in common to make great friends of them. They were of the same generation and upbringing, and both were aristocrats of the old school. They shared a horror of impracticality, at the political as well as the personal level, and both despised charlatanism, narrowness of outlook, and parochialism in any form. Neither one ever really learned to resist the temptation to speak one's mind, and occasionally, this led to minor clashes between them. Once Wellington, in speaking of a minor matter of state in Talleyrand's presence, made a passing reference to "the unfortunate revolution of last July"—whereupon Talleyrand promptly, and publicly, upbraided him for this thoughtless choice of words. Wellington, more delighted at his friend's sensitivity than offended at his readiness to take umbrage, cheerfully apologized and withdrew the remark. The two statesmen, in a word, understood each other thoroughly, and this understanding was a firm basis for mutual respect and friendship. Lord Aberdeen, the Foreign Secretary, showed a similar appreciation of Talleyrand. He and the prince had known each other well in Vienna. It was to Aberdeen that Talleyrand had written upon his appointment to London, and the answer, which came back immediately, was that Aberdeen was "eager to renew those friendly relations." The English minister had been born into a conservative class and, as a youth, had converted to liberalism under Pitt and Castlereagh.* His outlook was European rather than nationalistic in public affairs. With such men, Talleyrand could easily work in complete confidence of success. It was not an empty boast when he wrote to Madame de Vaudémont that he was "thoroughly convinced of the openness and loyalty of the English Cabinet."

As chance would have it, the first crisis of Talleyrand's ambassadorial mission in London arose, not from any difference of opinion between himself and the British government, but because his relations with his own government were less felicitous than those with Wellington's Cabinet. The understanding that had sprung up between the prince and Count Molé, France's Foreign Minister, in the afterglow of the July Revolution, had quickly dissipated. The fault, if truth be told, was not altogether that of Molé. Hardly had Talleyrand arrived in London when he was writing to Madame de Vaudémont: "One must cultivate the duke's [Wellington's] confidence if anything solid and lasting is to be accomplished. . . . I want the king and Mademoiselle† to be persuaded of this. As for Molé, I do not care what he believes. When he sees which way things are going, he will follow along quickly enough." This odd disregard by an ambassador of the man who was, at least theoretically, his superior was translated immediately into practice by the peculiar communications network that Talleyrand had established between the London embassy and the Palais Royal in Paris. Immediately upon Louis-Philippe's accession to the throne, a corre-

---

* Aberdeen's liberalism, however, like Castlereagh's, was a strange mixture of authentic devotion to the common weal and thoroughgoing self-interest. He was eager for popular reform, but only if such changes affected other people. This attitude gave birth to a saying, later in Aberdeen's career, to the effect that no government could be too liberal for his taste, so long as it did not forsake its conservative principles.

† Although Louis-Philippe's masterful sister was, and is, generally known as Madame Adélaïde, both Talleyrand and Dorothea invariably referred to her, after July 1830, as Mademoiselle—the title reserved, under the *ancien régime,* exclusively for the sister of the King of France.

spondence had sprung up between Dorothea and the king's sister; this was to continue, with few interruptions, during the whole of the prince's London sojourn. These letters, as well as those written by Talleyrand himself to his old friend the Princess de Vaudémont, who was an intimate of the royal family, served an extremely important purpose: to communicate to the king, through Madame Adélaïde and the princess, what Talleyrand did not want Molé, the Foreign Minister, to know. Dorothea was also in constant touch with Adolphe Thiers, and these letters were no less important, for Thiers was by then recognized as one of the most influential politicians of the July Monarchy, and Talleyrand expected great things of him.

Molé soon discovered, of course, that the foreign policy of France was being created and directed, not on the banks of the Seine by his own ministry, but on those of the Thames. He complained bitterly of this to Louis-Philippe, but the king, at his sister's bidding, ignored all such complaints. Finally, in a frenzy of frustration, Molé tried to resign, but this, too, Louis-Philippe ignored. The combination of Talleyrand and Mademoiselle was too strong for a simple Minister of Foreign Affairs to prevail against, and Molé, since he was being allowed neither to exercise his ministry nor to give it up, spent the remainder of his time in office complaining of the injustice being done him. Finally, on November 2, he was extricated from this impossible situation by the appointment of Laffitte to the presidency of the Council. Laffitte immediately turned over the office of Foreign Affairs to an old friend and collaborator of both himself and Talleyrand, General Sebastiani. Sebastiani was a solid, principled, and thoroughly honest soldier, who had not the vaguest notion of what was required of a Foreign Minister. He was therefore content, as Talleyrand and Laffitte had foreseen, to take his orders from his London ambassador, and for the next two years, Talleyrand's word was law in Louis-Philippe's Ministry of Foreign Affairs. The prince began by instructing his (theoretical) superior on the principles of French policy, the policies that Talleyrand himself had always advocated and that now, in his old age, he had finally been given the opportunity to implement:

> We must try to establish closer ties with those governments in which civilization has made the greatest advance, for it is with these that we have the most in common. This leads us quite naturally to regard England as the power with which we should be most closely associated. . . . England is the only power that shares our determination to have peace. The other powers still pretend to rule by divine right, but France and England no longer think in such terms. These powers support this right by the force of their cannons, but England and ourselves are supported by public opinion and by principles. Such principles are of universal appeal, while the range of cannon is limited.

The sentiments that Talleyrand tried to inculcate into Molé's successor had not really been the cause of his conflict with Molé himself. The point of difference between the two men was not principle, but the method of implementing principles. The first encounter had been over the question of Algeria. Talleyrand's personal inclination was to abandon the conquest of that country as a gesture of goodwill toward Britain, which, as always, opposed colonial expansion by any nation other than itself. Molé, however, was very apprehensive (with some justification) about the effect of such a move upon public opinion in France and was firmly opposed even to any discussion of the idea. Pozzo de Borgo reported to St. Petersburg: "M. Molé confided to me Prince Talleyrand's proposal for the abandonment of Algiers. When the minister would not accept the plan, the prince went to the king, and apparently, the king agreed with this proposal for the sake of pleasing England. M. Molé is absolutely opposed to it, and has assured me that he will make a report to the Council on the subject, and it is likely that the Council will be of the same opinion as the minister. . . ." In fact, so strongly did Molé feel on this matter that he threatened to resign if France considered abandoning Algeria. Talleyrand, who had always been able to distinguish between the essential and the merely convenient, and who moreover had no really strong opinion on the Algerian affair, gave way on this point in order to avoid provoking a crisis for the new regime. But he never quite forgave Molé for his opposition.

The battle that had been brewing between the ambassador and the Foreign Minister was joined in earnest over the question of Belgium and its struggle for independence from the Netherlands. To Talleyrand, it seemed the simplest thing in the world to resolve this matter in London, in collaboration with Wellington and the French ambassador to The Hague, Bertin de Veaux, who was an old friend and associate. He therefore proposed that Bertin send his reports directly to the embassy in London rather than to Paris. "It is thus that I carried on affairs for the emperor," he assured Molé, "as well as for Louis XVIII. You will find that I shall always tell you everything, except what I think is of no importance." But Molé would have none of this. He demanded that the reports be sent to him, immediately and directly, and he added a few uncomplimentary remarks concerning Talleyrand's behavior generally. "We are unhappy about the tone of M. Molé's dispatches," Dorothea complained to Paris.

Numerous small conflicts over procedure added fuel to the fire. Talleyrand had been piqued because Molé would not allow his address to King William to be published in the *Moniteur*, and he had offended Molé by sending the text to Thiers, who promptly published it in the *National*. He also wrote to Madame Adélaïde complaining of Molé's childishness [*un peu de jeunesse*] in attempting to communicate directly with the British government rather than going through the embassy. Even so, Talleyrand explained to the king's sister, Wellington promptly informed him of everything contained in Molé's "misdirected" dispatches. It was at this point that Molé lost his temper and attempted to resign. "Nothing," he told Louis-Philippe, "can persuade me to remain in office so long as M. de Talleyrand refuses to accept guidance and direction from me in the same way as the least of our ambassadors." But the king, prompted by Madame Adélaïde, refused to accept either Molé's explanations or his resignation. And Talleyrand, in an attempt to soothe the outraged minister, wrote a conciliatory letter:

> We know each other, we love each other, we desire the same things, we understand them in the same way, and we wish them to be carried out in the same way. Our approach is the same, and our goal is the same. Why, then, since we are on the same side, do we not understand each other? There is something here which is a puzzle to me, but which, I trust, is of a passing nature.
>
> Our correspondence is not friendly, and yet it is not official. I think that it should be otherwise between us, and I come to you, with all my old friendship, to beg you that it become so. Anything less than complete confidence and intimate understanding may seriously harm, impede, or delay affairs. Our friendship would suffer—and this would grieve me greatly. If my way of carrying on affairs is out of date, it would be better to tell me so frankly. Let us be quite open with each other. We can do no real good unless we treat affairs with that ease and candor that begets confidence.

Despite this no doubt sincere overture on Talleyrand's part, there was no peace between the embassy in London and the ministry in Paris, and no real possibility of peace, until Molé was replaced by Sebastiani in November, 1820.* And it was not until then that the Prince was able seriously to begin working at a solution to the Belgian question—a question that was the most critical, and the most potentially explosive, of the issues facing the July Monarchy.

In Vienna, Talleyrand had opposed the annexation of Belgium by Holland because it had seemed a violation of the sacred principle of legitimacy. He had not been surprised at the Belgian insurrection which had sprung up on August 25, and he had been profoundly disturbed by it. Even before his departure for London, Pozzo de Borgo had found him "very preoccupied with the Belgian question and determined to place it in the hands of the English so as to facilitate a solution. . . . 'The Belgian revolu-

---

* There was a two-week interval between Molé's resignation and Sebastiani's installation during which the Foreign Ministry was presided over by Marshal Maison. The marshal, however, proved so remarkably inept that he was summarily relieved of his office and sent as ambassador to Vienna. There he proved no more talented than in Paris, but it was felt that he could do less harm among the good-natured Austrians than in volatile Paris.

tionaries are pushing toward separation [Talleyrand said] and therefore toward a break.' " Talleyrand's words had been calculated to impress upon Pozzo di Borgo and upon his master in St. Petersburg the seriousness of the implications of the Belgian uprising. The annexation of that country to Holland had been determined in Vienna without reference to the wishes of the Belgians themselves, and yet it had been part of a settlement that was continental in scope. The refusal of the Belgians to accept their enforced submission to The Hague might be a direct, and perhaps mortal, blow to the European system inaugurated by the Congress of Vienna. It was perceived as such not only by Talleyrand, but in all the capitals of Europe. Everywhere—and especially in Berlin, Vienna, and St. Petersburg—it was greatly feared that the Belgian upheaval, coming as it did in the wake of the July Revolution, signaled the first stage of an international revolutionary (*i.e.,* liberal) uprising. The problem was enormously complicated for Talleyrand by the fact that many Belgians, vociferously supported by a sizable segment of the French population (the republicans, notably), were demanding that Belgium be united to France. To this, Prussia was naturally and resolutely opposed, since such a settlement would have given it France as a neighbor on the Rhine. Britain was no less opposed than Prussia, for it was determined to keep the great commercial port of Antwerp from falling into French hands.

In the face of this general alarm, Talleyrand's first move was to reassure the great powers by affirming France's determination not to intervene in the internal affairs of Belgium—that is, not to support the rebels.* It is to his credit that he was able to convince Wellington and Aberdeen of the sincerity of this declaration. Next, Talleyrand and Wellington jointly proposed that a conference be held to discuss and, if possible, to resolve the Belgian question. London, they added, was the most suitable place for such a meeting. The French republicans immediately sent up a howl of protest against the choice of London. Why not Paris? they cried. The answer was not difficult to discover. Paris, to Talleyrand's mind, was too restless, and a conference there might provoke demonstrations and a public outcry that could not fail to have an effect upon those attending the conference. Moreover, he felt that a meeting of the powers in London could probably be controlled by himself and Wellington jointly, whereas one in the French capital might open the door to interference by the French for-

* There seems to have been an interval in which Talleyrand considered urging the annexation of Belgium by France (although no mention of this is made in the *Mémoires*). His motive was not political, but economic. It had always disturbed him that Britain, from the Vienna treaties, had been placed in a position of economic domination over the rest of Europe, and he would have wished France to have Antwerp to offset, at least partially, this virtual hegemony. On more than one occasion, he expressed privately his concern "over the pejorative consequences of a universal commerce in the hands of a single Power."

eign minister* or, even worse, by Russia's ambassador in Paris, Pozzo di Borgo, who would be infinitely more difficult to handle than the innocuous Prince Lieven, who represented Czar Nicholas in London. Madame Adélaïde and Monsieur Thiers were enlisted on behalf of Talleyrand's choice, and the scales were tipped in favor of London. On November 4, 1830, therefore, the Conference of London was convened, comprising representatives of Britain, Prussia, Russia, Austria, the Netherlands, and, of course, France—even though, Talleyrand complained, "I had had no instructions whatever as to my line of conduct from M. Molé." †

The fact that Talleyrand, in the absence of instructions, was required to follow his own inclinations did not displease him, and at the first meeting at the house of Lord Aberdeen, he was careful to set the tone of informality which, he hoped, would prevail in the discussions. "I do not come here today to speak with the words of French diplomacy. There is no French diplomacy. I am merely a man of some experience who has come to sit down with old friends and discuss some matters of interest to us all." The Duke of Wellington addressed the delegates in the same spirit, pointing out that the sole purpose of the assembly was to find an acceptable way of avoiding bloodshed in Belgium and restoring peace to that land. Then, backed by Talleyrand, he pointed out that both humanity and policy required that these ends be achieved, and he suggested that an armistice be declared during the deliberations of the conference. To this, all the delegates agreed, and the session was adjourned until evening. At that time, Baron Flack, the ambassador of the Netherlands, informed the meeting that he accepted the proposed armistice and had transmitted it to the Dutch king. Simultaneously, the proposal was dispatched to the provisional government in Brussels.

According to the terms of the armistice, which had been carefully worked out beforehand between Talleyrand and Wellington, both the

* This proposal was made in October, while the Foreign Ministry was still headed by Talleyrand's antagonist, Count Molé.

† By the date of the opening of the congress the situation in Belgium had been somewhat stabilized. The Belgians had succeeded in ejecting Dutch troops from the whole of their country with the exception of Antwerp, and the troops of the two sides now faced each other along their frontiers. A provisional government had been established in Brussels and was administering, somewhat precariously, a new nation divided into factions: Catholics, who would not hear of any arrangement under which they would continue to be ruled by the Dutch, Protestant House of Orange; republicans, who, though a small minority, were loud in their demands for a "representative government" presumably to be organized by themselves; and the "French party," who were openly and effectively agitating for union with France. The situation had been further complicated by the actions of the Prince of Orange, heir to the Dutch throne, who, as a means of reconciling Belgium and Holland and yet maintaining the dominant position of his house in both countries, had offered to assume the crown of Belgium. This proposal was rejected with indignation by both the Dutch and the Belgians, and the Prince of Orange was, by the opening of the conference, in London, more or less in disgrace, while representing Holland.

Dutch and the Belgian armies were to remain undisturbed in their positions—a stipulation that amounted to recognition of Belgian independence. "The proposal," Talleyrand reported to Paris, "is advantageous in every way, and justice will be done to the intentions that brought it about."

The following day, November 3, the prince finally received the instructions that he had been waiting for. Happily, they coincided largely with his own convictions—a fact which prompted Talleyrand to conclude that they must have "been dictated by the king himself to Marshal Maison,* who was too little *au courant* with matters to have initiated and drawn them up." The points brought up in the dispatch were four, and reflected basic French—*i.e.,* Talleyrand's—policy:

1. Belgium must be separated from Holland and established as an independent state under a sovereign prince;

2. This prince should, if possible, be the Prince of Orange;

3. If it is not possible for the Prince of Orange to become King of Belgium, then the Belgians themselves should be asked to choose the prince who is to become their sovereign;

4. No fortress along the Franco-Belgian frontier, other than Luxembourg, must be turned over to any foreign power.

Talleyrand, acting jointly with Wellington in the first session of the conference, had already realized the first point for all practical purposes. The most important matter now remaining was to choose a monarch for the new kingdom that was about to be established from among Europe's reigning dynasties.† For the moment, Talleyrand inclined to King Louis-Philippe's view that the logical candidate was the Prince of Orange. "The situation is an extremely complicated one," he wrote to Paris, "and there is no doubt that the election of the Prince of Orange is the easiest solution."

Before this question could be seriously considered, an event occurred in Britain which Talleyrand found not especially surprising but nonetheless disturbing. The House of Commons, against the opposition of the government, voted by a fair majority to refer a minor, though controversial, bill to a special committee. Wellington's government chose to interpret this defeat (by a majority of 29 votes out of 437) as an expression of lack of confidence in themselves and submitted their resignation to King William.**

* At the same time as the instructions, Talleyrand received official notification of Maison's replacement of Molé in the Foreign Ministry.

† On November 10, a representative body, called the Congress, had been established in Belgium, which was, in Talleyrand's words, "the real exponent of national sentiment." On November 22, the Congress declared for a monarchical form of government by a vote of 174 out of 197. (Only thirteen members voted for a republic.)

** This minor defeat was only a pretext for the resignation. Wellington's steadfast refusal to consider parliamentary reform had caused great unrest. There were demonstrations in the streets of

The king then summoned Lord Charles Grey and asked him to form a government composed of moderate members of the Whig Party.

From a personal standpoint, Talleyrand sincerely regretted Wellington's departure from office. "I had long-standing and reliable relations with him, and he enjoyed the confidence of Europe to a greater degree than any other man." Yet, at the same time, the downfall of the Tories "might influence the result of our important negotiations [on Belgium] in various ways. . . . The presence of the Whig Party at the head of affairs, being more liberal in its general tendencies, offered hope that it might facilitate progress in our negotiations. This party was in no way responsible for the settlement of 1815, and having so frequently criticized and attacked these transactions, they could in no way feel themselves obliged to uphold them."

While waiting for Lord Grey to form his government, it was agreed that Wellington and Aberdeen would continue to represent Britain at the London Conference. This, in itself, was no great help, for after the initial success of the first meeting, as Talleyrand complained, "the plenipotentiaries met several times, without, however, making any marked progress, as we had not yet heard how the proposal for an armistice had been received at The Hague and Brussels." Nor did things go better when the conference's commissioners returned from Brussels in mid-November with the assent of the Belgian Congress. Both Belgium and the Netherlands protested against the frontiers proposed by the conference, in its armistice protocol,* as being prejudicial to their respective actions.

It was at this point that everything seemed to come undone and that all the groundwork that had been so carefully laid by Talleyrand and Wellington on November 4 was now threatened. The conference hurriedly dispatched commissioners once more to The Hague and to Brussels with two new protocols, one public and one secret. The first was essentially the same as that of November 4. According to the second, however, the commissioners were to try to persuade the Belgians to accept the frontier demanded by the King of the Netherlands, and if they were unable to do so, then the stipulations of the public protocol were to obtain.

Meanwhile, news of the squabbling over boundaries between the Belgians and the Dutch had become known throughout Europe, and this led

London and a drastic drop on the stock exchange. A member of the upper house, Lord Brougham, gave notice that he intended, on November 16, to introduce a motion for reform. Facing almost certain defeat on this most important issue, Wellington opted for early retirement. The Reform Bill eventually was passed in 1832 and did away with some 300 virtually nonexistent constituencies (the "rotten boroughs") while increasing the representation of urban centers.

* The protocol of November 4 gave as the frontier "the boundaries of Holland, previous to the Treaty of Paris of 30th May, 1814"—that is, the boundaries under the Napoleonic kingdom of Holland, previous to the First Peace of Paris.

to a rash of new and radical proposals for a solution to the Belgian question. Nicholas of Russia, with his customary candor, once more offered to send his Cossacks into Belgium to bring the Belgians to their senses. But, on November 29, the Poles revolted against Nicholas' regime, and to the relief of the Belgians and to the horror of Poland, the Cossacks had to be diverted into the latter country.*

Austria, likewise, alarmed by revolutionary unrest in several of the German and Italian states,† approached the King of Prussia with a suggestion of armed intervention in Belgium. But the Prussian monarch, "enlightened," as Talleyrand explained, "by his past experiences and by his profound knowledge of the state of men's minds in Germany and particularly in Russia—and, one must add, by the natural uprightness of his character —resisted all the influences and pressures brought to bear upon him." Metternich, Talleyrand noted, "far from making any concessions to the spirit of the times, was disappointed at not having been able to put it down, but he did not despair of being able to make up for lost time."

A more subtle and a more formidable obstacle to a just settlement of the Belgian problem came from a less expected source, France itself. The prince records the event with deceptive tranquillity:

> At the time the conference was beginning to discuss these important questions, there arrived in London an emissary from the newly constructed French ministry. . . . This was the Count de Flahaut. His mission was a somewhat complicated one, and the pretext given for his assignment was his earlier social and amicable relations with certain members of the new English ministry, Lord Grey and the Marquess of Lansdowne, among others. It was also supposed that, given the friendly protection I had accorded M. de Flahaut at the beginning of his career, I would find his presence agreeable under the circumstances.

The fact was that Talleyrand had, for many years, shown a high degree of affection for this handsome son of his by the seductive Madame de Flahaut (now Madame de Souza). With a bit of help from his father, young Flahaut had done fairly well for himself. He had risen, under the Empire, to the rank of general and had finally become aide-de-camp to the Emperor Napoleon himself. After Waterloo, he had gone into exile in England, where his charm, good looks, and family connections had endeared

---

* Almost the whole of Poland united under the command of General Chlopicki, but after a fierce struggle, Russia triumphed with the fall of Warsaw on September 7, 1831.

† In Italy, there were liberal revolutions in Romagna, Parma, and Modena, which Metternich suppressed with Austrian troops. The latter eventually were withdrawn upon the insistence of King Louis-Philippe, but descended again into the peninsula in 1832, at which point French troops were sent to occupy Ancona on Italy's eastern coast. In Germany, the people of Brunswick, Hesse-Kassel, and Saxony also rose up to demand constitutions and were successful in varying degrees.

him to one of that country's great heiresses, Margaret Elphinstone, daughter of Lord Keith. The events of the July Revolution had once again opened the door of advancement to M. de Flahaut, and with the stimulus of more than a little prodding from his wife, Charles de Flahaut had set his sights high. "I quickly extricated personal particulars from beneath the official covering that had been provided by his mission. . . . M. de Flahaut had come with the object of preparing the way to his becoming ambassador in London when circumstances should oblige me to resign that post."

This plan was not so absurd as it may have appeared. Flahaut had lived in England for more than a decade, and he knew everyone who was worth knowing. His wife, moreover, was related to many of the great Whig families and to more than a few of the Tories. In addition, Flahaut, being Talleyrand's son, was an attractive, amiable, and gifted diplomat. So much so that he had no difficulty in persuading the new Minister of Foreign Affairs, General Sebastiani, of the worth of his scheme. Prince Talleyrand, after all, had been sent to London on an extraordinary mission: to establish friendly ties between the July Monarchy and the British people and, as a result of circumstances, to represent France in the settlement of the Belgian question. Once the prince's mission was accomplished, given his great age, he would no doubt retire—and where else but in the prince's own family, so to speak, was Paris to find a man capable of replacing him?

All this was perfectly reasonable, and Flahaut's mission in London seemed to make great good sense to everyone concerned—except to Talleyrand and to Dorothea. Dorothea's objections were personal rather than professional. She had never been overly fond of this illegitimate offshoot of the Talleyrand tree, and perhaps she had resented the favor and advancement that the prince had showered upon Charles de Flahaut at a time when her own husband, an authentic Périgord, had been left to languish in obscurity as a mere regimental commander. It is also possible that possessive as she undoubtedly was, Dorothea feared competition of a sort for Talleyrand's affection with the Count and Countess de Flahaut. Dorothea's real enmity, however, was reserved for a foe worthy of it, Margaret de Flahaut, *née* Elphinstone. Margaret was as ambitious and as clever in many respects as Dorothea. She was, moreover, one of those women who regard virtue as a weapon rather than an embellishment, and that, Dorothea, who was unarmed in this respect, could hardly endure. Her sentiments were predictably returned in kind by Madame de Flahaut, who, in her more placid moments, referred to Dorothea as a "lying little devil" and a "horrid little serpent." Lady Granville, an amused spectator, reported that "Madame de Dino . . . and Meg meet and dine each other, but it is like the meetings in cock-and-bull fights." In these circumstances, Dorothea could hardly be expected to support the cause of the Flahauts in the

embassy. It suited her purposes very well to further a rift between Talleyrand and his son, and she did so with all the skill at her command.

Talleyrand, for his part, seems not to have taken so dim a view of Flahaut's ambitions. The count, after all, had come not to depose him, but to
emulate him by becoming his successor, and this may have been the sin-
cerest form of flattery. He was not so understanding, however, when it
came to, as he called it, "the official covering" of Flahaut's mission in London. The count was the bearer of a dispatch and of several letters from
General Sebastiani in which the new minister solicited his ambassador's
advice on various points. And this was routine. He had also received instructions to persuade his father to agree to a drastic solution to the Belgian question, and it was this that threw Talleyrand into a fury.

Early in November, the Belgian Congress, after voting to establish a
monarchy in their country, had queried Paris on the feasibility of offering
the crown to the Duke de Nemours, one of the sons of Louis-Philippe. The
king, upon Talleyrand's advice and fearing that acceptance of this honor
by a French prince might offend the British, had rejected the offer on behalf of Nemours.* Now Flahaut was attempting to persuade the prince
that since the Belgians would not accept the House of Nassau as their dynasty and since Louis-Philippe would not allow a member of his family to
become sovereign of the newly formed state, there remained only one way
of conciliating all parties: to divide Belgium into three parts, of which one
was to go to Holland, one to Prussia, and one (the largest) to France. England, lest it be offended, would be given the city and port of Antwerp.
"The Count de Flahaut's mission," Talleyrand explains, "was to induce me
to agree to accept this marvelous plan."

The "marvelous plan," was, of course, an absurdity, and it was immediately perceived as such. "It did not require much reflection on my part to
grasp how utterly senseless and dangerous such a project would be or how
completely it was in opposition to, and would prevent, the maintenance of
a permanent peace." The establishment of Britain upon the Continent,
"after what it had cost France, and how much bloodshed it had necessitated, to achieve their expulsion," was completely unacceptable. "I
vowed," Talleyrand said, "to cut off my right hand rather than sign any
document that should be the means of bringing them back." The proposal
to offer Prussia territory near France's northern frontier was no less objectionable. Flahaut's "solution" as a whole was "so suicidal to international

---

* Louis-Philippe was widely criticized in France for his caution in this respect, and paradoxi-
cally, the most vehement criticism came from the Bonapartists and the republicans. Talleyrand,
however, was enormously pleased at the king's willingness to sacrifice the glory of his house for the
good of France and wrote to Madame Adélaïde that he "was struck by the prudent judgment and
deep understanding of affairs" that had motivated Louis-Philippe's decision.

safety that it can be described as nothing more than an intrigue." With this reply, Talleyrand's son had to be content, and accepting injury on top of insult, he was compelled to carry it back to Paris with him. He had, in a word, been peremptorily dismissed by the prince, and given a good tongue-lashing into the bargain. The dispatch he bore ended up with a word of advice to Sebastiani: "As for Algiers, I have avoided speaking of it, and I should be happy if the same reticence were exercised in France. It is well that the world at large should accustom itself to the idea of the occupation, and silence is the best means to attain this end. I believe that in England, public opinion has undergone some change on this subject and that we shall experience no insurmountable difficulties over it." This was a far cry from the early days of 1830, when the British ambassador in Paris had expressed his government's indignation with such vehemence that Charles X had been forced to reply, "Mr. Ambassador, the best proof of friendship that I can offer your government at this moment is to pretend that I have not understood what I just heard." The overall message of Talleyrand's dispatch to Paris, carried by the hapless Count de Flahaut, was unmistakably this: "So long as you allow me a free hand in London and behave correctly at home, all will be well for France." Even the inexperienced Sebastiani could hardly misread it.

As Talleyrand was instructing his Foreign Minister not to meddle in foreign affairs, Wellington and his caretaker government were in the process of being replaced by Lord Grey's Whig Cabinet. Grey had not had an easy time of it. The Tories had been in power for virtually a century, and even the natural allies of the Whigs seemed less than enthusiastic about their assumption of power. The London *Times*, which acted more or less as the organ of the Whig party, summarized the situation in the following terms:

> General feeling is not very favourable to a Whig ministry, inasmuch as the Whigs, and the men of this party, do not possess that financial reputation to which public opinion attaches so great an importance; but it is difficult to see what other alternative remains. All practical men are of the opinion that a government could hardly be called to take office at a time beset with greater difficulties.

Despite these inauspicious beginnings, Grey was able, by November 20, to put together a government of formidable talents which included himself as Prime Minister and First Lord of the Treasury, Lord Palmerston as Foreign Secretary, and Lord Melbourne as Home Secretary. Talleyrand greeted the announcement of these names with optimism. "This government," he wrote to Madame Adélaïde, "will be strong and favorable to us. I have much friendly contact with the principal members who form it. . . . They wish that England and France may be in accord in all their dealings with other powers. They look upon the prosperity and strength of France as a necessity to the peace of Europe. And they all speak of the king [of the French] with the greatest respect."

It is true that Talleyrand was on terms of friendly intimacy with Lord Grey. Indeed, it was at the prince's suggestion that the new Prime Minister, in his first address to Parliament, stressed his government's sentiments of common purpose and common interests with France. Palmerston, however, with whom Talleyrand would have to deal ordinarily, was another matter. The new Foreign Secretary had the true Englishman's regard for "foreigners." He treated them all with carefully impartial contempt and with a truly democratic disregard for race, creed, or color. It appeared never to have occurred to him that Prince Talleyrand, because of his age, experience, accomplishments, background, and position, may have been entitled even to the courtesy that one gentleman ordinarily accords to another. The old prince was kept waiting for hours in the anterooms of the Foreign Office, summoned and dismissed peremptorily, and generally handled as though he were one of Palmerston's own civil servants rather than the illustrious representative of a great power. It may be that Palmerston's conduct toward Talleyrand was due, at least in part, to a widely publicized cartoon that appeared in France shortly after Grey's government took office. It showed the French ambassador in London leading the British Foreign Secretary by the hand, and carried the caption "The lame leading the blind." This, obviously, was not calculated to inspire affection for the ambassador in the heart of a man who tended to regard all "foreigners" as constituting a subspecies of the human race.

Whatever the cause of Palmerston's conduct, it kept the residents of the French embassy, especially Dorothea, in a state of constant rage. She came to despise Palmerston with all her heart:

> Seldom has a face revealed so much of a man's character. The eyes are hard and colorless, the nose turned up and insolent. His smile is bitter; his laugh, insincere. There is, in his features and his body, no dignity, no candor, no rectitude. His conversation is dry, but, I admit, not without wit. He has on him the mark of stubbornness, arrogance, and treachery, and this I believe to be a true reflection of his character.

Talleyrand himself was inclined to take a more lenient view:

> Lord Palmerston is certainly one of the ablest statesmen that I have met in my entire career, though not quite *the* ablest. He has all the talents and abilities that are most necessary to such a man in England: a wide and varied store of information, indefatigable activity, an iron constitution, inexhaustible mental resources, and great facility in speech. . . . Moreover, he has great social qualities and highly polished manners. There is one flaw,

however, which, in my opinion, entirely outweighs all these advantages and which will prevent him ever from becoming a true statesman. He allows his emotions to influence him in public affairs—so much so that he sometimes sacrifices the greatest interests to his personal feelings. It may be truly said that nearly every political question is, for him, transformed into a personal question; and, when he seems to defend the interests of his country, it is nearly always those of his hatred and revenge that he is serving.

Despite the almost natural antipathy between the statesman of the new school and that of the old, Talleyrand was far too subtle and experienced a diplomat to allow Palmerston's shortcomings, real or imagined, to interfere with his mission. It is possible, moreover, that given his relations with other members of the government, Palmerston's attitude was not a matter of much importance to Talleyrand. Princess Lieven probably described the situation correctly when she wrote to her brother that "Lord Grey adores him [Talleyrand]. Lord Palmerston detests him. And Lord Holland* passes along to him all the secrets of the government." So, braving Dorothea's articulate and righteous indignation, the prince succeeded in working with Palmerston with as much effectiveness, though perhaps with less enjoyment, as he had with Lord Aberdeen. "We worked together very amicably during the first months of the conference," he remarks, "and it is to this accord that the excellent results that were obtained may be attributed."

The excellent results to which Talleyrand referred were quickly forthcoming. At the first meeting of the conference under the presidency of Lord Palmerston, the new Foreign Secretary was able to announce that both the Netherlands and Belgium had formally accepted the armistice proposed in the protocol of November 4. This left the representatives of the powers free, or rather compelled them, now to turn their attention to a problem considerably more complex than that of a cease-fire: the selection of a sovereign for the Belgians who would be acceptable not only to the nation in question, but also, and perhaps especially, to the great powers of Europe.

Talleyrand's instructions from Paris had stated that the ambassador was to work for the election of the Prince of Orange, if possible. This choice had now been rendered virtually impossible by a majority vote of the Belgian Congress "excluding in perpetuity the members of the House of Nassau from all power in Belgium." The exclusion of this dynasty's heir, the Prince of Orange, was something of a blow to France and to Talleyrand

---

* Holland, as a nephew of the celebrated Charles Fox, former Lord Privy Seal and Chancellor of the Duchy of Lancaster in the Grey government, knew not only everyone, but everything, worth knowing. Whether or not he shared this knowledge with Talleyrand is a matter of conjecture, but the fact that Talleyrand was widely believed to be privy to "all the secrets of the government" was, for his purposes, almost as good as actually being so.

himself, who had regarded Orange as the means of conciliating the Belgians while rendering Belgian autonomy acceptable to The Hague. "My own government," he told the conference, "has recently given you conclusive proof of the sincerity of its intentions by trying to prevent the Belgian Congress from pronouncing the exclusion of the House of Nassau. I regret that we have not been more successful, and together we must now seek the means of compensating for this misfortune, if it be possible." It was therefore agreed during this session that an interval should be allowed in which the Belgian partisans of the Prince of Orange would attempt to persuade the Congress to accept their candidate. In the meantime, the ambassadors would occupy themselves with the comparatively minor questions of the adjustment of frontiers, the division of the national debt, and so forth. "Our affairs proceeded satisfactorily in London," Talleyrand recorded, "and even though the vexatious delays of the King of the Netherlands and the absurd demands of the Belgians* caused some difficulties at the conference, the good understanding which existed among the members assured us that these difficulties would eventually be overcome."

In Paris, however, affairs were proceeding less satisfactorily. The ministers of the former king, Charles X, were coming up for trial on a variety of charges, some of them justified, centering on their conduct in office under the Bourbon regime. At the same time, news reached Paris of the uprising in Poland, and there was a wave of popular emotion and loud demands for French aid to the beleaguered Poles. Louis-Philippe, however, held firm to his—that is, Talleyrand's—policy of nonintervention and resisted all pressures to the contrary. The government was equally determined that the former ministers of state would receive justice rather than vengeance and carried that determination to the point of protecting the accused from the onslaught of a mob on their place of detention. It seemed doubtful for a time whether the government would be strong enough to maintain order. "This was a matter of great anxiety in Paris," Talleyrand wrote, "and this anxiety, as well as its cause, did not tend to make the position of the French ambassador in London a comfortable one. It is not easy for a diplomat to adopt a high and firm tone when, at any moment, he may be asked, 'Does your government still exist today?' " Talleyrand's discomfort,

---

* Talleyrand, even though an advocate of Belgian independence, quickly lost patience with the Belgian demands for ever more territory—demands which he regarded as not only inopportune, but unjust and untrue. "The Belgians," he wrote candidly, "have falsified the frontier by the manner in which they represent it." As for the "vexatious delays" of the Dutch, Talleyrand was referring to a note from the ambassador of the Netherlands, in which the latter informed the conference that he was ill and would not be available for discussions for an indefinite period. The sole purpose of this indisposition, Talleyrand believed, was "to retard the work of the conference . . . which confirms me in the opinion that this prince [the King of the Netherlands] is endeavoring to throw all possible obstacles in our way."

however, as well as France's anxiety, was short-lived. On December 22, the ministers were tried before the Chamber of Peers, and although not a single sentence of capital punishment was handed down—despite public pressure to the contrary—there were no demonstrations and no rioting in the streets. "Here we are," Madame Adélaïde wrote from Paris, "past the crisis of this terrible trial. The great drama has ended in a manner worthy of our revolution and of the king who governs us." Talleyrand, who hated awkwardness of any sort, "received the news, I must confess, with immense satisfaction."

He was even more pleased with his accomplishments in London at a time when the situation in Paris had made his position, as he said, uncomfortable:

> I eagerly seized the opportunity afforded me by the obstinacy of the King of the Netherlands and the more friendly feelings of the Congress at Brussels to attain the end I was above all most eager to secure: the dissolution of the kingdom of the Netherlands. . . . I decided that there was only one way to put an end to our uncertainties—namely, to ask for the immediate declaration of the independence of Belgium. . . . The character of the King of Holland is an obstacle to everything, but this obstacle must be overcome, and I know of no better way to bring this about than to induce the conference to declare the independence of Belgium. I therefore intend to speak to Lord Palmerston about this before the meeting and then to lay the proposition formally before the plenipotentiaries of the four powers. If I am able to do this tomorrow—and I hope that I shall do so—then we shall have made a great step forward.

The following day, December 20, the powers met in a session lasting seven hours. "You will not be surprised," Talleyrand reported to Paris, "at the length of these discussions when you learn that only the English plenipotentiary and I were in agreement about the independence of Belgium and that we had to persuade the four other plenipotentiaries to share our opinion. But I attached too great importance to the king's wishes not to press forward, with as much determination as possible, a resolution so important." The combination of Grey and Talleyrand was more than the other representatives could resist, and one by one, they acquiesced in the proposed protocol which, under color of maintaining the balance of power in Europe, declared that "the conference will therefore occupy itself in discussing and arranging the best possible new arrangements, which will combine the future independence of Belgium with the . . . interests and safety of the other powers." The reference to Belgium's "future independence" was, as Talleyrand had intended, nothing less than a recognition of its present independence, and it was instantly recognized as such. The most determined opposition, predictably, came from the Russian ambassador, but even he, finally, was persuaded to sign—a fact which Talleyrand reported to Sebastiani with especial pride. Everything—the hours of arduous debate, the wrangling with Lieven—had been worthwhile for the advantages that would now accrue to France. The agreement, in effect, created a second Switzerland on France's northwest frontier. To Madame Adélaïde, Talleyrand wrote that "yesterday was one of those days that will always hold an important place in my life." And, from Paris, Mademoiselle replied that "the king is enchanted and very proud of the success of the ambassador *of his choice.*" Indeed, Louis-Philippe could hardly contain his elation and wandered around the palace describing to everyone "M. de Talleyrand's great *coup.*"

The declaration of Belgian independence was greeted with varying emotions in different countries. The Belgians, predictably, were delighted, and the Dutch, just as predictably, were indignant. "The King of the Netherlands," Talleyrand reports, "registered a most vehement protest against our decision." In France, despite Louis-Philippe's good humor, there was much dissatisfaction among the superpatriots—that is, the ultraconservatives—over France's loss of Belgium and over Louis-Philippe's open determination to reject the Belgian crown on behalf of the Duke de Nemours. Sebastiani, however, had learned his lessons well, and he wrote to London reassuring Talleyrand that "we cannot wish, in order to arrive at this, to place ourselves in such violent opposition as would oblige us to make war against the whole of Europe and to overthrow all social order, which is already trembling in the balance." The ultras, in other words, would be obliged to accept Talleyrand's solution to the Belgian problem whether they liked it or not.

In England, a very different spirit prevailed. Talleyrand, as the guiding spirit and inspiration of the conference, which had achieved this diplomatic triumph, this victory of principle over expediency, this bloodless substitute for Continental war, became the hero of the hour and the lion of the season. His carriage was greeted with hurrahs in the streets, and even Dorothea, as soon as she was recognized, was cheered by the people. The Lord Mayor of London hosted a great feast to which all of England's leading statesmen and political figures were invited. Among them, there was a single foreigner: Talleyrand, the guest of honor. Enormously moved by the affection of a people whom he so admired, he acknowledged, in his toast, "the rare happiness of being able to offer to Europe the prospect of freedom protected by law and guaranteed by the popularity of sovereigns who know all the advantages of peace and who bend all their efforts to its maintenance." The thunderous and sustained applause which greeted his statement was not so much for the words themselves, which were then as they are now, a political incantation, but for the man who spoke them, a figure who, in his extreme old age, was expending what energies remained to him in that pursuit of a peace that was, as it had always been, the most laudable passion of his life.

That peace, however, was not yet entirely assured. There still remained to be resolved the thorny question of a sovereign for the new nation. So far as Talleyrand's own choice was concerned, it had inclined, from the very beginning, toward a German prince, Leopold of Saxe-Coburg. "This prince," Talleyrand noted, "had addressed himself to me and I had hastened to assure him that, for my part, I should be very pleased if his candidature was successful. In fact, I knew of no other prince in Europe who was so well suited as he for such a delicate and complicated position. I had had the opportunity of becoming acquainted with him at the Congress of Vienna, where he had shown great intelligence and loyalty. . . ." Prince Leopold, it seems, had given proof of these qualities by seconding the position of France in those negotiations: "He supported the interests of the King of Saxony against Prussia and Russia." He had commended himself to Talleyrand particularly by his courage "in resisting the cajoleries, as well as the threats, of the Emperor Alexander." Leopold, in other words, having come forward as a man who supported France and opposed France's enemies, was to be France's—that is, Talleyrand's—choice for the Belgian throne. No one, however, could be trusted entirely, and it was proposed to hand Leopold not only a crown, but a queen as well, and one who could be relied upon to keep her husband firmly on the paths of righteousness: "Prince Leopold, as King of Belgium and married to a French princess, seemed to me the best possible choice that could be made to solve the difficulties with which we had to contend."

The English were brought around to Talleyrand's way of thinking by means reminiscent of the prince's dealings with Lord Castlereagh in Vienna fifteen years earlier. On December 14, an interesting exchange took place between Palmerston and Talleyrand on the subject of Belgium's sovereign. "The time has arrived," Talleyrand said, "to broach the important question of the future King of Belgium." Palmerston thereupon suggested several names, among them the Archduke Charles of Austria. All these Talleyrand rejected for various reasons. Lest Palmerston think that France had designs upon the new throne for itself, he added: "The Belgians think a great deal of the Duke de Nemours, but the king wishes to put aside this proposal. . . . He is, in fact, placed in a most singular position, for he is forced to employ all the skill he possesses to refuse that which others use in order to gain what they want."

"It would be difficult to persuade the other powers to consent to the Duke de Nemours," replied Palmerston. "Let us try to find someone else who, at least by marriage, might satisfy everyone."

"I consider," the prince suggested, "that by 'everyone' you mean you and us."

In this way, Talleyrand gradually worked the conversation around to Prince Leopold and to the possibility of a French bride for him, but in such a way that "Lord Palmerston himself brought forward the name. I exhibited some slight astonishment, as if this idea were quite new to me, but my astonishment rather took the form of a pleasant surprise. I had to say that I would immediately report the whole of this conversation to Paris, and we could then soon discuss it further. This is as far as we have got. It is evident that if Belgium were given to Prince Leopold (who would then marry a French princess), the English would be altogether pleased. I think, if you approve of this idea, that the proposal should be made at the conference by Lord Palmerston, and I will take it upon myself to persuade him to do it."

Despite this auspicious beginning, the New Year came and went, and still nothing had been done. Madame Adélaïde was writing from Paris complaining of "the dilatoriness of the London Conference," and Talleyrand was offering in explanation "the delays of the English, the vacillation of the Belgians, the obstinacy of the Dutch, and the necessity of having to deal with people who only acquiesce unwillingly in concessions opposed to their inclinations and often to their interests." The "dilatoriness" so often mentioned on both sides of the Channel consisted principally of Lord Grey's apparently unlimited patience in considering, discussing, and then allowing Talleyrand to reject, names other than that of Leopold of Saxe-Coburg for the Belgian throne: the Prince of Orange, Prince Charles of Bavaria, and Prince Charles of Naples among others. The real danger, however, was not from the unhurried approach of the English, but from the "obstinacy of the Dutch." Holland, in violation of the armistice arrived at under the auspices of the conference, had attained a stranglehold on Belgian commerce by blockading the Scheldt and the port of Antwerp. "The King of Holland," Talleyrand explains, "desired war above all things and hoped that it might lead to the restoration of his government in Belgium." The Belgians, in reprisal, laid siege to the town of Maestricht, and King William of Holland aggravated the situation by sending troops to relieve the siege and by inviting Prussia to intervene.

In this new crisis, Talleyrand moved quickly. Upon his motion, on January 9, the conference instructed the King of Holland that he must discontinue the blockade by January 20 and the Belgians that they must raise the siege of Maestricht. When this protocol was ignored by both sides, the conference, again at Talleyrand's instigation, reiterated its demand, adding that if the hostile nations did not comply instantly, the powers themselves would blockade their ports.

This served only as a temporary measure, and something more permanent was needed. For several days Talleyrand studied the problem and, on
January 20, submitted his solution to the conference, which adopted it immediately. That night, he reported to Paris: "We have succeeded in pro-
curing the recognition in principle of the neutrality of Belgium by the
plenipotentiaries. . . . The recognition of the neutrality of Belgium places
that country in the same position as Switzerland and consequently upsets
the political system adopted by the powers in 1815, out of hatred for
France." The importance of Belgian neutrality, however, was more than
diplomatic: "The thirteen fortresses of Belgium, by means of which our
northern frontier was perpetually threatened, will fall, so to speak, in consequence of this resolution, and we shall henceforth be free from
troublesome obstructions. . . . You will agree with me, M. le Comte [Se-
bastiani], as to the immense advantage that this resolution will afford to
the maintenance of peace."

The resolution of January 20 also settled, at least to the satisfaction of
the conference, the issue of the frontier between Holland and Belgium by
establishing the boundaries that had prevailed in 1790. Whether or not
King William was content with this arrangement was now academic, for
the resolution, in proclaiming Belgium "a neutral state in perpetuity,"
bound the signatory powers to "guarantee it this perpetual neutrality, as
well as the integrity and inviolability of its territory within the above-men-
tioned limits." It also obliged Belgium, under threat of intervention by the
same powers, "to observe the same neutrality toward all other states and
not to make any attempt to disturb their interior or exterior tranquillity."
Both Belgium and Holland, therefore, were faced with joint sanction by
France, Britain, Prussia, Russia, and Austria if they continued hostilities
between themselves, and on the horns of such a dilemma, there was nothing they could do but agree to lay down their arms. "The King of Holland," Talleyrand noted, "submitted with a very bad grace."

The point of Talleyrand's accomplishment, as he frankly states, was
"not to satisfy the impatient spirits in Paris, or the requirements of Brussels
and The Hague, but to maintain good relations between ourselves and
England and, by this means, to impose on other governments resolutions
as reasonable and fair as we should have done between ourselves. All else
was secondary, so far as I was concerned. I sought the true interests of
France where I hoped to find them, not in wild dreams that could lead
only to destruction."

The danger to which Talleyrand alluded was very real. If Prussia or Russia* had sent troops into Belgium at Holland's request, France could have

* The Prince of Orange was the husband of Czar Nicholas' sister, the Grand Duchess Anna,
and thus Russia had a vested interest, so to speak, in the well-being of the House of Nassau. This

responded only by a declaration of war, and such a war, Talleyrand concluded "would necessarily have been fatal to us, for it would immediately have developed a revolutionary character, which would have separated us from England." The declaration of the perpetual neutrality of Belgium had obviated that possibility—"but only on condition," he warned, "that we are the first to respect it."

Now that peace seemed virtually assured, the choice of a king for Belgium lost much of its importance for Talleyrand. "I felt sure from the first, since neutrality had been agreed to in London by the conference of great powers, that the chief interest of that sovereign, whoever he might be, must be to make friends with France and live in amicable relations with it." There were others who did not share the prince's tranquillity in this respect. In Belgium, the Congress was preparing to elect a sovereign, and though it was clear that whoever might be chosen must be acceptable to the powers represented at the London Conference, there was a great deal of agitation. The situation was not rendered more simple by the determination of the British—despite Lord Palmerston's earlier decision in favor of Prince Leopold of Saxe-Coburg—to make at least a show of supporting the candidacy of the one prince whom Belgium did not want at any price: the Prince of Orange. Yet Talleyrand, always the realist, had no serious objections to this bit of playacting on the part of London:

> I was perfectly convinced that dislike of the House of Nassau was too strong in Belgium for the Prince of Orange even to hope to reestablish himself there. Therefore, I saw no risk in allowing England to make the attempt. I knew that the Cabinet would have to convince Parliament that the claim had been considered, tried, and found impracticable and that a certain sense of shame obliged the English to extend this token of support to Holland* . . . and, finally, I felt that, later on, the English Cabinet would give me credit for the good faith we showed in not opposing openly the election of the Prince of Orange.

So, Talleyrand concludes:

> I decided not to concern myself so much with the choice of a sovereign for Belgium as with the purpose of widening and confirming the separation of that kingdom from Holland.

relationship, of course, was one of the reasons for Talleyrand's opposition to Orange's candidacy for the Belgian throne and one of the causes of his satisfaction that Orange was unpopular among the Belgians.

* In 1814, Holland had been given the Belgian provinces in exchange for those of its colonies—Cape Colony and various possessions in Guiana and Malabar—which Britain wished to retain after the Napoleonic Wars. It was the embarrassment of the British at keeping these colonies, even while being party to the dismemberment of the Netherlands, to which Talleyrand refers. This "shamefacedness," as the prince describes it, never became so acute, however, as to tempt London to return the colonies.

While Talleyrand was thus occupied, there arrived in London once more Charles de Flahaut, who had come, to Talleyrand's great disgust, "to re-open the famous question of the partition of Belgium, which I had believed to be buried in oblivion." Flahaut brought a letter from Sebastiani pointing out that the Belgian Congress had set January 28 as the date for the election of their sovereign, "and there is every fear that the choice will fall upon the Duke de Leuchtenberg," son of Eugène de Beauharnais, who was an idol of the Bonapartists and was regarded as anti-French. The French commissioner in Brussels, Sebastiani continued, had been ordered to inform the Congress that Leuchtenberg's election would not be recognized in France and, at the same time, to renew Louis-Philippe's refusal either to allow the election of the Duke de Nemours or to consent to the union of Belgium with France. "It is needless to write you a long letter," the message concluded. "M. de Flahaut will tell you everything that it is important for you to know."

What Flahaut told was that, in the impasse presented by the probable election of a candidate unacceptable to France, the only means to avoid war was to resort to a partition of Belgium. This, Talleyrand categorically rejected "in the strongest possible terms, as being both impolitic and impracticable." Then he sat down and addressed a letter to Sebastiani, repeating his earlier arguments against such a partition, and adding that "I am convinced, M. le Comte, that if you were plenipotentiary here, you would never sign your own name to an act which not even the longest and most unfortunate war could justify." He signed it with a flourish, handed it to the embarrassed Flahaut, and bid him begone to Paris. "And that," Talleyrand noted with satisfaction, "was the last I ever heard of the plan for dividing Belgium."

So confident was the prince in his own judgment that he could afford, he felt, lightly to dismiss the fears of others. He wrote:

> Fortunately, I did not allow myself to be upset or permit my plans to be thwarted by the intemperate emotions of others. My idea as to the choice of a sovereign for Belgium had never wavered. My candidate was, and always would be, Prince Leopold of Saxe-Coburg, and I was in no way disturbed by the noise and excitement which existed everywhere upon this question. I had high hopes. I knew, first, that King Louis-Philippe would certainly refuse the crown for his son; second, that the powers would reject the Duke de Leuchtenberg; and, third, that the Belgians themselves would never agree to recall the Prince of Orange.

Talleyrand's assurance, as it turned out, was entirely justified. On February 3, as was reported by Bresson, the French commissioner in Brussels, "H.R.H. the Duke de Nemours was nominated and proclaimed King of

the Belgians, at twenty-five minutes past four precisely this afternoon.*
. . . The greatest enthusiasm and the most perfect calm reign in the city."
An immediate dispatch went from London to Sebastiani in Paris: "I am
certain that the king will refuse immediately the crown which has been
offered to M. le Duc de Nemours. You must clearly understand that all
measures which may call for consultations with the powers will be regarded as delaying tactics and that only a firm and spontaneous refusal
will convince England, whose alliance we are now on the point of losing."
The following day this virtual command was followed by a threat of resignation unless Louis-Philippe's earlier, informal refusal of a crown for his
son was followed by a formal act: "I must repeat that, if this step is not
taken, my presence here will become useless, both to the king and to the
affairs of France." In any case, the prince explained, ambassadors would
be unnecessary, for the British Cabinet "agreed as to the necessity for immediate war should this election be recognized by France." But Talleyrand, as always, was determined that France, though necessity might dictate the refusal of a crown for one of its sons, would not be compelled to
witness the acceptance of that crown by a hostile prince. On February 7,
he had the pleasure of informing Paris that the powers had been persuaded
to declare they would not, on any condition, recognize any election which
might declare the Duke de Leuchtenberg to be King of the Belgians.†
Louis-Philippe and France had now been given the assurance that they required, and on February 17, in the presence of the Belgian emissaries who
had come to Paris with the intention of offering the throne of their country
to the Duke de Nemours, the King of the French solemnly and formally
renounced forever, on behalf of his dynasty, any claim to the crown of Belgium. Talleyrand was greatly relieved. "I must tell you," he wrote to Sebastiani, "of the effect produced here by the king's speech in reply to the Belgian deputation. It has made a most favorable impression, and this morning, at the grand reception at court, in honor of the queen's birthday, several persons spoke to me about it, and all were loud in its praises."

All the pieces in the Belgian puzzle were beginning to fall into place, just
as Talleyrand had predicted. The two leading contenders for the throne,
Nemours and Leuchtenberg, were now out of the running. The only remaining formal candidate of the original three was Charles of Austria, the
weakest of them all. To him, Talleyrand was naturally opposed, since the
presence of an Austrian prince in Belgium, now that the Duke de Nemours

* On the second and final ballot, the Duke de Nemours received 97 votes—the required majority. The Duke de Leuchtenberg had 47 votes; and the Archduke Charles of Austria, 21. Prince
Leopold, despite Talleyrand's confidence in his ultimate victory, had not even been nominated.

† Leuchtenberg's royal ambitions were eventually to be realized, after a fashion. In 1834, he
married Dona Maria, Queen of Portugal, and their union awakened great hopes for a revival of
the exhausted House of Braganza. These expectations were cut short, however, by Leuchtenberg's
death in the following year, at the age of twenty-five.

had been excluded from consideration, would have provoked great dissatisfaction in France. In conversation with Lord Grey, he dismissed Charles offhandedly as a mere offshoot of the Hapsburg dynasty which had, until 1797, ruled Holland and Belgium, and he concluded by quoting Pitt to England's Prime Minister: "A restoration is the worst form of revolution." With the field now virtually empty, the candidacy of Leopold of Saxe-Coburg could be seriously advanced. Those who were watching Talleyrand's maneuvering to accomplish this end were moved to admiration, and this number included his enemies. Pozzo di Borgo remarked to one of Talleyrand's correspondents, the Duke de Dalberg: "In all fairness, I must say that M. de Talleyrand has been the only one who has seen things in their true perspective." In truth, as Talleyrand observed modestly to Sebastiani,* the candidacy of the Prince of Saxe-Coburg now seemed more feasible than that of any other person. As proof of this assertion, he brought together Prince Leopold and the Belgian representatives in London and, rather like a father reporting on the courtship of a submissive son, sent periodic reports to Paris on the progress being made. On May 3: "The prince seems to have decided to accept the Belgian throne, but he is aware that to obtain the admission of the country among the European states, it is necessary that it be on friendly terms with the great powers. . . . His royal highness has frequently seen the [Belgian] deputies who are in London, and he always expressed himself to them in the sense I have just indicated." On May 9: "The prince has had frequent interviews with the deputies and is always perfectly frank and open with them. They, for their part, are gaining confidence in him and take every opportunity of expressing their desire to see him placed at their head, as they believe that only in this way will peace be restored to their country." On May 20: "Lord Ponsonby [British commissioner in Brussels] is still in London. He goes down to Claremont tomorrow to have an interview with Prince Leopold. I have reason to believe that the English government intends to further the prince's acceptance of the Belgian crown." On May 22: "We [the plenipotentiaries of the powers] met again yesterday, and I have drawn up protocol No. 24, a copy of which I send you herewith. You will see that Prince Leopold of Saxe-Coburg is mentioned in such a manner as to show the Belgians that, if their choice falls on this prince, the powers will give their consent thereto."

Finally, on June 4, to no one's surprise, Prince Leopold was elected King of the Belgians, by a majority of 155 votes to 44 and with the blessing of the London Conference. Talleyrand heaved a sigh of relief. To all ap-

* In mid-March, the government of Laffitte had fallen, and been replaced by that of Casimir Périer. General Sebastiani, however, had retained the Ministry of Foreign Affairs.

pearances, the Belgian question had been resolved. The nation's independence had been declared, its neutrality proclaimed and guaranteed by the great powers, and, as its first sovereign, it would have a prince acceptable both to the Belgians themselves and to France. Talleyrand's work, it seemed, was virtually completed.

But this was not to be. No sooner had news of Leopold's election reached the capitals of Europe than Belgium began loudly to demand "rectification" of her frontiers. There were reports that the Belgians had attacked the Dutch at Antwerp and fired upon the ships at anchor in the harbor. The Belgian deputation in London hastened to assure Talleyrand that there had been no attack launched by their side. "But," Talleyrand wrote to Paris, "if all accounts are true, it is clearly the Belgians who are the aggressors." A few days later, as the result of fatigue caused by the late and prolonged sittings necessitated by this "troublesome matter" as he called it, Talleyrand fell seriously ill and was confined to his bed. Even then, he did not rest. "I continued to take part in the deliberations of the conference, which now assembled at my bedside." It was also at his bedside that the Belgian delegation was treated to a careful display of anger and impatience at their "obstinate resistance" to the settlement dictated by the conference. "I even went so far," Talleyrand recorded later, "as to threaten them that if they persisted, I should be obliged to advise the partition of their kingdom, which could be effected without the war which their foolish conduct would most certainly bring about." Then, just at the moment when the Belgians, reacting to the prince's impatience, seemed on the point of acceding to the demands of the conference on all important points, a new and even more serious crisis presented itself. William of Holland, irritated at the demands of the Belgians and at the election of Prince Leopold, and hurt at his abandonment by all the great powers, decided upon a desperate measure, one designed, no doubt, to plunge the whole of Europe into war and to compel Prussia and Russia to come to his aid. On August 4, 1831, he publicly repudiated the armistice of the conference and sent his troops, under the command of the Prince of Orange, into Belgium.

Talleyrand acted immediately. At his suggestion, the conference drew up a protocol which, reflecting an official request of Leopold, authorized the entry of the French army into Belgium and permitted the British to send a squadron to defend the Belgian coast against Dutch attack.* Despite the calm with which Talleyrand relates the events surrounding the new protocol in his *Mémoires*, the decision of the conference raised a storm of protest in England. Lord Palmerston, despite Grey's adherence to the

* This protocol (No. 31, of August 6, 1831) stipulated that the French should confine their operations to Belgian territory, limit themselves to the expulsion of the Dutch, and withdraw as soon as hostilities had ceased.

protocol, wondered privately whether there had not been some secret agreement between Holland and France. In public, during a debate in the House of Lords, Lord Londonderry,* a Tory, launched a bitter attack on Talleyrand, deploring both his morals and his diplomacy in such terms as to horrify and disgust even the members of his own party. Two members of the government, as much out of personal outrage as from their duty to protect the representative of a friendly power, rose to defend the prince. Lord Goderich formally rebuked Londonderry for his intemperate attack. And Lord Holland, according to the *Times,* declared forcefully that his long acquaintance "with the noble individual who had been alluded to, enabled him to bear his testimony to the fact that, although those forty years had been passed during a time peculiarly fraught with calumnies of every description, there had been no man's character more shamefully traduced, and no man's public character more mistaken and misrepresented, than the private and public character of Prince de Talleyrand."

The noblest gesture of all, however, and the *coup de grâce* to Londonderry, came from a man who, though a Tory like Londonderry and the leader of the opposition, had never in his life allowed political expediency to cloud his judgment or to bridle his tongue. The Duke of Wellington rose and, in the most profound and respectful silence, addressed to the Lords his estimate of "that illustrious individual who had been so strongly adverted upon by his noble friend near him." He took the opportunity to remind Londonderry that his close relative, Lord Castlereagh,† now deceased, had had great esteem for Talleyrand:

> He had no hesitation in saying that in every one of the transactions that took place at the Congress of Vienna, and in every transaction in which he [Wellington] had been engaged with the Prince de Talleyrand since, from the first to the last of them, no man could have conducted himself with more firmness and ability, with regard to his own country, or with more uprightness and honour in all his communications with the Ministers of other countries. They had heard a good deal of Prince de Talleyrand from many quarters; but he felt himself bound to declare it to be his sincere and conscientious belief that no man's public and private character had ever been so much belied as both the public and private character of that illustrious individual had been.

Talleyrand was profoundly touched when these words were reported to him. An English peer who visited him the next morning found him moved to tears. To Dorothea, the prince confided that this had been the first time in his long life that any foreign statesman had spoken kindly of him.

* Londonderry's character and personality were immortalized for posterity by an expression of Greville's which gained wide circulation and followed the noble peer to his grave: "That ass, Londonderry."

† Londonderry was Castlereagh's half brother.

Actually, Lord Palmerston's suspicions of "an agreement" between France and Holland seem to have no foundation in fact. The same cannot be said, however, concerning the possibility of a private arrangement between Talleyrand and William of Holland. Papers from the Belgian archives, published for the first time in 1834,* indicate at least the existence of such a possibility. According to these documents, Talleyrand would have received a total of 35,000 pounds sterling from the Dutch king for showing consideration for Dutch territorial and financial claims in the discussions of the conference. Of this, 20,000 pounds may have been paid; it is not clear whether the remaining 15,000 pounds were ever forthcoming. The documents in question are not themselves entirely above suspicion with respect either to veracity or authenticity. It is worth noting that, at one point, Louise, Queen of the Belgians and daughter of Louis-Philippe,† openly accused Talleyrand of having accepted a bribe from the King of Holland. This complaint was, at the time, generally accepted for what it may well have been: the outburst of a woman who regarded herself, her husband, and her adopted country, perhaps rightly, as the innocent victims of the political necessity as interpreted by the great powers, particularly by France in the person of Prince Talleyrand. It would not, then, have been the first time, or the last, that such an outburst was given substance by being incorporated into official documents and corroborated by other documents relating circumstantial evidence. Nor would it be the last time that such documents, inflammatory as they were in chauvinistic sentiment, would be resurrected after many years, when their true context had long been forgotten, and presented as evidence of the victimization of one nation by another.

On the other side of the coin is the fact that Talleyrand had, not sporadically but consistently, throughout his entire life, used whatever means his considerable genius could devise to accumulate money. It is doubtful that he would have hesitated to accept a cash gift from the King of Holland while ambassador in London—particularly since that money would have been in payment for his support of a position which, one must admit, if one reviews his correspondence of the period with some objectivity, he had shown signs of supporting from the very beginning. The acceptance of "gifts" from all and sundry was, it must be recognized, a matter of habit with Talleyrand, as it was with many of his most distinguished contemporaries in public life. In the case of the prince, however, the habit was no longer a result of necessity. He was already a millionaire many times over, one of the wealthiest men in Europe, the ambassador extraordinary and

---

* *Mélanges*, pp. 190–192, ed. Professor Michel Huisman.

† The marriage between Louise and King Leopold was arranged in 1832 and celebrated in the following year.

plenipotentiary of the kingdom of France, an old man with one foot in the grave. Of money, he had no need. He accumulated it purely out of habit— just as other men continue to pursue, in their old age, the activities of their youth. Kant, when he was seventy-eight, was still taking his daily walks. Gladstone, at seventy-eight, was still chopping wood. It is not impossible that Talleyrand, at seventy-eight, was still taking bribes.

Be that as it may, the strategy devised by Talleyrand to meet the threat of a general war over Belgium was successful. The joint action of France and Britain was sufficient in strength and promptness to forestall intervention by any of the Eastern powers. Moreover, Holland's rash attack and the danger of a general war which it had at least momentarily created had had the effect of deciding the plenipotentiaries to impose a firm solution upon that country. And Belgians, "a little ashamed of their defeat and of the necessity of having had to accept France's protection," felt obliged now "to conclude matters and to emerge from its [Belgium's] painful state of uncertainty." It was therefore time to conclude a final treaty between the hostile nations. A month later, on October 22, affairs had progressed so far and so rapidly that Talleyrand was writing to Mademoiselle: "I hope we are at least approaching the end and that this difficult business of Belgium will soon be finished. The day on which I know it is decided will be the happiest of my life, for I shall have been of service in doing something which, in all respects, must be pleasing to the king and to Mademoiselle." The conference had now drawn up the basis for the formal separation between Belgium and Holland, in twenty-four articles. These were sent to The Hague and to Brussels with a firmly worded request for the consent of the two governments. On November 15, Talleyrand wrote in exhaustion and elation to the Princess de Vaudémont: "Our articles are signed! The Belgians will complain, but they are wrong. All has been done fairly, and I think in favor of the Belgians. . . . Belgium pays a much smaller share of the national debt than it did before the separation, so it cannot complain. Its population is increased, and its home commerce will benefit greatly by the facilities given it. . . . I am terribly fatigued. Yesterday our conference lasted until 5 A.M., and the day before until 4 A.M. I believe that I have obtained everything that it was possible to obtain." The government of France was of the same opinion, and congratulations poured into the London embassy, from Madame Adélaïde ("You have accomplished a great work") and from Louis-Philippe ("The Treaty of London of November 15, 1831, will be a great milestone in history. The more its consequences are clearly seen, the more France will appreciate the great service that you have just rendered it, and I hasten to testify to you how fully I join in this appreciation and in all the sentiments that this great success will evoke on your behalf.") Perhaps most surprising of all, a message of congratulation came from that ambassador *manqué,* the Count de Flahaut: "At last you have reached the end. . . . That you have succeeded in maintaining the peace, in the midst of all these revolutions and distractions, is a great achievement."

The solution of the Belgian question still had not, in fact, reached the end. There were still complications to be resolved, objections to be met, intrigues to be countered. There was an organized movement in the House of Lords to refuse to ratify the treaty of November 15—a movement that Wellington helped to defeat by coming out firmly on the side of the government. There were objections from the King of Holland, who, when he was finally convinced that the powers would not budge, swore that he would never accept the settlement; and when they still did not budge, he resigned himself to the inevitable and accepted. There were protests in France, where Talleyrand was attacked in newspapers by pundits who would never forgive him for preventing the union of Belgium with France, for having transformed Belgium into a monarchy rather than into a republic, or for having insisted that the Duke de Nemours renounce the Belgian crown. Innumerable caricatures of him were printed and distributed in Paris, all on the subject of Belgium and all equally venomous. One such carried a caption describing the prince as "a maker of muzzles, chains, and censorship. A writer of mots, epigrams, programs, and epitaphs. A buyer and seller of crowns, both new and used. A manufacturer of constitutions, charters, and restoration; a collector of cockades, flags, and decorations of all colors."

These problems Talleyrand met with a good humor indicative of his complete confidence in his ability to find appropriate solutions. And the criticisms he accepted with a resignation that amounted to indifference. He had been too long in public life to regard difficulties, condemnation, or praise as anything more than the everyday hazards of public affairs. He would have been more amused than indignant to read a letter from Princess Lieven to her brother written at this time, in which the princess, in the same breath, waxed ecstatic over Talleyrand's incredible diplomatic skill and over his "good and healthy principles" and, at the same time, ended by declaring that "he is, however, a great villain." For himself, he was content with the good will of his friends and did not look elsewhere for his reward. To the Princess de Vaudémont, after describing Wellington's noble defense of him in the House of Lords, he observed: "In Paris, for which I am working myself to death, no one would think of doing as much. They consider that enough has been done when you write me a few kind words —and I do believe that they are quite right."

Paris, in truth, and the whole of Europe had a great deal to be grateful for in the four years of Talleyrand's embassy in London. His masterpiece,

of course, was the Belgian settlement, which, in its complexity was the repetition and reflection, on a smaller scale, of the flexible and pacific genius
that had characterized his achievement in Vienna many years before. But
there were other successes, less striking and less important perhaps, but
nonetheless effective illustrations of Talleyrand's conviction that, when all
was said and done, nothing mattered except peace, and that the sole function of statesmanship was to assure the existence and maintenance of
peace. It must not be, however, peace at any price—but peace with honor,
so far as France was concerned. During Talleyrand's sojourn in London,
for example, no sooner had the Belgian question been settled once and for
all than a war seemed on the verge of erupting in the Iberian Peninsula; a
war which, because of the conflicting interests of the great powers, might
well have become general. After the death of the Spanish King Ferdinand
VII in 1837, he was succeeded by his daughter Isabella, with Dowager
Queen María Cristiana as regent. This government, of liberal tincture, had
the support of the liberals, but it was Don Carlos, the late king's brother
and head of the Spanish conservatives, who incited a civil war to place
himself upon the throne instead of his niece. Austria, Prussia, and Russia,
the conservative and absolutist powers, naturally favored the cause of the
insurgents, and Austria went so far as to send money and arms to Don
Carlos. The conflagration threatened to spread to Portugal, and both England and France were greatly alarmed. At this point, Lord Palmerston,
with typical abrasiveness and without bothering to consult Talleyrand, negotiated treaties with the legitimate governments of the two Iberian powers
and then had the effrontery, in Talleyrand's view, to invite France to adhere to these treaties. The prince categorically refused to consent. A great
power such as France did not "adhere" to the treaties of other powers, and
great statesmen did not acquiesce in decisions in which they had had no
voice. France must be one of the principals of the treaties—that is, a contracting party—or there would be no treaties. A whole year of wrangling
ensued, with Palmerston, in a frenzy over the presumptuousness of "foreigners," being forced to give way step by step. Finally, Talleyrand was
victorious, and in April 1834, the Quadruple Alliance was signed binding
together France, Britain, Spain, and Portugal in a pact of mutual support
and defense against external attack. The Eastern powers did not dare intervene, and the Spanish liberals and conservatives were left to determine the
fate of their own country.* The alliance was widely regarded as a great triumph of diplomacy and as a great victory for Talleyrand.

Such endeavors, however skillfully and energetically they may have
been undertaken and whatever credit they have reflected upon the prince,

* The Carlists, as the conservatives were called, were finally defeated in 1839.

were, in reality, peripheral to his mission in London. He had been sent to England for a dual purpose: to bind France and Britain together with the bonds of friendship and common interests and to settle the inflammatory Belgian question. By the middle of 1832 he had accomplished these purposes to his own satisfaction and to that of his king. Now, exhausted, and wanting nothing more for himself than a measure of the peace that he had once again given to Europe, he decided to return to France for a few months' rest. Then, as he and Dorothea were making the final plans for the voyage, a disturbing message arrived from Paris. Casimir Périer, president of the Council, had died of cholera on May 16.* A few days later, Talleyrand noted significantly in a letter to Madame de Vaudémont that "M. de Rémusat has arrived here with his wife and brought me some letters from Paris."

Charles de Rémusat was a nephew of Casimir Périer and himself a prominent member of the Chamber of Deputies. He belonged to the party of the *juste milieu,* the moderates, comprising, among others, Talleyrand's collaborators and friends Royer-Collard, the Duke de Broglie, Bertin de Veaux, and General Sebastiani. He had come to London bearing more than "letters from Paris." He had been instructed by those who sent him to persuade the prince to return to Paris and accept the presidency of the Council.

Rémusat was not necessarily the best possible choice for this mission. Despite his undoubted intelligence and talent, he lacked the sensitivity and tact required by what he was about to attempt. On the day of his arrival in London, Dorothea was already writing that she had "always found him, in particular, especially disagreeable, and I find it very unlikely that he will make a different impression upon me now." As though to prove that he could live up to her assessment of him, Rémusat began his mission by approaching Dorothea rather than Talleyrand himself. On May 25, he spent two hours with her, and predictably, he failed utterly to persuade her to use her influence with Talleyrand on his behalf. "We discussed a multitude of things," Rémusat recorded, "but the object of the conversation was for her to tell me this: 'So, you wish to transform M. de Talleyrand into a head of government? I beg you to spare yourself the effort. It would not suit him at all. He would refuse to do it. And, even if he were willing, I would prevent it.' . . . From this moment, I did no more than bring to bear on M. de Talleyrand the minimum of pressure that was required in order to demonstrate that I had not given up too easily." Dorothea, turning to her own diary, noted: "M. de Talleyrand is much too determined not to become in-

* There had been a serious epidemic of the disease toward the end of 1831, which reached London in January, 1832, and Paris in March. On April 3, Périer had become seriously ill, but until shortly before his death, it was thought that he was convalescing.

volved with any administration to be willing to give way on this point."

She was correct. The "minimum of pressure" that Rémusat was willing or able to exert met with stubborn refusal. "I am greatly flattered by their [Périer's friends'] opinion, but I have decided not to accept anything. I say this quietly and softly, as one must do when one's mind is quite made up." Far from having the slightest inclination to take on a position that was demanding and thankless, Talleyrand was determined, if not to retire, then at least to exact from life whatever of repose it might offer to a man of his position and age. Rémusat and his friends therefore had to seek elsewhere for a chief minister, and after much hesitation and many minor crises, the Duke de Broglie finally took over the presidency of the Council in October, 1832.

On June 20, Talleyrand left London for Paris, accompanied by Dorothea and followed by the best wishes of King William, and, perhaps surprisingly, of Palmerston, who wrote: "Good-bye once again. Give good advice where you are going; take care of your health, get over the fatigues of our long conferences as soon as you can, and come back here soon; but above all—come back." The Foreign Secretary, like the king, might have reservations concerning the prince's character, but he had none at all regarding the necessity of his presence if good relations were to be maintained between France and England and if the peace of Europe was to be secured.

Once back on the Continent, Dorothea spent a few days in Paris and then journeyed on to Switzerland and, later, to Rochecotte. The prince, however, had returned to France to rest, and he went to his favorite watering place, Bourbon-l'Archambault, where, he wrote to Madame de Vaudémont, he expected to be able "to go to bed early, to eat only what is good for me, and to avoid speaking a single word that might conceivably be of interest to anyone." Despite these high hopes, his stay was not entirely a success. He was alone, surrounded by the aged and the ailing, and soon depressed. In mid-August, he wrote to Royer-Collard that he had caught "a serious cold, for which they gave me an emetic yesterday. You see to what I have been reduced." Two weeks later he was at Rochecotte with Dorothea, and his spirits, as well as his health, were better. "I think," he wrote to Bacourt, "that I am getting stronger, and I am now sleeping better than I did. Madame de Dino is also in better health." A month later, on October 10, apparently both restored, Talleyrand and Dorothea left for the return trip to London.

Once there, however, the prince discovered, to his dismay, that the Belgian question had been reopened unilaterally by the King of Holland. That monarch, who had possession of Antwerp, had resolutely refused to surrender it to the new government of Belgium. On October 22, Talleyrand succeeded in persuading the British government to agree to allow French troops once more to enter Belgium. Early in December, Antwerp capitulated. William of Holland had now finally shot his last bolt.

It was another victory for Talleyrand, but one which he did not need and which he would have willingly forgone. He was now approaching his eightieth year, and the energies that he was required to expend in the interests of France left him quickly exhausted, despite his recent prolonged leave of absence. He had also, for the first time in his life, it seems, become ill-tempered and short with his subordinates. Adolphe de Bacourt, a young embassy secretary whose presence Talleyrand had specifically requested in London at the end of 1830 and whom the prince had, in the past, always treated with paternal affection, found this change so astonishing that he complained to Dorothea:

> I must tell you that the prospect of subjecting myself again to M. de Talleyrand's ill humor fills me with dismay. . . . I can, of course, forgive him the ill treatment I have endured at his hands because of his age, his ill health, and the pressure of affairs. Nonetheless, I have made up my mind to keep our relationship strictly that of employee and employer. Never again will I attempt to be to him what I once was.

The truth was that Talleyrand's unaccustomed bad temper and impatience were due only in part to the causes that Bacourt had charitably adduced—age, infirmity, and the press of business. Bacourt was young—fifty years younger than Talleyrand and ten years younger than Dorothea. He was, moreover, intelligent, affable, and charming. These were qualities that Talleyrand had always found pleasing. They were also traits calculated to impress a woman of Dorothea's rather passionate temperament. Before long and predictably, Bacourt and Dorothea showed signs of a strong mutual attachment. This, of course, did not escape the prince, nor did it particularly disturb him, at least at first. A man of his age and poor health was no longer subject to the burning passions of youth, and a man of his experience was too wise to believe that Dorothea, forty and still handsome, shared this immunity. He had winked at her discreet affairs during the Restoration, and he was perfectly willing to show her the same consideration on this occasion. Yet, with Bacourt living in the same house as himself and Dorothea, it became increasingly difficult to do so. There were doubtless times when Bacourt intruded, if not in person then at least by his presence in Dorothea's thoughts and conversation. Talleyrand apparently became jealous, and his behavior toward Bacourt revealed it. Yet, a short time later, tranquillity had been restored, and the prince was treating his embassy secretary with the affection and cordiality that had characterized the beginning of their relationship. What had happened? The answer cannot be known for certain. It seems likely that Dorothea, with her deep knowledge of her uncle and her intimate understanding of his nature, found some way to reassure him of her enduring love, a love which transcended the more pedestrian attachments and affections to which she was regularly subject and which would endure, immutable, until death, and beyond. It also helped, no doubt, that Bacourt, for all his good looks and winning ways, was a weak and pliable man. Despite his brave words, he no sooner caught sight of the prince upon the latter's return from France than he was once more what he had always been: a subordinate official in a demanding position, living in anticipation of a word, or even a glance, of approval from his master. Between two men such as these, Dorothea could have had no great difficulty in effecting a reconciliation.

As soon as Talleyrand and Dorothea were reestablished in London, life went on very much as before, at least superficially. Their dinners and receptions were as brilliant as ever, and everyone who was anyone in London flocked to them in impossible numbers. Talleyrand remained the lion of English society, and he and Dorothea set the fashions of the day. The prince's every word and act were commented upon and if possible imitated—though this was not always possible. Visiting Frenchmen were astonished to see one of their countrymen placed so high in a country where exclusiveness and snobbery were reputed to be the order of the day. Mérimée, who spent the winter of 1832–33 in London, wrote back to Paris that "The most amusing thing in the world is to see him [the prince] surrounded by the greatest lords of the land, who conduct themselves toward him in an obsequious and almost servile manner." An Englishman, the famous Charles Greville, was less frivolous in offering an explanation for Talleyrand's exceptional position:

> His age was venerable, his society was delightful, and there was an exhibition of conservative wisdom, of moderate and healing counsels in all his thoughts, words and actions very becoming to his age and station, vastly influential from his sagacity and experience, and which presented him to the eyes of men as a statesman like Burleigh or Clarendon for prudence, temperance and discretion. Here therefore he acquired golden opinions and was regarded by all ranks and all parties with respect and by many with sincere regard.

Despite this high esteem and universal respect, life in London had lost some of its charm for Talleyrand after his return from France. At the personal level, he suffered a great loss at the end of 1832 by the death of his good friend and correspondent the Princess de Vaudémont. For weeks, he was depressed by the loss of this lady, whom he had cherished for fifty years and with whom his relations had, from the first, been characterized by affectionate candor. He was also deeply affected by the death of another friend, the Duke de Dalberg, early in 1833. It was a time of his life when he was fated to see his old friends, one by one, disappear, until he was left standing virtually alone in a world to which, although he had helped create it, he had never really belonged. Once Mérimée asked him whether, in his opinion, the long-range effects of the French Revolution were good or bad. The prince's answer revealed, with some poignancy, his alienation from the era into which he had survived. "Before the Revolution," he said, "there was wickedness, but there was also elegance. There was malice, but there was also wit. Today there is only tasteless wickedness and the malice of stupidity."

Along with a sense of having outlived his time, there was another and perhaps more dangerous feeling: that of having outlived his usefulness. Immediately upon his return to England in October, 1832, Talleyrand had perceived a change in the political and diplomatic climate. Sebastiani, who had been the prince's willing disciple, had been replaced in the Foreign Ministry by the Duke de Broglie. The new minister and president of the Council was a different sort of man from his predecessor: authoritarian, austere, absolutely incorruptible, stern with superiors and subordinates alike. He had Molé's resolve to be master in his own ministry, but he had also the determination and the power to realize that ambition. Also like Molé, he was unwilling to risk an open conflict with his ambassador in London. This decision was perhaps dictated by prudence or by the fact that he and the prince had always been on amicable terms and had collaborated closely on various projects in the past and that he therefore had no wish to offend his friend. Whatever his motive, rather than handle British affairs, as his predecessor had done, through the embassy in London, Broglie entered into direct contact with Palmerston and bypassed Talleyrand. Wellington, when Molé had employed the same stratagem, had brusquely informed the prince of what was afoot, and that had been the end of the matter. Palmerston, however, had none of Wellington's uncompromising forthrightness. He was, in fact, delighted to contribute to the humiliation of the man whose political prestige he envied, whose personality he mistrusted, and whose "foreignness" he found a source of constant irritation. There was little that Talleyrand could do except complain to Paris, which he did to no avail. Broglie's government was too new, and the internal condition of France too unstable, for Louis-Philippe to be willing to risk offending the one or aggravating the other for the sake of a man who would, no doubt, soon be dead.

Palmerston, thus encouraged, redoubled his efforts to rid himself of Talleyrand. His lack of civility, always offensive, now reached such proportions that even the prince could barely bring himself to maintain his composure when in the same room with the man. Dorothea, needless to say, was equally outraged. Palmerston's manners were a source of deep embarrassment to Lord Grey, who was constantly forced to apologize for his Foreign Secretary's effrontery. On one occasion, he begged Dorothea to assure her uncle that Palmerston's intentions were of the best and that he really meant no harm. "I promise," Dorothea snapped, "to tell M. de Talleyrand that Lord Palmerston is as innocent as a newborn babe. But *I* do not believe a word of it!"

Late in September, 1833, Talleyrand and Dorothea left London for a visit to France. Their departure was the occasion for many rumors to the effect that they might never return. "I thought him greatly changed and enfeebled," Lord Grey said of Talleyrand, "and, at eighty, a man does not easily recover. There are those who think that Madame de Dino, seeing this, would not wish him to return." Throughout the autumn, at Rochecotte and later at Valençay, the prince and Dorothea meditated on what course to take. The position that he held was not to be surrendered lightly. A resignation at his age must necessarily mean the end of an active life, and he was not eager to give up either England or his established place in official society. "He is terrified," Dorothea wrote to Bacourt, "and I am terrified for him, of the isolation, the boredom, and the slow pace of life in the provinces or in the country. He is, moreover, certain that it would be impossible to live in Paris, where he would, so far as public opinion is concerned, have political responsibility, but without the benefit of it or the power that it confers." Dorothea, for her part, sensed that the time had come to retreat into private life while one's position still allowed one to do so gracefully. The situation in London, she feared, would be impossible, and retirement later might be more awkward than at present. On the other hand, there were loyal and well-informed friends of Talleyrand, such as Royer-Collard, who were convinced that the prince had nothing to fear either from Broglie or from Palmerston.

While these matters were being considered and discussed, first at Rochecotte and then at Valençay, a message arrived from Broglie, asking Talleyrand to meet him in Paris. At the interview, which took place on December 4, Broglie pressed Talleyrand to remain at his post in London, at least for the time being, but the prince would do no more than agree to give serious thought to the matter. It was not until he received, a few days later, a letter from Lord Grey urging his return to the British capital that he reached a decision: He would go.

The decision, as it happened, was a serious mistake. Princess Lieven, who, because of her intimacy with Lord Grey, knew more about the political undercurrents of London life than anyone else, described the prince's situation with great accuracy:

> He immediately discovered that the ministers would not deal with him and that all affairs were being handled between M. de Broglie and the British ambassador in Paris. . . . Although he might receive flattering letters from the Tuileries, his own Cabinet left him in total ignorance of their intentions. For a man of such ability and talent, such a position is unbearable. Madame de Dino weeps—and he no longer laughs.

And Dorothea confessed to Thiers early in February, 1834, that "I wish with all my heart that M. de Talleyrand had stayed at Valençay, for I can foresee nothing but grief and trouble for him here."

In this situation, Talleyrand obviously had a choice to make. Having virtually lost his usefulness to his own government and being unacceptable personally to the member of the British government with whom he had constantly to deal, he could resign. Or he could hope for a change of government either in England or in France that might reestablish him in his former position of authority with respect to both regimes. In fact, on March 28, Broglie resigned and was replaced by Admiral de Rigny. So far as England was concerned, the situation was even more encouraging. By the middle of 1834 Grey's government was tottering, and there seemed an excellent chance that it—and Palmerston—would fall from office. Very shortly, Talleyrand's and Dorothea's expectations seemed on the verge of being fulfilled. Lord Grey resigned—but Palmerston did not. Flabbergasted, Dorothea asked Lord Grey if it were not true that when a prime minister resigned, his Cabinet followed suit. It was not easy to explain British procedural mysteries to a foreigner. "Well, in theory, yes," replied Lord Grey gently. "But, in practice, no." Talleyrand's worst fears were soon realized. It was announced that King William had asked Lord Melbourne, a liberal, to form a government—and that that government included Palmerston as Foreign Secretary. "Lord Grey's example," Dorothea noted significantly on July 13, "is additional proof that the great figures of history should themselves choose their moment of retirement rather than wait for it to be thrust upon them by the mistakes and malice of others." At this point, her mind seemed made up. She would do everything that she could to persuade Talleyrand to retire of his own accord at the earliest possible opportunity.

A secondary cause of her decision was the disintegration of London's diplomatic society as they knew it. Their good friends, Prince Esterházy and his wife, the Austrian representatives, had returned to Vienna at the beginning of 1832. Now Prince and Princess Lieven were returning to their own country. This, too, was a result of Palmerston's poor judgment. The

Foreign Secretary had insisted, against all advice, on sending as ambassador to St. Petersburg a man whom he knew to be wholly unacceptable to Czar Nicholas, Sir Stratford Canning. The czar, in a rage, retaliated by ordering Lieven home. The entire diplomatic community—and the Lievens, most of all—felt the command as a crushing blow. The Russian prince and his extraordinary wife had been in London as long as anyone cared to remember. Their departure, which was interpreted as a result of Palmerston's malevolence, meant the severance of the closest social and professional ties. There was a farewell dinner for the couple, which Dorothea and the prince attended out of a sense of obligation and "solely for the sake of the princess." Dorothea has left a description of the uneasy and resentful assembly: "Lady Cowper was making a visible effort to appear at ease. Monsieur de Bülow [the Prussian ambassador] looked pale and embarrassed, like a pickpocket caught in the very act. And poor M. Dedel [the ambassador of Denmark] looked like an orphan at the funeral of both his parents."

Talleyrand planned to return to France for a visit in August, 1834; beyond that, he was as yet undecided on his future course. He knew that his own usefulness was at an end so long as Palmerston remained in office, but he knew, too, that a liberal government faced by a predominantly Tory Parliament could not endure. Perhaps he should remain in France, spend his remaining years in peace, surrounded by his friends and cared for by the woman whom he loved. But what if, after a few months of this idyllic existence, he should once more feel the need to participate actively in the affairs of Europe? It would then be too late. He was still in this indecisive frame of mind when, on August 18, the day before his scheduled departure, Dorothea handed him a long and thoughtful letter in which she carefully described her feelings on the subject:

> I have a grave obligation to you, which I never feel more acutely than when it seems to me that your reputation is at stake. . . . So let me write to you, and please be kind enough to forgive me if I say anything that may annoy you. It is my love for you that compels me to say it. . . .
>
> You did not come here four years ago to make your fortune, to find a career, or to enhance your fame. All these were secured long ago. . . . You came with only one intention: to render a great service to your country when it was in grave danger. At your age it was a perilous adventure to reappear after fifteen years of retirement and at the moment when the storm was at its height and to dissipate the tempest with a gesture. You have now done what you set out to do. Let that be sufficient. In the future, you can do nothing but detract from the significance of what you have already done. . . .
>
> This, and this alone, in my opinion, is a fitting close to your career. Any consideration which may lead you to think otherwise is unworthy of you.
>
> When one belongs to history, as you do, one can think of no future other

than that which history prepares for one. And history, as you know, judges the end of a man's life more severely than it does the beginning. If, as I am happy to believe, you value my judgment, as well as my love, you will be as candid with yourself as I dare to be with you. You will put an end to self-deception, illogical arguments, and considerations dictated by vanity; you will put an end to a situation which must soon harm you as much in the eyes of the world as it does in mine.

Do not cavil with public opinion. Dictate its judgment; do not have it thrust upon you.

Declare yourself to be old, so that others may not say that you are too old.

Say to the world in all its simplicity and nobility: "The time has come."

These thoughts Talleyrand weighed carefully, as he did all the opinions of Dorothea. Still, he arrived at no definite decision. It had always been his habit, so far as his personal affairs were concerned, to avoid precipitous judgments. Haste was but a manifestation of zeal, and zeal, even in one's own interests, he loathed above all things. He left, as planned, on August 19, after having formally taken leave of King William. Even the king had been touched by Palmerston's dislike and distrust of the prince. Before Talleyrand returned to France for a visit in 1832, the king had told him: "I have instructed my ambassador in Paris to inform your government that I shall insist on keeping you here." When he had gone on leave in 1833, William had said: "When are you coming back?" But now, he asked only: "When are you leaving?"

A few days later, when Dorothea joined Talleyrand in Paris, she found him sad, depressed, and somewhat bored. There was no one left in France, he complained; everyone was as old and as exhausted as he. Shortly, however, the prince and the duchess were at Valençay, where the sun, fresh air, and the almost feudal reverence that he was shown by his villagers and neighbors in the country restored his spirits. On October 26, the Duke d'Orléans arrived at Valençay for a three-day visit. He was courteous, thoughtful—and determined to speak his mind. "While staying in this very house," Talleyrand confided to Madame Adélaïde, "Monseigneur le Duc d'Orléans made it perfectly clear, in the presence of some English people who were also my guests, that, in his opinion, I was no longer in a position in London to be useful to the King." Orléans did point out, however, that Louis-Philippe himself did not share this view and, indeed, that the king was eager to see Talleyrand return to London. Still, the duke's words made a strong impression on Talleyrand. It was the voice of the new world of the nineteenth century speaking to the old world of the eighteenth. Talleyrand, with his sensitivity to the "spirit of the times" which he had himself so often invoked, listened attentively. At length, after Orléans' departure, he confided to Dorothea that so far as he could see, there was nothing more that he could do for France in London.

Taking this as a cue, Dorothea now redoubled her efforts to persuade her uncle to offer his resignation to the king, pleading, as before, that Talleyrand's true happiness and his place in history required that he do so immediately. To her arguments another voice was added, that of Royer-Collard, whom Talleyrand had always respected and whose opinions he had frequently sought. In 1833, Royer-Collard had urged Talleyrand to remain on as ambassador. But now he wrote to Dorothea to provide her with ammunition for her cause: "The proper time for him to have resigned was last year. And yet, from this same chair from which I am now writing to you, I was foolish enough to contradict you. . . . I was wrong."

Royer-Collard's letter, combined with the Duke d'Orléans' opinion and Dorothea's unrelenting arguments, seem suddenly to have brought Talleyrand to the verge of a decision. Early in November, a few days after Orléans' departure, he informed Dorothea that, having now considered all sides of the argument, he was more inclined to retire than otherwise. There remained one difficulty, he added, like a man grasping at a last, futile hope. He would find it difficult, if not impossible, to write the necessary letter to the king. Perhaps the prince was preparing to say that he must go to Paris and submit his resignation in person. Perhaps he hoped that, once face to face with Louis-Philippe and Madame Adélaïde, he would be persuaded, against his better judgment, to continue in public life. If so, he had not reckoned with Dorothea's determination. Within a half hour, the duchess handed him an excellent draft of the letter that he so dreaded. He read it carefully, made a few minor revisions, and then, at Dorothea's suggestion, sent the draft to Royer-Collard for his opinion. It was back within a few days, in a slightly altered form, with a note of sympathetic congratulations from Royer-Collard. On December 13, the letter was sent on its way to the king in Paris.

It was done. The struggle was over. But no one knew it for certain but Talleyrand himself. By return post from Paris, letters arrived from Madame Adélaïde and King Louis-Philippe urging the prince to reconsider his decision. Mademoiselle, always subtler than her brother, added that if the prince were really determined to relinquish his post in London, there was no reason why he should retire completely from public life: "There is nothing to prevent you from going to Vienna," she argued, "where you could be so useful to us." Dorothea worried that Talleyrand might succumb to the temptation, but her fears were groundless. Talleyrand had never made a decision in his life before considering every factor involved with infinite thoroughness. This made for delays, but it also had the effect of rendering his decisions irrevocable. He wrote back to Madame Adélaïde that of course, "England is out of the question so far as I am concerned. Vienna, no doubt, would please me in many ways, and it would also please

Madame de Dino, whose devotion to me is her sole consolation for having to give up London, where she was so highly regarded. But, at my age, one can no longer go looking for work so far from home. A permanent appointment would no longer suit me, and above all not in Vienna, where I was once, twenty years ago, the man of the Restoration."

Then, as though to make matters as difficult as possible at the last moment, news arrived from London, on November 19, that Talleyrand's expectations had been realized and that Melbourne's government had fallen, dragging Palmerston down with it. Wellington was now Prime Minister; moreover, he had immediately made known to Paris his desire to have Talleyrand in London once again. "You alone," Madame Adélaïde hastened to write, "were capable of bringing it [the understanding between France and Great Britain] to fruition, and you alone are capable of preserving it. . . . Of this, the king is certain, and my nephew [Orléans] has reached the same conclusion regarding your decision." On the same day, Louis-Philippe himself wrote, reiterating everything that Mademoiselle had said.

Here was indeed a very real temptation, but one to which Talleyrand seems to have given little or no consideration. The circumstances described in the letters from Paris and the reestablishment of Wellington in power meant only one thing to the prince: He had chosen the best possible time to withdraw. London was asking for him; Paris was virtually commanding him to remain as ambassador. He could now withdraw with no hurt to his pride or to his reputation and, with Wellington in power, with no hurt to France. On November 23, the prince informed Louis-Philippe and Madame Adélaïde once more that despite their kindness, he was firmly resolved to retire into private life immediately. Then he settled back to enjoy, as best he could, the pleasures of old age until death should claim him.

Part Seven

THE FINAL YEARS

(1834–1838)

Do not forget, I am a bishop.

—Talleyrand

TALLEYRAND, at the time of his resignation in November, 1834, was eighty years of age. He had still three and a half years to live, and these final years were to be a time of relative tranquillity and even of happiness. His health, it is true, was failing, and his legs, never very strong, were more troublesome than ever. His mind, however, was unimpaired, and his sight and hearing were as keen as ever. He seemed to possess virtually all that was needed to promote contentment in his last years. He was enormously wealthy. In Paris, he was the social lion of his time, the much sought-after and revered elder statesman of Europe, the quintessential *grand seigneur* of France. At Valençay, he was the honored lord, surrounded by family, friends, and servants whose overriding preoccupation was for his comfort. Talleyrand was, in other words, never more completely master of himself and of his circumstances than at this time, and he was able to devote himself to and to enjoy the three things that he prized most in life: the companionship of those he loved; the art of conversation; and his wealth.

So far as his considerable wealth was concerned, Talleyrand continued to spend without counting the costs, but only when the expense seemed justified by circumstances—that is, by his own enjoyment or by the demands of his position in society or by the needs of others. His money was spent generously, even lavishly, but it was never wasted. Opulence, such as reigned in the rue St.-Florentin and, on an even grander scale, at Valençay, Talleyrand regarded as a necessity. Lamartine, who was received at Valençay, remarked, accurately; "Opulence, for M. de Talleyrand, was a politi-

cal expedient as well as a requirement for an elegant life." Even so, his
household expenses were strictly budgeted, more out of an innate sense of
order than from necessity; and though of a legendary generosity where
friends and relatives were concerned, he never gave or spent thoughtlessly
or without counting the cost. On one occasion, when his niece Charlotte,
the Baroness de Talleyrand, and her daughter were to stay in the rue St.-
Florentin for several days, Talleyrand carefully instructed his butler to
provide all the necessities for his guests, but without extravagance:

> They will occupy the same apartment as last spring, and nothing more.
> . . . Charlotte's apartment should be cleaned thoroughly and furnished
> with linen, towels, candelabra, candlesticks and firedogs. You are to supply
> nothing more than that. Silver-plated candelabra and candlesticks will be
> good enough. So far as firewood and candles are concerned, it is up to
> them to provide for themselves. If they ask why, you are to say that you
> never supply such items. Say this as politely as possible, but without offer-
> ing any explanations. If she hires a carriage, the coachman must not be
> given lodging, and the horses must be sent back every evening.

Talleyrand was no less careful of the people around him than he was of
his funds. Even in the less happy epochs of his long life, he had never
lacked congenial company, for he had always possessed the gift of attracting those to whom he himself was drawn. Now he enjoyed as great a
measure of happiness in that respect as ever falls to those who reach extreme old age. Always at his side was Dorothea de Dino, the woman to
whom he had been devoted for twenty years and who still retained both
her beauty and those qualities of mind and character that had charmed
Talleyrand from the first. To complete his existence, there was also his
fourteen-year-old grandniece, Pauline, Dorothea's daughter, whom Talleyrand adored with a final, exquisite outpouring of passion. One of Talleyrand's severest critics, Ste.-Beuve, commented that "if M. de Talleyrand
has a good side in his old age, it is the purity of his affection" for Pauline.
Pauline had inherited her mother's grace and sweetness of manner. Her
soul was as unspoiled as only that of a sheltered child can be. Talleyrand
exulted in that crystal purity and spent every moment that he could spare
with her. In London, it had been one of the sights of the city to see Pauline
waiting, every evening, in a carriage outside the embassy for the prince to
finish his work and take her for a drive. Indeed, Talleyrand spent almost as
much time with Pauline as with Dorothea, and when they were separated
by circumstances, he wrote to her daily. When she was in Switzerland in
the summer of 1835, Talleyrand was miserable. "The house is completely
empty when you are not here," he wrote. "I find it difficult to accustom
myself to your absence, dear Minette"—his pet name for Pauline. When

the child was sent to "take the waters," as was the custom, at a spa, he wrote that "I am very eager to see you again, but, above all, I am eager for you to be in good health. If, therefore, a few baths will help you, you must take them." His letters to Pauline are a revelation not only of a deep and yearning tenderness, but of the ingenuity with which he, a man of more than eighty, could discern subjects to please and interest a young mind. From Paris, he wrote that "The Arc de Triomphe is superb. It is one hundred and fifty-two feet high, a hundred and thirty-eight feet wide, and sixty-eight feet deep." And on another occasion: "When you are in Paris, I must take you to see the King of Siam's elephant. This beast does all sorts of tricks with ease, and even though it is enormous, it is amazingly agile. You know that, when an audience likes an actor, it applauds until the actor comes back for a curtain call. This elephant, when the audience applauds after a performance, returns to center stage, where, using his trunk, he acknowledges the applause and thanks the people very politely. I am sure that you will enjoy seeing this. Good-bye for now, dear child. I love you tenderly, and I embrace you."

Talleyrand's love for Pauline did not confine itself to letters and to expressions of longing. He watched over her upbringing with a degree of care that only a man, an old man, who knew the world only too well could bring to the task. Above all, he, the ex-bishop, was anxious that she receive proper instruction in her religious duties, and he insisted that she use his own carriage for her frequent visits to her confessor and spiritual director, the Abbé Dupanloup. "He ended by taking great personal pride in Pauline's piety," Dorothea noted, "and he seemed flattered that, through his care, she was raised to be so religious."

Pauline's religious beliefs, Talleyrand insisted, must be reflected in her conduct and appearance. Here, however, good taste and virtue seemed almost indistinguishable. At the end of 1835, when Pauline was fifteen, she began to attend balls in the houses of close friends, and Talleyrand gave Dorothea strict instructions regarding his grandniece's dress—and especially her décolletage. With reference to the latter, he was explicit: "When what a lady shows is beautiful, then it is an offense against decency, and when what she shows is ugly, then it is very ugly indeed."

Dorothea de Dino began to keep a journal in 1831, and, beginning in 1834, she wrote in it regularly, if not daily. Her pages provide a thorough record of Talleyrand's and her own and Pauline's life during this period. They lived, as always, chiefly in Paris, in the rue St.-Florentin, while the summer months were spent at Valençay. Shorter periods were spent at Rochecotte, where Talleyrand assumed the role of guest and Dorothea that of hostess. At both places, entertainment was on a scale more in keeping with the reign of a *roi soleil* than with that of a bourgeois king. In the country, formal entertainments were relieved by gay interludes—plays such as *Les Femmes Savantes*, in which Dorothea and the younger members of the household played the leading roles. Talleyrand took special pleasure in such diversions, Dorothea assures us.

At Valençay, where life proceeded at a relatively leisurely pace, there were always visitors, old friends, men of letters, politicians—Royer-Collard, the Duke de Noailles, Decazes, the Prince de Laval, Princess Lieven, Montrond, and an innumerable flock of less notable guests. A visit by the Duke of Orléans was celebrated royally, with great bursts of martial music, a review of the village national guard, and a grand ball.

Lady Clanricarde, Canning's daughter and a great favorite of Talleyrand's, was there, as was John Hamilton, the son of Alexander Hamilton, Talleyrand's host of long ago in Philadelphia, and Henry Greville, younger brother of Charles, who was an attaché at the British embassy. During the first nine months that Greville was in France, Talleyrand's was the only house to which he received an invitation, and he was a visitor to Valençay late in 1834. He had left a description of a quiet—perhaps too quiet—day spent there:

> The day begins with *déjeuner à la fourchette* at half past eleven, after which the company adjourn to the salon and converse until two o'clock, when the promenades begin. Dine at half past five, and go to bed at any hour; but the early dinner hour makes the evening seem interminable. . . . Every evening at nine o'clock he [Talleyrand] drives for an hour, and on his return plays his rubber of whist until eleven o'clock, when the post arrives from Paris.

It was not to be expected that Casimir Montrond, *le beau Montrond*, Talleyrand's very good friend, would be at ease in such an atmosphere of tranquillity. He came to Valençay, nonetheless—to Dorothea's horror, and Talleyrand's delight. The duchess had long regarded Montrond as an evil influence on her uncle and had worked relentlessly to persuade the latter to end the relationship. Now, at Valençay, Montrond himself proved an unexpected ally in this cause. Unlike Talleyrand, he had aged badly. He was more rude, caustic, and difficult to please than ever. His congenital bitterness, rather than being softened by the years, had grown more pronounced, so that it was said of him that his wit lived on human flesh. The conversational skill that Talleyrand had admired had faded, leaving only malice in its place. Montrond had refused to accept the nineteenth century's ban on the indecent and the obscene in polite conversation, and his *mots* were as much a scandal in Parisian salons as they were at Talleyrand's table. Even worse, he had become a quarrelsome and irascible house guest. He cursed the servants, complained of the wine, sneered at the food, and, upon his return to Paris, dined out on his stories of the dullness and poverty of entertainment at Valençay.

Finally, Montrond's cantankerousness and Dorothea's entreaties moved Talleyrand to action. Accounts vary on what actually happened, but it seems that one evening at dinner Montrond made a remark that was, even by his standards, extraordinarily coarse. According to one guest's version of the incident, Dorothea rose, scolded the culprit at length, and ordered a servant to ring for M. de Montrond's carriage. Dorothea, however, tells us that Talleyrand himself ordered Montrond to leave his house. Whatever the truth of the matter, the fact was that Montrond's bad manners and gutter vocabulary had become intolerable, and Talleyrand's pleasure in his company had greatly diminished. This, combined with Dorothea's insistence, had finally moved him to sever the relationship.

Montrond's actions after the quarrel were characterized by that deviousness that Dorothea found so objectionable. First, before leaving the house, he promised Talleyrand to make no mention to anyone of what had happened. Then, he told everyone in Paris that Valençay was utterly "uninhabitable." As this story was making the rounds, Montrond was writing to one of Talleyrand's guests at Valençay, asking for news of events there, and, at the same time, he dispatched a letter to Dorothea expressing his gratitude for her hospitality during his visit. Even Talleyrand was annoyed—to Dorothea's great satisfaction.

Montrond was not missed. There was more than a sufficient variety of guests at Valençay to provide Talleyrand with conversation and distraction. Hardly had Montrond slammed into his carriage than Lady Clanricarde arrived with a numerous party of English friends. She found in the house, in addition to several house guests, and apparently on terms of familiarity with the prince, "a drawing-master, and several persons more or less concerned with Mlle. Pauline's education"; most remarkable of all was "a black gentleman," whose occupation even the curious Englishwoman was unable to discover. As for Valençay itself, she found the chateau "spacious and comfortable." She was pleased especially by the informal atmosphere there and uttered the highest compliment that her experience could devise: "It is quite like an English country house."

Not all of Talleyrand's guests found Valençay as congenial a place as did Lady Clanricarde. Princess Lieven came in June, 1836, and by the time she left the household would gladly have taken two Montronds in her place. The lady was bored to tears—or, as Dorothea put it, "she yawned to desperation." There were no other guests at the moment, and since Lieven could neither flirt nor hatch intrigues, she had nothing to occupy her time. Therefore, in order to distract herself, she manufactured complaints. Her room, she told Dorothea, smelled of paint. Dorothea, even though the room had not been painted since 1822, obligingly found her another. The new room, however, was no more acceptable than the first; its walls were "too thick," and it "gave her the spleen." Once more she moved, and once more the room had something (we are not told what) wrong with it. Eventually, Lieven ended up in the first room, the smell of paint having vanished as mysteriously as it had come. Even the gentle Pauline commented that "the princess is somewhat whimsical."

Talleyrand was a silent witness to such domestic crises. No doubt, they amused him, particularly since it was not he, but Dorothea, who was required to resolve them. Moreover, he enjoyed the company of the idiosyncratic Lieven. Perhaps her behavior held no mysteries for the man who had dealt with such men as Bonaparte and Alexander of Russia. In any case, Lieven seems to have felt that Talleyrand's friendship and Dorothea's amiable acquiescence in her foibles were sufficient to compensate for the smell of paint and even for an aggravated spleen. In a letter to Lord Grey, she described her visit as "perfectly agreeable" and commented that time had "flown by with astonishing rapidity."

There were guests more difficult to please even than Princess Lieven, and considerably more malicious. One afternoon, after a promenade in the park of Valençay, Talleyrand and Dorothea returned to the chateau to find a noisy group of strangers wandering through the rooms, inspecting the paintings, the decorations, and even leafing through Talleyrand's precious library of 10,000 volumes. The servants, when questioned, could say only that it was "a Madame Dudevant and her friends." One of Talleyrand's friends, who happened to be staying at Valençay, explained that this Madame Dudevant was actually the famous George Sand and that the people with her were her house guests at Nohant, the lady's country retreat nearby. Whereupon Dorothea greeted these unknown and uninvited guests warmly, offered them refreshments, and showed them through as much of the house as they had not already examined on their own initiative.

The consequence of this display of hospitality was not a letter of gratitude on George Sand's part, but an article, published a few weeks later, in which Talleyrand was compared, unfavorably, to a rabbit, a cat, a satyr, a reptile—"this man who was born for great vices and small acts." Talleyrand was "a dunghill," on which reposed "a white lily" (Dorothea). These were among the kinder sentiments expressed in the article. Dorothea was aghast, and for once, even Talleyrand was irritated. Needless to say, George Sand and her friends were never seen at Valençay again. "I receive people in my house for the first time if they bear a good name and wear decent clothes," Talleyrand explained. "The second time they are welcomed solely because of what they carry in their hearts and minds."

As a host, in fact, Talleyrand insisted not only upon a good heart and a good mind, but upon good manners as well. Usually, he was much too much the *grand seigneur* to betray, by so much as the flicker of an eye, when he had been displeased in that respect. On rare occasions, however, he abandoned his impassivity and corrected a guest to his face. In one such instance, he had served a guest a glass of superior cognac and silently watched him down it in one gulp. When the man smacked his lips, Talleyrand could no longer keep silent. "No, no, my friend. First, one holds the glass in the hollow of one's hands in order to warm it. Then one swishes the cognac around in the glass so as to release its bouquet. Next, one raises the glass and inhales deeply—"

"And then?"

"Ah, then one puts down the glass and continues talking."

Such incidents, whether occasioned by the deliberate bad manners of a George Sand or the innocent error of an inexperienced guest were comparatively rare at Valençay. Generally, life proceeded at an unhurried pace, and the established routine was seldom broken:

> Our life here [Talleyrand wrote] is very orderly, which makes the days pass rather quickly. At the end of the day, it seems that we have not been at loose ends for a single moment. This morning, for example, while we were reading, we were interrupted by the arrival of the body of a wolf killed by our guards. That was the most remarkable event of the day. I am working several hours a day, and I feel extraordinarily well.

Talleyrand, like his guests, rose fairly late in the morning. The increasing debility of his legs now prevented his customary walk in the park after breakfast, and he was forced to rely upon a peculiar vehicle given him by Louis-Philippe—a sort of armchair on wheels designed to carry the obese Louis XVIII about in the Tuileries. Afterward the prince had a glass of Madeira, and if there were guests willing to play, everyone assembled for a rubber of whist. Often Talleyrand simply retired to his study and spent the time in reading—the classics, mostly, as well as history and, above all, the funeral orations of Bossuet. Occasionally, when his guests hunted in Valençay's great park, Talleyrand followed the chase in an open carriage, pointing out with his cane, for his friends' benefit, a deer, or some other choice game. In the evenings, there was often music, for Talleyrand in retirement insisted, as he had in more active days, on having a musician in residence. At Valençay, there was a harpist, named Nedermann, who received the generous monthly sum of 600 francs to entertain the master of the house.

Valençay, for all its tranquillity, was not immune to tragedy. Death and news of death came often to shatter the contentment of the lord of Valençay and, as Dorothea observed, "to give warning of what the future holds."

The month of November, 1835, was particularly tragic for Talleyrand, who, more than most men, treasured friendship as a rare jewel. In the space of a few weeks, three of his cherished friends—the Countess Juste de Noailles, the Duchess de Mouchy, and the Princess de Poix—died. "How many there are around me who are dying!" Talleyrand wrote in agony. The greatest blow, however—and it came in that same unhappy November—was the death of Marie-Thérèse, Princess Poniatowski, whose loyalty and tenderness (for she had had nothing of physical beauty) had been sufficient to fascinate Talleyrand. An apartment was always kept in readiness for her at Valençay, and in Paris, she spent most of her days in the rue St.-Florentin. Talleyrand, when he learned of her death, was inconsolable, so much so that Dorothea feared the effect of this grief upon his health. He wrote to Lady Jersey:

> . . . her death is particularly hard to bear because of the absolute devotion that bound us for twenty-seven years. I knew for some time, of course, that the end was near, and yet the moment that marked our separation for all eternity has been difficult to bear. Affection is never prepared for the moment of relinquishment. Now I feel the need to share my feelings with someone whom I have loved for twenty years, and that is why I am writing to you today.

The princess was buried at Valençay, at her request, in the Chapel of St.-Maurice, and all of Talleyrand's household went into mourning.

To the sufferings of others were added Talleyrand's own. His leg, particularly after a fall from his wheeled armchair, pained him constantly and often prevented him from sleeping at night. On such occasions, he was too considerate to his family and his guests to ask anyone to stay up and play whist with him. He therefore developed the habit of writing, either working on the *Mémoires* or setting down, in the form of maxims and epigrams, his casual observations regarding human foibles and human nature. On parental authority: "Fathers always seem determined to spare their sons the pleasures of life." On the health and wealth of nations: "Financiers flourish only when nations decline." On manners: "A union of simplicity and elegance is the measure of nobility in every case and in every person." On sycophants: "I can easily forgive those who do not hold the same opinions as myself, but I find it difficult to bear with those who do not hold the same opinions as themselves." On marriage: "Matrimony is such a beautiful institution that one should spend one's whole life contemplating it." On public order: "Stability often adds something to perfection, but perfection has nothing to add to stability." On bourgeois kings: "Accessiblity on the part of rulers ends by inspiring love rather than respect, and love evaporates at the first sign of trouble." On detachment in public affairs: "In politics as elsewhere, one must not love too much. Love confuses. It lessens the clarity of one's vision. And it is not always counted to one's credit." On the future: "As for what will become of the world, I do not know. What I do see is that nothing is being replaced. Once something ends, it is finished. What has been lost is the only thing that one sees clearly."

Life in Paris during the winter, in the rue St.-Florentin, was more formal than at Valençay, and more demanding. As in the country, there was a constant flow of guests, for Talleyrand, social potentate that he was, felt obliged to hold court until the end of his days. Several times a week, he received friends and admirers and sometimes enemies in his salon. The list of those who were welcomed there transcends accidents of birth, post, or rank. Talleyrand had survived the Terror and he had flourished under the Directory, the Consulate, and the Empire. He had survived wars and revolutions, proscriptions and exile, astonishing successes and dismal failures. He had seen kings and princes made and unmade with almost whimsical facility. He was more aware than anyone else of how little, really, such things mattered in the long run. *Plus ça change, plus c'est la même chose,* he had preached. Now he lived that maxim.

Young and old alike were welcome in his house; parvenu noblemen and princes whose lineages, like his own, were lost in the dim recesses of antiquity; merchants and artists; writers and statesmen. It mattered not at all that a man might be minister to the King of France one day and in disgrace the next. So long as he was a friend or even an acquaintance, the gate in the rue St.-Florentin was never closed to him. He offered the compliment of friendship to skill, and grace, charm, and beauty, but he offered it also to virtue. Of Charles X, that most ineffectual of monarchs, he remarked: "It is true that Charles X was the least capable of French kings and the one who made most mistakes, yet I always esteemed him and loved him because he was the most faithful and one of the best men that I have ever known."

So they came. The young, in order to gaze upon a living monument of history, a legendary frame still endowed with life; and the aged and experienced, to listen to one whose wit and wisdom was of their own time, whose manners brought to life again the sweet era of their own youth, and whose memory, charged as it was with the details of his career, had become a beacon upon the past. Talleyrand received them all, seated in a huge armchair, his hair powdered in the old style, his cane tapping the floor, and his bad leg—his "horse's hoof," as the Countess de Mirabeau had called it—propped up on an ottoman. His blue-gray eyes, as keen as ever, were habitually half-closed, and his features were immobilized in a mask of indolence or indifference. He was the prince, always cool, unruffled, courtly, and always gracious. At times, one of his visitors reported, "he would suddenly come alive, as though out of a trance. His conversation would become lively, clever, brilliant, profound. His mind would flash like lightning. Everyone felt astonishment, delight, and listened in fascination. On such occasions, he always spoke loudly, and completely dominated the conversation."

Sometimes, his remarks turned upon history, particularly upon his own career. On such occasions, as often as not he sought to justify himself in the eyes of the rising generation of politicians. To M. de Montalivet, a young man regarded as a statesman of promise, Talleyrand said:

> Your father was a supporter of the Empire, and you dislike me because you feel that I abandoned the emperor. The truth is that I have always remained faithful to anyone who remained faithful to himself. If you judge all my actions according to this rule, you will have to admit that I have been extraordinarily consistent. Where could you find a man depraved enough, or a citizen vile enough, to surrender his own intelligence, or to sacrifice his country, for the sake of an individual—whoever that individual may be, and no matter how well-born or how highly gifted?

Not all his remarks were intended to edify or to instruct. His tongue was as sharp in old age as it had been decades before, and his mots—especially the unkind ones—were repeated throughout Paris as soon as they were articulated. Their target, as always, was bad taste, hypocrisy, and the ridiculous. Of one lady to whom nature had been unkind in a certain respect, but who, nonetheless, insisted on wearing the most outrageous décolletage, he said: "It would be impossible for her to uncover more or to reveal less." Pomposity inevitably drew a crushing rejoinder in Talleyrand's house. On one occasion a general was late to dinner and, when he arrived, offhandedly excused himself by saying that he had been detained by a Pekinese. In an icy voice, Talleyrand asked, "May I inquire, General, what you mean by a Pekinese?"

"Oh, 'Pekinese' is a word that we soldiers use for anything that is unmilitary."

"Ah, I see," Talleyrand answered. "Just as 'military' is a word that we use for anything that is uncivil."

When he was visited by a German diplomat who proved particularly garrulous, Talleyrand sat in complete silence, listening gravely but speaking not a word. Eventually, the German noticed the unusual silence and interrupted his harangue to ask, "What is the matter?"

Talleyrand answered: "Oh, I beg your pardon. I was waiting for you to say something."

Such reproofs were administered only when deserved. Ordinarily, Talleyrand treated his guests and servants with a consideration that bordered on paternal indulgence. He could not abide gossip of any kind, and he would not allow it in his presence or in his house. "I do not believe that there was a house in Paris," Dorothea noted, "where there was less back-biting or where gossip was held in so much scorn as in that of M. de Tal-leyrand." Talleyrand himself explained why: "Certainly, it is very easy to get involved in other people's affairs. I am as capable of doing it as anyone else. But what would it accomplish? It would complicate my life and create problems for me. Furthermore, I am too lazy to make the effort."

Talleyrand's caustic wit, although its targets were present in his own salon, seemed to attract rather than repel, and his house was always full. In a single day, for example, when Talleyrand's "door was open," as Doro-thea expressed it, the visitors included Jules d'Entraigues, the Duke de Noailles, Princess Schonberg, Alexis de Tocqueville, the Duchess d'Albu-fera, Adolphe Thiers, M. de la Redorte, and M. Mignet, the historian. And these are only a few of those who were sufficiently noteworthy to be named in Dorothea's *Chronique.* There were others, no doubt, who remain as un-known to us as they were to the political and social world of contemporary Paris. In the evening of the same day, Talleyrand indulged what Dorothea referred to as "his mania for dining out" and was a guest at the table of Louis-Mathieu Molé. This, we are assured, was a relatively unhurried day.

Many of Talleyrand's friends and visitors, of course, were politicians, and it was hardly conceivable that Europe's elder statesman, retired or not, could abandon politics so long as there was a breath of life in his body. In-deed, Count Molé described the rue St.-Florentin as "ablaze with political intrigue." That is an exaggeration. Talleyrand's role in the political life of France at this time was that of a man of great influence who uses that in-fluence cautiously. He had the ear of the king, through the monarch's sis-ter, Madame Adélaïde, with whom he was in constant correspondence, and he made use of that privileged position chiefly to support Adolphe Thiers in the long political rivalry that was just beginning between Thiers and Guizot. Thiers was Talleyrand's kind of man: His intellect was razor-sharp; his manners, impeccable; and his conversation, lively and entertain-ing. Moreover, Thiers was an old friend of the Duchess de Dino.* When Thiers was asked by the king to form a government in February, 1836, it was whispered everywhere that Talleyrand was responsible. And when he fell from power only six months later, it was believed that Talleyrand, by withdrawing his support, had brought about that fall. In neither instance,

* It was generally believed in Paris, and there is some evidence to support that belief, that the relationship between Thiers and Dorothea had, at one time, attained definitely sentimental pro-portions. There is a thorough and objective discussion of this relationship in Françoise de Bernar-dy's *Le dernier amour de Talleyrand, la Duchesse de Dino,* IIIᵉ partie.

however, had Talleyrand truly intervened. In fact, he was very disturbed
by all the talk of his influence. "M. de Talleyrand is in a very bad temper,"
Dorothea wrote. "The newspapers and public opinion all regard him as responsible for the new ministry. . . . He, however, has had nothing to do
with it, and as the sudden rise of M. Thiers has not met with universal approval, the English being particularly irritated, M. de Talleyrand is
aroused to great anger by all that he hears upon the subject." As for
Thiers' fall and his replacement by Count Molé, the first news was received
at Valençay, far from the hotbed of political intrigue that was Paris,
through a letter from Madame Adélaïde, on August 28. The fact of the
matter was that Thiers was preaching armed intervention in the affairs of
Spain. King Louis-Philippe refused to consent to this aggression, and Talleyrand shared the views of the king. He had opposed such intervention
under Napoleon. He had opposed it under Louis XVIII. He continued to
oppose it under Louis-Philippe. His influence, if any, in Thiers' fall and
Molé's appointment, therefore, was indirect—not by a withdrawal of his
support, but by an articulation of his views. Molé, of course, was in an excellent position to appreciate the weight carried by Talleyrand's views, and
his very first act on assuming office was to write to Talleyrand:

> As the new Cabinet has been formed upon a question, and with ideas,
> which M. de Talleyrand has wisely made his own, the new ministers should
> be able to congratulate themselves upon his approval. And for himself, he
> [Molé] trusts that it may be so, as he relies upon M. de Talleyrand's coun-
> sel and opinion.

The Duchess de Dino duly recorded the receipt of this "nice, deferential
little note," as she called it. The next day, after receiving a note, almost
flirtatious in tone, from Guizot, announcing his inclusion in the new ministry, she commented: "The friendship of the king for M. de Talleyrand and
the confidence with which he honors him forbid any minister to be on bad
terms with him."

The esteem in which the king continued to hold Talleyrand was an acknowledged fact of French political life. The prince was often a guest at
the Tuileries, where he was received sometimes by Louis-Philippe, sometimes by Madame Adélaïde. On one such occasion, the Chevalier d'Orsay,
a notable dandy and fop of the time, noted that Talleyrand's court dress
was hopelessly outdated. "His coat is too loose, and his hat too large,"
D'Orsay complained. But even he was forced to acknowledge the honor
and even the reverence with which Talleyrand was received, not only by
the king and his sister, but by the lords and ladies of the court. When the
sound of Talleyrand's cane was heard tapping in the distance on the parquet floors of the palace, the chevalier recorded, a great silence would fall

upon the assembled nobles, and a whisper would rustle through the room: "*Le prince! Le prince!*"

The king and the royal family, no less than their courtiers, were at pains to show their respect for the man who, whatever his political sins may have been in their eyes, was chiefly responsible for the restoration of the monarchy in France. Talleyrand was often singled out by Louis-Philippe for those small and sometimes uncomfortable honors by means of which kings express their esteem. During the winter of 1834–35, for instance, Talleyrand was obliged to accompany the king on a lengthy visit to Versailles, which Louis-Philippe intended to restore after forty years of abandonment. The palace, with its miles of corridors, waiting rooms and salons, represented an exquisite torture for a man afflicted both with weak legs and a strong memory. "My balance," he said, "is as precarious as that of Europe."

The Duke d'Orléans, heir to the throne, was married in the spring of 1837, at Fontainebleau, and Talleyrand was an honored guest at the wedding. While everyone else—including Dorothea and Pauline—had to share rooms, Talleyrand was given the splendid apartment that had belonged to Madame de Maintenon, morganatic wife of Louis XIV. "No one could have been surrounded with greater respect and attention than has been shown to M. de Talleyrand. He was quite overcome as he went away," Dorothea observed. She had been "trembling the whole time for M. de Talleyrand, who has been so incredibly rash as to subject himself to these exhausting trials." But Talleyrand himself, always sensible of the esteem of sovereigns, survived the days of festival and the nights of celebration and finally the torturously long marriage ceremony with a minimum of discomfort. "I was so pleased by everything at Fontainebleau," he reported, "that I quite forgot to be tired."

No less satisfying was his welcome at the Académie Française when Talleyrand attended the ceremony of Thiers' reception into that august body. He entered leaning on the arm of his great-nephew the Duke de Valençay and surrounded by the most elegant women in Paris: the Duchess de Dino, Lady Clanricarde, the Countess de Castellane, the Countess de Boigne, and several others. A dead silence fell upon the assembled notables when he entered. Here was the man who embodied the achievements of France and the history of Europe over the past half century. Spontaneously, the entire gathering of France's most eminent thinkers, writers, and leaders rose to their feet in homage to him.

Talleyrand, who had always despised public opinion, now had, ironically, the esteem of his contemporaries to a degree that perhaps only Bonaparte himself had surpassed. Yet, despite the influence he wielded with the king and the government, despite the respect and even affection shown him on every occasion, despite the comfort of his existence and the company of his family and friends, Talleyrand's mind was troubled. His mood centered not on the present, but on the past and on the future—that is, on his death. The fact that he had seen so many of his friends die in recent years and his own extreme old age contributed to make of death an impending phenomenon that was never far from his mind. The passing of his wife late in 1835, coupled with his increasing debility, no doubt brought home to him the ephemeral nature of human existence and caused him to begin looking beyond the grave. He himself, in fact, was in very ill health when word was brought to Dorothea in the rue St.-Florentin that Catherine, Princess de Talleyrand, lay dying in her house in the rue de Bourbon.* Dorothea's anxiety at the state of Talleyrand's health turned to acute alarm. She was not concerned so much with the shock of bereavement, for she knew, as did the whole world, that Talleyrand's "heart is not interested" in his wife. What she feared, wisely, was that the death of "a person much of his own age, with whom he had lived and of whom he had once been fond or who had been so indispensable to him that he had given her his name," would aggravate his condition. After much deliberation, she decided that she must prepare him for what was to come. Gently, she gave him to understand that Catherine was dying. He listened quietly, without saying a word. Then, when Dorothea had finished, he began to speak of some household affair. For the rest of the day, he did not mention his wife. The following day, however, he spoke of her incessantly. Not in sorrow— for he had never been a hypocrite—but calmly. Chiefly, he spoke of the arrangements that would have to be made when she died, of the funeral, of the cards to be sent out, of the mourning to be bought, and, concerning the latter, he repeated several times that "it will be an embarrassment to be in mourning." There was no sign that he felt an instant of grief or even of regret, and he was too proud a man to feign what he could not feel. Of the love that had bound him to Catherine years earlier, nothing was left. He felt only one emotion: relief. If Catherine died, he would be free of a burden, and the one scandal that he had never been able to live down would vanish. He would no longer be a married bishop. All day he was calm, serene. At moments he even seemed gay, and once Dorothea came upon him humming a tune. "Is it the fact that you will soon be a widower that puts you in such good spirits?" she asked mischievously. In answer, he gave her an amused smile.

The news that the Princess de Talleyrand was finally dead did not come until December 10, 1835. As so often happens, she had shown a dignity in

* The former rue de Lille. It had been renamed in honor of Louis XVIII's assumption of the crown.

death that she had lacked in life. After confessing to her curé and receiving the blessing of Monseigneur de Quelen, Archbishop of Paris, she asked the archbishop: "Am I indeed dying, my lord? Is there no hope for me?" The prelate answered gently, vaguely, but Catherine read the truth in his obvious distress. "Then I have a last favor to ask of you, my lord. Will you yourself recommend all who are in my service to the kindness of the Prince de Talleyrand? You yourself?"

"I will, my daughter."

"The Prince de Talleyrand. The Prince de Talleyrand," Catherine repeated softly, over and over again. Then, after receiving the sacraments of the church, she fell asleep. Early in the morning of December 10, she awoke. Her lips moved, whispered, "I am dying." Then she sighed, and she was dead.

When the news was brought to Dorothea that morning she told Talleyrand immediately. He showed no remorse, no agitation. "This simplifies my position considerably" was his only comment.

Catherine de Talleyrand, whom the church still called the widow of George François Grand, was buried at a solemn service, on December 12, in the Church of St.-Thomas-d'Aquin. Talleyrand did not appear at the rites. His agent, M. Demion, who had made all the arrangements for the services, represented him there and watched as the body of the woman Talleyrand had loved a half century before was lowered into a grave in the cemetery of Montparnasse. The inscription was simple: "Catherine, widow of George François Grand, known in civil law as the Princess de Talleyrand."

Catherine's death, the deaths of so many friends—death was too frequent a visitor for its dread presence not to be sensed by the master of the house. The disappearance of so many contemporaries not only foreshadowed Talleyrand's own approaching end, but also emphasized the fact of his great age and, concomitantly, the end of opportunity. What he had done, he had done, and there was nothing he could do now either to amend the past or to improve it. There were times now when he gave way to "an outburst of rage against Paris, against his age, against his position," or expressed "regret at having resigned his London embassy." Then, inevitably, resentment was followed by depression and agonizing doubts about his own achievements. On February 2, 1837, he wrote:

> Eighty-three years have passed! I am not sure I am pleased when I think back over how those years were spent. How many useless uproars there were; how many failures; how many outrageous complications; how much wasted emotion and energy, and how much wasted ability! Hatreds have been aroused, illusions lost, tastes jaded. And with what result? Moral and physical exhaustion, complete discouragement with respect to the future,

deep disgust with respect to the past. There are many people who have the gift, or the failing, of never understanding themselves. I, however, have been unlucky enough, or perhaps fortunate enough, to have received the opposite gift; and it increases with the passing years.

Dorothea, of course, noticed these moods of depression. "But," she wrote, "as soon as there are people present, his mind seems to take on new life, his conversation regains its vivacity, and the agility of his intellect and his intelligence astonish all who meet him." It was no doubt in an effort to relieve this recurring depression that she made no serious objection when Talleyrand was reconciled with Montrond. The two former friends met, by accident, in the house of a mutual acquaintance. Talleyrand, who could never allow any offense, real or imagined, to interfere with his manners, bowed politely to Montrond—who turned his back to the prince. Whereupon Talleyrand remarked in a sad voice—but loudly enough for Montrond to hear him: "He will not even say hello to me. I have done a bad job of raising him." Montrond, overcome, begged Talleyrand's forgiveness for his rudeness, and the two left together, arm in arm. They would remain friends now so long as life endured. They spent the autumn of 1837 together, at Valençay, where Dorothea learned to bear with Montrond for Talleyrand's sake. It was to be the final season that the two old friends were to spend together, and Talleyrand had a mysterious inner warning that this was to be so: "It causes me such an excessive and extraordinary pang of regret to tear myself away from Valençay this time that I cannot regard it as anything other than a presentiment."

The cause of Talleyrand's recurring depression, apparently, was his doubt concerning the verdict of posterity. He knew that that verdict was being written while he lived, and it is clear that Talleyrand, who had never cared what people might say of him, was now beginning to feel more than a little anxiety about what would be said of him after his death. He therefore set to work cultivating those men whose opinions, it seemed to him, would mold those of the future. Balzac, for instance, in *Le Père Goriot*, published in 1834–35, had referred to Talleyrand as the man who had saved France at the Congress of Vienna, the man to whom, above all, crowns were owed, but at whom mud was thrown. Balzac, therefore, was invited to Rochecotte in November, 1836. Dorothea found him "vulgar in appearance and manner, and I imagine his ideas are equally so. Undoubtedly, he is a clever man, but his conversation is neither easy nor light; on the contrary, it is very dull. He watched and examined all of us most minutely, especially M. de Talleyrand." Talleyrand, however, knew how important it was to win the good opinion of this fat, overdressed little man, and he was determined to win it. Balzac was greatly impressed. "M. de Talleyrand is astonishing," he wrote. "He had two or three outbursts of absolutely prodigious ideas. He has invited me to visit him at Valençay, and, if he lives, I shall certainly do so."

On another occasion, he opened his heart to Alphonse de Lamartine. He had been one of the earliest and most devoted admirers of Lamartine's poetry, and now he told him:

> Nature has made you a poet; poetry will make you an orator; and tact and reflection will make you a politician.* I knew the Mirabeau of the past; try not to be the Mirabeau of the future. He was a great man, Mirabeau; but he lacked the courage to be unpopular. In that respect, at least, I am more of a man than he. I abandon my reputation to all the misunderstandings and insults of the mob. It is said that I am immoral, Machiavellian, whereas I am only calm and placid. Never have I given bad advice to a government or to a sovereign, but when they fall, I do not share their fall. After a shipwreck, there must be pilots to save the survivors. I have presence of mind, and I guide these survivors to a port. It hardly matters what port it is, so long as it offers shelter. I have ignored public opinion all my life, and I can ignore it for forty years more in the grave.
>
> There are many ways in which a statesman can be honest. My way, I can see, is not yours. Nonetheless, one day you will think more highly of me than you do now. What people call my "crimes" are the illusions of imbeciles. What clever man has ever needed to commit a crime? Crime is the last resort of political half-wits. . . . I have had weaknesses, I admit; perhaps even vices. But crimes—nonsense!

Talleyrand's efforts to win the good opinion of those who might influence the future were not confined to men of letters. Women, too, especially those in places of importance, became the targets of his legendary charm. Long before, such difficult women as Madame de la Tour du Pin, Madame d'Arblay, Madame de Rémusat, and Madame Potocka had succumbed. Now, he turned his attention to a lady who was more formidable than any of them. This was Lady Granville, the British ambassadress in Paris, who was known habitually to refer to Prince Talleyrand as "the old lizard." Her aversion to Talleyrand was founded upon an antipathy for what she regarded as his "immorality," for in her very English way, she was a virtuous woman by her own standards, and she could not abide anyone less well established in the paths of righteousness. Then, one morning, Talleyrand arrived at her house to pay his respects. "Did I tell you," Lady Granville wrote to her sister, "Talleyrand paid me a long visit on Wednesday morning. I never knew before, as Mr. Foster says, the power of his charms. First of all, it is difficult and painful to believe that he is not the

---

* Talleyrand's prophecy was correct. Lamartine became Minister of Foreign Affairs in 1848.

very best man in the world, so gentle, so kind, so simple, and so grand. One forgets the past life, the present look. I could have sat for hours listening to him."

Lady Granville's good opinion, Lamartine's respect, Balzac's admiration, satisfying as they were, were not enough. Talleyrand knew it. All around him, he saw the Napoleonic legend, the myth that the days of the Empire had been France's Golden Age, taking possession of the minds of Frenchmen. He knew that for the future, the greater the fame of Napoleon, the darker would be his own infamy. Therefore, on October 1, 1836, at Valençay, he did what he had avoided doing all his life. He drew up a solemn declaration—a justification of his own actions—to be read to his heirs, relatives, and friends after his death. Passing over his role in the Revolution, he mentioned his secularization by the Pope and expressed the opinion that he had been thereby rendered independent of any allegiance. He had then decided, he explained, that he would serve France; France, under any government, for, whatever the form of government, there was always good to be done:

> Therefore, I served Bonaparte when he was emperor as I had served him when he was Consul. And I served him with devotion so long as I could believe that he himself was completely devoted to France. When, however, I saw him initiating those revolutionary enterprises which were to ruin him, I left the government, and he never forgave me for that. . . .
> Now, in my eighty-second year, recalling the numerous actions of my political life, which has been a long one, and weighing them by the strictest standards, I am able to conclude:
> That, of all the governments I have served, from none have I received more than I gave;
> That I abandoned none before it abandoned itself;
> That I put the interests of no party, nor my own interests or those of my relatives, in the balance against the true interests of France. These latter, in my opinion, have never been contrary to the true interests of Europe.
> This judgment that I pass on my own actions will be confirmed, I trust, by impartial men. If this justice is denied me when I am no more, then the knowledge at least that it is due me will suffice to ensure the tranquillity of my last days.

And then, a curious paragraph, designed, no doubt, eventually to pacify the partisans of the Empire:

> Placed by Bonaparte himself in the position of having to choose between France and him, I could only make the choice dictated by my primary duty, and yet I bitterly regretted that it was impossible for me to reconcile, as in the past, his interests with those of the country. Nonetheless, I shall remember, even in my last hour, that he was my benefactor, for the fortune that I leave to my nephews comes to me, in large part, from him. My neph-

ews should not only never forget this, but they should teach it to their children, and their children to their own children, so that the remembrance of it shall become perpetual in my family, from generation to generation. If ever a man bearing the name of Bonaparte shall be in a financial position where he has need of aid or assistance, he shall obtain from my immediate heirs, or from their descendants, whatever assistance that it may be in their power to render him.

The declaration also gave instructions that the *Mémoires* should not be published until thirty years after his death, and all his papers, including the memoirs, were left to the Duchess de Dino and, if she should die before the three decades were past, to Bacourt, who had been a member of the London embassy.*

The declaration, as explicit as it was, was addressed, primarily, not to the world, but to Talleyrand's immediate circle of relatives and friends. A wider audience was needed for a more formal justification, and that audience presented itself at the end of 1837, at the death of Count Reinhard, who had succeeded Talleyrand at the Ministry of Foreign Affairs under the Directory. Talleyrand decided to deliver a funeral oration at the Academy of Moral and Political Science, in memory of Reinhard. He would also take this opportunity to give to the world some of the conclusions he had reached as the result of his long political experience. In vain, his friends, especially Dorothea, anxious for his health, attempted to dissuade him. When his physician stated that he would "not answer for the consequences," Talleyrand replied: "Who asked you to answer for them?"

The ceremony took place on March 3, 1838. Early that morning, Dorothea wrote: "In two hours, M. de Talleyrand is going to the Academy in a cold and most unpleasant rain. I also fear the effect of the excitement upon him. There will be a large audience, but no women, as this Academy will not admit them." Her estimate of the size of the audience was correct. All

---

* The reason for this prohibition is not difficult to guess. The greater part of the *Mémoires* had been written early in the Restoration, in the aftermath of the Congress of Vienna, when legitimacy was the watchword of Europe. It would not do, therefore, to publish them under Louis-Philippe, whose regime was the embodiment of everything contrary to the principle of legitimacy. Dorothea, however, died in 1862, six years before the date decided on for the publication of the *Mémoires*. Bacourt died three years later, but before dying, he instructed his trustees not to publish them until 1888. By that year, however, the trustees were also dead; and the Duke de Broglie (a grandson of Madame de Staël), to whom the papers passed, did not publish them until 1891. It was, according to Talleyrand's intention, the worst possible moment. Waterloo and the decimation of France had been forgotten, as had the Second Empire of the ineffectual Napoleon III and its fall at Sedan, at the hands of Prussia, in 1870. In the 1890's the Napoleonic legend was in full vigor, and the reputation of Talleyrand, accordingly, had waned. Those who had known and appreciated Talleyrand in his old age—Royer-Collard, Barante, Balzac, Lamartine, Thiers, and Guizot in France, and, in England, Wellington, Holland, and the Grevilles—all were dead, and the generation that had known them and that might have contained his biographer had also perished. The biography and apologia could not be written until the *Mémoires* had appeared. Such are the accidents of history that decide whom posterity shall admire and whom repudiate.

Paris, at least all official Paris, seemed to be there. Talleyrand, always worthy of his audience, made an almost royal entrance, supported by two footmen in splendid livery. When the chief usher cried, "The prince!" the whole assembly rose to its feet as the old man slowly made his way to the chair reserved for him. He read the oration, without glasses, in a voice sonorous and firm as always, pausing occasionally to emphasize one or another point in his carefully prepared text.

He traced the not particularly distinguished career of Reinhard from its beginnings, laying stress particularly on the fact that he had originally studied for the church and pointing out that theological studies formed an excellent preparation for diplomacy. It was immediately clear to the audience, listening in fascination, that the oration was to be not about Reinhard, but about Talleyrand himself. He continued to follow, however, the career of Reinhard through the stages of first secretary, consul general, minister plenipotentiary, and, finally, Reinhard's brief tenure as Minister of Foreign Affairs. Briefly, the qualities required for each of these functions were described, and Reinhard's possession of them noted. There was one gift that was lacking in Reinhard, one "additional capacity" that prevented him from attaining true distinction:

> The clearness of his view and intelligence was admirable. He could write an excellent account of anything that he had seen or heard; his style was easy, clever, and attractive . . . but, admirably as he wrote, he could express himself orally only with difficulty. For action, his intelligence required more time than conversation could provide.

The audience could not, and did not, fail to note the contrast between the inarticulate Reinhard and the man who, in conversation, had never met his equal.

Talleyrand described the perfect Minister of Foreign Affairs:

> Such a minister must be endowed with a kind of instinct that gives him prompt warning and prevents him from compromising himself before any discussion begins. He must be able to appear frank while remaining impenetrable. He must be reserved and yet seem careless. He must discriminate even in the nature of his amusements. His conversation must be simple, varied, attractive, always natural, and sometimes candid. In other words, he should never cease, for a single moment in the twenty-four hours of the day, to be Minister of Foreign Affairs.
>
> At the same time, unusual as these capacities are, they would hardly be adequate if loyalty did not give them that foundation that they almost always require. I am bound to cite that fact here, in opposition to a generally current prejudice. Diplomacy is not the science of duplicity and trickery. If good faith is required anywhere, it is especially necessary in political negotiations, for good faith alone can make such transactions permanent and

durable. Attempts have been made to confuse reserve with duplicity. Good faith never authorizes duplicity, but it may admit of reserve, and reserve has the special quality of increasing confidence.

Dominated by a sense of honor, by his country's interests, by the honor and interests of his sovereign, by the love of liberty based upon a respect for order and uniform justice, a Minister of Foreign Affairs, when he is equal to his responsibilities, occupies the highest position to which any lofty mind may aspire.

These truths, the solemn and patently sincere manner in which they were spoken, the great age, astonishing career, and phenomenal prestige of the speaker produced a sensational impression on the audience, which burst into wild applause as the prince, surrounded by attendants, made his way out of the chamber. Victor Cousin, who was present, shouted that "it is Voltaire, only better." The press the following morning was, with a few exceptions, extremely complimentary. Talleyrand was delighted, and even Dorothea, who could not bear to hear the slightest criticism of her uncle, confessed that "the whole thing has come off better than I expected."

Talleyrand's eulogy on Count Reinhard was his final word to the people of Europe. It was, as he himself described it, "my farewell to the world." As always, his timing was perfect, for he had but three months left to live. Having turned from this world, he must now prepare for his reception in the next.

Talleyrand faced death as he had faced life, with the same tranquil demeanor and the same mastery of circumstances that had been one of the wonders of Europe for more than half a century. He would indeed surrender to death, but the terms of the surrender would be dictated by Talleyrand himself, and those terms would reflect the principles that Talleyrand had preached all his life: a concern for social order and propriety and submission to legally constituted authority. The final settlement of his life, therefore, must obliterate the last trace of resistance to such authority that existed in his own life. He would die, but not until he had negotiated a peace with the earthly arbiter of death, the Church of Rome. For Talleyrand was, above all, an aristocrat, and an aristocrat of his era did not die as a skeptic. The blessing of the church was as essential to a worthy end of a nobleman as armorial bearings on his tomb. Talleyrand himself had said it: "There is no sentiment less aristocratic than that of nonbelief." Moreover, Talleyrand was surely aware that Paris and all Europe were watching closely to see what his end would be. Madame de Broglie, a daughter of Madame de Staël and no friend of Talleyrand's, stated it with the bluntness that she had learned at her mother's knee: "And now, my dear, we shall see if he knows how to die."

Madame de Broglie and her friends, no doubt, would have been disappointed to learn that Talleyrand had already given much thought to that very question. A man who had spent his life observing the proprieties could not possibly face death without considering them under this different and final aspect. In addition, there were other reasons why it was virtually inconceivable for Talleyrand to end his days in a state of alienation from the church. For centuries, stretching back into the dim mists of the Merovingian age, his illustrious ancestors had been Catholic. His own family, particularly his mother, had been devout. He himself had spent his early years in a Catholic seminary. It is true that, at heart, he had never been a priest, that he had detested his enforced vocation, and that he had performed his sacerdotal duties reluctantly; it is equally true, however, in a way that it is perhaps difficult for later generations to appreciate, that in his heart he had always remained a Catholic. Talleyrand was the first to recognize and to confess that this was so. Those who knew him well—Dorothea, for one—could detect the symptoms of this continuing attachment even during the most active periods of his life. He always evidenced, for example, a strong attachment for the ministers of the church, and during the Revolution, he had done all in his power to protect endangered priests. Needy convents and monasteries were the constant recipients of his charity, and he always sought the honor of entertaining bishops and theologians in his house. In his later years he attended Sunday mass regularly, particularly at Valençay, where, as lord of the manor, he felt that to do otherwise would have been to set a regrettable example. Nor were his devotions confined to public displays of duty. At home he frequently read from the *Imitation of Christ*, and he recommended this classic to all his friends. He took great delight in Pauline's progress in piety, and he was not above offering religious instruction himself when the occasion presented itself. Once, he asked Dorothea what her favorite prayer was. "The *Pater noster*," she replied.

"But you should recite the *Salve Regina*, above all," Talleyrand corrected her. "Come, sit here, and I will teach it to you. Since I know it by heart, I will teach it to you in Latin and explain it as I go along." Dorothea listened as her uncle, with what can only be described as a sacerdotal air, recited the prayer. "*Salve Regina, mater misericordiae.* How exquisite those words are. *Vita, dulcedo et spes nostra*—'our life, our joy, our hope.' Learn these words, and say them often. You will see how much comfort you will derive from them." Then, Dorothea reported, "he made me repeat the entire prayer several times over, until I had learned it by heart. I remember it to this day, word for word."

This paradoxical piety in the ex-Bishop of Autun was known and provided the basis for hope among Talleyrand's more devout friends. He con-

stantly received messages from convents and monasteries—the beneficiaries of his alms—to the effect that masses and prayers were being offered
up "for his intentions." These letters he kept in a special drawer, and he
often spoke of them to Dorothea in these terms: "See? These good souls
have not given up on me. Perhaps I am not quite as wicked as some people
think."

All of these things, along with a catalogue of Talleyrand's devotions,
were recorded by Dorothea. She regarded them as evidence, as indeed they
were, that her uncle was "a good man; a very good man indeed," and that
he must, in one way or another, find his way back to the church. The truth
of the matter was that Talleyrand, several years before his death, had
begun thinking of defining more precisely his relations with Rome. The
manner in which he went about it, however, was consonant with the
thoughtful and sometimes maddeningly unhurried way he had always proceeded with matters of state. In the quiet of Valençay, he had spent long
hours meditating, evolving the act which was to be, from his point of view,
the climax to his career. Dorothea, however, did not know this, and though
she found signs of hope in Talleyrand's attitude toward the church and its
ministers, she was greatly troubled. Faith without action was, to her mind
as to that of all Catholic Europe, only a shade better than outright infidelity. It disturbed her to the depths of her soul that Talleyrand, to all outward appearances, was unwilling to take the steps necessary for a reconciliation with Rome, or at least that he seemed oblivious to the necessity for
such steps. "I have often been astonished," she wrote, "at the ease of my
uncle's bearing in the company of priests. I can only explain it by suppos-
ing that he was under a delusion—strange, but real and of long duration—
concerning his situation with respect to the church. He was quite aware
that he had dealt the church a blow, but he seemed to think that the process of secularization* that he had almost inadvertently stimulated had
been one of simplification rather than of destruction." What Dorothea
thought of as "a delusion"—that is, Talleyrand's assumption that his "secularization" had regularized his status with respect to the church—if it was
indeed real, had endured only so long as Talleyrand had been active in
public life. But this, too, she ignored, and determined to prod her uncle,
whom she regarded as puzzlingly reluctant, into the arms of the church,
she mounted a subtle campaign, one worthy of Talleyrand himself, to
achieve the end she desired.

Her opening gun had been fired years before, in June, 1835, on the occasion of Pauline's confirmation. Dorothea was then in regular contact with

---

* It will be recalled that, in 1802, as a reward for Talleyrand's role in the Concordat between the
church and the Empire, the Pope had addressed a letter to him, authorizing him in very vague
terms, to reenter civil life.

Hyacinth-Louis de Quelen, Count-Archbishop of Paris. This Quelen was a solemn, pious man, courageous and determined, but with little of those qualities Talleyrand prized most: humor, tact, and sensitivity. Dorothea, with her great good sense, had been quick to measure the archbishop's talents against the task that she would impose upon him:

> The trouble with the archbishop is that he has not quite the intellectual equipment to play the difficult role that circumstances impose upon him. However, he has many other good and noble qualities, and he has the greatest interest in all those who bear the name of Talleyrand.

Quelen, for all his faults, was the most powerful weapon at Dorothea's disposal. Talleyrand may indeed have been secularized, as he claimed, but not even the Roman Curia had been able to find a precedent for blessing the marriage of a bishop—even as reluctant a bishop as Talleyrand had been. It could be only through the intervention of an advocate as influential as the Archbishop of Paris that a reconciliation might be effected. At Dorothea's instigation, therefore, Quelen had written to Rome, asking what was necessary for the Prince de Talleyrand formally to be readmitted to the sacraments of the church. The answer came in due course. The Archbishop of Paris might absolve Prince Talleyrand and receive him back into the arms of the church on two conditions: First, the position of Talleyrand's wife must be resolved (the letter from Rome was written before Catherine's death) and, second, the prince must make an admission of guilt and a humble request for reinstatement. Finally, the archbishop was authorized "to inform the person in question of the Holy Father's grief and affliction and of the consolation he would derive from his return."

This, Dorothea knew, was impossible. Talleyrand, proud though he was, might retract, recant, and confess, but no one would ever be able to push him into doing so. She therefore refused to listen when Archbishop de Quelen proposed a direct overture to Talleyrand on the subject. Her role and the archbishop's, she insisted, would have to be "passive and cautious." She knew her uncle, and nothing else would do. The prelate was forced to acquiesce, and he suggested that, instead, he might call upon Talleyrand from time to time, as a friend, and—subtly, of course—do what he could to advance the cause.

The death of the Princess de Talleyrand at the end of 1835 had indeed, as the prince remarked, greatly simplified his position. In his own mind, it had removed the one great obstacle that blocked the road to Rome. The same thought had occurred to the archbishop, who regarded Catherine's death as the perfect opportunity for an opening visit to the rue St.-Florentin. Talleyrand professed himself delighted at the prospect and flattered, but, he said, the date suggested by Monseigneur de Quelen was impossible. Another date was proposed, but that, too, was inconvenient. Still another; with the same result. Dorothea may not have known what was in Talleyrand's mind, but Talleyrand obviously knew what was in hers. "M. de Talleyrand was well aware that I often had the honor of seeing the Archbishop of Paris," she remarked, somewhat ruefully, "and he had guessed that our relationship was actuated by one principal idea so far as M. de Quelen was concerned." It was clear that Talleyrand, though he had every intention eventually of being "converted," regarded the time as not yet ripe. Moreover, though he was prepared to make certain sacrifices in order to be readmitted to the church, he was wholly unprepared to be preached to by the clumsy Quelen. He would endure conversion, but he could never countenance boredom.

Dorothea, in the face of this reversal, adopted a new strategy. "I now take every opportunity of making obvious to him my own faith, in an attempt to stimulate his own. Yet I never do this until an opening presents itself. In such matters, a light touch is indispensable." True to her word, she missed no chance to point out to her uncle his equivocal position in the eyes of the world and of the church. Once, after she and Talleyrand had attended mass together, she asked: "Does it make you feel strange to attend mass?"

"Why, no," he answered. "Why should it?"

"I thought that possibly you might not feel the same as other people."

"But I feel precisely the same. Why not? I go to mass in the same way as you or anyone else. You forget that I have been secularized. That makes my situation perfectly simple."

"But, after all, you have ordained priests."

"Yes. But not many."

On another occasion, during a violent thunderstorm, Talleyrand asked Dorothea what she was thinking. "I am thinking," she replied, "that if there were a priest in the room, I would confess my sins. I am terrified of a sudden death. To die unprepared, to carry with one a heavy burden of sin —what a fearsome prospect this is. No matter how well one tries to live, no one can dispense with absolution and reconciliation." Talleyrand, Dorothea noted, made no reply.

Dorothea's new tactics were no less obvious to Talleyrand than her old ones. Yet he loved her too much and respected her intellect too well to take her efforts lightly or to dismiss her words as mere propaganda. For two years, she pursued her goal relentlessly and with such unselfish devotion that, by the end of 1837, even the immovable Talleyrand had begun to show signs of weakening. The turning point seems to have come in December of that year, after Dorothea had fallen seriously ill at Rochecotte.

"During the two days that I was so ill," she wrote to Bacourt, "it seemed to me that I could see something of the next world, and I realized that it was not so difficult as one might think to rise to one's Creator. Providence can soften all the trials which He sends up by giving us the strength to bear them." This "spiritual experience," as Dorothea described it, marked a new beginning in her life. She had arrived at Rochecotte a professed Christian; she left it a convinced Christian. From that time on, her *Chronique* and her letters would reflect a continuing acknowledgment of what she regarded as her small role in the "divine plan for the universe."

Talleyrand, who had observed his niece's illness with consternation, would not fail to note the subsequent reinforcement of her religious faith, nor, for the love he bore her, could he fail to be affected by it. "So," he said to her, "you have reached a new point in your life. Explain to me how you arrived there." He listened intently while Dorothea explained, as best she could, her spiritual progress, adding that, among the many other factors she had taken into account, was the obligation imposed upon her by her position in society. Significantly, this last observation seems to have impressed Talleyrand favorably.

Talleyrand's incipient response to Dorothea's urgent need for his reconciliation with the church came none too soon. From the beginning of 1838, the duchess' *Chronique* is virtually a daily record of Talleyrand's physical deterioration:

> I am very worried, and so is he; in short, I am greatly depressed, and everything weighs heavily upon my mind. . . . M. de Talleyrand is anxious about the state of his leg. . . . Want of fresh air and exercise, if this continues, may have serious consequences. . . . Yesterday, he stepped on the folds of Princess Lieven's dress and nearly fell . . . his knee gave way, his weak foot turned, and he twisted his big toe. . . . The sprained foot is weak and painful. I do not know if he will ever be able to walk again. . . . He is rather despondent and too farsighted not to realize all the possible implications of this. . . . I was awakened early this morning with the news that M. de Talleyrand was suffering from an inability to breathe. What I do not like is the fact that, for the past two days, he has been more or less feverish, and he will eat little or nothing. . . . I am far from optimistic concerning the result of this condition; it seems to indicate a general breakdown in his health.

The end was approaching. Talleyrand knew it. He knew, too, that there was little time left for lengthy and complex diplomatic maneuvers. Long before, in the autumn of 1836, he had dictated a declaration in which he had stated that "although I ceased to be her [the church's] minister, I never ceased to be her son" and a last will and testament, in which he had affirmed: "I die, as I have lived, a member of the Roman Catholic

Church." The moment had come for him to redeem those statements in the eyes of the world. On February 5 he asked Dorothea to invite the Abbé Dupanloup, Pauline's confessor and spiritual adviser, to dinner the following day. Dupanloup first accepted and then sent a message saying that he could not come after all. Talleyrand, who had been "sad and apprehensive" all day, was greatly disappointed. "He is less intelligent than I thought," he told Dorothea. "He should be eager to come here, for my sake as well as his own." Talleyrand suspected, and he was probably right, that Dupanloup was playing a waiting game or, more accurately, that he was playing Talleyrand as one plays a trout. To attempt to reel in a big fish, or a great sinner, too quickly, was a sure way to have him slip from the hook. Since Dupanloup was a man of some ambition and since Talleyrand's conversion would represent a large step forward in the fulfillment of his ambitions, he was taking no chances.* What Dupanloup apparently had forgotten was that he was dealing with the man who, in his day, had dictated terms to the kings of the earth. A bitter complaint was immediately lodged with the Archbishop of Paris, and the archbishop, who knew Talleyrand only too well, guaranteed that if the prince would condescend to repeat the invitation, he would guarantee Dupanloup's acceptance. Unexpectedly, Talleyrand consented. Once more Dupanloup was invited to dinner, and this time he came. Dorothea was ecstatic: "I cannot help ascribing his [Talleyrand's] excellent frame of mind to my own feelings during my last illness and to the words that I was then able to speak to him."

The dinner went off better than might have been expected under the circumstances. Dupanloup, who described the occasion in a letter to a friend in Italy, confesses that he had accepted Talleyrand's invitation with a heavy heart.

> I was seriously annoyed and even sad at finding myself condemned to leave my pious retreat for M. de Talleyrand's house. I, like the rest of the world, lacked faith in Prince de Talleyrand's good faith. I was aware of his ability and of my own lack of ability, and I found all this very embarrassing. Yet my conscience and the responsibilities of my ministry compelled me to go through with it. . . .
>
> The prince received me with the greatest kindness. He was seated in one of those high, wide armchairs that he favored. He dominated the whole room with his glance and with his rare, witty, and loud, but always courteous, speech. No king could be more a king in his palace than was M. de Talleyrand in his salon. . . .
>
> Though conversation at first was rather cold and hesitant and, though outwardly respectful, I felt nothing more than deep compassion at the sight

---

* Dorothea, who greatly admired Dupanloup, was not unaware of this aspect of the good abbé's character. "He is gentle, discreet, moderate . . . and has every quality that a spiritual director should have. But this does not exclude ambition." *Chronique*, entry of February 6, 1838.

of this aged man, I did not experience the slightest confusion or embarrassment. I learned later that he affects most people in this way, and that, of the distinguished men of the imperial court, only the emperor himself had sometimes been embarrassed by his wit, by the loftiness, promptness and soundness of his views, the coolness and sparkle of his ripostes, and by his perpetual calm. . . .

    I did not fully appreciate the greatness of his career. I knew only the bad side of his life. I had always been accustomed to look upon him as a great sinner and as a source of scandal. . . . You can imagine my astonishment at the conversation. I had expected propriety, but it was more than that. It was quite religious the whole time. M. de Talleyrand spoke a great deal of sermons and preachers of the present day, and he quoted many fine passages and beautiful axioms from preachers he had heard in his youth.

Talleyrand, for his part, had been impressed by the abbé. "He is a man who knows what it means to live," he told Dorothea, with approval in his voice.

The Duchess de Dino was now full of expectations after this good beginning, but once again, she was disappointed. Several weeks passed, Talleyrand's strength continued to ebb, and still he said not a word concerning his situation. By March 4, exhausted by his effort of the preceding day—he had delivered his eulogy of Count Reinhard on the third—Talleyrand was "very upset and very weak." Dorothea was frantic. At her request, the Abbé Dupanloup asked if he could call, and Talleyrand assented willingly. When the priest arrived, it was Pauline, Talleyrand's "angel," who led him to her great-uncle. When she left them, she went directly to her mother's apartment, where Dorothea and Pauline fell on their knees and asked God to grant the prince the grace of repentance and a happy death. In the meantime, Talleyrand had engaged Dupanloup in a lively discussion of his various afflictions and diseases and of the preposterous remedies that had been suggested. Nothing was said of retractions and recantations and confessions of guilt. Dupanloup, upon leaving Talleyrand, called upon Dorothea, and reported that her uncle, while he "did not speak of the subject directly," had "let fall some kind words." Therefore, Dupanloup felt, there were "grounds for hope." In any case, Dorothea noted, Dupanloup "has shown great discretion and tact, and I think he has handled the situation perfectly. So far, so good—provided we have sufficient time left. . . . But when dealing with such a mind, one cannot be hasty."

Even so, Dorothea was now determined to expedite matters. During the next two weeks, she spent much time with Archbishop de Quelen, preparing the draft of a letter to the Pope, which, if Talleyrand could be induced to sign it, would secure his reinstatement as a member in good standing of the church. On March 25, she recounts, she "defied an equinoctal storm to go and see the archbishop. By degrees, we now came to an agreement about the letter." Three days later, she had "a most important conversation with M. de Talleyrand and found him in a state of open-mindedness that seemed little short of miraculous" about the possibility of a written retraction.

The Abbé Dupanloup, informed of these encouraging developments, now rushed into the breach with a cautious letter to Talleyrand, in which he invoked, among other things, the memory of Talleyrand's beloved uncle, the Archbishop of Rheims, and the prince's responsibility for both Pauline's happiness and her edification through his good example. When the letter arrived, Talleyrand sent for Dorothea and handed it to her. "Do you know what this is about?" he asked suspiciously.

"No, monsieur, I do not."

"Very well, then. Read it aloud."

The duchess did as she was told. Several times during the reading, her eyes flooded with tears, and she was forced to pause until she had regained control of herself. "Come, come," Talleyrand said. "There is nothing to cry about. This is a serious matter."

When she had finished the letter, there was a deathly silence in the room. Then Talleyrand spoke, softly: "If I should fall gravely ill, I would send for a priest. Do you think that the Abbé Dupanloup would be willing to come?"

"I am certain that he would. But if he were to be of any use to you, it would first be necessary for you to be readmitted to the church that, unfortunately, you have abandoned."

"Yes, yes, I know. I must do something about Rome." And then, in the tone of a man revealing a great secret: "I have been thinking about it for a long time."

"Since when?" Dorothea exclaimed in astonishment.

"Since the last visit to Valençay of the Archbishop of Bourges.* Even then I wondered why the archbishop, who is supposed to be responsible for my soul, did not raise the question."

"Alas, monsieur. He would not have dared."

"But I would not have been at all angry."

Dorothea, with tears streaming down her cheeks, clasped Talleyrand's hand and said with great emotion: "But why must you wait for others to raise the question? Why should you not yourself take the step that is most in keeping with your honor and most gratifying to the church and to all people of good will? You will find Rome well disposed, I know. And the Archbishop of Paris is very fond of you. Why do you not try?"

* In early June, 1837, Talleyrand had left Fontainebleau and the Duke d'Orléans' marriage celebration at the earliest possible moment in order to return to Valençay for this visit. Valençay was in the archdiocese of Bourges, and the archbishop was Talleyrand's ordinary.

"I do not refuse to take this step. I know that I must do it. But I do not know what they want of me. Why do they not tell me?"

"Would you like me to tell you? I shall, if you are willing."

Talleyrand said softly: "I should be happy if you did so."

Dorothea immediately went to her desk and wrote out a list of the conditions that Archbishop de Quelen had insisted upon. Talleyrand read them, made one or two comments, but raised no serious objection to any of them.

On the same day, shortly after this conversation, a message was brought to Talleyrand and Dorothea that Archambaud de Talleyrand, the prince's brother, was dead.* Talleyrand was extremely upset. To make matters worse, Archambaud had died suddenly, without the opportunity to confess his sins or receive the sacraments. "It is yet another warning," Talleyrand told the Abbé Dupanloup, when the priest arrived later in the day to express his condolences.

A few days later, as Dorothea was preparing for a visit to Archbishop de Quelen, Talleyrand casually drew a folded paper from a drawer and handed it to her. "Here," he said, "is something that will get you a warm reception at the archbishop's. You will have to tell me what he thinks of it." It was the greatly desired retraction, his "submission" to Rome, "a sheet of paper covered on both sides, with erasures in several places." Upon her return, Dorothea told him that M. de Quelen "deeply appreciated the paper but wished the statements expressed therein to be presented in a more canonical form and that he would send him the proper ecclesiastical formula in a few days." This was hardly the reaction that Talleyrand had expected, but knowing the archbishop's intellectual handicaps, he contented himself with a few appropriately sharp words. Later in the day he told Dorothea that he intended also to write a letter of explanation to the Pope when he sent him the declaration. And he ended by saying, "What I am to write, however, must be dated in the same week as my speech to the Academy. I do not want people to say that I wrote it in my second childhood."

A few days after this, early in May, his health seemed sufficiently improved for Talleyrand to leave the house for a promenade, by carriage, in the streets of Paris. On May 12, however, while he was dining with the Count de Noailles, Princess Lieven, and Montrond, he was suddenly seized with a violent chill. He was carried into his room, put to bed, and given a cup of hot tea. After a few moments, he was himself again and continued the interrupted conversation—on Lamartine's *Chute d'un ange*—as

---

* Archambaud's title of Duke de Talleyrand passed to his son, Edmond, Dorothea's husband. Dorothea was thereafter known as Duchess de Talleyrand.

though nothing had happened. That night, however, he had another seizure, and his physician, Cruveilhier, diagnosed a gangrenous carbuncle in the lumbar region. The pain was intense, and Cruveilhier declared that surgery was necessary. The operation was prolonged and cruel. The only sound from Talleyrand during the entire procedure was a question addressed to the surgeon in a soft voice: "Ah, my good Cruveilhier, do you realize what pain you are causing me?"

No sooner had the operation been terminated than Talleyrand, still in excruciating pain and with a high fever, asked to be carried into the salon. There he began an animated conversation with the friends who had gathered to be with him, recounting, with great amusement, that one of the assisting physicians had brought his dog with him and that the animal had barked so much that it had been necessary to put him out of the room. This was his last recorded pleasantry.

That night the pain was still intense, the fever had not abated, and Talleyrand's strength was visibly waning. Dorothea, Pauline, the prince's friends, even the servants were in despair. The Abbé Dupanloup was hastily summoned, and Talleyrand received him immediately in his chamber. The priest found "this old man, this dying bishop," as he called him, greatly changed. The face seemed shrunken, the eyes half-closed. But the voice was still clear and firm. "My dear Abbé, it seems so long since we saw one another. I am very ill." Dupanloup now handed him two documents: the first, the text of Talleyrand's retraction as amended by Archbishop de Quelen; the second, the draft of a letter to the Pope. Both these, he explained gently, would have to be signed before the last rites could be administered. The tension in the room was almost unbearable as Talleyrand, with Dorothea and Dupanloup looking on, read the pages handed him. First, the retraction of his errors:

> Moved more and more by solemn considerations, and forced to consider impartially the consequences of a revolution affecting all things and lasting for fifty years, I find myself obliged, after a long life and much experience, to blame the excesses of the time in which I have lived, and heartily to condemn the grave errors which, in this long train of years, have so vexed and troubled the Catholic, Apostolic, and Roman Church—excesses to which I myself have unfortunately contributed.
>
> If it pleases Monseigneur the Archbishop of Paris, who has already assured me of the charitable disposition of the Sovereign Pontiff toward me, to present to the Holy Father, in accordance with my wishes, my confession and my entire submission to the doctrine and discipline of the church, and to the decisions and mandates of the Holy See in all the ecclesiastical affairs of France, I dare to trust that His Holiness will graciously deign to accept such submission.
>
> Being at one time exempted, by the venerable Pius VI, from the exercise

of ecclesiastical functions, I have sought during my long political career for opportunities on which to render to religion, and to many honored and distinguished members of the Catholic clergy, any services in my power. I have never ceased to consider myself a child of the church.

I deplore, afresh, those acts of my life which have offended the church, and my last prayers will be for her and for her supreme Head.

March 10, 1838

Without saying a word, Talleyrand put aside the retraction and took up the letter to Pope Gregory XVI:

MOST HOLY FATHER,

The young and pious child, who lightens my old age with the tenderest and most touching care, has just informed me of the benevolence with which His Holiness is inclined to regard me, and tells me of the joy with which she awaits the consecrated objects for which she has so fondly longed. I am impressed, as I myself was when the Archbishop of Paris first brought them to me.*

Before being enfeebled by the grave malady with which I am now afflicted, I desire, Holy Father, to express my feelings and to offer my submission. I dare to hope that His Holiness will not only deign to accept these favorably, but that, in his justice, he will remember the circumstances which have influenced my actions.

The *Mémoires*, finished some time since, but which, according to my wishes, will not appear until thirty years after my death, will explain to posterity my conduct during the revolutionary epoch. I must content myself today, in order not to fatigue the Holy Father, by simply drawing his attention to the general disorder of the time in which I lived. The respect which I owe to those who gave me birth does not, however, prevent my saying that all my youth was spent in preparation for a profession for which I was, by character, unfitted.

For the rest, I cannot now act more wisely, than by abandoning myself, as I have done in all things, to the justice and charity of the church and her venerable Head.

I am, Most Holy Father, with respect, Your Holiness' very humble and submissive son and servant,

All that was lacking was Talleyrand's signature, but he did not sign. Instead, he turned to Dupanloup and demanded to know why his own version had not been adequate. "I reflected carefully, M. l'Abbé, on what I had written. I put everything into those two pages, and those who know how to read them will find everything in them that is necessary."

Dupanloup was greatly embarrassed but somehow found the courage to reply that "those who know you, M. le Prince, will indeed find in these

---

* The Pope, through the Archbishop of Paris, had offered to send Pauline some relics of the saints, blessed by his own hand.

pages all that is essential. But you must admit that there are many people in this country who do not know how to read, and if you will allow me to say it, there are some who, where you are concerned, do not read very well."

This was the kind of reply that Talleyrand liked, and the kind that he understood. "Leave these papers with me, M. l'Abbé. I will read them again tonight."

Reluctantly, Dupanloup withdrew and reported to the archbishop the substance of his exchange with Talleyrand. The worthy prelate wrung his hands, raised his eyes to heaven, and whispered: "These obstacles are raised up by Satan!" Again, the archbishop showed that he did not understand the sinner with whom he was dealing. Montrond did, and his explanation of Talleyrand's procrastination is probably much nearer the truth: "At this time, he [Talleyrand] had two things foremost in his mind. First, not to cause a scandal by dying outside the church and, second, not to be converted until the last possible moment, so that he would not have to put up with the sarcastic comments of the whole world."

Talleyrand's evasive action was only the beginning of his struggle with the determined Abbé Dupanloup. The next day the priest was back. He found the prince propped up by pillows and supported by two footmen. The lower part of his body was paralyzed, and the pain from his surgical wound was too intense for him to lie flat in his bed. "The archbishop sends you his good wishes and his prayers," Dupanloup began. Then: "Will you now sign the declaration?"

"Please convey my thanks to my lord archbishop. And tell him that everything will be taken care of in good time."

Dupanloup went into the anteroom, where Dorothea and Pauline were waiting, and announced his failure. The duchess and her daughter were seized with panic that the prince would die, unreconciled, unshriven. A brief conference decided that a final, desperate effort must be made. Pauline, Talleyrand's "guardian angel," was commissioned to do what neither the priest's pleas nor the duchess' tears had been able to do. "My daughter," Dorothea said to Pauline, "you have been taught what you owe to the love of your uncle. The moment has come for you to prove your gratitude to him." The girl burst into tears and knelt at Dupanloup's feet for his blessing; then she went into the sickroom.

A few moments later she emerged, emptyhanded.

To her mother's questions, she replied that her uncle had assured her that he would indeed sign. When she had pressed him, asking, "Yes, but when, Uncle?" he had answered: "Tomorrow, between five and six o'clock in the morning."

"Tomorrow?" she had persisted.

"Yes, tomorrow, between five and six o'clock."

Thereupon Dupanloup reentered Talleyrand's chamber. "M. le Prince, may I tell the archbishop that he may hope to have your signature tomorrow?"

Impatiently, the dying man replied, "Do not say *hope*. Say *certitude*. It is definite."

Talleyrand's decision not to sign until the next morning plunged his family into an agony of suspense. It seemed hardly likely, as the night progressed, that he would last until the appointed hour. Once more, Pauline was sent to his bedside, this time with a pen in her hand, and once more she implored him, for the love he bore her, to sign. Once more, gently, he refused. "It is not yet six o'clock. I promised you that I would sign, and I promise you again that I shall—but between five and six o'clock."

By four o'clock on that morning of May 16, 1838, the Abbé Dupanloup, the Duchess de Dino, and Pauline were awake, dressed, and waiting. With them were the five witnesses designated by the Archbishop of Paris to attest to Talleyrand's signature: the Prince de Poix, representing the aristocracy of the *ancien régime*; St.-Aulaire, ambassador to Vienna, and Barante, ambassador to St. Petersburg, representing the diplomatic service; and Royer-Collard and Molé, president of the Council, representing the government. "It would have been impossible," wrote Dupanloup, "to find more honorable witnesses or men with greater authority." The priest, Talleyrand's family, and the witnesses entered the prince's room at five o'clock. They made not a sound. "We talked by signs," Dupanloup wrote. After a few moments, Talleyrand lifted his head, opened his eyes, and looked slowly around him. First, he greeted his visitors with his customary courtesy and with unusual feeling. Then he asked, "What time is it?"

"It is six o'clock, M. le Prince," someone answered. Dupanloup, however, could not allow this pious lie. "Not so," he said. "It is only five o'clock, M. le Prince."

"Good," breathed Talleyrand. And then he was silent, waiting. No one else ventured to speak.

A quarter of an hour passed, and then a half hour. The door of the room opened, and a small figure, dressed entirely in white, entered. It was Marie de Talleyrand, daughter of Charlotte, Baroness de Talleyrand. The child was about to make her first communion. She knelt next to Talleyrand. "Uncle, I come to ask your blessing."

"My child, I wish you great happiness in your life. If I can in any way contribute to it, I will do so with all my heart."

"You can," Dorothea interposed, "by giving her your blessing."

Talleyrand, extending his hands, blessed her.

The clock now struck six. The prince signaled, and the Duke de Valençay and M. de Bacourt approached to support him with their hands. Dorothea and Pauline knelt, while the witnesses stood. The duchess then read
the act of retraction in a clear, loud voice and handed it to her uncle. The
dying man took it and, without a moment's hesitation, signed it: *Charles-
Maurice, Prince de Talleyrand.* The letter of submission to Pope Gregory
was handled no less expeditiously. Both documents, according to Talleyrand's wish, were dated March 10—the week during which he had delivered his eulogy of Count Reinhard.

It was done. The papers were immediately carried to the waiting Archbishop of Paris, who dispatched them to Rome by a special courier.

Talleyrand slept. At eight o'clock, he was roused by a disturbance on the
floor below. The noise came closer. A royal herald burst into the room and
announced His Majesty, Louis-Philippe, King of the French. As Louis-
Philippe entered, followed by the Princess Adélaïde, Talleyrand, seated on
the edge of his bed, was once more, for the last time in his life, transformed
into the perfect courtier. It was the king who was embarrassed. "I am distressed, Prince," he stuttered, "to see you in such pain."

"Sire," Talleyrand replied in his sonorous voice, "you have come to assist at the last moments of a man who is dying. Those who truly care for
him can have but one wish: to see them come to an end."

Then Prince Talleyrand, once again the grand chamberlain of kings, cer-
emoniously presented to his majesty those who were in the chamber, not
forgetting to name his valet, who had been chosen to represent the household staff at his deathbed. When the king withdrew a few moments later,
Talleyrand, with almost his last ounce of strength, drew himself up and
made a deep bow. "Sire," he said, "today our house has received an honor
worthy of inscription in our annals, an honor that my successors will recall
with pride and gratitude." And to Madame Adélaïde, who lingered a few
moments: *"Madame, je vous aime bien."*

When the royal party had left, Talleyrand slept for a while. When he
opened his eyes again, the Abbé Dupanloup was standing next to him,
wearing the robes of his office. The moment had come for the prince to
confess his sins and be absolved. He had not received the sacraments for
almost half a century. The room emptied, and the two were alone for a
time. When the doors were opened again, Talleyrand's family, friends, and
servants filed in to watch as the prince received the eucharist and the sacrament of extreme unction—the final anointing. When the Abbé Dupanloup attempted to anoint Talleyrand's palms, however, the prince corrected him: "No, no, Monsieur l'Abbé. You forget that I am a bishop."
And Dupanloup was required to alter the ritual and anoint the tops of Talleyrand's hands rather than the palms, in accordance with the practice for

bishops. When he had finished, the prince closed his eyes and seemed to sleep.

In the meantime, the rooms and the street outside had filled with those who knew Talleyrand: statesmen, writers, friends; the sad and the curious, the indifferent and the weeping. The murmur of conversation filled Talleyrand's house, as it always had. Then, in midafternoon, the door to the prince's chamber opened and a servant stumbled out, half-blinded by tears, and approached the waiting physician. The doctor rushed to the open door, and everyone in the room followed him. They saw Talleyrand, seated on his bed and held upright by Bacourt and Dupanloup. He raised his head and looked around once; then his eyes closed, and he was dead. It was 3:55 on the afternoon of May 17, 1838. "We of his family were on our knees around my poor uncle, praying and weeping," Pauline recounted. "When the physician announced that he was no more, we all kissed his hand for the last time. It was already cold as death."

Instantly, the room was emptied, and Pauline and Dorothea were left alone with the dead man. Their only companion was a priest, who had been hired for the occasion to recite prayers for the repose of Talleyrand's soul. Everyone else had scattered throughout Paris to tell what they had seen and heard in the rue St.-Florentin.

By sunset there was not a citizen of Paris who had not heard it: "The prince is dead."

Bibliography

I. Talleyrand's Own Works

Talleyrand's many *Motions, Opinions, Réponses, Rapports,* and *Interventions* are preserved in the *Archives parlementaires* or the *Moniteur,* where they are indexed under his name. The works listed below are those which have been published separately. It may be noted, as one of the curiosities of modern historiography, that there exists no comprehensive collection of Talleyrand's vast correspondence. The individual collections listed below cover only particular phases of his career or include only his correspondence with one or another of his contemporaries. To them may be added G. Lacour-Gayet's *Talleyrand,* which cites, in whole or in part, many hitherto unpublished letters.

L'Assemblée nationale aux Français. Paris, n.d.
> Talleyrand's apologia for the policies of the National Assembly, delivered on February 11, 1790.

Communication faite au Sénat dans sa séance du 15 Pluviôse an XIII. Paris, n.d.

Compte de la dépense du ministère des Relations extérieures . . . Paris, an VII (1799).
> Talleyrand's accounting of expenditures by the Ministry of Foreign Relations for the period 1796–1799.

Compte de la dépense du ministère des Relations extérieures . . . Paris, an IX (1801).
> The accounting of expenditures by the Ministry of Foreign Relations for the period 1799–1801.

"Correspondance de Talleyrand avec le Premier Consul pendant la campagne de Marengo," Comte Boulay de la Meurthe, ed. in *Revue d'histoire diplomatique,* Vol. VI, p. 182.
> A collection of the letters exchanged between Talleyrand and Bonaparte during the Italian campaign of 1800. The relationship between the First Consul and his foreign minister was still in its honeymoon stage, and Talleyrand's letters are an interesting mixture of good advice and adulation.

"Correspondance de Talleyrand et de Bacourt," in *Le Correspondant,* March–July 1893.

Correspondance diplomatique de Talleyrand: Le ministère de Talleyrand sous le Directoire, edited, with introduction and notes, by G. Pallain. Paris, 1891.
> Talleyrand's official correspondence as minister of foreign affairs under the Directory. Some of the letters included in this collection (as well as in the two volumes following) are also found in Talleyrand's *Mémoires.* The text established by Pallain, however, is probably the more accurate of the two versions.

Correspondance diplomatique de Talleyrand: La mission de Talleyrand à Londres . . . , edited, with introduction and notes, by G. Pallain. Paris, 1887.

Talleyrand's diplomatic correspondence during the London mission of 1792, including letters to the Ministry of Foreign Affairs and to individuals, as well as the letters from the United States to Lord Lansdowne.

Correspondance diplomatique de Talleyrand: L'ambassade de Talleyrand à Londres, edited, with introduction and notes, by G. Pallain. Paris, 1891.

Talleyrand's official correspondence during the London embassy of 1830–1834.

Correspondance du comte de Jaucourt . . . avec le prince de Talleyrand pendant le Congrès de Vienne, edited, with introduction and biographical notice, by M. Le Visse de Montigny. Paris, 1905.

Correspondence and dispatches from Talleyrand to the Ministry of Foreign Affairs during the Congress of Vienna, 1814–1815.

Correspondance inédite du prince de Talleyrand et du roi Louis XVIII, edited, with introduction, commentary and notes, by G. Pallain. Paris, 1881.

The letters exchanged between Talleyrand and Louis XVIII during the Congress of Vienna, 1814–1815, and preserved in the Ministry of Foreign Affairs. There are only minor differences between the text established by Pallain and that given in the *Mémoires*, but the former is probably the more reliable of the two.

Des Loteries, par M. l'évêque d'Autun. Paris, 1789.

Talleyrand's argument, as Agent-General, against the national lottery.

Discours de M. le prince de Bénévent au Roi. Paris, n.d.

Talleyrand's address to Louis XVIII on May 2, 1814, upon the presentation of the Senate to the king.

Discours prononcé par le ministre des Affaires étrangères. Paris, n.d.

Talleyrand's address to the Chamber of Peers on September 8, 1814, regarding the adoption of new laws regulating state finances under the restored monarchy.

Éclaircissements donnés par le Citoyen Talleyrand à ses compatriotes. Paris, an VII (1799).

Talleyrand's statement on the Jorry affair, on the occasion of his resignation from the Ministry of Foreign Relations in 1799.

Éloge de M. le comte Reinhard. Paris, 1838.

The much praised eulogy of Count Reinhard, delivered before the Academy of Moral and Political Sciences of the Royal Institute, on March 3, 1838.

Essai sur les avantages à tirer de colonies nouvelles dans les circonstances présentes, M. d'Hauterive, ed., Paris, an VII (1799).

Talleyrand's paper on the desirability of establishing new French colonies, read to the Institut on July 3, 1797.

"Les États-Unis et l'Angleterre en 1795," in *Revue d'histoire diplomatique*, Vol. III, Paris, 1889.

The text of Talleyrand's paper on commercial relations between the United States and Great Britain, read before the Institut on April 4, 1797. It was published in London in 1805 under the title of *Mémoire sur les relations commerciales des États-Unis avec l'Angleterre*, and in Boston, in 1809, as *Memoir Concerning the Commercial Relations of the United States with England*.

"Intervention de Talleyrand sur l'article 6 de la déclaration des droits de l'homme," in *Archives parlementaires*, t. viii.

Talleyrand's proposal of August 21, 1789, in the National Assembly, concerning Article VI of the Declaration of the Rights of Man.

"Lettres à Madame Adélaïde," in *Nouvelle Revue rétrospective*. Paris, 1901–1902.
The letters addressed to the sister of King Louis-Philippe during the London embassy of 1830 to 1834.

"Lettres de Talleyrand à Caulaincourt," J. Hanoteau, ed., in *Revue des deux mondes*, 8th period, Vol. XXIX, p. 782; Vol. XXX, p. 142.
Correspondence with Louis de Caulaincourt, Duke de Vicence, during his embassy to St. Petersburg (1807–1811) and his tenure as Minister of Foreign Affairs (1813–1814).

"Lettres de Talleyrand à Madame de Staël," in *Revue d'histoire diplomatique*, Vol. IV, pp. 79, 290.

"Lettres de Talleyrand à Metternich," Jean de Bourgoing, ed., in *Napoléon*, No. 95, 1965.

"Lettres et billets du prince de Talleyrand et M. Royer-Collard," edited, with an introduction, by P. Royer-Collard, in *Mélanges de la Société des bibliophiles français*, Vol. I, p. 3, 1903.
Talleyrand's correspondence with the chief of the Doctrinaires during the last years of the Second Restoration and under the July Monarchy.

Lettres inédites de Talleyrand à Napoléon, edited, with an introduction and notes, by Pierre Bertrand. Paris, 1889.
Letters to Napoleon from the beginning of the Consulate until Talleyrand's "disgrace" and the loss of his position as Grand Chamberlain, in 1809.

Mémoires du prince de Talleyrand. Introduction and notes by the Duke de Broglie. Paris, 1891–1892. 5 vols. (Published in English as *Memoirs of Talleyrand*. Edited, with a preface and notes, by the Duke de Broglie, translated by Raphaël Ledos de Beaufort and Mrs. Angus Hall, with an introduction by the Honorable Whitelaw Reid. New York, 1891. 5 vols.)
A new French edition of the *Mémoires*, Volumes I and II, edited by Jean-Paul Couchoud, appeared in 1957. It is supplemented by useful documentation, and M. Couchoud's text is more accurate than that of the 1891–1892 edition.
Volumes I and II, covering the periods 1754–1808 and 1809–1814 respectively, are largely narrative and, so far as biographical material is concerned, incomplete. Volume III (1815–1830), Volume IV (1830–1832) and Volume V (1832–1834) are made up chiefly of official correspondence and contain only brief narrative passages, with the Congress of Vienna and the London embassy receiving the most detailed attention.
The *Mémoires*, in the form in which they were finally published some fifty-five years after Talleyrand's death, were probably retouched, to a certain extent, by Bacourt, Talleyrand's literary executor, but their overall authenticity, though occasionally questioned, has never been seriously challenged. (For a thorough discussion of the authenticity and credibility of the *Mémoires*, see the studies by P. Bertrand, G. Lacour-Gayet, and J. Flammermont listed in the bibliography of the present work.) They are concerned almost exclusively with political questions, and there is very little in them relating to Talleyrand's personal life—a fact which caused great disappointment and elicited great skepticism when the *Mémoires* were first published.

Le ministre des Relations extérieures au citoyen Camille Corona. Rome, 1798.
A letter signed by Talleyrand and dated Third Germinal, Year VI, congratulating the government of Rome in the name of the Directors.

Motion de M. l'évêque d'Autun sur les mandats impératifs. Paris, n.d.

Talleyrand's argument before the Assembly, on July 7, 1789, proposing the nullification of imperative mandates.

Motion de M. l'évêque d'Autun sur la proposition d'un emprunt faite à l'Assemblée nationale par le premier ministre des Finances, et sur la consolidation de la dette publique. Versailles, n.d.

Address of August 27, 1789, before the National Assembly, proposing proper measures to insure a loan to the state.

Motion de l'évêque d'Autun sur les biens ecclésiastiques. Versailles, n.d.

Talleyrand's address of October 10, 1789, proposing the confiscation by the state of ecclesiastical properties.

Opinion de M. l'évêque d'Autun sur les banques et sur le rétablissement de l'ordre dans les finances. Paris, 1789.

Talleyrand's report, on December 4, 1789, as examiner of the Bank of Discount.

Opinion de M. l'évêque d'Autun sur la fabrication des petites monnaies. Paris, n.d.

Talleyrand's address of December 12, 1790, on the recoinage of money.

Opinion de M. le prince de Talleyrand sur le projet d'adresse en réponse au discours du Roi. Paris, 1823.

The address, prepared for delivery on February 3, 1823, opposing the government's plans for war with Spain. (The address was never spoken, since debate was closured before Talleyrand was called. Nonetheless, it was printed in the records.)

Opinion de M. le prince duc de Talleyrand sur le projet de loi relatif à la répression des délits commis par la voie de la presse. Paris, 1822.

Talleyrand's argument before the Chamber of Peers, on February 26, 1822, against the Villèle government's proposed law depriving journalists and writers of trial by jury for offenses committed against the censorship laws.

Opinion de M. le prince de Talleyrand sur le projet de loi relatif aux journaux et écrits périodiques. Paris, 1821.

Talleyrand's famous address to the peers, on July 24, 1821, defending the freedom of the press against the government's proposed laws of censorship.

Opinion de M. le prince duc de Talleyrand sur le projet de loi relatif à la circonscription des arrondissements électoraux. Paris, 1821.

The argument of April 9, 1821, against the Richelieu government's proposed amendment of the franchise.

Opinion de M. le prince duc de Talleyrand sur une proposition de M. le comte Lanjuinais. Paris, n.d.

Talleyrand's address of December 26, 1820, regarding the duties and responsibilities of the Chamber of Peers.

Pétition de Maurice Talleyrand . . . à la Convention nationale. Paris, n.d.

The Philadelphia letter of 1795, to the National Convention, protesting Talleyrand's inclusion in the list of émigrés and requesting permission to return to France.

Le Prince de Talleyrand et la maison d'Orléans, Comtesse de Mirabeau, ed. Paris, 1890.

Talleyrand's correspondence with King Louis Philippe and Madame Adélaïde, 1830–1838.

Procès-verbal de l'Assemblée générale du clergé de France. M. l'abbé de Périgord, ancien agent-général, secrétaire de l'Assemblée. Paris, 1789.

Talleyrand's record of the proceedings of the Assembly of the Clergy of France of 1786, at which he was appointed secretary of the Assembly.

Projet des décrets sur l'instruction publique. Paris, 1791.

A draft of proposed laws implementing Talleyrand's *Report on Public Education.*

Rapport de l'agence contenant les principales affaires du clergé. Paris, 1788.

Talleyrand's report on the organization and goods of the church of France during the period 1780–1785, submitted by him, as agent-general of the clergy, in 1785. Though the document attributes authorship to "M. l'abbé de Périgord et M. l'abbé de Boisgelin"—Boisgelin being the other of the two agents-general—there is no doubt that the report is entirely the work of Talleyrand and that it was recognized as such at the time of its presentation.

Rapport fait au nom du Comité de constitution. Paris, n.d.

A report to the Assembly session of May 7, 1791, on a decree of the *département* of Paris, relative to religious freedom, of April 6, 1790.

Rapport fait au premier Consul, en Sénat. Paris, n.d.

Talleyrand's report to the First Consul on the settlement of indemnities with certain of the German states, delivered to the Senate in 1802.

Rapport sur l'instruction publique. Paris, 1791.

The famous *Report on Public Education*, presented on behalf of the Constitutional Committee of the National Assembly on September 10, 11, and 19, 1791.

Réponse de M. l'évêque d'Autun au Chapitre de l'Église Cathédrale d'Autun. Paris, 1790.

Talleyrand's justification, addressed to the chapter of the Cathedral of Autun, of the Assembly's decree of separation between church and state (April 12, 1790).

Talleyrand, ancien évêque d'Autun, à ses concitoyens. Paris, n.d.

Talleyrand's open letter to the National Convention, written from London on December 12, 1792, defending himself against the accusation of having conspired with Louis XVI against the people of France.

Talleyrand et Royer-Collard. Paris, 1927.

Unpublished correspondence, most of it not included in the collection edited by Paul Royer-Collard, between Talleyrand and Pierre-Paul Royer-Collard.

Talleyrand in America as a Financial Promoter, 1794–1796. Translated and edited by Hans Huth and Wilma Pugh. Washington, D.C., 1942.

Unpublished letters and other documents, by Talleyrand and others, concerning Talleyrand's commercial activities during his American exile.

Talleyrand intime d'après sa correspondance inédite avec la duchesse de Courlande. Paris, 1891.

A partial collection of Talleyrand's extensive correspondence with the Duchess of Courland.

II. Manuscripts, Published Documents, Letters, and Memoirs.

ABRANTÈS, DUCHESSE D', *Mémoires.* Paris, 1831–1838. 18 vols.

ALEXANDER OF RUSSIA, *Mémoires*, Countess Tisenhaus (Madame de Choiseul-Gouffier), ed. Paris, 1891. 3 vols.

ANGEBERG, COMTE D', *Le Congrès de Vienne et les traités de 1815,* Introduction by J.-B. Capefigue. Paris, 1864. 4 vols.

APPONYI, COMTE R., *Vingt-cinq ans à Paris: 1826–1850.* Paris, 1913–1926. 4 vols.

ARBLAY, MADAME D', *Diary and Letters.* London, 1846. 7 vols.

ARCHIVES DES AFFAIRES ÉTRANGÈRES:
   Correspondance politique: 363, 364, 586, 650, 651, 652.
   Mémoires et documents: 28, 32, 33, 320, 321, 650, 652, 655.

ARCHIVES NATIONALES:
   AF II: cts. 3, 9, 27, 77, 78, 212, 213, 214ᵃ.
   AF III: cts. 13, 15, 16, 23, 56, 57, 58, 60, 61, 69, 76, 77, 150ᵃ, 150ᵇ, 151ᵇ, 152ᵃ, 152ᵇ.

ARNAULT, A. V., *Souvenirs d'un sexagénaire.* Nouvelle édition. Paris, 1908.

AULARD, A., ed., *Recueil des actes du Comité de Salut Public avec la correspondance officielle des représentants en mission.* Paris, 1889–1950. 28 vols.

BACOURT, A. FOURIER DE, *Souvenirs d'un diplomate.* Paris, 1882.

BAILLEU, P., ed., *Preussen und Frankreich von 1795 bis 1807 Diplomatische Correspondenzen.* Leipzig, 1880–1887. 2 vols.

BARANTE, PROSPER DE, *Souvenirs, 1782–1866.* Paris, 1890–1901. 8 vols.

BARÈRE, B., *Mémoires.* Paris, 1895.

BARRAS, PAUL, VICOMTE DE, *Mémoires de Barras, membre du Directoire,* G. Duruy, ed. Paris, 1895–1896. 4 vols.

BEAUHARNAIS, PRINCE EUGÈNE DE, *Mémoires et correspondance politiques et militaires,* Vol. I. Paris, 1858.

BERTRAND, H. G., *Cahiers de Sainte-Hélène,* Paul Fleuriot de Langle, ed. Paris, 1949–1959. 2 vols.

BEUGNOT, COMTE CLAUDE, *Mémoires.* Paris, 1866. 2 vols.

BIANCHI, N., ed., *Storia documentata della diplomazia europea in Italia,* Vol. I. Turin, 1865.

BLANC, LOUIS, *Histoire de dix ans: 1830–1840.* Bruxelles, 1846.

BLESSINGTON, LADY, *The Idler in France.* Paris, 1841.

BOIGNE, COMTESSE DE, *Mémoires.* Paris, 1907. 3 vols.

BONAPARTE, NAPOLEON, *Correspondance inédite officielle et confidentielle de Napoléon Bonaparte.* Paris, 1819–1820. 7 vols.

BOURRIENNE, L. A. F. DE, *Mémoires de Napoléon Bonaparte.* Paris, 1830.

BRIFAUT, CHARLES, *Souvenirs d'un académicien sur la révolution, le premier empire et la restauration.* Paris, 1921.

British and Foreign State Papers, Vol. I, 1812–1814; Vol. II, 1814–1815. London, 1838–1841.

BROGLIE, DUC DE, *Mémoires, 1825–1870.* Paris, 1938.

———, *Souvenirs, 1781–1870.* Paris, 1886.

CAMPAN, MADAME, *Journal anecdotique.* Paris, 1824.

CASTELLANE, BONIFACE DE, *Journal du Maréchal de Castellane,* Vol. I. Paris, 1896.

CASTLEREAGH, VISCOUNT, *Correspondence,* edited by his brother, Vols. IX, X, and XI. London, 1852.

CAULAINCOURT, A. DE, *Mémoires du Général de Caulaincourt, Duc de Vicence,* edited, with an introduction and notes by Jean Hanoteau. Paris, 1933. 3 vols.

CHAMPAGNY, JEAN-BAPTISTE, COMTE DE, *Souvenirs.* Paris, 1846.

CHASTENAY, VICTORINE, COMTESSE DE, *Mémoires, 1771–1815.* Paris, 1896. 2 vols.

CHATEAUBRIAND, FRANÇOIS-RENÉ DE, *Mémoires d'outre-tombe.* Paris, 1948. 4 vols.

CLERCQ, A., ed., *Recueil des traités de la France.* Paris, 1864–1900. 21 vols.

COIGNY, AIMÉE DE, *Mémoires*. Paris, 1902.

CONSTANT (LOUIS-CONSTANT WAIRY), *Mémoires de Constant, premier valet de chambre de l'empereur, sur la vie privée de Napoléon*. Paris, 1830.

Corrispondenza inedita dei cardinali Consalvi e Pacca, G. Rinieri, ed. Turin, 1903.

Creevey Papers, The, Sir H. Maxwell, ed., London, 1903.

CZARTORYSKI, ADAM, *Mémoires*, Vol. II. Paris, 1887.

DALBERG, DUC DE, "Lettres inédites de Dalberg à Talleyrand," in *Revue d'histoire diplomatique*, avril–juin, 1937.

DEBIDOUR, A., ed., *Recueil des actes du Directoire exécutif*. Paris, 1910. 4 vols.

DINO, DUCHESSE DE, *Chroniques de 1831 à 1862*. Paris, 1909. 4 vols.

———, "Lettres à Adolphe Thiers," in *Revue de Paris*, juillet–août, 1923.

———, "Lettres à Madame Adélaïde," in *Nouvelle revue rétrospective*. Paris, 1901–1902.

———, "Lettres au comte Molé, 1830–1851," in *Revue d'histoire diplomatique*. Paris, juillet–decembre, 1947.

———, "Lettre à Talleyrand," in *L'Amateur d'autographes*, nouvelle série, Paris, 1909.

———, "Lettres à Vitrolles," in *La Duchesse de Dino et le Baron de Vitrolles: lettres inédites, 1817–1829*, by Louis Royer. Grenoble, 1937.

———, *Notice sur Valençay*. Paris, 1848.

———, *Souvenirs de la Duchesse de Dino, publiés par la comtesse Jean de Castellane*. Paris, 1908.

DUQUESNOY, ADRIEN, *Journal sur l'Assemblée constituante*. Paris, 1894.

ELLIOT, GRACE DALRYMPLE, *Journal of My Life During the French Revolution*. London, 1859.

FOUCHÉ, JOSEPH, *Mémoires*. Paris, 1945.

GAGERN, FREIHERR H. C. W. VON, *Mein Antheil an der Politik*. Stuttgart, Tübingen and Leipzig, 1823–1845. 5 vols.

GENLIS, MADAME DE, *Mémoires*. Préface de Lucas Dubreton. Paris, 1892. 2 vols.

GENTZ, F. VON, *Briefe an Pilat*. Leipzig, 1868. 2 vols.

———, *Dépêches inédites aux Hospodars de Valachie*, Vol. I. Paris, 1876.

GIRARDIN, STANISLAS DE, *Discours et opinions, journal et souvenirs*. Paris, 1828.

GOHIER, LOUIS-JÉRÔME, *Mémoires de Louis-Jérôme Gohier, président du Directoire au 18 brumaire*. Paris, 1824.

GREVILLE, HENRY, *Leaves from the Diary of Henry Greville*, Viscountess Enfield, ed. London. 1883–1905. 8 vols.

GRIOIS, GENERAL, *Mémoires, 1792–1822*. Paris, 1909. 2 vols.

GUIZOT, FRANÇOIS-PIERRE. *Mémoires pour servir à l'histoire de mon temps*, Vol. IV (*Talleyrand après Waterloo*). Paris, 1858.

HAUTERIVE, COMTE D', *Histoire de la vie et des travaux politiques du comte d'Hauterive*. Paris, 1839.

HOLLAND, LORD HENRY RICHARD, *Foreign Reminiscences*, 2d ed. London, 1851.

HOLLAND, LADY ELIZABETH, *Lady Holland to Her Son, 1821–1845*. London, 1946.

HORTENSE, QUEEN OF HOLLAND, *Mémoires de la reine Hortense*. Prince Napoleon, ed. Paris, 1927.

HYDE DE NEUVILLE, BARON, *Mémoires et souvenirs*. Paris, 1888–1892.

JACKSON, SIR GEORGE, *Diaries and Letters*, Lady Jackson, ed., Vol. II. London, 1873.

KIELMANNSEGGE, GRÄFIN, *Memorien der Gräfin Kielmannsegge über Napoleon I*. Dresden, 1927. 2 vols.

KLÜBER, J. L., *Acten des Wiener Congresses.* Erlanger, 1817–1835. 9 vols.

LA GARDE-CHAMBONAS, AUGUSTE, COMTE DE, *Fêtes et souvenirs du congrès de Vienne.* Paris, 1843. 2 vols.

LAMARTINE, A. DE, *Oeuvres complètes,* Vols. XXXVII–XL *(Mémoires politiques).* Paris, 1860–1869.

LAREVELLIÈRE-LÉPAUX, LOUIS-MARIE, *Mémoires.* Paris, 1873.

LAS CASES, E. A. D., *Mémorial de Ste. Hélène.* Paris, 1823.

LA TOUR DU PIN-GOUVERNET, MARQUISE DE, *Journal d'une femme de cinquante ans.* Paris, 1907–1911. 2 vols.

LAUZUN, DUC DE, *Correspondance intime du duc de Lauzun.* Comte de Lort de Sérignan, ed. Paris, 1906.

LICHNOWSKY, PRINCE FÉLIX, *Souvenirs.* Paris, 1844.

LIEVEN, PRINCESS, *Correspondence of Princess Lieven and Lord Grey, 1824–1841.* London, 1890. 3 vols.

———, "Lettres à M. de Bacourt," in *Le Correspondant,* août, 1893.

———, *Private Letters,* Peter Quennell, ed. London, 1937.

MACDONALD, MARÉCHAL, *Souvenirs du Maréchal Macdonald, Duc de Tarente.* Paris, 1893.

MALOUET, BARON DE, *Mémoires de Malouet.* Paris, 1868.

MARIGNY, MADAME DE, and UNDERWOOD, T. R., *Paris en 1814.* Paris, 1907.

MARTENS, F., ed., *Recueil des traités et conventions conclus par la Russie avec les puissances étrangères,* Vols. III, IV, VII, XI, XIV. St. Petersburg, 1875ff.

MARTENS, G. F., ed., *Nouveau recueil de traités d'alliance, de paix . . . conclus par les puissances et états de l'Europe.* Göttingen, 1817–1841. 16 vols.

———, ed., *Recueil des principaux traités d'alliance, de paix . . . conclus par les puissances de l'Europe.* Göttingen, 1817–1835. 8 vols.

MÉNEVAL, CLAUDE-FRANÇOIS, Baron de, *Mémoires pour servir à l'histoire de Napoléon I.* Paris, 1894.

METTERNICH-WINNEBURG, PRINCE C. W. N. L., *Mémoires, documents et écrits divers laissés par le prince de Metternich,* Vols. I and II. Paris, 1880.

———, *Lettres à la princesse de Lieven,* J. Hanoteau, ed. Paris, 1909.

MIOT DE MELITO, ANDRÉ-FRANÇOIS, COMTE DE, *Mémoires.* General Fleishmann, ed. Paris, 1881.

MIRABEAU, HONORÉ-GABRIEL RIQUETTI, MARQUIS DE, *Souvenirs de Mirabeau.* Étienne Dumont, ed. Paris, 1833.

MOLÉ, COUNT, *Mémoires du comte Molé,* Marquis de Noailles, ed. Paris, 1822–1830. 6 vols.

"Monseigneur de Quelen et la conversion de Talleyrand: documents inédites," in *Bulletin de littérature ecclésiastique,* no. 3, juillet–septembre, 1957.

MONTCALM, MARQUISE DE, *Mon journal (1815–1819) pendant le premier ministère de mon frère.* Paris, 1935.

MONTGAILLARD, J. G., COMTE DE. *Souvenirs du comte de Montgaillard, agent de la diplomatie secrète pendant la Révolution, l'Empire, et la Restauration.* Corbeil, 1895.

MURHARD, F., ed., *Nouveaux suppléments au recueil des traités et autres actes remarquables des puissances . . . depuis 1761 jusqu'à nos jours.* Göttingen, 1839. 3 vols.

MOREAU DE ST.-MÉRY. *Voyage aux États-Unis d'Amérique, 1793–1798,* S. L. Mims, ed. New Haven, 1913.

MORRIS, GOUVERNEUR, *The Diary and Letters of Gouverneur Morris*. New York, 1888.

NABONNE, B., ed., *La Diplomatie du Directoire et Bonaparte d'après les papiers inédites de Reubell*. Paris, 1951.

NAPOLÉON I, *Correspondance de Napoléon I, publiée par ordre de l'empereur Napoléon III*, H. Plon and J. Dumaine, eds. Paris, 1858–1870. 32 vols.

———, *Correspondance militaire de Napoléon I*. Paris, 1883. 32 vols.

NESSELRODE, CHARLES R., *Lettres et papiers du chancelier comte de Nesselrode*. Paris, 1908–1912. 11 vols.

NEUMANN, L., ed., *Recueil des traités et conventions conclus par l'Autriche avec les puissances étrangères depuis 1763 jusqu'à nos jours*. Leipzig, 1855. 32 vols.

O'MEARA, B. E., *Napoleon in Exile: or, a Voice from St. Helena*. New York, 1853.

ORLÉANS, DUC D', *Lettres, 1825–1842*. Paris, 1889.

ORLÉANS, LOUISE-MARIE D', *Lettres intimes*. Paris, 1933.

ORLÉANS, MARIE-AMÉLIE D', *Journal de Marie-Amélie, duchesse d'Orléans*. Paris, 1938. 3 vols.

OUVRARD, G.-J. *Mémoires*. Paris, 1826–1827. 2 vols.

PASQUIER, ÉTIENNE-DENIS, DUC DE, *Histoire de mon temps*. Paris, 1893–1895. 6 vols.

PITT, W., *The Speeches of the Right Honourable William Pitt in the House of Commons*. London, 1806. 4 vols.

POTOCKA, COUNTESS, *Mémoires*. C. Stryienski, ed. Paris, 1897.

RAIKES, ROBERT, *A Portion of the Journal kept by Robert Raikes, Esq., 1831–1847*. London, 1856–1858. 4 vols.

Réimpression de l'ancien Moniteur. Paris, 1847. 31 vols.

RÉMUSAT, CHARLES DE, *Correspondance de M. de Rémusat*. Paris, 1884–1886. 6 vols.

———, *Mémoires de ma vie*. Paris, 1958–1962. 4 vols.

RÉMUSAT, CLAIRE DE VERGENNES, COMTESSE DE, *Lettres de Madame de Rémusat, 1804–1814*. Paris, 1881.

———, *Mémoires, 1802–1808*. Paris, 1880.

ROEDERER, P. L., *Autour de Bonaparte: Journal du Comte P. L. Roederer*. Paris, 1909.

———, *Mémoires de la Révolution, le Consulat et l'Empire*. Paris, 1942.

ROVIGO, DUC DE, *Mémoires du duc de Rovigo (M. Savary)*. Paris, 1828. 9 vols.

SÉGUR, GENERAL COMTE PHILIPPE-PAUL, *Histoire et mémoires*. Paris, 1894–1895. 4 vols.

SHELLEY, LADY FRANCES, *The Diary of Lady Frances Shelley*, R. Edgcumbe, ed. London, 1912–1913. 2 vols.

THIBAUDEAU, A. C., *Mémoires, 1799–1815*. Paris, 1913.

———, *Mémoires sur la convention et le directoire*. Paris, 1824.

———, *Mémoires sur le consulat*. Paris, 1827.

THIÉBAULT, BARON PAUL, *Mémoires du général baron Thiébault, 1792–1820*. Paris, 1962.

VILLÈLE, COMTE DE, *Mémoires et correspondance*. Paris, 1888–1890. 4 vols.

VITROLLES, BARON DE, *Mémoires et relations politiques*. Paris, 1884. 2 vols.

WEIL, M. H., *Les Dessous du congrès de Vienne*. Paris, 1917. 2 vols.

WELLINGTON, FIELD-MARSHAL, THE DUKE OF, *Despatches*, Colonel Gurwood, ed., Vol. XII. London, 1847.

———, *Supplementary Despatches, Correspondence, and Memoranda*, edited by his sons, Vols. VIII, IX, X, and XI. London, 1860–1864.

III. Secondary Works (Selected List)

ACTON, H., *The Bourbons of Naples (1734–1825)*. London, 1956.
ACTON, LORD, "Essay on the *Mémoires* of Talleyrand," in *Historical Essays*. London, 1906.
ADAMS, E. D., *The Influence of Grenville on Pitt's Foreign Policy, 1787–1798*. Washington, 1904.
ALISON, SIR A., *Lives of Lord Castlereagh and Sir Charles Stewart*. London, 1861. 3 vols.
ANDERSON, M. S., *Europe in the Eighteenth Century, 1713–1783*. New York, 1961.
ANSCHÜTZ, G. and THOMAS R., *Handbuch des deutschen Staatsrecht*. Tübingen, 1930–1932.
ANTOINE, A., *Histoire des émigrés français depuis 1789 jusqu'en 1828*. Paris, 1828. 3 vols.
ARRIGON, L. J., "La Duchesse de Dino et la fin de Talleyrand," in *Revue des deux mondes*, mars–avril, 1955.
———, *Une amie de Talleyrand: la duchesse de Courlande*. Paris, 1945.
ATTERIDGE, A. HILLIARD, *Joachim Murat*. London, 1911.
AUCKLAND, LORD, *Journal and Correspondence*. London, 1862.
AUJAY, ÉDOUARD, *Talleyrand*. Paris, 1946.
AULARD, A., *Histoire politique de la Révolution française*. 5ᵉ ed. Paris, 1921.
———, *Paris sous le Directoire*. Paris, 1923.
BAC, FERDINAND, *Le Secret de Talleyrand d'après des témoignages contemporains*. Paris, 1933.
BASILY, CALLIMAKI, MADAME DE, *J.-B. Isabey, sa vie et son temps*. Paris, 1909.
BASTIDE, LOUIS, *Vie politique et religieuse de Talleyrand-Périgord*. Paris, 1838.
BERNARD, J. F., *Up from Caesar*. New York, 1970.
BERNARDY, FRANÇOISE DE, *Talleyrand's Last Duchess*, trans. by Derek Colman. New York, 1966.
BERNHARDI, T. VON, *Geschichte Russlands und der Europäischen Politik im XIXten Jahrhundert*, Vol. I. Leipzig, 1863.
BERTAUD, J., *Talleyrand*. Lyons, 1946.
BERTIER DE SAUVIGNY, G. DE, *Metternich et son temps*. Paris, 1959.
———, *France and the European Alliance*. Notre Dame, Indiana, 1958.
BERTUCH, CARL, *Tagebuch von Wiener Kongress*. Berlin, 1916.
BIBL, VIKTOR, *François II*. Paris, 1936.
BLEI, FRANZ, *Talleyrand, homme d'état*, traduit de l'allemand par René Lobstein. Paris, 1935.
BLENNERHASSET, LADY, *Talleyrand: eine Studie*. Berlin, 1894.
BLINN, H. E., "New Light on Talleyrand at the Congress of Vienna," *Pacific Historical Review*, Vol. IV, p. 143.
BOULAY DE LA MEURTHE, A., *Le Directoire et l'expédition d'Egypte*. Paris, 1921.
———, *Histoire de la négotiation du concordat de 1801*. Tours, 1920.
———, *Histoire du rétablissement du culte en France*. Tours, 1925.
———, *Les justifications de Talleyrand pendant le Directoire*. Angers, 1889.
BOURGEOIS, E., *Manuel historique de politique étrangère*. Paris, 1945–1949. 4 vols. (New edition.)
BOUTET DE MONVEL, ROBERT, *Les Anglais à Paris: 1800–1850*. Paris, 1911.
BRETT-JAMES, A., *1812: Eyewitness Accounts of Napoleon's Defeat in Russia*. New York, 1966.

BRIAN-CHANINOV, J., "Alexandre Ier et la paix," in *Revue d'histoire diplomatique*, XLVII, 1933.

BRINTON, CRANE, *The Jacobins*. New York, 1930.

———, *The Lives of Talleyrand*. New York, 1936.

BRUNN, GEOFFREY, *Europe and the French Imperium*. New York, 1938.

BUCKLAND, C. S. B., *Friedrich von Gentz's Relations with the British Government*. London, 1934.

———, *Metternich and the British Government*. London, 1932.

BURKE, EDMUND, *Reflections on the Revolution in France*, E. J. Payne, ed. Oxford, 1896.

BURNEY, MISS FANNY, *The Diary of Fanny Burney*, Lewis Gibbs, ed. London, 1950.

BUTTERFIELD, H., *The Peace Tactics of Napoleon, 1806–1808*. Cambridge, 1929.

CAMBON, J., *Le Diplomate*. Paris, 1931.

Cambridge Modern History, Vol. IX, *Napoleon*. Cambridge, 1906.

CAMON, H., *La Guerre napoléonienne*. Paris, 1903.

CAPEFIGUE, L., *Diplomates européens*. Paris, 1843.

———, *Histoire de la Restauration*, Vol. I. Paris, 1942.

CARION, HENRI, *La Mort d'un grand coupable*. Paris, 1938.

CASTELOT, ANDRÉ, *Napoléon*. Paris, 1971.

CASTELLANE, JEAN DE, *Talleyrand*. Paris, 1934.

CASTELNAU, J., *Madame Tallien*. Paris, 1937.

CASTILLE, HIPPOLYTE, *Talleyrand*. Paris, n.d.

CECIL, A., *Metternich, 1773–1859*. New York, 1933.

CHABROL, G., *Recherches statistiques sur la ville de Paris*. Paris, 1821.

CHANDLER, D. G., *The Campaigns of Napoleon*. New York, 1966.

CHARLES-ROUX, F., *Les Origines de l'expédition d'Egypte*. Paris, 1910.

CHRIST, YVAN, *Le Louvre et les Tuileries*. Paris, 1949.

CHUQUET, A., *Dumouriez*. Paris, 1914.

COBBAN, ALFRED, *Aspects of the French Revolution*. New York, 1968.

COLMACHE, M., *Reminiscences of Prince Talleyrand*. London, 1843. 2 vols.

COMBALUZIER, F., "Le Sacre episcopal de . . . Charles-Maurice de Talleyrand-Périgord, évêque d'Autun, 4 janvier 1789," in *Ami Clerge*, 1967.

CONNELLY, O., *Napoleon's Satellite Kingdoms*. New York, 1965.

COOPER, DUFF, *Talleyrand*. London, 1932.

COUDRAY, R. DU, *Metternich*. London, 1935.

CROZET, R., *Le Château de Valençay*. Paris, 1930.

DARD, EMILE, *Le Comte de Narbonne*. Paris, 1943.

———, *Dans l'Entourage de l'Empereur*. Paris, 1940.

———, *Napoléon et Talleyrand*. Paris, 1935.

DAUDET, E., *Les Émigrés et la Seconde Coalition*. Paris, 1886.

———, *La Princesse de Lieven*. Paris, 1903.

DE CONDE, A., *Entangling Alliance Politics and Diplomacy under George Washington*. Durham, N.C., 1958.

DESCHAMPES, J., *Les Îles britanniques et la Révolution française*. Paris, 1949.

DESLANDRES, M., *Histoire constitutionelle de la France: 1789–1870*. Paris, 1932–1933. 2 vols.

DESTREM, J. *Les Déportations du Consulat et de l'Empire*. Paris, 1885.

DEUTSCH, H., *The Genesis of Napoleonic Imperialism*. Cambridge, Mass., 1938.

DODD, ANNA BOWMAN, *Talleyrand*. New York, 1927.

DODGE, T., *Napoleon*. Boston, 1904, 4 vols.

DONTENVILLE, J., "La Catastrophe du duc d'Enghien," in *Revue des études napoléoniennes*, Vol. XXV, pp. 43–69.

DRIAULT, E., *La Chute de l'Empire*. Paris, 1927.

———, *Le Grand Empire*. Paris, 1924.

———, *Napoléon le Grand*. Paris, 1930. 3 vols.

———, "La Politique Extérieure de Napoléon I," in *Revue des études napoléoniennes*, Vol. VII, 1915.

DROZ, J., *L'Allemagne et la Révolution française*. Paris, 1949.

DUANA, M., "Napoléon et le système continental en 1810," in *Revue d'histoire diplomatique*, Vol. LX, 1946.

DUFOUR DE LA THUILERIE, SOSTHÈNE, *Histoire de la vie et de la mort de M. de Talleyrand-Périgord*. Paris, 1838.

DUNAN, MARCEL, et al., *Napoléon et l'Europe*. Paris, 1961.

DUPUIS, C., *Le Ministère de Talleyrand en 1814*. Paris, 1919–1920. 2 vols.

DUVERGIER DE Hauvanne, P., *Histoire du gouvernement parlementaire en France, 1814–1848*, Vol. I. Paris, 1857.

DYSSORD, J., *Les Belles Amies de M. de Talleyrand*. Paris, 1942.

EARL, J. L., "Talleyrand in Philadelphia, 1794–1796," in *Pennsylvania Magazine*, Vol. IX, No. 3, 1967.

EGRET, J., *La Pré-Révolution française, 1787–1788*. Paris, 1962.

ESPOSITO, V., and ELTING, J., *A Military History and Atlas of the Napoleonic Wars*. New York, 1959.

FABRE-LUCE, ALFRED, *Talleyrand*. Paris, 1969.

FAURE, ÉLIE, *Napoléon*. Paris, 1924.

FERRERO, GUGLIELMO, *The Reconstruction of Europe*, trans. by T. Jaekel. New York, 1961.

FERVAL, J., *Campagne de la Révolution française dans les Pyrénées orientales*. Paris, 1851–1853. 2 vols.

FISHER, H., *Napoleon*. London, 1913.

———, *Studies in Napoleonic Statesmanship: Germany*. London, 1903.

FLEURY, SERGE, *Talleyrand: maître souverain de la diplomatie*. Montreal, 1942.

FORNERON, H., *Histoire générale des émigrés*. Paris, 1887. 3 vols.

FOURNIER, A., *Der Congress von Châtillon*. Leipzig, Vienna and Prague, 1900.

———, *Die Geheimpolizei auf dem Wiener Kongress*. Vienna and Leipzig, 1913.

———, *Historische Studien und Skizzen*, 2d. ed. Vienna and Leipzig, 1908.

———, *Napoleon I, eine Biographie*. Vienna, 1886–1889. 3 vols.

FRANCIS, SIR PHILIP, *Memoirs*. London, 1867. 2 vols.

FRANZ, G., et al., *Bücherkunde zur Weltgeschichte*. Munich, 1956.

FUGIER, A., *Histoire des relations internationales: la Révolution française et l'Empire napoléonien*. Paris, 1954.

———, *Napoléon et l'Espagne*. Paris, 1930. 2 vols.

FUNCK-BRENTANO, F., *The Old Regime in France*. New York, 1929.

GAEVELLE, Y. R., *Vie de la princesse de Talleyrand*. Paris, 1948.

GAJE, J. A. DE ARAUJO, *Talleyrand et les négociations secrètes pour la paix de Portugal, 1798–1800*. Paris, 1950.

GEER, W., *Napoleon and His Family*. New York, 1927–1929. 3 vols.

GERSHOY, L., *The French Revolution and Napoleon*. New York, 1932.

GODECHOT, J., *La Grande Nation*. Paris, 1956. 2 vols.

———, *Les Institutions de la France sous la Révolution et l'Empire*. Paris, 1951.

GOOCH, G. P., *Germany and the French Revolution*. London, 1920.

——, and WARD, A. W., *Cambridge History of British Foreign Policy, 1789–1919*, Vol. I. Cambridge, 1922.

GOODWIN A., *The European Nobility in the Eighteenth Century*. London, 1953.

——, "Calonne, the Assembly of Notables and the Origins of the Révolte Nobiliaire," in *English Historical Review*, 1946, pp. 203–234, 329–377.

GOTTSCHALK, L. R., *The Era of the French Revolution, 1715–1815*. Boston, 1929.

GRANDMAISON, GEOFFROY DE, *L'Espagne et Napoléon*. Paris, 1908–1931. 3 vols.

——, "Les Princes d'Espagne à Valençay," in *Le Correspondant*, 25 mai 1900.

GREER, D., *The Incidence of the Emigration during the French Revolution*. Cambridge, 1935.

——, *The Incidence of the Terror during the French Revolution*. Cambridge, 1953.

GRIEWANK, K., *Der Wiener Kongress und die Neueordnung Europas*. Leipzig, 1942.

GRUNWALD, CONSTANTIN DE, *Metternich*. Paris, 1938.

GRUYER, PAUL, *Napoléon, roi de l'Île d'Elbe*. Paris, 1906.

GUEDALLA, P., *Wellington*. New York, 1930.

GULIC, E. V., *Europe's Classical Balance of Power*. London, 1956.

GUYOMARD, Y., *Le Secret de Talleyrand*. Cherbourg, 1934.

GUYOT, RAYMOND, *Le Directoire et la paix de l'Europe*. Paris, 1912.

——, *Du Directoire au Consulat*. Paris, 1912.

——, "Madame Grand à Paris," in *Feuilles d'histoire*, Vol. I, 1909.

——, *Projet de Talleyrand à la conférence de Londres, 16 janvier 1831*. Paris, 1907.

HANDELSMAN, M., "Napoléon et la Pologne," in *Revue des études napoléoniennes*, 1914, Vol. V.

HARDMAN, A., *Napoléon et la Pologne, 1806–1807*. Paris, 1909.

HARTMANN, L., *Les Officiers de l'armée royale et la Révolution*. Paris, 1910.

HAUTERIVE, E. D', *La Police secrète du premier empire*. Paris, 1908–1922. 3 vols.

——, *Le Contre police royaliste en 1800*. Paris, 1931.

HAWGOOD, J. A., *Modern Constitutions since 1787*. London, 1939.

HAYDEN, H. E., *French Revolutionary Pamphlets: a Check List of the Talleyrand and Other Collections*. New York, 1945.

HAZEN, CHARLES D., *The French Revolution and Napoleon*. New York, 1917.

HECKSCHER, E. F., *The Continental System: An Economic Interpretation*. London, 1922.

HERMAN, ARTHUR, *Metternich*. London, 1923.

HEROLD, J. C., *The Age of Napoleon*. New York, 1963.

——, *Mistress to an Age: A Life of Madame de Staël*. New York, 1958.

HERR, R., *The Eighteenth Century Revolution in Spain*. Princeton, N.J., 1958.

HEYMAN, N. M., "France Against Prussia: The Jena Campaign of 1806," in *Military Affairs*, 1966–1967, Vol. XXX.

HOBSBAWM, E. J., *The Age of Revolution: Europe, 1789–1848*. New York, 1962.

HILL, H. B., "The Constitutions of Modern Europe, 1789–1813," in *Journal of Modern History*, 1939, Vol. VIII, pp. 82–94.

HOLBORN, H. *A History of Modern Germany, 1648–1840*. New York, 1966.

HOLTMAN, R. B., *Napoleonic Propaganda*. Baton Rouge, La., 1950.

HOUSSAYE, HENRI, *1814*. Paris, 1888.

——, *1815*. Paris, 1898–1925. 3 vols.

HANOTEAU, J., "La Transformation sociale à l'époque napoléonienne," in *Revue des deux mondes*, Vol. XXIII, 1926.

JAURÈS, J., et al., *Histoire socialiste de la Révolution française*. Paris, 1901–1905. 4 vols.

JOELSON, ANNETTE, *Courtesan Princess: Catherine Grand, Princesse de Talleyrand.* Philadelphia, 1965.

KISSINGER, HENRY *A World Restored: Metternich, Castlereagh, and the Problems of Peace, 1815–1822.* London, 1958.

KLINKOWSTRÖM, A. F. VON, *Oesterreichs Theilnahme an den Befreiungskriegen.* Vienna, 1887.

KLUCHEVSKY, V. O., *A History of Russia,* trans. by C. J. Hogarth, Vol. V. London, 1931.

KORNILOV, A. A., *Modern Russian History from the Age of Catherine the Great to the Present,* rev. ed. New York, 1924.

KRAFT, J., *Prinzipien Talleyrand in der Aussen- und Innenpolitik.* Bonn, 1958.

KUSCINSKI, A., *Les Députés à l'Assemblée législative.* Paris, 1900.

LABROUSSE, C. E., *La Crise de l'economie française à la fin de l'ancien régime et au début de la Révolution.* Paris, 1944.

LACOMBE, BERNARD DE, *La Vie privée de Talleyrand.* Nouvelle édition. Paris, 1933.

LACOUR-GAYET, GEORGES, *Comment on devenait ministre sous le Directoire.* Paris, 1926.

———, "L'Enfance de Talleyrand," in *Revue de Paris,* 16 août 1926.

———, "Napoléon à Fontainebleau en 1814," in *Revue des études napoléoniennes,* 1922, Vol. XIX.

———, *Talleyrand.* Paris, 1928–1934. 4 vols.

———, *Talleyrand et la Pologne.* Paris, 1927.

LACRETELLE, J. DE, et al., *Talleyrand.* Paris, 1964.

LACROIX, PAUL, *Directoire, Consulat et Empire.* Paris, 1884.

LAFOURGUE, RENÉ, *Talleyrand, l'homme de la France.* Geneva, 1947.

LAJUSAN, M., "La Deuxième et Dernière Phase de la catastrophe napoléonienne, 1814–1815," in *Bulletin de la Société d'histoire moderne,* juin–juillet, 1952.

LANZAC DE LABORIE, L. DE, *Paris sous Napoléon.* Paris, 1905–1913. 8 vols.

LARIVIÈRE, C. DE, *Cathérine II et la Révolution française.* Paris, 1895.

LATOUCHE, HENRI DE, *L'Album perdu.* Paris, 1829.

LATREILLE, A., *L'Église catholique et la Révolution française.* Paris, n.d.

LEBON, A., *L'Angleterre et l'émigration française de 1794–1801.* Paris, 1882.

LEFEBVRE, A., *Histoire des cabinets de l'Europe pendant le Consulat et l'Empire.* Paris, 1845–1847. 3 vols.

LEFEBVRE, GEORGES, *Napoléon.* 4eme ed. Paris, 1953.

———, *La Révolution française.* 3eme ed. Paris, 1951.

———, *Quatre-Vingt-Neuf.* Paris, 1939.

———, *Les Thermidoriens.* 4eme ed. Paris, 1960.

———, *Le Directoire.* Paris, 1946.

LENOTRE, G., *Paris révolutionnaire.* Paris, 1894.

LESOURD, P., *L'Âme de Talleyrand.* Paris, 1942.

LEMMI, F., and FIORNI, V., *Storia d'Italia dal 1799 al 1814.* Milan, 1918.

LIMOUSIN-LAMOTHE, R., "La Rétractation de Talleyrand," in *Revue d'histoire de l'église de France,* Vol. LX, juillet–decembre, 1954.

LOBANOV-ROSTOVSKY, A., *Russia and Europe, 1789–1825.* Durham, N.C., 1947.

LOCKHART, J. G., *The Peacemakers, 1814–1815.* London, 1932.

LOKKE, C. L., "Secret Negotiations to Maintain the Peace of Amiens," in *American Historical Review,* Vol. XLIX, No. 1, October, 1943.

LONGFORD, ELIZABETH, *Wellington: The Years of the Sword.* New York, 1970.

LOTH, A., "Talleyrand et l'église constitutionnelle de France," in *Revue anglo-romaine*, Vol. X, 1896.

LOVETT, G. H., *Napoleon and the Birth of Modern Spain*. New York, 1965. 2 vols.

LUDWIG, EMIL, *Napoleon*. New York, 1926.

LUTOSTANSKI, K., *Les Partages de la Pologne*. Lausanne, 1918.

MACCABE, JOSEPH, *Talleyrand*. London, 1906.

MADELIN, LOUIS, *Le Consulat et l'Empire*. Paris, 1932–1954. 16 vols.

———, *Fouché, 1750–1820*. Two vols. 1900.

———, *Talleyrand*. Paris, 1944.

MADOL, HENRI, *Le Beau Montrond*. Paris, 1926.

MANN, G., *Secretary of Europe: the Life of Friedrich Gentz*. New Haven, 1946.

MASSON, F., *Le Département des Affaires étrangères pendant la Révolution*. Paris, 1889.

———, *Les Diplomates de la Révolution*. Paris, 1882.

MATHIEZ, A., *La Réaction thermidorienne*. Paris, 1929.

———, "La Réforme de la Constitution de l'an III après le coup d'état du 18 Fructidor," in *Annales historiques de la Révolution française*, Vol. VI, 1929.

———, *Les Grandes Journées de la Constituante: 1789–1791*. Paris, 1913.

———, *Rome et le clergé français sous la Constituante*. Paris, 1910.

MENTIENNE, M., *Histoire de deux portefeuilles de ministre du temps de la grande Révolution française . . .* Paris, 1924.

MICHAUD, L. G., *Histoire politique et privée de Charles de Talleyrand, ancien évêque d'Autun*. Paris, 1853.

MIKHAILOVITCH, LE GRAND DUC NIICOLAS, *L'Empereur Alexander Ier*. St. Petersburg, 1912. 2 vols.

MISSOFFE, MICHEL, *Le Coeur secret de Talleyrand*. Paris, 1956.

MORAN, C., *Black Triumvirate*. New York, 1957.

MORTON, J. B., *Brumaire: the Rise of Bonaparte*. London, 1948.

MOSSIKER, FRANCES, *Napoleon and Josephine*. New York, 1964.

MOWAT, R. B., *The Diplomacy of Napoleon*. London, 1924.

MÜNSTER, E. F. H., *Political Sketches of the State of Europe, 1814–1867*. Edinburgh, 1868. Revised and expanded version of the German edition of 1867.

NABONNE, B., *La Diplomatie du Directoire et Bonaparte*. Paris, 1951.

NICOLSON, H., *The Congress of Vienna*. London, 1946.

NOAILLES, MARQUIS DE, *Le Comte Molé*. Paris, 1922–1930. 6 vols.

NUSSBAUM, F. L., *Commercial Policy in the French Revolution*. Washington, D.C., 1923.

OLDEN, P. H., *Napoleon und Talleyrand*. Berlin, n.d.

OLLIVIER, A., *Le 18 Brumaire*. Paris, 1959.

OMAN, C., *A History of the Peninsular War*. Oxford, 1902–1930. 8 vols.

ONCKEN, W., *Das Zeitalter der Revolution, des Kaiserreichs und der Befreiungskreige*, Vol. II. Berlin, 1887.

———, "Lord Castlereagh und die Ministerconferenz zu Langres am 29 Januar, 1814," in *Raumers Historisches Taschenbuch*, Vol. VI, No. 3, Leipzig, 1884.

———, "Die Krisis der letzten Friedenverhandlung mit Napoleon I," in *Raumers Historisches Taschenbuch*, Vol. VI, No. 5, Leipzig, 1886.

ORIEUX, JEAN, *Talleyrand, ou le Sphinx incompris*. Paris, 1970.

PALÉOLOGUE, MAURICE, *Talleyrand, Metternich, et Chateaubriand*. Paris, 1924.

PALMER, A., *Napoleon in Russia*. New York, 1967.

PALMER, R., "Fifty Years of the Committee of Public Safety," in *Journal of Modern History*," 1941, Vol. XIII.

PARES, R., *King George III and the Politicians*. London, 1953.

PARISET, G., *Le Consulat et l'Empire*, Vol. III of *Histoire de France contemporaine*, E. Lavisse, ed. Paris, 1921.

PETRIE, SIR CHARLES, *Lord Liverpool and His Times*. London, 1954.

PHILLIPS, W. ALISON, *The Confederation of Europe*. London, 1914.

PICHEVIN, R., *L'Impératrice Joséphine*. Paris, 1909.

PLACE, CHARLES, and FLORENS, J., *Mémoire sur M. de Talleyrand, sa vie politique et sa vie intime* . . . Paris, 1838.

PONIATOWSKI, MICHEL, *Talleyrand aux États-Unis, 1794–1796*. Paris, 1967.

PORDEA, G. A., *Talleyrand et la couronne d'Espagne*. Bayonne, 1967.

RAIN, P., *L'Europe et la Restauration des Bourbons*. Paris, 1905.

———, *La Diplomatie française de Mirabeau à Bonaparte*. Paris, 1950.

RAMBAUD, A. N., *Popular History of Russia from the Earliest Times*, New ed. New York, 1904. 2 vols.

RAOUL DE SCEAU, PÈRE, *Guide historique de Valençay*. Châteauroux, n.d.

REINHARD, M., *Avec Bonaparte en Italie*. Paris, 1946.

REMACLE, COMTE LOUIS, *Relations secrètes des agents de Louis XVIII, 1802–1803*. Paris, 1899.

RENAUD, F., *La Onzième Heure, retouches à trois portraits: Mgr. Dupanloup, la duchesse de Dino, Talleyrand*. Paris, 1960.

RINIERI, I., *La diplomazia pontificia nel secolo XIX*, Vol. I. Rome, 1902.

ROBISON, GEORGIA, *Revellière-Lépeaux, Citizen-Director*. New York, 1938.

ROSE, J. H., *The Revolutionary and Napoleonic Era*, 7th ed. London, 1935.

———, *Life of Napoleon*. New York, 1907. 2 vols.

———, "Napoleon and Poland," in *Cambridge History of Poland*. Cambridge, 1941.

———, *Napoleonic Studies*. London, 1904.

———, *William Pitt and the Great War*. London, 1911.

RUDÉ, GEORGE, *The Crowd in the French Revolution*. London, 1959.

———, *Interpretations of the French Revolution*. London, 1961.

———, *Revolutionary Europe: 1783–1815*. London, 1964.

SAGNAC, P., *La Fin de l'ancien régime et la Révolution américaine, 1763–1789*.

———, *La Législation civile de la Révolution française*. Paris, 1898.

———, *Le Rhin français pendant la Révolution et l'Empire*. Paris, 1917.

SAINT-AULAIRE, COMTE DE, *Talleyrand*. Paris, 1936.

SAINTE-BEUVE, *Monsieur de Talleyrand*. Introduction and notes by L. Noël. Monaco, 1958.

SALLE, A., *Vie politique de Charles-Maurice, prince de Talleyrand*. Paris, 1834.

SAVANT, JEAN, *Napoleon in His Time*. New York, 1958.

———, *Talleyrand*. Paris, 1960.

SCHAUMANN, A. F. H., *Geschichte des 2er Pariser Friedens*. Göttingen, 1844.

SCHNERB, R., "La Dépression économique sous le Directoire," in *Annales historiques de la Révolution*, 1934.

SCIOUT, L., *Le Directoire*. 1895–1897. 4 vols.

SEE, H., *Histoire économique de la France: les temps modernes (1789–1914)*. Paris, 1942.

SEELEY, L. B., ED. *Fanny Burney and Her Friends*. London, 1895.

SIEBURG, F., *Napoleon: Die Hundert Tage*. Stuttgart, 1956.

SINDRAL, J., *Talleyrand*. 1926.

SIX, G., *Dictionnaire biographique des généraux et admiraux français de la Révolution et de l'Empire*. Paris, 1934. 2 vols.

SLOANE, WILLIAM M., *The French Revolution and Religious Reform*. New York, 1901.

SOREL, A., *L'Europe et la Révolution française*. Paris, 1885–1904. 8 vols.

———, *Essais d'histoire et de critique*. Paris, 1883–1884.

STENGER, GILBERT, *The Return of Louis XVIII*. London, 1909.

———, *La Société française pendant le Consulat*. Paris, 1904.

STOECKL, AGNES DE. *King of the French: A Portrait of Louis-Philippe*. London, 1957.

STRAKHOVSKY, L. I., *Alexander I*. London, 1949.

STRAUS, H. A., *The Attitude of the Congress of Vienna to Nationalism in Germany, Italy, and Poland*. New York, 1950.

TARLÉ, E., *Napoleon's Invasion of Russia*. New York, 1942.

———, *Talleyrand*, 2d ed. Moscow, n.d.

TATISCHEFF, SERGE, *Alexandre I*er *et Napoléon . . . 1801–1812*. Paris, 1891.

TESSIER, J., "Les Relations anglo-françaises au temps de Louis-Philippe," in *Mémoires de l'Académie nationale des Sciences*, Vol. LIX, No. 59, Caen, 1905.

THIERS, LOUIS A., *Histoire du Consulat et de l'Empire*. Paris, 1845–1862. 20 vols.

THIRY, J., *Le Coup d'état du 18 Brumaire*. Paris, 1947.

THOMAS, L., *L'Esprit de M. de Talleyrand*. Paris, 1909.

THOMPSON, D., *Europe Since Napoleon*. London, 1957.

TOCQUEVILLE, A. DE, *The Old Regime and the French Revolution*, new ed. New York, 1955.

TOUCHARD-LA FOSSE, G., *Histoire politique et vie intime de Ch. de Talleyrand, prince de Bénévent*. Paris, 1848.

TRIETSCHKE, H. VON, *History of Germany*, Vols. I and II. London, 1915–1916.

TURQUAN, JOSEPH, *Les Favorites de Louis XVIII*. Paris, n.d.

VANDAL, ALBERT, *L'Avènement de Bonaparte*. Two vols. Paris, 1903.

———, *Napoléon et Alexandre I*er*: l'Alliance Russe sous le premier Empire*. Paris, 1896–1903. 3 vols.

VARS, BARON DE, *Les Femmes de M. de Talleyrand*. Paris, 1891.

VATTEL, EMMERICH DE, *The Law of Nations*. Philadelphia, 1883.

VIEL-CASTLE, BARON L. DE, "Lord Castlereagh et la politique extérieure de l'Angleterre de 1812 à 1822," in *Revue des deux mondes*, 1 juin 1854.

VILLEMAREST, C. M. DE, *M. de Talleyrand*. Paris, 1834–1835. 4 vols.

VIVENT, JACQUES, *Charles X, dernier roi de France et de Navarre*. Paris, 1958.

———, *Monsieur de Talleyrand intime*. Paris, 1963.

———, *La Vieillesse et la mort de M. de Talleyrand*. Paris, 1964.

WALISZEWSKI, K., *Le Règne d'Alexandre I*er, Vol. II. Paris, 1923.

WALTER, GERARD, *Le Comte de Provence*. Paris, 1950.

WARD, SIR A., *The Period of the Congresses*, Vols. I and II. London, 1923.

WATSON, J. STEVEN, *The Reign of George III, 1760–1815*. London, 1960.

WEBSTER, C. K., *British Diplomacy, 1813–1815*. London, 1921.

———, *The Congress of Vienna*. London, 1919.

———, *The Foreign Policy of Castlereagh, 1813–1815*. London, 1931. 2 vols.

WEINER, MARGERY, *The French Exiles: 1789–1815*. London, 1960.

WEIL, H., *Le Revirement de la politique autrichienne à l'égard de Joachim Murat*. Paris, n.d.

————, *Talleyrand et la frontière ouverte.* Nancy, n.d.

WELSCHINGER, H., *Le Duc d'Enghien: l'enlèvement d'Ettenheim et l'exécution de Vincennes.* Paris, 1913.

WILKINSON, S., *The Rise of General Bonaparte.* Oxford, 1930.

YORKE, HENRY R., *France in Eighteen Hundred and Two*, J. C. A. Sykes, ed. London, 1906.

YOUNG, ARTHUR, *Travels in France During the Years 1787–1789*, C. Maxwell, ed. London, 1929.

ZELLER, G., "La Monarchie d'ancien régime et les frontières naturelles," in *Revue d'histoire moderne*, Vol. VII, 1933.

ZIEGLER, PHILIP, *The Duchess of Dino.* New York, 1963.

Index

Aachen, 424
Aberdeen, George Gordon, Earl of, 529
    and n., 541 and n., 545, 546, 548, 554
Aboville, Count d', 440
Acerenza, Jeanne, Duchess of, 365
Adams, John, 204, 205
Addington, Henry, 241, 242, 245
Adèle de Senange (Flahaut), 141
Affair of the Diamond Necklace, 57 and n.
Aiguillon, Duchess d', 235
Aix-la-Chapelle, Conference of, 455 n.
Albany, 160 and n.
Albigensian Crusade, 505
Albufera, Duchess d', 595
Aldini, Antonio, 409
Alexander I, Czar of Russia, 241, 260, 262,
    267, 268, 269, 272, 275, 276, 277,
    278 n., 289, 290, 291, 294, 295, 296,
    297, 303, 305, 307, 308, 309, 311, 323,
    324 and n., 325 and n., 328, 329, 331,
    332, 333 n., 334, 335, 336, 337, 338,
    339, 340, 341, 344, 348, 351, 352, 353,
    354 and n., 355, 356 and n., 357, 360,
    361, 362, 371–72, 383, 386, 389, 393,
    394, 395, 398, 399, 400, 401, 402, 403,
    404, 406, 407, 409, 423, 424, 431 n.,
    433, 450, 453, 454, 455 and n., 487,
    507, 528 and n.; quoted, 259, 292, 293,
    324, 326, 327, 336, 370, 375, 376
Alexander VI, Pope, 238
Algeria, 543, 552
Alien Act of 1793, 147
Alien Bill of 1782, 136 n.

Alien Bill of 1792, 136 n., 137
Alsace, 424
Alsace-Lorraine, 450
American Revolution, 63 and n., 81 and n.
Amiens, Treaty of, 243, 245, 246 and n.,
    258, 267
Andigné, Count d', 231
Angoulême, Duke d', 469 n., 494 n., 501,
    507
Angoulême, Marie-Thérèse, Duchess d',
    315, 469 n., 507
Anna, Grand Duchess of Russia, 361, 469,
    560 n.
Anspach, 263
Antibes, 414
Antwerp, 559, 565, 572
Arblay, General d', 145
Arblay, Madame d', 601
Arcola, 176
Armistead, Bet, 243
Arnault, Vincent, quoted, 200
Arnold, Benedict, 150
Arras, Bishop of, 51
Artois, Charles-Philippe, Count d'. *See*
    Charles X
Aspern, Battle of, 303 n.
Assembly of the Clergy, 40, 41, 45 and n.,
    53
Auerstedt, 270
Augereau, Pierre-François-Charles, Duke
    de Castiglione, 192, 193, 199
Augustus, King of Saxony, 390
Austerlitz, Battle of, 262, 263, 267, 349

Austria, 112, 113, 114, 115, 122, 147, 148, 176, 178, 188, 194, 197, 201, 202, 204, 205, 206, 214, 229, 232, 240, 258, 259, 260, 261–64, 266, 270, 271, 272, 274, 275, 277, 285, 290, 291, 293, 303–4, 305, 308, 309, 311, 313, 315, 332, 336, 343, 347, 348, 350, 351, 358, 359, 361, 368, 369, 375, 381, 383, 387, 388, 389, 392–93, 394, 396, 397, 399, 400, 401, 402, 403, 404, 405, 406, 410, 411, 415, 416, 417, 423, 443 n., 450, 465 and n., 477, 478, 488, 530, 536, 546, 558, 560, 570

Autun, 60, 61, 62, 66, 67, 69, 87, 90 n., 95, 170

Autun, Bishop of (Monseigneur de Marboeuf), 54, 57, 58, 59

Avaray, Duke d', 231

Bacciochi, Elisa Bonaparte, 409

Bacort, Adolphe de, 574, 576, 603 and n., 620; quoted, 573

Baden, 251, 252, 263, 266 n., 290

Badine (ship), 204

Bagration, Princess, 377 and n., 385, 387, 388

Bailly, Jean-Sylvain, 76, 78

Balzac, Honoré de, 600, 601, 602

Bank of North America, 101 n.

Barante, Prosper de, 501, 515, 516, 618; quoted, 13, 539

Barère, Bertrand, quoted, 130, 137

Barnave, Antoine-Pierre-Joseph-Marie, 106 n.

Barras, Paul-François-Jean-Nicholas de, 163, 171, 172, 178–79, 180, 181, 182, 183, 184, 186, 187, 190, 191, 192, 193, 194, 198, 204, 207 and n., 208, 211, 212, 215, 216, 218, 220, 221, 222, 223, 224 and n., 227, 335; quoted, 185, 186

Barthélemy, François, 179, 180, 181, 193 and n., 194, 217

Barthès, Joseph, 41

Basel, Treaty of, 345

Bassano, 176

Bassano, Hugues Maret, Duke de, 121 and n., 177, 478 and n.

Bastide, Louis, 207 n.

Batavia, 210, 240

Bathurst, Lord, quoted, 397

Baucort, Count de, 83 n.

Baudrand, General Count, 528 and n.

Bauffremont, Madame de, 463

Bavaria, 263, 266 n., 303, 380, 404

Bayonne, 286

Beauharnais, Alexandre de, 171–72

Beauharnais, Eugène de, 296, 325, 385, 562

Beauharnais, Hortense de, Queen of Holland, 199, 269, 270

Beauharnais, Josephine de (later Bonaparte), 171–72, 179, 198, 199–201, 220, 233, 239, 248, 258, 269, 270 n., 277, 294, 300, 306–7, 333 n.

Beaumetz, Count de, 132, 139, 143, 146, 148, 149, 152, 153, 156, 158 and n., 159, 160, 161

Beaumont, Archbishop, 42

Belgium, 123, 234, 247, 308, 345, 348, 418, 531 and n., 544–49, 551, 554–70

Bellerophon (ship), 433

Benevento, 265

Bénézach, M. de, 181

Bentham, Jeremy, 139

Berlin, 98, 187, 202, 203, 215, 269, 270, 278, 282

Bernadotte, General Jean-Baptiste; later King of Sweden, 216, 219, 249, 265, 305, 325

Berne, 227, 415 n.

Berry, Duke de, 361, 430, 469, 493–94, 523

Berry, Duchess de, 470, 480 n., 493–94, 494 n., 495 and n., 535

Berry, Mary, quoted, 459

Berthier, General Louis-Alexandre, 251, 303, 331, 440

Bertin de Veaux, Louis-François, 543, 571

Bessarabia, 261

Bessborough, Lady, quoted, 243–44

Bessières, Marshal, 440

Beugnot, Count, 427, 430; quoted, 426

Beurnonville, General de, 327 and n.

Beylen, 310

Bingham, Mrs., 153, 157

Biron, Duke de (Duke de Lauzun), 81 and n., 116, 117

Blacas, Count de, 411, 440, 499; quoted, 504

Blacons, Marquis de, 153

Blois, 318, 323

Blois, Bishop of, quoted, 39

Blücher, General, 356, 423, 424, 425

Bohemia, 380

Boigne, Countess de, 364 n., 530, 597; quoted, 364, 365, 447, 476 n., 503 n., 516, 531, 538

Boisgelin, Abbé de, 49 and n., 51

Boissy d'Anglas, François-Antoine de, 165, 440; quoted, 162–63

Bologna, 416

Bollman, Justus Erich, quoted, 139

Bonaparte, Caroline (Mme. Murat), 266, 410

Bonaparte, Elisa, Prncess of Lucca and Piombino, 259. See also Bacciochi

Bonaparte, Jérôme, King of Westphalia, 271, 290, 318, 507 n.

Bonaparte, Joseph, King of Naples, etc., 242, 243, 245, 259, 266, 275, 280 n., 284, 285, 290, 295, 318, 432 n.–33 n.

Bonaparte, Josephine. *See* Beauharnais, Josephine de

Bonaparte, Louis, King of Holland, 266, 269, 284, 290

Bonaparte, Lucien, 221, 223, 225, 226, 259, 431

Bonaparte, Napoleon. *See* Napoleon I

Bonapartists, 425, 431, 433, 439, 440, 441, 492, 502, 551 n., 562

Bonn, 404

Bordeaux, Archbishop of, 53

Bordeaux, Duke de, 495 and n., 523 and n.

Borgia, Cesare, 238

Boufflers, Madame de, 46, 173 n.

Bougainville, Louis de, 198 and n.

Bouillé, General François-Claude-Amour de, 107, 109, 137

Boullongne, Catherine de, Viscountess de Laval, 40 n.

Boulogne, 247, 260

Bourbon, Abbé de, 49 n.

Bourbon dynasty, 13, 73, 115, 175, 188, 231, 232, 233, 249, 250 and n., 251, 252–53, 254, 271, 272, 278, 282, 286, 303, 310, 315, 316, 317, 318, 325, 326, 328, 333, 334, 335, 336, 337, 338, 339, 340, 341, 349, 351, 359, 360, 375, 378, 393, 408, 410, 414, 417, 426, 427–28, 433–34, 436, 438, 441, 457, 469, 485, 486, 489, 494 n., 496, 498, 502, 512, 513, 515, 520, 521, 523–24, 527–28

Bourbon-l'Archambault, 467–8, 471, 504, 506, 572

Bourges, Archbishop of, 56, 613 and n.

Bourrienne, Louis-Antoine de, 220, 227, 232, 233, 252, 323; quoted, 220, 231

Bouvion, Marshal, 436

Braganza, House of, 563

Brazil, 283

Brest, 180

Breteuil, Louis-Auguste le Tonnelier, Baron de, 82

Brienne, Loménie de, 64, 87, 95 n.

Brionne, Countess de. *See* Rohan, Louise de

Brissot de Warville, Jacques-Pierre, 106 n., 120–21

Brivals, M., 165

Broglie, Duchess de, 475 and n., 483, 503; quoted, 605–6

Broglie, Duke de, 475 n., 509, 510, 529 n., 571, 572, 575, 576, 577; quoted, 505, 539

Bruix, Admiral, 223, 224

Brunswick, Duke of, 127 n.

Brussels, 423, 425, 460, 548, 560

Bulgaria, 261

Bülow, Baron von, 536, 578

Bulwer, Sir Henry, 452, 531

Burges, Sir James Bland, quoted, 131–32

Burghersh, Lord, 536 and n.

Burke, Edmund, 117, 136

Burney, Fanny, quoted, 143, 144, 145

Burr, Aaron, 152 n., 159

Cabarrús, Thérèse. *See* Tallien, Thérèse

Cadoudal, Georges, 250–1, 256

Calcutta, 159, 160, 212

Calonne, Charles-Alexandre de, 48, 55, 64, 80, 87, 152

Cambacérès, Jean-Jacques, 228, 252, 257, 280, 307, 503

Cambrai, 427, 428, 429, 431

Campo Formio, Treaty of, 197

Canclaux, Count de, 440

Candide (Voltaire), 42

Canning, George, 139, 278 n.

Canning, Sir Stratford, 578, 588

Canova, Antonio, 456

Cany, Marquis de, 21 n.

Capo d'Istria, Count, 400 and n., 405

Carrel, Armand, 512 and n.

Carignan, Princess de, 85

Carlists, 570 n.

Carlos IV, King of Spain, 272, 282, 283, 284, 285

Carlos de Borbón, 570

Carnot, Lazare, 179, 180, 181, 184, 190, 191, 193 and n., 194, 217, 335, 438; quoted, 177, 181, 186

Casalanza, Treaty of, 417

Caselli, Cardinal, quoted, 238

Casenove, M., 151, 156

Castellane, Countess de, 483 and n., 597

Castiglione. *See* Augereau

Castlereagh, Lord, 315, 316, 317, 325 n., 333 n., 335, 337, 344, 345, 349, 350, 357, 358, 361, 362, 369, 370, 371, 377, 378, 383, 386, 389, 391, 394, 395, 396, 397, 399 and n., 400–9, 411, 423, 427, 450, 455 n., 472, 541, 566 and n.; quoted, 332, 343, 350 n., 372, 374, 377 n.–78 n., 379, 381, 386–87, 452

Castlereagh, Lady, 385

Castries, M., 48

Catalonia, 284

Catherine, Grand Duchess of Russia, 295, 307, 354 and n.; quoted, 354–55

Catherine II, Empress of Russia, 112 n., 116

Caulaincourt, Marquis Armand de, 280,

298, 313, 315, 331, 431; quoted, 331, 332, 333
Cavanac, Madame de (Mlle. de Romans), 49 n.
Ceylon, 242
Chalais, 22, 23, 24, 26, 62, 75
Chalais, Princess de. See Rochechouart, Marie-Françoise de
Chambéry, 344
Chamfort, Sébastien, 42
Chamillard, Louis-Michel, 26 n.
Chamillart, Marie-Elizabeth, 17
Champagne, 127
Champagny, Jean-Baptiste Nompère de, Duke de Cadore, 280–81, 285, 478 and n.
Champs de Mars, 126
Chanteloup, 48, 49
Charles, Archduke of Austria, 558, 563 n.
Charles, Prince of Bavaria, 559
Charles, Prince of Naples, 559
Charles I, King of England, 129
Charles X, Count d' Artois, King of France, 78 and n., 79, 82, 83–84, 84 n., 85, 113, 133 n., 135, 159 n., 231, 250, 252, 304, 317, 330, 334, 336, 337, 428, 429, 473 n., 486, 487, 488, 489, 490, 491, 493, 494, 497, 501, 504–5, 508, 510–24, 533, 534, 535, 555, 593; quoted, 84, 335, 430, 514, 517, 520, 552
Charles Emmanuel IV, Duke of Savoy, King of Sardinia, 245 n.
Charles the Bald, 15
Charles, Hippolyte, 200 n., 220
Charlotte, Princess, 355
Charlotte, Queen of England, 117
Chateaubriand, François-René de, 207 n., 252, 425, 428, 435, 488, 499, 501, 503 n., 504; quoted, 498, 500 n., 503
Châtre, Duke de la, 133, 440, 472; quoted, 132
Châtre, Madame de la (later Madame de Jaucourt), 133, 140, 144, 440
Chaumont, Treaty of, 316, 372 and n., 416, 488
Chauvelin, François-Bernard, 119, 120, 123
Chénier, André, 164, 172, 177
Chénier, Marie-Joseph, 164
Cherbourg, 431, 432
Chérin, Louis, 193
Chevreuse, Marie de Rohan-Montbazon, Duchess de, 258
Chlopicki, General, 549 n.
Choiseul, Duke de, 26 n., 46 n., 48–49, 54, 90, 152, 175
Choiseul-Beaupré, Auguste de, 26 and n.,

27, 41, 43, 44, 46 n., 48, 54, 55, 81, 475
Christophe, Robert, 135 n.
Cisalpine Republic, 202, 234
Civil Constitution of the Clergy, 93, 94, 95, 97, 98, 106, 107, 109, 235
Civil Code, 503
Clairvaux, Abbot of, 50 n.
Clam-Martinitz, Count, 445, 446, 447, 448, 449 and n., 458, 481
Clancarty, Lord, 414
Clanricarde, Lady, 588, 589, 597
Clermont-Gallerande, Charles, Marquis de, 132 n.–33 n.
Club de Clichy, 180, 181
Coalition, 147, 148, 164, 165 n., 176, 188
Coblenz, 113, 132 n.–33 n.
Cochon, M. de, 181
Coigny, Aimée, 235; quoted, 76, 449
Colbert, Jean Baptiste, 17
Collège d' Harcourt, 25 and n., 26–27, 27 n., 30, 34, 41
Collège of St.-Sulpice, 33 and n., 34, 35, 36, 37, 38, 40, 41, 44
Colmache, M., 521
Cologne, 404
Committee of Public Safety, 152, 159, 162, 173, 216
Commune of Paris, 130, 131, 162
Compiègne, 338, 341
Concordat of 1516, 54 n.
Concordat of 1801, 236 and n., 238, 245, 249, 607 n.
Condé, Prince de, 424–25
Condé family, 251, 502
Condorcet, Nicholas de Caritat, Marquis de, 106 n.
Confederation of the Rhine, 264, 266, 290, 313
Congregation de la Vierge, 487 n.
Congress, U.S., 204, 205 and n.
Congress of Vienna, 325 n., 345, 347, 349, 359–66, 367–83 and passim, 405–6, 411, 414–15, 425, 428, 447 n., 451, 489, 530, 545, 600
Connecticut, 157, 158, 159
Consalvi, Cardinal, 389, 392, 409
Constant, Benjamin, 177, 178, 183–84, 200, 208, 248, 432, 487 n.
Constantinople, 203, 204, 277, 488
Constitutional Club, 177, 191, 248
Constitutions, French, 109–12, 132, 137, 147, 190, 191, 193, 194, 227, 228, 329, 339–40, 351, 352
Consulate, the, 220–55
Cooper, Duff, 118 n., 278 n., 448 n., 477 n., 489 n.
Copenhagen, Battle of, 241, 278

Cordeliers, 106 and n., 107, 108, 110
Corfu, 201, 332, 400 n.
Cornwallis, Lord, 243
Corsica, 199, 262, 332
Corsini, Neri, 409
Cossacks, 549
Coulmann, Jean-Jacques, quoted, 298
Council of Ancients, 165, 176, 180, 215, 216, 224, 225 and n., 226
Council of Five Hundred, 165, 176, 180, 221, 223, 225 and n., 226, 259
Courland, Anne-Charlotte-Dorothea, Duchess of, 296, 297, 298, 310, 311, 328, 334, 347, 363, 364, 456, 474, 476 and n.
Courland family, 296
Courier républicain, 170
Courtiade, M., 148, 156, 158
Cousin, Victor, 605
Couturier, Abbé, 37
Cracow, 399, 400, 403
Crawford, Madame, quoted, 476
Creevey, Thomas, 483, 488; quoted, 534, 540
Creutz, Count Gustave de, 47
Cromwell, Oliver, 129
Cruveilhier, Dr., 615
Cumberland, Duchess of, 244
Cussac, M. de, quoted, 39
Czartoryski, Prince Adam, 297, 399, 400 and n., 538, 539

Dalberg, Duke de, 327 and n., 363, 368, 503, 575; quoted, 564
Dalmatia, 277
Damas d'Antigny, Alexandrine-Marie-Victoire-Eléonore de, Countess de Périgord, 14, 18, 20, 25, 26, 28, 29, 30, 33, 38, 47, 59, 134 n.
D'Antigny, Marquis, 14
Danton (Christophe), 135 n.
Danton, George-Jacques, 106 and n., 107, 108, 109, 110, 127 and n., 128, 130, 134 and n., 135 n., 146, 164
Deane, Silas, 205 n.
Decazes, Élie, 458, 463, 471, 472, 477, 484, 486, 490, 491–92, 493–94, 588
Declaration of Pillnitz (1791), 112 n.
Declaration of the Rights of Man, 86 and n., 87, 88
Dedel, M., 578
Delacroix, Charles, 179, 181, 184, 210, 211, 217
Delacroix, Eugène, 210
Delacroix, Madame, 210, 217
De la Forest, Antoine, 159 and n.
Delille, Abbé Jacques, 42
Denmark, 169, 241, 277

Den Ny Proeve (ship), 166
Desmoulins, Camille, 106 n., 108
Desrenaudes, Borie, 61, 90 n., 134 n.–35 n., 163, 209, 225, 230
Dessoles, Augustin, 335, 492–93
D'Hauterive, Count Alexandre Blanc, 209, 230, 253; quoted, 253
Didier, M., quoted, 486
Dillon, Édouard, 211, 364 and n.
Dino, Duchess de. See Périgord, Dorothea, Countess de
Dino, Duke de. See Périgord, Count Edmond de
Directory, 165 and n., 166, 172–73, 175, 176–219
Dorinville, Dorothée, 36 and n., 37
Douai, Merlin de, 181, 194
Du Barry, Countess, 40 n., 48
Ducloux, Abbé, quoted, 60
Ducos, Roger, 216, 222, 224, 225 n., 226
Dumont, Étienne, 99 n.; quoted, 29, 120, 125
Dumouriez, Charles-François, 106 n., 121–23, 124, 125, 127 n., 170
Dupanloup, Abbé, 587, 611 and n., 612, 613, 615, 616, 619, 620; quoted, 616–17, 618
Dupont, General René-Antoine, 283, 310
Du Pont de Nemours, Pierre, 42, 475
Dutch East Indies, 358 n.

East Prussia, 272, 274
Egypt, 175, 201, 202, 203, 213–14, 217, 219
Elba, 332, 333 and n., 334, 401, 412
Elector of Bavaria, 260
Elector of Hesse-Kassel, 271
Elector of Trier, 112, 113, 121
Elphinstone, Margaret. See Flahaut, Margaret de
Empire, the, 256–81
Enghien, Louis de Bourbon-Condé, Duke d', 251, 252, 253, 254, 255, 256, 301, 424, 501, 502
England, 79, 112 n., 114, 115, 116–18, 119, 120, 122, 123, 128–29, 131–34, 138, 139, 140–49, 155, 163, 164, 174, 175, 176, 178, 187 and n., 188, 201, 204, 206, 211, 212, 229, 232, 240, 241–42, 243, 247, 258, 260, 267, 268, 269, 271, 272, 277–78, 283, 290, 316, 332, 336, 343, 347, 350, 351, 358, 361–63, 371, 375, 380, 382, 383, 387, 389, 393, 394, 396, 397, 401, 402, 404, 407, 410, 423, 427, 433, 440, 441, 450, 460, 488, 528, 531–81
Entraigues, Jules d', 595
Erfurt, 289–91, 294, 295, 298, 300, 303, 307, 348, 405

Essling, 304
Este, Archduke Francesco, 417
Esterházy, Prince Paul, 536, 577
Esterházy, Princess, 385, 535
Etruria, 392, 393, 396, 411, 417
Executive Council, 127, 130
Eylau, Battle of, 274

Fauchet, Joseph, 152, 153, 166; quoted, 156
Ferdinand, Grand Duke of Tuscany, 391, 392, 409
Ferdinand I, King of the Two Sicilies, 267, 410, 416, 474
Ferdinand IV. *See* Ferdinand I, King of the Two Sicilies
Ferdinand VII, King of Spain, 282, 283, 284, 289 n., 473, 498–99, 570
Fernsen, Axel, 109
Ferrand, Count, 499
Fesch, Joseph, Archbishop of Lyons, 57, 59, 199 n.
Feuillants, 106 n., 111, 112, 114, 121, 125, 133, 135, 405
Finland, 294
Fitz-James, Duke de, 239, 498
Flack, Baron, 546
Flahaut, Charles de (son of Talleyrand), 52, 269, 549, 550–52, 562; quoted, 569
Flahaut, Count de, 52, 101 n.
Flahaut, Countess Adélaïde de, 52, 55, 74, 96, 97, 101–3, 105, 114, 126, 141, 142, 144, 145 and n., 169, 170, 209, 235, 459, 477, 480, 549; quoted, 104
Flahaut, Margaret Elphinstone de, 550
Fontainebleau, 332; Treaty of, 285, 286, 333 and n., 334, 336, 469
Fouché, Joseph, Duke d'Otrante, 202, 217 n., 221, 222, 225, 228, 231, 233, 234, 249, 250, 251, 252, 278 n., 299, 300, 301, 304, 305, 307, 308, 309, 333, 431, 432, 433, 434, 436, 438, 441–44, 446 n., 463; quoted, 218, 280, 435
Fox, Henry. *See* Holland, Henry Fox, Baron
Fox, Charles James. *See* Holland, Charles James Fox, Baron
Foy, General, 509
Francis I, Emperor of Austria, 335, 344
Francis II, Emperor of Austria, 122, 263, 266, 295, 400
Francis, Sir Philip, 212
Franklin, Benjamin, 164
Frederick II, the Great; King of Prussia, 56, 269, 270, 275
Frederick Augustus, King of Saxony, 271, 380, 396, 402, 403, 406, 407, 408, 413, 414
Frederick William III, King of Prussia, 268,

269, 272, 275–76, 324, 335, 351, 352, 354, 361, 383, 385, 393–94, 396, 399, 406, 407, 431 n., 530
Fréjus, 219
French Army of the Interior, 172
French Guiana, 193 n.
Friedland, Battle of, 274, 275
Fuchs, Madame, 385
Funck, Ferdinand von, 532
Fürstenberg, Princess, 385

Gaeta, Duke of, 302
Garde-Chambonas, Count de la, 368
Génisson, M., 165
Genlis, Madame de, 32, 54, 140–41, 143, 145 n., 169, 170; quoted, 32–33
Genoa, Republic of, 259, 360, 391, 412, 415 n., 503
Gentz, Baron Friedrich von, 365, 371 and n., 381–82, 382 n., 390 n., 394, 447 and n., quoted, 375, 448
George II, King of England, 112 n.
George III, King of England, 117, 129, 229, 250, 267, 532
George IV, King of England, 532
George of Oldenburg, Prince, 354 n.
Germany, 161 n., 176, 214, 266 and n., 271 n., 303 n., 313, 315, 347, 410, 415, 416, 423, 464 n., 549 and n.
Gerry, Elbridge T., 204–5, 206
Ghent, 414, 418, 434 n.
Girac, Madame de, 51, 52
Girardin, Émile de, 512 n.
Girondins, 106 n., 120, 121, 162, 405
Gisors, 126
Giulay, General Count, 263
Gladstone, William, 568
Gnesen, 403
Goderich, Lord, 566
Godoy, Manuel de, 272, 282, 283
Gohier, Louis, 216, 224, 225 n.
Gontaut, Armand de, Duke de Lauzun, 41
Gordon, Duchess of, 138
Gould, Anna, 474 n.
Gramont, Madame de, 46
Grand, Catherine-Noël Worlée, Princess de Talleyrand, 211–13, 237, 238–39, 239 n., 240, 243–44, 265–66, 287, 288, 298, 363, 365, 458, 460, 461–63, 538, 598–99; quoted, 461
Grand, George François, 599
Grandchamps, Abbé de, 61
Granville, Lady, 534; quoted, 550–51, 601–2
Greek Orthodox Church, 488
Grégoire, Abbé, 81, 335
Gregory XVI, Pope, 616, 619
Grenville, Lord, 118 and n., 119, 122, 123,

124 and n., 136 n., 137, 138, 147, 229, 241, 267
Greville, Henry, 588
Greville, Charles, 566 n., 588; quoted, 574
Grey, Lord Charles, 356, 531, 532–33, 548, 549, 552–54, 556, 564, 565, 576–77, 590
Grey, Lady, 537–38; quoted, 538
Guadeloupe, 242
Guastalla, 392, 411, 417
Guiana, 223, 249, 561 n.
Guizot, François, 487 n., 529 n., 595, 596; quoted, 511
Gustavus III, King of Sweden, 56, 57, 112 n.

Hager, Baron, 377, 388; quoted, 389
Hague, The, 210, 543, 545, 548, 555, 560, 568
Hamburg, 166, 169, 170
Hamilton, Alexander, 151–52, 151 n.–52 n., 160, 588
Hamilton, John, 588
Hanau, 314
Hanover, 263, 336, 367, 368, 404, 533
Hapsburg dynasty, 176, 262, 263, 307, 359, 409, 564
Hardenberg, Prince Karl von, 317, 333 n., 369, 370, 372, 386, 387, 394, 399, 400, 401, 402, 405, 406, 407, 413
Hardi, Abbé, 26, 27 and n.
Hastings, Francis Fawdon-, Lord, 139
Haugwitz, Count von, 263; quoted, 270
Hawkesbury, Lord, 241, 246
Hébert, Jacques-René, 106 n.
Hélie I, 16
Hélie de Périgord, Count de Grignols, 15
Hénin, Princess de, 144
Hesse-Darmstadt, 405
Heydecoper, M., 156, 158, 159
Hincmar, Archbishop of Rheims, 32 and n.
Hoche, General Louis-Lazare, 172, 176, 180, 181, 190, 191
Hohenzollern-Hechingen, Pauline, Princess of, 365, 446
Holland, Charles James Fox, Baron, 114, 120, 123, 136 n., 139, 243, 244, 267, 268–69, 356, 554 n.
Holland, Lady Elizabeth, quoted, 335 n.
Holland, Henry Richard Vassail Fox, Baron, 544 and n., 566
Holy Alliance, 488 n., 499
Holy Roman Empire, 346
Hugo, Victor, quoted, 13
Hugues Capet, King of France, 16, 469
Hulin, General Pierre-Augustin, 251, 252
Humboldt, Baron von, 369, 370, 372, 374, 386; quoted, 381

Hundred Days, 412–18, 423, 434 n., 436, 438–39, 441, 450, 460
Hungary, 380
Hyde de Neuville, M., 231, 232

Île de France, 345
Impey, Sir Elijah, 243
India, 211, 212, 213
Infantado, Duke de, 311
Innocent III, Pope, 505
Institute of Sciences and Arts, 173 and n., 174
Ireland, 118 n., 176, 180, 242
Isabella II, Queen of Spain, 570
Issy, Seminary of, 60
Italy, 176, 178, 188, 189, 191, 195, 200 n., 201, 202, 203, 214, 219, 233, 234, 258, 259, 260, 261, 315, 332, 345, 347, 390, 391, 393, 412–18, 446

Jacobins, 98 n., 106 and n., 108, 111, 112, 113, 125, 126, 127, 130, 133, 135, 162, 177, 188, 190, 192, 202, 204, 213, 214, 215, 216, 217, 218, 219, 225, 234, 244, 248, 249, 438, 441
James II, King of England, 250, 513–14
Jaucourt, Marquis Arnail-François de, 132, 133, 143, 144, 146, 327 and n., 363, 378, 382, 436, 440
Jaucourt, Madame de. See Châtre, Madame de la
Jena, 270
Jesuits, 487 n., 506 n.
Jews in France, enfranchisement of, 90
Jiménez de Cisneros, Francisco Cardinal, 32 and n.
John XXII, Pope, 16
Jorry, M., 217 and n.
Josephine, Empress. See Beauharnais, Josephine de
Joubert, Barthélemy-Charles, 219
Jourdan, General Jean-Baptiste, 172, 176, 214, 216, 510
Journal (La Tour du Pin), 161, 314
July Monarchy, 115, 542, 544
July Revolution (1830), 518–20 and passim, 534, 535, 538, 541, 542, 545, 550
Junot, Marshal Andoche, 283

Kaunitz, Prince Wenzel Anton von, 122, 407 and n.
Keith, Lord, 550
Kelmannsegge, Countess, 309, 310
Knights of St. John of Jerusalem, 242
Knox, Henry, 156
Kurakin, Prince, 295–96

La Besnardière, Count de, 209, 363, 464

Labrador, Count de, 371, 372, 386; quoted, 373, 374
Laclos, Choderlos de, 81
Lacour-Gayet, G., 20 n., 36 n., 134 n., 377 n.
Lafayette, Marquis de, 81 and n., 82, 94, 97, 106 n., 112, 125, 432, 487 n., 509, 510, 520, 523
La Ferté-Alais, 190
Laffitte, Jacques, 509, 513, 529 n., 542, 564 n.
La Garde, Count de, quoted, 385
Lagrange, Joseph-Louis, 90 n.
La Harpe, Frédéric, 400 and n.
Lally-Tollendal, Marquis Trophime-Gérard de, 144
Lamartine, Alphonse de, 601, 602, 614; quoted, 585–86
Landau, 344
Lansdowne, Marquess of, 105, 114, 120, 138 and n., 139, 142, 152, 153, 549
Laporte, Arnaud, 134; quoted, 133
La Revellière-Lépeaux, Louis-Marie, 179, 180, 181, 182, 186, 190, 191, 192, 194, 216
La Rochefoucauld d'Enville, Duke de, 81, 126
La Rochefoucauld-Liancourt, Duke François de, 153, 235
La Tour du Pin, Marquise, quoted, 160 and n., 161, 314–15, 449, 601
La Tour du Pin, M., 160 and n.
Lauderdale, Lord, 267
Lauzun, Duke de. See Biron, Duke de; Gontaut, Armand de
Laval, Duke de, 249, 536 n., 588
Laval, Madame de, 208, 302, 310, 311, 444, 471. See also Boullongne, Catherine de
Lavoisier, Antoine-Laurent, 90 n.
Law, John, 160
League of Neutrality, 241
Lebrun, Charles-François, 228, 257, 280, 307, 328
Lefebvre, Marshal François-Joseph, 331
Legendre, Louis, 164, 165
Legislative Assembly, 110–14, 122, 125, 126, 128, 131, 134 n., 209, 211
Leipzig, 313–14, 406, 407
Leopold, Emperor of Austria, 109, 113, 122
Leopold, Prince of Saxe-Coburg, King of Belgium, 558–59, 561, 563 n., 564–65
Lessart, Antoine de, 113–14, 115, 118, 119, 120, 121 and n., 211
Le Tourneur, Étienne, 179
Leuchtenberg, Duke de, 562, 563 and n.
Lévis-Mirepoix, Duke de, 426
Liaisons Dangereuses (Laclos), 81
Lichtenstein, Prince Johann von, 263

Liechtenstein, 374 and n.
Liechtenstein, Princess, 385
Lieven, Count (later Prince), 354, 539, 546, 577–78, 590
Lieven, Countess (later Princess), quoted, 354 and n., 356 and n., 488 n., 534, 535, 539–40, 554, 576–77, 588, 589, 590, 614
Ligny, 424
Liguria, 234
Lille, 187 n.
Limoges, Bishop of, 16
Linge, Prince de, quoted, 367
Lisbon, 207, 283
Liverpool, Robert Banks Jenkinson, Lord, 345, 356, 377, 399 n., 433
Locke, John, 143
Lombardy, 176, 232
London, 114, 116, 117, 123, 124, 130, 131, 134, 138–39, 140, 149, 164, 211, 354, 370; Conference, 531–81
London, Treaty of (1831), 568
London Morning Chronicle, 131
London Times, 552, 566
Londonderry, Lord, 566 and n.
Lorraine, Princess Charlotte de, 48
Louis, Abbé, 42
Louis XIII, King of France, 16, 27
Louis XIV, King of France, 15 n., 17, 50, 63, 245, 301
Louis XV, King of France, 13, 26 n., 40 n., 49 n., 63, 175
Louis XVI, King of France, 39 and n., 40 and n., 46, 48, 54, 55, 58, 59, 63, 73, 78, 80, 81, 82, 83, 84, 85, 92, 93, 94, 95 n., 107, 108, 109, 110, 111 and n., 112 and n., 113, 114, 118, 120, 121, 124 n., 125, 127, 132 n., 137, 138, 140, 146, 178, 190 n., 235, 252, 315, 328, 342, 409, 433, 434, 435, 436, 469 n., 505, 507; quoted, 64
Louis XVII, King of France, 146, 190 n., 341, 352
Louis XVIII, King of France, 26 n., 78 n., 109 n., 113, 133 n., 190, 191 and n., 199 and n., 231, 232, 233, 250, 254, 304, 310, 325 and n., 326, 327, 328, 334, 336, 337, 339, 340 and n., 341 and n., 342, 351, 352, 353, 354, 361, 362–63, 382 n., 396, 397, 301, 402, 404, 407, 410, 411, 414, 415, 418, 425, 426, 427, 428, 430, 431, 433, 434, 435, 436, 437 and n., 438, 439, 440, 442, 451–57, 459, 463, 472, 473, 477, 482–87, 487 n., 488–91, 493–95, 497, 499, 501–2, 504–5, 509, 524 n., 596, 598 n., quoted, 15, 426, 429, 430
Louis-Philippe, Duke d'Orléans, King of

France, 47 n., 49 and n., 73, 77, 90–91, 85, 92, 140, 141, 170, 233, 239 n., 325, 341 n., 428, 483, 484–86, 495, 505, 509, 511 n., 513–14, 518, 521–24, 527–33, 541–47, 549 n., 551 and n., 555, 557, 562, 563, 567, 575, 579, 580–81, 591, 596, 597, 619; quoted, 568
Louisa, Queen of Prussia, 276; quoted, 276–77
Louise, Queen of the Belgians, 567
Louvel, M., 493
Löwenhielm, Gustavus von, 381, 390
Lucay, M. de, 287
Lucca, 259, 409, 417
Lucchesini, Girolanio, 268
Lunéville, Treaty of, 234, 240, 245 n., 313
Lusitania, 392
Luxembourg, 223, 234, 380, 404
Luynes, Duchess de, 311
Lyons, 414
Lyons, Archbishop of. See Fesch, Joseph

Macdonald, Marshal Jacques, 219, 223, 331; quoted, 243
Mack, General, 261
Madrid, 284
Maestricht, siege of, 559
Maine, 156, 157, 158 n.
Maintenon, Madame de, 597
Mainz, 266 n., 269, 270 and n., 380, 386
Maistre, Count Joseph de, quoted, 343 n.
Maitland, Captain, 433
Malabar, 561 n.
Malesherbes, Chrétien-Guillaume de La-moignon de, 48, 498
Malmaison, 428, 432
Malmesbury, James Harris, Lord, 178, 187 n.
Malouet, Pierre-Victor, 76
Malta, 201, 204, 242, 246
Mamelukes, 201
Mantua, 176, 232
Manuel, Jacques-Antoine, 487 n.
Marat, Jean-Paul, 92, 160 n., 107, 109, 110, 112 n., 164, 176
Marboeuf, Monseigneur de. See Autun, Bishop of
Marengo, Battle of, 232, 233, 234, 245
Marescaldi, Ferdinando, 409
Maret, Hughes. See Bassano, Duke de
Mareuil, Durand de, 209
Maria, Queen of Portugal, 563 n.
María Cristiana, Dowager Queen of Spain, 570
María Luisa, Queen of Spain, 272, 282, 283, 284, 285

Maria Theresa, Queen of Austria, 407 n.
Marie-Antoinette, Queen of France, 39, 57 and n., 74, 78, 92, 93, 101 n., 109, 112, 113, 114, 116, 125, 126, 127, 144, 146, 190 n., 211, 307, 342, 510
Marie-Louise of Austria, Queen of France, 307, 313, 316, 318, 323, 325, 332, 333 and n., 392, 408, 409, 411, 417
Marmont, Marshal, Duke de Ragusa, 323, 324, 328, 331, 332, 519–20
Marmontel, Jean-François, 42, 47
Marshall, John, 204, 205, 206
Martinique, 153, 242
Martignac, Jean-Baptiste-Sylvère Gay, Viscount de, 510
Massachusetts, 157
Maubreuil, Marie-Armand Guerri de, Marquis d'Oravault, 507 and n., 508 and n.
Maurepas, Jean-Frédéric-Phélippeaux, 48
Mazarin, Jules Cardinal, 32 n.
Meade, Lady Selina, 449
Médicis, Marie de, 181 n.
Melbourne, William Lamb, Viscount, 552, 577, 581
Melville, Lord, 148
Mémoires (Barère), 130
Mémoires (Marquis de Clermont-Galle-rande), 132 n.
Mémoires (Fouché), 278 n.
Mémoires (De Retz), 32
Mémoires (Talleyrand), 23, 24, 25, 28, 34, 36 n., 38, 39, 41, 62, 71, 83 n., 89, 90, 138 n., 141, 145 n., 153, 169, 173 n., 183, 185, 187 and n., 192, 198, 227, 236, 237, 238, 242, 252, 333 n., 343, 347, 363, 371 n., 426, 434 n., 437, 438, 454, 463, 477, 507, 536, 545, 565, 592, 603 and n.
Ménéval, Baron, 252, 301
Mérimée, Prosper, quoted, 539, 574, 575
Metternich, Prince Klemens von, 264, 303, 308, 315, 317, 332, 333 and n., 335, 336, 344, 351, 357, 358, 365, 368, 369, 371, 373, 376, 381, 385–88, 390, 391, 393, 395, 396, 397, 399, 400, 401, 402, 403, 404, 405, 406, 408, 409, 410, 411, 413, 414, 416, 417, 423, 427, 434 n., 447 n., 452, 477, 479, 488, 530, 549; quoted, 299–300, 336, 379, 380, 412
Metz, 109
Mignet, François, 509, 512, 513, 595
Milan, 172, 195, 214, 232
Millin, Chevalier, 461
Minorca, 242
Mirabeau, Count de, 42, 76, 77, 79, 80, 81 and n., 83, 85, 86, 88–89, 91, 98

and n., 99–100, 106 and n., 108, 129, 501, 528; quoted, 13, 78, 99
Mirabeau, Countess de, 593
Moldavia, 261, 291
Molé, Count Louis-Mathieu, 252, **444**, 445, 472, 492, 494, 529 and n., 541, 542, 543, 546, 575, 596, 618; quoted, 49, 306, 439 and n., 440, 447, 448, 471, 483 n., 530 n., 544, 595
Molé, Mathieu, 439 and n.
Moleville, Minister, 120
Moncey, Marshal, 335
Monge, Gaspard, 90
Moniteur, 134, 135 n., 163, 199, 206, 210, 222, 229, 232, 253, 311, **424**, 491, 502, 511, 519, 530, 543
Monneron, Louis, 211
Mons, 426, 427, 428, 429
Montagnards, 106 n.
Montespan, Marquise de, 15 n.
Montesquieu, Abbé de, 327 and n.
Montesquiou, François de, 177; quoted, 103
Montesson, Marquise de, 47 and n.
Montjoie, Madame de, 511
Montmorency, Alix de, 473 n.
Montmorency, Duke Mathieu de, 132, 139, 143, 144, 145, 146, 448, 499
Montmorency family, 17, 249, 302
Montmorency-Laval, Elizabeth de, Duchess de Luynes, 40 n.
Montrond, Count Casimir de, 208–9, 226, 227, 241, 509, 588–89, 600, 614
Moré, Count de, 153; quoted, 154
Moreau de St.-Méry, Médéric-Louis-Élie, 153, 165, 166, 169, 176, 219; quoted, 154
Moria, Lord, 147 and n.
Morris, Gouverneur, 74, 101 and n., 103, 114, 119, 126, 148, 158 n.; quoted, 52, 74, 100, 102, 105, 120, 138, 152
Morris, Robert, 101 and n., 158 n., 159
Morris, Mrs. Robert, 158 and n.
Mortemart, Duke de, 17, 21 n., 521
Mortemart, Marquise de, 258
Moscow, 278, 312
Mosloy, Count de, 241
Motte-Valois, Countess de la, 57 n.
Mouchy, Duchess de, 592
Moulin, General, 216, 224, 225 n.
Mounier, Jean-Joseph, 79
Mulhouse, 344
Münster, Count, 336
Murat, Joachim, 226, 266, 290, 359, 374, 379, 390, 392–93, 408, 410–11, 416, 417

Nancy, Bishop of, 55

Naples, 382, 383, 392, 395, 408, 410, 416, 417
Napoleon I, 13, 22, 97 n., 115, 147, 172, 176–77, 183, 346, 348–49, 370, 392, 393, 398, 450–51, 473, 478, 500, 549; during the Directory, 188–204, 206, 213–15, 217, 219; as First Consul, 220–55; as emperor, 256–81, 282–319, 327, 330, 331–32; abdicates, 333–41; and the Hundred Days, 412–18, 423–30, 453 n.; second abdication, 432; quoted, 201, 225, 226, 227, 232, 233–34, 243, 247, 251, 253, 256, 260, 267, 272, 277, 280, 281, 285, 286, 290, 291, 292, 294, 295, 301, 303–4, 306, 318–19
Napoleon II, 465 and n.
Narbonne, Count Louis de, 41, 81, 111, 113, 114, 120, 121, 132, 139, 140, 144, 145, 146, 148, 152, 200
Nassau, House of, 551, 555, 560 n., 561
National Assembly, 75–83, 85, 86 and n., 87–92, 93, 98, 99, 100, 106 and n., 107 n., 109, 110, 164; Constitutional Committee, 86–7, 90, 125, 126, 129, 130, 131, 215; Talleyrand elected President, 91–2. *See also* Legislative Assembly
National Convention, 134 and n., 135, 136, 137, 146, 147, 161, 162, 163–4, 165
National Guard, 82, 109, 112, 125, 506
Necker, Jacques, 46, 53, 64, 65, 74, 82, 87, 103, 104 n., 108, 111, 140, 155 and n.; quoted, 76, 105 n.
Nedermann, M., 591
Nelson, Admiral Horatio, 241
Nemours, Duke de, 551, 557, 558, 562, 563 and n., 564, 569
Nesselrode, Count, 296, 308, 317, 324, 326, 332, 369, 370, 372, 381, 386, 391, 399, 403, 413, 473
Netherlands, 109 n., 121, 156, 176, 214, 242, 246, 270 n., 284, 304, 348, 358, and n., 380, 418, 423, 455, 531 n., 543, 545, 546, 547, 548, 551, 555, 557, 559–60, 565–68
Neufchâteau, François de, 194
Neufchâtel, 263
Neuilly, 434, 435, 521
Neukomm, Sigismund von, 368, 409, 459
New York, 157, 159, 160 and n., 162, 166
Ney, Marshal Michel, 331, 333 n., 414, 463
Nicholas I, Czar of Russia, 528, 531, 539, 549, 560 n., 578
Nicholson, Harold, quoted, 447 n.
Niemen River, 275, 313
Noailles, Countess Juste de, 235, 592

Noailles, Count Alexis de, 363, 437, 614
Noailles, Viscount Marie de, 81, 91, 153, 588, 595
Noailles family, 296
Nogent, M. de, 341 n.
Noyon, Count-Bishop of, 44

Orange, House of, 347, 546 n., 547
Orange, Prince of, 355, 547, 554, 555, 559, 560 n.–61 n., 561, 565
Orléans, Adélaïde d', 140, 485, 495, 505, 511, 518, 521–22, 527, 537, 541 n., 542, 543, 544, 546, 551 n., 552, 557, 579, 580–81, 595, 596, 619; quoted, 556, 559, 568, 581
Orléans, Bishop of, 95 n.
Orléans, Duke d'. See Louis-Philippe
Orléans family and party, 485–86, 494 n., 495, 509, 512, 513, 514, 515, 522, 535
Orloff, Count, 323
Orsay, Chevalier d', 596
Osmond, Marquis d', 460, 531
Ottoman Empire, 292, 293
Oubril, Baron d', 268
Oudinot, Marshal Nicolas-Charles, 331, 335
Ouvrard, Gabriel, 224, 234

Paine, Tom, 86 n.
Palmella, Count de, 372
Palmerston, Henry Temple, Viscount, 531, 532, 552, 553–54, 558, 565, 567, 570, 575–76, 578, 579; quoted, 558–59, 572
Panchaud, M., 41
Papal States, 416
Paris, 61, 62, 63, 69, 78, 79, 82, 90, 91, 92, 93, 97, 98, 100, 101, 103, 107, 109, 112, 119, 120, 121, 123, 125, 126, 130, 135 and n., 140, 151, 156, 160, 161 n., 163, 165 n., 170–73, 175, 177, 178, 179, 188, 190, 191, 193, 198, 200, 201, 202, 203, 204, 205, 206, 211, 218, 219, 220, 221, 229, 232, 233, 242, 252, 268, 278, 288, 295, 299, 307, 311, 313, 316, 327, 329, 330, 334, 336, 337, 340, 342, 343, 345, 352, 358, 411, 413, 423, 424, 431, 432, 433, 434, 436, 438, 445, 449, 456, 458–60, 465 and n., 472, 475, 518–24
Paris: First Peace of, 344–45, 348, 349, 360–61, 362, 377, 382, 390, 404 and n., 405, 415, 450–51, 548 n.; Second Peace of, 455, 489
Parlement of Paris, 57 n., 64–65
Parma, 333 n., 391, 392, 408, 411, 417

Parma, Duke of, 391
Pasquier, Baron, 436, 444, 446, 472, 508–9; quoted, 445, 471
Paul I, emperor of Russia, 241, 330
Père Goriot, Le (Balzac), 600
Périer, Casimir, 509, 564, 571, 572
Périgord, Adalbert, Count de, 16
Périgord, Alexandrine, Countess de. See Damas d'Antigny
Périgord, Dorothea of Courland, Duchess de Dino, Duchess de Talleyrand, Countess de, 34, 35, 296–98, 307, 311–12, 334, 364–65, 368, 385, 424, 431, 445–49, 458–65, 468, 470 and n., 472–76, 479 and n., 480–85, 490–91, 496, 503 and n., 512, 515, 529, 530, 531, 534, 535, 536 and n., 537–42, 550, 553, 557, 566, 571–74, 586–92, 600, 603, 608, 610–20; quoted, 412, 501, 504, 533, 539–40, 543, 571–72, 576, 577, 578–79, 580, 587, 591–92, 595, 596, 606–7, 609, 617
Périgord, Count Edmond de, Duke de Dino, 162 n., 296, 297, 298, 311, 365, 445, 459 and n., 474–75, 479–80, 481, 482, 536 and n., 614 n.
Périgord, Abbé Maurice de, 19
Périgord, Pauline de, 480–83, 586–87, 589, 597, 606, 607, 612, 613, 615, 617, 618; quoted, 620
Perrey, M., 459, 461, 479 n.
Petiet, M. de, 181
Pétion, Jérôme, 112, 125, 126
Philadelphia, 151–54, 156, 157, 159, 165, 209
Philippe-Égalité (Talleyrand), 141
Phillips, Susanna, 143, 144, 148
Philosophes, 42, 49
Piacenza, 392, 411, 417
Pichegru, Charles, 180, 190, 191 and n., 193 and n., 250 and n., 256
Piedmont, 232, 234, 245 n., 246, 348, 391, 409, 455
Pinckney, Charles Cotesworth, 204–5, 206
Pitt, William, 65, 114, 118, 119, 120, 122, 124 and n., 136, 137, 147, 164, 178, 187 n., 207, 241, 242, 267, 532, 541
Pius VI, Pope, 56 and n., 95, 96, 97, 106, 615; quoted, 97
Pius VII, Pope, 236, 237–38, 257, 469
Platov, Count Matvei, 356
Poix, Mélanie, Princess de, 162 n., 592
Poix, Prince de, 618
Poland, 272–75, 310, 311, 357, 359, 362, 370, 382, 383, 386, 387, 388, 390, 393–94, 396, 397, 398, 399, 400, 401, 403, 404, 405, 406, 408, 410, 538, 549, 555

Polignac, Prince Jules de, 510–11, 512, 513, 514, 517, 519, 520–21, 534 and n., 535
Polignac, Princess de, 101 n., 510–11
Poniatowski, Prince Józef, 273
Poniatowski, Princess Marie Thérèse, 592
Ponsonby, Lord, 564
Pont-de-Sains, 460–62
Pontecorvo, 265
Portugal, 188, 207, 283, 285, 290, 294, 343, 347, 350, 370, 372, 375 n., 380, 392
Posen, 403
Potocka, Countess, 601; quoted, 298
Pozzo di Borgo, Count Carlo, 434, 435, 452, 531, 546; quoted, 436, 473, 487–88, 543, 544–45, 564
Pressburg, 408, 413, 414
Pressburg, Peace of, 263, 264, 270, 272, 274, 291
Priestley, Joseph, 139
Privy Council, 159 n.
Provence, Count de. See Louis XVIII
Prussia, 113, 115, 122, 127, 146, 148, 202, 206, 241, 260, 262, 267, 268, 269, 270, 271, 272, 274, 275, 276, 277, 285, 290, 303, 311, 313, 314, 315, 324, 336, 343, 345, 347, 350, 357, 358, 369, 371, 375, 377, 380, 382, 383, 386, 387, 388, 389, 391, 393, 394, 395, 396, 397, 398, 399, 400, 401, 402, 403, 404, 405, 406, 407, 413, 415, 416, 423, 424, 450, 455, 456, 464, 530, 536, 545, 546, 549, 551, 559, 560, 570

Quadruple Alliance, 455 n., 488–89, 570
Quelen, Monseigneur Hyacinth-Louis de, Archbishop of Paris, 503, 599, 608–9, 612, 614

Radziwill family, 273
Ragusa, Duke de. See Marmont, Marshal
Ramel, Dominique, 181, 193 and n.
Ratisbon, 304
Razoumoffsky, Prince, 403, 404
Récamier, Juliette, 171, 179
Redorte, M. de la, 595
Reflections on the Revolution in France (Burke), 117
Reinhard, Count Charles, 218, 227, 603, 604–5, 612
Reinhard, Madame, quoted, 266
Rémusat, Claire de Vergennes, Countess de, 247, 264, 291, 294, 318, 444, 476; quoted, 247–48, 485–86, 494–95, 601
Rémusat, Count Charles de, 318, 323, 572;
quoted, 446–47, 461, 469–70, 491–92, 571
Rennes, Bishop of, 51
Repnin, Prince, 396
Report on Public Education (Talleyrand), 90 and n., 134 n., 173
Restoration: First, 115, 135, 159 n., 193, 337, 342, 346 and passim, 358–60, 428, 436, 441, 500; Second, 436, 459, 490
Reubell, Jean-François, 179, 180, 181, 182, 184, 190, 191, 192, 194, 211, 215, 216; quoted, 187
Revolution, French, 25 n., 47 n., 51, 62, 71–92, 93–130, 132, 133–38, 141, 146–48, 152, 161–66, 171, 172–73, 174, 180, 188, 189, 190, 207, 209, 228, 231, 235, 286, 307, 335, 337, 340, 393, 398, 405, 413, 434, 444, 463, 485, 496, 498, 507, 518, 533
Revolution of 1648, 129
Revolutionary clubs, 106 and n., 107, 108, 109, 110, 111, 162
Revolutionary Tribunal, 162
Rheims, 30, 32, 35, 36, 37, 38, 39, 40, 44, 45
Ricci, M. de, 169
Richelieu, Cardinal, 14, 16, 27, 41, 75, 129; quoted, 17
Richelieu, Duke de, 19 n., 454, 455 and n., 456, 463, 468, 471, 472, 477, 486–97, 503; quoted, 18 n., 437, 453, 458
Rigny, Admiral de, 577
Rivoli, 176
Robespierre, Maximilien-François-Marie-Isidore de, 106 and n., 108, 109, 112 n., 146, 152, 161–62, 164, 172, 173, 176, 207, 215, 226; quoted, 216
Rocca, Madame. See Staël, Germaine de
Roche-Aymon, Charles-Antoine de la, 30 and n., 31 and passim, 43 n.
Rochechouart, Count de, 453
Rochechouart, Marie-Françoise de, Princess de Charles, 17, 21 and n., 22–25
Rochefoucauld, Sosthène de, quoted, 448
Rocher, Abbé, 504
Roederer, Pierre-Louis, 177, 222, 223, 225, 227
Rohan, Louis-René-Edward, Cardinal de, 50 n., 57 and n., 62
Rohan, Louise de, Countess de Brionne, 48, 56, 57, 85, 413
Rollin, Sandoz, 202; quoted, 206
Roman Catholic Church in time of Talleyrand, 31, 40, 49–51, 53, 88, 93–100, 107, 117, 235–36, 237–38, 391, 546 n., 605–6, 607, 609–11, 615–16
Rome, 94, 95, 96, 97, 98, 238, 259

Roosevelt, Franklin D., 20 n.
Rothe, Madame de, 31
Rousseau, Jean-Jacques, 464
Rovigo, Anne-Jean-Marie-René Savary, Duke de, 252, 309, 310, 311, 318, 501-3
Royer-Collard, Pierre-Paul, 466-67, 487 n., 509, 571, 572, 576, 588, 618; quoted, 467, 501, 580
Rulhière, Claude Carloman de, 42
Russia, 112 n., 113, 115, 122, 147, 148, 201, 204, 206, 214, 241, 259, 260, 262, 264, 268, 272, 273, 274, 275, 277, 291, 292, 293, 303, 308, 309, 311, 312, 313, 314, 315, 318, 323, 343, 345, 350, 351, 357, 358, 359, 362, 369, 370, 371, 375, 377, 380, 382, 386, 387, 388, 389, 393, 394, 396, 397, 399, 400, 401, 402, 403, 404, 405, 406, 416, 442, 444, 450, 530, 536, 546, 549, 560 and n., 570

Saar, 455
Sacred College of Cardinals, 38, 59
Sagan, Wilhelmina, Duchess of, 364, 377 and n., 385, 389, 446, 447, 449 n.
St.-Antoine, 125
St.-Aulaire, M., 618
St.-Cloud, 225, 229, 266, 519, 520, 522
St.-Denis, 434, 435
St. Helena, 17, 193, 253, 264, 273, 278, 286, 305, 433, 465, 476
St. Lucia, 345
St.-Marceaux, 125
St. Petersburg, 277, 289, 295, 296, 312, 387 n., 545
Sainte-Beuve, Charles Augustin, quoted, 19, 586
Sainte-Croix, Marquise de, 211
Salvandy, M. de, quoted, 515-16
San Carlos, Duke of, 288
Sand, George, 590, 591
Santo Domingo, 345
Sardinia, 332, 359, 393, 404
Savary, Anne-Jean. See Rovigo, Duke de
Savoy, 455
Saxony, 271, 277, 289, 290, 313, 314, 357, 359, 379, 380, 382, 383, 386, 387, 390, 394, 395, 396-97, 398, 400, 401, 402, 403, 404, 405, 406, 408, 410, 413, 414
Schonberg, Princess, 595
Schuyler, General Philip J., 160, 161
Schwarzenberg, Prince Karl Philipp von, 423, 445
Sebastiani, Count Horace-François-Bastien, 509, 529 n., 542, 544 and n., 550, 551, 552, 557, 562, 563, 564 n., 571, 575
Seine, Department of the, 125, 128
Senozan, Madelaine de, Countess de Talleyrand-Périgord, 161 and n., 162 and n.
September Massacres, 132, 133, 163
Septembrists, 130
Shelburne, William Petty, Lord, 139
Shelley, Lady, quoted, 466
Sicily, 266, 267, 268
Sieyès, Emmanuel-Joseph ("Abbé" Sieyès), 76, 77, 78, 79, 81, 91, 106 n., 177, 178, 215-16, 217, 218, 219, 220, 221, 222, 224, 226, 231
Silesia, 274
Sillery, Marquis de, 81
Simons, Madame (Mlle. Lange), 227, 308 n.
Simons, M., 308 and n.
Smolensk, 313
Sorbonne, the, 40, 41
Souvenirs (Dorothea, Duchess de Dino), 481, 483
Souvenirs de Mirabeau (Dumont), 99 n.
Souza, M. de, 169, 170
Souza, Madame de. See Flauhaut, Countess Adélaïde de
Spain, 112 n., 176, 187, 207, 242, 272, 282-86, 289 and n., 290, 294, 301, 303, 315, 343, 347, 350, 369, 370, 372, 375, 380, 396, 473, 498-99, 530, 570
Spinola, Cristofero, 212
Staël, Anne-Louise-Germaine de, 53, 94, 103, 104 and n., 126, 140, 142, 143, 145-46, 145 n., 148, 149, 155, 156, 160, 162, 163-64, 165 and n., 166, 170, 171, 173 n., 177, 179, 182, 183-84, 186, 198, 200, 205, 206, 207 and n., 209, 213, 235, 244, 248, 475 and n., 605; quoted, 104, 144, 185
Staël, Baron de, 104 n., 105, 140, 155 n.
Stafford, Lady, 138
Stanislaus II Poniatowski, 387 and n.
States-General of France (1789), 65, 66, 67 and n., 69, 73-82, 100, 101, 104, 109
Stein, Baron Heinrich Fredrich von und zum, 399-400
Strasbourg, 260, 261, 262
Stuttgart, 261
Suchet, Marshal, 495 and n.
Sutherland, Lady, quoted, 100
Suze, Count de la, 26 and n., 27 n.
Sweden, 155 and n., 241, 260, 272, 277, 311, 343, 347, 350, 372, 375 n., 380
Switzerland, 148, 155 n., 170, 336, 347, 390, 408, 412, 415 and n., 416, 455, 468, 559, 560, 572

Talleyrand, Catherine, Princess de. *See* Grand Catherine
Talleyrand, Charles-Daniel de, Count de Périgord, 14, 18, 20, 25, 26, 27, 28, 29, 30, 38, 58; quoted, 27
Talleyrand, Daniel-Marie, Prince de, 26 n.
Talleyrand, Gabriel de, Count de Périgord, 17
Talleyrand, Hélie de, Dean of Richmond, 16
Talleyrand, Henri de, Count de Chalis, 16, 27
Talleyrand, Baron Louis de, 162 n.
Talleyrand, Louis-Charles de, Prince de Chalais, 17, 21 n.
Talleyrand-Périgord, Alexandre-Angélique de, 18, 29, 30 n., 43 n., 45, 54, 65, 459
Talleyrand-Périgord, Archambaud de, 19 n., 30, 134 n., 161 n., 296 and n., 464, 474, 482 n., 614
Talleyrand-Périgord, Boson de, 20 n., 134 n.
Talleyrand-Périgord, Charlotte, Baroness de, 459, 586, 618
Talleyrand-Périgord, Marie de, 618
Talleyrand-Périgord, Mélanie de, 482 n.
Tallien, Jean-Lambert, 171, 172; quoted, 163–64
Tallien, Thérèse (Mme. Cabarrús), 171, 179, 237, 243
Talma (actor), 506
Talon, Omer, 153
Terror, the, 101 n., 132, 139, 155 n., 160 n., 163, 165 n., 172, 212
Thiébault, General, quoted, 239
Thiard, Marie de, Duchess de Fitz-James, 40 n.
Thiers, Adolphe, 467, 500 and n., 509, 512, 513, 527, 542, 546, 595; quoted, 522
Third Coalition, 267
Thugut, Baron von, 229
Thurn, 399, 400, 403
Thurn and Taxis, Princess, 385
Tilsit, 274, 275, 276, 277, 278, 289, 290, 291
Tobago, 122, 345
Tocqueville, Alexis de, 595
Tolentino, Treaty of, 346, 392, 411
Toulon, 147, 203, 204
Tournai, Battle of, 17
Tranquebar, 211
Transpadane Republic, 202
Treilhard, Jean-Baptiste, 216
Trier, 404
Trinidad, 242
Triple Alliance, 398–411

Truguet, M. de, 181
Turgot, Anne-Robert-Jacques, 48, 63; quoted, 63–4
Turkish Empire, 175, 201, 203–4, 214, 277
Tuscany, 332, 391, 392, 409
Tyrol, 263
Tyszkiewicz, Countess, 459, 466, 468

Ulm, 261 and n.
Undaunted, HMS, 334
United States, 63, 81, 101 and n., 148, 149–66, 204–6, 333
U.S. Constitution, 101 n.

Valençay, 286–87, 288, 289, 307, 461, 464, 465, 466, 467, 469, 473, 501, 514, 515, 576, 577, 579, 585, 587–93, 600
Valmy, 127 n.
Vaudémont, Princess de, 48, 514, 538, 541, 542, 568, 569, 571, 572, 575
Vendée, 146, 147, 188, 233, 246
Venetia, 263
Venice, 197, 261
Vergniaud, Pierre-Victurnien, 106 n., 137
Vienna, 113, 114, 119 n., 176, 261 n., 262, 266, 275, 303, 308, 357, 358, 384 and passim, 406–7, 414, 425, 445, 449 and n., 465, 477, 479, 570, 580–81. *See also* Congress of Vienna
Villèle, Count de, 494, 497–98, 499, 502, 503, 509–10, 514; quoted, 498
Vincent, Baron de, 274, 275
Virginia, 159
Vitrolles, Baron de, 83 n., 84 n., 328, 329, 331, 334, 434, 443, 466, 490 and n., 491; quoted, 317, 330, 435, 439, 440, 443, 486
Vittoria, Battle of, 285
Viviers, Bishop of, 95 n.
Voltaire, 42, 54, 115, 464
Vorarlberg, 263

Wales, Princess of, 355
Walewska, Countess Marie, 273–74
Walewski, Count, 273
Wallachia, 261, 291
Walpole, Horace, quoted, 140
Warsaw, 272, 273, 274, 277, 290, 310, 370, 383, 386, 387, 403, 549 n.
Washington, George, 81, 151, 152, 153, 156; quoted, 153
Waterloo, 13, 424, 428 n., 431, 453, 549
Webster, Sir Charles, 325 n.; quoted, 411 n.
Wellington, Arthur Wellesley, Duke of, 285, 401, 406, 408 and n., 411, 413, 414 n., 423–24, 425, 427, 431, 434, 435, 450, 452, 455, 470, 529, 531,

532–34, 537, 538, 540–41, 543, 544, 545, 546, 547 and n., 548 and n., 566, 569, 575, 581; quoted, 414, 541
West Indies, 204
Westphalia, 290
Whitworth, Lord, 246
Wilgrin, Count of Périgord, 15
William I, King of Holland, 559–61, 565, 567, 569, 572–73, 577, 579
William IV, King of England, 532, 533, 536–38, 547
William Penn (ship), 148–49, 150
Willot, Amédée, 193

Württemberg, 263, 266 n., 290
Würzburg, 392
Wycombe, Lord, 53, 105, 114

Ximenes. *See* Jiménez
XYZ Affair, 204–8

Yarmouth, Lord, 267, 268
York, Duchess of, 356

Zaignelins, Abbé de, 409
Zichy, Count, 395
Zichy, Countess, 385

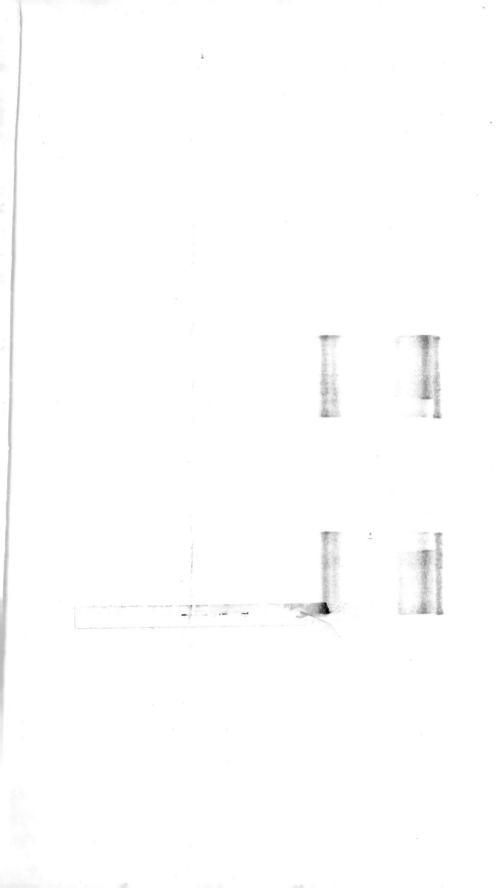